# MANAGING
# PLANNED CHANGE

# MANAGING PLANNED CHANGE

## *Paul C. Nutt*
Department of Management Sciences
College of Business
The Ohio State University

**Macmillan Publishing Company**
New York

**Maxwell Macmillan Canada**
Toronto

**Maxwell Macmillan International**
New York  Oxford  Singapore  Sydney

Editor: Charles E. Stewart
Production Supervisor: John Travis/Helen Wallace
Production Manager: Nicholas Sklitsis
Text and Cover Design: Jane Edelstein
Illustrations by Precision Graphics

This book was set by Publication Services, Inc.,
and printed and bound by R.R. Donnelley & Sons Co.
The cover was printed by R.R. Donnelley & Sons Co.

Macmillan Publishing Company
866 Third Avenue, New York, New York 10022

Macmillan Publishing Company is
part of the Maxwell Communication
Group of Companies.

Maxwell Macmillan Canada, Inc.
1200 Eglinton Avenue East
Suite 200
Don Mills, Ontario M3C 3N1

Library of Congress Cataloging-in-Publication Data
 Nutt, Paul C.
   Managing planned change / Paul C. Nutt.
       p.      cm.
   Includes index.
   ISBN 0-02-388685-4
   1. Organizational change. 2. Management. I. Title.
 HD58.8.N88 1992
 658.4'063—dc20                                                    91-21382
                                                                        CIP

Printing: 1 2 3 4 5 6 7 8   Year: 2 3 4 5 6 7 8 9 0 1

*To Margaret McLeese Brigham and Frank M. Brigham*

# FOREWORD

▲ ▲ ▲ ▲ ▲ ▲ ▲ ▲ ▲ ▲ ▲ ▲ ▲ ▲ ▲ ▲ ▲ ▲ ▲ ▲ ▲ ▲ ▲ ▲ ▲

All of us engaged in teaching students to train managers or to communicate with colleagues regarding planned change within complex organizations have faced great frustration. The past decade has been an era of richness and provocation; simultaneously, it has been a time of chaos within the planned change literature.

In my view the richness and provocation have been caused by:

1. Major experiments in the public and human service sectors that have produced planned change efforts of unprecedented scale. By and large, this critically important societal experience has not been integrated into the management literature, thus separating public administration studies from corporate studies.
2. Rational techniques have blossomed from decision sciences and the maturing computer age, but experience with these techniques is recorded mostly in the technical literature.
3. Numerous group techniques have been developed and tested in connection with planned change endeavors. This experience has been largely limited to organization development specialists and has not been easily available to managers concerned with planning.
4. A decade of experience with project planning in aerospace and defense has remained in a "project management, matrix management" subculture outside the mainstream planned change literature.
5. Studies of strategic and corporate planning, including attention to processes as well as concern with social-political realities, are increasingly a focal issue for research dealing with corporations in turbulent environments. This literature, largely labeled "policy studies" and "strategic management," has stood apart from the public sector studies, decision sciences, and applied group processes.

Clearly, there has been a need for a cogent encyclopedist who would bring these developments from diverse literatures (public sector, private sector; product producing, service producing; rational-analytic, social-political; policy level, project level) together in a single source book. Professor Nutt has undertaken this critical effort, and in this volume he provides clear conceptual overviews, careful documentation, crisp exemplification, and lucid schematic summaries integrating these fragmented but interrelated literatures. It is worth noting the comprehensive attention to human services, as well as of to business and engineering. This attention fulfills the long-standing need for a book equally useful to both sectors.

We have, finally, in one source book, a contemporary and holistic perspective on planned change. Managers responsible for planned change, organizational staff who facilitate the planned change processes, professors who teach planned change, and, above all, students who wish to understand planned change will find in this book an invaluable perspective on planned change concepts, processes, and techniques. It is not just a welcomed addition; it is a major contribution.

André Delbecq, DBA

# PREFACE

▲ ▲ ▲ ▲ ▲ ▲ ▲ ▲ ▲ ▲ ▲ ▲ ▲ ▲ ▲ ▲ ▲ ▲ ▲ ▲ ▲ ▲ ▲ ▲ ▲ ▲ ▲

Planned change deals with the creation and implementation of plans. Planned change is carried out by all types of organizations and on a scale that ranges from the trivial to the unmanageable. Despite the interest in planned change and its obvious importance, attempts to systematize prescriptions of how it should be done are surprisingly incomplete. *Managing Planned Change* attempts to rectify this problem by offering ideas on how to carry out and manage a planned change process. Although several books on planning and planned change are available, none deals with these issues in an interrelated way, and none tailors planned change methods to the needs of the user.

This book provides five key concepts that are not available in books on planned change. The first concerns *how to carry out* planned change. Techniques are drawn from a variety of sources, including systems engineering, behavioral science, systems theory, applied mathematics, sociology, and psychology. A greater variety of techniques is described in greater depth than has been done until now. The discussion of techniques stresses their step-by-step application using pertinent illustrations and case examples. The eclectic nature of these techniques and their integration into a planned change framework make the book unique.

Second, *hybrid methods* are created by merging techniques into planned change processes for various types of projects and strategic planning applications, depending upon the requirements imposed by a sponsor. The "requirements approach" to planning has not been previously addressed in books on the subject.

Third, the book integrates *implementation* into the planning process, stressing how to enhance the prospects of plan adoption. A framework is provided to permit the user to tailor implementation approaches to circumstances that a sponsor faces.

Fourth, the book presents planned change as a managerially guided activity. This presentation leads to two ideas often overlooked in planning books: process and process management. *Process* addresses what theoreticians contend should be done to plan and what practitioners actually do when engaged in planned change. Profiles of popular planned change approaches are presented to show where practice and theory diverge. *Process management* concerns the partnership between the sponsor and others that is needed to carry out planned change. The book shows first how the sponsor receives information to describe the results obtained from each stage of the process, and then indicates how a sponsor should use this information to manage the planned change process. Cases are provided to illustrate how sponsors actually manage various types of planned change efforts. Dysfunctional types of process management, called "pseudoplanning," are also described. Pseudoplanning occurs when the sponsor attempts to manage the process so a preferred alternative emerges, or to preserve the status quo.

Finally, planning books typically ignore various approaches to process management where sponsors take the role of a critic, or of a supporter, or of a neutral observer of the plan. The *planning dialogue,* in which sponsors and planners take up sides and debate the evolving plan, is played out in detail. Techniques that cater to sponsors and techniques that can improve results are offered for each sponsor role.

## Overview of Contents

The book is made up of 16 chapters and includes 29 cases drawn from my work experiences. Every case and example used in the book captures a planned change effort that an organization attempted to carry out. Exercises follow most chapters.

The book is organized into six parts. Each chapter begins with an outline of its contents and ends with a list of key points. Part One introduces the notion of planned change. In Chapter 1 the uses of planned change are described, indicating how planned change is practiced with cases and the lessons that can be drawn from practice. Chapter 2 describes approaches to planned change and the inquiring systems that lie behind planned change approaches. Chapter 3 introduces planned change as a process indicating the role of sponsors and planners, synthesis and analysis, and environmental conditions that influence strategic and project types of planned change.

Part Two describes 15 years of research into planned change in which the tactics used by practitioners and the success record of these tactics have been identified. Chapter 4 describes procedural recommendations found in the literature and compares them to the procedures of planned change used by practitioners. This chapter uses cases to illustrate how practitioners identify options that are considered in the planned change process. Chapter 5 describes how sponsors diagnose the need for planned change and manage the planned change process, indicating points where delegation and control as well as decision making take place. This chapter uses cases to illustrate how practitioners set planned change directions and implement their plans. Chapter 6 provides an evaluation of the tactics for direction setting, option identification, and implementation, indicating the extent of their success in practice.

Part Three deals with implementation, offering guidelines that show how planned changes can be made. Each chapter draws on cases and has exercises to build skills. Chapter 7 shows how sponsors can manage the planned change process. Chapter 8 provides implementation techniques that help a sponsor overcome barriers to planned change. Chapter 9 provides guidelines to select among these techniques and fashion an implementation procedure.

In Part Four the creative aspects of planned change are addressed. Each chapter has exercises and cases that can be used to build skill. Chapter 10 offers both a rationale and techniques for formulation in which directions are set. Chapter 11 provides techniques and the arguments that lie behind concept development in which options are identified. Chapter 12 offers techniques to detail and refine a plan.

In Part Five, hybrid methods for planned change are constructed by assembling techniques that set direction, identify options, and detail plans. In Chapter 13 guidelines based on expected results for the selection of direction setting, option identification, and plan detailing techniques are offered. Chapter 14 deals with the sponsor's style of process management and indicates conditions under which the best technique cannot be used. This problem points out how the style of process management used by a sponsor can force the adoption of less than ideal techniques and what can be done to improve things.

Part Six deals with choosing and reflecting. Choosing requires evaluation techniques. Chapter 15 describes subjective, qualitative, and quantitative techniques that can be used to select among options. Reflecting calls for an examination of what can go wrong during planned change and what can be done to cope. Chapter 16 shows planned change practices that lead to pseudoplanning and offers principles of planned change that improve the prospects of success.

An instructor's manual will be provided to textbook adopters. The manual gives tips on how to build skills in planned change process management and the use of techniques to support the process. Answers to all exercises are provided in the manual. It also offers suggestions in guiding group discussion.

## Text Usage

This book can be used in several ways. First, a *technique* orientation can be taken. Three kinds of courses could be taught around techniques and how to select and merge them into a planning method. A "project planning course" would use Chapters 1, 3, 7, 8, 9, 10, 11, 12, 13, and 15. A "strategic planning course" would use Chapters 1, 2, 6, 7, 8, 9, 10, 11, and 16. The third course could teach both project and strategic planning and use all of these chapters, which can be augmented by the cases in Chapters 4 and 5. These cases can be used as exercises for students to replan using the planning methods described in Chapter 13. Exercises and cases to drive home key points can be found at the end of most chapters.

Second, a *process* orientation can be taken. Such a course would be more advanced, addressing how managers do and should control the planned change process. The cases on Chapters 4 and 5 can be assigned to illustrate key points. Chapters 1, 4, 5, 6, 13, 14, and 16 could be used.

Other variations are also possible, including the study of *decision rules* and/or special topics, such as formulation and implementation. In the former, parts of Chapters 4 and 5 as well as Chapters 13 and 14 would be used. In the latter, Chapters 10 and 11 provide the substance and Chapters 4 and 5 provide cases to discuss relevant issues.

Finally, a *research* orientation can be taken. The prescriptions in Chapters 7, 9, 13, and 16 suggest hypotheses that can be explored in field or laboratory settings. The processes used by practitioners (Chapters 4, 5, and 6) can be correlated with measures of adoption, cost, and other factors. The propositions in Chapter 14, describing techniques that promote good sponsor relations, could be reconciled against the techniques selected on a requirements basis. Study of the trade-offs between quality (using the best methods) and acceptance (using methods that stimulate confidence) is needed if our understanding of planned change is to improve.

The cases at the end of most chapters pose useful questions that illustrate key points. Suggestions in using case material are provided in the instructor's manual.

This book has a variety of uses for classroom instruction; it also serves as a reference for organizations and individuals interested in planned change and for researchers. Moreover, it is sufficiently broad to be useful in teaching strategic management and planning. People interested in consulting or teaching in business, health administration, public health, public administration, industrial engineering, urban or regional planning, and architecture should find this book useful. It represents more than two decades of observation and study of planned change practice and the concurrent search for a better way.

Paul C. Nutt

# ACKNOWLEDGMENTS

▲ ▲ ▲ ▲ ▲ ▲ ▲ ▲ ▲ ▲ ▲ ▲ ▲ ▲ ▲ ▲ ▲ ▲ ▲ ▲ ▲ ▲ ▲ ▲

This book is built on ideas that were developed by many people. Particular recognition should be extended to those, such as Gerald Nadler, who have struggled to create planned change methods. The book also draws on a foundation of ideas laid by C. West Churchman, Kurt Lewin, Dan Schendel, A. D. Hall, Russell Ackoff, Igor Ansoff, André Delbecq, Ian Mitroff, Henry Mintzberg, Robert W. Backoff, and many others, regrettably too numerous to mention. Their friendship, ideas, and constructive criticism are deeply appreciated. I am also grateful to the following reviewers for their suggestions and comments: S. Robert Hernandez, the University of Alabama at Birmingham, School of Health Related Professions, and Henrik L. Blum, M. D., M. P. H., the University of California at Berkeley, School of Public Health.

My students at The Ohio State University and my experiences working in industry and in private nonprofit institutions provided cases that proved to be indispensable in thinking through how planned change is practiced and how it could be improved. Peggy Shields typed and edited the manuscript, providing invaluable help in improving the flow of ideas. I'm grateful for Peggy's extra effort as the book was taking shape. Cary Wasden, Steven Meese, and Susie Cinadr helped to put the manuscript in its final form.

Last but not least I am grateful to my family for their support and understanding during the many tension-filled times when deadlines had to be met. The book is dedicated to my grandparents who played a very important role in my life.

Paul C. Nutt

# CONTENTS

▲ ▲ ▲ ▲ ▲ ▲ ▲ ▲ ▲ ▲ ▲ ▲ ▲ ▲ ▲ ▲ ▲ ▲ ▲ ▲ ▲ ▲ ▲ ▲

▲  CASES

# *Part I*

# INITIATING PLANNED CHANGE

▲ ▲ ▲ ▲ ▲ ▲ ▲ ▲ ▲ ▲ ▲ ▲ ▲ ▲ ▲ ▲ ▲ ▲ ▲ ▲ ▲ ▲ ▲

*Part One presents the idea of planned change and how it seeks to capture the creation and the taking of action. To carry out planned change, a responsible leader takes charge of the planned change process and manages it. Cases in which planned change was attempted are used to describe the nature of planned change, its benefits, and when it is apt to fail, and offers some lessons from practice.*

*Several approaches to planned change are outlined, indicating the philosophy of science principles or 'inquiring systems' that are drawn upon.*

*Finally, several topics important to planned change, such as the role of sponsors and planners and how each uses systhesis and analysis during planned change, are discussed, as is how planned change efforts arise in organizations and how environmental factors limit or encourage strategic and project initiatives.*

# 1 | What Is Planned Change?

▲ ▲ ▲　　▲ ▲ ▲ ▲ ▲ ▲ ▲ ▲ ▲ ▲ ▲ ▲ ▲ ▲

"Planned change" is a process managed by a responsible leader that is used to modify or create strategies, policies, procedures, internal operations, products, or services for an organization. The challenge for managers and students of management is to master the demands posed by planning, change, the planned change process, *and* planned change process management.

## ▲ THE NATURE OF PLANNED CHANGE

*Planning* helps an organization to prepare for the future by making decisions and taking actions today. To master planning, managers must learn how to create a basis for action taking. This involves confronting several dilemmas. First and most important is the dilemma that stems from establishing a direction. Many managers spend little time questioning and exploring needs that have captured their attention. Resources are often allocated to deal with needs that are unimportant or are merely symptoms of deeper concerns. Also, opportunistic managers implement solutions that ignore underlying problems, making the rationale for an action obscure and possibly misguided. Successful managers explore needs before acting, questioning why action is needed, and then formulate directions as objectives. Second, managers must overcome the urge to limit the number of options that are considered, often developing a single remedy. Managers have more success when they identify and compare several alternatives. Third, plans must be detailed to specify how they are to work in practice. The workings of a plan also provide a means to appreciate the benefits, feasibility, and ethics of each. A comparison of benefits, feasibility, and ethics provides a means of identifying the merits of each plan and a basis to select one of the plans to put into use. Together, problem exploration, objective setting, developing multiple options, plan detailing, and evaluation make up essential activities needed to create a plan.

Planning is useless without change. Successful managers develop skills in putting the plans to use. To implement a plan, managers must understand the social and political forces that can arise in their organization and be able to manage these forces. This suggests that planning involves thinking about action and that change involves taking action while thinking. This interdependency is crucial. Both thinking *and* action are essential for beneficial change to occur.

Managers should have a working knowledge of several ways to sequence planned change activities. To organize a planned change effort, successful managers develop skills that help them explore the barriers to action and create beneficial actions, selecting a sequence of activities, or *process,* that matches situational needs and the manager's power to act as the agent of change.

The planned change process must be *managed* by an appropriate organizational leader. Successful planned change efforts stem from leaders who act as planned change sponsors. The sponsor is a manager with the authority to act who endorses the process, guides it, and gives it legitimacy. However, in practice process management is often delegated to one degree or another. For instance, some sponsors initiate projects and assign them to a subordinate, acting as gatekeeper by reserving the right to select the plan to be used. Others play an active role early in the process, for instance, by formulating objectives, and then become a gatekeeper. Planned change is more apt to be successful when the sponsor champions the process by shepherding it from beginning (setting directions) to end (implementation), drawing on staff support as needed.

This book provides managers and students of management with ways to carry out planned change, considering the situation that they must confront. These processes are designed to help the manager think about action and take action while thinking. Process offers a guide to thinking and taking action, not a substitute for either thinking or action. Managers can avoid thinking and/or taking action when process prescriptions are followed too rigidly or when they are viewed as a panacea. Ideally, the skilled sponsor, acting as an agent for change, applies the prescriptions that are offered to diagnose new situations. These prescriptions can help sponsors through sticky situations that often arise during a planned change effort by confronting ambiguous problems and developing useful responses.

## ▲ PLANNED CHANGE USES

Planned change is defined as a process, guided by someone in authority, that combines thinking about ways to resolve important problems and taking action to deal with the problems. This definition makes planned change a disciplined effort that shapes and guides what an organization (or work unit) does to deal with problems that merit action. If the process is adroitly managed, it facilitates communication among key people, accommodates diverse interests, provides a means of orderly decision making, and lays the groundwork for the successful implementation of a plan.

Planned change is carried out in all types of organizations. It has been used in the public sector to practice statesmanship, devise foreign policy, develop programs called for by legislation, design weapon systems, examine the merits of policy (such as national health insurance and educational reforms) and perform in many other ways.

Private firms and third sector organizations, such as not-for-profit hospitals and arts councils, apply planned change to initiate or modify products, services, internal operations, policies, and procedures and to respond to strategic initiatives.

This book makes no sector distinctions. The techniques and procedures for planned change can be applied in public, third sector (private, nonprofit), and private settings. And cases are drawn from all sectors to illustrate how the ideas presented in the book can be applied to all organizations.

Although the approach to planned change can be widely applied, some limitations should be noted. Planned change focuses on key decision makers who must find agreement through negotiation and bargaining before change can occur. The planned change process coordinates the activities that attempt to create the "buy-in" needed by key parties for a change to be accepted. A planned change process is also used when a change spans a number of work units and even an entire organization. However, when multiorganizational projects are undertaken, the prospect of success declines. The scope of action in such a project makes it difficult to reach all affected interests and deal with each individual's perceptions and needs. Much time is required organizing forums, involving various interests in planning groups, devising bargains and opportunities for negotiation, and coordinating these activities in multiorganizational planned change efforts. In these situations, attention is focused on collectives in which no one is in charge, making action more difficult to realize.

## ▲   THE BENEFITS OF PLANNED CHANGE

Organizations and work units within organizations engage in planned change to solve important problems. A process of planned change helps organizations (or work units) in many ways beyond providing problem solutions. The planned change process promotes careful thinking about important problems, clarifies what seems feasible, establishes priorities, considers future needs and folds them into current actions, provides a defensible basis for decision making, exercises control, seizes the initiative, coordinates across work units or organizations, and builds teamwork and skill in interested parties.

A planned change process can offer each of these benefits when procedures and techniques are selected according to the needs of a planned change effort. This matching, although helpful, does not replace knowledge of the situation and its idiosyncrasies. The procedures and techniques are not a substitute for canny leaders and staff who have knowledge of the change situation and its peculiarities.

### When Change Is Apt to Fail

Planned change may not be possible in several situations. Planned change can be ill-advised when the climate is hostile, when leaders treat the process as a gesture, when no one in authority will act, and when key players lack skill and expertise. *Hostile climates* arise when morale is low and when leaders have been heavy handed in implementing past change efforts. The resistance provoked by autocratic changes, and their residual effects, can make change difficult no matter what benefits a change may offer.

Some leaders treat the planned change process as a *gesture,* carried out to placate superiors or externals. University departments do strategic planning because accreditation reviewers demand evidence of planning, hospitals develop "long-range" plans because regulators will not approve an expansion without one, and managers in firms initiate planned change processes to create the aura of a well-run organization or department. In each case, the purpose is *not* to take action, but to give the appearance of action. Planned change efforts that are postures can destroy the credibility of future planned change. Whenever possible, astute leaders avoid "gesture" planned change efforts.

A planned change process requires *leadership* by someone with the authority to act. The leader must have the prerogative to make the required changes, even if this power is never formally applied. When prerogatives are lacking, key players sense that needed commitments are missing, making the planned change effort appear ill-advised or foolhardy.

Some organizations lack the skills and other *resources* to carry our planned change. Planned change in these situations must be limited and focused, or it will exceed the abilities of staff and others who must support the process or the financial support needed to realize a change.

## Avoiding Needed Change

In some instances, planned change is avoided when badly needed. Some organizational leaders believe that the cost of change outweighs its benefits and rely on intuition and experience to get them by. Others get overwhelmed by the demands of a planned change. Planned change should not be undertaken when its cost exceeds likely benefits. However, most studies show that the benefits of planning outweigh its costs (e.g., Thune and House, 1970; Hofer and Schendel, 1978; Armstrong, 1982; Nutt, 1984c). "Planning organizations" outperform nonplanning organizations when various performance indicators, including cost and revenue, are considered. Also, performance is more predictable in planning organizations. These conclusions hold for service industries and third sector organizations as well.

Eastlack and MacDonald (1980) have found that planning benefits are limited by the extent to which leaders are willing to devote time to the process. Bryson (1988) contends that effective leaders devote at least 10% of their time to planned change. This allocation seems clearly justified when viewing the benefits that planned change can provide. Leaders who avoid planned change will forgo substantial benefits for their organization.

Some leaders prefer intuition and avoid the "straitjacket" of formal planning. It is true that gifted leaders have the ability to make successful change without much process assistance. However, organizations are seldom populated with the gifted. Also, everyone can benefit from clear thinking about steps and procedures that can guide a complex long-term project, even if used only when special needs or circumstances arise, as when an impasse is reached. The steps and procedures in a planned change process offer this type of assistance.

Finally, some leaders prefer to follow an incremental process of change in which they muddle along. This type of leader responds only when needs and opportunities become clear and unequivocal. This approach seldom upsets key stakeholders, but it can miss significant opportunities and fail to deal with crucial needs in a timely manner. Muddling through is frequently ineffective (Miles and Snow, 1982; Bryson, 1988).

## ▲   THE PRACTICE OF PLANNED CHANGE

The experiences of real organizations in carrying out planned change are used throughout the book. Both desirable and undesirable practices provide messages of value. The poorly executed planned change effort provides a vehicle to explore what could have been done. This exploration can be particularly meaningful because it is based on what actually took place in an organization. Seeing how practice can be improved is a confidence builder. Also, by examining ill-advised practice, failures can identify pitfalls to be avoided. Successful planned change efforts offer prototypes of another kind, suggesting what can be achieved by good practice and the workability of the ideas presented in this book.

Several cases are now offered that have desirable as well as less desirable features to illustrate some of the pitfalls and opportunities that arise during planned change.

## The Renal Dialysis Case

The renal dialysis project was carried out in a large university hospital that had recently started a new outpatient clinic. The clinic design did not include a renal dialysis unit because such a unit was seen as cutting into the income potential of the medical faculty.

With the enactment of federal legislation, which financed most of the treatment cost for chronic renal disease, the demand for dialysis increased substantially. Historical planning decisions had left the university hospital with a single four-station unit. As demand grew, local physicians began to refer patients to a proprietary dialysis unit that had opened in the city. Compared with the proprietary unit, the university hospital's dialysis facility lacked many amenities, causing self-pay patients to prefer the proprietary center. Before long, the proprietary unit had absorbed nearly all the self-pay or third-party insured patients, leaving the indigent Medicare-Medicaid patients for the university. The result was not only lost revenues, due to patients being treated elsewhere, but also unreimbursed cost. (Medicare-Medicaid reimbursement to hospitals does not cover fully the out-of-pocket cost for the care of dialysis patients.)

Revenue opportunities triggered the planned change process. Analysis suggested that the capacity of the unit should be doubled—from four stations to eight—and that amenities should be improved. The achievement of improved amenities was expected to attract self-pay and third-party insured patients, which would result in improved revenue prospects.

The practices of the competitor served as a solution template. A list of features in the competition's dialysis unit was made to guide planning activities and the collection of information. A remodeling expert provide a layout that determined the changes needed to fit the competitor's dialysis unit into the clinic's building. Circulation technologists and nurses were asked to suggest staffing requirements and operating policies. All issues such as staffing configurations, policies, and procedures were drawn from the staff's experiences with other dialysis units. The features of the competitor's system were compared with current practices. Physicians were then asked to verify that these changes were acceptable. Acquiescence, if not support, by important groups was the dominant criterion used to determine acceptance. The hospital administrator judged the plan a success when all key groups ratified it. No formal evaluation was conducted. Memoranda publicizing the benefits of the new unit were prepared and circulated in the hospital's referral area. Performance was monitored by revenue changes, which continued to fall following installation.

To summarize, the steps in this planned change effort were

1. Recognizing declining revenues
2. Deciding to double capacity and improve amenities
3. Studying practices of competitor
4. Listing features of the competitor's service system
5. Comparing features to current system and selecting those that seem desirable
6. Having care providers critique plan by comparing it to renal units in which they had worked or trained
7. Publicizing the renal unit's availability
8. Measuring revenues for the renal unit. ▲

## *The Parking Case*

The parking project was conducted by a small company located in the heart of a student housing district, on the fringe of a large university. Rapid expansion of student housing in the area had gradually eroded parking places for customers, employees, and visitors, causing many complaints about parking. This led the firm's board of directors to authorize hiring a consultant to evaluate the parking situation. The consultant was to develop alternatives and supporting documentation.

The board directed the consultant to analyze the current situation by forecasting needs and proposing alternate solutions. The project began with an evaluation and then developed a proposal that was presented to the board of directors. To construct the proposal, surveys of employees, visitors, and customers were undertaken. No attempt was made to identify the cause of the complaints; the consultant merely asked each group where they usually parked. The second phase of the survey determined parking habits and was conducted the day of a huge blizzard. No attempt was made to repeat the parking habit survey on a more representative day. These data were then used to forecast future demands.

The information gleaned from the survey was coupled with the consulting firm's prepackaged solution for parking problems. The proposal consisted of constructing a parking ramp, with a temporary gravel-surfaced parking lot during ramp construction. In addition, the consultant proposed moving the company's main entrance to permit the construction of a pedestrian bridge from the ramp to a new entrance. The plan was buttressed with data to support it, describing costs-benefits, user convenience, and improved security.

The cost-benefit data that supported construction of the ramp were questioned because of the sloppy forecast. This allowed members of the board to sweep aside concerns of user convenience and security, which had not been affected by the analysis. The lack of credibility of the data was extrapolated to all other areas, rendering the conclusions questionable and the consultant's defense of a parking ramp vulnerable.

The board rejected the ramp, indicating their heretofore tacit belief that people prefer a surface parking lot and that the cost to construct, maintain, and secure a surface lot would be lower. Board members were also opposed to moving the front door, because the new door location would detract from the appearance of the building. They directed the consultant to make recommendations in accordance with these views and resubmit the proposal. This forced the consultant to prepare a plan for a surface lot, including the supporting documentation. The consultant revised the data that had been previously collected to support a surface lot plan. However, the sloppy and incomplete analysis made the "off-the-shelf" nature of the consultant's plans look foolish.

The consultant had originally been expected to aid in securing land for the parking lot. However, the consultant's poor performance led to its dismissal by the board. This action was taken before local property values and sale prospects had been determined. Subsequently, the board members attempted to make the necessary land purchases for a surface parking lot through its chief executive officer. At this point, property owners had gotten wind of the plan and increased their asking price severalfold, making the project economically infeasible.

To summarize, the steps in this planned change project were

1. Acknowledging complaints about parking
2. Hiring a consultant
3. Surveying parking habits of employees, visitors (e.g., vendors and suppliers), and customers
4. Forecasting future demand
5. Planning for parking ramp and temporary lot prepared from consulting firm's prototypes
6. Rejecting the plan in favor of a surface lot
7. Preparing plans for surface lot (also from the firm's prototypes) and fitting survey data to the surface lot plan
8. Appraising possible property for acquisition
9. Abandoning the plan due to unanticipated costs                              ▲

## The Materials Management Case

The materials management project took place in a medium-sized company located in a suburb of a major metropolitan area. The company had experienced exceptional growth in the past 15 years. During much of this period, management had heard negative reports about its materials management system. Complaints about stockouts and failure to monitor supplies adequately were common. The persistence of these reports prompted the vice president of finance to appoint a planning committee to investigate the organization's inventory control problems.

To initiate the project and to make other changes, the vice president hired an individual with recognized expertise in material management and named him the supervisor of a new "materials management" department and chairman of the planning committee. In effect, the planning committee had been delegated complete authority to revamp the system.

Frequent stockouts had been labeled as the problem meriting attention. The planning group agreed to analyze and rectify problems with the current system. Hence, problems in the current system guided the search for solutions.

The bulk of the activity occurred in detailing a plan. To search for ideas, current material management procedures used by each department were summarized with a flowchart. The flowchart pointed out current inventory control features and discrepancies between the way the policies were written and executed. The committee suggested modifications in procedures, which the staffers checked with the respective departments and incorporated into the flowchart. Several modifications resulted. The final flowcharts incorporated the best features drawn from these procedures.

When the chairman of the committee concluded that a workable plan had been created, it was installed and a monitoring system set in place. The planning committee continued to receive reports about the performance of the revised system, such as number of stockouts, ordering errors, and number of invoices in accounts payable. When problems were identified, the planning committee modified procedures and then implemented these procedures and monitored results.

The planning group became a permanent appendage to the organization, vested with control responsibilities. It met monthly to receive reports on the progress of the materials management control system.

To summarize, the steps in this planned change project were:

1. Deciding that stockouts occur too frequently
2. Modeling a current materials management system
3. Identifying current materials management procedures
4. Creating a flowchart of all steps, merging procedures
5. Assessing steps and proposing modifications
6. Demonstrating how new procedures can overcome stockout problems
7. Monitoring stockouts, safety stock, and complaints ▲

## The Branch Bank Case

A large urban hospital discovered that each payday an hourly employee was selected to cash the paychecks of a number of coworkers. The selected employee got all checks endorsed and then went to a nearby bank to cash them, returning to the hospital with a large sum of money. The hospital administration feared that theft was likely and worried that employees would demand that new checks be issued should a theft occur.

Discussion among the hospital's top management was used to verify the dimensions of the problem, such as the frequency of occurrence and the sums of money involved. This discussion then wandered to other issues, such as financial services to physicians that could help to ingratiate the hospital with its medical staff.

A staff member was asked to get proposals from local banks that would establish a branch bank in the hospital. A modified Delphi survey (see Chapter 10) was used to elicit ideas from the banks. Development was then delegated to the banks, which were asked to detail a branch bank proposal. Each branch bank carried out its stock market analysis and responded with a bid. Each bidder proposed to locate an automatic teller in the lobby.

The CEO gave the proposals a cursory review and rejected all of them, claiming that an automatic teller in the lobby "makes the place look too commercial." The banks were asked to rebid, with the location restriction considered in their new proposals. In the new bids, several banks dropped out, because an automatic teller in a "low-visibility" location would reduce their chance of getting lucrative physician business. The cost of the teller and ancillary services was based on getting some new, high-income physicians as bank customers, which now seemed more remote.

The staff person was assigned the task of evaluating the second round of proposals and proposing one to the board of trustees. The staffer checked all proposals for errors and omissions. Finding none, each proposal was evaluated, seeking the best proposal among those submitted considering cost, range of services, accessibility, ease of use, and several other factors. The staff person developed a visual aid that listed all banks in the second round of bids and how they met each criterion for presentation to the board. A contract was submitted by the staff person to the board of trustees for ratification, which led to the plan being severely criticized. The CEO of a local bank, who was a board member, objected to the bank selected, claiming that his bank had not been given the chance to make a bid. In fact, his bank had been contacted in the first round of bids and had withdrawn when a subordinate of the bank's CEO had applied a bank rule of forecasted additional business to decide against submitting a proposal. The action of the subordinate was not mentioned to avoid embarrassing the banker-board member. This led to a stalemate that aborted the project.

The steps in this planned change effort can be summarized as follows:

1. Identifying check cashing behavior of employees
2. Estimating frequency of occurrence
3. Suggesting an onsite bank and sending a request for proposal (RFP) to local banks
4. Having banks do a market analysis (based on prospect of garnering physician business)
5. Receiving automatic teller proposals from banks
6. Having CEO reject all proposals
7. Asking banks to rebid
8. Reviewing new bids
9. Checking for errors in proposals
10. Selecting criteria to judge the proposals
11. Listing attributes of each proposal using the criteria
12. Identifying best proposal
13. Drawing up a contract
14. Having board of trustees reject proposal                    ▲

### The Patient Registration Case

The patient registration project was carried out at a 600-bed hospital located in the center of a large city. In this hospital, the outpatient department was not centralized. Instead, each of the departments that offered outpatient services had a separate staff group to deal with patients. The registration of patients in which payment and other information was collected was done by department staff upon a patient's arrival.

The sponsor of this project was the director of patient services in the hospital. The sponsor initiated planning because his wife had received services as an outpatient several times over the course of a year and was not billed. A cursory search for information was made to validate the problem, concluding that centralizing outpatient registration would pay dividends for the hospital.

The sponsor visited several other institutions to observe their patient registration procedures. The visits verified that centralized record keeping was not only feasible but desirable. Several of the procedures picked up in the site visits were synthesized to propose a centralized record-keeping plan. The plan was presented to each department head to solicit their reactions. Most were positive, but some departments refused to participate. As a consequence, the sponsor initiated a pilot program.

The pilot test collected information on patient wait time and bill accuracy. The centralized record-keeping plan was initiated for the participating departments. A before-and-after analysis of the data was carried out in which patient wait time and the number of lost charges were compared before and after centralized record keeping. The pilot test suggested that wait time and lost charges were reduced by the plan. Nevertheless, the initial nonparticipants still refused to join in the centralized record-keeping system. They claimed the project was motivated by a selfish interest. They were put off by the sponsor's "grab for power" and pointed out how the anecdote had been used to justify the project. The project's origin (the wife's experience) lent credibility to their criticisms. Performance monitoring found that centralized outpatient registration was overly costly because of the nonparticipants, and it was terminated.

In summary, the steps taken in this project were

1. Failing to bill for outpatient services
2. Estimating scope of the problem
3. Proposing centralized outpatient registration
4. Making site visits to observe centralized patient registration procedures
5. Developing a centralized patient registration system from what was observed
6. Soliciting reactions of outpatient department heads
7. Encountering several department heads who refused to participate
8. Instituting a pilot system to demonstrate plan benefits
9. Finding that patient wait time and lost charges declined under centralized record keeping
10. Setting plan in place
11. Having nonparticipating department heads refuse to use system, claiming vested interests of sponsor were being served
12. Undertaking performance monitoring that found plan to be too costly and it was withdrawn. ▲

## ▲ SOME LESSONS FROM PRACTICE

Planned change failures occur when leaders do not take control of the process to endorse, guide, and legitimize the effort. Active involvement is desirable but, at a minimum, leaders must show key people that the project is important and what is expected of them. Leaders who act as champions of planned change are more successful, as illustrated by the materials management case. However, when a leader sends confusing signals, planned change efforts often fail, as illustrated by the parking case.

Additional difficulties that arise during planned change include (1) failing to understand the problems provoking action, (2) failing to agree on the need to act, (3) failing to appreciate the barriers to action, (4) relying on the practices of others, (5) failing to seek innovation, (6) misusing consultants, (7) failing to use participation, (8) ignoring ethics, (9) developing only one option, (10) emphasizing plan content at the expense of exploring needs, and (11) failing to look for options broadly defined.

1. *Mistaken or misleading problems.* The problems provoking action at the outset of a planned change project can be symptoms of deeper concerns, or misleading, or more urgent than important. For instance, the complaints in the parking case could have been caused by many factors that were not explored. Deeper probing may have found that the complaints were not parking related. Making unjustified assumptions has doomed many planning efforts.

Some problems are misleading. In the branch bank case, employee behavior was deemed undesirable, but no one made an attempt to determine whether an automatic teller would alter this behavior. Also, the urgency suggested by employee behavior was interpreted as creating an important need. The desirability of changing employee behavior does not suggest the importance of a planned change effort.

Problems create a window that directs all activity in a planned change project. Addressing the wrong problem looks out on a landscape that contains few, if any, solution cues *and* makes failure likely. Sponsors who buy into accepted or conventional notions of needs and/or opportunities make it hard to explore problems that appear to be provoking action. Projects that solve the wrong problem can discredit future planning, as the parking case illustrates.

2. *Failing to agree on the need to act.* People make different interpretations of the need to act. If key people see different degrees of urgency, the commitment needed to take action can be missing. For example, the need to act was made clear in the materials management case. The parking case and the patient registration case lacked this commitment to action because the need to act was neither clear nor compelling. Taking steps to justify the need to act and making clear expectations are crucial ingredients in a successful planned change. For example, in the materials management case, the sponsor demonstrated that periodic stockouts need not occur in a well-run inventory control system. This demonstration made needs clear and created a sense of urgency.

3. *Failing to appreciate barriers to action.* Successful implementation calls for an appreciation of critical factors that can derail a planned change. Had the CEO in the branch bank case taken control of the process the need to deal with the banker on his board of trustees would have been far more apparent. A phone call could have headed off problems by explaining what had happened. Another opportunity to bid by the bank could have negated the banks opposition. Insider knowledge of this type is both essential and seldom available to the staffer who was carrying out the project. Leaders who take control of planned change efforts can often head off political problems.

4. *Relying on the practices of others.* The most common source of ideas in planned change stems from current practices in the sponsor's organization or the practices of others. For instance, the idea in the renal dialysis plan was taken from a competitor. This approach is frequently adapted for major projects. Prior to a new construction program, executives often visit other facilities to determine how they operate. The billing system may seem adaptable from one organization and a materials handling system from another. These existing systems are then merged into a proposed design. This image gives the sponsor premises, which are offered as suggestions, but often become constraints. For example, architects incorporate and shape premises, defined by space demands of key people in the organization. They seldom challenge or modify them. The user's solution images become a requirement rather than a metaphor, which aids in the articulation of intentions and expectations.

The sponsor, after defining the problem, may delegate planning to outsiders. Consultants or vendors are asked to provide a ready-made solution, their stock answer to similar problems (as in the branch bank and parking cases). The supplier provides some minimal tailoring and sets its standard system in place. Again, this approach has the virtue of speed and may provide a quality solution, when the ready-made solution has a good fit to the problem. However, such off-the-shelf solutions may prove to be "off-the-wall." This is especially true when the problem-solution match is poor. However, economic considerations often coax the consultant or vendor to force fit their stock solution to the client's problem.

5. *Failing to seek innovation.* Organizations seldom seek innovative solutions to planning problems. Managers think it is clever to adapt the ideas of others, believing that such a practice reduces the costs of planning and provides an adequate, if not ideal, solution to the problem. This approach is quite sensible when a plan is readily transportable. For example, in the materials management project planning was inexpensive and relatively foolproof. The equivalent of a pilot demonstration had been conducted by the sponsor's former employer that showed that the system worked. However, when adaptability is less clear cut, planning costs can quickly escalate. In such a situation, delays and false starts occur in modifying the practice to be adopted that run up costs and lose credibility for future planned change efforts.

The materials management project also illustrates how the analysis of current practices tends to restrict innovation. Sponsors are often impatient, wanting tangible results early in the planned change process. Copying what others do is thought to have this "virtue," so it is often used in place of asking harder questions about purpose and options.

Some sponsors always attempt to adapt the ideas of others. The first thought after planning has been activated is to conduct a site visit. The visit reduces uncertainty but also sets up implicit constraints that inhibit new ideas. New images create uncertainties, so they tend to be discouraged. The failure to innovate is often traceable to introducing a solution prematurely during the planned change process.

6. *Misusing consultants.* People often push preconceived ideas. Low innovation results when leaders have been seduced by an idea that keeps them from giving careful consideration to their needs. In the parking project, the board had a preconceived notion of what was needed and consultants were hired to justify this view. The consultants did not talk with the board of directors before making their

proposal, leading them to propose a plan that was unacceptable. The consultants were required to revise both their plan and their data, raising questions about their credibility.

In other instances, consultants are brought in by a leader to verify the leader's pet idea. Frequently, the consultant is confronted with an idea and asked to evaluate it. Most consultants realize that repeat business may depend on rendering a positive assessment and feel pressure to provide one. Consultants used in this way provide little information and few insights of value.

7. *Failure to use participation.* Participation can be helpful in promoting ownership. Giving people an opportunity to comment as the plan evolves neutralizes their fear and offers insights into barriers to action. For example, the branch bank case failed to involve a key individual who saw himself as a stakeholder. Even a modest amount of involvement can neutralize criticism and get a critic to go along. If not, an inducement can be offered. Both inducements and "cooptation" could have been quite useful in the branch bank case.

8. *Ignoring ethics.* Planned change projects should seek plans that are politically acceptable, technically desirable, *and* ethically responsible. Ethical problems in planned change often arise innocuously through alternatives that are discarded or criteria that are not used. These ethical problems are more subtle than sole source contracting and conflicts of interest, although both do arise in planned change. For example, physicians on the medical staff of the hospital in the outpatient registration case opposed the centralization of billing information because it could be used by central administration to compute their income. Many physicians depend on the hospital as a vehicle to create their income. In this era of declining reimbursements to hospitals, the size of this income may entice hospitals to bill physicians in some way for facility use. Keeping their income under wraps allows physicians to plead poverty should such a proposal emerge. Ethical issues also arise when leaders push self-serving ideas or plans that benefit someone on whom the leader depends.

Dealing with ethical issues can be tricky. Taking an ethical position can be difficult without a planned change process with which to pose questions. For instance, Catron (1983) contends that asking how the organization or work unit would be seen if faced with an exposé helps to neutralize the ethically irresponsible action. Posing such a question to a group helps to deal with ethically questionable actions.

9. *Developing only one option.* Planned change calls for the development of several options. The competition among the alternatives suggests ways to combine them, blending the best features of each. Multiple options also provide a way to make comparisons to determine the merit of options, as in the branch bank case.

Planned change is typically carried out by detailing a single option, as the materials management and outpatient registration cases illustrate. The urge to limit the options that are considered stems from pragmatics and the visions of sponsors. It seems *pragmatic* to focus on a single option, particularly when one can demonstrate its workability. In the materials management case, the sponsor looked for an idea that worked to improve performance. However, a broader search may have yielded options with a better fit to the needs of the company or options with superior features.

Many planned change projects are dominated by a sponsor with an idea or a *vision*. The sponsor uses the planned change process first to test the idea's efficacy and then to fine-tune and shape it. The basic premise (e.g., centralized registration) is never questioned. For instance, the sponsor's assertion that patients are not billed for services was never verified. In fact, the departments may have extended "professional courtesy" to the wife by not billing her. In such projects, a sponsor's pet idea triggers the process and sets premises that are seldom questioned in the ensuing planning effort. Pet ideas severely truncate the search for options. Only one option is detailed, and the planned change process focuses on feasibility, such as the pilot test in the outpatient registration case.

10. *Emphasizing plan content at the expense of exploring needs.* There is an old adage that "people don't know what they want until they see what they can get." Sponsors who emphasize plan specifics at the expense of probing needs and identifying the remedies that each implies often behave in this manner. Sponsors who insist on specifics coax subordinates and staffers to select a specific plan quickly, allowing the sponsor to find out, as soon as possible, what can be done. Such a sponsor finds uncertainty about what can be done intolerable. There is a push to find a plan to eliminate this uncertainty. Such a sponsor forgoes exploring possibilities to show that the situation is under control. This preoccupation with plan specifics can lead to dealing with the wrong problems *and* limiting search to a single option.

11. *Failing to look for options "broadly" defined.* To avoid dealing with symptomatic and misleading problems, the shrewd planned change sponsor looks beyond the objective that has focused action. Both a broader and a narrower objective are then considered. Solutions are sought for each of these objectives. For instance, in the branch bank case, the focal objective of avoiding the problems of theft could be broadened to security questions and narrowed to behavioral change in employees. The security objective suggests direct employee check deposit, perhaps in the trustee's bank, instead of writing employees a check. Behavioral change suggests taking steps to help employees who are motivated to risk losses, to get quick cash. Probing may reveal that the employees who participate in the check cashing practice are being faced with wage garnishment or demands from creditors. Helping these individuals budget their pay or consolidate debt offer remedies.

Note how treating objectives in this way opens up new possibilities for taking action. Options "broadly defined," given by both larger and narrower objectives, emerge when this is done. Options narrowly defined (e.g., the proposals from the banks) cannot raise the larger scope of concerns noted earlier. As a result, the assumed problem provoking action is seldom reviewed to see if more pressing concerns may have been set aside.

## ▲ Key Points

1. The planned change process is managed by a responsible leader who initiates the process and regulates what is done. In this process both planning and change are essential. Planning creates action and change takes action.

2. Planned change can produce several *benefits* for an organization. They include careful thinking about important problems, clarifying what is feasible, setting priorities, considering future needs in today's actions, providing a basis for decision making, controlling what is done during a change, offering a means to take the initiative, coordination, and building both teamwork and an understanding of change making.

3. A number of difficulties can arise during a planned change effort that limits its effectiveness and may lead to failure. They include acting on mistaken problems or symptoms, creating conflict over the need to change among key people, failing to recognize social and political factors that pose barriers to action, ignoring the opportunities for innovation, considering but one alternative, failing to get the ideas of key people, and ignoring ethical issues posed by the plan and the changes needed to implement it.

## ▲ Exercises

1. Consider the cases presented in Chapter 1. What steps could have been taken by its sponsor (the individual who attempted to make the change) to manage the process? Speculate on how the outcome could have changed.

2. Discuss the misleading problems that initiated planning for the branch bank case. Why were they misleading?

3. Compare the imperatives to act in two of the Chapter 1 cases. Identify at least three stakeholders in each case. What problems might each have identified? Why are they alike or different?

4. Discuss the barriers to action in two of the cases. What actions seem needed in each case to overcome these barriers?

5. How did sponsors seek innovation in the cases? What other opportunities can you identify?

6. How were consultants misused in the cases? What would you recommend to overcome these problems?

7. How could each of the cases have used participation? Speculate on its effects.

8. Identify and discuss ethical problems that could arise in each case. What would you do to deal with each?

9. Identify and compare options broadly defined for one of the cases as illustrated in the discussion of the branch bank case.

# 2 Approaches to Planned Change

▲ ▲ ▲    ▲ ▲ ▲ ▲ ▲ ▲ ▲ ▲ ▲ ▲ ▲ ▲ ▲ ▲ ▲

This chapter describes several types of planned change approaches. These approaches fall into one of three categories: (1) intended application, (2) the values embraced, or (3) scope. Facility planning, merger planning, and service or product planning illustrate some typical applications. Scope depicts the ramifications of a planned change effort. Values are revealed when certain dictates are forced upon planned change. For example, in "community planning" citizen participation is required, often giving a voluntary citizen group the power to control the planned change process. Such a constraint reveals the values of advocates for this type of planning and sets the stage for a more fundamental discussion of the origin of values. In this discussion, the philosophical underpinnings of various planning approaches, called "inquiring systems," are discussed to point out the types of logic that have been used to develop planned change approaches.

## ▲ SOME PLANNED CHANGE APPROACHES

Planned change approaches are classified as application based or value based. Application types offer a planned change process to deal with a particular subject. Value-based planned change makes certain kinds of demands on the conduct of planning.

### Application Planning

The types of applications are defined by topics that planned change efforts frequently address. Specialization has led to fragmentation. For example, processes have been created to do merger planning, facilities planning, and product planning. These and other applications will be discussed.

#### *Merger and Acquisition Planning*

Mergers and acquisitions are on the rise in most industries. They are partially a response to a strategy that calls for divestiture or horizontal or vertical integration. Multiorganizational systems, such as conglomerates, grow and fragment in this way. Some organizations have lost their financial viability and believe that they will survive only if they merge with another. In the for-profit sector, mergers are prompted by the motivation to salvage asset value for investors. In nonprofit settings the motivation is to maintain the availability of a needed service. Viewed from the other perspective, the organization acquiring another may believe that the merger partner ensures growth in market share.

For example, in the hospital industry, regulation has all but eliminated growth through bed expansions. To obtain the efficiencies produced by economies of scale, a hospital may take on a financially troubled hospital to ensure future growth in admissions. Further, the out-of-state multihospital system, with its management contracts, can create an unwanted challenge to the local hospital that had a free rein over a local market. It may turn to acquisition as a means to keep new rivals from encroaching on its service area and "skimming" pay patients.

The way mergers and acquisitions have been carried out in the past offers guidance to others and suggests a planned change process. At some point, these ideas are compiled, and a prescription is offered to carry this type of project. Practitioner journals often publish a checklist to follow that all too often becomes dogma—prescribing the "one best way" to do mergers or acquisitions. Most specialized planning approaches tend to evolve in this way. The experiences of one institution, however, may be a poor guide for others in the industry. Even if tailored to fit local circumstances, such planned change approaches produce woefully little innovation.

### Corporate Restructuring

The hot topic of the 1980s has been corporate restructuring in which changes in fiduciary responsibility are aligned with new initiatives. Voluntary associations create for-profit ventures and seal them off from the parent organization to protect the parent from recourse by investors should the venture fail. For-profit organizations, such as consulting companies, create foundations to seek out donations and pursue government grants and contracts. Firms form divisions along new lines and shuffle responsibilities, creating the need to realign responsibilities and people with the new leadership positions. Mergers create problems of combining some functions and deciding who will be given new responsibilities, who will be demoted, and who will be discarded. Each poses legal issues so lawyers have been busy selling restructuring packages for handsome fees.

### Long-range Planning

Long-range planning (also called master planning) establishes goals for the institution, setting out its future role as a target toward which to plan. The time horizon can be set at any point in the future. However, 10 to 20 years is not unusual. Plans that contain activities that have various time horizons are also common. Merger or acquisition planning can be the product of a long-range planning process.

The long-range planning process deals with formative aspects of planning, goals, and development options, not details. Long-range planning programs conducted by consultants often include interviews of the concerned leaders to get their ideas for specific services and programs. A synthesis of their past engagements augmented by the programs and services offered by key competitors are submitted to the organization to ponder. Goals, if considered at all, are derived from the programs selected.

Long-range planning can be top down (goals to program) or bottom up (programs to goals). The advantage of the top-down approach is its inherent logic, but many participants, such as directors or trustees and CEOs, prefer not to deal with issues at a conceptual level because they tend to be intangible. The typical CEO, director, or trustee prefers to see a tangible aspect of a plan, which is a key advantage of the bottom-up approach. However, this approach is unlikely to be innovative, which is critically important in any long-range planning effort. Both top-down and bottom-up approaches can be found in the long-range planning offerings of consultants.

### Service and Product Planning

Long-range plans often lay out program areas to be developed such as open heart surgery, ambulatory care centers, health maintenance organizations (HMOs) in a hospital, or new models for a van and RV refinishing company. Product and service planning is used to add details and select a way to implement the program.

### Functional Planning

The functional plan is narrow in scope, often dealing with the operating features of a product or service plan. Examples include materials handling procedures, department sizing and layout, or allocating space among users of a new building. These plans become components of the product or service plan that, in turn, are part of the long-range plan.

### Facilities Planning

Facility planning devises the envelope that is to house service and other activities. The facility's appearance often takes on more importance than its functions. This is caused by a disproportionate emphasis on two of the three parts of facility planning, the feasibility study and the envelope, at the expense of how the facility is to be used. The feasibility study and envelope design activities are handsomely compensated, creating an emphasis in these areas.

The feasibility study is carried out to determine if the project is viable, and if it is, to create funds via bonds and other types of financing. The feasibility study required by bond rating agencies such as Moody's for the bond prospectus provides considerable information important to planning. The Bond Council, the feasibility consultant, and other parties to the study charge hefty fees for their services.

The architect specifies the physical features of the building, charging up to 7% of the project cost in fees. The functional aspects of the building's design, such as layout and procedures, are often done by underlings in the architect's firm. Facility planning tactics, applied by the client organization, often focus on scheduling the construction and occupancy steps of moving into the new building. Both the consultant and the client tend to deemphasize the design of the programs to be housed in the facility.

### Market Research

Organizations must continually search for new markets and ensure that their existing markets are well managed. Market planning is geared to study and interpret various types of utilization or sales patterns. This interpretation can be made in several ways. For example, in a hospital, medical staff admissions are the key causal factor in utilization. A few medical staff members can create the bulk of the admissions. These physicians must be pampered, managed, and monitored. Physician recruitment plans are essential long before the heavy admitters approach retirement age.

The "practice plan" is a variation on the market research approach. It is used in university medical schools to devise a way to compensate physicians. Each medical faculty member admits "his" or "her" patients to the hospital, creating revenue for the hospital, as well as teaching and research objects. The financial health of the hospital and medical school is dependent on the admission behavior of its full-time and courtesy medical staff. Medical practice plans split the revenue between the physician, hospital, and medical school. Tailoring such a plan to fit a particular setting has many marketing implications.

Unlike hospitals, firms market directly to the potential users of their products or services. Media are used to approach the potential consumer directly, selling the virtues of a particular product or service and coaxing them to purchase it. This approach can be quite impersonal, as in advertising to stimulate either beer or soap sales, or highly personal, as illustrated by the relationship of Boeing and other defense contractors to the U.S. Department of Defense. Planning and planned change plays an important role in developing marketing efforts.

### Regulatory Planning

In the past half century there has been a rapid increase in the regulation of many industries. Airlines have been subject to rate and route control and still must bid for gates at local airports. Airport authorities determine how available gates will be allocated, in part by considering the airlines' service plan for the community.

Public utilities are regulated by a variety of publicly appointed commissioners who serve on boards that rule on rates, power purchases, new construction and expansions, and sites, as well as monitor profits. Plans are frequently crucial in these negotiations. For example, a utility seeking to convert a nuclear power plant to a coal-burning facility must obtain permission from a regulatory body. The regulators can exclude conversion costs from the utility's rate base, making the project infeasible. The utility's plan would play a major role in the regulator's determination.

In health care all new services and capital expenditures for equipment and expansions above a few hundred thousand dollars are subject to review. The review agency gives a "certificate of need" (or CON) when a project has been approved.

The regulatory agency forces the applicant to plan by responding to regulatory materials that are required for a review. Consultants have quickly filled this void, offering planning services that satisfy regulators' requirements. Planning requirements in regulatory planning are often defined by the regulators' application forms.

### Areawide Planning

The notion of areawide planning was born from federal legislation passed in the 1930s and 1940s. Over a period of years, the planning role was taken from voluntary councils and given to quasi-public regulatory agencies with regions made up of one or more counties to manage. Government funding maintains planning agencies that deal with zoning and land use, roads and transportation, rivers and harbors, port authorities, airports, watershed management, welfare, aging, and many others. Well-known agencies such as the Army Corps of Engineers, the Bureau of Land Reclamation, and the Tennessee Valley Authority (TVA) are expected to plan services.

Areawide health planning provides an illustration of how such agencies plan. Areawide health planning was initiated by federal legislation to coordinate proposed services against some standard of need. This type of planning was conducted by inventorying health care resources in a region and the current CON applications, comparing them to norms such as beds per thousand population, to limit the growth of resources. By requiring the health institutions, such as hospitals and nursing homes, to submit a five-year plan with their application, areawide planners have forced health institutions to do intermediate-range planning. The five-year plan provides the regulators with a profile of current and future plans to compare with their need formulas.

## Value-Laden Planning

Value-based planned change puts certain types of demands on planning and change. The names of the planned change approaches suggest values held by their proponents. Examples include participatory planning, advocacy planning, and community planning.

### Participatory Planning

Participation is the key ingredient in many planning approaches (Delbecq, Van de Ven, and Gustafson, 1986). There are several merits to participation and many compelling reasons to involve people in a planned change process. Wholesale participation, however, can be undesirable. When used in this manner, the prescriptions for participation are misunderstood. People who have little knowledge or information to offer and lack the power to implement can be millstones for a planned change process to carry. Such individuals gradually create roles for themselves, such as historian or gatekeeper. Participation is costly, particularly when members of a planning group act as "gatekeepers" without the formal authority to behave in this manner. As a result, the planned change process is impeded and action-oriented people become frustrated. Rules for participation that overcome these problems are described in the section of this book devoted to implementation.

### Advocacy Planning

This form of planning was born in the turmoil of the 1960s and allows the planner to push a solution (e.g., Davidoff, 1965). The planner becomes the advocate for reform, calling attention to deficiencies in housing, rent control, health services, or what have you, and proposes new forms of low-income housing, rent control agencies, or tax-based subsidization of tertiary care services. The Environmental Protection Agency (EPA), the Occupational Safety and Health Agency (OSHA), health regulation agencies, and many other government agencies were created in an advocacy planning environment to force the adoption of certain practices by firms and other organizations.

### Community Planning

Advocates of community planning stress *citizen* participation (Blum, 1974). For example, participation is thought to be mandatory for all regional planning activities, whether it is carried out at the level of the neighborhood, service area, county, or even larger spatial groupings. Many planned change processes are steeped in citizens who are asked to pick objectives, priorities, and alternatives. The aspirations of people drive the planned change process in community planning efforts.

## A Critique

Both application- and value-driven planned change approaches have flaws. Application-driven approaches put content over procedure. Someone's perception of the state of the art in mergers, markets, facilities, and the like is stressed rather than new ideas. This problem becomes particularly apparent in the long-range planning packages that are sold by consultants as an assemblage of the wish lists of key people plus select ideas drawn from someone else's programs. Goals are inferred, a procedure that stifles the very outcome of what a long-range plan should demand: new ideas. Value-driven process can become so enamored with the end (the reform) or the means (participation) that good procedure is treated superficially.

# ▲ MODES OF PLANNING

Planned change approaches have various organizing themes. Three typical themes are shown in Table 2-1.

## A Forecasting Typology

A forecasting typology often encompasses a variety of approaches that ranges from antiplanning to a planned society. The organizing theme in this typology is the degree of forecasting that is demanded by each approach.

The *laissez-faire approach* is often viewed as antiplanning because it leaves all choices to market forces. The future is ignored. For instance, no interventions by government are seen as useful. Behind the adoption of such an approach is a Darwinian-like view that only the fittest should survive. Free choice and unplanned futures result.

*Incrementalism,* popularized by Lindblom (1965), proposes to make changes in small steps that follow the path of least resistance. Directions that appear to have positive effects are built on, until performance and/or acceptance falters. Plans are

### Table 2-1 ▲ Some Themes in Planning Approaches

| Forecasting | Problem Eradication | Scope |
|---|---|---|
| 1. Laissez-faire | 1. Problem solving | 1. Strategic |
| 2. Incrementalism | 2. Problem | 2. Managerial |
| 3. Allocative | 3. Coordination | 3. Operational |
| 4. Problem solving | 4. Allocation | |
| 5. Exploitative | 5. Creative | |
| 6. Explorative | 6. Design of standard | |
| 7. Normative | operating procedures | |
| 8. Comprehensive | | |

then modified by responding to pressure groups. As a result, obvious solutions to intolerable and immediate problems are stressed. The future implications of these plans are largely ignored.

An *allocative emphasis* shifts resources about to deal with problems. Notions of equilibrium run through this approach. For instance, firms frequently plan by allocations made in response to capital improvements suggested by divisions. The plans of these divisions are evaluated using such criteria as projected returns, fairness or equity, posturing for important interest groups, needed quality enhancements, or the actions of competitors. Available resources are allocated among the divisions according to this evaluation. Planning is made up of the decisions periodically rendered by corporate leaders. Similarly, when a hospital's high admitters make demands, funds may be shifted to meet those demands, balancing between the importance of the high-admitting physicians and other uses of these funds. As a result, an allocative approach has a short-run orientation, eliminating immediate problems.

The *problem-solving approach* takes problems as given and determines ways to eliminate them. Problem understanding is stressed. For instance, if sales in a particular region have declined, steps are taken to stimulate sales by marketing. If quality problems are encountered, quality enhancements are developed. If big admitters on the medical staff of a hospital are about to retire, a recruitment program would be developed. Little is done to look beyond the immediate problem or impending crisis. Because interventions that overcome the problem must be implemented into the future, the problem-solving approach has a short future time horizon.

The *exploitative approach* attempts to fill niches, defined in ecologylike terms. Unlike the problem-solving approach, exploitative planning contemplates the future. This approach tries to identify emerging needs and opportunities and the advantages to the organization that would accrue from their exploitation. As Blum (1974) puts it, "If we can predict a parade, let's...put our popcorn concessions at the right corners." But the exploitation approach doesn't question the desirability of the event being exploited, such as the parade. For instance, firms look for new market niches for their existing products and people's emerging desires that can be met with new products. The emergence of paid membership "athletic clubs" illustrates the latter and new exercise opportunities in these clubs the former.

Hospitals often use this approach to set up ambulatory care centers as feeders to their hospital in communities before they recruit physicians. This gives the hospital leverage. Physicians are put on the hospital's medical staff as they are hired to staff the clinic, which ensures that the sponsoring hospital will get all admissions.

*Exploratory planning* uses forecasts of possibilities and trends to suggest what may develop. The most likely future is an extension of the present, and plans are often based on its features. For instance, firms track sales by region, consumer characteristics, and sales tactics to detect trends that signal opportunities. Similarly, hospitals track proportions of Medicaid and self-pay patients. If the hospital has a growing percentage of Medicaid patients, its reimbursement rates are likely to decline. In both cases, a change in market focus may be signaled. New programs would be created that can improve revenues.

*Normative planning* is like the exploratory approach except that the attempts are made to change some undesirable aspects of a likely future. Much successful planned change creates a target of what is desired and works toward it. Massive expansion programs have this characteristic. The end result is specified, and resources over a certain number of years are allocated to achieve this end. Plans are made by working backward to trace the steps needed to set the program in place.

*Comprehensive planning* seeks to interrelate all the normative, exploratory, and exploitative activities within a single planning framework.

The typology is called forecasting because it moves along what might be called the future dimension. The approaches move from a total lack of concern about the future to an all-consuming interest in making the best possible forecasts, seeking to ameliorate the undesirable aspects of a likely future.

## A Problem Eradication Typology

The problem eradication typology stresses what to do to plan (Table 2-1). A problem-solving approach is problem driven and emphasizes evaluation techniques. Analysis is stressed, as in public health disease control or the analysis of product profitability.

*Program planning* implements a plan devised elsewhere, so it stresses implementation techniques. The federal-state-local relationship in programs for the aged and mental health are examples. Both use implementation planning at the local level to create programs within federal and state directives and constraints. Similarly, firms adapt the ideas of others, copying products that sell and sales practices that seem to work, and moving into markets that others find to be lucrative.

*Coordinational planning* is informational, carried out to interdigitate the planning activities of several entities, work units, or entire organizations. A firm's capital expenditure programs provide an example.

*Allocative planning* compares plan options or plans providing a decision structure. For instance, in areawide health planning, the state regulator may choose among several applicants to provide open heart surgery or some other services. In a firm, top management allocates resources among its divisions according to perceived needs.

*Creative planning* identifies a new order of things. A target complete with objectives is specified toward which the organization moves. For example, firms such as Disney and Intel devise innovative products to give them market leadership and the profits that strong sales of fresh ideas will bring. Designing procedures can also be a part of creative planning. For instance, the procedures to conduct cost-based reviews of work units in a company could be planned.

The problem eradication typology describes the component parts of a planning process. Accordingly, some planning activities are evaluative while others stress implementation or decision making.

## The Scope-Based Typology

The strategic, managerial, and operational typology is organized according to the scope of planning (Table 2-1). As shown in Table 2-2, the key distinction is between strategic planning and project planning, which can be either managerial or operational. An operational planned change process would consider functional planning problems, such as traffic flows, while managerial planning would deal with products, services, marketing, and the like. For simplicity, the planned change in these categories will be termed "project."

Most long-range planning is strategic in character. There are, however, several useful distinctions between long-range planning and strategic planning. Long-range planning tends to provide a linear extrapolation whereas a strategy is an idealized vision of what might be. Strategic plans call for creative leaps that deal with emerging concerns and do so in the ebb and flow of the political environment in

**Table 2-2 ▲ Distinctions Between Strategic and Project Planning**

| | Strategic Planning | Project Planning |
|---|---|---|
| Purpose | Provide direction | Accept direction |
| | Plan for long run | Plan for short run |
| | Engage in coordination | Engage in implementation |
| | Adapt to conditions | Form conditions |
| | Focus on future needs | Focus on current needs |
| | Make a comprehensive assessment | Make a narrow assessment |
| | Make strategic plans | Make tactical, managerial plans |
| Results (typical) | Accept risk | Avoid risk |
| | Undertake decision process | Find decision point |
| | Engage in ongoing planning | Engage in time-limited planning |
| | Take general action | Take specific action |
| | Offer range of alternatives | Offer single alternative |
| Typical stages | Define goals | Define problem |
| | Identify alternatives | Identify objectives |
| | | Search out alternatives |
| | | Detail solutions |
| | | Evaluate |
| | | Implement |
| Information | Seek subjective data forecasts | Seek objective data forecasts |
| | Offer values and indicate preferences | Make problem statements; provide technical and scientific information |
| | Offer visions | Offer structure |
| | Narrow problem statements | Broaden problem statements |
| | Require participation of top management | Done by organizational members |
| | Shape targets and direction | Respond to targets and direction |

which change must occur. Strategic planning is more apt to make quantum shifts in direction and consider the fallout associated with radical proposals.

Strategic planned change is done at the top of most organizations to devise a strategy that will guide the entire organization into the future. Project planned change is more limited in scope, often detailing projects that are part of the organization's strategic plan.

In Table 2-2, the distinctions between strategic and project planned change are drawn in terms of their purpose, intended results, stages, information used, and ways of dealing with the environment. The key *purpose* of strategic planning is to provide direction for project planning. It is conducted periodically by an organization to assess and revise its strategy or master plan. Project planning is short run and often takes its cues from the strategy articulated in the strategic plan. As a result, a strategic planning activity must be adaptive, future oriented, and comprehensive, while project planning is formative, with a short time horizon and narrow scope, dedicated to specific problems like acquisitions or facilities.

The *results* sought by strategic planned change are general, stemming from an ongoing process where decisions are periodic, to identify a range of alternatives that are broad and quite general. Risk is inherent and accepted. Project planned change makes a specific single recommendation at a point in time that attempts to minimize uncertainty.

The stages of strategic planned change set goals and identify alternatives. Subjective information, made up of values and preferences, as well as objective information, is desirable in this process that attempts to narrow problem statements. The strategic plan is part vision and part "best guesses" about how a vision can be translated into future action. Strategic planning is done at the top of an organization and tries to shape targets and direction.

Project planned change carries out a process that spans several stages from problem definition to implementation (Table 2-2). Objective information is sought from technical and scientific data whenever possible. An attempt is made to broaden problem statements, to avoid missing opportunities, yet, at the same time, add structure to make the plan tangible and specific. Project planned change is done at various locations in an organization and responds to targets and direction. Illustrations of the distinctions between strategic and project planning will be provided in the next chapter.

## ▲ INQUIRING SYSTEMS USED BY PLANNED CHANGE APPROACHES

The purpose of inquiry is to produce knowledge. An *inquiring system* (IS) specifies how knowledge is created. Planning creates a specific type of knowledge, seeking alternatives that best meet some objective.

Inquiring systems do not lay out steps in a planned change approach. Instead, they describe "warrants" that *justify* the procedures that are used. Every approach to planned change draws on one or more inquiring systems to construct its procedures. A discussion of inquiring systems is essential to expose the philosophical constructs that lie behind a planned change approach, and which provide an understanding of the crucial assumptions that are made. By stripping away all but the key assumptions, a better appreciation of the logic that drives a planned change approach is possible.

The epistemology of planning is the type of thinking and reasoning encouraged by following certain principles of logic. Each planned change approach uses somewhat different principles to determine what we know, how we know what we know, and what can be proven or demonstrated. Five types of inquiring systems that provide different rationales are described. These IS are named for the philosophers who proposed each approach to inquiry.

## Lockian IS

The Lockian system uses experience, facts, and judgment to derive inductively a plan or plan features. No notion of causation is needed because the plan is formulated by direct observation, tempered by experience. Heavy reliance is often placed on experts, as well as empiricism and consensus. Lockian planning approaches often advocate group processes, such as the nominal group technique and Delphi surveys (see Chapter 10), and some form of consensus. Both these group processes attempt to create a consensus among experts after a careful review of arguments. The use of statistics, data banks, and accounting reports also relies on Lockian principles. For example, the Lockian aspect of a statistical analysis stems from widely accepted generalizations made by people from the statistics.

The plan is validated by agreement. Plans that work are stressed. Expediency dominates rigor.

## Leibnitzian IS

The Leibnitzian approach to planning is axiomatic. A model or mathematical representation of the problem is constructed. The model is then solved to yield planning information. First, a basic theory is developed about the behavior of the problem/system under study. For example, if a waiting line is observed, a schedule can be devised using a queuing model. The ability of the mathematical model to represent the problem/system under study is critically important. A poor representation yields invalid plans and prescriptions.

Validity in a Leibnitzian IS is based on internal consistency, completeness of the representation, and precise specification. Both the Lockian and Leibnitzian IS are useful for well-structured problems, but often fail when problems are ambiguous.

## Kantian IS

Kantian IS can be described as multialternative planning. At least two plans are created. The Kantian approach presupposes at least two solutions (plans) for any problem are possible. The Kantian IS formulates each option by first extracting the inherent logic in two ways to create a plan using a Leibnitzian IS. The theoretical framework comes from the Leibnitzian IS and data from a Lockian IS. Different ways to carry out technological forecasting is one such example. Each plan is enriched by a Lockian generalization that seeks consensus on how the plan can be used. Planning theorists use this type of an IS to propose parallel planning processes. Each planning process elaborates an alternative to provide a basis for choice. From these alternatives one is selected that seems to be the best way to deal with the planning problem.

Validity stems from a comparison of the merits of several alternatives. The evaluation information that is created helps one to choose among the alternatives. The Kantian multioption plan is useful for the typical planning effort where modest uncertainty is present.

## Hegelian IS

The Hegelian IS is dialectical. For any problem at least two plans are created, but, unlike the Kantian IS, these plans are antithetical or opposite. They are created by surfacing assumptions and taking mirror images of these assumptions as a basis for planning. For instance, if the original plan assumes that sales will be declining, the other assumes that sales will increase. At least one other key assumption is also treated in this way. For example, consider a firm that identifies raw material availability and prices as key factors in its strategic plan. Both raw materials and pricing are governed by forces outside the firm's immediate control and can change from favorable to unfavorable in the future. A dialectic is formed by the best case (favorable availability and pricing) and the worst case (both unfavorable) or by the mixed cases. The choice depends on which pair produces the strongest tension. In other instances all four contingencies can be used to create multiple dialectics. Consider a hospital's strategic plan that identifies demand and financing prospects as key factors. A plan can be drawn that assumes that both demand and financing prospects will decline. Three additional plans can be created: high-demand, good-funding prospects; low-demand, good-funding prospects; and high-demand, low-funding prospects. The sponsor confronted with plans drawn by making these assumptions assesses them and seeks a synthesis.

A pure Hegelian IS begins with a model or a Leibnitzian representation of each position. Each model represents an opposing set of assumptions that is to guide each planning process. These models are developed using the *same* Lockian data sets and are developed by comparable groups of experts using similar information. This demonstrates to key participants how different assumptions can tease out dramatically different plans. It also points out that data can be made to support several positions. The sponsor observes these confrontations and builds a synthetic model that incorporates the best elements of each view.

Mason and Mitroff (1981) have developed a planned change approach that operationalizes the dialectic through "stakeholder" assessments. The positions of key stakeholders form the dialectic. The process uncovers the assumptions in each stakeholder's position to test their viability. These unique plans are then defended by supporting the assumptions that lie behind them.

Validation stems from conflict among the plans and their proponents that is believed to expose values. The conflict exposes expert biases in each plan, suggesting how to merge the best aspects of each. The dialectic in the Hegelian IS is particularly useful for ill-structured problems.

## Churchmanian IS

Churchman (1979), confronting the dilemmas of planned change in a complex society, notes that a plan, no matter how carefully constructed, will have critics. These critics tend to take four types of positions. They may oppose the plan for political, moral, ideological, and aesthetic reasons. Churchman calls for the sponsor to conduct a dialectic between each of these views during planning to tease out and deal with viable objections. These objections may offer a way to improve the plan or things to do to enhance implementation prospects. Unlike the previous inquiring systems that ignore implementation concerns, this IS deals with the issues posed by both planning and change.

### Politics

Churchman sees politics as *polis,* from the Greek word meaning the actions of people in a democracy. "Making polis" means the formation of a group around a common set of concerns to take action. A polis is issue based and often dissolves when an issue is resolved. Any plan may create a polis. The power of a polis can be compelling. The planner should seek out the group making polis and listen (and learn). If this approach fails to identify a compromise, the sponsor can create a "counterpolis."

### Morality

Plans can raise questions of morality in the form of "It seems feasible, but is it right?" Rightness is often defined in highly personal terms. Plans often stir people into many forms of dissent and counterdissent. For instance, a Catholic hospital's "birthing unit" is supported by some local community groups because it does not offer birth control services and is opposed by feminist groups for the same reason. Each forms a polis to set out its positions, but defines these positions in moralistic terms. Polis is often used to implement one's moral beliefs. Objections based on moral positions can create intense problems for a plan's proponents. Compromise is best. For example, offer referral for birth control and counseling services to all patients, because to counter a stance based on morality typically provokes violent opposition.

### Ideology

Plans can be opposed on ideological grounds. The doctrines and opinions of people dictate their views, often getting in the way of clear logic. Plan proponents who present logical arguments are faced with incoherent responses. The objection is rooted in the image the plan conjures to the individual. Plan proponents who appreciate this image may be able to recast the plan so it carries more acceptable ideological baggage. For instance, creating an advisory group in a Catholic hospital may negate the "abortion on demand" stand of women's rights advocates, which could scuttle the hospital's plan to become a referral center.

### Aesthetics

Finally, plans can be opposed on aesthetic grounds. The form versus function argument is best illustrated by problems that arise in the planning of facilities. A desirable form stresses uniqueness, which resists classification. Architects win awards with such a design. To others, quality is not measured by a visual gestalt. Serviceability is key. To be serviceable, a plan must grapple with details that make a plan work.

Facility planning in the space program provides a sharp contrast. Buildings are treated as "envelopes" that contain the functions that the facility is to house. An envelope is merely drawn around these functions. This leads to "functional looking" buildings, or as some claim, ugly architecture. Such buildings are often railed against by the "community beautiful" folks. In contrast, the architect begins with a design that has "appeal." Form follows function.

The intensity of the form versus function conflict can be illustrated by an architect who won an award for the design of a building for the Wisconsin Hospital Association, or WHA. The design created a "fortlike" building, with slanted walls and slits for windows. The air conditioner was located on top of the building in a structure (also with slanted walls) that blended into the overall look of the structure. Unfortunately, the architect placed the air conditioner on load-bearing building supports that transmitted its vibrations throughout the building and threatened the building's structural integrity. Because it had won an architectural award, the architect resisted moving the air conditioner, claiming it would destroy the integrity of the design. Provisions of the contract were cited that prohibited the WHA from changing the "look" of the building. A much more expensive option of reinforcing the roof was proposed. The dispute was finally settled when WHA was "allowed" to move the air conditioner to the rear of the parking lot and screen it from public view with landscaping, leaving the air conditioner's housing on top of the building. The WHA had to pick up all the associated cost.

The values exposed are instructive. The architect used "appeal" as a criterion. The sponsor used cost and moved the air conditioner off the building. The architect, however, using details in the contract, forced the sponsor to pay for reconstructing the air conditioner housing on the top of the building to preserve the aesthetics of the design. Losing a client's goodwill and the prospects of future business was not as important as losing the "appeal" of a past project. Never mind that the air conditioner made the building functionally unsafe. It looked good up there.

Most facility planning consultants have played out these arguments internally and fall somewhere along the form-function continuum. Buying a facility planner also buys an implicit emphasis on one or the other. CEOs would be wise to shop around, examining a few facility projects and walk through the planning process to judge the appropriateness of an architect for a given project.

A Churchmanian IS sets up a dialectic between these points of view. When planning is undertaken to overcome a poorly understood or ill-structured problem, a debate helps expose conceivable objections to the emerging plan.

## ▲ Key Points

1.  Application-based approaches tend to put solutions, such as a merger, before needs. Value-based approaches often displace important considerations, such as the need to act and barriers to taking action. Planning procedures should have generic rather than specific applications. Also, planners should confront ethics and ethical considerations rather than advocate planning approaches that cater to people's urges but do little to meet their needs.

2.  Scope-based distinctions differentiate two types of planned change efforts: strategic and project. A generic planning approach that can deal with each type of planned change will be developed in this book.

3.  Inquiring systems identify the logic and rationale that lies behind planned change approaches. The practitioner should look for key assumptions that expose how the proponents of planned change approaches are justifying what they recommend.

# 3 Planned Change As Inquiry

▲ ▲ ▲   ▲ ▲ ▲ ▲ ▲ ▲ ▲ ▲ ▲ ▲ ▲ ▲ ▲ ▲ ▲ ▲ ▲ ▲

Planned change is defined as a form of inquiry that requires managerial direction and involvement. Managers direct inquiry to search for ideas and ways to implement them to make change in an organization. The role of planners and sponsors is discussed in this chapter to show how staff specialists, who act as planners, and managers support a planned change process. Planned change calls on planners and sponsors to engage in both the synthesis and analysis of information to produce ideas and bases for action.

Three types of planned change are discussed to distinguish between strategies, policies, and plans. Strategic and nonstrategic planned change captures the crucial distinctions among application types. Features of the environment in which planned change is attempted determines the kinds of outcomes that can be realized and the types of strategic and nonstrategic efforts that will be encouraged and discouraged. This assessment helps organizational leaders who carry out planned change to form realistic expectations and appreciate the need for situational diagnosis.

## ▲ VIEWS OF PLANNED CHANGE

A planned change method must include an orderly procedure that makes explicit the steps to take in planning and change. The procedure should also encourage reflection and yet be rooted in the behavior of individuals who carry out the process and have a future orientation and yet be sensibly bounded. The views of planned change described in Chapter 2 are reviewed to determine the extent to which each meets these tests.

### Inquiry Related to Planned Change

Some see planned change as *forecasting* (Bennis and Nanus, 1985). Various forecasting tools, such as exponential smoothing, are offered as planned change methods. The behavior of several parameters, such as utilization or revenues, is extrapolated to judge the implications of trends. Forecasting meets the future "test" but fails to meet either the reflective or the behavioral requirements. Forecasting is a part of a planned change process, but not a dominant theme. Planned change is more than just "future thinking."

Executives often treat planned change as *problem solving,* the removal of barriers and obstacles. The symptom is treated. If, for example, costs have increased, one is expected to poke around the cost problem to discover causes. Once a cause is found, a solution is inferred. Clever administrators are thought to provide eurekalike solutions aided by group problem solving (Maier, 1970). Planned change is treated this way in much of the organization behavior literature. It meets the reflective and behavioral tests but fails to offer an explicit framework to guide action.

Planned change can be seen as *programming,* taking cues from another process to articulate and justify needed action. Programming is a way to detail the plans of an organization, elaborating what is to be done and when. For instance, a building plan must have a "program" to move departments from the old to the new building. This is a useful but far too narrow conception of planned change.

Planned change has been described as *design*. Design is what Simon (1969) and Nadler and Hibino (1990) contend that colleges of engineering, architecture, and other professional schools should teach, but do not. For example, Simon contends that engineering schools teach science, emphasizing chemistry, electronics, or what have you, rather than how to make changes *using* science. According to Simon, all engineers are designers, but to keep engineering "scientific," the design process has been largely ignored. Definitions of design meet all the tests (explicit framework, reflective, future orientation, and behaviorally grounded) but tends to be narrow, focusing on creation of artifacts: hydroelectric power plants, automobiles, and so on. The outcome of planned change is often broader than an artifact.

*Policy analysis* (e.g., Laswell, 1974; Wildavsky, 1979) starts with an "answer" (the policy) and works backward to assess its implications. The process calls for assessment and then reformulation to be repeated in several cycles. For example, proposals for national health insurance have been tested by estimating their cost and benefits. This analysis found that the costs of all proposals were excessive, which suggested that a "catastrophic" plan, one limited to ailments such as end-stage renal disease whose treatment costs would bankrupt the typical American family, might be a viable alternative to a comprehensive national health insurance plan. Various catastrophic proposals were then assessed, again estimating costs and benefits. Policy analysis begins with evaluation and poses new ideas at the margin of proposed policy ideas which prove to be infeasible. The policy (e.g., national health insurance) tends to constrain the plan and makes few, if any, provisions to generate new ideas.

Planned change can also be seen as an inherent part of a *decision* process (Mintzberg et al., 1976). Much of the organization theory literature tends to mix planned change and decision making. For example, Snyder and Glueck (1980) contend that planned change determines in advance actions and resources needed to meet an objective by identifying and selecting among alternatives. Mintzberg (1981) calls this same process decision making. This view merges decision making activities of diagnosis, design, and choice with implementation.

In this book, planned change will include the diagnostic and choice activities that are carried out by a decision maker to provide information that is collected as the process unfolds. Merging planning (design and implementation) and decision-making (diagnosis and choice) activities in this way allows the book to show how the planned change process can be managed by an appropriate decision maker. The formal link between planning and decision making will be discussed in several chapters, most notably Chapters 4 and 5.

## Activating Planned Change

Planned change is one of several responses that managers make to problems that they have diagnosed (Mintzberg et al., 1976). Planning is used when current performance falls below norms and both performance and norms are clear (March and Simon, 1958). Planned change is a tool that, with a given amount of skill, resources, and support, can transform an undesirable state into a better one, using the norm as a target to guide the effort (Nutt, 1979).

As shown in Figure 3-1, the current problem state can be recognized by *performance gaps* such as preventable infant mortality, declining sales, or escalating costs. Norms specify an attainable mortality level or a target for sales and cost. The difference between the current and ideal state is called the performance gap. Planning is used to devise or revise an organization's strategies, policies, products, services, or internal operations seeking to close the performance gap by improving performance factors such as client satisfaction, revenue, costs, or quality. This view of planned change is broader than creating artifacts, begins with a problem and not a policy, and uses an explicit rather than an implicit process or procedure. Specifying targets or objectives, creating alternatives, and choosing among them suggest process stages. To eliminate the performance gap, planned change must also deal with the conversion of plans into action. An implementation stage is required to meet this qualification, which attempts to create an environment in which change can occur.

The stages of the planned change process are shown in Figure 3-2. In stage I, formulation, the manager who initiates the process looks for ways to understand the performance gap. A search for causal connections that have a fresh perspective is conducted. Stages II and III, concept development and detailing, deal with creating alternatives and documenting their features. Several alternative plans are created. The competition among these alternatives tends to reveal assumptions about each and raise the level of debate as stakeholders explore the merits of the alternatives. In stage IV, procedures that aid in a selection among these alternatives are carried out. Stages I and V (problem finding and conversion to action) are the most important because they determine what is to be done and take steps to promote plan use, respectively.

The process manager can enter or exit at any stage of the planned change process shown in Figure 3-2. Further, emphasis can be placed on some stages at

| Perceived Performance Gaps → | Transforms → | Solutions → | Consequences |
|---|---|---|---|
| Profit Levels | Planned change methods | New products or services | Innovation |
| Mortality rates in surgical intensive care unit | | Changes in agency operations | Quality |
| | | | Cost |
| Innovations by competitors | | "Fact-finding" (the process as an end in itself) | Satisfaction of sponsors |
| Policy statements by a discretionary body | | | Acceptance by clients |
| Market share | | | Sales or revenue |

**Figure 3-1**　▲　**Planned Change as Transformation**

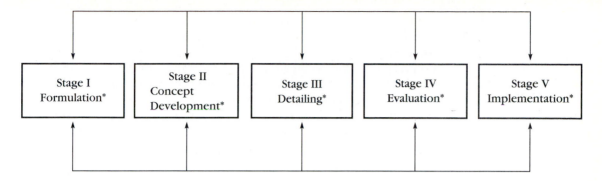

* Any sequence of stages can be used.

Figure 3-2  ▲  The Stages in a Planned Change Method (A General Transformation Process)

the expense of others, depending on the specific needs that a project encounters. In Chapter 4 the activity called for by each stage will be discussed, along with the various processes (stage sequences) used in practice and found in literature.

## ▲  PLANNERS AND SPONSORS

There are two types of actors in a planned change effort, called *planners* and *sponsors*. Planners are often delegated the responsibility to collect information called for by the process stages. Planners typically have either content or process skills, offering either solutions or ways to conduct planning. Planners can be drawn from inside or outside the organization. The "inside planner" can act as an agent for the sponsor and may be given considerable authority to manage the planned change process. If skilled in carrying out process, such an individual can be effective as a facilitator. Planners that have only a rudimentary knowledge of process find planned change frustrating and prone to failure. Staff specialists, such as financial analysts, are also used as planners, and they, too, often lack the needed skills. This book seeks to overcome such a deficiency by adding skills in planned change to the armament of capabilities of staff specialists who take on a facilitator role in planned change.

Planning services are also provided by many consulting firms. The consulting organization likes to deal in specifics, typically offering a solution rather than a planned change process. The management of consultants doing planning poses a difficult problem for many organizations. This book offers guidelines that a manager can use in monitoring the consultant, seeking to improve the value of their services to the organization.

The individual who activates a planned change process will be called its sponsor. The sponsor interprets the organization's needs, which leads to the problem stipulation that the planned change process is to consider. The sponsor can also act as a planner, posing both problems and solutions. Mixing these roles can be unwise, particularly when the problems are complex, broad in scope, or poorly understood. In such situations the insights of several people often prove to be the key factor in planned change success.

The sponsor guides the planned change process by periodically comparing its findings with his or her understanding of the organization's needs. Some sponsors are comparatively active and others passive in process guidance.

The sponsor's role is critical to the success of planned change. Unlike other forms of managerial inquiry, such as evaluation, the sponsor should be involved in *all* stages of the process. Successful planned change hinges on sponsors who maintain active involvement to *learn* from the information that they acquire. For instance, the planned change process may determine that an initial problem diagnosis is misleading. When the sponsor acts on this new level of understanding, new problems are recognized that can change directions. If this new information is not considered, the plan may deal with a symptom rather than a cause. The best way to ensure that a diagnosis is thoughtful, and leads to a better understanding of the problem, is to forge a viable partnership between the planner and sponsor. Prescriptions for this dialogue and ways to manage it are vitally important issues in the conduct of planning. This book offers prescriptions for the dialogue and "transactional models" which show that the sponsor can manage a planned change process as described in Chapters 4 and 16.

## ▲  THE ROLE OF SYNTHESIS AND ANALYSIS IN PLANNED CHANGE

Planned change is more than an analytical process. A crucially important activity is synthesis: putting things together. The deductive nature of synthesis brings together ideas and principles to create a new plan. Analysis is used to judge the merits of the plan, making it a reactive aspect of planned change.

Successful planned change is often mysterious to both the manager who carries it out and the researcher who studies it. The successful planned change process often takes creative leaps that draw on mental processes that people find hard to articulate. These creative leaps are stimulated by synthesis, which draws on intuitive rather than analytical skills. Synthesis skills, which include the creation of novel ideas, seem to be located in the right hemisphere of the brain (for right-handed people).

In one relevant study, Doktor and Bloom (1977) wired executives up to an EEG to measure their brain activity as they solved analytic and synthetic problems. Synthetic problems caused right-side activity and analytic problems left-side brain activity (in right-handed people). Relying on these findings and other studies, researchers now believe that holistic and novel thinking take place in the right hemisphere. The left hemisphere of the brain deals with logic and controls thinking, which is orderly and sequential. The right side of the brain provides art appreciation, skills in listening to music, and interpretive capabilities, with the left side doing art, playing music, and engaging in mathematical and accounting skills that provide information for others to interpret. In other words, the right hemisphere favors the implicit and creates a synthesis to form an argument. The left is explicit and uses logic to provide an analysis. As Mintzberg (1979) points out, the nature of policy-making is dynamic, irregular, and discontinuous, calling for a groping interactive process, with an emphasis on synthesis. A groping-interactive process is more likely to trigger a flash of insight. A good many of the techniques used in planned change are geared to encourage groping and bring out the intuitive side of people through group interaction. In creative activities analytic activity is subordinated to synthesis.

Analysis and synthesis have both strengths and weaknesses. Analysis is often bound by its own dimensions, categories, and classifications. This emphasis on depth gives up breadth. Synthesis gropes for meaning by using new configurations to foster creative leaps. But emotionally inspired responses tend to address surface concerns by reacting rather than probing. Action becomes short run, superficial, and suboptimal—sometimes even wrong. Incrementalism may result in which the organization takes small, shortsighted steps into big problems. Also, the broad brush loses its meaning when a sufficient number of categories are blurred. But analysis is inflexible, imposing excessive structure that can limit and drive out innovation. In short, analysis is useful for breaking something down into its parts and synthesis in putting them together. There will be no attempt in the book to choose between extinction by instinct and paralysis by analysis. As Polanyi (1966) points out, "Intuitive people tend to act before they think, if they ever think, and analytical people think before they act, if they ever act." Clearly, planned change is not just another analytical activity. Both synthesis and analysis have a role in each stage of the planned change process.

## ▲ STRATEGIES AND POLICIES AND PLANS

Strategy, policy, and plans describe three distinct types of products (outcomes) of a planned change effort. Strategy has broad, organizationwide, implications; policies are often multiorganizational in character; and plans are created by projects, carried out by an organization.

### Strategy

Strategy depicts the nature of the organization's markets, products, services, and other activities (Ansoff, 1984), capturing the "key idea" embodied in these activities (Schendel and Hofer, 1979). For instance, a firm may address issues such as the role of growth, its product profile, markets to be exploited, and ways to create vertical and horizontal integration to lay out its strategy.

Strategy provides a way for an organizational leader to define and navigate the organization's "domain." Domain is defined by service or market area, key benefactors, sources of funds, customers, regulators (e.g., OSHA, the EPA), competitors, and the like. The choice of domain determines which markets are sought, benefactors stroked, competitors recognized, and so on. Domain choice often stems from a strategic plan or may be imposed by market conditions, or by each. Domain "navigation" refers to a stream of choices made about domain: the revision of a strategic plan in light of external change, such as the intrusion of a competitor or new Medicaid reimbursement rates. Newman's (1971) "propitious niche" and Selznick's (1957) "distinctive competence" both illustrate the need for careful timing and creative exploitation in strategic planning. Many organizations go "niche prospecting" with their distinctive competence to seek out an unserved market they can exploit with their capabilities to form a strategy.

Strategy is the driving force of the organization. Not surprisingly, there is much debate about its origin. Several views of strategy are highlighted to define the parameters of this debate.

### The Emergent View

Mintzberg (1978) takes the position that strategy tends to emerge from a stream of choices made by key people in an organization. According to this view, strategies become "realized" rather than created. The stream of decisions pushes the organization in a particular direction. When the choices exhibit coherence, a strategy emerges. Strategies in this context have a seminal quality: Once the seed is planted and it takes root and grows, it is difficult to root out. For example, Volkswagen continued with the "Bug" long after it had played out its market. This strategy was continued in the face of financial crisis, and even after dramatic changes in the organization's leadership.

Strategy is shaped by the interaction of bureaucratic momentum, leadership, and the environment. Environments pose changes in demand: VW's Bug no longer sells. However, bureaucratic momentum constrains change. Organizations seek stability. A new strategy is resisted because it will cause perturbations that the organization must smooth. Volkswagen resisted the retooling that would be required to modify the Bug's design because retooling required that new materials be purchased, new people be hired, new procedures devised, and so on. Further, management had become psychologically committed to design for symbolic reasons. The Bug's image as the people's car had long been the symbol of success for Volkswagen. Furthermore, owners' psychological commitment to the Volkswagen Bug was truly astounding. People extolled its virtues in the face of engines that routinely failed at 40,000 miles, heaters that never worked, and floor boards and fenders that literally rusted away. When the market for the Bug had finally played out, it took two changes in leadership to initiate a new strategy (an Audi copy). Rather than planning, Volkswagen groped for a new strategy, taking a series of small steps that finally led to a new line of automobiles. The groping continued until a workable strategy emerged that became the basis that guided future operations. Bureaucratic momentum again takes over so that the bureaucracy can again run like an elephant.

Mintzberg's (1987) studies found that strategy does not take shape using a plan, created by formal methods or by the acts of key management. According to the emergent view, strategies result neither from planned change nor from charismatic leadership, but rather from an accumulation of incremental decisions.

### The Environmentalists

Environmental adaptation is another view of strategy. Miles and Snow (1978) believe that organizations define their product-service market domains by scanning the environment for opportunities and marshalling the organization's resources and ca-pabilities to take advantage of these opportunities. Strategic managers make strategy as they adapt to new realities. These adaptations were found to have four patterns called (1) defender, (2) prospector, (3) analyzer, and (4) reactor. Within each type entrepreneurial, engineering, and administrative tasks are carried out. The en-trepreneurial task is to identify domain: the product (service) line and its market niche. The engineering task is to create a means of manufacture for products or a means of delivery for services. Administrative tasks ensure that needed activities are carried out efficiently.

Strategic managers become *defenders* when they try to maintain current prod-ucts (services) and markets. Steps are taken to close off a portion of the market or to protect turf. Entrepreneurial tasks take shape as lobbying, selling or seeking fran-chises, import barriers and taxes, advertising and promotion, and trade associations that defenders use to protect a domain. Miles (1982) shows how tobacco companies used these tactics to maintain their tobacco products in the face of governmental studies that linked smoking and premature death and disability. Engineering tasks stress efficiency in production and distribution that leads to huge investments in production and distribution capacity. The tobacco industry, for example, is well known for its highly efficient automated manufacturing and sophisticated distribu-tion systems. Control tasks ensure that this efficiency is realized.

Strategic managers following a *prospector* strategy seek out new product (ser-vice) and market opportunities. Being an innovator becomes an important aspect of the organization's culture. The Limited and Hewlett-Packard provide examples. The entrepreneurial task is to create new products that fill needs in particular market segments. To use this approach the strategist must invest heavily in people with creative energy to come up continually with new ideas and match the innovations with market niches. The engineering task is to maintain flexibility that permits rapid response to new initiatives. Administration is loose and is designed to facilitate and coordinate many projects in various stages of compilation.

Some organizations combine prospector and defender approaches, creating what is called an *analyzer* strategy. The strategic manager with an analyzer perspec-tive attempts to lower risk and increase opportunity, combining the strengths of a defender (domain defense) and a prospector (domain offense). The entrepreneurial task is to look for new product-market opportunities *and* maintain current cus-tomers. Analyzer strategy is based on imitation, adopting products and services that prospectors have initiated with good results. Engineering and administrative tasks deal with creating a balance between the demands for control and flexibility. For old products or services, standardization and mechanization are stressed, and for new ones, fluid arrangements, such as venture management teams, are used.

The pattern of adjustment to environmental shifts can be inappropriate and in a constant state of flux. *Reactors* represent an ineffective form of strategy in which adaptations either miss markets or select products (services) that the organization is ill equipped to provide. Failure leads to passive postures when aggressive be-havior is needed, and overly bold initiatives lead to unwarranted risk taking. The reactor strategy evolves from failing to act effectively as a defender, prospector, or analyzer.

Acar (1987) and Nutt and Backoff (1992) extend the typology to show how some of these strategies have negative features that stem from overreacting to competition or markets. These new strategic types are called custodian, developer, stabilizer, and entrepreneur.

A custodian strategy replaces the reactor strategy. *Custodians* maintain distinctive competencies and markets. The custodian takes a position that defends historical commitments without being as reactionary. The U.S. steel industry has used custodian strategy successfully for decades. *Stabilizers* replace defenders. The stabilizer takes steps to respond to important environmental clusters, much the way the U.S. automobile companies have adjusted to slow growth in traditional lines of business with renewed emphasis on efficiency in all product lines. The *developer* is used in place of a "dreamer" strategy that clings to tradition long after the products (services) have lost their vitality, such as Volkswagen's commitment to its Bug. The developer applies benchmarks of competition, such as market share, to signal when innovation seems needed. IBM's response to competitors illustrates this posture. An entrepreneurial posture is preferred to that of a prospector. Prospectors cling to weak market signals and change strategy too often, creating chaos. *Entrepreneurs* balance signal reading with developmental activities. This type of strategy has been pursued by Intel, Disney, and Apple and lead to rapid growth and excellent profitability for each organization.

Even more broadly framed kinds of environmental adaptation have been used to describe strategy. Lawrence and Dyer (1983) develop a framework in which available resource and rate of change are used to capture shifts in the posture of entire industries. The movements of steel, railroads, real estate, hospitals, retailers, mining, shipping, and others are tracked to find successful and unsuccessful adaptations.

### Negotiations as Strategy

Murray (1978) believes that strategy is created by negotiations carried out with external centers of power. The negotiations try to determine what types of actions will be permitted. Negotiation is seen as essential when the environment contains several regulatory agencies and many special interest groups. Murray's work was conducted for public utilities, a highly regulated environment much like the health industry. For instance, to expand, a health organization must submit plans to regulators for approval. Hospital rates are also regulated, in this case by third-party payors such as Blue Cross. But regulatory decision bodies are often made up of community groups, representatives of their competition, and people who control sources of funding, among others. Before proceeding, the applicant is (implicitly) told to conduct behind-the-scenes negotiations with these key groups.

### Analytic Approaches

Analytic approaches stress some form of portfolio analysis. The analysis is carried out to determine how well various product or service lines fit the organization's strategy and to make resource allocation decisions. The most widely used approach was developed by the Boston Consulting Group (BCG).

Developers of the BCG matrix argue that all business costs follow a "one-third rule" in which unit cost falls one-third as volume doubles (Henderson, 1979). This "experience curve," as it has come to be known, suggests that increased market share will pay significant dividends. Profits will increase because unit cost falls. Therefore, gaining market share becomes a generic strategy. The BCG matrix classifies businesses, product lines, products, and still other units of analysis by how its market is growing and the size of its market share, as shown in Figure 3-3.

Four categories emerge called stars, cash cows, dogs, and wildcats. The *star* category has products or services with high growth and high market share that produce substantial cash and require continuing investment to maintain this position. The *cash cow* product or service has low growth but high market share that produce large cash flows with little investment. Cash cows often produce a profit (margin in nonprofit organizations) that is siphoned off to be used elsewhere in the organization. The *dog* category has low-growth and low-market-share products or services. There is little cash flow and little prospect of increasing market share. *Wildcats* represent high-growth and low-share products or services. They are risky ventures that require considerable investment to grow into either a cash cow or star. The likelihood of this growth creates a measure of risk.

To apply these ideas, the strategist looks at the growth of a product or service relative to the market share of an industry leader. If a product or service is the market share leader, it will be located on the far left of the horizontal axis of Figure 3-3. High growth puts the product or service toward the top of the vertical axis of the figure. The usual prescription calls for taking revenues from cash cows to fund the growth for stars, selling off wildcats that seem too risky.

### Competitive Models

Porter (1980, 1985) has developed a competitive analysis model using industry norms. The forces that shape an industry are used to predict the success of strategy. Porter and others (Harringon, 1981) identify six key forces that shape an industry. Success is influenced by the relative power of customers and suppliers, the threat of competitors or new entrants, the competitiveness or rivalry among key players in the market, and exit barriers that keep organizations from leaving a market. Porter claims that strong forces lower financial returns for both the industry as a whole and the organizations that make up the industry.

|  |  | Stars | Wildcats |
|---|---|---|---|
| INDUSTRY GROWTH | High | Stars | Wildcats |
|  | Low | Cash cows | Dogs |
|  |  | High | Low |

RELATIVE MARKET SHARE

**Figure 3-3 ▲ Portfolio Analysis**
Adapted from D. Miller and P. H. Friesan (1978) and Nutt (1984a).

### The Creationist View

The corporate planning and other literatures contend that strategies should be created by using formal methods (e.g., Steiner, 1979; Lorange, 1980; Wheeler and Hunger, 1989). Strategic plans are then set in motion to achieve goals drawing on organizational resources to deal with priority concerns. For example, strategic planning often precedes product changes. This view has led to fashioning normative approaches to strategic planned change.

### A Consensual View

Strategies can stem from formal planning, negotiation, competition, analysis, assessing environmental opportunities, and caprice, among other things. While many organizations in a variety of industries undoubtedly become the victims (or beneficiaries) of unintended strategies, there are many forces that suggest that planned change can and should be done to create strategy. Thus, the creation of strategy is a desired outcome of the planned change processes discussed in this book.

## Policy

The policymaker often takes a multi-institutional perspective. For instance, policies are prescribed to suggest how the United States should control inflation or how a state should regulate the expansion of public utilities. Policies take on a public character. In one sense they are public strategies. However, policies are typically too narrowly conceived to be accorded this distinction. All manner of public issues are phrased in unidimensional terms. For example, periodic debates on public school funding invariably focus on how the funds are to be raised, tending to ignore how the funds are to be allocated and used. Like strategy, it is unclear if policy is created by planning or is merely assessed by an evaluation process.

The dilemma of policy information is posed nicely by Laswell (1964). The rise of techniques like policy analysis assumes that a policy exists that can be analyzed. This suggests that planning is evaluative and that policy formation is (or should be) outside the realm of the planned change process. Others go so far as to contend that proactive policy should not create objectives, because the objectives of public policy should evolve through debate (e.g., Alexander, 1977). Lindblom (1965) contends that the policy itself *must* evolve. Small disjointed and incremental steps are proposed and taken that move toward implicit objectives. According to Lindblom, formal policy planning is unwise and potentially evil.

Despite these views, contingency planning is possible, and even desirable. Various plans (policy initiatives) with certain assumptions about objectives are constantly being proposed in the public arena. Why not make them innovative and structurally sound? Wildavsky (1979) fears that selfishness, passivity, and irrationality will reduce such efforts to shambles. But, why not try? Well-posed options for public school funding or the regulation of utilities can sharpen the debate and expose vested interests, stimulate comment, and reduce caprice. Clearly, this is a role for planning in policymaking. This book will show how planned change can be used to aid in the creation of policy.

## Planned Change Projects

The planned change projects of an organization deal with subjects that are narrower in scope than strategy or policy. Nonetheless, projects of this type represent a large part of the creative activity of most organizations. Whether taking its cue from a strategic plan or from a performance gap articulated in a conventional way, such as by a routine report on costs, planned change projects represent the bulk of an organization's planning activities. By their sheer number, these activities are important and absorb most of the resources spent on planned change. Also, in many instances, planned change projects deal with vitally important issues in an organization.

Because of their importance, planned change projects will be given emphasis in this book. Procedures will be described to illustrate how to deal with several distinct types of planned change projects. These procedures differ somewhat from those used to conduct strategic planned change, but are similar to those used for policy. Prescriptions for planned change methods will be provided for both projects, used to create plans and policies, and strategy.

## ▲ HOW THE ENVIRONMENT INFLUENCES PLANNED CHANGE

Strategic, and, to a lesser extent, project planned change, are influenced by their environment. The environment intervenes to create growth opportunities, pose retrenchment demands, or to suggest the continuation of basic themes as a strategy. In strategy making, the sponsor scans the environment to cull out problems and create opportunities. As problems are dealt with several policy and/or project type efforts are initiated. The imposition of environment poses constraints and creates opportunity. Several archetype environments are described to illustrate how each can influence planned change.

### Environmental Types

Miller and Friesan (1978) and Nutt (1984a) describe environments that enhance or retard the prospects of planned change success. Prescriptions are offered for private, public, and third sector organizations and are summarized in Table 3-1.

An organization's environment can be dynamic or stable. A dynamic environment would have rapid innovation (e.g., new products or services), changes in reimbursement or budgetary allocations, and major competitors that enter or leave a market or change their strategy. Environments can also be munificent or hostile. For example, environments become "hostile" when capital markets dry up, when labor shortages occur, and when business taxes increase. Stability and favorability are key features of the outer environment.

Environments internal to an organization can also influence planned change prospects. Relevant factors include perceptions of past performance, the amount of delegation and power sharing, types of controls, both financial and human resources, esprit de corps of key administrators, the clarity and fidelity of information channels, percentage of staff specialists to total employees, differentiation (congruence among

**Table 3-1  ▲  The Environment's Impact on Planned Change**

| | Key Environment Features | | Influences of Environment on Planned Change | |
| --- | --- | --- | --- | --- |
| *Successful Archetypes* | *Outer Environment* | *Inner Environment* | *Strategic Planning* | *Project Planning* |
| 1. The franchised organization | Stable and favorable | High resources and strong leadership | Extrapolation of current ideas | Controlled by executives to be consistent with strategy |
| 2. The coping organization | Shifting and hostile | Strong intelligence and communication with delegation | Search at all levels | Analysis of all feasible alternatives |
| 3. The multiorganizational system | Shifting and becoming hostile | Delegation and planning stressed | Growth focus | Support both strategic and traditionally defined efforts |
| 4. The innovative organization | Stable and hostile | Expertise and creativity stressed | Visions of CEO | Many proactive attempts to produce innovation |
| *Unsuccessful Archetypes* | | | | |
| 1. The bold organization | Shifting and hostile (sought out) | No controls over differentiation | Risk seeking | Low direction, stressing the fashionable |
| 2. The inflexible organization | Stable and neutral, becoming hostile | Centralization of intelligence | Traditional | Discouraged and few successes |
| 3. The leaderless organization | Various | Decentralization and poor intelligence | Decentralized | Merged with decentralized strategy making |
| 4. The groping organization | Stable and hostile | Centralized and low resource availability | Grafting on historical strategy | Discouraged |

Source: Adapted from D. Miller and P. H. Friesan (1978) and Nutt (1984b).

organizational units as to their mission, methods, and styles), and conflict and the tenure of upper management. Some of these factors are set by management, for example, delegation; others are reactions to a management philosophy such as esprit de corps. Information channel clarity illustrates a factor that is partially set and partially manipulated. Finally, several of the factors, such as resource availability and conflict, pose constraints.

Organizations respond to their inner and outer environments through their planned change activities. Environments color and shape the development of these strategies and plans. Studies by Miller and Friesan have identified successful and unsuccessful tactics and strategies that were used by organizations that faced particular environments. Successful approaches can be built on and the unsuccessful approaches changed when possible, giving the organization cues on when to initiate and how to manage planned change.

## Successful Tactics

### The Franchised Organization

Organizations with a "franchise" dominate a market (see Table 3-1). For instance, some hospital clinics become national referral centers such as M. D. Anderson for cancer or the Mayo Clinic. Xerox and IBM's behavior during the 1960s illustrates firms that act as though they have a franchise. Successful organizations, acting as though they had a franchise, have a stable and favorable external environment with strong leadership, considerable resources, and a strategy rooted in past practices. In such organizations leaders become powerful because they are perceived as having created a highly successful strategic plan.

In this type of environment an "extrapolative" approach to planned change is used. Strategic planning is futile, except to operate at the margins of what the organization is currently doing. Planned change is used to modify the strategy incrementally as new opportunities arise or as the organization improves its expertise. Planned change projects are done at comparatively high reaches of the organization. To make it acceptable to management, the projects must pay homage to the organization's strategy in all plans.

### The Coping Organization

The franchise can gradually (or rapidly) lose its vitality when the environment poses new demands. The experience of the automobile industry in the '70s and early '80s illustrates this situation. Past strategies enabled growth and profits, but the external environment became unstable and then hostile. Large and luxurious automobiles were no longer affordable in the face of increased gasoline prices and rampant inflation. As soon as gas supplies stabilized, consumer demand shifted back to gas-guzzlers just as the industry had downsized. For example, the sales of Toranados, Rivieras, and Eldorados dropped by two-thirds leaving General Motors with a fleet of unsalable cars and a five-year lead time to make changes in the design. In the interim, Honda and other foreign automakers introduced upscale luxury models and began to take significant market share from General Motors, which G.M. has yet to win back. The other U.S. automakers made less extreme adjustments and fared better.

Similarly, many a "downtown" hospital today finds its environment becoming hostile as patient mix becomes largely Medicare–Medicaid, its growth is limited by regulators, and its medical staff leave to work in suburban hospitals. Under these conditions, financing can become so poor that the very survival of the hospital is threatened. The environment now resists changes, such as capital improvement or location shifts, that would draw back its customers (the physicians) and reduce its number of nonpaying users.

The internal environment is also shaped by these events. Delegation tends to be widespread so many people are involved in the search for opportunities. Keen intelligence, sensitive controls, and clear internal communications are emphasized (see Table 3-1).

Planned change in a troubled environment is incremental, adapting to opportunities as each surfaces. Strategic planned change is seldom used because the CEO's scanning replaces it. A formerly successful organization that faces a troubled environment starts many policy and projectlike planned change efforts that test and elaborate the merits of ideas from several sources.

### The Multiorganizational System

In the past few years, several multihospital systems have emerged through merger, acquisition, and the initiation of management contract services. The large individual hospital may also have grown by acquisitions, purchasing nursing homes, office buildings, laboratories, and the like. These organizations are similar to conglomerates like LTV, TRW, Textron, and Gulf and Western in the late 1960s, which attempted to shape their environments rather than respond to them.

To be successful, this type of organization attempts to compartmentalize. New activities help the organization to buffer a shifting environment that appears to be becoming more hostile. These activities are carried out to absorb uncertainty. Firms begin to differentiate horizontally (e.g., buy key suppliers). Office buildings are purchased in physician neighborhoods to connect the hospitals with a new source of physicians for their medical staff. Office rent subsidies offer incentives to the physicians to become committed to the organization's hospitals and nursing homes.

Strategy is quite important to this type of organization because of their expansionist aims. Strategic planned change is active, with periodic updates to gauge progress toward environmental safety. (All organizations would like to sink into the comfort of the franchised setting.) Project planned change is often used to support the strategic activity. This gives planned change considerable credibility. Executives in such an environment tend to see planned change as a valuable tool that can be used in several ways by the multiorganizational system.

### The Innovative Organization

Innovative firms find a niche(s) where no competition exists, new product (service) ideas, or both. Planned change is devoted to finding opportunities, such as new products with potentially good markets, that have not been exploited by others. Such organizations avoid competition. Polaroid with its instant photography is an example.

There are fewer clear counterparts to the innovative firm in the public and third sector, in part because executives have difficulty operating with enough discretion to behave in this way. Also, innovative organizations tend to be centralized with strong leadership, an anathema to public and many third sector organizations. The environment for this type of organization has moderate instability and hostility, just what many U.S. hospitals face today. In the future, the aggressive third sector organization and some public agencies may be able to act more as an innovator, particularly when a viable strategy is requisite for action. For instance, departments of natural resources have used license and other user fees to underwrite initiatives in conservation that state legislatures will not fund. The leader who has a vision of what the organization can accomplish by moving in a given direction can be successful in pursuing an innovative tactic.

The innovative organization is the project planner's paradise. Being proactive is essential so many potentially viable innovations are initiated to judge their merits. Strategic planned change is done mostly in the head of the CEO, with the help of trusted associates.

## Unsuccessful Tactics

### The Bold Organization

Bold organizations can become impulsive, which leads to taking on complex and little understood environments. These new environments are often more hostile and unstable than are those in which the organization has been operating. Such a move also creates internal demands in which projects that bring in new technology and define new ways to compete are initiated.

Hospitals adopting a malpractice self-insurance program or expanding into HMOs, long-term care, and the like create such an environment if the hospital's leadership has done little to ready the organization for these new responsibilities. The intelligence system (which is made up of the scanning, control, and communication systems) cannot deal with the new environment. Top management becomes overloaded because they cannot coordinate all the new activities.

Because attention is lost, no measure of outcome is made and the strategy may continue to emphasize failure-prone activities. Planned change projects became disjointed and responded to many conflicting signals. Projects often mirror the organization's strategy, exploring fashionable activities in a helter-skelter manner.

### The Inflexible Organization

Inflexible organizations are usually found in stable environments that see no imperatives to change. Prerogatives tend to be centralized in just a few people. Leaders see little need to change past practices because they fail to detect the hostile forces looming on the horizon. Eastern Airlines under Rickenbacker in the 1960s fit the inflexible archetype. Other examples include the state-funded mental health hospitals and their reaction to deinstitutionalization of their patients and the concomitant loss in funding. Lower levels of management in the mental health system saw the need for change, but their limited power made it impossible to present these rationales. This situation leads to high conflict and low esprit de corps.

The conservative nature of the organization makes planned change very difficult. Old procedures are emphasized, even though they are no longer useful. In this environment, project planned change is attempted, but seldom finished.

### The Leaderless Organization

Organizations often experience an era of drifting when their founder dies (e.g., Pan American Airlines) or when a key figure departs abruptly. Without leadership, the organization drifts. Work units become increasingly autonomous, due to the implicit delegation that occurs during the search for permanent leadership. Intelligence gathering declines and each unit begins to evolve a strategy independent of the others. Strategic and project planned change tend to merge and focus on resolving the perceived performance gaps in each work unit.

### The Groping Organization

Organizations with a history of success struggling through a difficult period are termed groping. Examples include the housing industry in the early 1990s.

In the groping organization, resources are usually thin and reputation is in eclipse (see Table 3-1). The organization sees the need to take decisive action but must do so facing an environment that is hostile with limited funds. Such organizations often centralize strategy making with an individual who is brought in to "turn things around." The absence of funds forces a grafting approach in which the organization can afford only minor variations on their current strategy. Projects are seldom encouraged, unless they support the "turnaround" program. The CEO has neither the time nor the energy to sanction many such efforts and lacks the funds to allow others to initiate projects.

## ▲ Key Points

1. Planned change is defined as a process with formulation, concept development, detailing, evaluation, and implementation stages. The process is carried out by a responsible manager who becomes its sponsor or by delegating to a planner (staff specialist) who facilitates one or more of the process stages.

2. Planned change processes can have strategic or nonstrategic purposes. The formation of plans and policies with a planned change process is particularly important because this type of application occurs frequently, capturing how most organizations are changed. Strategic planned change is carried out to establish new directions for an organization and initiates many policy and project efforts.

3. The features of the environment in which planned change occurs determines whether strategic efforts will arise and how strategic efforts govern projects in which planned change is attempted. Some environments encouraged planned change and others stifle it. Sponsors should make environmental assessments to form realistic expectations of the prospects for strategic and project planned change efforts.

# *Part II*

▲ ▲ ▲ ▲ ▲ ▲ ▲ ▲ ▲ ▲ ▲ ▲ ▲ ▲ ▲ ▲ ▲ ▲ ▲ ▲

# PLANNED CHANGE IN THEORY AND PRACTICE

▲ ▲ ▲ ▲ ▲ ▲ ▲ ▲ ▲ ▲ ▲ ▲ ▲ ▲ ▲ ▲ ▲ ▲ ▲ ▲ ▲ ▲ ▲ ▲ ▲

*In Part Two the distinctive features of process and technique are addressed. Process describes the phasing of activity, and technique provides ways to identify information and ideas that are needed as the process unfolds.*

*First, the stages and steps of planned change are identified as a morphology that is used to show how planned change should be carried out and how it is carried out in practice. The strong and weak points of practice are indicated. Then principles of process management are discussed, identifying process management tactics. Finally, lessons drawn from practice are offered. The tactics used by practitioners to set direction, uncover options, and implement plans, and the record of success of these tactics, is described.*

# 4 Methods of Planned Change

▲ ▲ ▲   ▲ ▲ ▲ ▲ ▲ ▲ ▲ ▲ ▲ ▲ ▲ ▲ ▲ ▲ ▲

Planned change methods have two distinguishing features: process and technique. *Process* spells out the sequence or order in which stages are to be carried out. *Technique* offers ways to carry out the activities called for in one or more of the process stages. A planned change method can be fully defined in technique and process terms. For instance, the program planning method (PPM) has five stages: (1) problem exploration, (2) knowledge exploration, (3) priority development, (4) program development, and (5) program control and evaluation (Delbecq and Van de Ven, 1971). The "nominal group" technique is used to identify problems in stage 1 and possible solutions in stage 2.

This chapter lays out several planned change methods to provide an overview of planning thought. Prescriptive methods specify what theorists believe should be done. A comparison of methods will be made to see how process and technique differ. Attention is directed toward gaps in the methods, issues ignored by the methodology, and strengths and weaknesses. Also, the method prescriptions will be compared to what organizations actually do when carrying out a planned change. Case studies will be used to illustrate distinctive practice types. The cases provide "exemplars" that illustrate the sequence of steps and techniques frequently applied by practitioners. Gaps between prescription and practice identify the strengths and weaknesses in current practice and suggest ways to improve the conduct of planned change.

## ▲ SOME DISTINCTIVE PERSPECTIVES

There are many planned change methods in the literature, created by architects, urban planners, social and behavioral scientists, engineers, and systems scientists, to name just a few. As one should expect, these methods are quite different. Because of their number, no attempt will be made to summarize all available planned change methods. Instead, discussion will concentrate on profiling and then comparing methods drawn from four distinct perspectives: research and development, problem solving, social change, and design. These methods are compared in Table 4-1 to reveal differences in approach.

### Research and Development

The research and development or diffusion approach is typical of the methods taught in many engineering schools (e.g., Asimow, 1962; Hubka, 1982). The process moves through an orderly sequence, beginning with problem identification and moving to solution development and finally to diffusion and adoption by users. Initiative rests with the planner. The process has five stages: (1) basic research, (2) applied research, (3) development and testing of prototypes, (4) mass production, and (5) packaging (Table 4-1).

The research stages are used to conduct scientific inquiry, investigate the problem, and/or gather data. The development stage engages invention, design, testing, and evaluation activities. Production and packaging consider manufacturing or service process steps and the marketing and promotion of the product or service. Dif-

Table 4-1 ▲ Stages in Distinct Types of Planning Methods

| Research and Development | Social Change | Problem Solving | Design |
|---|---|---|---|
| 1. Research (basic definition and applied) | 1. Awareness | 1. Need | 1. Problem |
| 2. Development | 2. Interest | 2. Development of relationships | 2. Objectives setting |
| 3. Production and packaging | 3. Evaluation | 3. Diagnosis | 3. Synthesis |
| 4. Diffusion | 4. Trial | 4. Intentions | 4. Analysis |
| 5. Adoption | 5. Adoption | 5. Translation | 5. Optimization |
| | | 6. Generalization and stabilization | 6. Selection |
| | | 7. Termination | 7. Implementation |

fusion can deal with providing information, demonstrations, trials, pilot programs, training, and helping or nurturing. It can inform or create widespread awareness. A demonstration or trial stage is often used in diffusion that stresses pilot testing. Adoption involves installation and institutionalization of the plan.

The last stage is dominated by users. For instance, a new drug moves from the laboratory to the drug company's production facilities and finally to use. Use is created by the drug company's "detail men" who attempt to convince the physician (the user) of its merits. The physician is approached using rational arguments (cost or pharmacological benefits). If convinced, the drug is adopted, becoming institutionalized. In the research and development model, the user or target group is passive. If adoption appears logical, it is assumed that users will accept the plan. For example, in education a user population is acted on and influenced, often with a mass dissemination.

The research and development model stresses the scientific development of ideas. It is widely used in industry, agriculture, defense and space, and education. The process relies on a rational sequence of activities, which moves from discovery to use. Stages are divided according to major actors: (1) the researchers, (2) the producing organizations, and (3) the users.

The early stages in the research and development approach are carried out by specialists. This type of process is planner directed because signals flow from the process to a passive client. The focus is on the planner as he or she devises a solution to the problem. As a result, emphasis is placed on coordination among planners, researchers, and engineers.

## Social Change

Social change theorists, led by the pioneering work of Lewin (1958), advocate focusing on the individual or the group to implement the change sought. The process proposed by the social change school was based on the stages individuals go through as they accept a plan. Some label these stages differently and others disagree on ordering. The process described here typifies the way the social change process has been conceptualized.

A five-step process is often suggested: (1) awareness, (2) interest, (3) evaluation, (4) trial, and (5) adoption (Rodgers, 1962). The process is shown in Table 4-1. The *awareness* stage is used to expose the target of change to new ideas and possibilities. The target is passive during stage I.

The *interest* stage is used to get the target to see the value of the idea in the prospective user's setting. When the prospective user begins to ask questions about application, involvement and thereby interest increases. Prospective users may become antagonistic or supportive, based on how they perceive the answers provided to their application questions.

*Evaluation,* in the social change approach, is a "mental trial." The individual considers the plan as it appears to function in current and future circumstances the target believes are (or would be) relevant to his or her situation. Evaluation can range from the implicit to the explicit so this decision may or may not be informed. The goal is to coax the target into a commitment to try.

The *trial* stage is engaged if the evaluation is favorable. The trial applies the idea on a small scale to demonstrate value or provisionally installs the plan pending a performance assessment. In the *adoption* stage, a decision is made to accept or reject the plan.

The social change process stresses several types of information sources: introspection, interaction, the actions of rivals' mass media, and research, which can be translated to practice. Introspection dominates the awareness stage. During the interest stage, interaction, such as contact with an expert and with others, particularly colleagues and rivals, provide information. Evaluations are introspective. Trials rely on objective information.

The social change approach was originally derived from studies in agriculture done by rural sociologists (Havelock, 1973). The process of successful innovation served as a model to extract stages for the planned change process. The means to form a plan are left implicit. The method stresses sources of information that will move clients to adopt a plan. The client in this process is expected to react to plausible/rational arguments for change, launching a process to adapt readymade plans or to modify existing practices.

## Problem Solving

A problem-solving process uses extraindividual sources to find solutions. Key proponents have been Maier (1970) and Simon and Newell (1970). The process captures the relationship between the problem solver and a client. The problem solver can be an internal or external consultant skilled at bringing about change, often called a change agent. The agent is a "sender" and the client a "receiver." The sender engages in diffusion activities and the receiver in adoption reactions. The relationships between sender and receiver during this process are depicted in Figure 4-1. The seven stages in this process are (1) need, (2) change relationship, (3) diagnosis, (4) intentions, (5) transforming intent to action, (6) generalization and stabilization, and (7) termination as shown in Table 4-1.

The *need stage* is used to determine what must happen to create stress in the system so change is possible. People are made aware of problems that cause

Sender                                                    Receiver

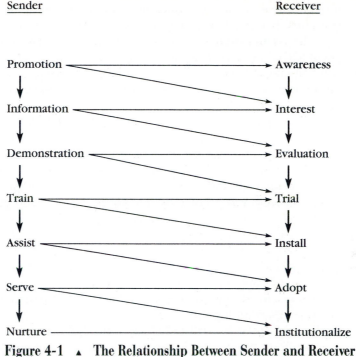

**Figure 4-1** ▲ **The Relationship Between Sender and Receiver in Problem Solving**

Adapted from Havelock (1973).

tension in the organization. After problems have been recognized, the prospects for improvement are presented that reinforce the need for change. Change agents present both problem and change prospect types of information.

In stage II, the change agent takes pains to establish a positive relationship with the client. Needs are communicated after trust and mutual understanding are created. Trial working periods are helpful in this relationship-building process.

The *diagnosis stage* begins with the collection of detailed information and ends with its analysis and interpretation. The interpretation may be rejected, causing more data to be collected and analyzed, or negotiations may develop to find a target of inquiry acceptable to the client. Ultimately the client may be faced with a diagnosis that changes his or her notions about the needed scope of effort.

In the *intentions stage,* the diagnostic insights are translated into alternative solution concepts. These options may be innovative and/or threatening. The change agent retains as many potentially viable ideas as possible as he or she moves to stage V.

The *translation* of intentions to action puts plans into operational terms, adding specifics to each alternative. The client must be shown how each option can be made viable in practice to avoid scuttling the plan.

The *generalization and stabilization stages* enlarge the scope of application of the plan and work out operating problems. Once a viable plan gains a foothold, it often spreads by sheer momentum. In other cases, operational problems must be overcome before adoption becomes voluntary.

The *termination stage* is reached when the plan has penetrated all relevant client activity. In this stage, dependency of the client on the change agent is gradually reduced and normal operations are begun. The change agent severs client ties but remains available as a consultant to help in making minor modifications and to fine-tune operations.

The problem-solving approach focuses on the client. It is drawn from the social psychology literature and stresses ways to coax clients to adopt plans. The client can be active or passive. If passive, the solution is presented by a change agent and shaped by both the client's desires and prescriptions. Less often, the solution is custom-made to fit the client's specifications. Active clients take over the planned change process and become its sponsor, monitoring and guiding planning efforts.

## Design

Design methods (Simon, 1969; Nadler, 1981; Nadler and Hibino, 1990), like the research and development approach, stress the development of solution details. In all other ways, the design and the research and development approaches are markedly different. Discounting semantic disagreements and minor sequence differences, a method proposed by Hall (1977) is typical of many design approaches. This design method calls for a process with seven stages and numerous steps and substeps that have time relationships. The stages are (1) problem definition, (2) objectives and criteria, (3) systems synthesis, (4) systems analysis, (5) optimization of each option, (6) selection, and (7) implementation (Table 4-1).

The stages are linear, each building on the information provided in the previous one. The problem definition stage creates information about needs and the environment. This information is used to specify values useful in setting objectives. Objectives provide a basis to derive criteria to judge performance. The objective guides systems synthesis in a deductive manner. This stage invents, collects, and synthesizes alternative solutions to the problem defined in stage 1. Systems analysis is used to decide the pros and cons of each alternative, consistent with the objectives identified in stage 2. These conclusions are used by the optimization stage to enhance the positive features and ameliorate the negative features discovered in analysis. With this information one alternative is selected and an implementation plan devised to install the solution.

Program planning describes how the various types of projects to be pursued are identified. The project planning phase details a solution to a specific problem, terminating when a system has been defined for further development. This phase provides a way to implement a plan, often including specifications and drawings. Production planning lays out the service or production system that is to create the product or service. It includes buildings, equipment, service delivery procedures, or production lines. Distribution planning considers how the product or service will reach its customers or users. Marketing and demonstrations are often used. Operations or consumption planning deals with optimizing the use of existing capabilities, such as use of service facilities and equipment in off hours. Finally, plans are drawn to retire the system. The phaseout of one plan to make room for another can be quite important if one is to use resources wisely.

The array of stages and steps is shown in Figures 4-2 and 4-3. Figure 4-2 shows the morphology and Figure 4-3 depicts the logic of the process as it moves through time to refine the plan. The morphology shows how information plays into each stage of the process and how the stages draw on specific issues depicted by the phases. The stages depict the logic of the process, which Hall calls the "fine structure." Phases depict the time dimension, called the "coarse structure." The planner moves across a given phase in the coarse structure by carrying out the stages of planning. A given project may activate any of the cells (row-column interactions in Figure 4-2) in the morphology, drawing on one or several information sources (the dimension into the page in Figure 4-2). The morphology permits the planner to distinguish between project and program planning and between operational planning and planning for retirement or phaseout. The morphology also describes how a large, multiphased project would be carried out in practice.

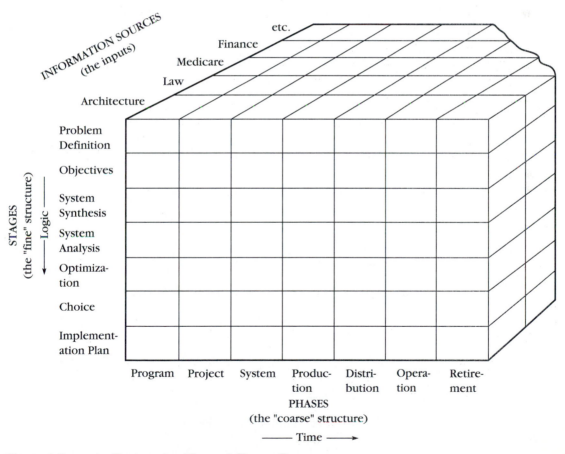

**Figure 4-2 ▲ An Engineering Planned Change Process**
Reprinted from Hall (1977). Copyright ©1977, IEEE.

(a) Cornucopia model

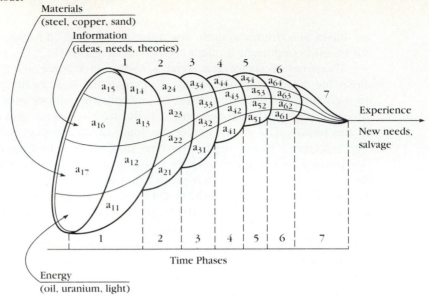

Materials
(steel, copper, sand)

Information
(ideas, needs, theories)

Experience

New needs, salvage

Time Phases

Energy
(oil, uranium, light)

(b) Hyperfine structure

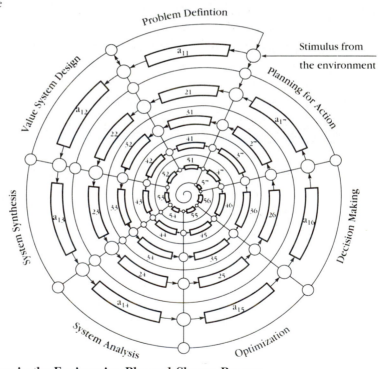

**Figure 4-3 ▲ Steps in the Engineering Planned Change Process**
Reprinted from Hall (1977). Copyright ©1977, IEEE.

Figure 4-3 illustrates how specific cells in the three-dimensional morphological box can be mapped into a specific planning process. The cornucopia shows the iterative and converging nature of the proposed process. It depicts how the process should move from general to specific concerns. The two-dimensional representation in Figure 4-3 is called the "hyperfine structure." It is created by turning the cornucopia on its transverse axis and showing planning activities as tasks, assigned an "a" and a subscript. The a's shown in Figure 4-3 depict specific tasks. For instance, "$a_{365}$" concerns choice in the development phase concerning legal issues.

The process is used to track needed tasks for complex problems. It aids the planner in plotting out a process that can discover (or uncover) needed actions and information. In addition to complexity reduction, the process acts as a filing system to store, and later integrate, across stages.

## ▲ THE PLANNED CHANGE MORPHOLOGY

To make comparisons of planned change methods, a generic process was constructed that captures the range of activities called for by planned change methods (see Figure 4-4). A number of planned change methods, like those described in the preceding section, were reviewed to identify stages. Activities required by each method were distilled. This distillation suggested formulation, concept development, detailing, evaluation, and implementation as process stages. This same test was applied to identify the steps required to carry out a given process stage. This assessment revealed that steps of search, synthesis, and analysis were typically used to provide the information required by each process stage. Combining the stages and steps creates the morphology shown in Figure 4-4. The planned change morphology describes the form and structure of planned change, identifying what should be considered when carrying out a planned change effort.

The morphology has two purposes. First, it identifies how planning *should* be carried out by enumerating the types of activity that are required. The prescription implied by the morphology is based on consensus or a Kantian warrant (see Chapter 2). A composite of the views of individuals who have proposed methods for planned change was used to fashion the process of planned change used in this book. Second, the morphology will be used to profile how planned change is carried out in practice and how various methods that appear in the literature propose to carry out planned change. The prescriptive and descriptive profiles that result will be used to reveal what is done, which will be compared to what is recommended. This comparison provides insights into the strengths and weaknesses of practice and avenues for improvement.

### Planning Stages

The stages of planned change identify bundles of activity that are essential to engage in planning *and* change. In the discussion that follows, each stage is briefly described along with techniques that are useful in identifying, combining, and selecting information called for by each stage.

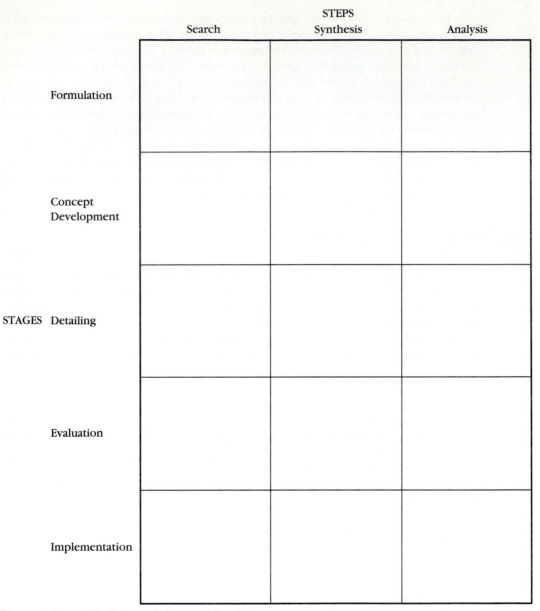

Figure 4-4    ▲    The Planned Change Morphology

### *The Formulation Stage*

The formulation stage is carried out to determine direction for a planned change effort. To establish direction, one must verify and clarify problems that initiated action, applying the insights gained in problem exploration to identify an objective that will guide the effort.

Need and/or opportunities that provoke action are *stipulated* by the sponsor considering the views of stakeholders and other claimants, such as users/customers, judicial renderings, industry associations, and regulators. These stipulations take shape as key players pose essential conditions and demands. These stipulations come from many individuals who have viewpoints that can be contradictory, self-serving, symptomatic of deeper concerns, or misleading. As a result, steps are taken to tease out the problems that are embedded in these needs and opportunities. The priority problems that are identified specify an arena of action that the organization will address. For example, the Environmental Protection Agency may claim that a firm engages in environmentally dangerous dumping of waste materials. This claim is interpreted by the union, management, the board, and others to pose needs that the company should address. Similarly, a trade journal may disclose a new product, suggesting a new initiative by a competitor. Key people in the firm may identify opportunities to beat the competitor and close off a market previously overlooked.

To translate diverse need and/or opportunity into coherent problem statements, the sponsor gathers information by applying planning techniques. Table 4-2 summarizes useful techniques that are described more fully in Chapter 10. The sponsor can respond to these problem statements in several ways, depending on the expectations for the plan. The context of action can remain "problem reactive," attempting to solve priority problems. Well managed planned change efforts call for a more proactive approach, in which objectives are set to guide the search for solutions.

### The Concept Development Stage

The concept development stage is used to create options that respond to the problems and objectives identified in the formulation stage. Beginning with Dewey (1910), most planned change theorists call for multiple options to be developed. The competition among solution ideas is thought to improve the plan that is ultimately adopted. Note how this view is supported by the warrants of Kantian and Hegelian inquiring systems (see Chapter 2).

A second demand posed by concept development is innovation. At least one of the options should represent a new idea, one that has not been previously used by the organization. Some pose a stronger test, calling for "radical innovation," seeking ideas that will be new to the industry. Radical innovation is credited with giving many organizations a decisive advantage in the marketplace. Michelin dramatically increased its market by introducing radial tires, a complete break with the bias tire design used throughout the tire industry. Xerox ran over companies making carbon paper for copying with its Xerography dry copy product.

Techniques useful in fashioning both innovative and conventional options are summarized in Table 4-2 and described more fully in Chapter 11. The sponsor initiates activity in which these techniques are applied, such as hiring consultants or assigning staff specialists. In other instances, a sponsor may wish to control what is done with minimal disclosure or commitments to act, carrying out these techniques without assistance.

**Table 4-2** ▲ **Planning Techniques and Their Relationship to the Planning Process**

| Stages in the Planning Process | Planning Techniques |
| --- | --- |
| Formulation | Exception reports |
| | Brainstorming (Osborn, 1957) |
| | Nominal group technique (Delbecq et al., 1986) |
| | Delphi surveys (Dalky, 1967) |
| | Brainwriting (Gueschka et al., 1975; Nutt, 1984b) |
| | Function expansion (Nadler, 1970a; 1981) |
| | Kiva (Nutt, 1989a) |
| Concept Development | Morphology (Zwicky, 1969) |
| | Synectics (Gordon, 1961) |
| | Relevance trees |
| | Check lists |
| | Attribute listing |
| | Relational algorithm |
| | Lateral thinking (de Bono, 1972) |
| | Input-output analysis |
| | Scenarios |
| Detailing | Block diagram (Wilson and Wilson, 1970) |
| | Flow charting (Gregory, 1966) |
| | Systems design (Nadler, 1970a, b; 1981) |
| | Graphical analysis (Watts, 1966) |
| | Interpretative structural modeling (Warfield, 1976) |
| | Operations research |
| | General systems |
| | Systems analysis (Quade and Boucher, 1968) |
| | PERT/CPM |
| Evaluation | Subjective techniques (e.g., ranking and rating) |
| | Assumptional analysis (Mason and Mitroff, 1981) |
| | Multiattribute utilities (Huber, 1980; Nutt, 1989a) |
| | Decision trees (Raiffa, 1970) |
| | Elimination by aspects |
| | Balance sheet (Janis, 1989) |
| | Stakeholder analysis (Freeman, 1984) |
| | Field experiments (Cook and Campbell, 1979) |
| | Multiple regression |
| | Operations research |
| | Simulation |
| | Operations research models |
| Implementation | Change agent |
| | Unfreeze-refreeze (Lewin, 1958) |
| | T-groups (Greiner, 1970) |
| | Participation-cooptation (Mayo, 1933) |
| | Consortium (Nutt, 1979b) |
| | Game scenario (Bardach, 1977; Nutt, 1982a) |
| | Edicts and power (Dalton, 1970a) |
| | Persuasion (Parsons, 1960) |

### The Detailing Stage

The detailing stage is carried out for both refinement and elaborative purposes. Potentially viable options are developed to indicate how to put them into practice. Detailing identifies what procedures, training, and the like are required to be specific about plan operations. These activities are often very time consuming, so just a few options are carried forward to this stage of the process. Solution concepts in stage II are winnowed with just a few selected for further refinement.

To sketch the operating features of a plan, "constructive" techniques are used (see Table 4-2). These techniques, described in Chapter 12, include systems design and analysis and general systems theory. To refine a plan, "interrogative" techniques, such as simulation and other mathematical techniques, are applied to reveal ways that the plan can be improved. These techniques allow its user to explore how changes in assumptions, resources, and the like influence the efficiency, effectiveness, and acceptability of the plan. Interrogative techniques are also discussed in Chapter 12.

### The Evaluation Stage

The evaluation stage is used to assess the options with several criteria to judge the fitness of each option. Evaluation identifies the costs, benefits, acceptance, and other factors that influence the adoptability of each option that survives stage III. Evaluation information provides a basis to select among the options or to rule out all of them as unacceptable. In Chapter 15, techniques that can provide evaluation information will be described. (See Table 4-2 for a summary.)

### The Implementation Stage

Implementation is applied to devise a social environment in which change can occur. Steps that encourage plan acceptance are considered. Acceptance can be promoted by using client representatives in planning groups or by canvassing clients early in the planned change process. These techniques stress cooptation and partial involvement of claimants and stakeholders (e.g., Delbecq, Van de Ven, and Gustafson, 1986). They are applied as an integral part of the earlier process stages.

Organizational design (OD) techniques approach implementation as a housing for the first four process stages. Each calls for a "change agent" that guides stakeholders and users through a process that alters their objectives, social ties, and self-esteem and reinforces the positive aspects of the evolving plan.

Edict and persuasion techniques are often used to create change. Persuasion marshals arguments to adopt the change, dramatizing its benefits. An edict prescribes the behavior necessary to implement the plan. These techniques are summarized in Table 4-2. In Chapters 7, 8, and 9 a scheme to manage change by selecting appropriate techniques and procedures is described. The scheme provides rules that the sponsor can use to select among unilateral action, persuasion, ad hoc planning groups, or change agents for particular types of planned change implementation.

## Planning Steps

The planning *steps* of search, synthesis, and analysis are performed for *each* stage of the process.

### The Search Step

Search is used systematically to gather information pertinent to one or more process stages. For instance, search procedures can be used to identify problem statements in stage I or possible solutions in stage II. Techniques that promote creativity aid the search for new or innovative ideas in stage II using techniques such as synectics (Gordon, 1971) and lateral thinking (De Bono, 1970). Obtaining statements of need from clients, soliciting expert opinions, or discussing problems with responsible administrators can be used to search for information in stage I. Techniques such as nominal group technique (NGT), brainwriting, and the nominal-interacting technique are often used to promote search.

### The Synthesis Step

The synthesis step is used to identify generalizations, patterns, and themes in the information produced by the search step. After search, this information is often redundant and lacks organization. Synthesis techniques assemble or put together the information into a relational format. For example, morphological expansion (Zwicky, 1968) identifies novel components for a system that can be combined in new ways to create options in stage II.

### The Analysis Step

Analysis is applied to test a synthesized result for a given stage. At each stage of the process, some form of ranking and sorting is used to prune ideas to a manageable number. For example, paired comparisons and other ranking techniques can be used to select among objectives or prioritize problem lists, in stage I; options in stage II; aspects of plans, such as staffing procedures, in stage III. In stage IV, a more detailed exploration of the relationship among important concepts or variables is often required, and more elaborate kinds of analysis, such as stakeholder analysis or decision trees, can be applied. The analysis step in stage IV may require something as elaborate as statistical analysis—to verify cause and effect relationships in proposed solutions—or something as simple as a vote.

## ▲ EXAMINING PRESCRIPTIVE PLANNED CHANGE METHODS

In the discussion that follows, the morphology (Figure 4-4) will be used to contrast three planned change methods. The methods selected represent three distinctly different views of planned change. Comparisons point out how the emphasis and assumptions in process and preferred techniques create distinctive strengths and weaknesses for these methods. This assessment is used to justify an approach that combines the best features of each method.

## The Program Planning Method: A Behavioral Approach

In Figure 4-5 the approach used by the program planning method or PPM (Delbecq and Van de Ven, 1971) is summarized using the morphology in Figure 4-4.

PPM uses planning groups made up of users or clients, content experts, and administrators who control resources. The results from each group are passed to the next group by representatives. Clients present priority problems to the experts who, in turn, aid clients in presenting possible solutions to resource controllers.

Phase 1 of PPM, "problem identification," corresponds to stage I, *formulation*. The nominal group technique (NGT) is used in phase 1 to help clients identify their priority problems. First, problem lists are written down individually by the clients. This corresponds to a search process. Each person then contributes a problem from their list, one at a time. After all problems have been recorded, they are discussed by the clients. These two steps provide some *synthesis*. Following discussion, the clients select high-priority problems. A "rank-discuss-rerank" process is used to specify these priorities, which correspond to step 3, *analysis*. In *concept development,* the nominal group technique is used by an expert group to list solutions to the priority problems, after client representatives have interpreted their problem definitions to the experts. Search, synthesis, and analysis techniques are provided by the NGT and its ranking procedures.

In PPMs phase 3, "priority development," client and expert representatives present their solution ideas to an administrator that controls needed resources. The administrator is asked to verify the feasibility of the solutions. This corresponds to an *implementation* tactic (stage V). In PPM, emphasis is placed on gaining acceptance. Early involvement enhances the prospects of acceptance. Thus, phase 3 of PPM is used to identify the reservations and qualifications to the solution (search) so that adjustment (synthesis) can be made to permit administrators to assess (analyze) the concept to determine if they can endorse it.

Phase 4 of PPM, "program development," is identified but no techniques are described, suggesting that any technique for detailing a solution component can be adopted. PPMs phase 4 corresponds to the *detailing* stage.

Phase 5 of PPM is "program control and evaluation." Representatives from the client, expert, and resource control groups are assembled to hear the planner's report. The report details features of the proposed solution. The link between the solutions and the priority problem is described, pointing out necessary compromises. The key criterion in this evaluation is solution acceptance. Thus, plan quality is judged by its implementation prospects. Phase 4 in PPM provides an *evaluation* structure that, in part, corresponds to stage IV in the generic model. No evaluation techniques were described.

## Work Systems Design: A Systems Approach

Like others with a systems orientation, Nadler's (1970, 1981) approach attempts to create "what should (or could) be" a new scheme. Solution quality is emphasized, which can be contrasted with the emphasis on acceptance in PPM. Figure 4-6 profiles the method. Note that the steps unfold linearly, moving through each stage in order and performing the steps required in that stage sequentially.

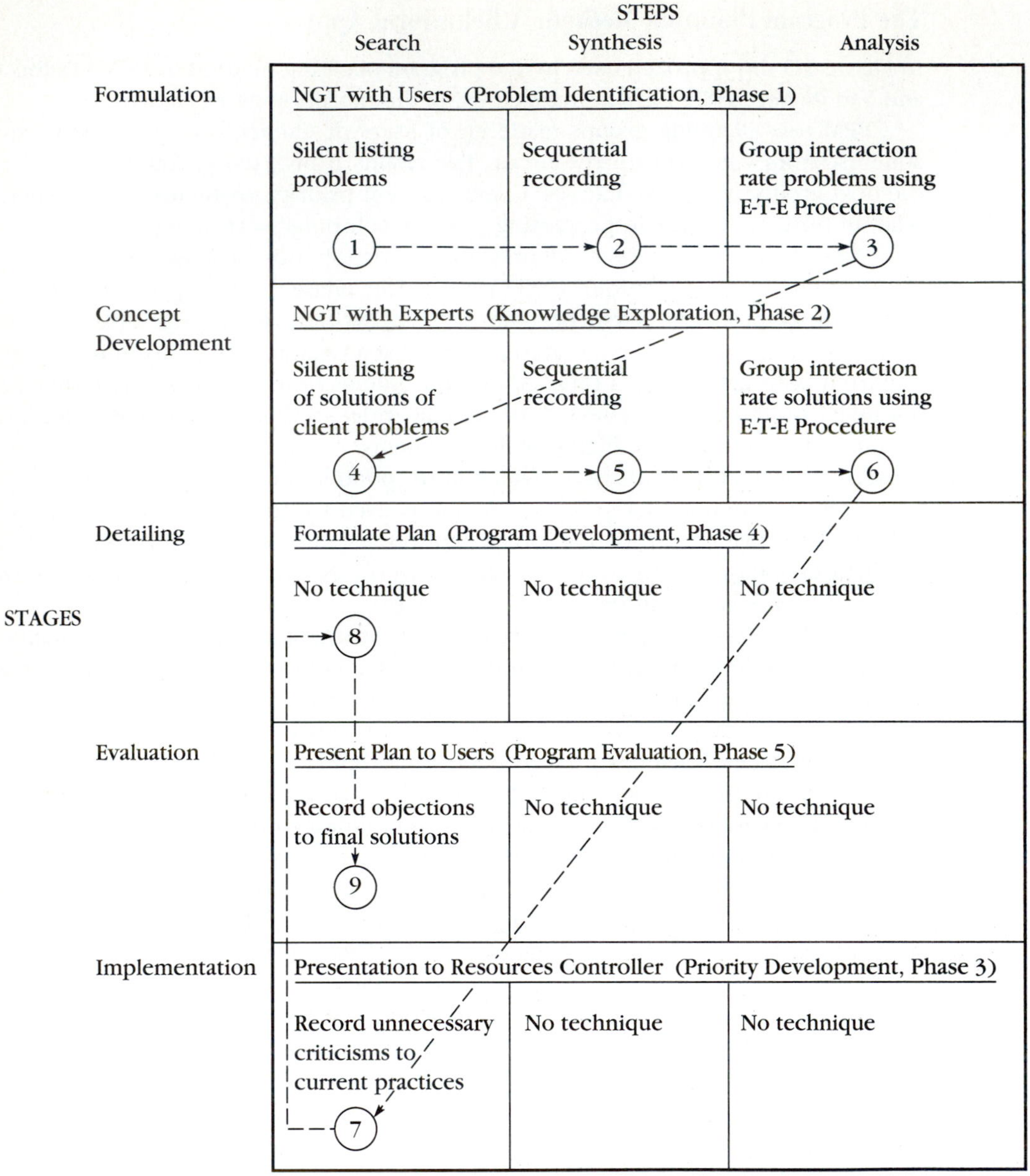

STEPS

|  | Search | Synthesis | Analysis |
|---|---|---|---|
| **Formulation** | NGT with Users (Problem Identification, Phase 1) | | |
|  | Silent listing problems ① | Sequential recording ② | Group interaction rate problems using E-T-E Procedure ③ |
| **Concept Development** | NGT with Experts (Knowledge Exploration, Phase 2) | | |
|  | Silent listing of solutions of client problems ④ | Sequential recording ⑤ | Group interaction rate solutions using E-T-E Procedure ⑥ |
| **Detailing** | Formulate Plan (Program Development, Phase 4) | | |
|  | No technique ⑧ | No technique | No technique |
| **Evaluation** | Present Plan to Users (Program Evaluation, Phase 5) | | |
|  | Record objections to final solutions ⑨ | No technique | No technique |
| **Implementation** | Presentation to Resources Controller (Priority Development, Phase 3) | | |
|  | Record unnecessary criticisms to current practices ⑦ | No technique | No technique |

STAGES

Note: Iteration (repeating stages and steps) often occurs.
One iteration is described.

**Figure 4-5 ▲ The Morphology for PPM**

72

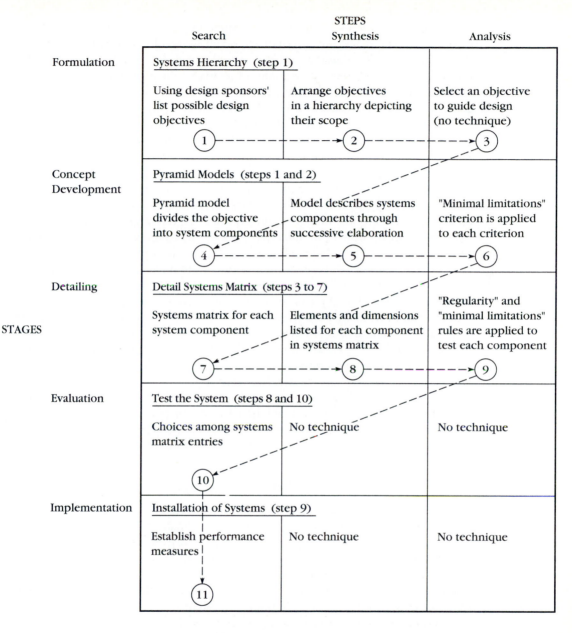

Note: Iteration (repeating stages and steps) often occurs.
One iteration is described.

**Figure 4-6 ▲ The Morphology for the Systems Approach**

Nadler uses a ten-step process: determine objectives, develop an ideal system, gather information, suggest alternatives, select workable system, formulate system details, review system design, test the system, install the system, and establish performance measures. Step 1 determines objectives, which correspond to the *formulation* stage. The sponsors and/or beneficiaries of the project are assembled in a group to identify a hierarchy of possible *objectives*. Each objective in the hierarchy indicates a system that could be designed, thereby defining the scope of a possible project. The group or the sponsor selects the most appropriate system, defined by its objective. *Search* is conducted by brainstorming possible objectives. *Synthesis* occurs when these objectives are arranged in a hierarchy. The sponsor uses *analysis* to select an appropriate scope for the project, which defines its objective.

Also, in step 1, *functional components* are identified by building a pyramid model to elaborate the objective selected for large, complex systems. The pyramid model breaks down the objective (or system) to identify its components. The procedures used to build pyramid models correspond to the concept stage.

A description of each component using a system matrix is developed in step 2. The matrix defines each component in terms of its objectives, outputs, sequence, inputs, environment, and physical and human catalysts along four dimensions: current and future features, performance measures, and control systems. A component is designed by filling in the matrix. Completing the systems matrix corresponds to the *search* and *synthesis* activities. An "ideal system" is constructed by eliminating all unnecessary restrictions or constraints from the systems matrix. Eliminating limitations corresponds to the *analysis* step.

Steps 3 to 7 can be compared to the detail design stage. The systems matrix is used to elaborate further the solution by adding pertinent information to cells in the matrix. Steps 8 and 10 are related to evaluation, and step 9 deals with implementation. Little in the way of techniques is provided.

## Action Research: An OD Approach

Action research is one of several organizational design or OD approaches proposed for planned change. The OD approach seeks to make full use of the most up-to-date innovations by modifying or managing the organization's climate. Like most OD approaches, action research was evolved from Lewin's (1958) three stages of change: (1) unfreezing, (2) moving, and (3) refreezing. Unfreezing creates problem awareness in the client, moving provides a way to solve the problem, and refreezing reinforces the positive features of the new system.

Action research approach has ten steps (French, 1969), which are summarized as follows:

Step 1    Perception of problems by sponsor
Step 2    Selection of change agent
Step 3    Data gathering (using one or several standard instruments devised by OD interventionists)
Step 4    Preliminary diagnosis by change agent
Step 5    Data presentation to client

Step 6      Client and change agent jointly diagnose problems
Step 7      Goals and objectives set jointly
Step 8      Action planning
Step 9      Performance assessment
Step 10    Client review

A recycle can occur after step 10, repeating steps 4, 8, and 9 until acceptable performance is observed. Action research is profiled using the morphology in Figure 4-7.

Step 1 in action research corresponds to formulation-search cell in the morphology. Problem awareness arises through exception reports or other mechanisms of recognition in the organization. When a potential sponsor senses that a problem must be attended to, the process moves to stage V, implementation.

Implementation is emphasized in action research. Search in stage V corresponds to step 2 in action research. During problem recognition, the sponsor selects a change agent, from within or outside the organization, who will guide the planned change process.

Synthesis in stage V is based on data gathering. Three techniques are used: interviews (e.g., Cannell and Kahn, 1953), questionnaires (Likert, 1967), and observation (Selltiz et al., 1959). The survey approach often uses several standard instruments. For instance, Likert inquires about performance characteristics and motivating forces, as well as communications, interactions, decision making, goal setting, and control processes. Some of these issues can be elaborated and others skipped, depending on the application. A representative sample (or all) of the people who control implementation prospects are asked to complete the questionnaires.

Interviews by the change agent have both set and open-ended questions. The interview, like the questionnaires, may seek specific detailed information. These structured and unstructured interviews are used to allow members of the organization to express their views about needs and what should be done about them (Margulis and Wallace, 1973).

Process observation is used to watch groups in action to see who interjects and whether questions are asked or assertions are made. The information helps to assess the organization's climate. Data gathering has two purposes: identify key actors that must be influenced and seek out viable solutions held by these actors. According to Huse (1975), the change agent should

1. Identify people's problems with change.
2. Determine who is involved and his or her influence.
3. Identify his or her prerogatives and resource.
4. Lay out preliminary objectives.

Margulis and Wallace (1973) call this process "organizational sensing." It seeks to identify widespread notions about how well the organization is functioning, important problems, and people's ideas of how to solve them. "Sensing sessions" are held by supervisors spanning several levels under their control to draw out views on these issues followed by problem-solving sessions.

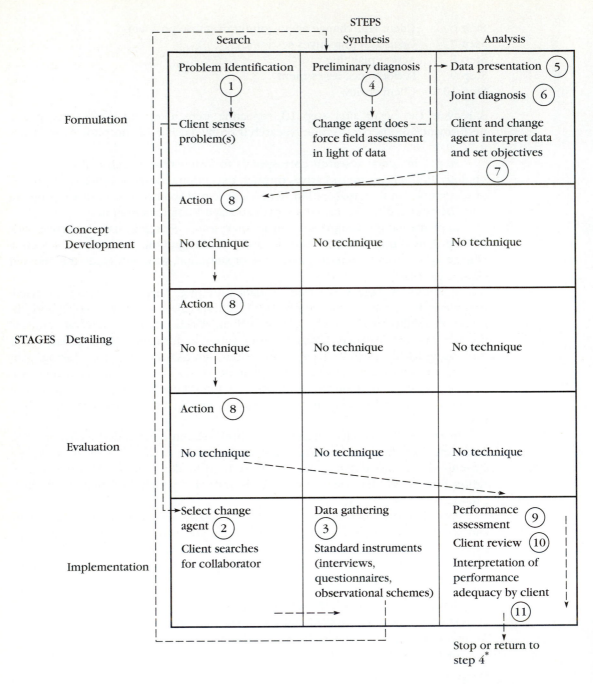

STEPS

|  | Search | Synthesis | Analysis |
|---|---|---|---|
| **Formulation** | Problem Identification ①<br><br>Client senses problem(s) | Preliminary diagnosis ④<br><br>Change agent does force field assessment in light of data | Data presentation ⑤<br>Joint diagnosis ⑥<br>Client and change agent interpret data and set objectives ⑦ |
| **Concept Development** | Action ⑧<br><br>No technique | No technique | No technique |
| **Detailing** | Action ⑧<br><br>No technique | No technique | No technique |
| **Evaluation** | Action ⑧<br><br>No technique | No technique | No technique |
| **Implementation** | Select change agent ②<br>Client searches for collaborator | Data gathering ③<br>Standard instruments (interviews, questionnaires, observational schemes) | Performance assessment ⑨<br>Client review ⑩<br>Interpretation of performance adequacy by client ⑪ |

STAGES

Stop or return to step 4[*]

\* Note: Cycling is between steps 4, 8, and 9 after the first interaction.

**Figure 4-7 ▲ The Morphology for "Action Research"**

76

Table 4-3 ▲ Attributes of a Problem Solver

| Task Roles | Facilitating Roles |
|---|---|
| *Information Giver* | *Harmonizer* |
| Offers facts and generalizations | Mediates differences between members |
| *Information Seeker* | *Encourager* |
| Asks for needed facts and generalizations | Accepts diverse points of view |
| *Opinion Giver* | *Participation Seeker* |
| Offers beliefs about alternatives | Keeps communication of all going |
| *Clarifier* | *Recorder* |
| Shows or illuminates relationships among ideas to synthesize | Record keeper |
| *Elaborator* | *Compromiser* |
| Illustrates ideas with examples | Seek to resolve conflicts |

Source: Adapted from Havelock (1973) and Nutt (1984b).

Sensing groups are formed and observed to find people that play task and facilitator roles (see Table 4-3). The change agent selects people that have either task and facilitative abilities because these behaviors are needed to build and maintain effective problem solving in a planning group. Devices such as the "organizational mirror" use a reference organization as a benchmark to compare performance with internal norms, so the organization can better judge its own performance.

Next, the action research process reverts to the formulation stage search step in which a preliminary diagnosis is made. A technique called "force field analysis" is used (Lewin, 1951). The technique graphs the influence of those opposing and favoring a given type of change with two sets of vectors. These forces can represent the viewpoints of people, work units, or even organizations. The length of the vector represents the magnitude of force behind each point of view. To avoid stalemates, two tactics can be used. People can be persuaded to drop their objections or positive forces can increase the commitment to change.

In the formulation-analysis cell, action research carries out three steps: data presentation (step 5), joint diagnosis (step 6), and objective setting (step 7). The change agent withholds his or her diagnosis and reviews data from step 3 with the client. This leads to a joint diagnosis of the problem through collaboration and discussion. From this discussion, objectives for change are set. The client must feel he or she has "ownership" over the direction chosen.

Action, step 8, spans the concept, detailing, and evaluation stages, as shown in Figure 4-7. The "action" is assumed to arise spontaneously, be known to those interviewed, or be provided "off-the-shelf" by the change agent. No techniques are offered.

Action research terminates in the implementation stage-analysis step, through performance assessment (step 9) and client review (step 10). Either a demonstration or actual field test provides the assessment. The client is left to interpret the performance adequacy, perhaps cycling through steps 4, 8, and 9 to revise the plan.

### Comparing the Planned Change Methods

Comparing the PPM, work system, and action research procedures in Figures 4-5, 4-6, and 4-7 reveals several interesting differences in their methods. Each of these methods has both strengths and weaknesses. Each has an insightful process and interesting techniques, and each ignores or treats superficially the requirements of several planned change stages. Distinctions arise from the order and selectivity of activity.

Planned change methods move through the stages and steps in the morphology by following *unique paths*. These paths, which identify the order of required activities, define the process used by a given planned change method. PPM sets the stage for detailing, which is the last activity in the process. Detailing becomes relevant when the ramifications of several types of solutions to priority client problems have been explored and tacitly approved by the plan sponsor. The systems approach stressed solution development with the planner in a leadership role. Implementation is the final stage in the process. Action research interrelates the formulation and implementation stages. Problem definition depends on what a client (or client group) comes to recognize as a legitimate topic for planned change and as potential solutions. Objectives are discussed to be sure the project is feasible. The change agent coaxes the client to take a broad view. Within this realm, planning takes place. The means to produce the "action" is not discussed. Solution development is largely ignored and assumed to spring spontaneously from the merger of stages I and V.

In each of these methods, some stages are skipped. When a planned change method skips the formulation stage problem definition is believed to be given, making it an input to the process. In other planned change methods, implementation is ignored, skipping stage V, making change someone else's responsibility.

Each of the planned change methods profiled in Figures 4-5, 4-6, and 4-7 ignores sections of the morphology, suggesting that no single method can be universally applied. A "hybrid method" that brings together concepts and ideas drawn from several sources seems more desirable. As a result, the planned change methods presented in this book will draw on a wide diversity of sources to provide a sponsor with a repertoire of techniques and processes.

## ▲ EXAMINING THE METHODS USED IN PRACTICE

Case studies of planned change were obtained through interviews with the individual responsible for the project. The sponsor described the effort, and the case was then profiled using the morphology. Planned change activities and supporting techniques (when used) were identified and located in the morphology, indicating the order in which activities were carried out. The case studies were then classified according to type of method. Four types emerged, called template, search, nova, and appraisal (Nutt, 1984a, 1984c, 1992). Each truncates the planned change process, some in desirable and others in undesirable ways. Each type is illustrated in the discussion that follows, using a representative case. The types of approaches and key variations are summarized in Table 4-4.

Table 4-4 ▲ Planned Change Approaches and Variations

| Type and Variations | Stages Activated | Themes |
|---|---|---|
| Template | 1, 3, 5 | Adopt the practices of others |
| Provincial | | Single sources |
| Enriched | | Multiple sources |
| Search | 1, 3, 4, 5 | Aggressive and overt search |
| Extended | | Evaluation criteria defined by attributes of the alternatives |
| Truncated | | Generic criteria used |
| Appraisal | 1, 4, 5 | Seeking a rationale |
| Covert | | Deflecting criticism |
| Overt | | Shaping the plan's features. |
| Nova | 1, 2, 3, 4, 5 | New ideas sought |
| Internal staffers | | Carried out by organization's staff |
| Outside consultants | | Specialist from outside the organization used |

## Template Methods

### The Process

Templates guide plan development by using concepts drawn from the practices of others, activating the formulation, detailing, and implementation stages. This planned change process can be summarized as

$$1–3–5$$

(formulation–detailing–implementation)

Concepts drawn from the practices of others guide solution development. The sponsor visits an organization or recalls an experience that offers a way to deal with or further specify an opportunity. For example, an organization hired a key executive from a competitor to find out how the competing organization priced their product and billed for sales. Policies, procedures, and staffing patterns were identified by having key people recall practices in places where they had worked.

The template allows the sponsor to visualize actual operations, which demonstrates that action is feasible, and puts solution development on a tangible basis at the outset. The warrant applied is one of demonstrable workability, like that called for by the Lockian IS (see Chapter 2). Because costs are modest and the process appears to be foolproof, sponsors thought this approach clever. The equivalent of a pilot project has been conducted that demonstrates workability. The concept development stage is skipped because the planned change process is not used to provide ideas. The evaluation stage is also skipped. The plan functioned elsewhere, so it was assumed that it would work in the new setting.

### The Renal Dialysis Case

The development of a renal dialysis center described in Chapter 1 will be used to illustrate "template" planned change. Declining revenues triggered the process (Figure 4-8). Analysis, which was quite implicit, suggested that a capacity should be doubled and that amenities should be improved. Improved amenities should attract self-pay and third-party–insured patients, which should result in improved revenue prospects. It was proposed to double the capacity, increasing the number of dialysis stations from four to eight.

Detailing the practices of the competitor provided the sponsor with a list of features. These features were enumerated to guide planning activities. A remodeling expert provided a layout that determined the changes needed to fit the competitor's dialysis unit into the clinic building. Circulation technologists suggested types of dialysis equipment. Nurses from the sponsor's dialysis unit were asked to suggest staffing requirements and operating policies and physicians responded to medical issues. All issues, such as staffing configurations, policies, procedures, and the like, were template based, being drawn from the staff's experience with renal units where they had been trained or knew about. The features in the competitor's plan were compared to current practices. Users of the system (the physicians) were then asked to verify that these changes were acceptable. Acquiescence, if not support, by important groups was the dominant criterion used. The sponsor judged the plan a success when all key groups ratified it. No formal evaluation was conducted. The plan ownership promoted in detailing and the memoranda publicizing the benefits of the new unit were sufficient to secure adoption. Field performance was monitored by revenue changes. ▲

### Variations

The template approach had two variations that used the same sequence of stages but differed in the nature or intensity of key activities. The template was either provincial or enriched.

*Provincial template.* The *provincial* variation occurred when the practice or procedure of a single organization or work unit, thought to have high prestige, was used as a template for plan development. For example, in one of the cases, when the organization's inventory control system failed, an executive was hired who had installed a similar system in an organization thought to be highly prestigious. In this situation, the installed system becomes nearly a carbon copy of the practices used by the high-prestige organization.

Finer distinctions were made by observing plan development tactics in the detailing stage. Five approaches were identified by comparing the detailing activities that were used in plan development. These approaches could be summarized as hiring a system, making site visits, using past experience, assessing outside requirements, and using the literature. One-third of the provincial projects were carried out by hiring a key individual to install a program. For instance, in a management information system (MIS) project, the CEO hired a manager known to have a good track record from a competitor. In a burn unit project, a burn specialist was re-

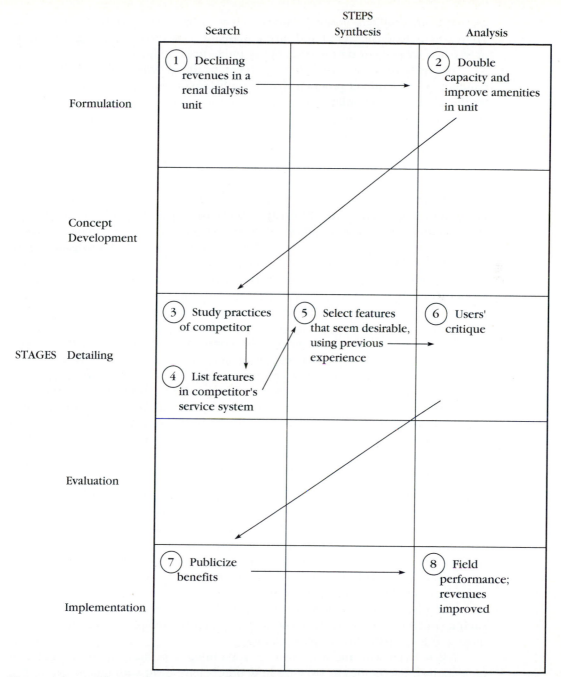

Figure 4-8 ▲ The Development of a Renal Dialysis Center

cruited from a military hospital known to have a high-quality burn care program. These key individuals were hired on the basis of their credentials (e.g., where he or she had trained) or on the basis of the individuals' abilities.

Site visits were also used in 30 percent of the provincial cases. Visits were conducted to identify a program that fit with implicit and unstated criteria used by the sponsor. A subordinate was then asked to copy the features of the favored site. Executives were also prone to copy a program that they knew about, without a site visit. Less frequently, the guidelines of a funding agency were used to specify operating features or the idea was drawn from the literature.

*Enriched templates*. The *enriched* variation occurred when the practices of several organizations or work groups were collected to cull out the best features from each. Before purchasing major equipment, such as CT or MRI scanners (diagnostic equipment that creates extraordinarily clear cross-sectional pictures of the body), staff members from some hospitals visited several sites of care to compare types of equipment and treatment procedures. The hospitals then used an amalgamation of the practices and procedures from the sites visited.

Key plan development tactics for the enriched template stemmed from site visits or bids by contractors. Site visits were used in most (80 percent) of these projects. For instance, staff members visited institutions similar to their own to identify the best features of programs to carry out personnel policy, inventory control, MIS, and organizational restructuring. The contractor-bidding approach is similar to the procedure used by several federal agencies. Ideas are solicited by requesting multiple bids for each phase of a project. Contractors are compensated for their efforts, and the resulting ideas are used to rewrite the requirements (contract-end items) for the next phase of the project. This approach is much like visiting a site, because it solicits ideas for the purpose of synthesis. For instance, the Department of Defense uses this process when developing large projects, such as the B-1B bomber.

### Implications

Many planned change sponsors attempt to adapt the ideas of others, believing that a template provides an adequate, if not ideal, solution. Sponsors think it is pragmatic to adapt the ideas of others, believing that they can avoid most of the costs of planning. This approach is quite sensible when a plan is readily adaptable. For example, in the renal dialysis project, the template was easy to acquire, making planning inexpensive and relatively foolproof. The equivalent of a pilot demonstration had been conducted by the competitor that showed that the system worked. However, when adaptability is less clear cut, planned change costs can quickly escalate. In such a situation, delays and false starts in adapting the template occur that run up costs and lose credibility for planned change.

When faced with the need to plan something new, many sponsors will visit high-status organizations to visualize how others have dealt with this problem. The physical features and procedures are adapted to fit the sponsor's situation. If the adaptation is thoughtful, a workable idea can be rapidly constructed. The need to be timely provides the essential motivation. In the vernacular, "Why reinvent the wheel?" Another motivation is the need to reduce uncertainty. Sponsors often visit an operating system to form an impression of how things are done. Seeing that someone else has dealt with the problem implies that a solution is feasible. Although pragmatic, this approach stifles innovation. New ways to deal with the planning problem must fight through a maze of precedents, so they seldom surface.

Consider a major university hospital's attempt to revise its governance. Rather than introspect about their needs, the executives visited several university hospitals to determine the features of their corporate structure: how long-range decisions are made to set policy, establish their domains, select their clients, and the like. The visits enumerated specific functions of trustees and their prerogatives as a controlling entity. However, a composite of the functions performed by the board of trustees offered little guidance in creating a structure because factors that played a role in forming the structure of a given university hospital are obscure. For example, some universities have monopoly power over tertiary care and free services, giving them control over the referrals statewide. Fee structure is also important. Physicians whose incomes hinge on patient charges have more interest in governance than does a research-oriented medical faculty. In addition, the size of the state's appropriation and level of the research funding of the medical faculty are important. Each creates a series of pressures to which the administration must be responsive, creating imperatives. These imperatives become formalized as procedures that respond to the constraints and prerogatives imposed on the organizations.

The governance of a given university hospital is little more than a reaction to environmental pressures and opportunities. It is difficult to find practices to adapt unless monopoly power, fee structure, state appropriation, research funding, and so on are comparable. Even if such an organization can be found, one must detail why the observed structure is effective and which features (e.g., strong or weak deans or department chairs) make it so. For instance, a sponsor may be envious of Iowa's grip on tertiary care, but may fail to see the undesirable aspects of state control. The state that grants monopoly power also feels the need to play watchdog, which can be seen in the makeup of the governing structure. Thus, relying on the practices of others has several limitations. What appears to be a fast and insightful way to find workable ideas may merely introduce many side issues that distract a planned change process. Rather than explore why Iowa's structure works in its university hospital, the sponsor would be better off considering what options can work locally and their pros and cons.

## Search Methods

### *The Process*

Search approaches look for canned ideas. The sponsor believes that there must be a solution "out there" because others must have had a similar problem. A search is mounted to find these solutions, activating the formulation, detailing, evaluation, and implementation stages. As a result, a four-stage process is used:

$$1-3-4-5$$

(formulation–detailing–evaluation–implementation)

The search approach attempts to identify the best available ideas. The warrant assumes that competition among ideas will produce a superior decision suggesting a Kantian IS (see Chapter 2).

Search is aggressive and overt. Search aids, such as a request for proposals (RFPs), are often used. In response to the needs stated in the RFP, vendors or consultants select one of their prepackaged solutions and tailor it to fit the organization's statement of need. A small-scale repeat of the detailing stage is used to tailor and rationalize the prototype for its new user. The sponsor evaluates the plans submitted to select the one that seemed best suited to the needs of the situation. Evaluation is an important part of the search process as compared with the template process, in which this stage is not used. An RFP is prepared in the formulation stage, concept development is skipped, detailing is used to shape the plan, and evaluation is used to pick the best plan from those submitted.

A consultant, vendor, or supplier offers "turnkey" planning, spanning activities needed to develop a plan. Developmental costs are included in the charges for each new application of the turnkey plan. Charging clients in this way creates considerable profit for the consultant or vendor and thereby incentives to market ideas that solve certain types of problems.

### The MIS Development Case

A small firm had decided to move from its current downtown location to the suburbs. The CEO, who acted as the sponsor of this planned change effort, believed that the impending relocation offered an opportunity to introduce computerized information handling into the company. The CEO believed that machine information processing would be more cost efficient, reduce the redundancy of incoming information, provide faster access, increase turnaround, and compile data needed for decision making.

Little activity of a technical nature occurred during the formulation stage. The sponsor wanted to mechanize the company's information handling and gave this mandate to staff. In step 1 (see Figure 4-9) the sponsor articulated the opportunity to mechanize information flows. In step 2 the planner established a task force that identified options to create the MIS. Three options were considered: in-house development, contracting with a consultant, and using a turnkey plan of a vendor. In step 4 the task force evaluated these options. The sponsor received a report describing the pros and cons of each of these options. The sponsor selected the consultant option (step 5) in which staff would work with a vendor during development to tailor the vendor's off-the-shelf system to meet the company's needs. (In a turnkey plan the user is more passive, merely looking for usable ideas.) In step 6, the RFP was sketched by the planner and submitted to the sponsor for his approval.

The planner, with the assistance of a task force made up of potential users and operators of the system, began to detail the RFP in step 7. The task force had representatives from each line department involved in manufacturing, sales, data processing, materials management, accounting, R&D, and quality control. This group reviewed the planner's systems analysis of the current information system and applications that were envisioned for the new system (step 10). The task force

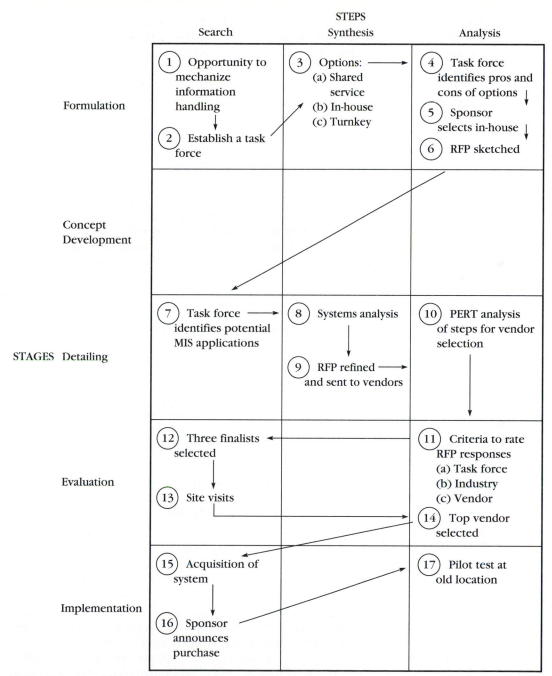

STEPS

| | Search | Synthesis | Analysis |
|---|---|---|---|
| Formulation | ① Opportunity to mechanize information handling ② Establish a task force | ③ Options: (a) Shared service (b) In-house (c) Turnkey | ④ Task force identifies pros and cons of options ⑤ Sponsor selects in-house ⑥ RFP sketched |
| Concept Development | | | |
| Detailing | ⑦ Task force identifies potential MIS applications | ⑧ Systems analysis ⑨ RFP refined and sent to vendors | ⑩ PERT analysis of steps for vendor selection |
| Evaluation | ⑫ Three finalists selected ⑬ Site visits | | ⑪ Criteria to rate RFP responses (a) Task force (b) Industry (c) Vendor ⑭ Top vendor selected |
| Implementation | ⑮ Acquisition of system ⑯ Sponsor announces purchase | | ⑰ Pilot test at old location |

STAGES

**Figure 4-9 ▲ Management Information System Development**

suggested additional applications. The applications were prioritized for inclusion in the RFP. An RFP was prepared and sent to MIS vendors (step 9), and their responses were collated. The planner then prepared a schedule of steps for vendor selection (step 10).

Evaluation criteria were extracted from several sources to analyze the vendor proposals. Each task force member rated each vendor proposal on each criterion. Industry ratings of the vendors were determined by data published by the Datapro Corporation. A vendor's overall assessment was determined by combining these ratings to rank the vendors. Site visits were conducted for the top three vendors (step 13). A top vendor was recommended to the CEO in step 14.

The sponsor signed a contract with the recommended vendor in step 15 and announced the purchase of the system by a memo in step 16. The CEO then called for an implementation of the system at the current site. He treated the implementation as a pilot program to suggest ways the system could be improved in the new building. There was considerable opposition to setting the system in place and then having to dismantle it and set it up again at the new site. These concerns were swept aside by the CEO.

A memo was used to initiate the changes called for by the new information system. The pilot test of the system allowed the CEO to monitor the cost, redundancy, speed of access, turnaround time, and extent that decision-making needs were met to judge the system's value to the company.                                                   ▲

## Variations

The key variations were linked to the scope of search. Some projects *truncated* and others *extended* search. Search was extended when the sponsor was unsure of potentials, and it was truncated when standards to judge a vendor's idea seemed clear. For example, if a chief financial officer believed he or she had knowledge of the state of the art in financial analysis packages, a search would be stopped when a package was identified that met his or her expectations. Other CFOs may accumulate several competing packages and study them at length before making a choice.

*Extended search.* An extended search is used to extract criteria from the features of the competing ideas (note the Kantian IS). This type of approach was used when the controller in a city government patiently sought out proposals from a score of electronic data processing (EDP) manufacturers in an attempt to learn what constituted an adequate system.

Tactics used in the detailing stage of extended search projects were RFPs and matching, although most projects relied almost exclusively on RFPs. Search without an RFP involves knowing the requirements but not the options that could be matched to these requirements. When an option was uncovered it was rigorously evaluated to compare it with norms.

*Truncated search.* Generic criteria are used to select among vendor proposals in a truncated search process. The criteria are applied to evaluate the ideas offered in consultants' off-the-shelf programs.

Tactics used in the detailing stage of truncated search projects included RFPs and sole-source contracting. The sole-source contractor is frequently used in planning change projects. Apparently architects, auditors, and the like cultivate organizations until they achieve "consultant loyalty" much like the brand loyalty promoted by advertisers. Many executives seemed to overstate their ability to recognize a good system when they saw one. Using a sole-source consultant suggests that the scope of ideas considered is limited, creating some potential problems for organizations that apply satisficing (March and Simon, 1958) criteria.

The remaining third of the truncated-search projects solicited competition among consultants and vendors. RFPs were used to solicit ideas or to find someone to carry out the project. For example, RFPs were sent to architects to initiate building renovations and to vendors to identify equipment options.

## Appraisal Methods

This type of approach begins with a plan of unknown or contentious value. Appraisal activates formulation, evaluation, and implementation stages. The process is

$$1-4-5$$

(formulation–evaluation–implementation)

The approach resembles the scientific method. The warrant is similar to the norms of science (a Leibnitzian IS).

Evaluating findings are used to win the support needed to implement. The appraisal process builds a strong motivation for action, but does so at the expense of fine-tuning the idea, as in the template and search processes. Detailing considers only issues that make an assessment feasible. All other detailing activities are assumed to be carried out on the job, during a shakedown period, as the plan is put into operation. Operators, department heads, and other management personnel often have to make procedural refinements to make the idea work.

### The Pharmacy Case

Faculty members in a department of pharmacy had discovered ways to individualize drug dosage. The procedure established a mathematical relationship between the dose of certain drugs and the plasma concentrations in people. This procedure created an opportunity to reduce the hospitalization cost due to drug dosage problems and improve care quality. For instance, 20 to 30 percent of the patients who use digitalis experience toxicity due to overdosing. Eleven percent of the patients receiving these same drugs experience underdosing. In both instances, preventable hospitalization occurs.

To determine dosage for an individual patient required a total of two hours of a pharmacist's time, which was priced at $20.00. Charging for the service seemed reasonable because of the potential for reductions in hospitalization for digitalis toxicity, which could save third-party payors over $50,000 annually at just one university hospital.

This savings was based on 3.7 percent of all hospital admissions (or 260 patients out of 7017) that have adverse drug reactions. Of these 16.9 percent stemmed from digitalis toxicity. Proper dosing spared the patient an average hospital stay of 5 days. These 46 patients would represent 130 patient days, at $220 per patient day, for a projected savings of $50,600 at the time of the study. Other toxic drugs also had potential savings. For example, annual savings of $144,840 were estimated for Gentamicin.

After viewing the potential cost savings of the drug dosage system, the university hospital pharmacy decided to seek third-party reimbursement for a $20 pharmacy charge to make the dosing calculations. The planned change process was initiated, recognizing that a pharmacy charge would be precedent setting for Blue Cross. The case is profiled in Figure 4-10.

The search phase in formulation recognized the value of the individual dose system (Figure 4-10). The synthesis phase identified drugs with toxicity problems. A simulated analysis was conducted to document the cost of the service and the potential savings.

The administrator of the hospital pharmacy (the sponsor) chose to update a proposal that was successful in previous negotiations with third-party payors. Blue Cross rejected the revised proposal, contending that this service fell within the usual day-to-day functions of the pharmacist and did not justify a special fee. This led to lengthy negotiations with Blue Cross. Finally, it was decided that a careful cost justification would be accepted. Field trials were conducted to document further the costs and benefits of individual dosing.

The revised proposal was based on evaluation information. The pharmacy initiated the evaluation to document savings carefully, which took a year to accomplish. This documentation of the savings and benefits of individual dosing was included in the new proposal. After extensive negotiations, Blue Cross approved the plan supported by field trial data. The costs and benefits of the new procedure eventually overturned the precedent of not reimbursing pharmacists for specific activities.

Implementation occurred through the routine billing of fees as they were incurred. Details of the billing system were proposed, and the billing procedure was established. The pharmacy department created monitoring systems to ensure that reimbursements were being made according to the arrangements.          ▲

### Variations

The appraisal can be covert, carried out to devise politically defensible arguments to support the idea, or overt, attempting to remove real uncertainty about a plan's value. A *covert* appraisal is carried out to justify implementation. The idea is modified to blunt the attacks of its adversaries. An *overt* appraisal is less defensive, more inquisitive, and more open to change.

Covert approaches are used to verify the costs and benefits or to make current and proposed system comparisons. Some appraisals are used to structure arguments and gather support. Other appraisal efforts are postures, undertaken to placate key constituencies rather than to produce new information. Still others are merely verifications, which produced just enough information to ensure that current under-

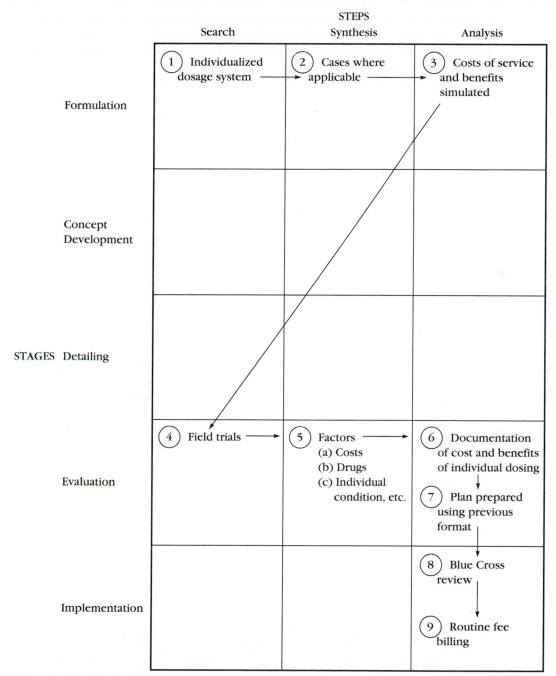

Figure 4-10  ▲  The Pharmacokinetic Dosing System

standings are accurate. For instance, initiators of the pharmacological dosing project already knew the costs and benefits but did an evaluation to be doubly sure that the numbers were defensible. Defensive evaluations are undertaken when the costs or benefits are not so clear.

Overt appraisals are carried out to document unknown benefits and, often, to assess through consumer input the reaction of potential users. For instance, the framework of benefits for government programs for the aging are fixed through legislative mandate and bureaucratic rule making, but programs from a cafeteria of options can be selected to meet local needs, revealed by an evaluation. Public hearings are mounted to hear user views of proposed service. Such an approach is widely used in service organizations, such as public utilities commissions and power-sitting boards, which hear the views of interested citizens before granting rate increases or licenses to expand.

### Implications

Two features of the appraisal methods case should be noted. First, only one alternative is considered. Second, evaluation is used to initiate the process, but may not be used to validate the plan. The perceived need for speedy results sacrifices both multiple alternatives and the careful assessment of a favored option. The sponsor of the drug dosing project was an academic department within a university so it is not surprising that analysis was stressed. However, success hinged on Blue Cross' willingness to overcome precedents in light of the cost justification submitted in the proposal. The sponsor believed that this decision would depend on rational arguments. The initial turndown prompted another evaluation to produce more data to make the arguments *more* rational. In such cases, rationality had little to do with an approval. Giving Blue Cross a face-saving way to increase rates would have speeded up the plan's adoption.

## Nova Methods

A nova approach attempts to fashion a plan through developmental activities. All process stages are activated. As a result, the process is

$$1-2-3-4-5$$

(formulation–concept development–detailing–evaluation–implementation)

A nova approach attempts to create an innovative plan. The warrant of innovation is applied. New ideas are created to challenge approaches in use by organizations. These new ideas are sought without specific reference to the practices of others. Concept development, in which options are identified and pursued in subsequent stages, is particularly important. The nova method is the *only* approach with activity in the concept development stage.

A nova approach can be supported by internal staff or outside consultants. Internal support is drawn from the organization's staff. The outside consultant is usually selected from among individuals or organizations known to the user, often on a sole-source basis. Consultants are often drawn from the firm that provided auditing services, from an old-boy network of friends and former associates, or from organizations thought to be high in prestige as in the search approach. The approach differs from the search because the consultant sells process, not a product, and because the sponsor asks for or tolerates innovation-seeking activities.

## The Medical Records Case

The medical records plan was initiated during a large construction program for a thousand-bed university hospital. In the construction program, the clinic was designed to be the most progressive and fully equipped facility of its kind providing ambulatory care for 11 specific patient care services.

The philosophy of the clinic, which followed that of the medical school, allowed each physician to work independently with support services provided centrally. Historically, each physician had kept his or her own medical records and supplied only summary information to the hospital. Individual physician offices delivered patient records to the clinic at the time of a visit. Coordinating the movements of hundreds of records back and forth from physician offices to the clinic created considerable cost and frequently lost records (step 1, Figure 4-11).

A clinic planning committee had been overseeing the overall clinic building program. The CEO (the sponsor) charged this committee to develop a system to store patient records in a central file (step 2). The committee was made up of administrators and influential members of the medical staff. The committee also believed that the current medical record system was chaotic and that the new building provided an opportunity to improve the system. The clinic planning committee stated an objective of using the latest technology in their medical records system, as shown in step 3, Figure 4-11.

The planning committee set out to automate and centralize the record system. The committee contacted the data processing department in the university and asked them to develop a medical records system (step 4). This system was to house all patient records in a central file, to be retrieved one day prior to a patient's visit. The system was also to have a computerized appointment, scheduling, and billing system. Input and output terminals were to be located in patient care areas so a clerical person could type a code number on a CRT terminal and obtain appointment scheduling and other kinds of information. After a lengthy design process, a fully computerized plan, termed the medical records library system (MRLS), was developed (step 8).

The planning committee did not review the system but, instead, called for a pilot test of the MRLS in one department, at the old clinic site (steps 9 and 10). During the pilot, time pressure became extreme as the clinic's opening day drew near. Simultaneously, the pilot was uncovering several problems in the operation of the MRLS system (step 11). The CEO, however, ignored these problems, claiming that the test was run in a single dissimilar site (department) that gave little indication of what to expect if the MRLS was implemented on a large scale. The CEO decided to attempt to install the MRLS in the new clinic and rectify problems as they were encountered.

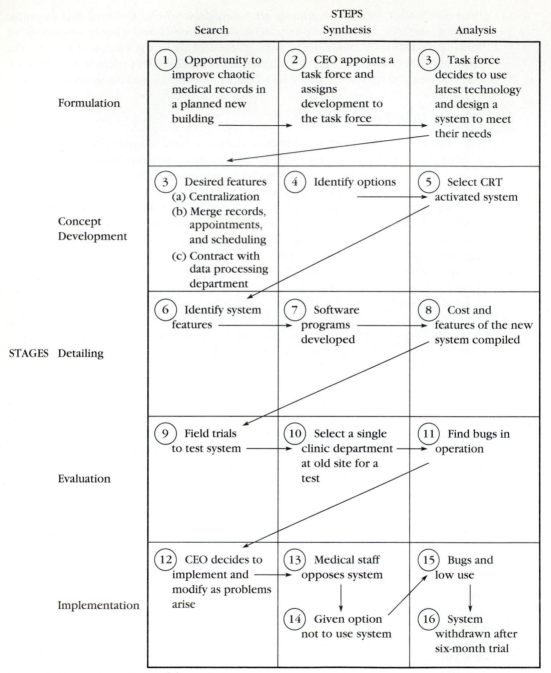

**Figure 4-11** ▲ **The Medical Records System**

The MRLS system was installed before it was thoroughly debugged. During implementation, physicians staged a boycott, claiming that the system violated the confidentiality of their records (step 13). Because of the CRT access to the computer files it was felt that confidential information describing both physician and patient could be accessed by the university. At this time, the university was engaged in a delicate negotiation for a practice plan with the medical staff, who were being asked to give a portion of their private practice income earned on patients treated at the university hospital clinics to the university. The CEO decided not to push the MRLS and give physicians the option of whether or not to use it (step 14). Monitoring MRLS performance uncovered several operational problems and a high proportion of physicians who refused to use it (step 15). Six months after the system had been installed, it was withdrawn and junked (step 16).  ▲

### Variations

The tactics used to identify solutions were either problem corrective or innovative. The corrective tactic responded to complaints and proposed a modification to overcome the identified malfunctions. Outside consultants are prone to be problem reactive, perhaps fearing that they may offend a client by attempting to redefine the problem. Staff members were also reluctant to challenge the sponsor's definition of the problem and often limited their scope of inquiry to the immediate neighborhood of the problem symptoms.

Innovation-seeking projects were more than twice as common for internal staff consultants, compared to outside consultants. Apparently outside consultants feel more constrained than internal staff to offer ideas that depart from the traditional programs and policies used by the organization. This suggests that sponsors should be more attuned to the outside consultants' unwillingness to challenge stipulations of needs and should encourage them to offer new ideas.

### Implications

Many advocate nova approaches. Such a planned change process is engaged to provide what Mintzberg et al. (1976) called a "custom-made" solution. Those who advocate custom-made solutions also call for innovation. Theorists contend that having multiple options, which are detailed and winnowed to select options that are then formally evaluated, leads to the best results. This permits a comparison among potentially viable courses of action, which often leads to a superior synthesis, according to Kantian IS. But perceptions of time constraints and high costs drastically limit the number of alternatives developed by a nova process, and multiple alternatives are seldom developed. Also, techniques that stimulate creativity are seldom applied to develop new ideas in planned change, making innovation difficult. As a result, nova methods can produce faulty plans, just like any of the other approaches to planned change.

Many people in staff roles would prefer, because of their inclination and training, to devise a new system. The staffer hopes that the sponsor's premise allows for innovation in operations, just as an architect hopes a building project will permit originality in creating the building envelope. When premises give staff or consultants room to maneuver, innovation is possible.

Innovation creates custom-made solutions to the planning problem. For example, to plan a county home care system, one can draw on current services (e.g., a visiting nurse service or meals-on-wheels) and use this service profile as a model. Alternatively, the planner can deal with more basic questions, such as profiling the target group's needs and ask how to respond to the questions that these needs pose. The answers can lead to innovative ideas. Innovation can lead to better plans and has the disadvantage of apparent (if not actual) higher costs and delays. The cost can be offset by the possible benefit of innovative plans. The sponsor's perceived need to be timely can also present problems. Custom-made solutions often take longer. However, when a solution does not have a good fit to the sponsor's problem, the planned change effort must backtrack, which is both time consuming and costly.

## ▲ PRACTICE AND THEORY

Three major conclusions can be drawn from the practice of planned change (Nutt, 1984b, 1991a). First, the methods applied by practitioners have little resemblance to the prescriptions for planned change. Instead, an amalgamation of ideas drawn from several sources seem to be used. Second, many planned change stages and steps are skipped in practice. Third, much planned change is done informally, without the benefit of planning techniques.

### Hybrid Methods

In practice, planned change applies techniques and processes drawn from several sources. Processes found in the literature may seldom, if ever, be used. This may be due to gaps in these processes, where they fail to deal with important issues, or because the experienced practitioner likes to extract and synthesize planning ideas. The synthesized process evolves and may even become *contingently* based, where different procedures are used to deal with certain types of problems. Practitioners seem to want to fit method to problem. But even the best practitioners have counterproductive preferences and outright biases. This suggests that practitioners should be exposed to hybrid methods in a contingency framework, selecting methods according to the requirements the sponsor wishes to impose on the planned change process.

### Process Truncation

The planned change methods used by practitioners skip several stages and steps. Stages and steps may be deleted because practitioners see them as unnecessary for particular applications or for all applications. Time pressures and limited budgets may also cause stage skipping. The stages skipped may also suggest that practitioners believe that they are not essential, particularly when stringent deadlines must be faced. Stages devoted to option creation are skipped more often than any other. Also, formulation and implementation are frequently carried out in a superficial manner. The importance of these stages suggests that this practice is undesirable.

## Simplistic Techniques

Much planned change activity is informal. The information required by planned change stages and steps is provided by sponsor demands, opinions, or intuition, not formal planning techniques. For instance, many planned change efforts were activated by a sponsor's stipulation which contains or implies a solution. Some of these stipulations can be misleading. The sponsor describes a solution, often in detail, in an attempt to be specific about needs or opportunities. The planner takes the stipulation too literally and details what the sponsors' intend as an illustration.

In other cases, the sponsor's preconceived ideas are introduced to coax the adoption of a pet idea. Still other sponsors introduce ideas, hoping to speed the process. A plan is stipulated (e.g., an operating system or policy) as a template that the planner is expected to use. It is hard for the sponsor to imagine that an adaptation can be both incomplete and costly, which is often the case. Stipulations that contain a solution obviate the need to use techniques in formulation and concept development. Most theorists believe that planned change results would be improved if formal techniques were used in each process stage.

Sponsors may also force premature closure by adopting the first solution that appears viable. Early closure often coaxes the sponsor to issue implementation decrees when more subtle techniques are called for to implement the plan.

## ▲  Key Points

1.  Prescriptive planned change methods were compared to the methods applied in practice. Two conclusions were reached. First, the prescriptive methods found in the literature are not used. Practitioners typically apply a variety of procedures and techniques, drawing them from several sources. However, this repertoire is quite limited and techniques with very little sophistication are typically used. Such behavior suggests that a hybrid planned change method, which combines process and technique notions from several sources, is both needed and desired by practitioners. Hybrid methods should appeal to the practitioner and also should improve the practice of planned change.
2.  There is a need for contingency-based methods. Rules to select among competing procedures and techniques for given types of planned change efforts are seldom found in the literature and seem badly needed.

## ▲  Exercises

1.  Construct a morphology for one of the cases in Chapter 1. Carefully review the case and then fit the steps to the morphology. Note that not all cells will be

filled. Trace the sequence of events with an arrow, as shown in Chapter 4. Note how the renal dialysis case was transcribed as a guide (see Figure 4-9).

2. Gather information to construct a morphology for two planned change efforts carried out by the *same* sponsor. Select a project that was adopted (a success) and one that was developed but not implemented, or implemented and later withdrawn (a failure). Compare the two projects. Speculate on the causes of failure from a procedural point of view.

# 5 | Process Management

▲ ▲ ▲   ▲ ▲ ▲ ▲ ▲ ▲ ▲ ▲ ▲ ▲ ▲ ▲ ▲ ▲ ▲

This chapter describes the management of planned change efforts. As in the previous chapter, a comparison of process management practices with theory yields insights into what works and why.

Process management activities are divided into two blocks, one describing decisions and the other plan development and installation. Decision making involves recognition and the choices made during development and installation. Recognition takes place when an organizational leader finds performance shortfalls to be significant and decides to take action. The choices made during development guide the evolution of a plan and its adoption. To describe the flow of these activities, situations that can activate a planned change effort are identified, and alternative ways to guide a planned change process are presented.

In practice, process management often differs from the requirement of sponsor involvement in each process stage. Cases of planned change are used to describe the tactics used by sponsors to steer the process. Discussion is devoted to the tactics applied to carry out formulation, which sets directions for planned change, and implementation, which attempts to deal with forces that could block plan adoption. Formulation and implementation tactics are illustrated by cases in this chapter and are evaluated in the next chapter.

## ▲  ACTIVATING PLANNED CHANGE

When accumulated stimuli reach some threshold level, resources are mobilized to initiate change. An organizational leader sorts through acknowledged stimuli by identifying the claims made by key people, coupled with the leader's own observations. Claims accumulate until a threshold is reached that demands action. The needs or opportunities that are recognized stem from performance gaps, formed by comparing perceived performance to a standard or expectation for that performance. For example, a product becomes suspect when its cost and its rate of returns due to quality problems exceed those in comparable organizations, suggesting the need to cut costs and improve quality. This process is called managerial diagnosis (Nutt, 1979b).

Claims can arise from internal, external, or both internal and external actors and organizations. Claims with an external origin can stem from users or customers, consultants, competitors, regulators, accreditation agencies, endowers, legislatures, or the courts (e.g., lawsuits). Internal claims can spring from top or middle management, boards of trustees or directors, and staff. Claims that have both internal and external features include subsidiary agents (e.g., physicians in a hospital), subsidiary organizations, and consultants. Various surveillance mechanisms in the organization, such as a management information system (MIS) or people in liaison roles, recognize and attempt to document claims. For example, physicians in a hospital make claims about the needs for ultrasound equipment to pulverize kidney stones; welfare rights groups call for the restoration of cuts in WIC (Women Infant Children food supplement) programs; and managers argue for increased capacity or improved accounting capability using documentation stemming from information systems, personal discussions, and interpersonal networks.

Claim types include unsatisfied demands, new patterns of activity, problem and policy statements, criterion checks, and goal conflicts. Each can have an internal or external origin. Unsatisfactory demands can stem from dissatisfaction expressed by managers, users, clients, customers, regulators, or subsidiary agents, such as procurement officials with defense contractors. Demands can arise when claims are thought to be treated superficially, ignored, or deferred. For instance, the mayor of a township without a health care facility pressured a neighboring hospital to open an intermediate care center, claiming the township was deprived. Employee turnover can provide a claim that alleges turnover causes, such as low or inequitable pay between male and female employees. Coalitions can be formed to bolster these claims, taking the form of community associations, legislation, or litigation that prompts sponsors to recognize and classify these signals.

New patterns of activity can take two forms: adaptations and innovations. Adaptations typically stem from technological advances. The claim arises from the expenditures needed to adapt the technology for local use. When proposed adaptations are rejected, they can become unrecognized demands in a subsequent decision. Innovations arise from claims that the organization must devise a fresh perspective in their service, products, markets, or internal operations. The claim carries with it an imperative to act in ways that are new to the organization or to the industry. A radically innovative claim is made when the organization seeks to be an industry leader. Hewlett-Packard's approach to product design is an example. The radically innovative posture is rare.

Criterion checks stem from control activities inside or outside the organization. Inside the organization, claims may involve inadequate space, low census, falling revenues, poor cash flow, or excessive downtime. Outside the organization, regulators or accreditation agencies can call for certain targets to be met. Building code violations and accreditation denials illustrate external claims based on criterion checks.

Goal conflicts stem from two or more actors that make claims and counterclaims. Disputes over the needs for service functions, such as computer support in a university, can emerge between faculty and administration, triggering a planned change process. Similarly, physicians and administrators may have different views of the need to expand services, such as severe burn care. The physician views the service in terms of its benefits and the administrator in terms of its reimbursable costs.

## Managerial Diagnosis

Either rational or political diagnostics can be applied by a manager (sponsor) to initiate planned change. A "rational diagnostic" relies on performance gap measurements. When performance measures differ sharply from norms, action is mandated; if not, action is deferred. A "political diagnostic" relies on how key people perceive both performance and norms. Action is called for when these individuals *believe* that a performance gap exists.

Information describing the performance gap, whether based on rational or political factors, can stimulate four kinds of behavior. Claims can be *ignored,* because to recognize them might highlight past failures that can lead to a loss of power for the sponsor. For example, if the sponsor was responsible for initiating a practice that now has a negative performance gap (performance below norms), planned change may not be initiated because it could draw attention to the unacceptable practice. Second, the sponsor can *distort information*. Various kinds of ancillary considerations can be introduced that alter expectations, making the performance gap seem insignificant. Third, information can be *withheld*. In this case, information can be routed or summarized so those in a position to make a diagnosis are unaware of current performance levels. Finally, the performance gap can be called insubstantial, treating it as less important than other concerns within the organization.

The process of managerial diagnosis sets out the basic assumptions that guide planned change. These assumptions stipulate key considerations that the sponsor will use to frame the questions stipulated for the planned change process to consider. Assumptions may also indicate the type of results the sponsor expects from the effort.

### Rational Diagnostics

People react to stimuli by making claims based on a comparison of performance indicators to norms. The diagnostic process begins when a sponsor faces these claims with incomplete information. First, available information sources are consulted to clarify performance and norms. Information seeking can lead to the accumulation of considerable data, some of which can be contradictory. For example, when a respected member of a board of directors claims that the organization is run ineffectively because it lacks a strategic plan, the CEO may reflect on the remark, discuss it with a trusted colleague, seek out and read a strategic plan, or even brush up on strategic planning approaches to assist in judging its value. These assessments may or may not support the contention of low effectiveness for the organization.

The diagnostic process assembles information from several sources. Indicators of innovation, support levels, efficiency, and the like are collected for both expectations and performance. An expectation identifies a desirable and seemingly attainable state of affairs. Expectations are formed by performance trends in comparable or respected organizations, the experience of key constituents, and theoretical models.

To diagnose, norms are compared to performance. There are four possible outcomes, as shown in Table 5-1. In situations 2, 3, and 4, performance is found to be ambiguous or unsatisfactory, calling for action. As shown in Figure 5-1, recognition of a performance gap leads to a stipulation that prompts inquiry. When inquiry has

### Table 5-1 ▲ The Disposition of Claims

| Situation | Outcome | Response |
|---|---|---|
| 1 | Performance exceeds norms. | Defer action. |
| 2 | Norm exceeds performance. | Undertake planned change. |
| 3 | Norm is uncertain. | Evaluate norm. |
| 4 | Performance is uncertain. | Evaluate performance. |

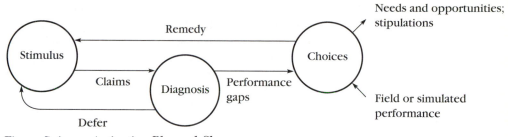

**Figure 5-1** ▲ **Activating Planned Change**
Adapted from Nutt (1979b).

been completed, performance indicators are checked to ensure that the remedy is sound. Diagnosis may lead to a deferral or provide stipulations that initiate a new round of inquiry.

### Nonplanning Responses

*Deferral.* Situation 1 in Table 5-1 results in a deferral. The sponsor does not feel a need to act because expectations have been surpassed. Current practices are ratified. The absence of a performance gap forms the basis for public statements that rationalize keeping things as they are. Only changes in the sponsor's aspirations (March and Simon, 1958) can alter norms. However, expectations can increase when the sponsor sees that others outperform the organization in terms of quality, turnover, and the like. When this occurs, situation 1 can shift to situation 2, calling for planned change.

*Evaluation.* Evaluative activity arises out of uncertainty. A diagnosis calling for evaluation is predicted when uncertainty clouds either norms or performance. Managers respond to uncertainty by seeking information. A diagnosis leading to evaluation occurs in situations 3 and 4 (Table 5-1).

In situation 4 in Table 5-1, an operation, program, or policy has unknown performance. In such a situation, sponsors feel compelled to seek information that documents performance. Performance evaluation is initiated to clarify the unit cost, outcomes, and other features of the programs, such as counseling services in a mental health center, or internal policies, such as rules for sick leave. If the performance evaluation finds that performance is below expectations, the diagnosis will shift to situation 2, which makes planned change the predicted response.

In situation 3, performance is clear but expectations are not. Evaluation seems needed because uncertainty clouds expectations. Diagnosis calls for a "norm evaluation" to determine performance information that can be used to form norms for the sponsor. Norm evaluations often precede major commitments, such as firms considering vertical or horizontal integration by purchasing suppliers and sources of raw material or buying out a competitor. The prospects of improving profit and other performance features are unknown, making the decision to proceed with such plans fraught with uncertainty.

Experience influences perceived uncertainty. When a sponsor believes that his or her experience is relevant, uncertain information states may be explained away.

To illustrate, the CEO may compare the organization's performance to that in other organizations the CEO has managed. If the organizations seem comparable, norms can be extracted from the previous experience. Expectations are based on acceptance, cost revenues, and other performance levels obtainable, in a situation thought to be analogous. When this occurs, situation 3 shifts to situation 1 or 2, as dictated by the norm inferred by the sponsor. Also, rationalizations can change norms. A norm can be revised downward until performance seems acceptable (situation 1). This occurs when sponsors search for an organization or situation with low performance, and use the performance as a norm. If this occurs, situation 4 reverts to situation 1, and the sponsor ratifies current practices.

### Planned Change Responses

The diagnosis in situation 2 finds that performance falls below expectations (see Table 5-1). The failure to meet expectations calls for a planned change. The rational sponsor sets out stipulations based on his or her understanding of norms and current performance to define a performance gap. The stipulation often identifies performance expectations and new ways of operating that can meet these expectations.

### Political Diagnostics

Planned change is also initiated by political activity. Politics characterize the process of maneuvering by various groups or individuals, to promote needs or opportunities. The sponsor, as before, must deal with a variety of stimuli, but in this case, the stimuli can produce claims that seem contradictory. Some claims suggest a large performance gap, but claimants may cite different types of gaps that call for different kinds of action. Others may find the same gap to be insignificant and not meriting attention. Information stemming from the views of people takes on increased importance. The beliefs of key people often reveal many contradictions. Political diagnosis follows a five-step process of activism, trial alliances, recognition, coalition, and stipulation, as summarized in Table 5-2.

*Activism.* During the activism phase, many people interpret norms and performance. Each determines if a performance gap is large enough to call for action. For example, the delays in information processing, such as billing, may be interpreted as grossly inadequate by those with high expectations or merely undesirable by those with modest expectations about the time to process and send out a bill. These views create conflicts over the need for planned change and its urgency. Various positions are expressed by arguments that support modest and high expectations. To justify these positions, the bill processing time in a respected competitor may be cited. To counter this argument, another may use improvements in the state of the art to justify expectations that call for faster processing. In this example, both a large and modest performance gap are thought to exist by key people. The relative importance of the individuals who are pushing for change, and the information sources they use, help to sort out the importance of each person's claim.

### Table 5-2   ▲   Political Diagnostics

| Steps | Key Activities |
|---|---|
| 1. Activism | Triggering through both rationally and politically defined performance gaps |
| | Information gathering |
| 2. Trial alliances | Formation of tentative coalitions |
| | Use of hardball, media, and interorganizational relationships |
| 3. Recognition | Exploration, diplomacy, and rationalization activities in the trial alliance activities |
| | Scanning and solicitation |
| 4. Coalition | Confrontation via problem definition and "red herrings" |
| | Resolution |
| 5. Stipulation | Statements of needs and opportunities |

Adapted from Lyles (1980) and Narayhan (1980)

In Table 5-2, triggering and information-gathering activities occur during the activism phase. Triggering takes place via the various interpretations of a performance gap. For example, consider the situation where occupancy in a university hospital plummets following the initiation of an unpopular practice plan, which calls for physicians on the medical school faculty to share income they earn from treating patients in the hospital with the medical school. The medical school dean seeking advice on how to improve the occupancy of a university hospital may find that the performance gap can be interpreted in several ways. For example, marketing experts may see needs in terms of recruiting physicians for the medical faculty who are likely to be high admittors. An organization behaviorist may identify needs in terms of decisions not to participate by the physicians. An accountant could describe needs in terms of financial incentives, and an economist in terms of the supply and demand for physician services. These conflicting interpretations of the performance gap imply conflicting remedies and would trigger information gathering by the sponsor to size up the situation.

Sponsors continue to read performance gap claims made by key people until they have a "language" that describes a need or an opportunity. Pondy and Mitroff (1979) contend the concept of language is basic to understanding these performance gap claims. Language provides categories that allow the manager to classify the behavior of protagonists as they offer their performance gap definitions. Language has four distinct roles: filtering, categorizing, exchanging, and influencing. Language provides a filter that eliminates events the sponsor cannot classify. Performance gap claims are then categorized to give them meaning according to the sponsor's experience. These categories are used to exchange ideas in an attempt to influence others. In short, language allows a manager to read and reconcile performance gap claims made by key people.

The plan sponsor's ability to frame planning needs or opportunities with metaphors that create compelling imagery improves his or her prospect. For instance, descriptions of a practice using an anecdote can often convey the urgency to act. Statistical charts do not have much imagery without a verbal interpretation. A medical staff member describing the consequences of treating a head injury in an emergency room without a CT scanner can provide a vivid image of the need for this equipment. Statistics depicting who has CT scanners will pale beside such an anecdote.

The sponsor attempts to describe a performance gap so it will resonate to power figures in the organization. The sponsor who devises a language that can reconcile various performance gap claims and counterclaims demonstrates leadership in resolving conflicts and framing planned change questions.

Myths and stories are important vehicles to use when framing a planning question. Administrators who use the organization's history and origins, triumphs over adversity, and tangible symbols (e.g., logos) are quite successful in making various types of performance gap claims, including those for planned change. For example, the traditions of community service can be used by a hospital CEO to justify new and risky tertiary care services, such as open heart surgery. When making new proposals, the CEO who has made a firm profitable, emphasizes his or her past success in turning the organization around. In this case, profit-related criteria would be used to define all performance gaps. Each performance gap claim suggests metaphors that can be used to define various kinds of norms. Thus the sponsor, in reconciling conflicting demands for change, draws upon and rephrases the traditions of the organization.

*Trial Alliances*. The second step in political diagnosis is forming trial alliances. Once the sponsor has a language that captures the performance gap, it is fine-tuned by seeing who supports it. Those who are pushing for change are often required to ratify the importance of a need or opportunity. The sponsor attempts to mobilize support by drawing on centers of power inside and outside the organization. Initially, the sponsor identifies networks of people who think alike, seeking support to act. This group is then expanded to include key people who are potentially useful in promoting a solution.

According to Jerrell (1980), hardball politics, media scrutiny, and interorganizational relations shape the coalition as it evolves. Plan sponsors must recognize and assess each factor as the coalition is forming. Plan environments often contain tough, ambitious, and calculating competitors who vie for status behind a public veneer of idealism. Their behavior can be described as "survival of the most shrewd." Each competitor develops attitudes and game plans. While the manager need not respond to ruthless behavior in kind, he or she must recognize that political action is essential to prevent total control by an adversary who engages in *hardball politics*.

Government regulatory agencies and special interest groups often operate under hardball norms. For instance, to pressure hospitals, Blue Cross agencies can deny rate increases, the Medicare-Medicaid program can delay payments, and regulators can refuse to initiate reviews of capital expansion proposals. Similarly, activist groups often form in a community and demand that firms stop dumping toxic waste, end discrimination, and allow local leaders to participate in institutional decision making. Increasingly, such groups seek capitulation, not compromise.

The *mass media* looks for controversy, because controversy stimulates interest. For example, when a company presents its case to close a downtown division and build a new one in the suburbs, the media will look for controversy, not the logic (or lack of it) in the case presented. Inconsistencies in the argument will be dramatized. For example, if people disagree on the merits of relocating the division, the media sense an expose. They will draw attention to inconsistencies among the arguments made, and away from points that each of the debating parties seeks to make. Charges of bias, negativism, oversimplification, and outright hypocrisy often follow.

Politics is also played externally to balance the competing goals and interests in the community. Interorganizational relations often become important, in which pluralistic politics create problem definitions for planned change. Organizations have many constituencies, and often these constituencies have incompatible interests. When these interests demand representation, conflict is ensured. For example, the governance of some hospitals is made up of providers, consumers, third-party payors, critics, and those with the express intention of tearing down the current health system. Each possible alliance has vested interests that can influence planned change. The CEO grapples with this situation by balancing the conflicting demands. The analysis of factors that has led to conflict among the interest groups is carried out to assess the needs or opportunities that can be identified by the sponsor. When faced with supercharged issues, sponsors seek both political and personal types of advice. One set of information stems from analysis, the other from a desire for self-preservation. Each helps to assess whether dealing with a need or opportunity is feasible.

*Recognition*. The recognition step considers the reciprocal effects of exploration, diplomacy, and rationalization activities to propose and then test the viability of various alliances (Table 5-2). Diplomacy identifies who thinks what about the issue. It assesses how power centers in the organization are aligned vis-à-vis a need or opportunity and if they support a planned change effort. Diplomacy has two components: scanning and solicitation. To scan, the sponsor assesses the beliefs of key people to determine whether these beliefs must be a part of the need or opportunity stipulation. Preserving personal power for the sponsor is often an integral part of the stipulation. Managers spend much of their professional lives involved with the acquisition of power and authority and will go to great lengths to avoid giving it up. During the solicitation phase, the sponsor attempts to gather support for his or her understanding of needs or opportunities. Scanning and solicitation form the basis for the sponsor's exploration and lead to a rationalization of available information, suggesting how to form a coalition (Table 5-2).

*Coalition*. In step 4, coalitions (Thompson, 1967) are formed. The sponsor forms a group that can agree on a need or opportunity that seems politically feasible to address. Bargaining is used to determine the payoff demanded by various people who are affected by needs or opportunities as they are being defined. Two types of gambits are used. One deals with the resources required to initiate planned change, and the other introduces "red herrings" to divert attention. Political diagnostics initiate a planned change effort to deal with the preconceived notions of the coalition. The coalition can call for postponement, avoidance, competition, accommodation, or the adoption of a pet idea. Thus, many planned change processes begin with some notion of the preferred outcome that accompanies the stipulation of need or opportunity.

The rationalization settled on offers a need or opportunity that often creates some form of confrontation. Confrontations take place by debates, discussions, and a whole host of other information exchanges in which the sponsor coaxes others to adopt his or her view of a need or an opportunity. Resolution comes from consensus and mandate. If no consensus emerges, the planned change effort is aborted before it can begin.

*Need or Opportunity*. Resolution in Table 5-2 ends with a stipulation of needs and/or opportunities acceptable to a coalition that initiates a planned change process.

## ▲ TWO VIEWS OF PROCESS MANAGEMENT

Some approaches to planned change delegate developmental activities, as shown in Figure 5-2. The sponsor's decision making consists of offering a need or op-

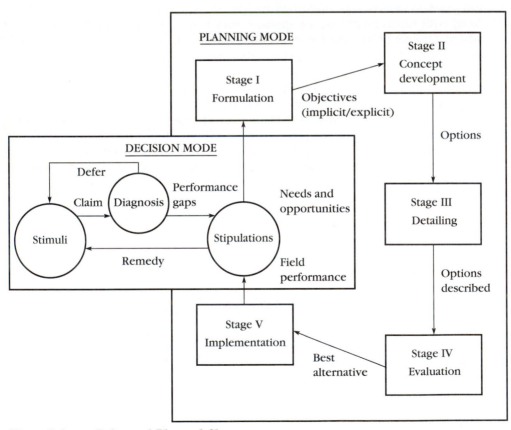

Figure 5-2 ▲ Delegated Planned Change

portunity stipulation and accepting or rejecting a remedy. When performance is below expectations, a stipulation is made to activate a planned change process. The sponsor then delegates process management and waits for a remedy, reserving judgment until its merits and degree of opposition can be determined. Meritorious plans that do not provoke opposition are adopted. The rest are rejected or held up until modifications that overcome objections, questionable benefits, or both can be made.

Delegation can be intentional or unwitting. An intentional delegation occurs when the sponsor compares the planned change effort to other responsibilities and finds that it has priority. Unwitting delegation results when sponsors have their decision-making prerogatives taken over by experts and staff specialists who have taken on the manager's role. Many (but not all) experts and staff specialists prefer, and even try, to keep a sponsor at arm's length as the planned change process unfolds. The loop shown in Figure 5-2 describes the *path* preferred by planners, an orderly procession moving from one stage to the next and terminating in some form of a field test. The sponsor waits until planning is finished to see if a field test or simulated performance indicates the performance gap has been closed.

The sponsors of planned change should not merely accept or reject the planner's vision of what can or cannot be done. To take a more active role, sponsors must steer the planned change effort. Sponsors in an active management role can identify concerns as the process unfolds. Concerns that frequently arise identify the nature of the transactions and information exchanges that should occur as a planned change process is carried out.

## ▲ THE TRANSACTIONAL APPROACH TO PROCESS MANAGEMENT

Sponsors guide a planned change process by calling for key information, as shown in Figure 5-3. As a result, the sponsor and planner (e.g., staff specialist) are expected to interact throughout the process. This interaction calls for the planner to provide information to a decision-making process that is external to the planned process. The sponsor makes decisions for each stage of the process. The nature of the transactions in each process stage suggests ways in which the process can be managed.

The sponsor may take on the role of a planner, moving to the planning mode in Figure 5-3, or delegate these activities to staff or experts who are brought in to support the planned change effort. A partnership between the sponsor and individuals who take on a planner role in one or more process stages produces the best results.

### Formulation

The sponsor is experiencing the frustrations of declining revenues, unacceptable declines in plant capacity, or complaints about ineffective operations. This experience shapes the sponsor's notions of what's needed or required and fashions need or opportunity stipulations that provide direction.

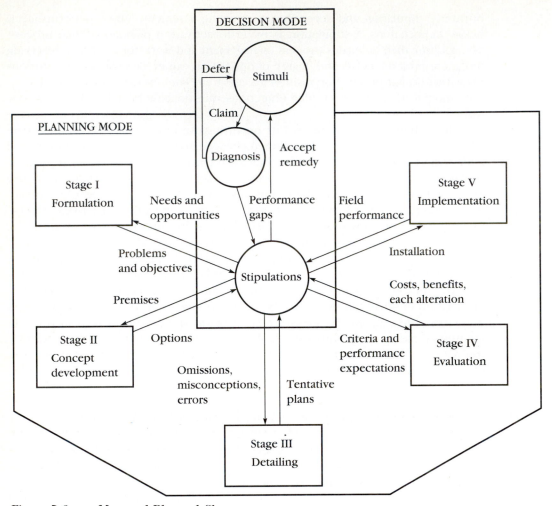

**Figure 5-3** ▲ **Managed Planned Change**

Adapted from Nutt (1986).

During formulation, the sponsor reconsiders his or her views of needs or opportunities and the directions that are implied. This activity, if it occurs at all, is frequently carried out by a sponsor without the assistance of others. Ideally, someone in a planner role should be involved in these transactions. The sponsor stipulates needs or opportunities that the planner interprets, using one or more planning techniques to identify priority problems and objectives (see Figure 5-3). The sponsor tests the problems and objectives to see if they offer new insights into process direction. In this exchange the sponsor can provide too little or too much leeway. Either can lead to poor results.

Repeated unsuccessful attempts to define problems can signal unrealistic sponsor expectations or misunderstandings between sponsor and planner. For example, in consulting, the client often demands a proposal that provides definition of the planning problem and suggests a solution. But defining the problem and offering a way to solve it captures much of the creative act in consulting. It also sweeps away a good deal of the uncertainty surrounding the project with noncompensated work. The Department of Defense (DOD) use of a recursive bidding process to select a contractor provides another example. Bidding is repeated several times, permitting the DOD to use the information gleaned from past bids to restipulate performance requirements for the next round of bids. The defense contractors regard this practice as unethical, but it does provide the DOD with considerable information about the feasibility of various weapon systems.

Too little stipulation can also create difficulties. Sponsors may be afraid to show their ignorance and provide only vague or ambiguous stipulations. This makes the arena of action unclear, and implicity delegates direction to someone in a planner role. Planners, left to their own devices, may have little insight into what can or should be done, which leads them to take unproductive directions.

## Concept Development

Once an objective has been selected, the sponsor offers "premises" for the concept development stage. These premises provide notions of causality and/or interventions that the sponsor believes can be helpful in dealing with the performance gap. Limits to the scope of inquiry are also specified. Armed with a definition of the planning arena and some solution concepts, the planner attempts to construct options, as shown in Figure 5-3. The sponsor may take on this role, developing options or proposing them. However, better results are produced when provincial ideas are avoided and a search for ideas is carried out by several knowledgeable individuals.

The options that surface may change the arena or suggest a solution tactic that challenges the premises initially offered. Sponsors may reject one or more of the options when a sufficient number of their premises are left out. From the planner's vantage point, some sponsors do not allow the planner enough latitude to interpret the sponsor's wishes and views and offer remedies.

This interaction can lead to cycling. Cycling occurs when the arena of planning is progressively altered to incorporate a sponsor's objections. This dialogue may serve to stimulate high-quality solutions or may degenerate into an acrimonious debate.

## Detailing

The detailing stage is expected to provide a tentative plan. Sponsors may attempt to dominate detailing by offering a canned solution or may delegate development to a planner. Again, a partnership is encouraged in which the sponsor tests the plans suggested by experts and staff specialists for omissions, misconceptions, and errors.

Following widely held views of planning, individuals in a planner role should attempt to introduce several competing plans for the sponsor to consider. However, the typical planning effort develops very few alternatives with distinct features (Mintzberg et al., 1976; Nutt, 1984a). To illustrate, prior to the outbreak of hostilities in Korea, only one distinct alternative was considered by government study groups. Armed intervention was the key ingredient in all "options" that were considered (Snyder and Page, 1958). Allison's (1969) study of the Cuban missile crisis revealed that policymakers considered two distinct options: armed intervention and blockade. In each case, government policymakers believed that a wide range of alternatives had been considered.

When competing alternatives are introduced, the sponsor may react unfavorably. As the list grows, the sponsor may see only the difficulties in sorting out a preferable plan and not the benefits that come from competing ideas and hold these new alternatives to higher standards. More refinement is required in the new options, and omissions and errors tend to be overstated in their review. The dialogue between the sponsor and the planner can focus on the appropriateness of these judgments and not the sponsor's attempts to comprehend each alternative.

## Evaluation

In the evaluation stage, the options are subjected to an assessment. Sponsors can make intuitive judgments about merit or ask for assessments by users, experts, and staff specialists. Again a partnership in which sponsor intuition is augmented by the assessments of others is preferred. The sponsor, with the help of users and other interested parties, identifies costs, benefits, acceptance, and still other criteria to determine the best plan. Planners carry out an evaluation to determine how each of the alternatives meets each criterion. The sponsor compares predicted performance expectations. When these expectations are not met, cycling often results.

If the choice is not clear cut, most sponsors will repeat the evaluation to confirm their norms or to verify the accuracy of the evaluative information. If no option emerges as a clear winner, the sponsor may call for new or revised alternatives. After several such cycles, the sponsor's norms may change.

The dialogue between the planner and the sponsor in the evaluation stage stems from the nature of the decision rule that is applied. Thompson (1967) contends that the explicitness of performance criteria and the extent to which cause-effect or producer-product relationships in the plan are understood defines the best decision rule. In order of their power, these decisions rules are optimizing, satisficing, instrumentality, and social tests. An optimizing test can be used when both cause-effect relationships and criteria are known to compare plans, following a Leibnitzian IS (Chapter 2). A social test is used when both are unknown and applies a Lockian IS. In the remaining tests only one of these factors is understood. A satisficing test has known criteria and the instrumentality test has known causal relations. A "satisficing" sponsor would select the first plan that meets the objective selected in stage I, and an instrumental sponsor would select the first plan that seems to work.

Well-informed planners expect the sponsor to use the most powerful decision rule feasible. But as Mintzberg et al. (1976) point out, choices among plan options are often based on imitating high-status peers or organizational traditions. Such sponsors rely on social tests, comparing their plans to the practice of others, and tend not to use analytical evaluation information.

Sponsors who lack control over needed resources will bargain with those who have resource control. In this type of situation, a sponsor may adopt an alternative merely because it has powerful supporters (Cyert and March, 1963; March, 1981). Planners who are unable to see these motivations often find such a choice to be arbitrary and capricious. Cynical views of the sponsor's motives result. Planners who question a sponsor's motives may attempt to control the process by pruning and distorting evaluation information.

## Implementation

In stage V, the sponsor installs the plan. Performance factors like cost and satisfaction are gleaned from actual or simulated operations and used to measure success. Performance measurements are monitored by the sponsor until the plan is functioning at the anticipated level. Poor performance can suggest the need for a better implementation approach or a return to stages I, II, III, or IV to rectify the problems encountered in the field.

Plan revision also occurs for reasons that are not performance related. These include politics, information control, the actions of dissidents, and a failure to understand the plan.

Planners may be told to revise a plan for *political* reasons. A sponsor can seek to satisfy organizational needs through the attainment of personal goals, believing that personal achievement and organizational growth are synonymous. To such a sponsor, a plan is implemented only if it can enhance the sponsor's prestige. If the plan has a neutral or negative impact on the sponsor, the plan may be rejected and the planner told to return to an earlier stage to revise it. In such a situation, the reasons cited by the sponsor to modify the plan will seem flimsy and evasive to the planner. Sponsors are unlikely to reveal what will be acceptable because their expectations would be couched in personal terms.

Sponsors may resist implementing a plan that reveals *information* they control. Information is power (Huber, 1982). Sponsors will not relinquish control of important information sources, even to obtain a high-quality solution. For example, oil company executives, well trained in quantitative methods, resisted using linear programming to allocate crude oil to refineries. Linear programming provided an optimal solution to the allocation problem, but also revealed the executives's allocation rules. Intuitive approaches to allocation were retained until competitive factors forced the adoption of analytical methods. The implementation of inventory control models and computer-aided diagnosis is often blocked for similar reasons. Sponsors do not want uncontrolled information flowing in their organizations. As before, the rationale for blocking a plan is seldom shared. The planner is merely told to seek another solution or to abandon the project.

Implementation may be delayed while the sponsor consults with potential *dissidents* or groups to comprehend the consequences of the plan and/or its implementation. The sponsor must justify the plan to its users and to power centers in the organization, so full *understanding* is essential. If resistance develops, the project may be abandoned or started again with new objectives. For example, a manager may find that an automated record system, while efficient, seems unacceptable to the accounting department and the chief financial officer. The astute manager carefully measures the lengths to which he or she will go in pushing for the system's adoption. If a modest amount of persuasion fails to convince the CFO of the system's merits, the manager may retain the manual system. A positive balance of social credit must be retained to deal with such a center of power in the future.

Under these conditions, planners seldom understand the need to revert to an earlier stage. The rationale is not shared when implementation is blocked by the sponsor for personal reasons. And planners seldom participate in the negotiations orchestrated by sponsors to win over powerful constituents. Legitimate reasons for a new plan or revised plan may develop, but may be considered "sensitive" by the sponsor. Thus, the needs for refinement may be distorted (by the sponsor) or misunderstood (by the planner). Communication between the planner and the sponsor breaks down and conflicts may result.

## The Planning Path

When the sponsor draws the planner into the decision mode shown in Figure 5-3, they may emerge in any stage. The sponsor may apply a test or ask for information that has little to do with the results the planner seeks to report. For instance, the planner may suggest an objective, only to find the sponsor unwilling to reconcile this objective against his or her view of needs and opportunities, insisting that the planner propose a solution. If the planner fails to offer a solution, the ideas of the sponsor may be introduced. The planner must then move to stage III to detail and stage IV to evaluate the sponsor's idea. The outcome of this evaluation may call for the problem to be redefined, reverting to stage I, or the sponsor may choose to implement, shifting to stage V. Patterns of movement through the transactional model identify the "planning path" that profiles how a sponsor manages the planned change process.

Interrupts and time pressure also cause movement between stages. *Interrupts* stem from environmental factors (Mintzberg et al., 1976). They force the sponsor to halt the project to consider the views of important patrons, benefactors, or constituents, causing attention to shift from one stage to another. For example, a powerful member of the board of directors may insist that an expansion plan incorporate a waste management program in which he has an interest. The vested interest is known but hard to discuss. A community group, contending that the expansion plan would destroy their neighborhood, may block the expansion plan in the courts. The process pauses to take in this information and then shifts to the stage best able to deal with these events. Interrupts also occur when the sponsor attempts to understand the results from any stage (comprehensive recycles) or when the sponsor or planner tries to overcome failures (repair recycles).

*Time pressure* can truncate the process. Sponsors with a "crises orientation" may force planners into shortcuts that lead to stage skipping. Such an orientation can cause poor results and has given rise to the adage, "There is never time to do it right, but always time to do it over."

## ▲  PROGRESS MANAGEMENT TACTICS

The transactional model in Figure 5-3 was used to profile the nature and sequence of steps in planned change efforts carried out by practitioners. The transactions between key participants were gleaned from interviews with sponsors and others who worked on the project. The interviews asked the participants to spell out the steps that were taken and the order in which the steps were carried out. The profile captured consensual views of what had transpired. The case profiles were sorted into categories that had different steps and step sequences. Frequently occurring patterns of step sequences were identified as tactics. To show how practitioners manage planned change, the tactics applied by sponsors to carry out formulation and implementation will be presented.

Three formulation tactics called target, idea, and problem emerged from this analysis (Nutt, 1992). Four implementation tactics were identified called intervention, participation, persuasion, and edict (Nutt, 1986). Each tactic is illustrated with an example.

### Formulation in Practice

Three types of formulation procedures, each using two different tactics, are presented. Each formulation procedure resolved claims into a performance gap. The distinguishing features stemmed from the steps taken to form a coherent statement about how to proceed. The features of these procedures and tactics are summarized in Table 5-3.

#### Formulation with Targets

This type of procedure responds to performance gaps drawn from claims with a target (e.g., a statement of objectives, missions, aims, or goals) that is used to guide developmental activities. Directions stem from desired performance, such as reduced costs or increased capacity. The objective could specify a specific target (e.g., decrease cost by 20 percent) or a general target (e.g., decrease cost), identifying the two *tactical* variations that managers used to deal with objectives. Because

Table 5-3  ▲  Formulation Tactics

| Tactic Type/Variations | Features |
|---|---|
| *Target processes* | *Target* are used to focus development. |
|   Specific target tactic |   Target have specific targets. |
|   General target tactic |   Target have general targets. |
| *Idea process* | *Idea* ultimately used is available at outset. |
|   Concept tactic |   Process is used to fine-tune idea. |
|   Inferred problem tactic |   Analysis is used to link problems to idea before fine-tuning. |
| *Problem processes* | *Problems* are used as focus to identify solutions. |
|   Inferred solution tactic |   Problem analysis is used to infer solution. |
|   Arena search tactic |   Arena identifies where to search for solutions. |

a means is not suggested or implied, there is considerable freedom to search for a way to meet stated aims during development, encouraging innovation but also potentially lengthening the process and increasing its costs.

The steps in formulation are claims, performance gap, stipulations of needs or opportunities, and a statement of an objective with a specific or general target, as shown in Figure 5-4. (In the figures, circles indicate decisions; boxes, planning activities.) Specific targets identify specific expectations for profit, cost, revenue, and the like. The general target created expectations such as needs to improve cost and profit performance, without indicating an expected amount of cost or profit.

### The Answering Service Case

The stimulus for the planned change project profiled in Figure 5-5 was prompted by a need for space. (The direction of the arrows in the figure show the sequence of actions and decisions as the planned change was carried out.) A new chief operating

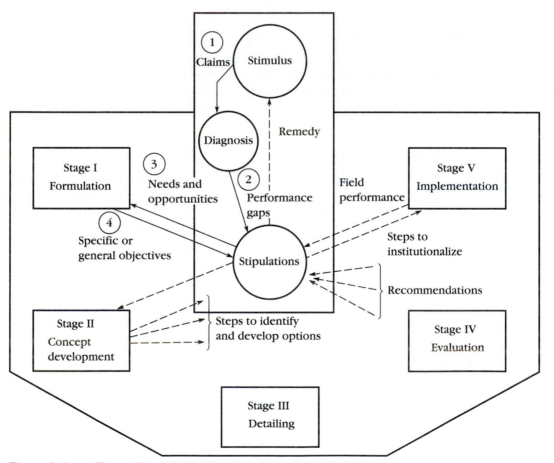

**Figure 5-4** ▲ **Target Formulation Processes**

officer (COO) had just been hired by a large real estate company with 800 agents. The COO had been given a mandate to trim costs and improve operations. The COO was searching for space to house computers that he had just purchased when he found a heretofore unknown answering service for agents in a large room adjacent to the company's switchboard. The operator informed the COO that she had worked for the agents for 13 years, taking important messages and routing appropriate calls to their home or car phones.

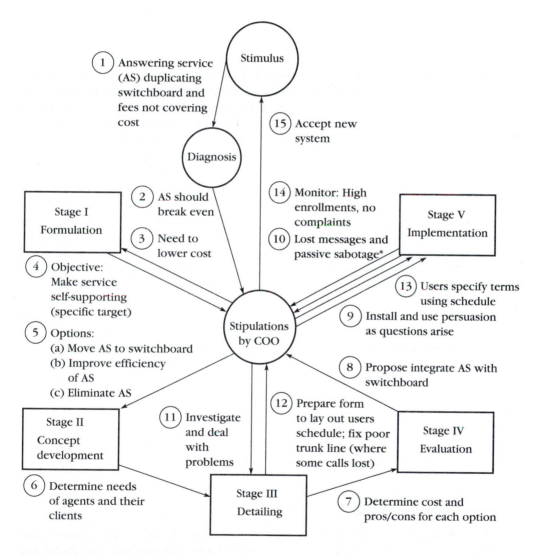

* By former AS operator (refused to interpret binder of instructions, e.g., where to call and conditions)

Figure 5-5 ▲ Answering Service Case

The COO looked into the arrangements, finding that the agents paid $50 per month for this service, and 50 of them were currently enrolled. This provided a revenue of $2500 per year, which covered less than 10 percent of the $30,000 cost of the service (step 1, Figure 5-5). The remaining cost was paid by the company, who paid the operator's salary and benefits and rented the equipment. This led to the diagnosis (step 2) that subscription services, such as this, should break even. Development began when the COO stipulated the need to lower the cost of the answering service. The need to relieve space problems was left as an implicit reason behind the project. The COO set an objective of making the answering service self-supporting (a specific target).

In step 5, the COO stipulated that three options be considered: (1) moving the answering service to the switchboard, (2) improving the efficiency of the answering service, and (3) eliminating the answering service. In step 6, a survey was carried out to determine the needs of agents and their clients. In step 7, the cost and pros and cons for each of the three options was determined. Integrating the answering service with the switchboard could produce a break-even situation without an increase in charge to the agents. In step 9, installation was attempted through persuasion in which the COO would answer agent questions as they arose. The answering service operator was offered a new part-time position. She resisted changing duties or being given a job that was seen as less important and resigned.

In step 10, several performance problems cropped up as measured by lost messages and the passive sabotage by the former answering service operator. The former operator had refused to interpret a binder in which she had compiled agent instructions, such as where to call to reach them and conditions under which calls should be taken or messages transcribed. She contended that these instructions had been largely memorized, and she kept only partial documentation. She refused to recall or transcribe these arrangements.

In step 11 the COO began a redesign of the answering service. A form was prepared to document agent instructions regarding calls. The information was organized and the switchboard operator trained. In addition, it was found that messages were being lost due to a poor trunk line, which periodically would not ring through to the switchboard. This problem was rectified with the local telephone company. In step 13, agents were allowed to specify terms for calls being forwarded. In step 14, the COO monitored agent enrollment in the service and complaints. All former users had enrolled, an additional 50 agents had signed up for the service, and no complaints had been lodged. In step 15, the COO accepted the redesigned answering service because revenue was now covering company costs.                    ▲

### Formulation with Ideas

Idea procedures had three steps: the reconciliation of claims, performance gap recognition, and an application of preexisting ideas. The sponsor had an idea in mind before the effort begins and imposes this idea on the planned change process. Analysis is focused on the idea to verify its virtues and to determine the reactions of key people. Developmental activities are used to refine the idea. Such an approach limits innovation, but reduces uncertainty about the nature of the plan. Risk for the sponsor is lowered because there are no surprises that could mobilize unexpected opposition. Also, time is not taken up in idea finding, just idea exploring. Two tactics are used to carry out idea processes, called "concept" and "inferred problem."

### Concept Tactic

The concept procedure has three steps: claims, performance gap, and idea (see Figure 5-6). The idea imposed on the planned change process becomes the focus of all subsequent inquiry. For example, the success of a tax checkoff option used by the state of Minnesota in its income tax regulations was adopted by Ohio as a means to support "natural areas" and "wildlife protection" programs. The tax checkoff idea promoted developmental steps to ensure passage of the required legislation. No attempts were made to evaluate the success of the Minnesota program. It was merely borrowed and used as the idea in a planned change process that took more than a year to carry out.

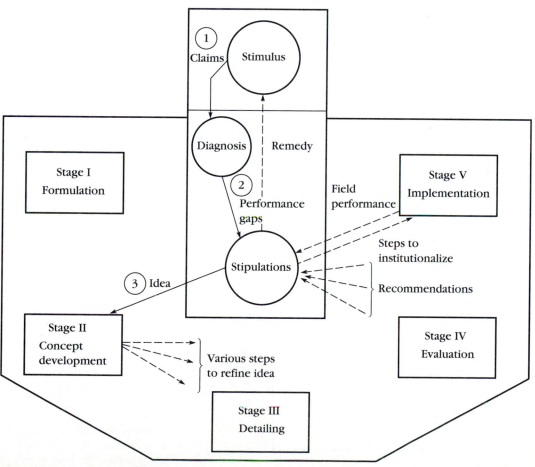

**Figure 5-6** ▲ **Concept Tactics**

### The Solar Energy Case

Figure 5-7 profiles a planned change case dealing with solar energy. A solar heat pump was devised during the mid-1970s when the escalating cost of energy was thought likely to continue indefinitely (stimulus). The CEO of an air conditioning manufacturer was approached by the developer of a solar heat pump

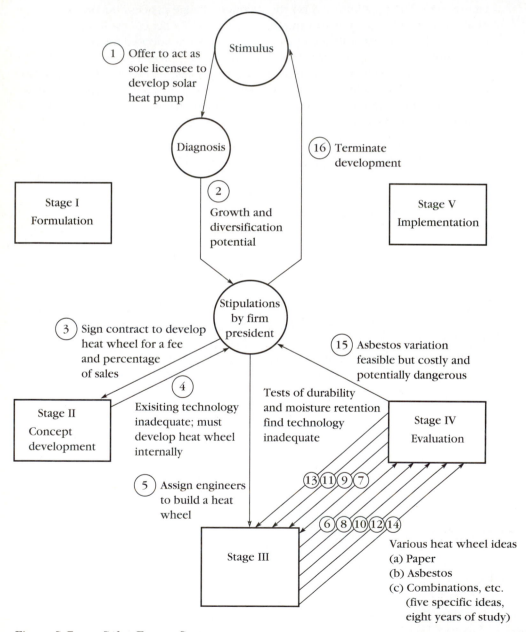

Figure 5-7   ▲   Solar Energy Case

who offered the firm a license for its manufacture (step 1). Exploration of the idea (diagnosis) revealed growth and diversification potential (step 2). A 30 percent increase in sales was thought to be possible (performance gap) through a new heating and cooling device that could be sold to homes. The firm's president signed a contract to develop a heat wheel, an integral part of the solar heat pump that licensure had yet to develop, for a fee and a percentage of the ultimate sales (step 3).

A search revealed that existing technology was inadequate and the firm must develop the heat wheel internally (step 4). In step 5, the firm's president assigned engineers to build the heat wheel. This resulted in an eight-year effort in which the engineers devised five specific heat wheel ideas and tested them for durability and moisture retention (steps 7–14). The first four of these ideas lacked either durability or moisture retention, or both. After eight years, an asbestos heat wheel was created that met the durability and moisture retention requirements (step 15). However, the material was also found to be costly and potentially dangerous. Recently disclosed environmental studies had linked asbestos to health hazards. This report was made to the president, who terminated development as the final step. ▲

### Inferred Problem Tactic

The inferred problem has steps of performance gap, idea, analysis, and stipulation of opportunities derived from the idea analysis (see Figure 5-8). The search for confirming evidence follows the recognition of a solution. Analyses are carried out to find problems that justify the solution. For example, the National Aeronautics and Space Administration (NASA) sought to broaden use of their hyperbaric oxygen treatment program (pressurized oxygen used for decompression) developed for astronauts and make it more cost effective by giving it to a local hospital. The Florida hospital that was offered NASA's program carried out analyses to determine its reimbursability as a treatment modality for various medical diagnoses.

### The Community Laboratory Case

The vice president of finance (sponsor) of a 500-bed suburban community teaching hospital hit on an idea of marketing the services of the hospital laboratory to compete with commercial labs in the community (the claim). The sponsor believed that considerable margin (excess revenue over costs) could be created by such a move. The "profits" would then be used to fund other initiatives (performance gap).

The idea of competing with commercial labs triggered three assessments shown in step 4, Figure 5-9. First, in the past year the hospital had purchased a satellite facility of 150 beds, 8 miles from the base hospital. A physician office building had been erected to serve the satellite hospital. The vice president of finance thought this group of physicians would be likely to use the lab because of their association with the hospital. Second, tests being done by commercial labs charged much more than the hospital's bookkeeping (real cost) charge for the same tests. As a result, the hospital could increase its prices and thereby increase its revenue. Third, it was

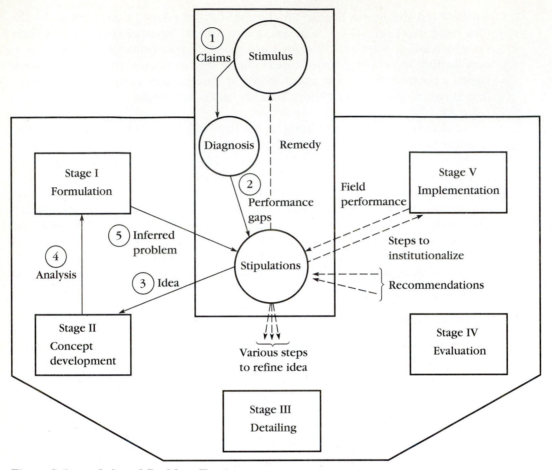

**Figure 5-8** ▲ **Inferred Problem Tactic**

felt the hospital's lab was superior in quality to the commercial labs and could be easily sold on that basis. The stage I–stage II loop in Figure 5-9 closed when the vice president of finance decided that increased revenue created an opportunity for the hospital, as shown in step 5.

The sponsor then delegated the project to an assistant vice president who was to carry out the details of planning, coordinating with the lab manager and others. As a first step, the assistant vice president conducted interviews with prospective users, moving to the evaluation stage. A series of interviews were carried out, involving a meeting with each physician who was to move into the physicians office building. The interviews had two purposes: to inform the physician about the new service and to find out what a physician looks for in a lab service. Stages 4 and 3 were connected by a "requirements analysis" that created a profile of the expected services.

These meetings suggested that the lab service should be sold as an "expansion to meet physician desires for a high-quality source of laboratory tests" to make

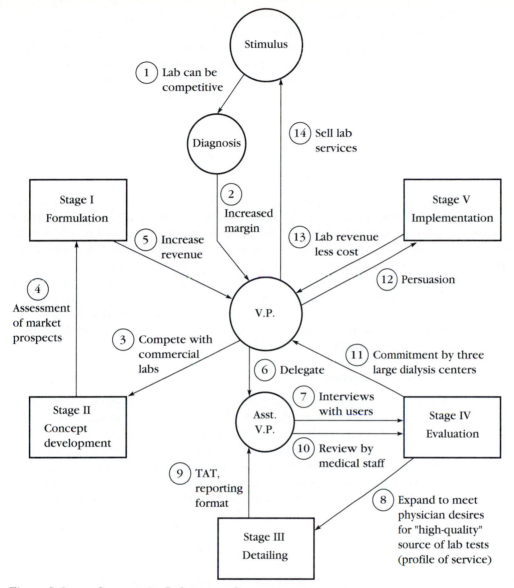

**Figure 5-9** ▲ **Community Laboratory Case**

the hospital appear charitable rather than profit seeking. Two key requirements were turnaround time and recording format. This led to a guarantee of a one-day turnaround time and a new format to report lab results. Other physician preferences were reviewed and judged according to their practicality and cost. (One preference, not adopted because it appeared too costly, was to alter the reporting format so test results and the normal range for that indicator could be listed.) It was generally agreed that cost should be minimized to ensure feasibility.

The looping of the sponsor between evaluation and detailing led to a second evaluation phase in which the plan was reviewed by the medical staff. This review produced a serendipitous outcome. One of the physicians, who owned three large kidney dialysis centers, had become quite unhappy with his commercial lab service. This physician agreed to shift all of his business—over $3000 a month—to a new system once it became operational. The single physician's commitment was sufficient to justify the plan, which the vice president of finance then installed. Performance monitoring compared lab profit to expectations.  ▲

### Formulation with Problems

In this type of procedure, a problem is analyzed to identify options. Sponsors become problem solvers, attempting to tease solutions from problems. This approach can be effective if important problems are recognized. If not, symptoms may be attacked that direct inquiry away from important concerns that lie behind the symptoms. Further, the problem suggests the nature of a solution. For instance, morale problems imply a morale-type solution, cost problems a cost-type solution, and marketing problems a market-based solution. A solution is implied by the problem, compared to target processes that are open to any solution that has favorable performance. Two tactics are used as attempts are made to extract solutions from problems: "inferred solution" and "arena search."

### Inferred Solution Tactics

The inferred solution tactic traces a path that goes in the opposite direction of the inferred problem tactic (see Figure 5-10). The steps are claims, performance gaps, stipulation of needs, analysis of needs, and inferring a solution that deals with these needs. For example, the appeals process in a department of claims could not deal with the volume of social security benefit cases. After considerable debate, a backlog of 18 months in dispositions was termed excessive. The need to reduce the backlog led to a pooling idea that grouped similar cases for mass handling.

### The Data Processing Case

A medium-sized company with many specialized products, selling to diverse customers, had been experiencing problems with its data processing. The system operated at very close to 100 percent capacity. Any downtime is very costly and causes many other problems. In addition, new ideas for the use of computer time are constantly arising and being rejected due to lack of capacity. This resulted in conflicts between data processing management and user departments, the engineering department and R&D. The data processing case is profiled in Figure 5-11.

Planned change was triggered by claims of inadequate capacity (step 1, Figure 5-11). These claims were brought to the CEO (the sponsor) who acted on the capacity needs of current data processing needs (step 2, performance gap), ignoring the new projects that required data processing support. The CEO conducted a search for ways to solve the capacity problem (steps 3 and 4). Two options materi-

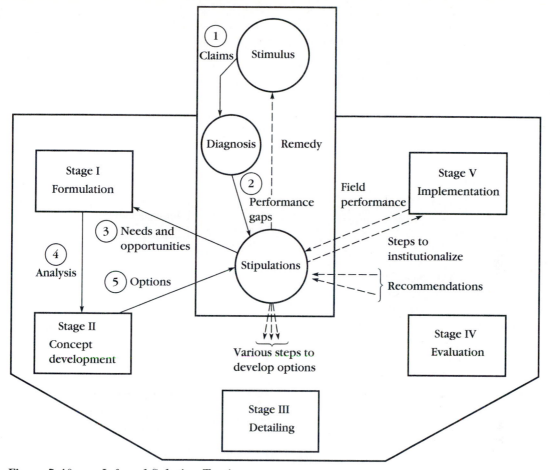

**Figure 5-10** ▲ **Inferred Solution Tactic**

alized: prioritize all current uses and allocate computer time, thereby assuming the risks of operating at 100 percent capacity, or purchase a new system (step 5).

The CEO preferred the "expanded system" option and hired the Ernst and Young consulting firm to evaluate the system's current status and make recommendations about each option (step 6). Predictably, the consultant found that the present system was inadequate for current and future operations (step 7). This re-activated the *formulation* stage, and the need for increased capacity was defined as the problem requiring solution (step 8). The sponsor looked for ways to increase capacity and lower operating costs, repeating problem-solving tactics (steps 8–10). This analysis determined that a new system should be created. This task was delegated to the data processing department (step 11). The department's staff linked concept development with detailing by making flowcharts of the present system and identifying options, described as various profiles of the system's features. For a period of time the system's features were gradually refined, resulting in three cycles with detailed plans in the detailing stage.

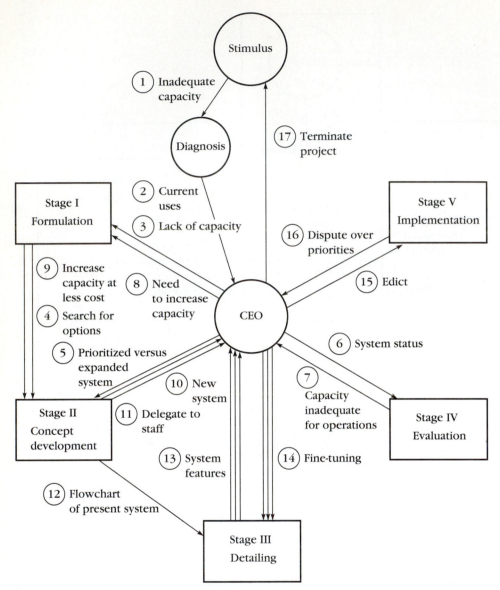

Figure 5-11 ▲ Data Processing Case

    The sponsor did not consult with other users and decided to implement the system by an edict in step 15. This led to an interrupt caused by disputes over priorities in the use of the new system. Ultimately, these disputes scuttled the project. ▲

### Arena Search Tactics

The arena search tactic provided a guide to search for solutions instead of a problem. The steps are claims, performance gap, arena of search, and arena-bound responses.

The procedure looks like the one for targets (Figure 5-4), except that arenas of search are stipulated by sponsors instead of needs or opportunities and solutions replace objectives. Sponsors seldom delegate solution search, relying on their powers of intuition to produce solution ideas. For example, in one of the cases, claims of inequities in salaries between males and females suggested potential problems of discrimination to an organization. The need for equity became the performance gap, leading to stipulating a search for ways to *overhaul the compensation system*. The arena (overhaul the compensation system) identified features of the solution. Sponsors stipulate an arena of action to be used to identify an idea, rather than a problem to be overcome, as in the inferred solution tactic.

## Implementation in Practice

The nature and degree of a sponsor's involvement in planned change management can be used to distinguish between implementation tactics. The tactics are called intervention, participation, persuasion, and edict. Each tactic had important variations. Table 5-4 summarizes the features of each tactic. The steps used in each of these implementation tactics will be illustrated with case examples.

### Intervention Implementation

Sponsors who apply an intervention tactic take control of the planned change process, as shown in Figure 5-12. To initiate planned change, sponsors become protagonists, justifying the need for change in the minds of key people. Applying new norms (step 1, Figure 5-12) and then appraising performance with these new norms (step 2) creates the justification to initiate a planned change effort. For instance, a new norm could be applied to the unit cost performance of a product by showing that a competitor has lower cost. These new norms can be bogus, applying anecdotal information or making ad hoc comparisons (e.g., the competitor has access to a low-cost work force), or they can suggest a real opportunity to make a positive change.

In step 3, intentions are stated based on the performance shortfall. This stipulation is followed by an identification of plausible causes for the performance gap, or showing what could be done to improve current practices. If suggestions are made, options are created that the planned change process must consider during development (steps 4 and 5).

Committees and task forces are sometimes asked for ideas or used as a sounding board, offering a commentary on the plan as it evolved. Sponsors, however, have the power to veto or modify any recommendation. All planned change activities are regulated by the sponsor, making it clear to all participants who has control. After a plan is devised, the sponsor demonstrates how changes called for by the plan overcome performance deficiencies in step 6. Performance monitoring follows plan installation (step 7).

Implementation steps following the intervention tactic can be summarized as

1. Assume the sponsor role and establish new norms to judge performance.
2. Apply new norms to identify performance inadequacies.

## Table 5-4 ▲ Implementation Tactics

| Tactic | Key Features | A Summary of Key Steps[a] |
|---|---|---|
| Intervention | 1. Sponsor acquires authority to guide the planned change process. <br> 2. Groups are used to offer advice that the sponsor can veto. | 1. *New norms are used to identify performance problems in system(s) that the sponsor is to change.* <br> 2. *New norms are justified.* <br> 3. *Illustration of how performance can be improved is given.* <br> 4. Develop plan.[b] <br> 5. *Show how plan improves performance.* |
| Participation | 1. Group can specify plan features, within prestated constraints. <br> 2. Staff is assigned to support the planning group. | 1. Sponsor stipulates needs and opportunities. <br> 2. *Sponsor forms planning group by selecting stakeholders.* <br> 3. *Sponsor delegates planning to the group and states intentions (objectives and constraints).* <br> 4. Planning group develops plan.[b] <br> 5. *Key people are coopted.* |
| Persuasion | 1. Demonstrations of value <br> 2. An expert manages the planned change process. | 1. Sponsor stipulates needs and opportunities. <br> 2. *Sponsor authorizes an expert to develop ideas responsive to the strategy.* <br> 3. Expert develops plan.[b] <br> 4. *Expert uses persuasion to sell manager on plan's value as a response to a strategic priority.* |
| Edict | 1. The sponsor and staff share process management responsibility. <br> 2. Sponsor uses position power to implement the plan. | 1. Sponsor stipulates strategic needs and opportunities. <br> 2. Sponsor develops plan.[b] <br> 3. *Sponsor issues a directive that calls for plan adoption.* |

[a] Steps in italics were found to differentiate the implementation tactics.
[b] Several additional steps are taken to develop the plan.
Adapted from Nutt (1986).

3. a. Justify new norms.
   b. Demonstrate feasibility of improving practices.
4, 5. Develop plan.
6. Demonstrate improvement in performance.
7. Monitor performance.

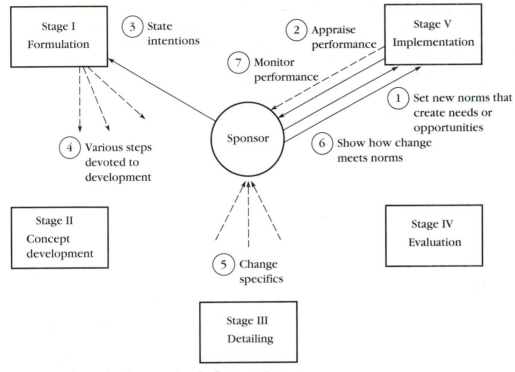

**Figure 5-12 ▲ Implementation by Intervention**

Information flows with solid lines depict implementation-related activities and dashed lines nonimplementation-related activities; circles represent decisions, boxes developmental activities. Reprinted from Nutt (1986).

### *Variations*

Tactical variations arise in the degree of justification that managers used. The justification step involved validating new norms, showing that change is possible, or both. These variations will be called feasibility tests, norm tests, and dual tests.

*Feasibility tests* indicate how organizational practices could be improved. For example, the sponsor in a firm demonstrated how the organization's materials' management procedures differed from up-to-date practices of inventory control.

*Norm tests* occurred when new standards to judge performance are established. For example, a hospital CEO phased out a decentralized approach to the management of patient care. Under the decentralized system, an administrator located in each hospital ward coordinated its use of supplies and of ancillaries, like X ray; its contact with admitting, billing, and other wards; and so forth. To phase out this department, the manager-sponsor contended that the administrative costs of competitors are lower because they avoided the duplication of effort and diffused the accountability inherent in a decentralized system.

Some sponsors addressed *both* norms and ways practices could be improved. For example, fiscally concerned hospitals were wary of providing burn care services because third-party payors, such as Blue Cross and Medicaid, did not cover all of the costs incurred. To overcome this objection, a demonstration was made of how the cost of burn care could be covered by using a combination of sources—endowments, governmental care cost reimbursements, private insurance, and a cheap resident work force. This sponsor integrated the demonstration of financial feasibility with a description of how successful burn units were operated.

## The Cash Flow Management Case

The project profiled in Figure 5-13 was initiated to deal with a cash flow problem in a company making shoes located in a large urban area. The company had just finished a $34 million construction project. The inconveniences caused by the construction had resulted in a significant drop in production. The large debt, coupled with decline in revenues, had caused a negative cash flow. To dramatize the problem, the entire management staff took a 5% salary reduction. At this point, the situation was labeled as having crisis proportions.

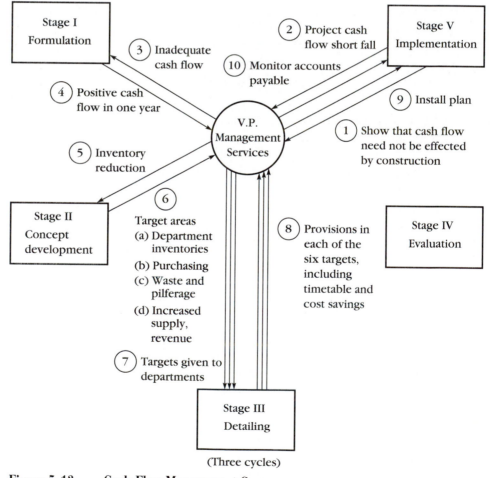

Figure 5-13 ▲ Cash Flow Management Case

A new vice president of management services (sponsor) was hired to deal with the company's financial problem. The sponsor determined the magnitude of the problem by monitoring cash flow and then demonstrated that construction is carried out in many companies without creating cash flow problems (step 1, Figure 5-13). Construction projects with larger disruptive effects in other shoe manufacturing companies were described to drive this point home to key people. The sponsor then stipulated a need to increase cash flow and set an objective of having positive cash flow within a year (steps 3 and 4).

Three distinct programs were initiated by the sponsor: reduction in accounts receivable, cost containment, and a reduction in accounts payable. For simplicity, just the last program is described here. To reduce accounts payable, the sponsor mounted an inventory reduction program. An objective of reducing accounts payable from $1.8 million to $800,000 was established. The inventory control program selected four target areas: reductions in departmental inventories, reductions in the cost of purchasing, reductions in waste and pilferage, and increased revenues from accounting for the use of supply items.

The features of the plan were preordained. The sponsor was hired because he had successfully implemented a similar plan at another shoe company. To initiate the detailing stage, targets were given to each department that had any involvement in stores, inventory control, departmental inventory control, purchasing control, supplies dispatch control, central processing control, and forms control. Each department head was to propose a way to reduce his or her share of the $1 million accounts payable reduction target. The departments were to respond with provisions in each of the six target areas, including timetables and projected cost savings (step 6). The sponsor examined details of these proposals in weekly meetings with each of the department heads. There were three cycles in the detailing phase as the sponsor made various modifications to the department head's plans (steps 7 and 8).

The sponsor imposed firm expectations, but allowed considerable latitude in how to meet them. This increased the prospect that the final plan would be supported by the departments. After the plan had been set in place by the sponsor, accounts payable were monitored to watch movement toward the target level (step 8), closing the process. ▲

### Participation Implementation

In participation implementation the sponsor initiates planned change by stipulating needs or opportunities (step 1, Figure 5-14) and then delegates development to a group. For example, a sponsor could cite the need to reduce excessive sick time or opportunities to acquire the space vacated by another department. As needs and opportunities are described, expectations with varying degrees of explicitness are set (step 2). In step 3 the sponsor selects task force members. The delegation to the group specifies constraints and expectations and identifies support staff assisting the group during development.

The group members are carefully selected so that key points of view and information would be represented. As a result, planning groups are often made up

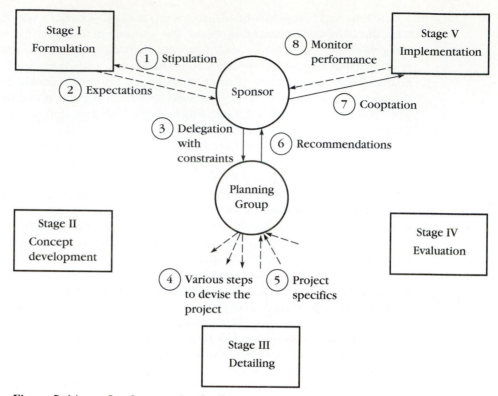

**Figure 5-14 ▲ Implementation by Participation**

Information flows with solid lines depict implementation-related activities and dashed lines nonimplementation-related activities. Boxes represent developmental activities; circles represent decisions. Reprinted from Nutt (1986).

of two types of people: individuals that have either vested interests or the knowledge to offer ideas.

Under the participation tactic, both the sponsor who initiates planning and a planning group share responsibility for guiding the process. The planning group makes suggestions and decisions, aided by staff who provided the information requested by the group. If the group has the authority to make decisions about the features of the plan, the implementation tactic is participative. The group leader cannot have veto power. As long as constraints are adhered to, it is understood that the plan proposed by the group would be adopted.

In steps 4 and 5 the task force arrives at a consensus about a plan or a proposal. In step 6, a recommendation is made. The cooptation implicit in this delegation becomes a vehicle to promote adoption and compliance in step 7, with performance monitoring in step 8.

Steps using implementation by participation are as follows:

1. Sponsors stipulate needs, opportunities, or both.
2. Sponsors set objectives.

3. Task forces are formed by sponsors who
    a. Identify stakeholders.
    b. Delegate responsibility with a statement of expectations and constraints.
    c. Assign staff support.
4, 5. Plan is developed.
6. Recommendations are made to sponsor.
7. Acceptance is promoted through cooptation.
8. Performance is monitored.

### Variations

The extent of involvement and the role of the task force identify the key variations in participation implementation. *Comprehensive participation* calls for delegation of development to fully representative task forces. This approach has the greatest cooptative potential owing to the breadth of the role and extent of participation that it allows. Task forces, whose memberships include all important stakeholders, such as users and power centers, create considerable commitment that makes implementation likely.

*Complete participation* also calls for full participation but asks task forces to frame rather than specify developmental details. Members might be asked to set directions or offer ideas, with staff specialists responsible for developing changes in line with the directions set or ideas offered. Completed participation is less cooptative than the comprehensive type because it restricts the role of a task force. Changes that have long-term effects and require broad-term commitments use this type of participation. For example, all users could be involved in critiquing proposed physical structures or procedures.

*Delegated participation* has stakeholder representatives suggest solutions. Strategic planning groups with members drawn from organizations' boards of directors and key executives illustrate this type of participation. Organizations selected benefit packages, designed laboratories, made contingency plans for strikes, carried out renovations, and planned operating procedures in this manner. In delegated participation, participants are often coopted, but their ability to persuade others to go along with changes hinged on whether the prerogatives of nonparticipants seemed threatened. Delegated participation is less effective than the complete type.

The least cooptative form of participation is called *token participation*. Both the use of representatives and their limited role hampers implementation. For example, surveys may be used to frame users' problems. But problems can be misunderstood unless carefully developed sampling procedures are followed. If not, those surveyed may be unaware of stakeholder needs or misrepresent them. Moreover, the members of a task force, although personally committed to changes, may fail to convince others. These two limitations suggest that token participation will be the least successful type of participation.

### The PBX Case

The PBX case (profiled in Figure 5-15) began when the organization's telephone operators filed a series of grievances concerning work load (step 1). Discussion with

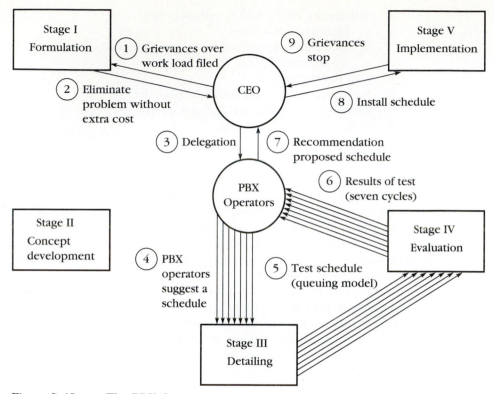

**Figure 5-15 ▲ The PBX Case**

Arrows trace the flow of information from authorization, designated by circles, to development, designated by boxes. Reprinted from Nutt (1986).

Bell System technical staff revealed the work demands made on the operators were 20 percent below that expected by Bell for their own operators. With this information in mind the sponsor, who was the CEO, asked an operations research staff specialist to rectify the situation. The specialist could make any change that did not increase operating costs (step 2). At the specialist's request, the sponsor delegated the choice of the terms of work to the PBX operators, making them a decision maker (step 3). The specialist asked the operators to identify schedules, with the understanding that any schedule could be adopted as long as it did not increase costs. A queuing model was used to evaluate the cost of each proposed schedule in step 5. The seventh option proposed was found to have accepted levels of both cost and satisfaction; no attempt was made to find the least cost or optimal schedule. In step 6, this recommendation was presented to the CEO. In step 7, a disgruntled supervisor who had not been involved, reluctantly put into effect the schedule the operators and management had agreed on. After the new schedule was set in place, the grievances stopped (step 8).

In the PBX case the delegated form of participation was used. Not all of the operators were involved, but task force members were allowed to dictate the terms of the new schedule, as long as it adhered to the preset constraint. ▲

### Persuasion Implementation

In persuasion implementation the sponsor makes little effort to guide the planned change process due to disinterest, lack of knowledge, or persuasive experts. The process begins when the sponsor or experts stipulate needs or opportunities (step 1, Figure 5-16). Sponsors allow experts to control development with little review. The path moves around the periphery of Figure 5-16 showing the independence of the experts who develop options and develop justifications in steps 2, 3, and 4. In step 5, experts present their plans for approval. Attempts are made to sell an option that seems best, using projected benefits to argue for adoption (step 6). Some sponsors become aggressive as they weigh the imperatives to act, demanding extensive documentation and even field trials. If convinced, the sponsor uses the same arguments to win over others during plan installation.

In persuasion implementation, the delegation of idea development to technical staff or consultants can be implicit or explicit. When this delegation is explicit, the sponsor assigns development to the expert. An implicit delegation occurs when an expert approaches a sponsor and garners the authority to develop an idea. The expert uses the sponsor's implied authority to carry out planning and then attempts

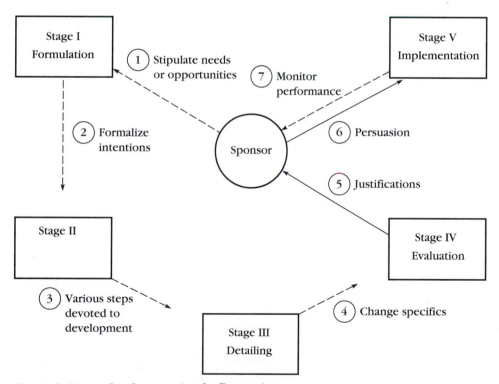

### Figure 5-16 ▲ Implementation by Persuasion

Information flows with solid lines depict implementation-related activities and dashed lines nonimplementation-related activites. Boxes represent developmental activities; circles represent decisions. Reprinted from Nutt (1986).

to "sell" the resulting plan. The plan's ability to help the sponsor realize a strategic aim is used by the expert to argue for its adoption.

Steps in implementation by persuasion are as follows:

1. Sponsors stipulate needs, opportunities, or both, or accept need or opportunity stipulations from experts.

2, 3, 4. Plan is developed.

5, 6. Interested parties uses persuasion tactics to sell ideas.

7. Performance is monitored.

### Variations

The key variation in implementation by persuasion stemmed from the type of expert, with two types of distinctions. The first is a distinction between the content and process expert. Content experts are familiar with topics or systems; process experts sold procedures describing how to carry out planned change and had no specific outcomes in mind. Content experts include consultants who sell turnkey plans to sponsors. Process experts are used when development is entrusted to organizational staffers thought to be skilled in procedure.

The second distinction was between consultants and internal staff. Internal staff carries out development in 70 percent of the persuasion cases (Nutt, 1986). When internal staff are involved, sponsors believe that the organization has experts skilled in either procedure or content. For example, a sponsor may ask a staff member to study existing supply management programs and recommend one to the organization. Internal staff purchased equipment, developed management procedures, planned construction and renovations, and designed accounting and other systems in this way.

Organizations hired consultants to carry out processes in 30 percent of the persuasion cases. Consultants who are experts in specific content areas are used when sponsors have little knowledge of or expertise in the planned change topic. Organizations also use consultants for projects that involved new technology. Consultants with process expertise are often used to develop construction plans and carry out specialized developmental activities, such as site selection and evaluations.

### The Scanner Case

The case profiled in Figure 5-17 deals with the initiation of a Magnetic Resonance Imager or MRI scanner service at a large osteopathic teaching hospital. The hospital has formal affiliations with colleges of osteopathic medicine in two different states. There are 42 residents and 26 interns as well as 5 medical students from one university and 25 from the other.

The hospital's first executive director had just passed away. This individual supplied most of the needed funds to establish the hospital. In turn, he was named the hospital's chief executive officer and had a relatively free hand in operating the hospital. Although some of the founding fathers were also shareholders and board members, they had delegated most decisions to the CEO. The CEO guided the hospital through difficult times, seeing it grow from its humble beginnings to its current status.

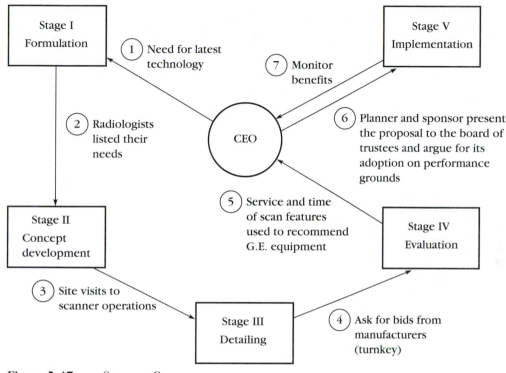

**Figure 5-17** ▲ **Scanner Case**

The new administrator had been in an "acting" capacity during a long hospitalization of the founder and, after the founder's death, was named his successor. During this phase, the physicians sought to establish more control over operations. One of the demands was for the latest technology, in this case an MRI scanner.

The MRI scanner rationale was compelling. MRI scanning provides radiologists with the latest means of making very clear cross-sectional pictures of the body, highly useful in diagnosis and treatment. Without such equipment, the osteopathic hospital would not be competitive with allopathic hospitals in the community, nor would the hospital be able to provide an adequate teaching site for its medical school affiliates. Although the project would require regulatory approval, these factors suggested that approval was likely. The planned change process proceeded with little or no discussion between the planner and the sponsor (the CEO). Instead, the radiologists acted as planners and carried out planning through discussions, listing their needs and how the scanner could meet them. These discussions linked stages I and II. Stages II and III were linked by site visits conducted by radiologists to visit other hospitals with MRI scanners. The visits enabled the radiologists to visualize the operation of an MRI service. Each was assessed to suggest desirable features in an MRI operation.

The link between stages III and IV was carried out by asking for bids. Manufacturers were given a very general mandate and asked to suggest an MRI operation for the hospital. After the bids were received, two criteria were used to assess them:

time of a scan and type of service contract that would be provided by the company. Radiologists reviewed the proposals and selected a preferred one, submitting it to the CEO.

The radiologists sold the plan using persuasion (step 6). The administration prepared a Certificate of Need application and submitted it to regulatory agencies for their review. Subsequently, a CON approval was received. In step 7, monitoring was carried out by measuring whether the scanner performed at the level expected.

▲

### Implementation by Edict

Edict implementation draws on the sponsor's power and authority. This tactic has three features. First, sponsor's control of the planned change process is intermittent with no underlying theme (see Figure 5-18). There is no recognizable pattern in monitoring and no formal delegation to gain insight into ideas or barriers to action. Experts and users are not consulted. Second, the sponsor does not discuss the plan with users or attempt to demonstrate its feasibility or need. Third, sponsors issue adoption directives. They merely announce the change and prescribed the behavior expected with a memorandum, formal presentation, and on-the-job instruction that

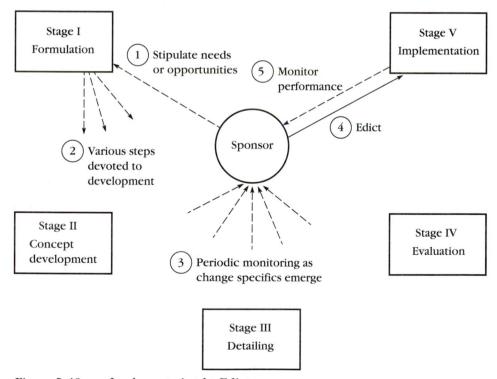

**Figure 5-18** ▲ **Implementation by Edict**

Information flows with solid lines depict implementation-related activities and dashed lines nonimplementation-related activities. Boxes represent developmental activities; circles represent decisions. Reprinted from Nutt (1986).

specifies who is to do what. For example, to introduce a new fringe benefit policy as part of a strategic plan, its sponsor prepared a memo that listed benefits and co-pay requirements and sent it to all employees.

Edicts were used when a sponsor attempted to show that his or her visions provided a way to deal with priority directions called for in the strategic plan. Sponsors with a vested interest often used these tactics. Edicts are also used when a plan has special significance or high visibility in contributing to a priority strategic direction. Building programs and other costly undertakings often conjured up sufficient importance to prompt the use of an edict.

The steps associated with edict implementation in planned change processes are as follows:

1.  Sponsors stipulate needs or opportunities.
2, 3.  Plans are developed.
4.  Sponsors issue directives.
5.  Performance is monitored.

### Variations

There are three notable variations in the use of edicts. These variations are based on whether changes have individual or organizational significance, or both. Sponsors can have a personal, vested interest in a change. The change is identified with a sponsor to the extent that a failure to adopt it would have hindered the manager's upward mobility. For example, a CEO, hoping to deal with a recent rash of injuries to employees in manufacturing incidents, announced a safety department by having the head of this new department make a presentation to key executives. Other sponsors saw themselves as acting in their organization's best interests by issuing edicts because they thought the changes had special significance. For instance, a sponsor used a memorandum to announce a new pricing policy, hoping to stem recent losses of business to a competitor. Still others believed their interests and their organization's interests synonymous. For example, a hospital started a helicopter transport system because the CEO was interested in flying and wanted to get his flight instructor a job. Additionally, a key competitor was about to offer the same service. Both the motivation to preempt the plans of the key competitor and the CEO's pet idea provided the imperative to act.

## ▲ LEVELS OF PLANNING

Planned change takes place on several levels, ranging from broad institutional or multi-institutional issues to the operating concerns of departments. For instance, a firm's strategic plan may involve several outside organizations (e.g., bankers and regulators) who aid in the development of a plan that is composed of broad options, such as product-market possibilities. Operational plans often deal with modifying the internal procedure or practice of a department. Three levels of planning are defined to capture planned change that has a broad, intermediate, and narrow scope.

## The Strategic Level

Strategic planned change is done in the upper reaches of an organization. The process is carried out to frame or discover a strategic posture for the entire organization (see Chapter 3). Objectives and the creation of broad options is stressed. Stages III and V are ignored. Evaluation (stage IV) is often cursory. Typically the analysis step in stage II is adequate, making stage IV (evaluation) cursory in strategic planning. Detailing and implementation are carried out in subsequent planning efforts at the project level. Examples of strategic planning include mergers and acquisitions, product or service initiatives, corporate restructuring, and foundations deciding on their funding priorities.

## The Managerial Level

The purpose of the managerial layer in an organization is coordinational (Thompson, 1967). Managerial plans often spring from indigenous sources, identified by needs within the organization, and less frequently from options defined by a strategic planning process. Managerial planned change projects can become strategic, if issues are redefined in sufficiently broad terms in stage I. Similarly, strategic processes may revert to the managerial level to detail options and test implementation prospects.

All planning stages can be important for this type of planning. The first four planning stages define an objective and create viable responses. Implementation is stressed because managerial projects tend to cut across several departmental boundaries. Frequently, steps must be taken to convince key stakeholders of the merits of the plan to the organization.

The sponsors of managerial planned change projects tend to be highly placed executives in the organization who have proven their ability to deal with large complex problems. Their most important attribute is past successes: Executives become plan sponsors when they have developed a track record. Success with small projects leads to large responsibilities. The CEO often takes control of projects that have particular importance to the organization.

Most of the planned change in an organization comes from the managerial layer. Examples include building programs, expanding services, new practices, creating internal services (e.g., industrial engineering), contingency plans for a strike, financial planning, information management, and the like.

## The Operational Level

Planned change at the operational level deals with projects that have few spillover effects into other departments. Typically, just single departments are involved. Structural changes required by the plan tend to be localized within that department. Often operational plans are undertaken to improve service to others. For example, revamping information management in a company creates many changes in its operations to produce faster and higher quality service at lower cost to its users.

Sponsors of operational planned change projects tend to be the department head or his or her immediate superior. All planned change stages are activated, but the detailing and evaluation stages are stressed. The key to success is the plan's viability. Only viability will sell the plan to higher-ups. Acceptance is somewhat less important than the managerial level, because fewer potentially conflicting parties are involved.

Like the managerial plans, operational plans tend to arise within the organization and search for a sponsor. Occasionally, operational plans begin at the strategic or managerial level and filter to the operation level for detailing and feasibility assessment. Only rarely do issues that originate at the operational level become accepted as managerial planned change efforts.

## The Integrated Process

On occasion, planned change spans all three levels. A strategic plan can activate the managerial level, which, in turn, calls for detailed plans from several operating departments. Processes that span all levels are complex, making it difficult to represent their path. For example, the path can move from strategic to managerial, and then to operational before returning to the strategic level for approval. (Plans will always revert to the highest level that has been involved for all approvals.)

Figure 5-19 illustrates how a planned change effort can span all three levels. In this example, a strategic plan was mounted that framed basic options, such as alternative visions of a firm's future. Objectives were set and visions formed in stages I and II, with seemingly viable concepts delegated to the managerial level for further exploration. For instance, a goal for a hospital to become a referral center can be sent to the managerial level to determine the feasibility of a major building project. Managerial planned change further conceptualizes the options by adding features, or options within options. For instance, various types of building plans can be considered: tertiary care, secondary care (e.g., adding acute care beds), or community services (e.g., alcoholism or drug abuse centers). These alternatives are partially detailed and assessed, with the best option sent to the operational level for detailed planning. An alcoholism treatment plan, for example, may be given to specialists to come up with a functional layout, a staffing plan, and a budget.

## Shifts Between Levels

Figure 5-20 illustrates the types of movements that a planned change process can make between levels. Type I process describes a process that begins and ends at the same level. These processes are typical of most planned change efforts, with managerial planning characterizing most of the projects carried out in the field. The answering service case, community laboratory case, and cash flow management cases discussed in this chapter provide illustrations.

Type II projects shift downward one level: strategic to managerial or managerial to operational. The solar energy, PBX, and MRI scanner cases provide illustrations. These projects crop up when the plan is thought to impinge on interests and prerogatives that span levels in an organization or when the higher levels lack information thought to be available at a lower level. Such processes are (1) strategic-managerial-strategic or (2) managerial-operational-managerial, reverting to the original level for approvals.

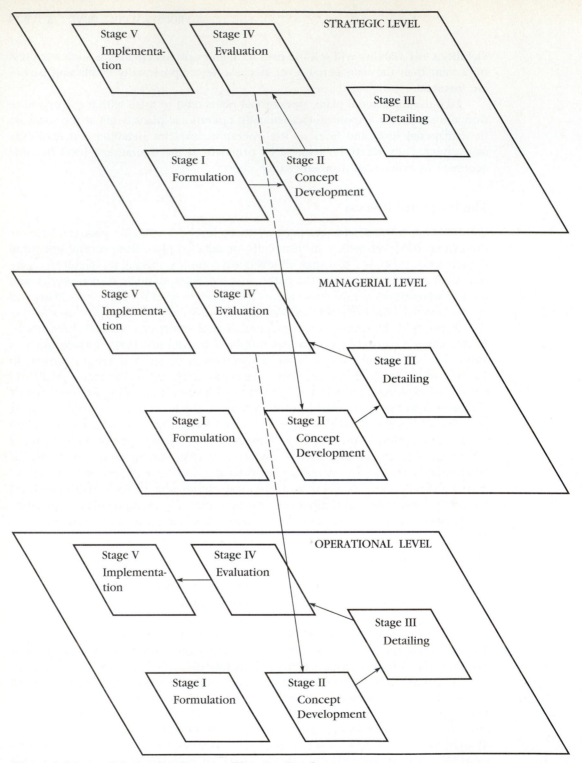

Figure 5-19 ▲ Relationship Between Planning Levels

140

|  | MOVEMENT TO | | |
|  | Strategic | Managerial | Operational |
| --- | --- | --- | --- |
| Strategic | Type I*<br>process | Type II<br>process | Type IV<br>process |
| MOVEMENT FROM   Managerial | Type III<br>process | Type I<br>process | Type II<br>process |
| Operational | Type V<br>process | Type III<br>process | Type I<br>process |

* A planning process that stays at the strategic level.

**Figure 5-20 ▲ Planned Change Processes That Move Between Organizational Levels**

The remaining shifts occur far less often. Type III processes try to shift to a higher level, attempting to get this level to take responsibility. This action is taken when the current sponsor recognizes he or she lacks the authority necessary to guide the process. Sponsors at the lower levels are reluctant to make such a request, so many of these projects are abandoned. When approached, the new sponsor may reject the request for legitimate (e.g., other priorities) or frivolous reasons, such as the "not discovered here syndrome."

A Type IV planning process moves from the strategic to the operational level. This shift is unlikely because the managerial layer would be, as a matter of course, consulted. Type V processes are rare because they call for an organizational "short circuit." The operational sponsor skips his or her superiors and goes over their heads to ask for someone at the strategic level to become a sponsor. Such behavior is dangerous and therefore rare.

## ▲ Key Points

1. The transactional model of planned change captures patterns in the sequence of choices during a planned change effort, illustrating how sponsors control and influence the process. Formulation and implementation tactics can be identified from the pattern of choices made by sponsors.

2. Formulation in planned change takes place when sponsors impose ideas, infer problems from an idea, attempt to analyze problems, look for solution cues in problem statements, or set specific or general objectives to guide development. These tactics characterize how formulation is typically carried out by managers during planned change.

3. Implementation is carried out by sponsors through intervention by renorming expectations for the practice to be changed, participation by having people influenced by the change determine some of its features, persuasion by demonstrating benefit, and edict in which power is applied to secure the compliance needed for a change to be successful. These tactics describe how implementation is typically carried out by managers during planned change.

▲  **Exercises**

1. Construct a transactional model for one of the projects in Chapter 1. Carefully review the case and then indicate with arrows the transactions between sponsors and others who support the planned change process, such as staffers, subordinates, or R&D departments. Note that sponsors do not assign all the activities called for in a stage. When this occurs the arrow connecting the sponsor (the decision maker) with a stage can depict reflection or the sponsor's pet ideas or visions. Not all stages will be activated. The arrow describing the planning path should be continuous, but need not go to all stages. To check your logic, trace the path to be sure it does not jump between stages without a connecting activity.

   Carefully review the case you have selected and then fit the steps to the transactional representation, noting the definitions of activities offered in this chapter (see Figure 5-3). Trace the sequences of steps with an arrow, as shown in this chapter. Note how the cases in this chapter were fit to Figure 5-3 as a guide.

2. Gather information to construct a transactional representation for two planned change efforts carried out by the same sponsor. Alternatively the projects profiled for Chapter 4 can be selected. To select projects, find one that was adopted (a success) and one that was developed but not implemented, or implemented but later withdrawn (a failure). Compare the two profiles. Speculate on the causes of failure, drawing on the formulation and implementation and process management ideas discussed in this chapter.

# 6 | Learning from Practice

This chapter presents an evaluation of the tactics used by sponsors of the planned change effort. Case histories of planned change, like those described in Chapters 4 and 5, are profiled to identify the tactics applied to set directions, develop options, and implement change. Indicators of success for each tactic are presented to identify tactics with the best track record. Both learning from practice and guidelines for practitioners emerge for the evaluation of tactics. Successful tactics are highlighted and recommended for wider use. Planning techniques can be substituted for practitioner tactics that have a poor track record. This assessment provides the basis for suggesting techniques and procedures found in Parts Three and Four of the book.

## ▲ ACQUIRING PLANNED CHANGE CASES

Planned change cases have been collected from a wide variety of organizations. Interviews with the sponsor of the project revealed the steps taken during the planned change and provided indicators of success (Nutt, 1984a, 1986, 1992).

### Participating Organizations

Table 6-1 provides descriptive information about the cases, the organizations represented in the cases, and the informants who provided the information. The prime informant (the sponsor) was often well placed in the organization. Thirty-four percent were CEOs and two-thirds were top executives (CEOs, COOs, or CFOs). The secondary informants were line managers, subordinate to the primary informant, in 45 percent of the cases, a staff person in 48 percent of the cases, and a task force member in seven percent of the cases. The most frequent type of observed planned change in the cases involved technology and controls, closely followed by products or services. In all, seven types of planned change efforts were included in the cases (Table 6-1).

### Identifying Tactics

Interviews with the sponsor and other project participants were conducted, asking each informant to spell out the sequence of steps that were taken during development, following procedures described in Nutt (1984a, 1986, 1991a, 1992). These steps were documented with the morphology, the transactional model, and a narrative.

### Determining Success

Determining the success of planned change is difficult because the value of its outcome can be controversial. To some the outcome may be beneficial, but to others it may be useless, making it difficult to separate the good from the bad planned change. For instance, plans that serve an individual's interest may be seen as good, those that do not as either neutral or bad. Also the downstream effect of a planned change can be crucial. What seems to be a poor plan when adopted may

## Table 6-1 ▲ Planned Change Types

|  | Percent |
|---|---|
| *Plan types* | |
| Service/product | 20% |
| Support services[a] | 17 |
| Personnel policy[b] | 7 |
| Technologies[c] | 23 |
| Reorganizations[d] | 4 |
| Controls[e] | 23 |
| Domains[f] | 6 |
| Total | 100% |
| *Organizational setting* | |
| Public | 26% |
| Private | 16 |
| Third-sector | 58 |
| Total | 100% |
| *Sponsor* | |
|   *Primary informants* | |
|   CEO | 34% |
|   COO | 25 |
|   CFO | 4 |
|   Middle manager | 37 |
|   Total | 100% |
|   *Secondary informants* | |
|   Subordinates | 45% |
|   Staff | 48 |
|   Task force member | 7 |
|   Total | 100% |

[a] Material management, parking, telephone, records, purchasing, laboratory, et cetera.
[b] Time off compensation, wage and salary, retirement, dismissal, et cetera.
[c] Equipment purchases, construction, space renovation, et cetera.
[d] Mergers, organizational restructuring, et cetera.
[e] Data processing, planning financial management, staffing, et cetera.
[f] Public relations, marketing, et cetera.

pay dividends in the future, such as the Dulles Airport. Others that seem to be good plans may fail and be withdrawn.

Adoption, merit, and duration measures identify three important aspects of a successful planned change. Pragmatics suggest adoption as a success measure. Success for a manager is bound up in use. If a plan is put to use, it meets this test. Applying the "put to use" criterion, a management information system (MIS) would be considered adopted if the organization stopped using the old system, and a merger would be adopted if it were completed. However, planned changes can evolve. For example, the merger may meet with initial resistance that holds up adoption but ultimately is carried out. Some departments may refuse to participate in the MIS, while all departments may use some of the capabilities of the MIS, ignoring other features. Planned actions can be initiated but later withdrawn. For instance, a new service or product can be withdrawn after performance monitoring.

Delays in use, proportion of use, and terminated use suggest important qualifications that suggest important downstream changes in the status of the plan. Two measures apply. In the first, "initial adoption" separates planned changes that have been tried out from the rest. The initially adopted plan has the potential to produce value for the organization, as contrasted to the plan for which implementation failed. "Initial adoptions" determine the proportion of plans that were initially put to use. The second measure captures downstream use. Projects were followed for two years to determine changes in use. Several kinds of modifications were observed. First, some plans were only adopted in part due to limited scale of use. Other plans experienced substantial delays before adoption. Finally, some plans were withdrawn after performance monitoring, becoming ultimate rejections, and some initially rejected plans were ultimately put into use. An "ultimate" adoption measure was created by calling partial adoptions and ultimate rejections "failures" and ultimate adoptions "successes." Because partial adoptions were treated as failures, the ultimate adoption measure provides a stringent test of use, as well as a determinant of sustained use.

The merit of the plan provides another success indicator. Plans with considerable merit may not be pragmatic. Merit can be determined by objective data, describing economic returns or benefits from the plan. However, most organizations are reluctant to provide information, such as money lost or gained, and others claim that reconstructing economic benefits and the like for a particular project or effort is prohibitively expensive. In some instances, data are creatively lost to avoid facing embarrassing questions. As a result, measures of perceived value are used. Informants other than the sponsor evaluated each plan. First, the plan's impact was assessed by the informants in terms of improving organizational capability. In the second, intrinsic value was assessed by the informants. The sponsor provided a final measure, indicating his or her satisfaction with the plan. These measures were combined into an overall measure of merit by averaging the rating for impact, merit, and satisfaction. A plan with a value rating of 5 was called "outstanding" because it made a decisive contribution, provided exceptional perceived quality, and produced sponsor satisfaction. Decisions with a value rating of 1 were termed "poor" because the plan had no impact, no merit, and produced sponsor dissatisfaction. The remaining scale points for the merit were termed "good" for values of 4, "adequate" for values of 3, and "disappointing" for values of 2.

Timely planned change efforts are also desirable. Sponsors want fast answers. A meritorious planned change may be carried out but only after an extended duration. This suggests that the time required to carry out the planned change is an indicator of success. Time was measured in two ways. For the formulation and option development tactics, the elapsed time from recognition to a decision to adopt a particular plan was determined to capture the developmental time. For implementation tactics, the time included both development and attempts to secure full use of the planned change.

## ▲ ESTABLISHING DIRECTION

Formulation tactics indicate how sponsors establish direction for a planned change effort. Chapter 5 identified three tactics called idea, problem, and target. The target tactic uses either a general or a specific objective to guide development. Idea tactics apply the visions or pet ideas of the sponsor that both constrain and structure development, using concept and inferred problem tactical variations. Problem tactics use problem solving and apply arena and inferred solution tactical variations. The features and frequency of use of these tactics are shown in Table 6-2. The tactic's variations shown in Table 6-2 had different steps, as discussed in Chapter 5, but applied a similar approach and have similar success.

### Idea Tactics

The ideas of sponsors directed planned change efforts in 37.5 percent of the cases, making it the most frequently used tactic by practitioners. Sponsors prefer to use existing ideas because they can rapidly couple the need for action, symptoms, apparent causes, and justifications to a specific way out of the dilemmas posed by out-of-control situations. Ideas emerged from the visions and beliefs, educational activities, the literature, vendors, RFPs, joint venture opportunities, the notions of key people, and staff proposals. The sponsor then imposed the remedy implied by the idea on the planned change process. Analysis is applied to verify the idea's virtues and to determine the reactions of the stakeholders. Developmental activities are used to refine the idea.

Table 6-2 ▲ Features of Formulation Tactics

| Tactic/Type Variation | Frequency of Use[a] | Features |
|---|---|---|
| *Targets* | 32.6% | *Objectives* are used to focus development; target guides development. |
| Specific target tactic | (22.2%) | Objectives have specific targets. |
| General target tactic | (10.4%) | Objectives have general targets. |
| *Ideas* | 37.5% | *Idea* ultimately used available at outset. Idea directs development. |
| Concept tactic | (9.7%) | Process is used to fine-tune idea. |
| Inferred problem tactic | (27.7%) | Analysis is used to link problems to idea before fine-tuning. |
| *Problems* | 29.9% | *Problems* are uncovered and are used to identify solutions. Problem solving directs development. |
| Inferred solution tactic | (21.5%) | Problem analysis is used to infer solution. |
| Arena search tactic | (8.3%) | Arena identifies where to search for solutions. |
| Total | 100.0% | |

[a] Percentage of all cases.

Idea tactics produced "good" plans (see Table 6-3). However, idea-guided planned change was not particularly timely, taking 12.0 months to carry out. The idea typically required tailoring, which lengthened the planned change process. An initial adoption occurred in 67 percent of the plans produced by idea tactics. Adding qualifications, the ultimate adoption rate for the idea tactic fell to 50 percent. The concept and inferred problem variations had similar success.

## Problem Tactics

A problem solving tactic was used 29.9 percent of the cases by its sponsor (see Table 6-2). In these cases a problem (concern or difficulty) is analyzed to find a way to respond. The sponsor carries out a form of problem identification. Analysis is then used to explore the nature of the problem and its distinctive features, hoping to uncover cues that suggest a remedy. Developmental activities are applied to fine-tune and then implement the remedy.

Problem solving is the least successful formulation tactic. The problem tactic produced plans with the lowest initial adoption rate, 57 percent, the lowest ultimate adoption rate, 39 percent, and the lowest merit rating. The 11.4 months required to carry out the problem tactic was not timely and comparable to the idea tactic. The plans created by problem tactics had the lowest merit rating (between adequate and good) of any formulation approach. The arena and inferred solution variations of this tactic produced similar results.

## Target Tactics

Targets were used 32.6 percent of the time, making it the second most frequently used tactic. This tactic developed an objective or goal, indicating desired aims or ends to be sought, to guide the planned change process. The target identified performance expectations such as increases in capacity, reductions in cost, or improved utilization. Both specific and general targets were observed (see Table 6-2). The specific target called for a specific level of performance, such as an 80 percent increase in utilization, and the general target indicating the type of performance sought (need to improve utilization). Subsequent steps in the planned change process search for ways to respond and developed and implemented these ideas.

Table 6-3 ▲ Formulation Tactics and Success

| Tactics | Initial Adoption Rate | Ultimate Adoption Rate | Merit[a] | Time[b] |
|---|---|---|---|---|
| Ideas | 67%[c] B/C[d] | 50% B/C | 4.0 B | 12.0 A |
| Problems | 57% C | 39% C | 3.4 C | 11.4 A |
| Targets | 71% B | 60% B | 3.9 B | 8.6 B |

[a] Scale points: 5 = outstanding, 4 = good, 3 = adequate, 2 = disappointing, 1 = poor.
[b] Time measured in months.
[c] Percentage of plans implemented.
[d] Duncan Multiple Range Test letter codes indicate means that differ ($p \leq .05$).

The target tactic is much more successful than the idea or the problem-solving tactic and produced good results (see Table 6-3). Using targets led to plans rated as good (3.9), with a 71 percent rate of initial adoption, taking 8.6 months to carry out. Applying targets led to a 60 percent ultimate adoption rate. The type of target (general or specific) had no effect on the success of a planned change effort.

## ▲ IDENTIFYING OPTIONS

Four option development tactics, two having key variations, were identified from the practices or sponsors in Chapter 4. Table 6-4 summarizes these tactics according to the focus of option development, the developmental activities carried out, and the frequency of use by sponsors. The appraisal approach uses an "adaptation" tactic in which a preexisting idea is imposed on the planned change process. The template tactic looks for options in the practices of others. Search tactics seek options by reviewing prepackaged ideas. The nova tactic creates options that have innovative features. Table 6-5 summarizes the adoption rates, merit ratings, and development time associated with each tactic.

### Adaptation Tactics

Adaptation was used in 26 percent of the cases, making it the tactic used most frequently by practitioners to identify options in planned change. Developmental

**Table 6-4 ▲ Features of Option Identification Tactics**

|  | Frequency of Use | Focus of Development | Developmental Activities |
|---|---|---|---|
| *Tactic* | | | |
| Adaptation | 26% | Preexisting idea | Validate and demonstrate merit of an idea. |
| Template | 26% | Practices of others | Tailor practices to the new situation. |
| Search | 30% | Understanding needs | Use needs to guide search. |
| Nova | 18% | Innovation | Design a plan. |
| Total | 100% | | |
| *Variations* | | | |
| Single search | 24% | RFR writing | Limit search. |
| Cyclical search | 6% | Framing needs according to what is available | Undertake repeated searches. |
| Subtotal search | 30% | | |
| Single template | 19% | A single practice | Tailor to fit. |
| Synthesized template | 7% | Synthesis of several practices | Amalgamate best ideas from several sources. |
| Subtotal template | 26% | | |

#### Table 6-5 ▲ Option Identification Tactics and Success

| Tactic | Initial Adoption Rate | Ultimate Adoption Rate | Merit | Development Time (months) |
|---|---|---|---|---|
| Search | 80%[a] A[b] | 48%[c] B | 3.8[d] A | 9.7 B |
| Adaptation | 63% B | 46% B | 3.9 A | 9.4 B |
| Template | 69% B | 69% A | 4.1 A | 10.0 B |
| Nova | 60% B | 52% B | 3.8 A | 15.3 A |
| *Variations* | | | | |
| Single search | 78% B | 50% C | 3.9 B | 10.4 B |
| Cyclical search | 100% A | 37% D | 4.1 B | 6.8 A |
| Single template | 64% C | 64% B | 3.9 B | 10.1 B |
| Synthesized template | 90% A | 90% A | 4.6 A | 9.7 B |

[a] Percentage of plans implemented.
[b] Duncan Multiple Range Test letter codes indicate means that differ ($p \leq .05$).
[c] Percentage adopted, treating delays and partial adoptions as failures.
[d] Scale points: 5 = outstanding, 4 = good, 3 = adequate, 2 = disappointing, 1 = poor.

activities were used to fine-tune and to promote an idea that had captured the attention of the sponsor. The solar heat pump case in Chapter 5 used this tactic. Developmental activities in the air conditioning manufacturer were confined to refining the solar heat pump idea and selling it to investors who were approached to provide venture capital.

The adaptation technique had a 63 percent initial adoption rate, which fell to 46 percent when ultimate adoptions were measured, one of the lowest rates of adoption observed (Table 6-5). The plans produced were judged to be no better than those produced by the other tactics. Development took 9.4 months, suggesting that the use of preexisting ideas does not lead to quick responses.

### Template Tactics

The template tactic identifies options by exploring the practices of other individuals and organizations. This tactic was used in 26 percent of the cases (Table 6-4). An organization or an individual is visited or an experience is recalled to deal with the sponsor's perceived need. In contrast with adaptation tactics, templates are not available at the outset and must be recalled or collected in some way. Developmental activities are carried out to find and then tailor these practices to fit the new situation. For example, Chapter 4 described how a renal dialysis center was developed by visiting a successful dialysis operation recording policies, procedures, staffing, and building features. Development modified these practices to fit the hospital's situation, such as nursing turnover, building features, and budgets.

Template tactics are carried out by following the provincial and enriched tactical variations described in Chapter 4. Provincial tactics use a *single template*. The practices of a single organization or work unit are used to produce an option. Developmental activities are confined to making changes that allow the template to be successfully applied by the borrowing organization. In the enriched template variation, more than one template was examined. Developmental activities were directed at creating an amalgamation of the best ideas from two or more sources, producing a *synthesized template*. For instance, in one of the cases, organizational restructuring was carried out by examining organizational arrangements used by similar successful organizations, incorporating the best feature pertinent to the particular circumstances being faced by the adopting organization. The template is created by using a composite of features culled from several sources. Practitioners used single templates to create options in 19 percent of the cases and reframed templates in 7 percent of the cases (Table 6-4).

The synthesized template produces very good results. Both the initial and the ultimate adoption rates were 90 percent (Table 6-5). The options were judged to be somewhat below outstanding (4.6). Development took just 9.7 months to carry out. The "single template" had substantially lower initial and ultimate adoption rates (64 percent), ideas judged to be "good" (3.9), and a developmental time of 10.1 months.

## Search Tactics

Development in the search tactic begins with attempts to understand needs. Needs then guide the search for options. Requests for proposals (RFPs) are often used to search. Vendors, consultants, and manufacturers respond by selecting one of their prepackage solutions that seem responsive to the RFP. For example, needs for information storage and retrieval can be interpreted by a computer manufacturer as a computer system that includes one or more software packages. Sponsors were found to use search tactics 30 percent of the time.

This tactic was carried out with a truncated or extended search (Chapter 4). Many sponsors selected the best response to their RFP, or other search aids, by comparing the features of the proposals. For instance, a controller in one of the cases selected among software packages for automatic billing by comparing the costs and capabilities of proposals submitted in response to bid requests. A *single search* was used. In a *cyclical search,* the initial search is carried out to learn about available ideas and subsequent searches exploit this knowledge by rewriting RFPs to recognize cutting-edge capabilities. The Department of Defense uses this approach to identify the next generation of military hardware. Bids are requested from defense contractors for "concept designs" of planes, radar, submarines, missiles, and the like that can outperform hardware currently in use. DOD learns from these concept designs and rebids the hardware using an RFP that incorporates a sophisticated understanding of pertinent development in metals, propulsion, and electronics. Practitioners apply a single search 24 percent of the time and a reframed search 6 percent of the time.

Search tactics produced results nearly as good as the template tactic, with some important qualifications. The single search tactic had a 78 percent initial adoption rate, results judged to be good (3.8), and developmental time of 10.4 months. Ideas for the reframed search had the same merit (4.1) but were much more timely, requiring 6.8 months for development, and had higher initial acceptance—

100 percent were adopted. However, both of these tactics had poor ultimate rates of adoption: 37 percent for reframed search and 50 percent for single search.

### Nova Tactics

Some development emphasizes the design of new options without any reference to available ideas, the practices of others, or searches for a vendor. Staff groups, such as R&D or engineering, or consultants are asked to devise a new way to deal with a need or an issue confronting a sponsor. Many internal operations of a firm are developed in this way, such as devising new software packages for inventory control and material management, marketing initiatives, promotion and appraisal procedures, sales promotions, and products or services. Sponsors apply nova tactics 18 percent of the time.

Nova options had a 60 percent initial adoption rate, which fell to 52 percent for ultimate adoptions. The options produced were judged to be good (3.8), but took 15.3 months to develop, making innovation the least timely tactic applied by sponsors. These results suggest that innovation is costly and time consuming and not apt to produce breakthroughs. However, when innovation does produce a breakthrough, its impact creates huge advantages that the relatively crude measure of value would be unable to capture. Consider the value of radial tire for Michelin, the 707 swept-wing aircraft designed for Boeing, or dry copying for Xerox (Foster, 1986). Typically, nova tactics do not have this kind of impact, making innovation higher risk and more costly than the other tactics.

## ▲ IMPLEMENTING CHANGE

Implementation tactics are used by sponsors to cope with the barriers to change. Sponsors were found to use tactics called intervention, participation, persuasion, and edict. The features of these tactics are summarized in Table 6-6. These tactics were illustrated with cases in Chapter 5 to show how each can be carried out in practice.

### Intervention Tactics

When applying an intervention tactic, the sponsor acts as a lightning rod. The planned change process is energized when the sponsor justifies the needs for planned change and the opportunities that planned change would bring. To install the plan, the sponsor then demonstrates how the changes called for by the plan address these needs and opportunities. The cash flow case described in Chapter 5 illustrates how sponsors use intervention.

Intervention tactics are rarely applied by sponsors, being used only 16 percent of the time, but are much more successful than any other tactic. When sponsors use an intervention tactic, all of the planned changes were initially adopted (Table 6-7). After a period of two years, 81 percent of these plans were still in use. Also intervention was very efficient, taking an average of 11.2 months to gain full acceptance. This

Table 6-6 ▲ Features of Implementation Tactics

| Tactic | Frequency of Use[a] | Features |
|---|---|---|
| Implementation by intervention | 16% | Key executive justify need for change with new norms to judge performance and ways performance can be improved. |
| Implementation by participation | 20% | Stakeholder representatives determine change features: |
| Delegated | | Solution specification with partial participation. |
| Complete | | Solution framing with full participation. |
| Implementation by persuasion | 35% | Experts attempt to sell a change they devise. |
| Implementation by edict | 29% | Sponsors issue directives requiring adoption. |

[a] Percentage of all cases.
Reprinted from Nutt (1987). By permission, John Wiley and Sons, Ltd.

time is just over half of that of the next most successful tactic, participation. Wider use of intervention is highly desirable. For this reason, many of the implementation techniques featured in this book will call for intervention.

## Participation Tactics

Sponsors apply participation by stipulating needs, an arena of action, and/or priority options and then delegate planning to a task force. Task force members are selected so they represent viewpoints and have the expertise needed to recommend and critique a plan. The PBX case discussed in Chapter 5 illustrates this tactic. Only the delegated and complete variations of the participation are used with any frequency by sponsors (Nutt, 1987). These tactics had comparable use and success. The participation tactic was used to implement planned change in 20 percent of the cases.

Participation, like intervention, is used sparingly, but provides a very good way to carry out implementation. Eighty-one percent of the planned changes were initially adopted when participation was used. The ultimate adoption rate, adding qualifications in which short-lived and partially used planned changes are termed

Table 6-7 ▲ Implementation Tactics and Success

| Tactic | Initial Adoption Rate | Ultimate Adoption Rate | Merit Scale | Time to Install or Withdraw (months) |
|---|---|---|---|---|
| Intervention | 100 % A[a] | 82% A | 4.4 A | 11.2 A |
| Participation | 80.6% B | 71% B | 4.4 A | 19.0 B |
| Persuasion | 65 % C | 49% C | 3.9 A | 20.0 B |
| Edict | 51 % D | 35% D | 4.0 A | 21.5 B |

[a] Duncan Multiple Range Test letter codes indicate means that differ ($p \leq .05$).

failures, was 71 percent. The average time to install a planned change is 19.0 months, longer than that required for intervention but less than that required by other tactics. Although sponsors seem reluctant to relinquish control to the extent called for by participation, this tactic presents a very good alternative for situations in which intervention cannot be used.

## Persuasion Tactics

The persuasion tactic calls for the sponsor to delegate, implicitly or explicitly, development consistent with priority directions to experts, such as technical staff or consultants. The expert uses the sponsor's stipulation of priority directions, carries out development, and then attempts to "sell" the changes based on the plan. The plan's ability to help the sponsor realize an aim is used to argue for its adoption. The sponsor weighs imperatives to act. The MRI scanner case in Chapter 5 illustrates the persuasion tactic.

Persuasion was used 35 percent of the time by sponsors, making it the most commonly applied implementation tactic. Persuasion had an intermediate level of success (Table 6-7). Sixty-five percent of the planned changes were implemented when persuasion was used. Ultimate adoptions were 49 percent. Implementation took an average of 20 months to complete. Note that participation is just as timely as persuasion, suggesting that this tactic can be substituted for persuasion without any loss in timeliness.

## Edict Tactics

An edict is used when directives for planned change adoption are issued. The use of power is the dominant theme. The sponsor announces the change and prescribes the expected behavior using a memorandum, formal presentation, or on-the-job instruction. Also, the sponsor attempts to show that his or her ideas provide a way to deal with priority directions called for by organizational aims or goals. Edicts are often used when a planned change has special significance in contributing to a strategic direction or when the sponsor has a vested interest.

Edicts were the second most frequently used tactic to implement planned change, being observed 29 percent of the time. Edicts are the least successful tactic that can be used for implementation. Only 51 percent of the planned changes are adopted when edicts are used. When qualifications were considered, adoptions plummeted to 35 percent. These low rates of adoption were observed for planned changes judged to be of comparable merit to those carried out by intervention, participation, and persuasion. Edicts were also inefficient, taking an average of 21.5 months to carry out. The use of edicts was no more timely than participation and much less apt to be successful.

## ▲ Key Points

1. Tactics that set direction for planned change are particularly important because they can constrain or open up the process to possibilities during development. The most successful tactic—targets—opens up search. The least successful

constrained what the planned change process could consider by imposing ideas or directed the search by attempting to solve problems that are inferred from the claims of important people.

2. Sponsors seem to prefer idea tactics to set directions because uncertainty about the nature of the plan is eliminated. This lowers risk because the sponsor can identify who may object to the plan and anticipate opposition before it can mobilize. Idea tactics also seem pragmatic and timely to sponsors because money is spent on idea development and *not* on idea finding. However, idea tactics have none of these benefits. Ideas are an undesirable way to direct a planned change process.

3. The "synthesized template" tactic provides a good way to identify options during planned change. However, this tactic is seldom applied, suggesting that planned change success could be improved with its use. The "cyclical search" tactic that carries out a repeated search to learn about possibilities is also quite successful and infrequently applied. Nova tactics seeking innovation had substantial rejections and led to long development. Techniques that enhance creativity should help practitioners improve the merit of innovations and shorten development (see Chapter 11). Although widely applied, adaptation tactics that applied preexisting ideas are failure-prone and no more efficient than the template and search tactics.

4. Success is strongly influenced by the tactics used to implement a planned change. The intervention tactic is the best way to promote planned change. The superiority of the intervention tactic and its infrequent use suggest that sponsors should become more involved with managing a planned change process. When sponsors take charge of the process and create an environment in which plans that help to realize a change can be justified and understood, adoption is likely.

5. Although some planned changes may not lend themselves to involvement, participation also seems underused, given its superior track record. The efficiency arguments that have been advanced not to use participation do not hold up. Participation took much less time than persuasion and edicts. There seems no motivation to reserve edicts for short-fuse decisions. The resistance engendered by edicts seems to create delay that produced considerable inefficiencies in installing planned change.

## ▲ Exercise

1. Review the cases presented in Chapters 1, 4, and 5, indicating, where not already specified, the tactic that was used for formulation, concept development, and implementation. Defend your choice by noting the distinguishing features of the tactic using specifics drawn from the case.

# *Part III*

# SELECTING IMPLEMENTATION PROCEDURES

▲ ▲ ▲ ▲ ▲ ▲ ▲ ▲ ▲ ▲ ▲ ▲ ▲ ▲ ▲ ▲ ▲ ▲ ▲ ▲ ▲ ▲ ▲

*The chapters in Part Three present implementation procedures and guides for procedure selection. An implementation procedure is fashioned by first considering process management and then implementation approaches. Process management options identify ways to organize and manage the planned change process. The sequence of planning stages and steps are shaped so they respond to opportunities and limitations imposed by the organization on the plan sponsor, providing a way to manage the process. A process management option is selected by considering the sponsor's freedom to act and need for consultation.*

*Implementation approaches are made up of techniques coupled with ways to apply power. The sponsor uses an implementation technique and various types of power to deal with dissenters and to offer incentives that encourage the adoption of the plan. To select an implementation tactic, the sponsor considers how individuals are affected by the plan and the climate of the work group or organizational unit in which change will occur. If the climate is favorable, the sponsor offers incentives and uses tactics that differ from those preferred when the climate is unfavorable.*

*This view of implementation calls on the sponsor to take an active role in planned change, both in shaping the process and in participating in plan development.*

# 7

# Managing the Implementation of Planned Change

▲ ▲ ▲ ▲ ▲ ▲ ▲ ▲ ▲ ▲ ▲ ▲ ▲ ▲ ▲ ▲ ▲ ▲ ▲ ▲ ▲

The purpose of implementation is to deal with perceived problems that arise in the minds of individuals affected by a planned change as well as coping with deficiencies in the plan. To initiate a planned change, its sponsor must make a realistic appraisal of his or her prerogatives. This appraisal identifies the planned change sponsor's freedom to act and need for consultation.

In this chapter guidelines are offered to help a planned change sponsor select from among several approaches that can be used to manage the planned change process. To set the stage, various types of planned change are identified. The type of planned change and the conditions thought to be surrounding the planned change effort are determined by the prospective sponsor. These situational determinants narrow the choice of process management tactics and offer guidance in its selection. This chapter provides a potential plan sponsor with the means to make these assessments.

This chapter also lays the groundwork for the chapters in Part Three by discussing problems that arise during planned change. These difficulties show the importance of implementation and why it is a crucial activity in a planned change process.

## ▲ THE IMPORTANCE OF IMPLEMENTATION

Poor implementation practices with a good plan often lead to failure, as discussed in Chapter 5. When implementation is poorly carried out, the plan is often thought to be deficient, resulting in good ideas being discarded or dismissed and the plan's benefits forgone. In other cases, lingering doubt, stemming from the impression created by a botched implementation, influences people's impressions of the plan. For example, when Republic Airlines was acquired by Northwest Airlines implementation problems nearly doomed a well-conceived merger plan (Houston, 1986). Traffic exceeded expectations and swamped the merged airline's computer system, resulting in lost reservations and several passengers being ticketed for the same seat. Baggage transfer became hopelessly confused as the former Republic baggage handlers learned a new system leading to a sharp increase in lost bags. Both airlines had an on-time departure rate of 85 percent before the merger, which fell to 25 percent. The complaints lodged with the U.S. Transportation Department increased by 250 percent in the first month of joint operation. Although Northwest anticipated some problems, the company was not prepared for the magnitude of difficulties that were encountered. Many still consider the merger ill-advised.

An implementation debacle, like the Northwest merger, has sensitized an increasing number of managers to the importance of implementation. A recent survey of top managers (Alexander, 1985) identified the most troublesome implementation problems that were encountered in making planned change as follows:

1. Inadequate leadership
2. Underestimated the time required
3. Failing to see major problems that can block or delay action
4. Poor coordination of implementation activities
5. Lack of skill in individuals who are carrying out implementation

6. Uncontrollable outside events
7. Failure to treat implementation as a process that deals with social and political factors upset by the change
8. Incomplete monitoring of process steps

To deal with these problems managers must take charge of the planned change process and manage it with the barriers to planned change in mind. The chapters in Part Three offer a series of steps, that can be organized into an implementation procedure, which have been shown to increase the prospects of planned change adoption (Nutt, 1983, 1987, 1989b).

## ▲ BARRIERS TO PLANNED CHANGE

Organizations that seek to implement a planned change must amass the assent of individuals who can block the changes called for by the plan. Acceptance is enhanced when individuals see such factors as achievement, self-esteem, and recognition as favorable. The manner in which a change is introduced can influence each of these factors.

Planned change goads affected parties to take action. As these influence attempts are played out, a situation is created that may be conducive or resistant to the change required by the plan. Each individual tends to see the changes proposed by the plan in personal terms, drawing positive, neutral, or negative reactions. For example, the plan could be seen as lowering an individual's security, altering desirable social relationships, posing a personal threat, or placing a valued procedure or practice under the control of others.

To illustrate, the security of employees can be threatened when changes in the rules governing early retirement are discussed. Employees with health problems and other motivations to consider early retirement will strenuously resist plans to change rules and may not share their reasons. The number and intensity of these reasons frequently catches management by surprise.

The prospect of a personal threat and the power of social relationships also tend to be overlooked during a change. For example, a sharp increase in grievances by kitchen employees was noted after a new work schedule was proposed. The cooks and the other kitchen workers had worked together in one kitchen for many years and had formed friendships that went beyond work-related associations. The new schedule called for flexibility and assigned the cooks and employees each day to one of several kitchens to reduce costs. The employees resisted the new schedule and filed grievances seeking to block it. Resistance grew to the point that the attempts to implement the new schedule were abandoned. At this point it was discovered that one of the cooks was illiterate and relied on coworkers to read menus to her in "her" kitchen. Switching kitchens posed a threat that the illiteracy would be discovered. Coworkers blocked the planned change because of their loyalty to a friend who seemed threatened by the proposed change.

Executive offices have special status. Plans to create the "Kodak office building" in New York City posed a threat to the status of all executives to be housed in the new building. The executives had become quite adept at counting tiles to estimate the square feet in the offices so they could link space to perceived status. The office layout was redrawn over and over and never did satisfy all the executives. After years of frustration the plan to develop the office building was abandoned using expense as a justification.

As the planned change process unfolds, expectations are formed. Attempts are made to shape the plan so valued resources and relationships are retained. People who believe they will be adversely affected can be seen engaging in outright resistance, manipulation, and bargaining, or merely expressing distrust. These acts heighten the conflict. Others are coaxed to take sides, either joining a "palace revolt" or jumping on the implementor's bandwagon.

Zaltman, Duncan, and Holbeck (1973) contend that people's views about the need for planning and how it is conducted lead to an appraisal of their own urges and needs. If prerogatives seem threatened, insecurities and anxieties can mount to the point that opposition is voiced. Eichholtz and Rogers (1964) have identified several types of rejections and the behavioral basis of each. In Table 7-1 these arguments are extended to describe some of the typical reasons people express for opposing a plan. In each case, the projected behavior is drawn from information that is shaped and validated to form a rationalization about the plan, the process, or both. These bases for rejection are not always logically consistent, but they are nonetheless used to vigorously defend the position taken. Destroying the rationale of an opponent seldom gets the opponent to change his or her position from one of opposition to one of support. Showing that the basis for rejection of a planned change is invalid or inaccurate is insufficient. Stronger measures are needed to implement planned changes successfully.

Out of the milieu of large and small dislocations, a sentiment develops that can be largely favorable, unfavorable, or mixed. The size of the dislocations and the intensity of perceptions about them create a climate in which implementation must take place. Peoples' reactions to the change implied by the plan create incentives for some to use "gamesmanship" tactics. Games are played to maximize the advantage of the player and to block (or modify) plans perceived not to benefit the player.

## Table 7-1 ▲ Basis for Plan Rejection

| Basis for Rejection | Origins | Information | Behavior |
|---|---|---|---|
| Ignorance | Inability to appraise change | Absent | Contend that information is too hard or too costly to obtain. |
| Wait and see | Case not clear | Dismissed | Wait for others to confirm. |
| Situational | Other ideas as good | Comparative | Contend that comparisons must show superiority. |
| Personal | Offended by the plan | Alienating | Dismissed as being irrelevant. |
| Experimental | Trials | Empirical | Claim past experience shows plan won't work. |

Source: Adapted from Eichholtz and Rogers (1964) and Nutt (1984b).

## Basis for Involvement

The basis for involvement in a planned change stems from the reactions of people who are affected by the plan. The addition of a task or role may be seen in a positive or a negative way, depending on the benefits thought to be associated with it. For instance, a task that carries with it a budget with slack may be sought, and a task that seems contentious and difficult to carry out may be avoided.

A person's role is enhanced when it includes highly valued tasks and excludes tasks that create problems and/or offer no opportunities. A person's role is diminished when valued tasks are eliminated and problematic tasks added. Within an organization, people rally to support a plan that creates valued roles and rail against a plan that detracts from their role. Thus, the implementor of planned change controls the destinies of people who are both adversely and positively affected by the plan.

The plan itself may strip some people of authority over some tasks, giving the authority to another. Changes in the task responsibility milieu also create a preponderance of support or opposition within the ranks, giving rise to implementation problems. A sponsor must consider whether the plan creates tasks that serve people's basic interests. If these individuals perceive that the emerging plan weakens their position, opposition can be expected. The tactics adopted by the individuals affected by the plan are typically quite rational, given a clear understanding of their vested interests (Mackenzie, 1976).

## Behavioral Treaties

The expectations of people in an organization establish "behavioral treaties" (Mackenzie, 1978a). The treaty identifies people's expectations of the routes that should be followed in making changes. Insisting that a representative committee must be used is an example. This emphasis on process is evoked when an authority gap exists. Process is used to protect turf. As the process unfolds, individuals can sort out how change influences them and make suggestions that protect their interests. Such processes help to stabilize the organization or unit that is being strained by the prospects of a change.

Successful plan sponsors seem to be aware of these treaties and avoid violating them during implementation (Nutt, 1983). When expectations (such as involvement) are violated, new tasks are dreamed up, which bring more people with vested interests into the fray. As the situation becomes more complicated, delays can be expected. A delay gives the opposition time to form a coalition to thwart the plan.

# ▲ TYPES OF PLANNED CHANGE

A change can deal with two kinds of plans: the implementation of an existing plan and the development of a plan. Existing plans call for the fine-tuning and then the implementation of ideas that are imposed on planned change process. Planned change with existing ideas can occur in both public (for example, government) and private organizations. An example of public sector planned change with an existing plan is the translation of legislation into programs. Planning details the program outlined in the legislation. When employees are asked to implement the visions or pet ideas of a manager in the private sector, the planned change process is carried out in the same manner.

Planned change with an existing idea gathers support, animosity, or both as the process unfolds. The planned change process may or may not create sufficient rationale to justify the plan. Planning is needed to minimize distortion of legislative or managerial intent and to create an environment in which change can occur.

The plan that stems from existing ideas often requires additional planning to assemble the elements of a program that will detail how it is to operate. Other stages of the planned change process are used to detail these mechanisms and select among alternative procedures. For example, most legislation defines problems and objectives (formulation) and offers the broad parameters of a solution (concept development) but not the details of service provision. Thus, detailed planning and implementation are done by bureaucrats who write guidelines that tell field personnel how to render services.

Those with a vested interest often tailor the guidelines. As a result, distortion can occur. The plan can be shaped to benefit a somewhat different clientele or buttress a personal interest held by field or agency personnel. For example, Job Corps was implemented by local agencies to target somewhat different groups than intended by legislation. If services seldom reach the program's clients, another type of distortion occurs. For example, Bardach (1977) describes a California state law designed to protect the civil liberties of people labeled as mentally ill, pointing out that fewer than one-third of these patients were ever exposed to the legislatively mandated services.

The movement of plans between levels of government and levels of a large multinational firm or federated organization develops similar problems. Key people in both settings can have limited power to make demands on lower levels. Implementation can be blocked when the authority required to make demands seems to be (or is) missing. Planned change can also be blocked in the courts. Implementation becomes failure-prone when the plan's sponsor resorts to persuasion or the power in his or her position to push for plan adoption.

Organizations create plans with a planned change process as well as implement known ideas. Both innovative and conventional plans are derived from a planned change process as described in the introductory chapters. Innovation implies that the plan proposes something new to the organization, which may or may not be new to others. Change refers to the installation of something that is merely different. Defined in this way, all innovations require change, but not all changes are innovative. From an implementation viewpoint, the distinction between new and different conveys no special meaning.

In public organizations, a planned change process can also be used for plan development. The product of the formation and concept development stages can be seen when an agency testifies to a legislative committee, proposing legislation to deal with a problem identified by the agency, its constituency, the legislative body, or others. Both preexisting and process derived plans can be blocked and shunted aside. Both types of planned change require formal implementation to improve the prospect of the plan's adoption.

Comparison of planned change in public and private settings can be instructive. In the public sector, more people can (and often do) object to an evolving plan. Users may rise up and make demands or articulate needs that mandate an exchange during planning. In the private organization, users tend to be more passive. For example, a firm fills a niche (provides a new product to a new market) and makes a rational assessment of the response: Was the product sold and to what extent did we make money? The prospect of extreme political polarization over a plan is always a possibility for both the private and public organization, but somewhat easier to predict in the former than the latter. The constituencies in the public sector are often amorphous and seldom understood. Because public and private settings pose similar sets of implementation problems, the same approaches will be used to promote plan adoptions.

## ▲ SUCCESSFUL AND UNSUCCESSFUL IMPLEMENTATION

Studies of implementation attempts illustrate some of the problems in getting plans adopted. Greiner (1970), for example, sorted implementation attempts into successful and unsuccessful categories and then identified factors that stood out in each category. Antecedents, tactics, use of facilitators, and the permanency of results were found to be key considerations.

The features associated with successful and unsuccessful implementations are shown in Table 7-2. In successful attempts, many people felt the pressure to change

Table 7-2 ▲ Comparing Implementation Failures and Successes

| Key Features of Successful Implementation | Key Features of Unsuccessful Implementations |
|---|---|
| 1. Need to change is recognized. | 1. Disagreement arises about need for change. |
| 2. Change agent takes charge and key people commit. | 2. Process lacks a recognized leader. |
| 3. The following process characteristics are exhibited: | 3. Process fails to move through formulation, option generation, and evaluation steps. |
| a. Change agent consolidates information defining need and opportunity to create a mutually understood diagnosis | 4. Unilateral approaches are used. |
| b. Ideas offered | |
| c. Ideas tested for credibility | |
| 4. Several levels of the organization are involved. | |
| 5. Success is gradual. | |

Source: Adapted from Greiner (1970) and Nutt (1984b).

and saw it as stemming from both inside and outside the organization. The pressure usually came from claims of low performance, which often causes low morale. This tension was lacking in the failure cases. Tension came from inside or outside the organization, but not both. Outsiders created less persuasive motivations to change than organizational insiders, but internal pressure was not fully persuasive until it had been validated by outsiders. Alleging poor performance was not sufficient without confirmation.

"Change agents" were active in successful implementations. Such an individual was perceived to have an outstanding track record and had the authority to make changes. This suggests that managers, not planners, should lead the implementation process. The change agent, called a "sponsor" in this book, can play one of two roles: a facilitator, offering new ideas to the planned change process, or an activator, involving subordinates in a planned change process carried out by an expert. As a facilitator, the sponsor exploits the situation. If tension is not present, it can be created to mobilize the level of support needed to make planned change possible. The sponsor then initiates a planned change process to define or to ratify a plan of action. Successful plans were preceded by the commitments of key people at several levels of the organization. Failures were found to use unilateral tactics and were less concerned about building a commitment to act and reinforcing success.

Some of the features in Table 7-2 act as constraints. Disagreements over the need to change can be legitimate and hard to resolve—organizational insiders and outsiders may have incompatible expectations. The recognition of power is another key feature. Plans must be tailored to respond to legitimate complaints and to fit the demands of power figures. In all other instances, features that limit success can be managed with an appropriate implementation procedure.

## ▲ WHAT THE PLANNED CHANGE SPONSOR MUST DO

Situational diagnosis precedes all other activities in a planned change. The planned change sponsor examines the situation he or she must confront to select among options to manage the contemplated planned change effort. This examination is guided by a series of questions or queries that helps the sponsor appraise the situation being confronted. From this assessment tactics emerge that meet the demands posed by the anticipated planned change effort. This assessment identifies people who can act as a sponsor and tactics that the sponsor should use to manage the process. Potential planned change sponsors are managers who have the prerogatives to make changes called for by the plan. The sponsor must be selected from these individuals. Diagnosis also determines how the sponsor should activate and manage the planned change process. The sponsor's freedom to act and need for consultation are key factors in the selection of a process management approach. The individual sponsoring the effort must assess the environment to determine how people are likely to react. This assessment suggests whether he or she can act or must get a superior to guide the process. In summary, there are two key steps in diagnosis:

1. Identify an appropriate planned change sponsor.
2. Determine how to manage the planned change process.

## ▲  LOCATING A SPONSOR

To an observer, implementation often appears anarchistic. Plans appear to seek someone to deal with them and managers seem to be seeking situations to demonstrate their managerial skills. Plans are looking for a champion and managers are looking for action. It is essential to find the appropriate plan champion. Inconsistencies between the authority to act and the need to implement a specific plan lie behind many implementation failures (Lippitt and Mackenzie, 1976; Nutt, 1989b). Matching planned change efforts with people who can guide their implementation is the key to success.

An organization's authority system can seldom be fully described with its organization chart. For example, authority usually flows downward in the organization chart. There are many exceptions in practice (Mackenzie, 1978b). Because of tradition or expertise, a subordinate may exercise control, sometimes without official sanction. Subordinates can gain sufficient information on systems operations to discourage changes that do not seem to be in their best interest. For example, if the information needed to change a computer system in a government agency is vested in one person, that individual can thwart change by merely delaying action until a new administration sweeps in a new group of political appointees. By making the time for planned change appear to extend beyond the supervisor's expected tenure, the personal benefits that can accrue to the new supervisor for making a change can be made too remote to pursue.

Authority limits can make it impossible for someone to have the leverage needed to implement a plan. These limits grow out of lapses in control, tradition, usurpation, expertise, as well as errors in assignments within an organization.

Dual or shared responsibility for implementation by people at the same level can create two supervisors for the same task. Problems stem from duplication or joint responsibility to carry out one or more tasks. Such a relationship often limits prerogatives.

These relationships complicate an organization and lower its ability to respond to change. They are signaled by power struggles and refusals to accept responsibility, giving rise to games being planned by key people to thwart planned change. Unneeded committees tend to be spawned, which lowers morale and stifles leadership. These problems make an implementation costly and time consuming.

The basis for selecting a change agent stems from gaps in authority. A gap arises when a planned change falls under the jurisdiction of two or more individuals. Gaps also arise when authority is not clear. Ambiguous authority can make it impossible for a sponsor to act. For these sponsors, obtaining the needed authority may lag or may never be granted. Such gaps complicate the implementation process. When authority is not clear, adversely affected individuals can block the plan by merely failing to take action.

## ▲  PROCESS MANAGEMENT OPTIONS

Implementation is treated as a stage of the planned change process, which is carried out by its sponsor. The sponsor selects among persuasion, intervention, participa-

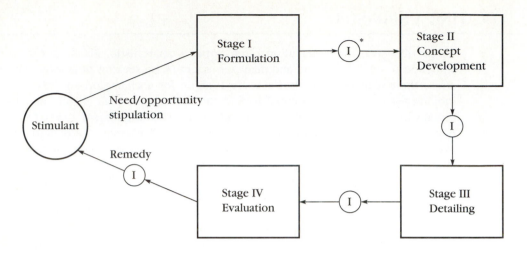

* Denotes an implementation screen.

**Figure 7-1** ▲ **The Participation Managed Process**

tion, and edict approaches to process management. Each shapes the sequence of planned change stages in a unique manner.

## Participation Managed Processes

Figure 7-1 describes the participation managed planned change process. A feasibility screen is provided at each stage of the process. This type of planned change is cooptative in nature. As a result, planned change techniques such as nominal group technique, brainwriting, or nominal-interacting technique with clients or users are often used to define problems in formulation, and the same techniques with experts to propose solutions in concept development and detailing (described in Chapters 10, 11, and 12). Evaluative techniques can be used to help sponsors select from among the alternatives (see Chapter 15). A participative planned change process can develop a substantial momentum that makes plan adoption likely.

## Intervention Managed Processes

Intervention managed planned change makes implementation the first stage in the process (Figure 7-2). Implementation tactics act as a guide to the remaining stages, managing the process. The sponsor, acting as a change agent, takes those affected by the plan through a process that demonstrates the necessity for planned change. The sponsor paves the way for change by exploiting or manipulating the situation to create an environment in which change can occur. Plan development is shaped by the claims of allies and dissidents. Legitimacy and clout determine the extent to which a plan must be modified to be implementable.

The sponsor shepherds stakeholders through a process that justifies the need for change and then reinforces the desirable features of the plan. The sponsor

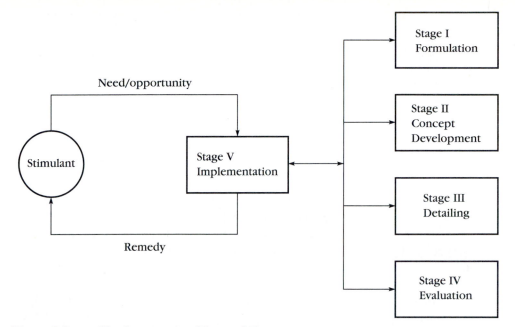

**Figure 7-2 ▲ The Intervention Managed Process**

provides information, initially about problems diagnosis and later, regarding plan feasibility.

## Persuasion and Edict Managed Processes

Both persuasion and edict planned change processes carry out formulation, concept development, detailing, and evaluation before turning to implementation concerns. They differ in their approach to implementation. Persuasion follows development with an attempt to sell the plan (see Figure 7-3). An expert takes a leadership role. The plan's logic and rationale are used by the expert to argue for its adoption. The sales approach to implementation calls for the expert to prescribe and then lay out the behavior necessary to implement. Edicts also follow development with implementation. In this case, the sponsor issues a proclamation calling for plan adoption. The edict can take the form of a memo, on-the-job instruction, or hiring someone to install the planned change.

Unlike participation and intervention, neither of these processes frames the developmental activities of planned change. Implementation follows plan development or plan recognition, for existing plans.

## ▲ MANAGING THE PLANNED CHANGE PROCESS

### Implementation Tactics

Table 7-3 summarizes the tactics available to the sponsor and links them to process management options. The *consultation tactic* calls for an expert managed process.

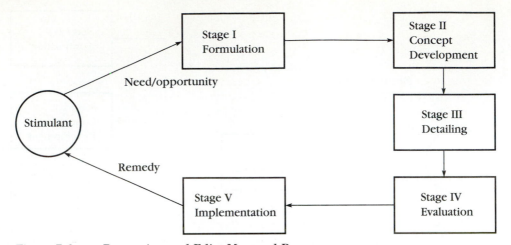

**Figure 7-3  ▲  Persuasion and Edict Managed Processes**

Sponsors can bring in experts to validate a preconceived plan or to help to create a plan. Two types of expertise can be used: the content expert and the process expert. The "content expert" is used to verify the veracity of an existing plan, commenting on its costs and benefits. A content expert must be familiar with the plan's subject matter. Sponsors use a "process expert," when they delegate planning responsibility to someone expert in planning procedure. The process expert helps the organization create a plan to meet aims that can be stipulated by a sponsor or identified by the planned change process.

The *implementation committee tactic* shapes an existing plan to make it acceptable to the organization. An ad hoc group is formed. Its members represent centers of power that must be managed and/or people who will be affected by the plan when it is installed. Either intervention or participation can be used. Intervention is preferred when the sponsor has considerable freedom to act, and participation is preferred when power is dispersed among several organizational

**Table 7-3  ▲  Process Management Tactics**

| Tactics | Congruent Implementation Process |
|---|---|
| 1. Seek leadership | Recycle to select |
| 2. Abort | None |
| 3. Consultation | Expert |
| 4. Form an implementation committee to shape the plan | Intervention |
| 5. Form a planning group | Intervention or participation |
| 6. Ask a standing committee to monitor | Participation |
| 7. Act as change agent | Intervention or edict |

Source: Adapted from Nutt (1989b).

actors. When power centers must be managed, cooptation through participation, indicating how the plan is to be modified, can help to win over potential dissidents.

The *planning group tactic* is used to develop a plan, as contrasted with the implementation committee, which is used to shape an existing plan. Planning groups are ad hoc, with their members selected to represent sources of knowledge and information. Planning groups can be managed by either participation or intervention, following the rationale outlined in the last paragraph.

*Standing committees* are sanctioned organizational bodies that have or claim to have jurisdiction over the plan or its development. All organizations have expectations of process. The steps deemed necessary in making a change often include checking with key power centers and individuals and adhering to formal and informal rules for making change within the organization, called "behavioral treaties." If groups with perceived (or real) prerogatives are not involved in planned change, conflict is inevitable, often leading to recalling or even scuttling the plan. Foul play is expected and the stakes escalate. When the plan is finally placed under the standing committee's jurisdiction, their attitude can be quite jaded. Had the standing committee been used from the outset, suspicion would have been put aside and the stakes lowered. The "standing committee tactic" can be used to either devise or modify a plan. In each case a participation tactic is required to encourage its members to "buy into" the plan as it evolves.

Either an intervention or an edict managed process can be used by a sponsor acting as a *change agent*. Edicts are pragmatic when the sponsor has some leverage, time is short, and experts are not available to help. An intervention process is preferred in all other circumstances because it is more likely to be successful (Nutt, 1987, 1989b).

## Selecting Tactics

The list below identifies the queries to be made by sponsors as they work through the decision tree, shown in Figure 7-4, to select a way to manage the planned change process. Answers to the queries identify the planning context, defining conditions under which the sponsor must operate.

*Queries Made by the Sponsor*

1. Does implementation exceed the sponsor's authority to act?
2. Will the problem disappear with inattention?
3. Does a technically sound plan exist?
4. Are there sufficient resources to activate planning?
5. Can the plan sponsor shape the plan so it falls under his or her control?
6. Is the problem recurring?
7. Can plan acceptance be negotiated with affected parties?
8. Can the sponsor pass the problem to a superior?
9. Does a standing committee appear to have jurisdiction?
10. Should consultants be used?
11. Do time constraints exist?

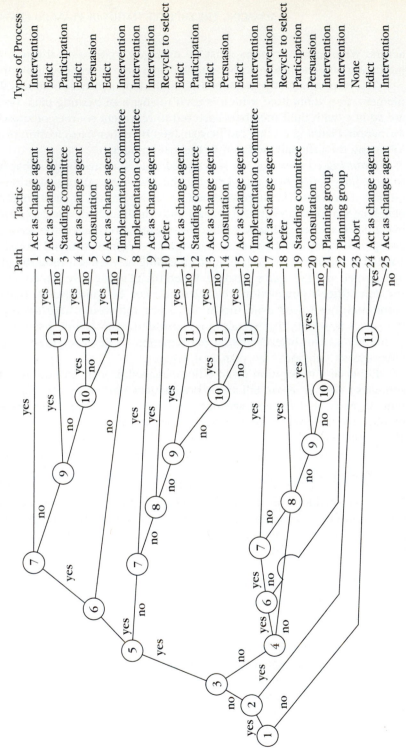

**Figure 7-4 ▲ Selecting Implementation Tactics**
Adapted from Lippitt and MacKenzie (1976) and Nutt (1989b).

Question 1 determines if the manager can preempt the steps that must be taken to implement a plan or initiate a planned change process. To answer this question the sponsor reflects on whether he or she has the authority to control these activities. If authority is insufficient, the plan sponsor should not use an edict and must resort to a more subtle approach.

Question 2 considers whether the performance gap is likely to disappear if no action is taken. This question often arises as planned change is being activated. To abort the effort its sponsor must show that the planned change process has or will become ill advised.

In question 3, the sponsor determines if a plan exists that is technically sound. Paths 1 to 16 in Figure 7-4 are activated when a technically workable plan exists. Off-the-shelf plans that meet minimal technical standards are often pushed because they are timely and seem pragmatic even though some degree of formal planning may be needed to detail some of its features. Paths 17 to 22 in Figure 7-4 are activated to create a plan.

The next question asks whether the sponsor believes he or she has the resources, such as time or budget, to act (question 4). For instance, if planned change demands people and resources that are busy elsewhere, the sponsor may not act. With the exception of path 18 (Figure 7-4), plans will have sufficient resources to activate paths 17 to 24.

Question 5 considers whether the sponsor can identify a modified version of the plan that falls within his or her authority to implement. The sponsor attempts to shape the plan so it deals with activities and people over which he or she has control. A committee can be formed or consultants brought in to sanction the sponsor's actions. If the plan cannot be altered to bring it under sponsor control, attempts to implement it can produce a power struggle in the organization. The sponsor can be seen as either breaking a treaty or trying to renegotiate its terms. Treaty violations arise when the plan unknowingly demands an action that violates long-standing rules of operation or conduct.

Next, the recurring nature of the problem that stimulated the effort is considered (question 6). If the problem recurrence seems unlikely, the sponsor's stakes are lowered. If not, the problem may spread and arise again with more sweeping consequences. Recurring problems often involve many people spread throughout the organization. Such problems often spawn a temporary organization, such as a venture management team or a formal planning group, which is outside the regular organizational structure.

Acceptance is considered next (question 7). The sponsor asks whether subordinates and others seem likely to attempt to block implementation and their prospects of success. The sponsor assesses the motives and status of key people. If the sponsor believes he or she can persuade key people to accept the plan, or the process needed to create a plan, a successful negotiation can be imagined. If not, the key people must be involved in shaping or developing the plan. Involvement in the process is more likely to demonstrate necessity than persuasion.

The sponsor should shed the role of change agent if he or she does not have preemptive power. To determine if you (the sponsor) have sufficient leverage to implement, a superior is often consulted (question 8). If the superior believes that the plan has importance and has control of the needed resources, such as people and support services, he or she should take over process management and become its sponsor.

The sponsor also checks to see if a "standing committee" has a mandate to deal with issues raised by the plan or the steps needed in its implementation (question 9). Failing to involve such a committee would be seen as a violation of organizational rules and is likely to create resistance. A standing committee with jurisdictional rights will always have the right to preempt the plan sponsor.

The prospects of bringing in outside process and/or content expertise is considered in question 10. Outside consultants usually require discretionary funds which provide alternatives to the outside consultant. In both cases, an expert is used to provide another point of view.

Finally, the sponsor considers time constraints (question 11). The need to act may prompt the sponsor to skip over unresolved conflicts and negotiations. Tactics differ depending on whether the sponsor believes he or she can act to sort out conflicts within time constraints.

## Implementation Options

Specific combinations of the eight factors in Figure 7-4 identify 25 conditions or contexts in which planned change can take place. Justifications that support the matching of a process type to each context or set of conditions are offered. Several distinctions are drawn. In the first, conditions that call for an intervention or an edict managed planned change process are identified. Second, distinctions among types of involvement are made. Tactics that call for stakeholder involvement can be carried out using ad hoc groups such as implementation committees, standing committees, and planning groups as vehicles for participation. Conditions that call for each of these modes of involvement are delineated to identify where each should be used. Third, some conditions are found to be equally amenable to using either participation or intervention. Finally, justifications for matching persuasion to just a few well-defined planned change contexts are offered.

### Conditions Calling for Intervention

Huse (1975) and others argue that a "change agent" tactic should be adopted whenever implementation-related actions are required. The change agent tactic calls for an intervention process to be used by the sponsor. Organizational development (OD) prescriptions call for consultants to act as change agents and play on tensions stemming from alleged performance failures, identifying and adapting the ideas that people believe can improve performance (e.g., Lewin, 1947; Schein, 1964a; Likert, 1967). In using the intervention process the sponsor takes on several of these roles but displays a far more aggressive posture toward renorming the system to be changed. In nearly one-third of the conditions described in Figure 7-4 the sponsor is called on to act as an interventionalist. Nine of the paths through the decision tree (designated conditions 1, 7, 8, 9, 16, 17, 21, 22, and 25 in Figure 7-4) allow the sponsor to take an interventionist role, either to initiate a process to devise a plan (paths 1, 7, 8, 9, and 16) or to set in place a known plan (paths 17, 21, 22, and 25). The intervention tactic is called for in these situations because it is feasible and because it has the best success record of any of the implementation tactics (Nutt, 1986, 1989b).

### Conditions Calling for an Edict

In eight of the paths (2, 4, 6, 11, 13, 15, 24, and 25) conditions arise in which time constraints, the inability to negotiate, or the lack of expertise allow for the use of an edict. The sponsor can use an edict to implement either an existing plan or to devise and then implement a plan under this set of conditions.

The distinction between conditions calling for edict and intervention processes must be carefully drawn. For example, in conditions specified by paths 24 and 25 (Figure 7-4), the sponsor would have clear-cut authority to act. Applying this authority by using an edict is recommended only when severe time constraints arise (path 24). Intervention (path 25) is preferred in all other circumstances because intervention has a far better success rate than using edicts (Nutt, 1986, 1987). In the other conditions, ambiguities about the sponsor's authority call for intervention. If a plan does not exist, the sponsor uses the intervention process to guide planned change. If a plan exists, the intervention process is used to guide its implementation.

### Conditions Calling for Participation

For the conditions identified by paths 3, 12, and 19 in Figure 7-4, the sponsor must rely on existing organizational decision bodies. In each case, a *standing committee* has or claims to have jurisdiction. Participation advocates (e.g., Delbecq, Van de Ven, and Gustafson, 1986) call for these stakeholders to create or comment on the plan. The participation tactic is used to coopt the members of the standing committee. Under the conditions identified by paths 3 and 12, a planned change process will be used to create a plan that the standing committee wants to monitor. Path 3 identifies conditions in which the sponsor can preempt with an existing plan, but the recurring nature of the problem implies that precedents will be set that the standing committee must endorse before implementation can proceed. In path 12 the same situation is present, except that the problem is a one-time incident. Nevertheless, the jurisdiction of the standing committee dictates that its approval is needed, as the conditions identified in path 3. In each situation participation is required to review and possibly modify the plan, as well as to specify the terms of implementation. Participation is used as the committee moves *back* through the planned change process. The standing committee modifies the plan and then assesses the implications of their changes. The standing committee is also given jurisdiction over the planned change process for the conditions identified in path 19. The sponsor cannot activate planning without the standing committee's approval. Thus, for the conditions specified in paths 3, 12, and 19, the standing committee is asked to take control of the planned change process.

### Conditions Calling for Either Participation or Intervention

Both participation and intervention processes can be used in conjunction with implementation committees and planning groups. *Implementation committees* are ad hoc groups formed so that the sponsor can observe the objections of stakeholders who are affected by the plan before it takes on its final form. Members have a reactive rather than proactive role, suggesting ways to shape the plan, but do not provide basic direction. Paths 7, 8, and 16 in Figure 7-4 identify conditions that call for such an approach. In paths 7 and 16 the sponsor lacks the leverage to negotiate acceptance and no standing committee has jurisdiction. The existing plan is fine-tuned by an implementation committee. The intervention process calls for proactive behavior by the sponsor to forge a plan that is acceptable to those who are affected by it, using the implementation committee as a sounding board. The participation process is used when the sponsor chooses to retain his or her social credit for the future. The sponsor delegates responsibility to the implementation committee. The group reviews and then modifies the plan until it can overcome objections posed by stakeholders.

In path 8 the sponsor has a technically acceptable plan for a nonrecurring problem. The plan falls under the sponsor's sphere of influence, so it can be modified to deal with the objections posed by stakeholders. Under these conditions implementation by intervention is both feasible and effective. However, people realize that the sponsor has the power to act so they would be pleasantly surprised when he or she chooses participation.

*Planning groups* are initiated to develop a plan in path 21 for recurring problems, and in path 22 for unique problems. The sponsor asks the planning group to develop a technically sound plan. Planning groups differ from implementation committees in one key aspect: the planning group starts with a problem and creates a plan, while the implementation committee has a plan that is shaped to fit the problem as well as people's objections. In path 21 the recurring nature of the problem justifies more investment in planning than path 22, which deals with a one-time planning problem. In all other aspects these planned change processes are the same, and either intervention or participation processes can be used.

### Conditions Calling for Persuasion

Persuasion is congruent with a "consultant" approach to planned change. Persuasion and demonstration are tactics often recommended for experts to use when they become proactive in implementation (Schultz and Ginsberg, 1984; Churchman, 1975). In paths 5, 14, and 20 expertise is used. Paths 5 and 14 have a plan in hand. In path 5 the sponsor uses the "content expert" (e.g., a merger specialist for a planned change involving a merger) to validate and/or modify the plan, so that it gives the sponsor the legitimacy to proceed with implementation. The recurring nature of the problem calls for assurances that the plan will prove to be beneficial. A validated plan provides these assurances, which eases its implementation. In path 14 the sponsor cannot modify the plan to bring implementation strictly under his or her control so a consultant is brought in to defend the plan. According to Ritti and Funkhouser (1987), consulting firms are often hired merely to help managers, acting as planned change sponsors, to demonstrate the merits of their preferred plans. Because the sponsor cannot act without the sanction of expertise, a persuasion tactic is desirable for paths 5 and 14.

In path 20 the sponsor activates a planned change process and delegates leadership to a "process expert," someone with expertise in planning procedure. A persuasion tactic is used. Because plan acceptance is not negotiable, a premium is placed on developing quality ideas. The persuasion tactic is used because it can focus on plan features, emphasizing innovation and cost-benefit concerns rather than the social environment in which the plan is to function.

## ▲ Key Points

1. Planned change begins with an assessment of the barriers to implementation. The planned change sponsor is called on to make an appraisal of his or her freedom to act and need for consultation. This appraisal is then used to select a way to guide the planned change process.
2. To make an appraisal, a sponsor works through a series of queries to identify the conditions surrounding the planned change. A process management tactic is selected that matches situational factors that define the context in which the planned change effort must occur.
3. A match between the process management tactic and the situational factors defining context increases the prospect of a planned change adoption.

## ▲ Exercises

(Cases are located at the end of Part Three on pages 232–235.)

1. Take the role of the sponsor who is appraising the planned change situation described in one of the cases. Answer the queries in the text and enter them in the decision tree (Figure 7-4). What ambiguities did you encounter? How would you choose among process management tactics that result when one or more of the queries is unknown? Compare the approach you selected to the one that was used.
2. Repeat for another case. Compare the process management approaches that you selected. Account for the differences.

# 8 Implementation Techniques

▲ ▲ ▲   ▲ ▲ ▲ ▲ ▲ ▲ ▲ ▲ ▲ ▲ ▲ ▲ ▲ ▲ ▲

This chapter presents five techniques that can be applied to deal with the social and political forces that often arise during planned change.[1] Edicts, persuasion, game scenario, unfreezing-refreezing, and participation techniques are described. Plan sponsors also have the option of applying *power* with some techniques or in place of them. Each source of power can be associated with an implementation technique to promote the adoption of a planned change, forming what is called an implementation approach.

Implementation techniques can be characterized by the amount of leverage that the implementor must apply, causing them to fall into unilateral, manipulative, or involvement categories, as shown in Table 8-1. A high-leverage technique calls for the implementor merely to announce the change and to specify the compliance behavior that is expected. Manipulative techniques are more subtle, seeking to coax and lead. Participation calls for the sponsor to give up some of his or her prerogative to act and assign it to a group of stakeholders, hoping for stakeholder support of the plan that results. Unilateral techniques call for high leverage. Manipulative techniques have moderate risk and involvement. Participation has little risk, if the sponsor is prepared to accept what a planning group will recommend.

## ▲ EDICT AND PERSUASION TECHNIQUES

To apply an edict, the implementor prescribes the behavior expected to install a plan. This approach can move through phases of decree, replacement, and structural change (Table 8-1). A given phase is enacted if the previous phase fails to achieve the desired results. The implementor begins by issuing an official decree by memoranda, formal presentation, or on-the-job instruction. Decrees assume that people are rational and will look to see how the plan benefits the organization before passing judgment. If problems are encountered, attempts are made to show the reticent how the plan falls within the authority of its sponsor. Proclamations have little cost, but also can have little effectiveness when the interests of key people are threatened. However, such a demonstration can be successful, as well as efficient, when the target of the influence attempt has a large zone of indifference and the plan falls within the sponsor's prerogatives. For instance, the manager of a management information systems (MIS) department can institute new procedures if those who are to carry out the procedures have no interest in how that aspect of the job is done and if the change falls within their notions of the sponsor's prerogatives.

When people become reticent, or fail to comply, stronger measures are required. A *replacement approach* follows that removes people who are blocking plan implementation. There are two types of premises behind replacement. First, making examples of a few may coax others into line. Second, problems may be centered in just a few people who will irrationally resist the plan. If the plan has sufficient importance, it may be necessary to remove the resisters.

---

[1]  Some planned change processes define implementation in terms of installation. Installation techniques provide ways to set the plan in place. Flowcharting and PERT techniques are particularly useful in this activity. An example of using PERT as an implementation control device is described in Chapter 12.

Table 8-1 ▲ Types of Implementation Techniques

| Leverage and Risk | Behavior Required | Techniques |
|---|---|---|
| High | Unilateral | Decree, replacement, and structural change |
| | | Demonstration |
| Modest | Salesmanship | Persuasion |
| Intermediate | Manipulative | Game scenario |
| | | Unfreeze-refreeze |
| Low | Delegated, shared, or indirect involvement | Participation |

If replacement fails to overcome implementation problems, the manager, using a unilateral approach, resorts to *structural changes* in the organization. The sponsor redesigns the formal organization's or unit's structure and moves people likely to support the plan into key positions within the structure. This tactic requires the application of considerable managerial power and is often quite time consuming. The implementor continues to assume that he or she is justified in pushing the organization toward policies, products, services, or internal operations thought to be beneficial.

## The Limitations of Unilateral Techniques

Applying unilateral techniques to implement planned change can create several types of problems. Problems that frequently arise include encountering power limits, rebellion against being forced, entropy, and authority responsibility gaps.

### Power Limitations

Unilateral techniques assume that a demonstration of benefits is sufficient to make a plan acceptable. When the demonstration is not sufficient, it is assumed that the implementor is justified in replacing the opposition and making sweeping changes in the organizational environment. Clearly, as the implementor moves from decree to replacement to structural changes, vast increases in power must be applied, and the prospect of success becomes more problematic. Managers in autocratic environments are more likely to be successful when they issue a decree. Both replacement and structural changes, however, can undermine levels of trust and confidence needed to function on a day-to-day basis, even when subordinates have been conditioned to accept autocratic leadership. Long-term problems stemming from the use of unilateral approaches crop up in terms of effects on morale, measurable by high turnover and absenteeism rates.

### Rebellion Against Force

People often oppose a plan because the changes it requires, although perhaps good for the organization, seem to have undesirable consequences for them. These consequences can be real or imagined. Some plans that are justified from an organizational perspective can create problems for particular individuals. For example, a strict allocation system for typing services in a consulting company may seem equitable, but will create real hardships for the high performer. Also, plans calling for a change in office location may be perceived negatively because they alter symbols important to people in the organization.

Even when the plan has obvious merit or when people favor it, forcing, or the appearance of forcing, people to accept it may create opposition. People resist unilateral implementation tactics by opposing the plan. This problem is magnified when there is a rational basis for resisting the plan. This type of behavior is often observed when professionals are required to adopt a new practice.

### Entropy

As with many forces in nature, an edict tends to lose its momentum (energy) as it moves between agencies or within levels of an organization. Increased entropy often makes adoption of an edict incomplete or problematic.

Entropy is caused by several factors, including incompetence and organizational memory. Society seems to protect the inept, at least the marginally competent seem to be everywhere, often in key positions. People rising to their level of incompetence is a very real problem in most organizations (Townsend, 1970). Rules on hiring and dismissing further exacerbate the situation, protecting the productive and the incompetent alike. Entrenched in positions of importance, unproductive individuals act as barriers to progress and to the upward mobility of more effective people. Also, there is ample evidence of trained incapacities. Such people resist acquiring skills and by doing so avoid new assignments that would make feather-bedding difficult.

Diminished organizational memory occurs when there is a frequent turnover of key people in the organization. For instance, the Bureau of Health Planning in the U.S. Department of Health and Human Services initiated the same study five times in four years, in part because the change in personnel had been so pervasive that completed studies went unrecognized. A meddling medical school dean caused a complete turnover of a university hospital staff four times in twice as many years. Each new group of recruits attacked the same set of problems without the benefit of prior efforts, giving rise to organizational drifting. Organizations with diminished memory display bizarre behavior, often making irrational commitments or ignoring legitimate projects. In one such instance, obsolete equipment was purchased long after its proponent had departed because the organization had no memory of the origin and rationale surrounding the request.

### Authority-Responsibility Gaps

An edict assumes that people have the leverage to get a plan adopted. In some instances, a sponsor may lack the authority to work effectively for the changes demanded by the plan. For example, when a new procedure is suggested by an engineer, the departmental manager may or may not have the authority to implement a new system. Users may also fail to take needed or prescribed action. Examples include the failure of patients to heed early warning signals of incipient health problems, the low compliance of people to managerial instructions, and states that do not enact legislation to secure matching federal funds.

Bardach (1977) notes that plan sponsors are called "statesmen" by people who agree with them and "czars" by those who do not. Enticing people from various organizational units who disagree to work together in promoting a plan can be quite difficult. The implementor must seek out people, activities, and even organizations that can work together. The successful implementor does not always select the most competent or visible people to become key participants, but the most compatible. Outsiders often fail to see the logic in these selections. They see the importance of the project and wonder why the most competent people are not involved.

For example, to start a community health center, the successful implementor matches the views and predilections of prospective clients, service providers, and locals. Without such precautions, clients who take a reformlike posture would perpetually be at the physicians' throats. Similarly, conservative communities may attempt to rescind abortion, birth control, and other controversial services demanded by providers with "a mission."

## Persuasion

Sponsors with less leverage, who have expertise in the subject matter of the planned change, rely on demonstrations to promote a plan. The implementor can also be an expert who has been assigned planned change responsibility by a sponsor, as discussed in the last chapter. If the argument to adopt a plan seems clear and defensible, a *persuasion* approach can be used. To use persuasion, one cites the anticipated benefits or goes further and shows how the benefits would be realized, using a demonstration. The demonstration can engage users in operating a mock up. For instance, an MIS proponent could take a potential user through the steps needed to operate the information system, pointing out benefits along the way. Most formal presentations have this character. Effectiveness is dependent on overcoming resistance to planned change by showing that the plan works, that it offers demonstrable benefits, and that a potential user can cope with it.

## ▲   THE GAME SCENARIO TECHNIQUE

Implementation can be construed as a game (Bardach, 1977; Nutt, 1983). The metaphor of a game is used to identify the players so their stakes, strategies, resources, conditions for winning, definitions of fraud (which indicate notions of fair play), uncertainty, and communication tactics can be visualized. Any or all of these factors may come into play during a particular implementation attempt. Games are described to dramatize opportunities to distort the process of implementation and to provide insight into how to deal with each game.

Games can be used for existing plans and plans that are in the process of development. Attempts can be made to manipulate the process by managing the detailing and evaluation stages of the "program assembly process." More often, games are mounted by persons to counter a plan whose features appear not to be in their best interests. In this case, games are also used to deflect objectives and to resist control after the planned change process has been completed.

Games can be classified as resource based, objective modifying, evasion of control, and incomplete adoption. Each game is described by potential players, stakes, and rules in Table 8-2.

## Resource-Based Games

### Easy Money

A plan can be distorted by various games that divert resources. One such game manages the exchange of payments for services so the provider receives more than the fair market value for these services. A "utility surplus" is created for the service provider. In other instances, a surplus can be created by outright fraud. For instance, in the Medicare-Medicaid program, patients were charged on a fixed-fee-for-service basis but the providers were able to lower the comprehensiveness of the services that they provided without fear of audit. Another type of utility surplus was created through a vertically integrated monopoly. To exploit the Medicare-Medicaid program, physicians put patients into nursing homes that the physician owned. Pharmacists had to give physicians a kickback to provide drugs to patients in the nursing home. Patient visits are routinely billed whether the physician shows up at the nursing home or not (Mendelson, 1984).

Consultants use a variation of the resource-based game by selling their services with the most experienced people but assigning the newest recruit to do the work. Hospital contract management organizations recruit the administrator after the contract has been sold. The contractee has no idea what qualifications the administrator will have.

### Spend More—Get More

The "budget game" was first identified by Parkinson (1962) who discovered that performance is often inversely related to budget demands. A manager can never afford to show a budget surplus because it will be taken as a signal of potential waste. This has given rise to the adage, "To those who spend more, more shall be given," in public funded organizations.

In the private organization, similar incentives are created. Middle managers become budget maximizers. Success in the organization is linked to control over resources. As a result, all managers have incentives to ask continually for more money than they actually need to operate a new internal operation or carry out a policy from a planned change process. Bloated budgets intended to create slack can result, which can doom the cost effectiveness of an otherwise workable plan.

### Easy Life

Program managers and implementors have incentives to shape a plan to suit their aspirations and work habits. For example, the Job Core Program was set up to get low-income youngsters to finish high school. By selecting dropouts who had

**Table 8-2 ▲ A Summary of Implementation Games**

| Type | Potential Players | Stakes | Rules |
|---|---|---|---|
| **Resource-Based Games** | | | |
| 1. Easy money | Service providers who see a way to offer services by cutting quality | Size of the utility | Utility surpluses are taken by the cleverest |
| 2. Spend more, get more | Managers without clear performance expectations | Potential slack in allocated funds | Though possibly unethical one must play to ensure budget is maintained |
| 3. Easy life | Bureaucrats and others who can dictate own work environments | Workload and prerogatives | Regulate capricious environment (e.g., budget cuts) by rationing services |
| 4. Pork barrel | Politicians and those who can bargain in organizations | Discretionary resources | The end justifies the means |
| **Games That Modify Objectives** | | | |
| 5. All things to all people | Problem solvers | Posturing that a problem has been dealt with | Some problems are unsolvable so deflecting attention is legitimate |
| 6. My program | Potential plan beneficiaries | A slice of the resources to be allocated | One group is as needy as another |
| 7. Peace keeping objectives | Zealots | Status and power | Mission to root out evil |
| **Evasion of Control Games** | | | |
| 8. Gesture | Managers and bureaucrats charged with implementation | Protecting the easy life | Token cooperation hoping for plan failure |
| 9. Pitched battles | Managers and bureaucrats charged with implementation | Protecting the easy life | Protect vested interests by power monopoly |

## Incomplete Adoption Games

| | | | |
|---|---|---|---|
| 10. Delay | All | Meet players' terms | Withold support till terms met |
| 11. Turf | Those with legitimate or quasilegitimate program linkages | Setting operational guidelines | Seek modifications before a program becomes institutionalized |
| 12. Someone else's problem | Anticipated program managers | Dumping a controversial or demanding program | Responsibility can be shifted to those better equipped |
| 13. Odd man out | Those with something to lose | The amount that can be lost (e.g., discretionary funds) | Minimize losses |
| 14. Reputation | All | Various | *Adopt games of* <br> 1. Spend more—get more <br> 2. All things to all people <br> 3. My program <br> 4. Peace-keeping objective <br> 5. Odd man out <br> *To fight games of* <br> 1. Easy money <br> 2. Easy life <br> 3. Pork barrel <br> 4. Gesture <br> 5. Pitched battle <br> 6. Delay <br> 7. Turf <br> 8. Not our problem |

Source: Adapted from Bardach (1977) and Nutt (1983).

a B average, the prospect of program success was enhanced, making the program manager look good with less effort than what would have been needed to seek out and motivate all dropouts. The same tendency exists in the private sector. The middle managers of firms who will supervise an activity have incentives to make the activity easy to administer. Procedures are simplified regardless of the consequences. In both settings, easy life is a game played against a clientele that lacks power.

### Pork Barrel

Modifying program coverage and eligibility requirements is a favorite game to divert resources from a program. Elected officials have incentives to make everyone eligible, which dilutes program resources. Private sector managers can use the program to "professionalize" their team, hiring people with skills beyond that needed. These highly skilled people can provide services that help out in other areas that are poorly funded or poorly staffed. This practice has several consequences. First, it bleeds off resources, lowering the number of services that can be offered. The program appears to have excessive costs, making it appear less feasible than an evaluation would suggest. Second, a tendency to have overqualified staffs creates inappropriate cost norms as well as unchallenged, and often unhappy, subordinates.

## Games That Alter Objectives

The objective of the plan, even one that is off-the-shelf, can always be renegotiated. These changes may expand, contract, or even refocus the plan's intent. This game is particularly insidious because most planners are conditioned to accept the need to rethink objectives.

### All Things to All People

Preliminary successes of a plan may attract a host of new missions. Broadening objectives can be a clever tactic. For instance, the American Medical Association feared that the Medicaid program would signal the wholesale intrusion of government into medicine. They were right! The program was used as a vehicle to usher in a host of programs ranging from quality monitoring to cost control.

In other instances, the "all things to all people" game can spell disaster for the program. Expanded objectives can be used to scuttle a program. Health planning programs were required to move from identifying and filling gaps through voluntary efforts to becoming both planner and regulator, and finally to oblivion. Health planning agencies were unable to shift roles quickly and found that their watchdog and innovator roles were incompatible. Adding regulation drove out planning. Regulative activities lost credibility for the planning programs.

A similar problem arises in private settings. The old adage of giving tough problems to the busiest people illustrates this point. The most successful manager or staff department often inherits thorny organizational problems, leading to an overtaxed staff and a dissolution of their effort.

Ideological baggage can distort plans. For example, "educational opportunity" has degenerated into quotas that ensure racial balance within a public school. No one cares that minority children read at a level far below that of their peers. To deal with these reading deficiencies would create reading groups composed largely of minority children, so such practices are discouraged. "Let each child achieve at his or her own level" was one school's official response. A checkerboard array of faces in a classroom is now taken as a proxy for educational success. Regrettably, minority students in integrated schools still fail to acquire the skills needed to make them fully competitive in the job market.

### My Program

Some problems develop a clientele that can drive it in unexpected directions. Legislators and managers are often faced with a "do something even if it's wrong" mandate and provide a program that is intended to be a gesture (see Chapter 14). For instance, a hospital pastoral care program may be set in place to appease a trustee. The program may have a budget and a manager, but no clear objective. It becomes fodder for activists inside and outside the organization to shape. As a result, the pastoral care program may emerge with a drug abuse or suicide prevention mandate, or something even further from the intentions of its founder.

Similarly, legislation often identifies social problems without any idea of how to attack them. Some of Johnson's War on Poverty programs, the Tennessee Valley Authority, and the Professional Standards Review Organization (PSRO) are examples. The PSROs were established in communities across the United States without a clear notion of how to audit physician services. So clever county medical societies could have taken over the local PSRO and shaped its mission to suit their own ends. At the same time, watchdog groups that supported the PSROs could have seen to it that bureaucrats implemented the program. However, many medical societies became reactionary. They confronted the PSROs, seeking to restore the status quo by limiting the scope of agency actions.

Implementing agencies are often confronted by legislators, administrators, and consumer groups who make contradictory demands. Agencies like the Environmental Protection Agency (EPA) and the Occupational Safety and Health Administration (OSHA) can be seen engaging in one type of action on one day and abandoning it the next. Many of their actions result in charges of unethical behavior or dereliction of duty by one group and charges of irresponsible activism by another. As a result, the EPA and OSHA periodically promulgate and rescind regulations. The organization behaves irrationally, in part because no one stays long enough to develop a consistent implementation plan. At this extreme, the turnover of agency staff can lobotomize an organization.

Regulatory programs are often captured by those they seek to regulate: the Food and Drug Administration (FDA) by drug companies, area-wide planning committees by developers, and PSROs by local medical societies. This problem can lead to redefining the aims of regulation so the regulators can become friends rather than antagonists.

### Peace-Keeping Objectives

Legislation is often designed to root out real or imagined evils. The Office of Economic Opportunity (OEO) community action programs, the EPA, and OSHA are examples. Both the EPA and OSHA have been kept at arm's length by several administrations—close enough to restrict their freedom of action but far enough to be held publicly responsible for controversial actions or inactions. This results in a periodic changing of agency objectives without apparent reason. The ombudsman in a university and the chaplain in a prison have similar problems, finding that they are asked to be an advocate for both the individual and the institution.

## Evasion of Control Games

To resist control, people either fail to take the planned change seriously, at one extreme, or deliberately thwart it at the other. Similar problems occur when plan users feel abused and try to show that the plan is ill conceived, if not downright evil. Evasion of control games are pervasive within and outside organizations.

### Gesture

A common game involves procrastination or minimal effort, making the program appear ineffective. Examples of gestures range from some states' enforcement of the 55-mile-per-hour speed limit to bureaucrats in the departments of Justice and Education who take the busing of school children as synonymous with providing educational opportunity. The gesture game is used when refusal or outright defiance is infeasible, but players have the power to regulate some of the terms of what's done. For example, when the users' wishes are ignored, in, for instance, equipment selection, token cooperation may be mounted in the hopes that a system failure will result. Department managers can deliberately slow reports to demonstrate that the selected equipment was inappropriate.

### Pitched Battles

The opposition may be sufficiently strong so that the key people can refuse to act or comply. Noncompliance can often make program plans ineffective. For instance, had massive numbers of physicians refused to treat Medicare patients, the program would have been rendered unworkable. The framers of the legislation counted on greed to overcome philosophical objections, and it did. Within a firm, long-standing animosities between key people can create pitched battles. All programs are opposed if they are supported by or appear to benefit the other antagonist. A pitched battle is both overt and dangerous, demanding positional security and a podium to defend one's actions.

## Incomplete Option Games

Another type of game designed to thwart implementation stems from incomplete adherence to the plan. Implementation failures stem from turf battles, postures to enhance someone's career, and evasion of responsibility more often than poor plans.

### Delay

A common game is to hold back on commitment to the plan in order to extract concessions. These concessions state the terms under which key actors or agencies will become active participants. For instance, managers have been known to use this game when they discover a new initiative in areas totally outside their sphere of interest. They seek not to block the plan, but rather to extract support for a pet project of their own.

Public sector implementation faces a more complex situation. Representatives of state and local governments, the insurance industry, professional societies, consumer groups, and others barter to establish quid pro quos. For example, Bardach (1977) details the lengthy dispute between the Department of Labor (DOL), the Department of Health and Human Services (DHHS), and others over how to conduct manpower training under the Manpower Training Act. All agreed on the need for the program, but could not agree on how to train, operate, or even fund the program. Private agencies were seen by DHHS as playing the easy money game; others believed that they should turn aside power grabs for program control by local and state agencies. Ultimately, the program collapsed because no one stepped in to manage the bargaining process.

### Turf

Multiple jurisdictions often make responsibility ambiguous. In some instances, there is an overlapping of jurisdictions. In others, it is perceived or contrived. The heads of agencies or organizational units that seek to grow may claim a program merely to increase their control over resources. Intraorganizational rivalries between staff also stem from assumptions about their sphere of influence. Agency conflicts in the public sector also stem from notions of turf. In instances where the implementor can examine qualifications and make a selection, competition can be wholesome because it can be used to improve performance. Competition can be destructive when jurisdiction is in reality fuzzy and no one is willing (or able) to make a selection among competitors. This results in persistent haggling and no decision.

Disputes among implementors can literally dismember programs. For instance, disputes between California's Department of Social Welfare and the Department of Mental Hygiene (DMH) centered on the state's attempt to expand its turf (Bardach, 1977). The state department sought to add to its role of placement the supervision of the mentally retarded in the deinstitutionalized setting. The patient advocate role, sought by the state agency, clashed with the prerogatives of local mental health agencies that were set up by federal funds and administered through DMH.

Within an organization, clashes over turf are common. Higher levels preempt lower levels and staff departments clash over prerogatives. For example, management information systems implementation can be delayed because accounting, data processing, and others seek to control MIS resources and claim the MIS function.

### Odd Man Out

The "odd man out" game is played to cut losses. Support is withdrawn or the program is dumped. When federal funds for health planning were withdrawn the support of the state medical societies and hospital associations (and others) quickly evaporated. The "partnership for health" was unable to survive because its constituents merely sought federal funds and did not embrace the commitment to reform the health care delivery system through local initiative.

## Reputation: The Composite Game

The reputation game is partly an end in itself and also is used as an instrument of change. It is used as a bluff, to climb the latest hurdle created by "easy money," "turf," and other games (see Table 8-2). Reputation also stems from setting oneself up as being good at playing games that garner resources for the organization. Managers try to demonstrate that they can play the "spend money—get more," "all things to all people," "turf," "peacekeeping," and "odd man out" games. Bureaucrats write memos to the record to cover their tracks, and become experts at "odd man out." Politicians excel at "pork barrel." All avoid being linked to "easy life," "easy money," and "not our problem."

Several reputation games are played at one time. For instance, managers promote their turf-holding ability with subordinates and "pork barrel" with superiors.

### Reputation Games and the Sponsor

Reputation is based on past implementation successes. Sponsors are pulled from the pool of reputation-seeking managers. This motivates managers to create the aura that their performance meets these high standards. Life being what it is, failure plagues us all. However, to advance, the manager creates an image that success is a *fait accompli*. If his/her reach does not exceed his/her grasp, or if it can be made to appear that way, the reputation game has been well played in that episode. But more episodes will follow. A string of contrived and real successes is the stuff that a chief executive officer and leaders of all kinds are made of.

The aspiring CEO cannot be satisfied with past successes: He or she is seduced into making assurances about the future. The wake of successes that lies behind the career of successful mangers is not sufficient. Metaphorically, they must create a wake in front of their boat. Assurances about the outcome prior to starting a project are demanded by higher-ups. The manager "on the move" quickly learns that he or she must create, at all costs, the aura of success.

In one sense, the reputation game marks the leader. He or she who plays, and is not caught, displays the cleverness to succeed in the rarefied atmosphere that surrounds a CEO. At this level, there are many clever game players. Survival is to hold one's own. Success is measured by building a list of implementation claims faster than one's competition.

## Coping with the Game Players

To deal with games, two key steps are taken: countering the game and, if this fails, fixing the game.

### Game Countering

To counter a game, the players' strengths are sized up. If the player has a monopoly, either the gesture or the resistance game can be played. Both games can be countered by using certain tactics.

*Countering the Gesture.* Obstructionist tactics by monopolies often create delays or partial compliance. These tactics can be countered by a variety of measures including doing without, competition, cooptation, and using countervailing power.

Doing without is common in public organizations. For example, noncooperation within universities leads faculty to ignore services or to create a service that can be controlled. For instance, university administrators who control graduate admissions are both inefficient (slow) and ineffective (unable to collect information used as criteria in decision making). Parallel admissions procedures allow faculty to collect needed information, bypassing the uncooperative service departments. One who does without a service in effect pays for it twice.

Competition can often be stimulated. If the supervisor of a custodian department is uncooperative, attempts to sell the notion of cost centers, where everyone buys from the lowest bidder, can be pushed by those not well served. Local firms offering janitorial services can be asked to bid on providing services. In the public sector, vouchers were proposed to liberate the poor from the public hospital. Big users can force quick reform with these tactics. If the competition tactic is feasible, quick reform often follows because the department can ill afford the loss of business.

Cooptation, which occurs through participation, often creates a sense of commitment and deflects unwarranted criticism. (A complete discussion of cooptation is presented later in this chapter.)

Antagonistic organizations, such as Common Cause, or units, such as an ombudsman in a university, can confront the implementing monopoly with countervailing power. These watchdog groups can be quite effective, but often experience a decay in their zeal over time and tend to lose their effectiveness.

*Countering the Pitched Battle.* In a pitched battle, key people refuse to act or comply. Tactics of persuasion, automatic control, incentives, and punishment can be used to promote compliance.

The tactic of persuasion can be used to show the reticent how well the plan works. When a successful demonstration is made, acceptance often rises. Proclamations have little cost, but also little effectiveness when important centers of power are threatened.

Contracts drawn between the sponsor and organizational members provide several automatic control options for the sponsor. Federal research grants require equal opportunity hiring, the Hill-Burton hospital construction funding program stipulated that hospitals must provide free care, and universities agree to ratchet class size because of structures to flood the market with people in order to drive down their earning power and drive out the marginally competent. The first dollar of federal support brings with it all the federal strings, even when the strings are contradictory. (Sears recently sued the federal government asking that its myriad guidelines for hiring minorities be reconciled.) Agreement of all kinds within an organization have a similar intent: trading support for future consideration, financial and otherwise.

Bureaucratic incentives can be used to create rivalries among agencies or work units, enticing them to bid for desirable programs. Subsidies to the agency and work units to encourage them to take on a difficult assignment can be used. Output-based incentive systems can be used, but they can be subject to manipulation. For instance, particular types of job placements can be easy for some employment commissions and hard for others. Devising suitable measures for desired outcomes is always challenging and frequently impossible. Often, inputs are used as proxies. For instance, physicians are reimbursed for services, not for the patient's health status.

Outright *threats* can be used. They include removing a license or accreditation, warnings that funds will be cut off, systematic harassment, and disfavor. These tactics can be risky. The individual threatened must see the threat as legitimate, within the power of the executive to administer, and likely to be carried out if behavior does not change. To secure compliance, a dissident must first be made aware of what can be done. For instance, federal agencies are within their rights to cut off funds when certain conditions are not fulfilled. Other agencies have the power to revoke a license. However, the promise of sanctions can be hollow unless the threat is seen as likely to be delivered if there is no compliance. For instance, DHHS singled out several hospital expansions, approved under the Capital Expenditure Review Program, as unwarranted. However, applicants were aware that the DHHS had the power to overturn, but never did. As a consequence, these threats had little value in changing either applicant or review agency behavior.

In some instances, dissidents can be systematically harassed into compliance, such as being compelled to fill out seemingly endless forms. Ritti and Funkhouser (1987) show how calling an early morning meeting for noncooperating subordinates without a clear agenda created an incentive to work out their problems and terminate the inconvenient meeting. Disfavor also has limitations because the agency, work unit, or individual that has fallen from grace may be seen as a victim of bias or caprice.

Figure 8-1 illustrates one set of reward-punishment tactics. Applying positive or negative incentives is well known; however, removal creates some new tactics. Removing a reward is called omission. It can be used by sponsors to convey a subtle message. For example, a person is bypassed when rewards (such as pay increases) are dispensed. The message can be public, which creates a heavier-handed reaction. When penalties are skipped, a person is allowed to escape. People are often grateful to be removed from situations in which they inevitably lose. For example, individuals repeatedly bypassed for promotions may welcome a lateral move in which comparisons to others is less direct.

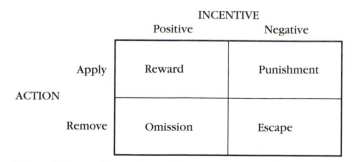

Figure 8-1 ▲ Reward-Punishment Tactics

## Fixing the Game

Successful implementors develop ways to negotiate with game players. These negotiations are complicated by technical problems in the plan, forcing the sponsor to act on two fronts: the perceptual and the operational.

Operating problems are real, tangible malfunctions in the plan. They can be caused by misconceptions and incomplete specifications made during planning. For example, a new billing practice, such as 15-day remainders, can make several incorrect assumptions about the behavior of late payors, the ability of employees to absorb the changes, and the clarity and completeness of procedures to implement the plan.

The sponsor takes responsibility to correct operational problems. He or she conducts training, devises a marketing program or a demonstration, and/or engages in more detailed planning to make the plan complete. Considerable plan detailing may be required in the implementation phase as field conditions reveal unattended contingencies and exceptions.

Perceptual problems are derived from consequences stemming from the plan. Individuals influenced by the planned change may see opportunities to be exploited or imagine situations that could develop that would cause them difficulties. For example, people have a mental image of a fair day's work, which becomes a local norm. Changes in procedure (stemming from a plan) can be seen as trying to ratchet performance expectations, leading to resistance. People also resist the mechanization of their assigned tasks when skill has been acquired through experience. When the task to be changed implies expertise to coworkers, modifying the task is often resisted because any change is seen as potentially diminishing the individual's job. Routinizing or mechanizing activities, which may imply that expertise and experience are no longer needed, downgrades the unit's or the performer's image of their importance, often leading to resistance.

Dealing with operational problems eliminates the factual basis for objections. This is an essential first step in dealing with perceptual problems. Two approaches can be used to deal with perceptions: intermediaries and closing off options.

### Intermediaries

When a planned change is blocked, mediation through third parties can help to find areas of compromise. Also, the third party can often point out unreasonable fears or concerns with greater ease than someone believed to have a vested interest in a plan's implementation. Mediation is encouraged and even sponsored by many government agencies.

The Lewin-Schein "change agent" is a mediator who works within an organization (Lewin, 1958; Schein, 1964). The change agent has a track record that has created prestige and respect with peers and subordinates. This aura permits the change agent to negotiate on behalf of the organization. The change agent often paves the way for change by finding adaptations that allow the plan to be implemented.

### Foreclosing Options

When plan sponsors, acting as change agents or mediators, find persuasion ineffective or unlikely to succeed, a somewhat more devious tactic can be used. The administrator limits opponents' maneuverability, forcing them into a path consistent with that called for in the plan.

The "bandwagon effect" is created when the plan sponsor sets a new course and calls it the "wave of the future." Some people will be enticed to support such an effort, fearing isolation should the plan become successful. The sponsor, seeking to create a new wave, must have considerable faith in the plan. For this tactic to be successful, the plan must be vigorously sold, necessitating the sponsor to invest considerable amounts of his or her social credit.

Making opponents play the "odd man out" game is the reverse tactic. The sponsor removes supportive resources from those blocking the plan and gives them to plan proponents. Often the mere threat to remove resources can coax the reluctant party into line. This tactic can also backfire when a confrontation between the sponsor and the participants is created. The relatively greater power of the sponsor dictates the outcome in most, but not all, of these confrontations.

The situation may preclude foreclosing all the options of managers and others who are resisting the change. For instance, department managers who do not seek further advancement often need nothing further from the organization, making them invulnerable to many organizational incentives. In other situations, the sponsor cannot legitimately withhold resources. For example, in a service setting, withholding funds can result in lowering the number or quality of services. As a result, it may be impossible to cut off all options, or even make them look less attractive than cooperation to the recalcitrant department manager. In other cases, department managers can have special sources of power through their connections or nepotism, which protect them.

## The Game Scenario

To prepare the scenario, four types of game-related issues must be considered: who is playing, the likely perceptions of players, the player's expected behavior, and the player's power.

### The Players

Traditional antagonists and vicious department managers are easy to spot. But the lure of power, or money, or both may attract new players to claim turf or easy money. Proponents and opponents can be flushed out by announcing one's intention to create, for instance, a new division in a company or by inference through using the nominal group technique or a similar group process (see Chapter 10). Within an organization, the players can be less visible and must be enumerated with care. Again, group process can be helpful.

### Player's Beliefs

Each player must be contemplated to sort out his or her perceptions. Knowledgeable people are helpful to suggest the values and rationales that lie behind each player's position.

### Player's Behavior

The intensity of play represents another key factor in the scenario. Those with experiences in dealing with each actor provide invaluable help in assessing whether they will be active or passive in their support or opposition of a given plan and what triggers such a response. Questions include what games are likely and the intensity of the resistance. In short, what is the prospect of the player being outraged?

### Player's Power

A player may seek to block the plans but may lack the power to do so. These players will seek allies so collective action can have clout. The plan sponsor tries to keep such coalitions from forming, or offers incentives to break them up. A few people will have the power to act on their own. If also motivated to do so, they represent the key set of individuals to whom negotiations are brought.

## Scenario Writing

The steps used in implementation scenario writing are:

Step 1    Restate the plan and its objective.

Step 2    Inventory affected parties.

Step 3    Identify areas of compromise that lower resistance and identify implementating units that are compatible.

Step 4    Determine if resistance is likely to stem from low-effort games (delay), resource diversion games (e.g., easy money), objective modification games (e.g., my program), evasion games (e.g., gesture), or incomplete adoption (e.g., turf).

Step 5    Identify the players and the stakes in each likely game. Find natural allies and decide whether they are likely to be supportive of the plan. Measure prospects of success by determining who must be confronted and their power.

Step 6    Fix the game: offer incentives to participate which create a manageable coalition supportive of the plan (or a modification).

First, the sponsor looks for games that might be played, identifying the players and their stakes. The approach is similar to the scenario writing procedure described for concept development (Chapter 11). The consequences of plan adoption to key groups are traced out to identify who might object and why, identifying what must be changed to make the plan acceptable to various parties.

Delivering Medicaid services to those eligible for Medicaid in a community health center will be used to provide an example of scenario preparation. In this

CHC, the administrator sought ways to minimize expected losses. Because CHCs are capitated, dropouts can dramatically reduce revenue, creating operating losses. To deal with this prospect, a CHC administrator first seeks to limit the welfare subscriber's prerogatives to drop out of the plan. However, consumer-sovereignty principles, articulated by welfare rights groups, limits the prospect of success when using this tactic. Next, the administrator tried to have Medicaid programs guarantee per capita funding for Medicaid enrollees for a year. Finally, the administrator sought the right for the CHC to be selective in the enrollment of Medicaid and Medicaid eligibles, rejecting those likely to have long-term, expensive health problems.

The scenario forces the implementor to consider carefully the incentives of various parties to destroy or block the plan. Each party is described in terms of the games that they are motivated to play, as shown in Table 8-3. For instance, Medicaid watchdogs should anticipate that CHC management will play easy money, exploiting both Medicaid subscribers and the federal treasury. Not our problem is played by DHHS if they insist on a first-come, first-served enrollment for the Medicaid population in the CHC. The local university may play pork barrel when asked to staff the CHC, seeing it as an opportunity to underwrite some of their educational and research expenses. The activist members of the consumer board of the CHC can play the all things to all people game, adding vogue but medically questionable services, such as stress management. Keeping the peace may be created by the antics of the local medical society whose members see the CHC as a threat. Blue Cross and other private third-party payors may engage in delay, insisting on a role, but offering low-quality contribution and delaying on key arrangements to hamstring the effort. These delay tactics may be a precursor to a takeover. The Blue Cross representatives may engage in turf games, claiming jurisdiction over the CHC. All parties can be expected to play reputation.

Table 8-3 ▲ A Game Scenario Illustration

| | Players | Games | Stakes | Intensity | Barter |
|---|---|---|---|---|---|
| 1. | U.S. Department of Health and Human Services | Not our problem or easy life | Retaining integrity of the reimbursement practices regardless of enrollment problems | High | None |
| 2. | University medical school | Pork barrel | Covering research expenses | Moderate | Size of budget |
| 3. | Consumer board of directors | All things to all people | Control over terms of service | High | Sizable |
| 4. | Local medical society | Keeping the peace | Philosophical control over medical practice | High | Moderate |
| 5. | Blue Cross | Delay | Gain a foothold by controlling board membership | High | Membership criteria |
| | | Turf | Jurisdiction over reimbursement mechanism | High | Dicker over budget |

## Using the Scenario

There are two basic strategies in game fixing: using the scenario to identify a coalition and determining who must be bribed.

### Coalition Building

Thompson's (1967) notion of a dominant coalition is similar to the coalition of game players that emerges. People who share a common interest make up the coalition. It is the sponsor's task to manage this group. Management takes place by defining plan objectives agreeable to the coalition or shaping the view of planning to be consistent with the coalition's emerging consensus. Objectives may change, calling for the planner to change the plan accordingly.

### Bribery and Incentives

Bribery is an ugly term. Nevertheless, the essence of the actions of a successful manager draws on this notion whenever plan implementation is both important and difficult. On occasion, to create a coalition, something must be offered. The barter can be covert or quite open, depending upon circumstances (Mitroff, 1987). It is common for people to express their dissatisfaction in dollar terms. Productive staff dissatisfied with their current assignment are given a salary increase. Providing perks in the form of "work" vacations to tour Europe, house subsidies, and the like for CHC administrators are other examples. The implementing manager identifies available resources and divides them up in such a way as to maximize support.

Bardach (1977) sees these "fixes" in somewhat more genteel terms. His ideas include letting staff have a role in setting a line manager's budget, thereby giving staffers watchdog roles. The staff person (e.g., planner) with budget prerogatives creates some interesting dilemmas for recalcitrant managers. A shift of values toward innovation is one likely outcome.

Staffers as watchdogs have somewhat murkier implications. The staffer or planner will find it hard to be both idea stimulator and regulator. The health planning movement is an example of regulation driving out planning, perhaps with federal encouragement following the easy life game. For-profit organizations with a poor history of innovation may benefit the most from such an arrangement. However, considerable line-staff conflict should be expected.

## ▲ THE UNFREEZE-REFREEZE TECHNIQUE

The "unfreeze-refreeze" technique has been taken from the work of Lewin (1947, 1958) and Schein (1964). This research led to the establishment of a discipline called organizational development (OD), which applies behavioral science concepts to help an organization adjust to change. From this beginning, OD has gradually embraced the aim of organizational self-renewal, which has planninglike purposes. The unfreeze-refreeze technique and the associated notion of a change agent have remained key constructs in OD. Although many adaptations have been made (see Chapter 4), its precepts provide a useful implementation technique.

Table 8-4  ▲  The Change Process

| Unfreezing | | Change | Refreezing |
|---|---|---|---|
| Tension created that signals the need for change. | Change is advocated by a change agent | Users develop or test the plan | New behavior and skills reinforced and internalized |

Source: Adopted from Dalton (1970a).

The unfreeze-refreeze technique is used to overcome the resistance to planned change. The procedure has three steps: unfreezing, changing, and refreezing. Unfreezing exploits existing tensions or introduces a disequilibrium into the present situation, which is seen by members of the organization or work group as stable. The change step provides new information and ideas offering new perceptions, new skills, and a new set of behavioral patterns. To refreeze, these new perceptions, skills, and behaviors are reinforced to create a new stability. The steps in the technique are summarized in Table 8-4.

The unfreeze-refreeze technique orders events and draws attention to contextual factors and situations. The sponsor acting as a change agent must understand the disrupted values and dashed expectations to appreciate fully the context that surrounds the planned change process. Resistance to change is lowered when events that preceded a definition of the need for planned change have been recognized and understood.

## The Procedure

*Step One: Unfreezing.* The first step calls on the sponsor to take advantage of dissatisfactions with current conditions or to create dissatisfaction. Unfreezing is begun by critiquing (or by failing to support) the value of the organization's products, services, internal operation, or policies. Cues are provided that suggest that past practices are no longer effective. Performance is compared with that achieved by others, or with what is theoretically attainable. Guilt, anxiety, or the implied inability to meet expectations aids the unfreezing process as new norms are set.

During unfreezing, the sponsor must recognize that people often ignore negative information when that information has even minor ambiguities. Blunt or heavy-handed presentations are apt to relegate critical information to a "special case" category, so it can be ignored. The failure to meet expectations is rationalized by special circumstances or problems that are not likely to recur. When critical information is ignored, the sponsor's view can be seen as unreliable, a highly undesirable situation for a sponsor's career.

In summary, the sponsor establishes and justifies new norms that get key people to recognize the need to change. When this occurs, people are more willing to consider adopting new skills and the new behaviors these skills require. The unfreezing step creates the impetus for change.

*Step Two: The Change.* During the change phase, the targets of planned change are exposed to the new procedures and what will be required of them, such as acquiring new information, altering behavior, or developing new skills. During this step, a group of users can be guiding each stage of planned change, or the group may be testing outcomes from a concurrent evaluation process. The change step either

Table 8-5  ▲  The Unfreeze-Refreeze Technique

| Change | Tension Within the Organization (antecedent conditions) | Unfreezing Phase | Change Phase | Refreezing Phase |
|---|---|---|---|---|
| 1. Objectives | Objectives and norms questioned | → General objectives selected | → Growing specificity of the objective | → Settling on specific norms |
| 2. Social ties | Stress induced in existing social ties | → Prior social ties interrupted or changed | → Formation of new alliances centering around new activities | → Reinforce new social ties by new behavior |
| 3. Esteem | Self-doubt encouraged | → Begin esteem building by assurances of change agent | → Esteem building through task accomplishment | → Recognition for meeting norm builds sense of accomplishment |
| 4. Motives | Motives questioned | → External motive for change (opportunity to innovate or planning results) | → Field testing | → New norms serve as basis to judge performance (norms internalized) |
| | ↑ | ↑ | ↑ | ↑ |
| 5. Change agent's role | Promote tension | → Offer ideas | → Training and guidance | → Demonstrate accomplishment |

Source: Adapted from Dalton (1970a).

reacts to a planned change process by shaping and modifying the plan or guides the planned change process, as shown in Table 8-5. When an implementation group guides planned change, project teams are often spawned to provide information for each process stage. The implementation group, with the sponsor as its leader, monitors the diagnostic phase (unfreezing and formulation), develops or responds to options (concept development and detailing), and selects the preferred option for implementation (evaluation).

Implementation groups can function as an evaluative body and participate in criteria selection and weighting to carry out an evaluation. The values of the group dictate the criteria that will be used to find a favored alternative. The group may also play a role in reviewing and suggesting modifications for alternatives as they emerge, to make them acceptable to various constituencies.

*Step Three: Refreezing.* Reinforcement through practice occurs in the last step. The plan becomes integrated into the "attitude systems" as well as the formal procedures of the organization. Feedback control mechanisms, which compare performance against the new norms, provide a basis for determining success. The sponsor often prunes this information to ensure that an early success is reported. For example, if early cost information is not favorable, it is kept under wraps during what is termed a learning phase.

## Four Mechanisms of Change

Four change mechanisms are used. The sponsor, acting as a change agent, alters the implementation group's objectives, social ties, self-esteem, and motives (Table 8-6).

Table 8-6  ▲  Mechanisms of Change

| Away From | Toward |
| --- | --- |
| Generalized objectives | Specific objectives |
| Old social ties | New social ties which support the plan |
| Lowered self-esteem | Heightened self-esteem |
| External motives | Internal motives |

Source: Adapted from Dalton (1970a).

To carry out the unfreeze-refreeze technique, the sponsor deals with each of these factors during each step of the procedure, as shown in Table 8-5.

### Objectives

Initially, objectives are quite general. Objectives are made increasingly specific as the sponsor guides an implementation group through the planned change process. During planning, the objectives should take on increased immediacy and specify increasingly tangible results (Table 8-5). For instance, Dalton (1970) found that objectives in successful implementations moved from the general to the specific. In these case studies of inspection and accounting, general directives caused managers to engage in setting weekly schedules with increased specificity of target dates and budgets during planned change, which ultimately improved inspection methods and accounting procedures. Management by objectives (MBO) programs use a similar approach.

Outside the organizational setting, a similar phenomenon can be observed. During successful therapy, the initial objective set by the therapist and the patient is often quite general and becomes increasingly specific as the treatment process proceeds. Explorations begin with the patient examining past relationships and feelings and then moving toward specific instances that cause trouble.

If the plan is to have lasting effects, this movement from general to specific objectives is accompanied by the individual giving up past practices and becoming more open to adopting new ones. These steps can be seen when an individual is converted from one set of views to another. The general to specific movement of objectives probably represents an ingrained social need in people and will occur with or without a planned change process. For instance, the movement toward concrete objectives seems inherent in the behavior of subordinates, who demand that a problem should be managed.

### Social Ties

Social ties must be loosened for change to occur. Behavior is often deeply rooted, based on years of past associations. People are comfortable, if not ecstatic, with this relationship and fear new ones. Work groups, whether formal or informal, shape behavior. By merely introducing a new individual into the group, a new equilibrium must be sought, which makes change more likely. To change an individual, one must separate the person from his or her normal social support systems and routines. Convents and monasteries exercise this tactic, but prisons do not because prisoners continue to be reinforced by the antisocial values of their fellow prisoners.

Colleges and universities use distance from home and work load to cause a partial breaking of ties, thought to be necessary for learning. During college, students frequently adopt some of the views of other students and faculty, while somewhat discarding those of their parents (Newcomb, 1958). Experimental results also support the impact of breaking social ties. When subjects are placed in a group in which the other members are coached not to agree or support the subject's views, the subject will begin to doubt his or her own position (Asch, 1951). In experiments where the group was supportive, resistance to social pressure increases.

These studies help to explain the lack of influence of training programs. Dalton (1970) reports case studies at International Harvester and at Tampa and Sigma (disguised companies), to improve their training programs. These programs became effective only after the supervisors agreed to make the changes in procedure taught to their subordinates. Without this commitment, the contact with supervision and peers is so pervasive that people quickly abandon new skills and return to old habits after the program is over. For example, the drug prescribing behavior of physicians can be measurably changed by pointing out the dangers of drug interactions and better substitutes in a pharmacology lecture. However, the old drug prescribing behavior will resurface in less than six months without reinforcement (Nutt, 1984a).

Breaking social ties was an integral part of the "brainwashing" techniques used by the Chinese in the Korean conflict. New prisoners of war (POWs) were placed with POWs who had made confessions so that newcomers were steeped in the "reformed" attitudes. The Chinese measured progress by the least reformed member, pressuring the strongest to conform. Schein (1961) concluded that pressure from other members became so great that this tactic became the most effective device in enticing POWs to make bogus confessions. New social ties help to secure the conversion. This approach was unsuccessful in Vietnam, in part because POWs overcame their isolation with elaborate support systems and maintained codes to keep in continual contact with one another. New ties have been found to be essential in religious conversion as well as alcoholism and drug abuse programs.

### Self-Esteem

Changes in self-esteem were found to facilitate change. The desired movement is away from self-doubt toward heightened self-esteem (Table 8-5). First, old patterns of behavior are dropped; then new ones are adopted.

Stress is a precondition for change. The sponsor plays on existing tension, magnifying it and focusing on it. The communication may be implicit or explicit. Failure to reach targets can be presented directly, via meetings and other forums. When the situation is well known, subtle approaches are more appropriate. For instance, expressing confidence in people to do better recognizes that self-esteem is already low and begins to rebuild it. This gives the sponsor the legitimacy to make the change called for by a plan. Externals (consultants) can be used as change agents when the situation demands firmness and resistance is expected. The outsider can afford to lose his or her social credit whereas a sponsoring manager may not; managers must retain a balance of credit with their key people so that they will accomplish other tasks.

As a planned change is introduced and success is experienced, the sponsor attempts to build self-esteem. The sponsor's role is to recognize and encourage better performance. The Hawthorne experiments found that coworkers with heightened self-esteem improve their productivity (Mayo, 1933).

### Motives

Motives for change initially are external, but should gradually become internalized (see Table 8-5). Internalization occurs when the new behaviors are seen as intrinsically rewarding. This internalizing process has three aspects: new structure, application and improvisation, and verification.

The new structure provides a new way to think about one's contributions and the organization's response to these contributions. Both a language and an associative set are required. The language provides a means to recognize new concepts, and the associations indicate how new behaviors and skills create benefits for the individual *and* the organization.

Application often leads to improvisation, which creates an identification with the plan. Identification permits the user to make an application to personal problems, testing the veracity of the new scheme on his or her home turf. Application is often an essential ingredient before an idea will be fully accepted. Research in social psychology has demonstrated the application-improvisation effect in many studies, showing that opinion change is enhanced by improvisation. When people are given an opportunity to modify a statement to incorporate personal issues they are more inclined to adopt the statement, even if it implies a change in opinion. Studies of brainwashing revealed that the most effective break occurred when the POW wrote his own confession.

Experienced-based verification is the key to successful implementation. If the plan is tested and found to work on the performer's turf, it gains enormously in acceptance. Defense contractors use this tactic by operating a new system along with Air Force personnel for an extended period, partly to train them but what is more important, to demonstrate that the system works. The implementor should take such a role whenever possible, not merely delivering a set of manuals to the program manager. Dalton's (1970) case studies also show the pervasive impact of the demonstration effect. Companies that had managers serve as contact men, coordinating research and sales, increased the acceptance of the research department's ideas. Managerial participation in devising plans greatly aided the implementation rate for cost reduction schemes.

## Ethics

The unfreeze-refreeze technique can be critiqued in terms of the ethics of its manipulative elements. The coercive aspects of the process do have ethical implications. In one sense, the sponsor provides leadership but in another, opportunities for demagoguery are rampant. Manipulation does occur. The sponsor acting as a change agent must recognize the fine line between influencing and manipulating, using the former tactic and avoiding the latter.

## ▲   THE PARTICIPATION TECHNIQUE

Planning groups are formed to get their members to see the need for change by going through steps of problem recognition and solution development. Representatives of important points of view are permitted to make plans for the organization. The participation of people affected by the plan in its development enhances the prospects of plan adoption while retaining some degree of control over the process for the sponsor. Participation works because absorbing people one hopes to influence into a policy-making body of the organization coopts them (Thompson, 1967). Cooptation increases the likelihood of plan acceptance, averts threats from potential adversaries, and gathers support for the plan and the planned change process.

Some planned changes cut across several disciplinary boundaries or organizations that have overlapping charters and prerogatives. The Highway Safety Program is an example. A *consortium* planning group is formed to deal with problems or issues, such as traffic accidents, that exceed the mandates and expertise of a single organization. The consortium is made up of representatives of the organizations needed to take action. The sponsor of a planned change asks the leaders of these organizations to select representatives for the consortium. Hospital shared services and the National Kidney Foundation provide examples. Firms also cooperate in this manner. Eastman Kodak and General Electric introduced the instamatic camera worldwide in the early 1960s, capturing the small camera and accessory market for nearly a decade. A consortium of Kodak and G.E. people designed the camera and flash cube in a joint effort.

Consortiums are used because they provide information and represent centers of power that must be managed if planned change is to occur. Venture management teams used by firms to stimulate innovation are a special type of consortium that assembles interests and expertise within an organization (Galbraith, 1971; Galbraith and Kazanjian, 1986). *Venture teams* assemble these interests and expertise to tackle thorny interdepartmental problems or issues, such as overseeing new product development. Consortium planning groups drawn from within an organization are called venture groups. Planning groups that involve external experts and interests are called consortiums. In each case, a planning group is assembled because the cooperation of several departments or organizations is needed.

Consortium or venture group members are drawn from departments or organizations that have (1) resources influenced by the plan, (2) leadership required to implement the plan, and (3) mandates to deliver services or act in certain ways. A consortium or venture group attempts to marshall the resources, leadership, and mandates of these organizations or departments by offering representatives of these organizations a chance to participate in the planned change process. Involvement is believed to enhance both the quality and the acceptance of a plan. Experts from cooperating organizations are expected to bring fresh perspectives and new ideas to the planned change process.

Cooptative planning groups, and particularly consortiums, can be difficult to manage, making their benefits elusive. Organizations or viewpoints represented in the group often have conflicting objectives. Some members may find that attending to these objectives keeps them from disclosing information useful in planned change. Other members may seek personal goals, like prestige. Still others may seek advocacy of a personal viewpoint or the interest of a professional group. As a result, some members support innovative ideas and others push traditional points of view.

Despite these drawbacks, studies show that consortiums that represent several organizations produce plans with higher quality that were more acceptable, compared with conventional groups (Nutt, 1979b, 1984b). A consortium that represents several organizations or viewpoints improves the plan and makes it more implementable. Also, member conflict, rather than positive reinforcement by peers from another organization, was prevalent in studies of consortium planning groups. Conflict is likely when a group's members have status differentials, unique frames of reference, different views, or dissimilar objectives and beliefs. Conflicts among a group's members eliminate "participation effects" and lead to lower acceptance.

Cooptation is effective when new members are solicited one at a time. Introducing a new member to a core group, whose members are committed to the sponsor's point of view, subtly pressures the new member to conform to the standards, goals, and expectations of the group. Thus, cooptation occurs when a planning group gradually builds its power and influence with its members. Also, group process techniques (discussed in Chapter 10) help to bring out the benefits of a planning group and manage its shortcomings.

## Participation Approaches

A planning group can have a delegated, shared, or indirect role in plan development (Table 8-1). To delegate, the sponsor has individuals affected by the plan formulate its terms, hoping to coopt them. The shared approach uses representatives of key power centers in a planning group to formulate some of the plan aspects. Indirect approaches canvass plan users, experts, managers, and others early in the process to identify their concerns or demands that may or may not be acted on. In each case, suggestions from stakeholders are sought hoping to get their acquiescence, if not wholehearted acceptance. In the delegated form of participation, the group is asked to develop a plan. The plan is outlined by the planning group in the shared type of participation, laying out key premises, but not details. This form of participation offers valuable ideas, but less cooptation of participants occurs. The delegated form of participation has the best prospects for implementation success.

Participative techniques can be applied in all stages of planning, as described in Chapter 7. The type of participation depends on what the planning group is asked to do and the degree of involvement in the process of people affected by the plan, as shown in Figure 8-2 (Nutt, 1986). Type IV or *comprehensive* participation calls for delegation to a planning group, which is fully representative, charged with specifying plan details. The group is made up of all important users and power centers. The Likert "System IV" illustrates this approach. Type IV participation creates considerable commitment making implementation likely.

The type III or *complete* approach to participation calls for full participation, but asks the planning group to frame rather than specify the details of the plan. Clients or users are asked to set a direction. Staff specialists create a plan that is responsive to the directions set. The PPM approach discussed in Chapter 4,

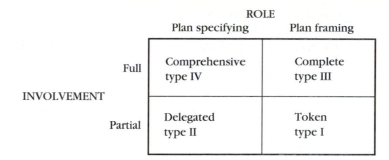

**Figure 8-2** ▲ **Types of Participation**
Adapted from Nutt (1986).

illustrates this type of participation. Participants are asked to identify the problems to be addressed, but not plan details. Type III participation is somewhat less effective than a type IV because the role of the group in planning is somewhat restricted.

The type II or *delegated* approach has representatives of power centers and users create the plan. A strategic planning group, with its membership drawn from board members and key executives, uses the type II participation. Much of the social planning initiated by the "Great Society" programs of the 1960s implicitly used type II participation notions. This type of participation is found in most community planning efforts. To make this type of participation effective, the planning group members must sell the plan to others who make up their constituency. The participants are often coopted, but their ability to persuade others to adopt the plan hinges on whether prerogatives seem threatened and on the degree of professionalization in their constituency. Professionals are not inclined to adopt plans devised by colleagues because it sets a precedent of unilateral action. These constraints make complete participation more effective than delegated participation.

The least effective form of participation is a type I or *token* approach, which uses representatives to frame the plan. Implementation effectiveness is hampered by the participant's role as well as the use of representatives. An example is the Delphi survey, discussed in Chapter 10. The frame that is set (e.g., problems identified in the survey) can be misleading unless the sampling procedure is carefully developed and explicitly followed. If not, those sampled may not be aware of needs, or they may misrepresent these needs. The views, needs, or wants of the representatives may dominate. The role of framing limits the effects of cooptation. As in delegated participation, the representatives often fail to convince others to adopt the plan, further limiting the effectiveness of token participation.

### Selecting Members for a Planning Group

There are several views on member selection. Some believe that expertise is key whereas others insist on user or citizen representation. For instance, federally funded planning agencies have been required to include consumers, providers, and community leaders as planning group members. These requirements stem from legislation that, over the past two decades, has gradually refined its definitions of who should be participants in a planned change process (Parker, 1970; Nutt, 1984b). Experts, the controllers of key resources, the users of products or services, and activists or reform leaders have been required as participants in planning groups. Those with technical knowledge of the planning are experts. For example, an expert could be a nephrologist for a project concerning renal disease, a computer specialist for a project involving a management information system, a financial expert for a project involving an acquisition, or a lawyer for corporate restructuring. Experts are particularly helpful in bringing viable solution ideas to the planned change process. Thus, content area specialists often become members of planning groups to give technical insight.

Resource controllers have a grip on needed resources or authorizations. Voluntary agencies and accreditation bodies have control over standards of practice, administrators deploy resources, and insurance carriers must authorize changes in important parameters associated with service provision. Resource controllers are involved in a planning group to increase their understanding of the needs for changes, to identify the feasibility of plans, to secure the authorization to implement, and to specify relevant constraints, such as budget limits. Unnecessary challenges to existing systems can be reduced by giving resource controllers membership in the planning group so these concerns have an outlet. Thus, the involvement of key decision makers is justified through their sanction of the planned change process and their contribution of problem-related information.

The involvement of clients in planning has a long history. In the public sector, the rationale for such involvement stems from egalitarian arguments: in a democratic society, people should have a role in articulating their needs. Moreover, as Delbecq (1968) notes, "Calcified bureaucrats often ignore the needs of their clients when planning programs." Client involvement is also justified because consumers are in the best position to specify their needs. A program built on legitimate needs produces greater benefit for the client group and thus satisfies utilitarian criteria. A number of case studies demonstrate that organizational innovation is strongly related to recognizing and understanding its clients' wishes (Utterback, 1971; Souder, 1987). For these reasons, client involvement is often advocated.

Consumers are *users* of the products or services one seeks to initiate or change. For example, Delbecq, Van de Ven, and Gustafson (1986) define users as the beneficiaries of the services to be planned. The user of a health program may be the public at large, such as a community's consumers of emergency health care services, or those who will consume a particular type of service, such as the users of an MIS in a firm. A renal program might involve those with end-stage renal disease and a hypertension program those with high blood pressure. As Delbecq and Van de Ven (1971) view it, the users of the services being planned are in the best position to specify what services they need, as well as some aspects of the mode of delivery of these services. According to this view, to effectively plan products for a firm, the consumers of the products should participate in the planned change process.

Power groups based on the concept of consumer participation, such as "welfare rights" organizations, often organize to articulate their needs or the needs of a reference group. Social issues have been a common stimulus for the formation of activist groups. It is not uncommon for an activist group to seek out and secure formal sanction from local government or sponsorship from a federal program, such as OEO, and become a quasi-permanent voluntary organization. As a result, members of activist organizations often obtain considerable knowledge of a product or service and become important spokespersons. Representatives from these activist organizations are often drawn from the decision-making body of the activist organization to become members of a planning group. Representatives of activist groups are placed on planning groups to obtain the sanction and approval of the activist organization and, to a lesser extent, because they have knowledge of the needs of their reference group or solution insights (Nutt, 1976a).

### Why People Accept Planning Group Membership

Membership in a planning group is accepted for several reasons (Nutt, 1989a). Members may see the group as a means or an end in which they can fulfill social or task needs (Figure 8-3). When the group serves as a means to achieve social needs, membership is accepted for status reasons. Participation can be satisfying, and some people accept membership with this end in mind. Task-oriented members seek control by manipulating the group's processes or by dictating choices.

Mixing people with these diverse motivations creates tension in the group and should be avoided. In particular, people with task and social needs may clash because people with social needs seek a pleasant atmosphere whereas people with task needs must, on occasion, be contentious to achieve their goals. Means-ends clashes are signaled by members who stress procedural matters while others are seeking action on important issues. Members of a group that seek prestige are careful not to antagonize because to do so puts them at risk of losing their status. They contribute little to the process and have little influence on the outcome.

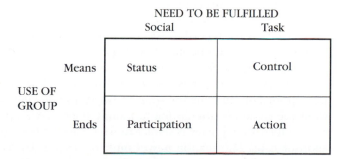

NEED TO BE FULFILLED

|  | Social | Task |
|---|---|---|
| Means | Status | Control |
| Ends | Participation | Action |

USE OF GROUP

**Figure 8-3  ▲  Member's Attitude Toward Planned Change Groups**
Adapted from Filley, House, and Kerr (1976).

# ▲ USE OF POWER WITH AN IMPLEMENTATION TECHNIQUE

The sponsor can draw on various types of power to assist an implementation. The power bases are used in conjunction with or independent of the implementation techniques previously described.

## Bases of Power

Sponsors can apply power to pave the way for a change. French and Raven (1959) identify types of power that plan sponsors can use to improve the prospects of implementation. The guidelines that follow have been adapted to make them useful for the implementation planned change (Nutt, 1983).

Five bases of power can be identified: (1) reward, (2) legitimate, (3) expert, (4) informational, and (5) referent. Reward power stems from providing rewards or removing noxiants. For instance, the escape tactic discussed previously can be a noxiant, as can undesirable peer relations. Reward power draws its strength from the importance that many people attach to certain kinds of rewards (e.g., money). Coercive power is a special type of reward power where punishments are administered or rewards are skipped (e.g., the omission tactic). A plan sponsor can monitor behavior and administer rewards when behavior is supportive of the plan and can act in a coercive manner when behavior is not supportive.

Legitimate power stems from beliefs by the implementation targets that the sponsor has the right to influence them and that they are required to conform. Legitimate power comes from cultural norms. For instance, some Asian societies give power to their senior citizens; younger people conform because elders have legitimate power over them. A person's position in an organizational structure is another source of legitimate power. Supervisors are granted power over their subordinates by virtue of their position. Agents are also given legitimate power. Examples include the executors of an estate and unions acting as bargaining agents. Legitimate power is always restricted in scope. A supervisor, for instance, can influence the work but not the leisure time activities of his or her subordinates.

Expert power develops when the sponsor is seen by those he or she seeks to influence as having unique knowledge and skills. The sponsor must be seen by those being influenced as both credible and trustworthy. To be credible, the sponsor must have a track record of successes. Trust stems from a reputation of honest and candid dealings with people. Expert power fits well with the activities of a change agent applying the unfreeze-refreeze technique.

Information power is defined as the ability to offer insights, which alters the perceptions of someone the sponsor hopes to influence. The information is tailored to fit the situation, attempting to modify the target's preconceived ideas about the plan. Information power is similar to what Parsons has called "pure persuasion." The sponsor using information power must be seen as trustworthy, but not necessarily as credible. To use information power, the sponsor cites a relevant anecdote, which must be seen as well intended but may or may not be seen as relevant.

Some sponsors can create (or have) some form of attraction or identification that draws people to them, called referent power. The charismatic leader is said to have referent power. Such leaders have power because people are drawn to their style or to other attributes. The ability of researchers to define factors that predict who will be seen as charismatic ("great man") has been unsuccessful (Nutt, 1989a). Referent power has limited value in implementation because a plan sponsor has little to go on to identify change agents that have referent power traits.

## Using Power to Implement Planned Change

The power bases have cumulative effects. For instance, both reward and coercion power can strengthen legitimate power. Those with reward prerogatives are also often seen as legitimate change agents. Expert power enhances information power. Thus, when applied together, several of the sources of power increase the prospects of implementation. In addition to applying power in a cumulative fashion, the sources of power can be applied in conjunction with the implementation techniques to create an implementation approach that is used to promote the adoption of planned change. Reward, legitimate, referent, expert, and informational power can be applied with edicts, persuasion, the game scenario, the unfreeze-refreeze, and participation techniques. In the next chapter, conditions under which each power type and implementation technique can be profitably applied will be identified.

## ▲ Key Points

1. Edict and persuasion techniques can be applied to obtain the compliance needed to implement a planned change. These techniques can be effective when time is short, when the sponsor has the prerogative to act, and when stakeholders are minimally affected by the planned change.

2. Manipulative techniques (the game scenario and unfreeze-refreeze techniques) alter the perceptions of stakeholders by managing the situation. Although more risky than participation, these techniques work well in difficult situations that have wary stakeholders.

3. Participation is tied to the use of planning groups. Participation is an effective way to promote the acceptance of change, when stakeholders are powerful and apt to be threatened by a planned change effort.

4. An implementation approach is made up of power bases used in conjunction with one of the implementation techniques.

## ▲ Exercises

For each exercise, take the role of the sponsor who is attempting to implement the plan called for by one of the cases. Select the same case for each question. (Cases are located at the end of Part Three.)

1. Prepare an edict calling for the implementation of the plan called for by the case. Include a description of who is apt to resist the plan and the prospects for his or her replacement. Suggest a structural change that would remove your

resister. How feasible is your new structure? Consider the limitations of the unilateral implementation techniques. Which are you apt to encounter? Why? Appraise your prospects of success if unilateral techniques are used to promote adoption of the plan in the case.

2. Prepare the best argument that supports the adoption of the plan in the case. Identify key stakeholders. Which stakeholders are apt to buy your arguments and which will not? What assurances would the latter group of stakeholders need to move them to a neutral or positive posture? Appraise your prospects of success if persuasion is used to promote adoption of the plan in the case.

3. Apply the game scenario to identifying players, games, stakes, and intensity of play, and barters or incentives that you could use in the case. Indicate game countering tactics that you could use. Evaluate incentives or barters. Appraise your prospects of success if the game scenario is used to promote the adoption of the plan in the case.

4. Apply the unfreeze-refreeze technique to the case. Identify objectives, social ties, self-esteem, and motives pertinent to this case. State general objectives and how they can become more specific. Provide two examples of specific objectives that could be considered for the case. What social ties will be broken by the plan? Identify opportunities for new social ties. How would you promote them? How can self-esteem be lowered by the plan? Identify two actions that can be taken to increase esteem. Identify external motives for the plan. How can these motives become internalized? Arrange your responses using the framework in Table 8-5. Appraise your prospect of success if the unfreeze-refreeze technique was used to promote adoption of the plan in the case.

5. Contrast the implementation plans suggested by your answers to questions 1, 2, 3, and 4. Which technique would you use? Why?

6. Apply the game scenario or the unfreeze-refreeze techniques to another case. Compare your recommendations. How are they alike and how do they differ?

# 9 Selecting an Implementation Approach and Fashioning Implementation Procedure

▲ ▲ ▲   ▲ ▲ ▲ ▲ ▲ ▲ ▲ ▲ ▲ ▲ ▲ ▲ ▲ ▲ ▲

▲ **Predicting Implementation Prospects**
  *Environmental Assessments*
  *Key Environmental Characteristics*
  *Environmental Limits to Power*
▲ **Selecting an Implementation Approach**
  *Collegial Environments*
  *Professional Environments*
  *Nova Environments*
  *Consultative Environments*
  *Liberated Environments*
  *Abdicated Environments*
  *Delegated Environments*
  *Trust Environments*
  *Suspicious Environments*
  *Neurotic Environments*
  *Overmanaged Environments*
  *Control Environments*
  *Totalitarian Environments*
  *Standardized Environments*
  *Distributive Environments*
  *Rigid Environments*
▲ **Creating Implementation Procedures**
  *Fashioning a Procedure*
  *Reconciling Contradictory Diagnoses*
▲ **Key Points**
▲ **Exercises**
▲ **Cases**

This chapter provides a way to select an implementation approach, made up of an implementation technique and the types of power that can be applied by a sponsor. An assessment of the *climate* in which implementation is to take place provides the basis for selecting a technique and for specifying the type of power that can be applied. Environments with a favorable climate place fewer demands and allow the use of a low-cost technique (e.g., edict or persuasion) with the position power of the sponsor. An unfavorable climate creates an environment that requires more elaborate tactics. Key features of the environment that specify its climate are described and related to power options and implementation techniques.

# ▲ PREDICTING IMPLEMENTATION PROSPECTS

Climate stems from views and beliefs about the environment in which a planned change is to be made. These views and beliefs are created, in part, by the actions of key people in the organization or work unit. Environments with a positive climate are open to change and, in extreme cases, can become change prompting. The climate in hostile environments makes the introduction of even modest changes time consuming and costly, with considerable chance of failure.

Traditions of participation in decision making, the mix of disciplines, activities (e.g., products or services) that stress quality or quantity, and cost-consciousness concerns are key factors that make up an organization's climate. A particular combination of these factors defines a climate that ranges from supporting to limiting change. For example, change can be difficult in an environment made up of homogeneous skills that do not participate in organizational decisions, stressing quantity and cost consciousness. An unfavorable climate calls for more effort to be directed toward implementation.

## Environmental Assessments

Organizational or work unit characteristics have been found to influence the prospects of plan adoption (March and Simon, 1958; Burns and Stalker, 1981). These characteristics have been used to predict the rate of innovation in these settings. The prospects of implementing a change called for by a plan will be treated as synonymous with the prospects of implementing an innovation. The organizational characteristics found to be useful for implementation are defined in Table 9-1 (Hage and Aiken, 1970; Nutt, 1983). The relationship of these characteristics to implementation prospects is shown in Table 9-2.

### *Complexity*

Complexity is defined in terms of skill mix. It is measured by the number of occupations that have a well-developed knowledge base within the organization or work unit. The number of distinct licensing and certification processes represented in the organizational or work unit provides a convenient measure of complexity. Some occupations, like physician and social worker, differ widely in terms of the period

**Table 9-1 ▲ Organizational Factors That Influence Implementation Prospects**

| Factor | Definition |
| --- | --- |
| Complexity | Number of distinctly different professions or jobs |
| Centralization | Degree of participation in decision making |
| Formalization | Number of rules that regulate behavior |
| Stratification | Differences in pay or prestige between top and bottom of organization or work unit |
| Production | Preference for quantity (as opposed to quality) |
| Efficiency | Degree of cost consciousness |
| Job satisfaction | Morale |

Source: Adapted from Hage and Aiken (1970).

of training and skills acquired. Others (e.g., accountants and engineers) are similar. Hospitals and universities are organizations with high complexity whereas social work agencies have low complexity. Departments with low complexity include R&D laboratories and accounting.

As complexity increases the prospects for implementation also increase (see Table 9-2). Hage and Aiken (1970) find that the rates of adoption of new programs in public schools were directly related to the level of the teacher training. In community hospitals, departments with many subspecialties such as medicine were far more innovative than homogeneous departments like surgery. Professionalism

**Table 9-2 ▲ Relationship Between Implementation Prospects and the Organizational Factors**

| Factors | Implementation Prospects |
| --- | --- |
| Complexity | Many diverse disciplines *encourage* implementation prospects |
| Centralization | Low participation in decision making *retards* implementation prospects |
| Formalization | Many rules that govern behavior *retard* implementation prospects |
| Stratification | Considerable differences in pay *retard* implementation prospects |
| Production | Quantity emphasis *retards* implementation prospects |
| Efficiency | Cost consciousness *retards* implementation prospects |
| Job satisfaction | High morale *encourages* implementation prospects |

places considerable emphasis on knowledge acquisition and skill maintenance. An organization or work unit that draws from many diverse places to acquire knowledge is more likely to be receptive to change. This is due to the positive value accorded knowledge and its implicit demand for change. Thus, high complexity enhances the prospects of a successful implementation.

### Centralization

Centralization describes the distribution of power in the organization or work unit. Power is defined as one person's ability to direct the activities of another. Organizational elites have considerable latitude and act somewhat independently of others. Sometimes elites are created by delegation, and sometimes by the nature of the skill, as in the case of physicians. Organizations with a few elites tend to function in a highly centralized environment. Those with a higher proportion of jobs that participate in decision making are less centralized (see Table 9-1).

Centralization tends to lower the prospects for a successful implementation (Table 9-1). When comparatively few people in a work unit or organization participate in decision making, implementation prospects decline. By concentrating power, a veto is more likely as often to demonstrate power as to reject a plan. Change may create subtle erosions of power. The powerful will try to restrain change until its power implications become clear.

Centralization also makes group action more difficult. There are fewer people with comparable status to draw on, and groups become tiresome to the frequent participant. Also, democratic principles encourage conflict, which is feared by a power elite. Conflict may change a previous set of boundaries, which alters the status quo in unacceptable ways. With few people in a power elite, there are fewer ideas. With fewer ideas, there is less interplay between them, making synthesis less likely. Centralized organizations require lengthy communication to sell an idea, which makes a definitive demonstration of need difficult. Support for this relationship stems from studies of centralized and decentralized public schools matched on other characteristics. These studies revealed that decentralized schools adopted more new programs and revised teaching materials more often. Medical research organizations in the United States or Germany are far more decentralized and have far higher rates of discovery than do those in England and France.

### Formalization

Formalization stems from rules (Table 9-1). Organizations or work units run with rules or master plans specify guidelines for decisions (Nutt, 1981). Formalized work units also have highly codified jobs with formally written job descriptions in elaborate personnel manuals. These rules define what each job holder is to do and implicitly what he or she can (or must) avoid doing. All job descriptions can be interpreted as a constraint on behavior, identifying those activities that the job holder lacks the prerogatives to carry out. The most formalized organizations check behavior against these norms to ensure that people do not exceed their authority. When jobs give little leeway in modifying or adapting procedures, they encourage formality. In extreme situations, job performance can become ritualistic.

Jobs with low formalization give the individual considerable latitude to search for appropriate procedures. Continued modification of procedures can lead to inefficiency, but also innovation, which is quite unlikely in a highly formalized job environment. The tradition of uniformity enshrines the status quo, making implementation difficult in formalized settings (Table 9-2). The more rules an organization has, the more likely that a suspicious elite will interpret them so they can act as a gatekeeper. For example, Hage and Aiken (1970) studied welfare organizations with a "job specification" scale. The scale sought to measure the sheer number and pervasiveness of regulation and the diligence of their enforcement. Highly codified environments appeared to retard innovation, but environments that were lax on rule enforcement did not.

### Stratification

Stratification concerns rewards (Table 9-2). The difference in pay and in symbols, such as office space and other prestige-based rewards, between people in a work unit measures stratification. As these differences increase, stratification increases. Status is the formal rank assigned to a job. It is usually measured by its salary. Prestige can also be assigned by the difficulty of gaining appointment to a position. The ease of movement between levels of the organization or work unit suggest the prestige assigned to various levels. Some high-prestige positions may pay poorly (e.g., public school teachers).

Increased stratification reduces the prospects of innovation (Table 9-2). Large differences in salary and/or prestige between the top and bottom layers of the unit make change in that unit more difficult. Those who have gained power are inclined to block a plan because it may lead to a reduction between the gap in social or financial rewards. The plan is reviewed by the elite, first, to determine its impact on stratification and, then, for its merits.

Highly stratified settings also have clear lines of promotion. Plans may propose a change that implicitly criticizes a superior who devised the procedure and set it in place, a deadly trap for the ambitious. Implementation can be very difficult in such settings. Ben-David (1982) examined 125 years of medical research in France and England. Little progress was observed when one individual dominated a specialty. For example, the European "chair system" in universities does not exist in the United States, and the United States leads the world in discovery of new ideas. Ben-David found that many of these same ideas were discovered in England and France, but they were blocked by key people! These findings are also supported by small-group research that shows that status differences retard the effectiveness of planning groups (Collins and Guetzkow, 1964).

### Production

Production defines whether outputs of the organization or work unit in which the plan is to be implemented emphasize quantity or quality (Table 9-2). For example, within a hospital, the cafeteria and housekeeping departments expect volume, whereas the hospital outpatient department stresses service, such as ordering tests and procedures tailored to meet specific patient needs. Even within service categories, variations exist. A standard treatment and follow-up plan can be used for orthopedics, minor surgery, and obstetrics. Within these parameters, a choice can be made between volume (patient days) and quality (patient care).

Settings that stress volume inhibit innovation (Table 9-2). Quantity-stressing organizations or work units are reluctant to change practices for fear that their volume of output will be reduced. Such organizations see training and setup periods to install a plan as substantially lowering productivity. The promise of downstream productivity increases are viewed as speculative, which breeds conservatism. Quality-stressing organizations find their aims are elusive, which creates an environment more conducive to change. Comparing the research budgets of volume- versus quality-seeking organizations shows that the latter makes a far larger investment in research and development. The automotive, cigarette, and chemical industries, which all stress quantity, invest far less in research and development than do the aircraft and electronics industries.

### Efficiency

Efficiency measures the importance attached to cost in key activities (Table 9-1). Attitude toward cost is another basic organizational or work unit characteristic. Some settings emphasize cost cutting far more than others.

An efficiency emphasis tends to reduce innovation (Table 9-2). The effort expended to conserve resources is incompatible with the unpredictable costs that accompany a new product or procedure. Settings that stress cost control are unlikely to support radical, or even modest, departures from the status quo. For example, the more innovative public schools were found to have a higher cost per pupil and stressed programs that gave students more individual attention. Schools that have a quality emphasis introduce more programs but have higher unit costs.

### Job Satisfaction

The level of job satisfaction is suggested by morale (Table 9-1). Morale sums up the job holder's view of salary, pace, freedom, and other factors inherent in the job. All organizations or work units must exceed a threshold level of morale to function. As morale increases above the mandatory level, change becomes feasible.

High morale enhances implementation prospects (Table 9-2). Change induces stress in any setting and high morale is needed to deal with tension. In situations with low morale, the inherent tension of a change will be amplified, distorting its true proportions. Coch and French's (1948) classic study documents the impact of job satisfaction. They found that implementation attempts were more readily accepted when morale was high, although the changes in procedure they studied were small. Allowing workers to participate in decisions about working conditions increased both the prospects for implementation and satisfaction. Blau's (1985) study showed that implementation was enhanced for job-satisfied people in welfare agencies. Job satisfaction is a precondition for the introduction of change, particularly when the change will have a disruptive effect.

## Key Environmental Characteristics

Some of the environmental characteristics are correlated whereas others seem independent. Centralization, formalization, and stratification measure related aspects of an organizational (or work unit) environment (Nutt, 1983). A centralized organization needs rules to maintain control. The controller is often paid relatively more than those controlled. The top of such organizations or work units will tend to acquire prestige and status to differentiate it from other layers. The centralization characteristic seems the best way to represent such organizations. A highly centralized organization will also have many of the features of a highly stratified and codified environment.

A second simplification can be made by deleting morale. Environments with low morale make poor candidates for planned change initiatives. The sponsor must first raise morale to a level that makes people at least neutral, if not positive, about their jobs. Low morale is a barrier to change and must be attended to before important planning efforts are mounted.

The remaining four characteristics are used to identify implementation environments. Some of these environments are favorable to change and others unfavorable. Environments are determined as shown in Figure 9-1. Paths through the figure iden-

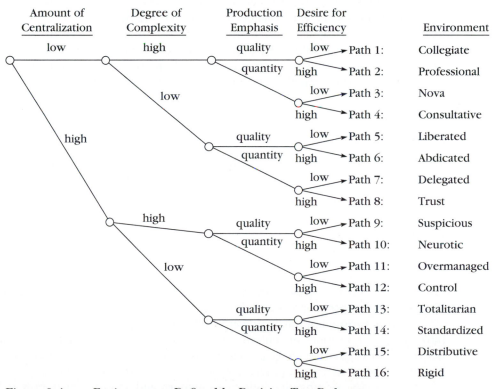

**Figure 9-1** ▲ **Environments Defined by Decision Tree Pathways**
Adapted from Nutt (1983).

**Table 9-3** ▲ **Plans with Good Implementation Prospects**

| Path | Environmental Characteristics | | | | |
|------|------------------|------------|------------|------------|------------------|
|      | *Centralization* | *Complexity* | *Production* | *Efficiency* | *Environmental Type* |
| 1 | Low | High | Quality | Low | Collegial |
| 2 | Low | High | Quality | *High* | Professional |
| 3 | Low | High | *Quantity* | Low | Nova |
| 4 | Low | High | *Quantity* | *High* | Consultative |
| 5 | Low | *Low*[a] | Quality | Low | Liberated |
| 6 | Low | *Low* | *Quantity* | *High* | Trust |

[a] Undesirable characteristics italicized.

tify 16 unique environments. Tables 9-3, 9-4, and 9-5 summarize the characteristics of environments that have good, problematic, and fair implementation prospects, respectively. Table 9-4 identifies an implementation approach that is best suited for each environment, considering planned change efforts that involve single or multiple work groups or organizations.

The environments can exist for multiple organizations, several work units in a single organization, or a single work unit doing planning. Intraorganizational implementation is carried out by "venture management" teams when several units are affected (Zand, 1974). For instance, a firm can bring people from several areas to form a venture management group for the purpose of devising a strategic plan. The plan can also be carried out by a particular work unit. A consortium is used for interorganizational efforts. The Kodak and G.E. joint effort to produce the instamatic camera and emergency medical service councils are examples of consortium planning groups.

## Environmental Limits to Power

The bases of power indicate the tactics that the sponsor uses in conjunction with an implementation technique. In summary, the power bases are

▲ Reward (coercive)
▲ Legitimate
▲ Referent
▲ Expert
▲ Informational

The linkage between these power bases and the organizational characteristics is discussed in the paragraphs that follow.

*Centralization.* Legitimate power is influenced by centralization. Sponsors who have high-level positions in centralized organizations will have legitimate power. In decentralized organizations (e.g., matrix organizations) sponsors often lack such power. All other sources of power can be used in centralized settings.

*Complexity.* Complexity influences expert and informational power bases. Expert power may have limited use because of the difficulty in demonstrating both credibility and trust to many diverse disciplines or skills. For instance, in a firm,

Table 9-4 ▲ Implementation Tactics for Planned Change Environments

| Path | Project Environment | Implementation Team | Type of Power | Implementation Technique |
|------|---------------------|---------------------|---------------|--------------------------|
| 1 | Collegial | Consortium | None | Participation |
|   |           | Venture management | None | Participation and persuasion |
| 2 | Professional | Consortium | Expert | Participation |
|   |              | Venture management | Expert | Participation |
| 3 | Nova | Consortium | Expert | Participation |
|   |      | Venture management | Reward | Participation |
| 4 | Consultative | Consortium | Referent | Participation |
|   |              | Venture management | Reward | Participation |
| 5 | Liberated | Consortium | Expert | Participation |
|   |           | Venture management | Expert or informational | Participation |
| 6 | Abdicated | Consortium | — | Infeasible |
|   |           | Work unit | Expert or informational | Unfreeze-refreeze |
| 7 | Delegated | Consortium | — | Unlikely |
|   |           | Work unit | Reward | Unfreeze-refreeze |
| 8 | Trust | Consortium | Informational | Persuasion |
|   |       | Venture management | Informational | Persuasion |
| 9 | Suspicious | Consortium | — | Unlikely |
|   |            | Venture management | Legitimate | Game scenario with participation |
| 10 | Neurotic | Consortium | — | Infeasible |
|    |          | Work unit | Legitimate | Persuasion |
| 11 | Overmanaged | Consortium | — | Unlikely |
|    |             | Work unit | Legitimate and reward | Unfreeze-refreeze |
| 12 | Control | Consortium | — | Unlikely |
|    |         | Intraorganizational | All | Game scenario |
| 13 | Totalitarian | Consortium | None | Participation |
|    |              | Work unit | Legitimate | Edict and persuasion |
| 14 | Standardized | Consortium | — | Unlikely |
|    |              | Intraorganizational | Legitimate | Unfreeze-refreeze |
| 15 | Distributive | Consortium | Expert | Persuasion |
|    |              | Intraorganizational | Legitimate and reward | Persuasion |
| 16 | Rigid | Consortium | — | Unlikely |
|    |       | Intraorganizational | Legitimate and reward | Game scenario |

Source: Adapted from Nutt (1983).

**Table 9-5　▲　Plans with Problematic Implementation Prospects**

| | Environmental Characteristics | | | | |
|---|---|---|---|---|---|
| Path | Centralization | Complexity | Production | Efficiency | Environmental Type |
| 9 | High[a] | High | Quality | Low | Suspicious |
| 14 | High | Low | Quality | High | Standardized |
| 15 | High | Low | Quantity | Low | Distributive |

[a] Unfavorable characteristics italicized.

a consultant may be accepted by management but rejected by the research and development staff. The ability to use an informational power base will also decline in a complex environment. The message tailoring must be variegated, designed to fit each discipline. The cost and complexity of this task often renders information power of little value. Similarly, a person with referent power in one discipline may hold little attraction to another. Only reward and legitimate power are useful in complex environments.

*Production.* The ability to use rewards is drastically limited when quality of production is stressed. Reward (coercive) power is dependent on the ability of the sponsor to monitor behavior, offering incentives that encourage plan adoption. Quality monitoring is much more difficult than monitoring quantity. Organizations that stress quantity are in a better position to use rewards to reinforce useful implementation behavior. All other power bases can be used in this type of environment.

*Efficiency.* Rewards are far easier to administer in a cost-conscious environment, again to reinforce behaviors that enhance implementation prospects. An environment that does not stress efficiency will have to search for a measure that can be monitored, rendering reward power less valuable. All other power bases can be used.

## ▲　SELECTING AN IMPLEMENTATION APPROACH

Implementation approaches are made up of power bases and techniques applied to gain plan acceptance. Each of the environments in Figure 9-1 will be described, identifying an implementation technique and power bases best suited for that environment.

### Collegial Environments

A collegial environment stems from a high degree of professionalism (high complexity) in a decentralized setting, reinforced by a strong emphasis on quality and little emphasis on efficiency (Table 9-3). Hospital medical staffs and university faculties are excellent examples of collegial environments. For example, university faculties have considerable freedom to pursue their own interests, as long as they can demonstrate quality (get published). No one monitors cost (e.g., faculty time) to get an article published or, indeed, even considers it.

In such an environment, participation is mandatory (Table 9-4). Planning pre-rogatives are delegated to representatives of the work unit. The sponsor guides the work group representatives through a participation managed process, as shown in Figure 7-1. In this environment, participation in all of the stages of planned change is essential because the environment is composed of diverse people with high levels of expertise, each of which is needed by the plan. If properly involved, participants readily accept the result and will be prepared to advocate the plan to nonparticipants. Planned change in collegial environments can take place within an organization, or it may involve several organizations. A consortium must also adopt a participative approach to implementation (see Table 9-4). The need for participation is paramount because those serving on the planning group represent powerful interest groups. Each sponsoring organization must sanction the planned change process *before* it can begin. Plan sponsors cannot use power in a collegial environment.

## Professional Environments

The professional environment has many diverse skills. Managers who have accom-modated the desire of these disciplines for independent action and control cost and quality by delegation create a professional environment (Table 9-3). For exam-ple, major book publishers largely delegate future title decisions to experts. The publisher's executive committee selects topics and authors, but relies heavily on consultants' recommendations obtained by department chiefs specializing in each field. To make a profit, the books must be of sufficient quality to sell, and they must be able to be produced efficiently, that is, have minimal symbology and other cost-inducing features. Authors are selected who can produce a quality product that conserves the firm's resources.

Participation is the preferred implementation technique in professional envi-ronments (Table 9-4). The delegation in such environments makes participation nearly mandatory. Similarly, the consortium composed primarily of representatives from professional organizations will demand that planned change responsibility be delegated to a group. Participation can be supported by expert power, both for internal and consortium planning bodies in a professional environment. If the plan sponsor or his or her agent or representative are seen as experts, their support of the plan can aid implementation.

## Nova Environments

Environments that stress output volume, with less emphasis on cost controls, de-manding a diverse skill mix, often force its manager to decentralize (Table 9-3). Such environments are termed "nova" because the diversity of disciplines and simplistic nature of the task (volume) create a climate in which innovation is fostered. Ex-amples include outpatient clinics and same-day surgery centers. Both deal with the comparatively routine health problem and can use charges to cover inefficiencies in operations. The professionalism and skill mix is high, leading to loose managerial control.

Nova environments stimulate change. Plan sponsors in such settings will find planning groups forming spontaneously to look into ways of increasing volume. The administrator must gain control over these planned change processes (become their sponsor) by offering staff services. Participation is mandatory, but the impetus comes from the bottom up, forcing the sponsor to use tactics that ensure that the planned change is cost justified (Table 9-4). The sponsor needs no implementation technique beyond controlling the propensity of people in these environments to make change for the sake of change. Consortia formed by people from nova environments also need the structure of a planned change process. Participation is mandatory, as shown in Table 9-4. Reward power, though not essential, can be useful to support implementation when internal planned change is attempted. The sponsor can often create an incentive scheme, based on volume, to encourage use of the plan. Also, implementation prospects improve when someone who is seen as an expert endorses the plan, drawing on expert power.

## Consultative Environments

Environments demanding high volume at low cost and requiring diverse skills should be decentralized (Table 9-3). These environments are naturally consultative. Consultation is needed to understand the diverse mix of skills and the role of each in maintaining a favorable unit cost picture. Examples include manufacturers with several complex production stages that must be linked, such as manufacturing photographic film. Quality control in such an organization is less important than unit costs. Film emulsion making, packaging in a low-light environment, and the distribution of the perishable film product call for vastly different skills. Consultation among these manufacturing stages is essential to ensure that one does not, inadvertently, influence the costs of another.

Participation is essential in consultative environments to manage the boundaries between work groups (Table 9-4). The venture management team calls for membership from each different skill or knowledge base. A consortium that merges distinct organizations to develop plans calls for the careful selection and management of the participants who represent each organization. Participation is essential when a consortium is used. Reward power can be used to augment participative techniques, for use in internal planning in a consultative environment. Because volume and cost are emphasized, a unit cost criterion of performance can be constructed. An incentive scheme using unit cost measure can be used to encourage plan implementation. A consortium made up of mutually dependent organizations is susceptible to referent power. Getting someone whom the participating organizations respect to endorse the plan enhances its chance of being adopted.

## Liberated Environments

Environments that do not control a homogeneous work group that is required to provide quality services or products, with little cost emphasis, are called *liberated* (Table 9-3). Examples include psychiatry departments, behavior modification centers, and others offering professional services, such as physical and speech therapy organizations and home nursing services. The origins of a liberated environment stem from traditions in the dominant discipline that provides the service. Control attempts are evaded by keeping the patient care process mysterious. This environment demands that each service be adapted to the individual patient's needs. Service tailoring is often inherent. The environment is liberated by permitting decentralized decisions, because a centralized approach would be more cost effective. Decentralized decision making, which extends to all organizational activities, is common in professional service organizations.

People in a liberated environment will insist on participating in all planned change efforts mounted by a plan sponsor. The participation provides guidance, as in the nova environment (Table 9-4). Formal planning, however, is relatively more important in the liberated environment because change is less likely to percolate from skill mix interactions. Consortia follow the same strictures as venture groups. Both types of implementation teams are made up of those affected by the planned change effort. Either information or an expert power can be used by the sponsor to aid an internal participative planned change process in a liberated environment. Because the environment is homogeneous, the sponsor can argue from the vantage point of trust, or trust and competence. The consortium can also use both approaches but prefers expertise, because trust is harder to develop when several organizations are involved.

## Abdicated Environments

When a relatively homogeneous skill mix creates a product or service that demands both cost and quality, with comparatively little direction, the environment is termed abdicated (Table 9-6). This situation calls for considerable scrutiny because the expectations are stringent, demanding both quality and cost-effective products or services. Delegation in such an environment implies that managers are not exerting sufficient controls. Examples where this could occur include research and development departments, hospital laboratories, and some staff units.

The hospital laboratory typically creates a profit so that efficient operations are essential. Hospitals often use this source of funds to offset losses elsewhere. Quality is also essential as key decisions hinge on the precision of laboratory information. Surprisingly, many hospitals leave laboratories to function independently. They do not even check on the lab's revenue less cost contribution against norms (e.g., this

**Table 9-6 ▲ Plans with Fair Implementation Prospects**

| Path | Environmental Characteristics | | | | Environmental Type |
|------|----------------|------------|------------|------------|-------------------|
| | Centralization | Complexity | Production | Efficiency | |
| 6 | Low | *Low*[a] | Quality | *High* | Abdicated |
| 7 | Low | *Low* | *Quantity* | Low | Delegated |
| 10 | *High* | High | Quality | *High* | Neurotic |
| 11 | *High* | High | *Quantity* | Low | Overmanaged |
| 12 | *High* | High | *Quantity* | *High* | Control |
| 13 | *High* | *Low* | Quality | Low | Totalitarian |
| 16 | *High* | *Low* | *Quantity* | *High* | Rigid |

[a] Unfavorable characteristics italicized.

same figure in comparable laboratories). Similarly, staff units, such as accounting and engineering, have enormous impact on a firm and yet they are seldom evaluated.

In the abdicated environment, the plan sponsor must first gain control before initiating a planned change process (Table 9-4). Intraorganizational planned change is best preceded by the unfreeze-refreeze technique to reestablish control. Consortiums cannot develop in an abdicated environment. Work groups are inward looking and lack the motive to consider the benefits of boundary spanning planned change. No one in the group would have the prerogative needed to initiate a viable consortium. The use of incentives is often rendered impossible when the performance criteria must stress both cost and quality. Expert and information power are recommended for the reasons cited in the previous discussion. Both expert and information power fit well with the unfreeze-refreeze technique and should be useful in helping to ensure plan adoption.

## Delegated Environments

Delegated environments do not mirror the abdicated environment. The needs for managerial monitoring are less stringent because volume is the required outcome (Table 9-6). Complexity is low, which allows for centralization, but management chooses to delegate rather than control, because the unit can be monitored by a quota-filling strategy. Also, other departments or activities may take precedence, so a sponsor may elect to spend more time dealing with units that are not cost effective and monitoring products that stress quality. A delegated environment can occur when purchasing departments are expected to keep inventories for supply items filled.

Delegated environments develop a tradition of independent action. The plan sponsor must reassert his or her control to establish the need for change in a work unit and initiate a planned change process. The unfreeze-refreeze technique sets the stage for planning and reestablishes the sponsor's control, making change prospects favorable (Table 9-4). A consortium, formed by members from delegated environments, is highly unlikely. As with the abdicated environment, the incentive to form a consortium does not exist. Reward-based power can be used to aid implementation in a delegated environment. Incentive schemes that measure volume can be used to entice plan use.

## Trust Environments

Only centralization can be changed by managerial prerogatives in a trust environment. The other characteristics (volume, efficiency, and complexity) are all fixed in the short run. This allows management the choice of establishing a centralized or a decentralized organization. The centralized structure is the more common. When delegation occurs it is called a trust environment. An environment stressing trust delegates in the face of efficiency and volume demands (Table 9-3). The relative homogeneity of job holders in the work unit is a neutral factor.

A trust environment is generally supportive of change and change becomes problematic only when key people exploit the trust situation. Examples include the relationship between a contract management service and the trustees of the managed hospital. The contract management services uses a cadre of professional managers and is expected to improve the hospital's bottom line, demanding attention to both volume and costs. Typically, persuasion is all that is needed to implement in a trust environment (Table 9-4).

The participation of several organizations in a trust environment has no influence on the preferred tactic. Both intra- and interorganizational implementation can use persuasion because the members of a consortium or a venture management team have similar relationships with superiors. A trusting environment fosters trust in the participating organizations. In such an environment, informational power bases are preferred, for both internal and multiorganizational projects. This approach fits well with the persuasion implementation tactic. Elaborate implementation techniques are not required in a trust environment.

## Suspicious Environments

Decentralization is the preferred tact when complexity is high and the product demands quality with less emphasis on cost (Table 9-5). When such environments are found to be centralized, they are called suspicious. Examples include research and development organizations, such as RAND and Battelle, that use a matrix structure to carry out projects, but impose several layers of managers above the project level hoping to maintain control. These hopes are futile because the quality dimension of the consultant's work makes it hard to monitor, except on an anecdotal basis.

Other examples include consulting organizations and government "think tanks." A matrix structure is used to form a project team. The product (often a feasibility study or an evaluation) is controlled by managers who dictate who will serve on the group, as well as the group's budget and its leadership. Monitoring is carried out by cost progress toward completion dates, using techniques like milestone charts and the program review and evaluation technique (PERT). Control is imposed, which stifles professionalism and individual initiative in an environment that calls for just these qualities.

Sponsors seeking to induce change in a suspicious environment are faced with a difficult task. Past battles over turf make persuasion unworkable and edicts undesirable. The game scenario with participation in planning is recommended (Table 9-4). The game scenario can be used to identify key people who should be persuaded to make the changes demanded by a plan. The game scenario–participation approach is not useful in a consortium setting. A consortium made up of suspicious organizations would be unlikely to form, let alone function as a planning group. The centralized nature of the suspicious environment calls for the use of legitimate power to implement. A sponsor is selected who can act for the organization. If the sponsor is properly selected, he or she will have the legitimate power to encourage plan adoption. Such power is often needed because plans developed in suspicious environments tend to have problematic adoption prospects.

## Neurotic Environments

Some environments make stringent demands, requiring both quality and cost effectiveness, and have heterogeneous skills managed by centralization (Table 9-6). Such environments are called neurotic because control is a totally inappropriate tactic. The work force prefers a professional approach and the nature of the work also calls for this approach. A manager who imposes tight controls despite the need for decentralization shows the anxieties in his or her leadership. A compulsion to control often stems from phobias about being unable to account for the natural variations in performance. A neurotic environment is created by the manager so any professional setting can be subjected to control. For instance, an insecure manager can be found in publishing, consulting firms, accounting and other staff departments, and other settings in which professionalism should be stressed.

Edicts are apt to be used in this environment, but persuasion is preferable. No other approach will work without an environmental change shifting the prescription to that for a professional environment (Table 9-4). A consortium cannot arise in neurotic settings.

Legitimate power can be used in the neurotic environment. In a centralized setting, a sponsor can be selected that has sufficient prestige to use legitimate power. Legitimate power works well in tandem with the preferred implementation technique: persuasion.

## Overmanaged Environments

An overmanaged environment results from centralizing a diverse work force charged with providing volume. The environment is potentially innovative (see Table 9-6), but the manager has stifled innovation. Such an environment tends to create control tactics, such as rule codification and complex procedures, and creates differences in prestige and pay between organizational layers. For example, stringent controls placed on a research and development unit will tend to shut down its innovative urges.

To plan in an overmanaged environment, the need for change must be introduced. The unfreeze-refreeze technique is best for this purpose (Table 9-4). A consortium will not develop in an overmanaged environment. Overmanaged work units seldom find sufficient impetus internally for interorganizational planning, and the manager finds such a group foreign to his or her control tactics.

Power can be useful in the overmanaged environment because the prospects for implementation are only fair. Both legitimate and reward power can be used to aid the implementation of internally created plans. The centralized structure allows the selection of a sponsor from high enough in the organization that his or her recommendation must be heeded. The sponsor can also offer volume-based incentives to ensure that key people will work toward plan adoption.

## Control Environments

In this environment, attention is directed toward optimizing unit costs. Control is stressed to keep the many skills in line (Table 9-6). The diversity of employee views can be hard to appreciate. This diversity provides the impetus to instigate generic control procedures to homogenize the situation, thereby simplifying control. The control mentality justifies a centralized organization, under the unit cost monitoring guise. Examples include departments charged with making travel disbursements and contractors specializing in large-building construction. Travel-monitoring departments publish elaborate rules and apply them religiously to maintain expenditure control. Even justifiable deviations are disallowed because the department fears that other travelers will exploit any exception. Further, the myriad justifiable exceptions are hard to appreciate fully. They stem from an assortment of reasons, justified by the unique circumstances operating in each disciplinary area. Similarly, the successful contractor carefully monitors completion dates and budgets to keep the subcontractors under control.

Plan sponsors in control settings must use elaborate tactics. The game scenario technique is recommended (Table 9-4) for finding peoples' incentives to block or support the plan. Formation of a consortium made up of control type organizations is unlikely. Consistent with the previous arguments, legitimate and reward power can be used. (Incentives in this case are based on unit cost measures.) However, all sources of power may be needed because implementation prospects are only fair in a control environment.

## Totalitarian Environments

A controlled environment, with natural urges to be liberated (see Table 9-6), is called totalitarian. The manager who imposes control tactics (rules and procedures with artificial status differentials) on a homogeneous work force seeking quality, with relatively few cost restraints, creates such an environment. Examples include the relationship between house staff and departmental chiefs in a university hospital and the European system of higher education with its chairs. Fiefdoms are created in university hospitals where the service chief controls the care given through his or her orders, often administered in a Byzantine fashion. These power differences are reinforced by enormous differences in pay and status during the house staff person's educational process. The pecking order in the university hospital creates a very tall organization in which change is difficult to induce without the chief's backing. Universities in Europe are run much like services in a university hospital. Each department has a "chair," which everyone else aspires to occupy because the occupant has nearly absolute control over curriculum, promotion, and the like. The pecking order created by these arrangements makes innovation difficult, as evidenced by the slow pace of curriculum changes in European higher education.

An edict is used in such environments (Table 9-4). The leader has the power to make unilateral changes and can severely punish noncompliants. Edicts are fast but reinforce a negative image of a leader. An edict coupled with persuasion can be helpful in illustrating the leader's rationale, if not his or her consideration. A consortium can form in such an environment, but will be made up of service chiefs or department heads from various institutions. People who create totalitarian environments will nonetheless demand participative planning when among their peers. Consortium planned change, when its members come from totalitarian environments, will demand collegial environments. No source of power will be useful. Internal planned change relies exclusively on legitimate power. If change agents have sufficient standing in the organization, they can issue decrees. Because implementation prospects are only fair in a totalitarian environment, the sponsor should moderate the negative features of an edict by using persuasion to demonstrate the plan's value.

## Standardized Environments

A centralized setting with a homogeneous work force, demanding a cost and quality emphasis, is called standardized (Table 9-5). When both quality and cost are demanded, a clear understanding of the parameters surrounding the product or service is essential. This leads the manager to seek ways of standardizing the delivery to ensure that both quality and cost requirements are met. Examples include firms that sell data processing services and printing companies. Each must provide quality at a competitive price, and each typically has a centralized structure with a comparatively low skill mix to make standardization easier.

Standardized environments are poor candidates for change unless there is a clear need for change that is widely apparent. The unfreeze-refreeze technique is recommended to guide plan implementation (Table 9-4). It is unlikely that standardized organizations or work units would form a consortium. Implementation in a standardized environment benefits from the use of legitimate power. The sponsor that has clear-cut powers will be far more effective in using the unfreeze-refreeze approach for internal planned change efforts.

## Distributive Environments

A centralized setting characterized by high volume and low concern for cost, with a homogeneous skill pool, creates a distributive environment (Table 9-5). The emphasis is on meeting consumer demands. Examples include companies scrambling to bring a new technology to market. Profits stem from big volumes, obviating the need to be overly concerned about costs. Organizations with a new product and the need to make a market create a distributive environment, such as Xerox in the 1960s. Counseling services that have United Way or tax support to cover their cost have a similar mandate and so they try to bring as many services to people as possible.

Such environments are change oriented. Any plan that has the promise of increasing volume will be considered. Implementation in this setting merely requires a demonstration of how the plan can increase volume. Persuasion is usually adequate to bring off an implementation. A consortium whose members are motivated by distributive concerns would also be responsive to a demonstration based on persuasion techniques. Legitimate power and reward power can be used as implementation aids for internal planned change in a distributive environment. Both mesh well with persuasion. Incentives, tied to a volume criterion, can be used to create rewards that encourage plan use. However, the use of power has much less value in this environment because of its change orientation. A consortium made up of people drawn from distributive environments can aid implementation by using expert power in conjunction with persuasion tactics.

### Rigid Environments

Rigidity stems from the centralization of authority with rules and procedures that allow the unit's or organization's leadership to exert tight control (Table 9-5). The demand for volume and efficiency gives such an environment a single criterion of success (unit cost). The criterion acts as a constraint: All change must demonstrate that unit costs will be enhanced, even during a period when a plan is being installed. There are few countervailing forces because of the relatively homogeneous skill and professional mix. Departments providing janitorial and food services in a firm are examples.

The best technique for this environment is the game scenario. This technique encourages the plan sponsor to identify and bargain with key actors during the planned change process (Table 9-4). Intraorganizational planning in a rigid environment must also use the game scenario. Consortium planning, in which the participating organizations all have rigid characteristics would be infeasible. Power is needed as an implementation aid in a rigid environment because all of its characteristics point toward problems during plan implementation, as shown in Table 9-4. Both legitimate and reward power should be used. Incentives use unit cost improvement in this environment.

## ▲ CREATING IMPLEMENTATION PROCEDURES

Two steps are required to select an implementation procedure for a planned change effort. A process management approach is selected according to the sponsor's latitude to act, as described in Chapter 7. An implementation technique and power base are then matched to a climate that characterizes the environment in which planned change is to take place, as described in this chapter. These assessments yield two distinct appraisals: one indicating the sponsor's personal leverage and the other suggesting the difficulty of implementing a planned change, considering the work group or organization that the planned change will affect.

### Fashioning a Procedure

Implementation procedures made up of a process management approach and an implementation technique, augmented by power bases, should be compatible. Some implementation techniques are compatible with all process management approaches and others less so.

Intervention managed planned change processes can apply any of the implementation techniques. The flexibility of an intervention process stems from the case made for a change by the intervention. If the sponsor has the leverage to apply norms that show performance is substandard, he or she also has the latitude to use any implementation technique that seems best according to assessments of the climate in the organization or work group affected by the change (see Table 9-7).

Participation managed processes have a more restricted list of compatible implementation techniques (Table 9-7). The unfreeze-refreeze technique can be used to organize a planning group's efforts, and the game scenario is helpful in iden-

Table 9-7 ▲ Fashioning Implementation Procedure

| Process Management Determined by Sponsor's Freedom to Act | Techniques Determined by Climate in Which Change Is to Occur |
| --- | --- |
| Edict managed (compatible with) | Persuasion |
| | Game scenario |
| | Unfreeze-refreeze |
| | Decree, replacement, and/or structural change |
| Expert managed (compatible with) | Persuasion |
| | Unfreeze-refreeze |
| | Game scenario |
| | Indirect or shared participation |
| Participation managed (compatible with) | Unfreeze-refreeze |
| | Game scenario |
| | Shared or delegated participation |
| Intervention managed (compatible with) | All techniques |

tifying barters that the group could refine. The partial and full delegation of plan development approaches are also options that have the group oversee some or all of a planned change process. Participation is incompatible with unilateral techniques and indirect participation, such as a survey, unless the survey will be interpreted by a formal planning group.

Expert managed processes frequently use persuasion. To use persuasion, the plan sponsor attempts to show that the plan will produce benefits for the organization. Some experts are adept at applying the unfreeze-refreeze technique with or without a group of stakeholders. Indeed, the OD literature calls for the involvement of an outsider to sanction a planned change. Often the sales pitch for a plan presented to the sponsor includes how to secure compliance as well as plan benefits. Experts can use the game scenario to augment persuasion tactics by identifying barters and incentives that can move key stakeholders and barriers to a change that can be removed by adroit action. Experts can also marshall expertise and insight into barriers to change by the indirect or shared participation of key people in a group.

Edicts tend to be incompatible with expert managed planned change processes. The expert typically lacks the formal authority to issue a decree or to take the more extreme measures called for by replacement and structural change.

Edict managed processes can apply persuasion and any of the unilateral techniques. Sponsors following this approach can also use the game scenario to sniff out opposition. The game scenario helps the sponsor to anticipate objections and cut off the maneuvering of stakeholders who are apt to resist the implementation attempt. Although feasible, the unfreeze-refreeze technique is seldom used because opportunities to show the need for change are lost when a sponsor waits until a plan is ready for implementation before acting to manage potential opposition. The opportunities for participation are lost for the same reasons.

### Reconciling Contradictory Diagnoses

In some instances, a sponsor's freedom to act can be incompatible with the demands posed by the climate of the work group in which change is to occur. This occurs when a process management approach and an implementation technique cannot be used together. Two possibilities exist. First, the sponsor's diagnosis of his or her freedom to act, or situational factors indicating climate, or both can be mistaken. This can occur when answers to some of the queries that specify a process management approach or factors specifying climate are ambiguous. To deal with this situation, the ambiguity is accepted each time it occurs, which leads to two paths in the decision trees (see Figure 7-4 and Figure 9-1). Finding compatible process management approaches and implementation techniques among the paths suggests one way to proceed. A sponsor should trace the choices in the decision trees several times to ensure that a thoughtful diagnosis has been made. Second, a sponsor may find that some of the queries regarding freedom of action cannot be answered or that some work unit features are unknown. The best the sponsor can do in this situation is to narrow the choice of implementation procedure to a few process management approaches and implementation techniques.

Environments that are apt to resist change pose the biggest threat to a successful implementation effort. Bad climates must be carefully managed by an appropriate implementation approach. This takes precedence over situations in which sponsors have considerable freedom to take action. The demands posed by a poor climate are given priority. A technique called for by a difficult environment is selected and then a compatible process management approach is identified when the diagnoses of a sponsor produce an incompatible process and technique. In all other cases, the sponsor should select a management approach that has the best track record. If the choice is between intervention and edict processes, choose intervention. Intervention is preferable to participation, participation is preferable to expert managed processes, and expert processes are preferable to edict processes (see Chapter 6).

## ▲ Key Points

1. Implementation techniques can be direct, as in an edict, or indirect, as in cooptation via participation. In between these extremes, more subtle techniques (unfreeze-refreeze and game scenario) can be used to create an environment conducive to implementation. The unfreeze-refreeze and game scenario techniques are called manipulative because they manage the situation so people are predisposed to support the plan.

2. An implementation approach is made up of techniques and types of power that sponsors can apply. An implementation approach is selected by appraising the climate that makes up the environment of the work group or organization in which change is to occur. Sixteen distinct implementation environments were defined for organizations (work units) in terms of their tendency to be centralized and/or cost conscious, their quality or quantity orientation, and their skill mix. Implementation approaches (techniques and types of power) best suited to the demands of each environment were identified.

3. An implementation procedure is made up of desirable power bases, which can be drawn on by a sponsor, an implementation technique, and a way to manage the planned change process. The sponsor, acting in concert with one of these processes, applies power and uses implementation techniques to pave the way for plan adoption.

4. Selecting an implementation procedure calls for reconciling two distinct diagnoses. In the first, the sponsor determines his or her freedom of action, and in the second, the environment in which change is to occur is assessed to determine the kind of implementation technique that is needed. Sponsors are encouraged to manage the planned change process with implementation processes and approaches that match their diagnoses and have the best track record. Difficult environments, indicated by poor climates, take precedence over a sponsor's freedom to act.

## ▲ Exercises

1. Take the role of a planned change sponsor who must confront the environment depicted in one of the following cases. Determine the centralization, complexity, productivity, and efficiency environmental characteristics for this case. Which climate is suggested? What ambiguities did you encounter? How would you choose among the implementation techniques and associated power types when one or more of the four environmental characteristics is ambiguous? Compare the techniques used to those recommended. What differences did you detect?

2. Compare the implementation technique you selected in question 1 with the process management technique you identified for this case in a past assignment. Are they compatible? If not, what would you do to reconcile the techniques and the process management approach that are recommended?

3. Select another case and select a process management approach and an implementation technique using the guidelines. Under what conditions could the recommendations be incompatible? Select an implementation procedure and defend it for this set of conditions.

## ▲ Cases

### The Supply Management Case

The supply management project was carried out in a 400-bed inner-city hospital. The administrator, who acted as the plan sponsor, had received considerable notoriety for his inventory control and supply management system. The plan called for the elimination of all unofficial floor inventories, and went so far as to have new patient wards constructed without any storage closets or shelves. A cart system was used to provide nursing supplies for 24-hour periods. Supplies remain on the cart until they are actually used. To charge a patient for the supplies, a card that bears a name and price code for the supply item is taken from the cart. The number of items used is coded and placed in a compartment on the cart labeled "used." After a 24-hour period, the cart is returned and restocked. The cards are counted and reconciled against the actual inventory remaining on the cart. The difference between accounted and unaccounted use is tabulated. A lost charge report is distributed monthly to each department as a control device.

Two departments in the hospital would not participate in the supply cart system: surgery and anesthesiology. When each surgical case was finished, the scrub nurse tallied from memory supplies that were used. This prompted the sponsor to claim that charges are lost. Control could be improved by the supply cart system. Without such a procedure, lost charges were deemed inevitable.

Interviews were conducted to determine how surgery and anesthesiology could be integrated into the current system. Key service department heads were also interviewed. They included the material manager, the department managing the cart system, the fiscal officer, and the data processing director. The user departments (surgery and anesthesiology) were not involved in the initial discussions.

The sponsor presented the modified patient charge card system to the surgery and anesthesiology department heads. Each questioned the plan's merit. Both claimed that there was no evidence that charges were being lost under the current memory system. (The sponsor had not verified that charges were actually lost in these departments.) The departments also claimed that charge cards were redundant and called for more time than they had available to complete the required paperwork.

User departments were asked to make suggestions to make the plan workable. Blank cards were recommended. The cards were to be placed on the cart and filled out when items were used, marking the first time objections to the plan were seriously considered. The cart department manager opposed this change in the system, claiming it would create an audit problem. This debate led to a further modification of the plan to reduce the amount of information recorded on the cart, without making blank charge cards available.

The revised system was installed by the sponsor who wrote a memo describing how the system was to operate and when it was to begin and sent it to the appropriate departments. The system was promptly sabotaged by nurses in the surgery department. The surgical nurses discarded all the charge cards and continued to prepare charges using the memory system. Incidents of system failure, such as sterility compromise of a supply item by staples used to attach the charge cards, were displayed in prominent places (e.g., hospital bulletin boards). The sponsor responded, modifying the system by attaching charge cards with rubber bands. A faintly veiled threat of replacement was made followed by a written procedure that dictated how the cart system was to be used. Resistance continued, calling for more extreme measures. ▲

## The Community Health Center Case

Community health centers (CHC) are used to provide an entry point for low-income people into the health system. These centers typically provide some primary care services and act as a referring agent. The best centers have hospital backup.

The mayor of a large metropolitan community, while attending a national mayor's conference, discovered that private grants could be used to augment the federal monies that initially set up community health centers. When the mayor returned, he formed a consortium with the people from the local (federally funded) health planning agency. The consortium was charged with preparing a proposal that expanded CHC funding for submission to the Robert Wood Johnson (RWJ) Foundation. The local planning agency was allowed to appoint the members of the planning group. The consortium was assigned to manage the grant preparation process. The consortium identified premises for the plans from the request for proposal (RFP) used by the RWJ Foundation. The planner detailed current provisions in the city's operational community health center, and how they can or do meet the RWJ Foundation's constraints and requirements.

A simulation was prepared to show how these requirements would influence three key actors to the plan: the city health department, the community health center, and the two hospitals that provided backup to the CHC. This tactic forced the consortium to recognize that they did not represent the key interests affected by the plan. As a result, the consortium delegated review to the health department, the CHC, and the two hospitals. Reactions were sought in the form of critiques from each party. The city health commissioner objected to the service expansion proposed in the plan, questioning how services would be continued when grant funds expired. The CHC wanted more services to be added. The hospitals objected to several points. Also, they were unwilling to provide 24-hour backup, which was a requirement in the RWJ guidelines. The planner noted these objections and submitted a modified draft of the grant proposal to the consortium. The consortium approved a compromise proposal and submitted it to the mayor.

The mayor, feeling that the city's financial commitment was too large, caused a delay. During this period, the RWJ Foundation was asked to respond to several "what if" questions, drawn from the objections and concerns of the key constituent groups. This tactic prompted RWJ to make some unusual commitments. These commitments were incorporated in the final proposal.

The final proposal made provisions to expand the hours and services at each neighborhood CHC, provided for 24-hour backup emergency care at each center, made select dental services available, provided for health education services at each center, provided for select outpatient services, and strengthened the CHC-hospital relationships for patient services. The project has been submitted to RWJ by the mayor.

▲

## The Telecommunication Case

A large division of a company embarking on a substantial capacity expansion project noted that its phone service expenses had increased by 300% in a ten-year period. Phone costs were in excess of $1 million a year. High cost and poor performance, coupled with Bell's unwillingness to work within the new building's design, raised questions about continuing with the Bell system. Due to construction deadlines, the planned change process had to offer a viable option prior to the completion of the building project, so planning was conducted under considerable pressure.

The company is known for giving autonomy to its divisions but demanding profit accountability.

Four vendors submitted their plans, which were reviewed by the division manager (sponsor). Several revisions were required to increase the number of prestige phones (phones with buttons) and the capacity of the computer equipment that backed up the system. These revisions were misunderstood because the vendors did not take the division's desire for a large number of phones with buttons seriously. As this was a major source of cost, it was a key feature in the vendor's approach to keep costs down. Finally, the number of button phones was established as a constraint and new bids were requested.

To initiate the evaluation, the sponsor dictated that cost, manageability, service capability, and maintainability be used as criteria. However, only cost was dealt with in sufficient detail to be taken seriously. With the cost data provided by consultants, a variety of cost analyses were conducted, including total operating cost and net present value of each alternative. After this information was reviewed, all four options were still acceptable. The evaluation process was repeated for two reasons: first, to determine the basis to select among the proposals and, second, to include the Bell Centrex system, even though it was an unacceptable alternative. Political considerations made it advisable not to rule out Bell prior to the detailed evaluations.

The second evaluation checked with other companies using each of the vendors' systems to be sure that no massive failures had occurred. After this evaluation, there was still no basis to select among the proposals. The sponsor concluded that there were serious methodological problems in the cost analyses and asked for the evaluation to be repeated a third time. The division's management felt that before Bell could be ruled out, evaluation must be clear, without any loopholes or methodological problems. After this evaluation, a superior system seemed to emerge. This proposal was submitted to the company's hierarchy for review.

New criteria were added at each level as the proposal rose up the chain of command to the vice presidents, the president, and finally the board of directors. The evaluation was repeated to measure performance against new criteria that were introduced at each level. As the proposal rose in the hierarchy, evaluation focused less on financial and more on political factors. After four additional evaluation cycles, the division had yet to receive the authorization to proceed.                ▲

# *Part IV*

▲ ▲ ▲   ▲ ▲ ▲ ▲ ▲ ▲ ▲ ▲ ▲ ▲ ▲ ▲ ▲ ▲ ▲ ▲

# THE CREATIVE ASPECTS OF PLANNED CHANGE

▲ ▲ ▲ ▲ ▲ ▲ ▲ ▲ ▲ ▲ ▲ ▲ ▲ ▲ ▲ ▲ ▲ ▲ ▲ ▲ ▲ ▲ ▲ ▲

*Part Four presents techniques that can be used to satisfy the creative demands of the formulation, concept development, and detailing stages of planned change.*

*The importance of formulation is described and techniques are provided to uncover problems and identify planned change objectives. Concept development calls for multiple options and techniques that can be used to uncover options with innovative features. Techniques that fashion and fine tune a plan are presented for the detailing stage.*

# 10 The Formulation Stage of Planned Change

▲ ▲ ▲　　▲ ▲ ▲ ▲ ▲ ▲ ▲ ▲ ▲ ▲ ▲ ▲ ▲ ▲ ▲

This chapter provides techniques that can be applied to carry out the formulation stage of a planned change process. The formulation stage is devoted to identifying problems that are used to set objectives. The techniques presented in this chapter help sponsors carry out formulation by applying search, synthesis, and analysis steps to uncover problems and to set objectives.

As described in Chapter 5, sponsors initiate planned change when performance falls short of expectations creating a "performance gap" that seems large and cannot be explained away. Sponsors react to the performance gap and identify needs or opportunities that offer imperatives for change. In some instances, sponsors may respond to misleading or symptomatic cues, and may have no clear notion of what constitutes a desirable and attainable level of performance. For example, by contending that "we must do something about our sales," the sponsor seems to be calling for an increase in sales to some unspecified level. The merit of the implied need to increase sales is tested by making expectations explicit and by exploring what lies behind poor sales. Examining needs and opportunities ensures a more accurate diagnosis of the situation and more appropriate expectations. By testing diagnoses and norming in this way, the direction and motivation for planned change become clear and defensible. The formulation stage can lead to project abandonment, a revision of direction, and/or a stronger rational for the need or opportunity.

Three phases of activity are required. During Phase 1, discovery, sponsors test their understandings of the situation by uncovering problems. Techniques that help the sponsor search out, synthesize, and select priority problems are presented. The discovery phase helps the sponsor determine if a change problem domain would be useful. For instance, in the sales example, domains could be morale building, training, or promotion. The second phase establishes direction. Sponsors use the domains suggested by priority problems to establish objectives for the planned change effort. In the choice phase, which follows both discovery and direction, sponsors or participants in the process use techniques that help set priorities for problems or objectives.

## ▲  WHY FORMULATION IS ESSENTIAL

The need for formulation is prompted by the paradoxes associated with the identification and verification of ways to direct a planned change process. For any direction that is selected, there will be a number of potentially relevant directions that must be ignored. As the branch bank case (see Chapter 1) illustrates, attending to directions that were ignored would have created significant opportunities and advantages. As a result, managers (sponsors) are admonished to avoid solving the "wrong problem," which Raiffa (1968) calls the "error of the third kind." This error occurs when sponsors stipulate directions based on symptomatic or misleading problems. For example, consider a Toyota dealer who, after a long period of sales growth has been getting disturbing signals. Declines in the closing ratio (a measure of lost sales) were noted, and profit had leveled off. The dealer judged these signals to be important and linked them to staffing problems. Growth was thought to have forced the addition of salespeople who were not enculturated into the dealer's approach to the car business. A sales manager position was created to train and supervise the sales force. After a year, profits remained unchanged, and closing ratios continued to fall. The sales manager was fired and the dealership was back to square one. In this case, the linkage of lost sales and leveled profits to sales force training and enculturation proved to be incorrect. Uncritically accepting statements of needs or opportunities is a prime cause of failure in planned change.

There are several other rationales for formulation. *Pragmatists* stress understanding the sponsor's expectations, not altering them. An example is the procurement process used by the Department of Defense, or DOD. To develop a new aircraft, DOD outlines its needs and requests bids. Each defense contractor's bid is to specify "contract end items," the performance features of the systems or weaponry to be provided. Many other governmental agencies operate in the same way. For instance, a request for proposals from U.S. government departments asks for a description of the expected product, which is used to evaluate each bidder's proposal. This type of contracting requires the sponsor to define expectations in precise terms. These expectations are often accepted as stated by consultants and others who believe that attempts to refine the sponsor's stipulations will cost them credibility and be unacceptable to the sponsor. The necessity for a mutually understood product can force expectations to be prematurely specified. Clear expectations allow the planner (or consultant) to cost the product and be specific about completion dates. However, rapid closure on expectations is seldom desirable, except for a routine (unambiguous and low-uncertainty) efforts. Premature agreements make it difficult for consultants and planners to act outside the domain implied by the expectations, no matter what opportunities a broader search might bring.

The pragmatist contends that user's expectations should be documented as the first step in a planned change process (Archer, 1989). Without such understandings, the sponsor's expectations may shift as the planned change effort clears away uncertainty. This shift in expectations may cause dramatic changes in the time and resources needed to complete the effort. The sponsor may not see how these changes increase resource commitments and draw out completion dates, leading to a breakdown in confidence between consultants or internal staff and the sponsor. Consultants, acutely aware of the need to stay on time lines and within budget often get their planned change clients to draw up a contract that makes expectations clear. However, such an agreement can result in the sponsor making premature judgments about needs. Perceptive sponsors and consultants create contracts that call for joint problem exploration before expectations are specified.

Differences in *perception* among key people are also common, with each view having its own rationality. For example, Churchman (1979), in attempting to plan a system to improve the flow of goods to and from U.S. ports, found that each affected party had a different view of needs. The longshoremen were using wildcat strikes to protest job selection practices by the union. The union's leadership worried about mechanization that they believed would result in the loss of jobs. Congress defined needs in economic terms, responding to charges of union corruption and disruptions of commerce that stemmed from periodic wildcat strikes. The port authorities saw needs in terms of their operating costs. Accepting any of these needs without considering the others would have led to badly underpricing the costs of planned change and understating the time for completion. Also, all the key parties (longshoremen, unions, Congress, and port authorities) would resist plans that did not deal with their notion of need. Formulation is used to find a domain of action (defined by problems and objectives) that is acceptable to important interests.

*Diagnostic* failures also occur, as the car dealer case illustrates. Solving the wrong problem is both costly and common error. After careful scrutiny, what appears to be a crucial problem may prove to be symptomatic of an underlying problem. For instance, in a hospital a sponsor asked a planner to deal with complaints of "excessive" waiting time in an emergency room. If, after triage, emergencies are expediently handled but the patients put in a "convenience care" category resist being referred to an after-hours clinic, the wait time problem is misleading. If the planner takes the problem statement literally, and tries to reduce the emergency patients' waiting time, a more important problem will go unattended. Cues can be found by asking why convenience care patients refuse transfer and become testy after they choose to wait. In this case, addressing the wait time problem would direct planned change to deal with a symptom rather than a root cause.

Formulation techniques are applied to provide a better understanding of the situation and avoid solving trivial problems. Sponsors often believe that they do not have the luxury of reexamining their initial understandings. By seeing that these early understandings frequently prove to be economically unsound or politically unwise, sponsors become aware of the risks in prematurely selecting directions for a planned change effort. The appropriate *scope* of a planned change effort is often unclear at the outset. For example, Nadler and Hibino (1990) describe a case study in which the sponsor stipulated the need to improve the operation of a warehouse loading dock. Rather than accepting this problem statement, the planner guided the sponsor through a formulation process that led him to sell the warehouse.

Wildavsky (1966) notes that managers (plan sponsors) often don't know what they want until they see what they can get. Such a sponsor has little tolerance *for uncertainty* and fears disclosing his or her ignorance. The sponsor is enticed to specify a need or opportunity even though he or she does not understand the source of the problem well enough to provide even approximate specifications. To illustrate, the military, alarmed by the frequency of tank breakdowns under enemy fire during World War II, ordered a redesign of tanks. The reinforcement of the forward portion of the tank was ordered. The breakdowns continued. Finally, hospitalized tank commanders were consulted, who revealed that enemy soldiers waited until the tank passed before firing. This led to a reinforcement of the aft portion of the tank and a decline in breakdowns (Delbecq, 1967).

## ▲ TECHNIQUES USEFUL IN FORMULATION

Techniques are used in formulation to uncover problems and to specify hoped-for results. These techniques can be classified by their orientation and by who

PHASE

| | | Discovery | Direction |
|---|---|---|---|
| **PARTICIPATION** | Group | Nominal group<br>Brainwriting<br>Delphi<br>Brainstorming<br>Kiva<br>NI<br>Focus group<br>Interacting group | Function expansion<br>Objective components<br>MBO techniques<br>Snowball |
| | Dyad | Dialectics<br>Dyadic silent reflection | Stakeholder analysis<br>MBO techniques |
| | Individual | Problem analysis<br>Need assessment<br>Decomposition<br>Dimensional analysis<br>Organized random search | Function expansion<br>MBO techniques |

Figure 10-1  ▲  Classifying Planning Techniques for Formulation

participates. Two orientations can be identified: reactive, specifying problems, and proactive, specifying objectives. The participation categories are group, dyadic (two person), or individual (one person). The orientation and participation categories offer a number of ways to carry out formulation, which are shown in Figure 10-1. Planning techniques that apply to formulation are also listed in Figure 10-1. Note that some techniques span several cells and others do not, indicating their lack of generality. The techniques discussed in this chapter are drawn from those listed in Figure 10-1 that have particular value in planned change activities.

The procedure for the formulation stage is made up of strings of techniques that are useful to set directions. These techniques strings are summarized in Figure 10-2. Each creates a *hybrid* that is made up of particular techniques for the discovery, structure, and choice phases of formulation. The discovery phase can be carried out by one of the reflective group techniques such as the nominal group technique (NGT), surveys (such as Delphi), or interactive approaches (such as brainstorming). The structuring techniques are snowball and function expansion. The group process options can be used in conjunction with snowball, adding synthesis to problem lists and to objective setting in the structural phase. The analyses step in formulation helps people to make choices among candidate problems and objectives. The choice mode provides a way to organize these activities. Two modes were identified: vote-discuss-vote (VDV) and Q-sort. The ranking techniques are anchored rating scales (ARS), paired comparisons, rank-weight, direct assignment, and pooled rank. A choice terminates both the structure and discovery phase, so these techniques are used in both phases.

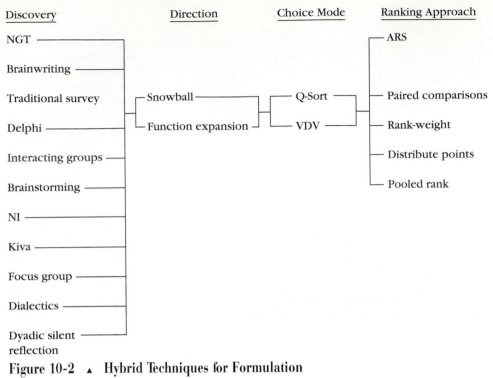

**Figure 10-2** ▲ **Hybrid Techniques for Formulation**
Adapted from Nutt (1982a).

In all, there are $(11 \times 2 \times 2 \times 5)$ 220 hybrid planning procedures identified in Figure 10-2. These hybrids offer many useful ways to carry out the formulation stage of planned change.

## ▲ THE DISCOVERY PHASE

Groups are often used to bring in fresh perspectives when uncovering problems. To manage a group, a "group process" technique is used to promote both efficiency and effectiveness. A group process aids the group in developing ideas, making judgments, bringing forward information, and exchanging views. A variety of group processes has been developed—many have similar features. The techniques presented here have two distinctive features. Each can be learned with modest effort, and each has useful procedures that set it apart from the others.

Group processes are classified as synthetic, interactive, and silent reflective. Within these categories there are several techniques that have comparable benefits so they can be used somewhat interchangeably or applied in situations that can benefit from special features of the technique. Group processes rely on a Lockean inquiring system (IS) and the warrants of consensus and agreement among informed individuals (see Chapter 2).

## Synthetic Groups

A synthetic group pools the judgments of people without a face-to-face meeting. Two ways of creating a synthetic group are discussed in this chapter: survey approaches and the Delphi technique.

### *Survey Approaches*

Pooling responses from a survey is one way to create a synthetic group. In planned change a survey is used to determine the views of consumers, experts, and the like and to test sentiments in important categories of people. Two types of surveys are often conducted by sponsors and their staff. The first targets a specific set of individuals who have a certain attribute, such as expertise or leverage. The survey could determine how centers of expertise or power, inside and outside the organization, view needs or opportunities. Second, surveys can be used to provide a barometer of opinion that describes a general reaction to various planned change–related issues such as needs, opportunities, problems, and objectives. In other planned change stages, the survey could explore reaction to options, plan details, and barriers to change. Respondents are often selected by a random sample. An analysis of respondent views provide a starting point for a discussion. A wide variety of surveying techniques is available that can produce desirable statistical properties in survey responses. Techniques for survey research will not be discussed in detail in this chapter. For more information, see Sudman and Bradburn (1982).

### *The Delphi Technique*

The Delphi technique draws its name from the Greek Oracle of Delphi. A Delphi survey (Dalky, 1967; Delbecq, Van de Ven, and Gustafson, 1986) systematically solicits and collates judgments to form a synthetic group. A series of questionnaires is used. The first questionnaire solicits ideas, information, opinions, or viewpoints and may ask the panel members to state the rationale behind their ideas, proposals, and recommendations. Subsequent questionnaires consolidate and feed back the ideas and the associated rationales to the Delphi panel members. The initial Delphi questionnaire asks broad questions, and subsequent questionnaires are built on responses to the preceding questionnaire. Each panel member can review the logic behind the arguments of others, which is believed to stimulate consensus. The questionnaires continue until consensus is reached, sufficient information has been obtained, or it can be terminated with a vote to prioritize the information that has been collected (Nutt, 1984b).

Delphi was devised to do technological forecasting. The Department of Defense applied it to provide up-to-date technological information not readily available in a literature search. It also has value when used prior to a meeting, allowing the members of a group to clarify and share views efficiently.

Time, skill, and motivation are essential ingredients. Delphi participants must have time, writing skills, and the motivation to set out their views carefully. Staff competence is also essential because a Delphi survey places a heavy burden on staff members who must interpret survey responses. The survey can be time consuming. About 45 days is usually required for three rounds of the survey. This time can be cut to two to three weeks if just the initial round of Delphi is used to gather information. The procedure has steps of development of Delphi questions, participant selection, survey development, analysis and feedback, and prioritization.

1. *The Delphi Question.* The Delphi question specifies the query that the panel will consider. Examples are (a) listing problems in meeting the new quotas for a worldwide sales force, (b) noting the strengths and weaknesses of various prospective reimbursement schemes for hospitals, and (c) indicating the barriers to equal educational opportunities in America. Each question calls for different information. The first and last illustrative Delphi questions concentrate on eliciting problems. The remaining Delphi question poses a solution and seeks a preliminary evaluation, indicating how Delphi can be used to identify and prioritize solutions to priority problems. The first Delphi survey concentrates on getting ideas, with the second and subsequent surveys elaborating and adding to the ideas. The final surveys can evaluate the feasibility of ideas and establish priorities. The Delphi question must be carefully selected to ensure that the panel has an appropriate focus.

2. *Participant Selection.* Both expertise and motivation are key criteria in the selection of panel members. Often, motivation can be ensured only by some form of payment or by a personal interest in the outcome of the planned change. The feeling of personal involvement may offset the lack of monetary rewards, particularly when members have views they wish to share. The needed expertise for the participants is usually suggested by the content of the Delphi question. For example, salespersons, academics, insurance specialists, financial management experts, and education reform advocates suggest expertise useful in dealing with the three Delphi questions. Selection begins with information about prospective members, often provided by planners and local experts. Nominations by others are solicited. The list is then pruned, and the participation of prospective panelists is solicited. The individual soliciting participation should fully explain the Delphi procedure, including the number of steps and time requirements, before asking someone to serve. Between 10 and 15 members is a manageable panel size.

3. *The Survey Instrument—Analysis and Feedback.* The survey instrument is developed and pretested to eliminate possible biases. The Delphi question is usually posed succinctly, with plenty of space for detailed responses. A sample first round form is shown in Figure 10-3.

The participants are told when the next questionnaire will arrive and are given a deadline within which to respond (usually a week). A week may be required to analyze the initial responses. Using the example in Figure 10-3, staff would interpret and combine the strengths and weaknesses of the quota system. The consolidated strengths and weaknesses make up the next questionnaire. A minimum of three days is usually required to summarize the results and return them.

In the second round, members are asked to critique each response, adding still other strengths and weaknesses they may think of. These steps are repeated until

Name _____

Please indicate the strengths and weaknesses of our current quota system for salespersons in the company.


STRENGTHS                                                    WEAKNESSES


Figure 10-3 ▲ First Round Delphi Questionnaire


both the critiques and new ideas stop or until a predesignated number of rounds is completed. Staffers consolidate the information to find areas of agreement and disagreement and items needing verification. Subsequent questionnaires may take the form of lists with a consolidated commentary of the panel under each.

4. *Prioritizing.* Prioritization can be done by voting. Voting usually accompanies the third and all subsequent surveys. Each panel member is asked to prioritize the list of ideas. Average scores are fed back for reconsideration by the participants in the final round of the survey. The final votes are taken to elicit the views of the Delphi panel. In some cases, no final vote is needed. The procedure is stopped when no new information is obtained or when panel views seem to have been adequately explored. (Techniques for voting and making choices in Delphi and the other group processes will be discussed later in this chapter.)

Figure 10-4 illustrates responses to an intermediate round of a Delphi questionnaire dealing with barriers to primary care in rural America. Participants could be experts in various aspects of primary care provision and use. The current vote tally is shown in the second column. The vote represents the average panel ranking from the previous round. The list of barriers taken from the first round, and the

Instructions:

1. Review all items on list

2. Select the top five priority barriers to primary care in rural America

3. Give the most important a vote of 10 and the least important a vote of 1, with other votes reflecting the relative importance of each barrier

4. Return by _____ to: _____

| NEW VOTE | OLD VOTE | BARRIER | COMMENTS |
|---|---|---|---|
| | | The most important barriers are | |
| — | 10 | 1. Travel distance | (a) Is this generally true? |
| | | | (b) For what type of services? |
| | | | (c) |
| — | 8 | 2. Cost of care is generally higher in rural areas because of time and cost of commuting | (a) Does this mean travel would be underwritten by insurance? |
| | | | (b) |
| — | 7 | 3. Diagnosis often delayed leading to more costly and less successful treatment | (a) What is the evidence? |
| | | | (b) |
| — | 2 | 4. Physicians less competent | (a) Doubt this is true. |
| | | | (b) Not true for those in general practice. |
| | | | (c) How is this a barrier? People will go to anyone because there are so few resources available. |
| — | — | 5. | (d) |
| — | — | 6. | |

Figure 10-4 ▲ Intermediate Round Delphi Questionnaire

barriers added in subsequent rounds, is shown in the third column. The last column lists the comments made by panelists in the previous rounds. Some take the form of questions, which one or more panel member is encouraged to answer. Other comments take a position on the merits of a barrier. The next round may provoke still further questions or new barriers to which the panelists will respond. Another survey that abstracts these issues is then prepared.

One form of a final round survey is shown in Figure 10-5. In this survey, issues, not barriers, have been abstracted and voted on. The last vote keeps the members aware of each barrier's importance to aid in the final ranking of each issue. The comments become heavily annotated, indicating the way to deal with objections and answers to questions about feasibility. The final vote is then taken in the last survey.

Instructions:
1. Review issues and comment
2. Select the five most important issues
3. Voting instructions (see Figure 10-4)
4. Return instructions (see Figure 10-4)

| ISSUE VOTE | BARRIER VOTE | BARRIERS | ISSUES | COMMENTS * |
|---|---|---|---|---|
| 8 | 10 | 1. Travel distances | 1. Systems of ambulatory care centers must be created | (a) Who will staff them? |
| | 8 | 2. Cost of care in rural areas | | (b) What about federal subsidies? |
| | 7 | 3. Delayed diagnosis | | (c) How will they be located? |
| 3 | 2 | 4. Physician's competence | 2. Determine measures of competence | (a) Why can't we measure competence by family practice board certification? |
| | | | | (b) What can be done if competence is missing? |
| — | — | 5. Cost of care in rural areas | 3. | . . . |
| — | — | 6. Delayed diagnosis | 4. | |
| | | . . . | . . . | |

* Under each comment answers to the question are summarized to aid the ranking. The rejoinders are provided by panelists and summarized by staff, along with other information that the sponsor believes to be necessary.

**Figure 10-5** ▲ **Final Round Delphi Survey**

A minimum of five surveys are used in Delphi, one to get the list of barriers and two each to get barrier comments and comments on the issues abstracted by staff. When new questions arise, they must be summarized and sent out for the panelist's commentary, drawing out the process. For the simple form of Delphi pro/con analysis, three surveys are minimal: one to list and two to react and prioritize.

### Delphi Uses

Delphi is an excellent information dredge. It is also useful when confidentiality is essential, because group members can remain anonymous, and when meetings are too costly because of travel distances. But Delphi can be cumbersome, time consuming, and arbitrary. There are no generally accepted rules for summarizing results. Staff must have (or acquire) considerable knowledge to reduce the information derived to manageable proportions. During information reduction, unconscious staff views and preconceived notions can creep in to bias or manipulate the results. A large number of surveys may be needed before disagreements become apparent. Finally, closure forced by a vote can be artificial.

## Interactive Group Processes

An interacting group meets face to face and conducts an open-ended discussion. Rules or procedures that are used to guide this discussion are minimal. Four types of interacting groups are considered called traditional, brainstorming, focus, and dialectic groups.

Formal planning groups, regardless of their structure, require an appropriate introduction to frame the planned change question and to give the leader legitimacy in regulating the group's efforts. This introduction should define the problem, provide the procedural orientation, and introduce the leader. A format useful in the initiation of a planning group is shown in Table 10-1.

### Traditional Face-to-Face Groups

Traditional planning groups have a conventional discussion format. Discussion is free flowing and open ended, and little in the way of procedure is used. Structure stems from the agenda and from the leader, who maintains a focus on the issue.

The benefits of interacting groups are obtained only when full and candid participation from all members is realized. However, interacting groups often become inhibiting to its members. Members divide their time between the task and maintaining the social relationships in the group. Performance can be improved when the leader recognizes and deals with the interpersonal obstacles that may crop up in the group's social environment (Collins and Guetzkow, 1964; Nutt, 1989a). Some typical problems and remedies are the following:

1. Some members of a group will tend to withhold information they know to be relevant. Social rewards, like praise and solicitous requests for contributions, will help to overcome this reluctance to share information.
2. Inferior group members have a depressing effect on the group's performance. A group can come to grips with planning problems that cause some mem-

## Table 10-1 ▲ Introduction to Participants of a Planning Group

The following presentation should be made at the start of a planned change project by the sponsor.

*Introduction*

The sponsor thanks members for attending this meeting, pointing out that each person's participation and ideas are essential for success. The purpose of the meeting is defined as getting the members' recommendations and ideas.

*Problem Description*

The sponsor should describe the planning problem, and its origins, and indicate the expected outcome from the group (e.g., to improve coordination, make recommendations). Next, the sponsor should indicate that the group was assembled because its members are thought to have information and knowledge crucial to dealing with the problem. This gives the members a purpose and provides a general expectation for a member's individual contribution. Finally, the sponsor describes how the information provided by the group will be used. For instance, recommendations for changes in the retirement system could be given to the board of directors and its staff for further study.

*Procedural Description and Leader Introduction*

The sponsor introduces the group leader who may also be the planner. The sponsor's introduction should stress the leader's skills and accomplishments giving the leader legitimacy. The leader describes the procedures to be used in managing the group's activities.

bers of the group to lose something when all members view each other as competent. Demonstrations of competence in which the leader cites the past accomplishments of each member are useful when group members are not acquainted.

3. Group members will experience participation penalties when their views are not readily accepted or when they are rejected outright. A leadership style that stresses the need for full participation and ameliorates tactless remarks, should they occur, helps to overcome these problems.

4. Groups become inhibited by large status distinctions. Members who perceive themselves as "high-power" will talk with "low-power" members until their status is clear, and then they restrict their communication to other "high-powered" members. This behavior creates needless tension and conflict in the group, suggesting the need for groups that are homogeneous in competence, but not point of view.

5. The behavior of some members can be inhibiting to the group. Nonparticipants have a chilling effect, as do isolates (people without a clear role). The leader should attempt to draw out nonparticipants and seek ways for the isolate to participate.

6. A group member seeking personal power (gratification from serving) and one seeking issue power (changing the course of events) are incompatible and should not serve in the same group.

7. The members of a planning group who support their views with logical arguments and show how their views are consistent with past experiences of the other group members have the most influence.

### Brainstorming Groups

Brainstorming is a particular type of interacting group, specifically geared to planning. In brainstorming, the leader challenges the group into a rapid-fire generation of ideas, inviting modified and new ideas. Brainstorming used during formulation seeks ideas that help to define the problem. In concept development, brainstorming can be used to identify solution options.

Brainstorming works best when the fact-finding and problem-finding activities are separated (Osborn, 1963). Facts highlight issues. New ways to define problems are based on integrating and extrapolating known facts. Premature evaluation keeps the integrative and extrapolative steps from occurring, so early criticism is ruled out. To encourage integration and extrapolation of facts, considerable latitude in problem search is essential. These requirements lead to the two principles of brainstorming: "deferment of judgment" and "quantity breeds quality."

The need for deferment stems from the distinction between the judicial and the creative mind. The judicial mind carries out the analysis and comparisons that are required to make a choice. The creative mind makes forecasts to visualize new ideas. These mental processes are incompatible. Making judgments is not compatible with the free association one needs to be creative. The judicial mind tends to dominate. As a result, a brainstorming group must defer all types of judgment. The leader must create an environment in which the members of a brainstorming group will verbalize their ideas about problems without any concern for the idea's acceptability or importance.

The second dictum is that many ideas are needed. The notion that quantity breeds quality stems from the view that a person's thoughts have a hierarchical structure. The dominant thoughts in the hierarchy are conventional. To transcend these conventional notions of problem definitions, considerable effort is needed to create new associations. The quantity dictum forces the members to exhaust their conventional notions to get at the creative ones.

*Brainstorming Rules.* The deferment and quantity-quality principles suggest four rules for a brainstorming group (Stein, 1975; Nutt, 1984b).

1. *Eliminating criticism.* All criticism is ruled out. Participants are told that a subsequent session will be used to evaluate. When criticism occurs, some leaders become self-critical (attempting to deflect the judgmental effects) or use a device, such as a bell. The leader can get the group to agree that he or she can ring the bell when one member is critical of another's contributions.
2. *Unconventional ideas.* Participants are made to feel that they are expected to offer unconventional problem definitions. This gives the adventuresome members the sanction they need to participate and helps the more inhibited relax. A plant or two—people prepared with unconventional problem definitions—can help get the session moving.
3. *Many ideas.* Participants are told that they should come up with as many ideas for problem definitions as they can. Encouraging quantity increases the chance that later suggestions will be original.
4. *Integration of ideas.* Problem definitions should be combined and improved whenever possible. When a member shows how problems can be integrated, the leader should reinforce this behavior. If this does not occur early in the session,

the leader can give an illustration. This rule also helps those who contribute later in the session to mark out a distinct role for themselves. The notion of "hitchhiking," in which a member gives a variation on a theme of a past problem definition, encourages both integration and refinement.

*Group Management.* Several actions must be taken to establish and manage a brainstorming group. First, a group size of about 12 members is recommended, involving people with either problem knowledge or experience. People who tend not to see each other in their day-to-day activities should participate. Second, the leader should be committed to the technique and be familiar with its steps and the rationale behind the steps. The leader should have an outgoing, gregarious personality. Third, steps are taken to maintain a record of the ideas. Tapes, chalkboards, flip charts, and many other devices can be used.

The leader begins with a "warm-up session" using a sample problem, such as improving the hospital gown or dealing with computerized telephone solicitations at home. The humor and good feeling that result provide a springboard from which to tackle a more substantive problem.

To begin the problem session, the leader states the problem and spells out the technique's steps. A rapid-fire list of suggestions is encouraged, but members are limited to one idea each time they are recognized. The leader must be careful to let everyone participate. During slow periods, the leader can offer his or her ideas and call for hitchhiking. The typical session lasts between 30 minutes and an hour.

*Pitfalls.* Brainstorming has several pitfalls. The most common is the failure to get proper sanction. For brainstorming to work, its participants must believe that the session is needed and that it is approved by upper management. A second pitfall is poor preparation. Expectations should be reasonable, and the participants must be fully indoctrinated into the technique's steps. Finally, follow-up is often a problem. Most forms of ideation that fail do so because the planned change process was not completed. Management blames the most visible step (brainstorming) for the failure, not recognizing that the process was stopped prematurely.

### Focus Groups

In the focus group technique, outside experts are brought together to describe problems or opportunities to organizational leaders. The experts can be brought in one at a time or as a panel, with the intent of provoking a dispute over their differing positions. Focus groups can be useful in informing the sponsor or helping a planned change group focus on the most pertinent questions.

### Dialectic Groups

The systematic examination of an idea from several points of view produces a dialect (Mason and Mitroff, 1981; Emshoff, 1980). For instance, subgroups of a planning group can be asked to develop ideas based on radically different assumptions about the environment, constituencies, and strategic positioning. Each subgroup presents its ideas, and members of the planning group debate the merits of the ideas. The purpose of the debate is to spell out the implication of each need or opportunity to challenge it by exposing weaknesses in its underlying assumptions. Discussion of two competing alternatives is not a dialectic. A dialectic involves discussion of ideas that are based on *different* assumptions. For example, an opportunity can be discussed under assumptions that call for budget increases and budget cuts.

Dialectics have several benefits. First, the debate forces a sponsor or planning group to consider a wide range of information. Pet opinions can be subjected to careful and systematic scrutiny in which the sponsor or group members note how internal and external stakeholders would view the situation. This leads the listener to develop fuller appreciation of the rationales behind each position, which may lead to synthesis and innovation. Dialectics may not work, however, for well-structured planned change or when there is preexisting conflict between certain group members.

The dialectic group draws on a Hegelian inquiry system (IS) and its warrants that call for debate between opposites to produce a consensual view (see Chapter 2).

## Silent Reflective Group Processes

Silent reflection is advocated to overcome the barriers to group participation, to encourage disclosure, and to promote thoughtful consideration of the planned change task. During the silent reflection phase, group members feel a certain tension that promotes competition for good ideas. This helps the group avoid superficial arguments, tired diagnoses, and pet ideas that can stifle innovation. There are several group processes that use silent reflection principles: nominal group technique, or NGT; brainwriting; the nominal-interacting technique, or NI; Kiva; and dyadic silent reflection.

### The Nominal Group Technique

The nominal group technique (Delbecq and Van de Ven, 1971) was derived from the behavior science literature, tempered by experience. Most planning groups have an ideation phase and an evaluative phase. Ideation provides a search for ideas, and evaluation screens and merges ideas into a coherent picture. A different type of group process is best for each phase: silent reflection for ideation and interaction for evaluation. NGT can also control individuals who try to dominate the group, which lowers both productivity and satisfaction. The NGT technique controls this behavior, encourages reflection, and allows equal participation.

The NGT group is small, composed of seven to ten members who are seated so each can view the other. The leader introduces the group and outlines all steps in the process. It is important that each group member understands the steps and agrees to follow them. When the leader is unknown to the group members, an outside source of authority is often essential to get process acceptance (see Table 10-1).

The nominal group technique has the planning group initially work without discussion to encourage reflection. This reflective phase is followed by a systematic consideration of results. The leader begins by stating the purpose of each step in the NGT technique. Next, the need or opportunity that provoked action is described.

Each member is asked to write his or her ideas (e.g., problems) on a pad of paper, *without discussion*. Those who wish to talk during this phase are discouraged in a friendly but firm manner. The silent listing phase proceeds until all the members have stopped writing or until a given time period has elapsed, preferably the former. The leader should resist all but process questions and work silently to be a role model for the group.

In step 2, the leader solicits and records the ideas of each member. This phase is useful in depersonalizing the ideas and allowing each member equal time to present his or her views. It also provides a written record. Each individual is asked to give one idea from his or her list, which the leader then records on a flip chart. The leader should be sure the member agrees with the written version of the problem before proceeding. The leader rotates among the members, getting their ideas one at a time until members confirm that their ideas are exhausted. At this point, several sheets should be taped to the wall in full view of the members. Between 20 and 25 ideas (e.g., problems or solutions) are usually listed by an NGT group.

In step 3, each idea is discussed. The leader asks first for clarification and then for the merits and demerits of each idea on the list. Considerable discussion may result, and the leader should make notes on the flip chart indicating significant elaborations. The leader should avoid focusing on one idea and should tease out the logic in each listed idea by asking for clarification, recording differences of opinion. Consolidation attempts follow in which the leader merges similar ideas, asking for consent of the members. The leader should avoid arguments, leaving both options when a consensus to merge them does not develop.

In step 4, the group is asked to create a consensus by selecting the most important ideas. Several voting techniques, which can be used for this purpose, are explained in the next section.

In summary, the four steps in NGT are (1) silent recording of ideas; (2) listing ideas, giving each member a turn, one at a time, until the ideas are exhausted; (3) discussing the ideas to consolidate the list and sharing information about the merits of each idea; and (4) voting to select a priority list.

### Conducting an NGT Session

The leader begins an NGT session by thanking participants for coming to the meeting. These remarks should be linked to the sponsor presentation, shown in Table 10-1. The leader should also stress the need for each member to participate.

The leader reviews the NGT steps (see Table 10-2) and then answers questions. In the first step, group members are asked to think like consumers or users and (e.g., dealing with formulation) list problems that they, or people they know, have encountered. Problems of *any* type can be considered. But they are often divided into personal and organizational. Personal problems stem from the individual's wants and needs. All other problems tend to be imposed on the individual by the organization.

Members take between 15 and 20 minutes to record their ideas, without discussion. Next, the members are expected to offer ideas one at a time, which the leader records on a chart. Listing continues until all ideas are recorded. During the recording of ideas, each idea should be discussed fully so that an understanding is

**Table 10-2  ▲  Leader Guides for Meetings with Silent Reflection**

Step 1:  Silent Listing
1. Present written problem statement and a written outline of all process steps
2. Resist all but process clarifications
3. Maintain atmosphere by leader also writing in silence
4. Discourage members who attempt to talk to others

Step 2:  Round-Robin Recording
1. Indicate purpose of step 2 (to create a record of the meeting)
2. Ask members to present their problem briefly and clearly
3. Accept variations on a theme but discourage duplicate items
4. Ask if idea has been correctly recorded to gain approval before proceeding
5. Keep list visible to all members by taping it on the wall

Step 3:  Interactive Discussion
1. Indicate step's purpose (to explain and consolidate)
2. Skirt arguments but accept both opinions when a difference arises
3. Give all items some consideration
4. Encourage elaborations from everyone without reference to who proposed the item
5. Gain the group's agreement to merge similar ideas, keeping the ideas separate when the group objects

Step 4:  Prioritization
1. Establish purpose (to set priorities)
2. Explain technique to be used

Adapted from Delbecq, Van de Ven, and Gustafson (1986).

shared by members of the group. After a break, the members are asked to rank the top five ideas (e.g., problems) from most to least important.

### The Brainwriting Technique

Brainwriting (Gueschka, Shaude, and Schlicksupp, 1975) is another group technique that uses silent reflection. In the "cued" variation (Nutt, 1984b) of brainwriting, the leader initiates the session by placing sheets of paper that contain several written cues (e.g., problem suggestions that focus the group's attention) in the center of the table. The participants are asked to take a sheet, read it, and silently add their ideas to the list. When members run out of ideas, or want the stimulation of another's ideas, they exchange their current list with one in the center of the table. After reviewing the new list, ideas are added, and the procedure continues until ideas are exhausted.

A variation called "structural brainwriting" induces more synthesis (Nutt, 1984b). Members are asked to list their ideas in particular categories. Cues are provided for particular themes, such as personal and organizational problems. After two items have been added in each category, a work sheet is exchanged for another member's work sheet in the center of the table. This process continues without discussion, with members exchanging their work sheets until ideas are exhausted or time is called. The "structured" brainwriting approach creates synthesis around the themes initially selected and allows members to sort themes within theme options, creating a second form of synthesis. These steps improve the quality of ideas and provide some innovation as constraints implied by the cues are considered.

The round-robin recording step of NGT is used to list ideas. (In the structured form of brainwriting, several listing steps are carried out at the same time.) Each member is asked to describe one item on his or her current work sheet. The leader records the ideas one at a time, moving from one member to the next. This listing continues until all members pass. A discussion phase follows, permitting members to comment and elaborate on their ideas or the ideas of others. Prioritizing is the final step.

In summary, the steps are

1.  Silent recording and elaborating
2.  Round-robin recording
3.  Discussion
4.  Prioritizing

A typical session can produce 60 to 80 ideas that are more thoughtful than are those that stem from interactive meetings. This technique is both efficient and effective for the ill-structured planned change effort.

### Nominal-Interacting Technique

An adaptation of the nominal-interacting technique (Souder, 1980) is particularly useful in providing a forum for "anteroom lobbying" during a group process (Nutt, 1984b). Group meetings are carried out using NGT or brainwriting steps. The procedure is truncated at several points to allow for lobbying. A special room is provided with refreshments, ostensibly for a break. Between 30 and 45 minutes are allocated for group members to share views and lobby each other.

The lobbying can be implicit or explicit. When implicit, the purpose of the break is not discussed. Under certain conditions, members can be asked to seek accommodations, much the way that the "second chance sessions" of the Roman Senate were carried out (Nutt, 1989a), allowing small groups to meet in a social setting to work out their differences.

These steps are particularly valuable when considerable accommodation among members is needed, due to conflict. The procedure is shown here:

| Round 1: | Step 1: | Silent reflective listing (NGT or brainwriting) |
| --- | --- | --- |
|  | Step 2: | Round-robin recording |
|  | Step 3: | Anteroom lobbying |
|  | Step 4: | Group discussion |
|  | Step 5: | Anteroom lobbying |
|  | Step 6: | Initial prioritization |
|  | Step 7: | Anteroom discussion |
|  | Step 8: | Final prioritization |
| Round 2: |  | Repeat steps 3 to 8 on another day |

The NI technique introduces informal lobbying into the idea generation and ranking procedures. Meetings use NGT or brainwriting, but the procedure is broken off at several points to allow for lobbying to occur. After a substantial number of ideas has been generated, the leader calls a break of 30 to 45 minutes; members go to another room. This step allows the natural urges that people have to share views and lobby each other to emerge. The leader or facilitator can be more direct, asking members to share opinions, exchange facts, challenge views, and bargain during the break. Members can ask for one another's priorities and their justification. These informal exchanges create mutual understanding and help the group avoid premature closure. Three lobbying sessions typically are needed before final vote on priorities can represent the level of consensus possible in a particular group. Typically, the first session identifies the diversity of opinions. In the second, members begin to adopt or reject ideas. After the third, judgments can emerge based on new understandings.

This approach is particularly useful for ill-structured and obscure planned change efforts that have little precedent that can be used as a guide. The anteroom discussion teases out the information that leads to the group making thoughtful judgments about priorities.

### The Kiva Technique

A Kiva procedure was devised by the Hopi Indians to make important tribal decisions. The Kiva technique is drawn from the structure used by the Hopi in their deliberations (Nutt, 1989a).

The Kiva technique begins with the key decision body, such as the tribal elders, that conducts an open discussion that leads to making preliminary judgments. This key body is surrounded by several rings of tribal members who listen to the discussion. The ring adjacent to the tribal elders is made up of individuals who have status just below that of the inner ring. The last ring has only adolescents. After discussion, the tribal council moves to the outer ring and then all groups move one ring toward the center. The group now in the center discusses what its members *think they heard*, with all others listening. This process repeats until the tribal council is again in the center ring. The tribal elders, aided by reflections on the reflections of others, then reconsider their views. This type of group process is useful for strategic management and high-importance projects carried out in decentralized organizations, to involve many groups or levels in the organization's structure. A Kiva arrangement allows representatives of various groups or levels to reflect on what a planning group proposes to do and permits a sponsor (or planning group) to gather an in-depth appreciation of reactions, and reactions to reactions, before setting priorities. NGT, brainwriting, NI steps, or an interactive discussion can be used to uncover the views of each circle.

### Dyadic Silent Reflection Technique

A variation on the silent reflection theme can be introduced into sponsor-planner discussions (Nutt, 1984b). In a planned change project, the planner is often confronted by the sponsor with a statement of need or opportunity that is discussed in a classic interactive fashion. The planner often leaves this meeting unsure of what is to be done and unwilling to ask, being afraid to appear imperceptive. The sponsor, believing he or she has communicated, is less willing to be helpful in subsequent meetings. Questions in subsequent meetings can be seen as challenges to prerogatives rather than attempts to clear away the planner's confusion.

Paragraph writing at an intermediate point in such meetings can provide silent reflection. Both the planner and the sponsor write a brief paragraph defining the issue as they currently understand it and exchange them. The final discussion is focused on clearing up mutual misunderstandings. Tests of this technique find that it provides results that are superior to the interactive approach.

## The Benefits of Group Processes

Guidelines based on the benefits obtained from using types of group processes are beginning to emerge from the extensive group process studies conducted in the past four decades. These studies find that no single group process is best for all applications. Interacting face-to-face groups promote innovation and acceptance better than synthetic groups. However, synthetic groups serve as useful sources of information when all affected people would make an interacting group too large and unwieldy.

Studies of the merits of brainstorming rules have been instrumental in evolving improved group processes. For example, people were asked to compose clever titles for stories with and without evaluation. The titles composed by the "without evaluation" group were both more novel and more appropriate (Christensen, Guilford, and Wilson, 1957). This study is typical of many that find that deferred judgment increases the quality of a group's efforts.

The link between quality and quantity has been studied in "eureka"-like tasks, such as exploring various uses for hangers and brooms. As the number of ideas increases, the quality of ideas also increases (Parnes and Meadow, 1959). People are more likely to make clever observations when they are *asked* (Maier, 1970). The mere act of telling people to be creative has been found to promote more novel ideas. Implicit in the quantity argument is that better ideas will result from integration, which tends to occur later in the session. Generally, the quality of ideas is higher in the second half of the meeting (Parnes, 1961; Nutt, 1984b).

Brainstorming has been used for nearly half a century. Although there is a decided bias toward reporting successful and not unsuccessful applications, a large number of reports cite impressive results. For instance, Bell Telephone found ways to increase the demand for long-distance phone calls by using brainstorming. And the National Association of Social Workers implemented a large number of ideas that came from a brainstorming session. Other successful applications range from improving a city's bus service to making a community more livable.

Secondary effects of improved morale and attitudes of group members are also widely reported. Being selected for group membership can be a powerful motivator. The increased attention paid to the group to initiate the session also improves morale and attitudes. It is hard to separate the effects of the session from the effects of being asked to participate.

Brainstorming groups are better than a synthetic group for developmental tasks (Herbert and Yost, 1979). But many researchers (e.g., Bouchard and Hare, 1970; Vroom, Grant, and Colton, 1969; Nutt, 1976b) also find that brainstorming and interacting groups can inhibit creative thinking. Members' inhibitions and hasty evaluations shut off valuable lines of inquiry. This reduces the innovativeness and the acceptance of new ideas. Furthermore, people in interacting and brainstorming groups prefer to react to someone else's idea rather than offering one of their own (Delbecq and Van de Ven, 1971). This is called the "focus effect," which inhibits creativity. The silent reflection phase in NGT and similar group processes overcomes some of the barriers to creative thinking, making these group processes quite useful in planned change. Compared to an interacting group, silent reflection produces more ideas and better quality ideas as well as more candor, member acceptance, and innovation (Nutt, 1977). The effectiveness of NGT and Delphi have been compared in several studies. Recall that both have a form of silent reflection, a means to expose members systematically to the views of others to stimulate synthesis, and pooled judgments. Delphi has the advantage of anonymity but lacks timeliness. An NGT session can be completed in one evening while Delphi takes up to two months. NGT has more spontaneous feedback, which can help or hinder a group. Groups under extreme stress find that NGT promotes conflict.

Studies that controlled leadership, which can have a decisive effect on the performance of a group, also found NGT groups to be superior to interacting groups in terms of innovation, acceptance, and quality of results for planned change efforts (Nutt, 1976b). The silent reflection portion of the procedure permits a member to conduct a broad search for information that has been found to stimulate new ideas. NGT is clearly superior to other group processes in its ability to generate new information.

## Tailored Group Processes

The group processes described in this chapter should be regarded as flexible procedures that can be tailored to fit a given application. The needs of the task and the benefits of each process step can suggest minor, or even major, alterations in steps that are desirable. Examples already discussed include adding NGT procedures to brainwriting and using NGT or brainwriting to enhance the Kiva technique. Changes can be made to cope with logistics or factors inherent in the problem under study. A match between task needs and group process benefits should be sought when a group process is tailored. A tailored group process can be developed to exploit the beneficial features of the group processes described in this chapter, with the new procedure composed of steps that seem needed for the task at hand.

## ▲  THE DIRECTION PHASE

Direction setting is used to organize the priority problems into a coherent statement that indicates aims of a planned change project. Techniques specify direction by drawing on the performance gaps identified in the discovery phase. Two techniques will be described: function expansion and snowball.

## The Snowball Technique

The snowball technique is similar to the "storyboarding" approach applied by the FBI in kidnapping cases. The FBI has its agents bring all information regarding a kidnapping to a room and organize it according to categories such as motives and MOs. These categories and the information each contains are periodically updated by agents as they gather new information about the case. The room becomes a repository of information that is organized into categories that gradually reveal characteristics (themes) of importance in solving the case. Storyboarding is also used by firms to sum up competitor intelligence and market information.

Snowball is like the storyboard approach, specifically devised for use by groups. Applying NGT, brainwriting, Kiva, and other silent reflective group processes to generate problems often creates long lists of partially integrated and overlapping problem suggestions. The snowball technique (Greenblat and Duke, 1981; Backoff and Nutt, 1989) can be used to find labels that identify themes or generalizations that sum up bundles of problem ideas, such as low public awareness, poor public relations, need for new clients or customers, updating products, services, or new products/services.

To delineate themes or categories, a group sorts cards (or sheets of paper) that list the individual problem ideas identified in the discovery phase. Each card or sheet describes one of the problems that were identified. The group members are asked to tape the cards or sheets to a wall, grouping similar problem ideas, and then to label the resulting categories. No ownership of problem ideas or categories is allowed; anyone can change any label or exchange cards or sheets among categories. The group members study the labels and the category or theme that each implies and reorganizes them without discussion. Stable patterns often emerge after three or four attempts at labeling and content modification. These classifications provide a more general set of categories than the initial pool of problem ideas, identifying important themes or generalizations in any problem set. This procedure can be added to any one of the silent reflective group processes to create a synthesis of problems before prioritization is attempted.

The snowball technique is similar to the gallery and pin-card techniques devised by the Battelle Group in Germany (e.g., Gueschka et al., 1975). The procedure allows group members to browse through ideas as they would move through an art gallery. A more elaborate version of this technique calls for different colored cards to be prepared for each theme or category. Problems are then attached to the color-coded cards and pinned to the wall.

The steps in a snowball procedure are

1. A problem list is recorded on flip chart paper and taped to the wall of the room. (This type of list is typically left from a silent reflective group process.)
2. Members of the group peruse the problem list and take notes (5–10 minutes).
3. The group silently examines the list and looks for categories or themes that capture the problems listed (10–20 minutes).
4. The group members attempt to rephrase problems to make improvements or add new problems (10–20 minutes).
5. Group members round-robin list themes and categorizations (20 minutes).

6. Each member silently adds problems related to a theme or category by taping a sheet of paper to the wall until the category and sheets below it contain all problems that fit the category.
7. Group members browse the categories and problems.
8. Without discussion new categories are created, categories are renamed, and problems are shifted among categories by individual members.
9. Browsing continues until all members return to their seats (10–20 minutes).
10. Disagreements are discussed and compromises are sought.

The snowball technique avoids semantic difficulties that can block the synthesis of ideas, which is required in all silent reflective group procedures. People find it easier to write their ideas. Also people are more creative when physical activity is combined with mental activity.

Difficulties with the technique arise if the members of a group disagree about categories and problems continue to shift between categories. There is no easy way to resolve these disputes should they become intense. To manage disagreements the leader can allow several synthesis attempts to unfold with duplicate problems in each.

## The Function Expansion Technique

According to Nadler (1970, 1981), the first requirement of any planning activity is determining purpose. The purpose indicates the objective or aim of the planned changed effort: its reason for being. An objective also links the desired outcome to resource demands. The objective can change when resources do not match the intended scope of the effort. The objective is also linked to a plan or system. The system represents an interconnected junction of inputs, outcomes, and processes designed to achieve the objective. The plan specifies what is to be done and how it is to be carried out. The plan has a two-way effect that influences both objectives and resources. To illustrate, planning a new quality-control procedure for a company may lead to personnel retraining, which hikes resource needs. Managers of the line departments may resist the disruption that they expect to flow from this training, which may lead to modifying the initial objective. The pattern of interactions among objectives, resources, and systems or plans is shown in Figure 10-6. The diagram shows how a plan is shaped by both objectives and resources. Objectives, plans, and resources exist conjointly. What gets included in the plan depends on how a sponsor permits objectives and resources to change with emergent needs and insights.

Nadler defines function as the aim of the planned change effort that emerges from the interplay of objectives, resources, and plans. (The notion of a function is synonymous with that of an objective.) Function refers to intended outcomes, whereas an "output" indicates how the function or objective is to be achieved. For example, assume that the objective is to bill people who have purchased a product with a credit card. The output is the bill sent and its features. The features could include the use of sanctions, such as late payment charges, and the terms of payment that will hike portions of the balance due after particular time intervals.

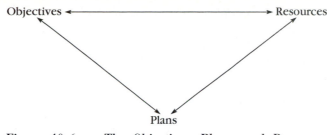

**Figure 10-6** ▲ **The Objectives, Plans, and Resources Relationship**

Adapted from Nadler (1981).

## The Need for Objectives

Establishing an objective is a crucial step in planned change. The objective directs the search for solution alternatives by indicating an arena in which to search. Objectives that lack clarity suggest that several arenas can be considered at the same time, which leads to unfocused inquiry. Without a clear arena for search, alternatives are hard to identify and may have little to do with the problems prompting planned change. Also, most criteria to judge merit of alternatives are derived from objectives. Clear objectives make criteria easy to identify. Unclear objectives lead to fuzzy and contradictory criteria.

Consider, for example, the development of an alcoholism treatment program. Planned change guided by an objective of "making people aware of alcoholism problems" is substantially different from planned change intended "to ameliorate alcoholism problems." The objective of making people aware implies a case finding plan. Alternatives could be sought that encourage self-assessment acts by at-risk individuals. Criteria to judge the merit of these alternatives would measure costs and the extent to which at-risk individuals have been reached by the program. In contrast, treatment objectives to ameliorate alcoholism problems suggest alternatives such as adapting AA substance abuse programs. Criteria that measure an individual's abstinence, recovery rates, changes in the level of family tension, and job problems, as well as cost, would be used to judge the merits of such alternatives.

Another example can be provided by a firm that is manufacturing plastic bags (Nadler and Hibino, 1990). During fabrication, a problem arose with die-cutting a sheet of cardboard into the desired shape, like a Kleenex box, to hold the plastic bags made by the company. The complexity of the pattern was producing 25 percent rejects. Die-cutting problems suggested two different objectives: "cut holes in a sheet" or "provide the customer with a bag container." Alternatives for the "hole-cutting" objective would deal with modifying the machinery or alternating how the machinery is operated. The alternatives for providing "customer packaging" would consider new materials and shapes that accomplish the purpose of holding bags and dispensing them one at a time. Criteria to judge the success of the hole cutting would deal with altering the reject rate, at an acceptable cost. Criteria for the customer packaging options are quite different and would determine if customer needs were met at a reasonable cost.

These examples illustrate the importance of an objective. Identifying the scope of a planned change effort is a key consideration. For instance, plans concerning people's alcoholism awareness (case finding) are subordinate to and precede treatment. Cutting holes is subordinate to satisfying customer packaging needs.

## The Structure and Semantics of Objectives

Objectives contain statements calling for action that have a particular structure (Nadler, 1970, 1981). Note that objectives in the examples considered thus far have an infinitive-action-verb form, immediately followed by a direct object. Recall the objectives "to make people aware" in the alcoholism example and "to provide customer packaging" in the packaging example. Sometimes this form is extended to add qualifiers, such as "to make more/most people aware" in the alcoholism project or providing flexible and waterproof packaging in the packaging example (Warfield, 1990). The qualifiers can become complex, laying out a host of probable causes, consequences, contingencies, conditions, and targets. Such an objective could take the form of "to make unserved people aware, by removing barriers to getting care, caused by ignorance and fear, thereby improving a person's prospect of seeking care, within budget and time constraints and the limitations imposed by work force turnover, etc." The simpler and less qualified form for an objective is preferred because it has more focus and less clutter, leading to fewer restrictions that overly focus subsequent inquiry (Nutt, 1984b). Also, note that the qualifiers do *not* include means. An objective lays out ends, not means.

The semantics of an objective is also important. The words used can bring meaning or take it away. *Qualifiers* can be changed and, by doing so, add or take away constraints that set boundaries. Altering the objective "to reduce budget overruns by 10 percent" by dropping the qualifier (10 percent) has a similar effect. The response to an unqualified objective elicits a search for the broadest possible range of alternatives. (Qualifiers are treated as norms in the next section of this chapter.)

Alterations in the *verb* can also have important effects (Volkema, 1986). The action "maintain" is quite different from "enhance" or "maximize." Within an implied action type, semantics can have subtle effects that alter how objectives are interpreted. For instance, people are apt to view "maintain competence" and "keep competence" differently, perhaps by giving the former a neutral interpretation and the latter an interpretation that competence is slipping.

The *object* has the greatest potential to refocus inquiry. A change in object can create very different impressions of needed action, ranging from very narrow to very broad searches for ways to resolve problems that the organization is confronting. For example, the objective "to get new budget forecasts" points to looking for a specific set of techniques compared with "to improve budgeting," which opens up inquiry to consider the entire budgeting process, thus allowing the planned change process to look for a wider range of alternatives. Experienced managers know that failed planned change efforts often stem from dealing with lower-level objectives at the expense of more pertinent higher-level objectives. Finally, changing from a negative to a positive context is desirable. For example, changing "to eliminating budget problems" to "to improving the budget system" moves inquiry from attaching blame to finding productive responses.

## The Scope of an Objective

Objectives always have a hierarchical relationship in which one objective provides the means to accomplish another. For example, the alcoholism project could embrace an objective "to make people aware" or "to motivate people needing help." Awareness is a means to motivate. Broad-scope objectives lead to expanded lists of alternatives that consider wider courses of action, unless the objective becomes grandiose (Volkema, 1983). For example, the objective of "to engender growth and development" may not be helpful in stimulating ideas for planning alcoholism programs.

The arena of search is set by the scope of the objective in a hierarchy. The scope of the intended planned change effort is crucial, and sponsors are encouraged to explore the implications of several objectives before selecting one to guide the process.

The steps in the function expansion technique are (1) identifying possible objectives, (2) arranging objectives in a hierarchy, and (3) selecting an objective to direct the search for solutions. Either a group or the sponsor working alone can use the technique. Group process techniques that can be used carry out the objective listing steps.

### Step 1: Identify Possible Objectives

To begin, the sponsor or leader of a group reviews problems that have prompted the planned change effort. This review can include background about organizational concerns, imperatives for change, and the listing of priority problems from a group process. Also, the sponsor or leader should note support from key leaders for planned change. The sponsor (or group leader) then reviews an example of the outcome of this technique that provides a hierarchy of objectives, like those shown in Figures 10-7 and 10-8.

First, the sponsor or group identifies possible objectives that can deal with the priority problem. For example, in dealing with the packaging project, someone may suggest an objective "to provide openings in a box." The "verb-object" form should be noted. The verb is "provide" and the object is "openings in a box." Objectives that have this format are sought. As they are suggested or uncovered, they are recorded.

Next the objectives are reviewed. Limited or qualified objectives are deleted. For example, "to treat alcoholics within budget constraints" is trimmed to "to treat alcoholics" (Figure 10-7). Statements such as "reduce costs," are disregarded because they suggest a criterion to measure an objective rather than offering direction.

### Step 2: Arrange Objectives in a Hierarchy

In step 2, the pruned list of objectives from step 1 is ordered in a hierarchy. First, a search is conducted for the most immediate, direct, and irreducible objective in the list. In Figure 10-7 this objective in the alcoholism project was "to provide operational definitions of alcoholism." For the packaging project, this objective was "to cut holes in cardboard." The intended result is a vertical arrangement of possible

To provide operational definitions of alcoholism

↓

To identify people suffering from alcoholism

↓

To make people aware of alcoholism problem in general

↓

To make people aware of own alcoholism problems

↓

To motivate people to take some form of positive action

↓

To assist recovery

↓

To assist the person to ameliorate or eliminate alcoholism problem

↓

To assist the person in dealing with problems associated with alcoholism

↓

To meet person's needs

↓

To meet needs of social, vocational, and personal adjustment

**Figure 10-7** ▲ **Hierarchy of Objectives for Alcoholism Project**
Reprinted from Nutt (1989a).

objectives in which each higher-level objective encompasses all other objectives that are lower in the hierarchy.

As the expansion proceeds, objectives are sought that result in the smallest possible increase in scope. Levels can be elicited by asking two types of questions. In the first, the sponsor/leader asks: What is the objective of the last objective stated? For example, What is the objective of defining alcoholism? The answer could be to identify people with alcoholism problems. Or one could ask: What is the objective of identifying people with an alcoholism problem? An answer could

To cut holes in cardboard

↓

To provide openings in the cardboard

↓

To provide openings in a box

↓

To package and dispense plastic bags

↓

To deliver bags one at a time to customers

↓

To provide customers with plastic bags

↓

To provide customers with a flexible and watertight container

**Figure 10-8** ▲ **Hierarchy of Objectives for Packaging Project**
Adapted from Nadler and Hibino (1990).

be to make people aware. A second type of question asks: What is gained by defining alcoholism, or what does a definition of alcoholism permit us to do? A possible answer is to identify people with an alcoholism problem.

If a jump between objectives is too large, the gap is filled. Small increments are sought, for example, by asking in the packaging example why do we cut an opening in the box, which can trigger the next objective "to package and dispense bags" (Figure 10-8). Before a new objective is added, one checks the hierarchy to ensure that each objective is larger in scope than the one immediately lower in the hierarchy. For example, in the alcoholism example, two objectives could be "to identify alcoholics" and "to provide alcoholism treatment." However, "to identify alcoholics" is a part of treatment; therefore, it is a smaller scope objective and would be listed first (Figure 10-7). When two or more objectives seem to deal with the same issue, the objective that seems best is selected.

The highest-scope objective should appear so grandiose and expansive as to have little value. For example, the objective to meet personal adjustment needs of alcoholics may require more than treatment services. These objectives are retained to illustrate the magnitude of the problem and to ensure that the sponsor's thinking about the nature of the plan will be sufficiently broad.

### Step 3: Selecting an Objective

In the final step the sponsor or the group selects an objective. The objective with the largest feasible scope is preferred because most planned change efforts take an overly restrictive view of possibilities, which limits what can be found in a search for alternatives. Selection should be preceded by a full consideration of the implications of adopting an objective with a broad or a narrow scope, as discussed in Chapters 1 and 5. The selection process can be carried out by applying one of the ranking techniques discussed later in this chapter.

### A Leader's Guide to Carrying Out Function Expansion in a Group

To carry out function expansion in a group the leader begins by introducing participants and the purpose of the meeting, following the sponsor's presentation shown in Table 10-1. The leader goes over the steps to be taken and answers questions, noting that determining objectives is important because the objectives will guide all subsequent aspects of plan development.

An example is used to illustrate what the meeting will produce, as shown in Figures 10-7 and 10-8. The leader acts as the group facilitator and records suggestions. One of the group processes discussed in this chapter can be used to uncover and list possible objectives. To make suggestions, each member is asked to identify objectives that should be considered in dealing with the planning problem. For example, in dealing with an alcoholism project, an objective could be "to identify persons with alcoholism problems." The "verb-object" form is pointed out. For example, the verb is "identify," and the object is "persons with alcoholism problems."

When the suggestions have been listed, the leader helps the group arrange objectives in a hierarchy. First, the most immediate, least inclusive, or unique objective is located. Subsequent objectives can be elicited by asking the following questions:

1.  What is the objective of the last objective? For example, what is the objective of defining alcoholism? The answer could be to identify those with alcoholism problems. Or the group could be asked; What is the objective of identifying people with an alcoholism problem? And the answer could be to make people aware.
2.  The leader can ask the group what is gained by defining alcoholism, or what does a definition of alcoholism permit us to do? A possible answer is to identify people with an alcoholism problem.
3.  Participants could be asked to identify the next most inclusive objective.
4.  Finally, participants could be asked to define what larger objective contains the last objective on the list.

The most immediate and more inclusive objective is selected next—proceeding in this fashion until an objective is listed with a scope that is clearly beyond the interest of the sponsor.

Attempts should be made to avoid the following pitfalls:

1.  Sequence problems that arise when processing in flowchart terms are identified by the group. To overcome this, the leader should reemphasize the hierarchical nature of the result.
2.  When more than one objective is identified at a given level, the most frequently occurring objective is selected, ignoring the rest. The group should be encouraged not to identify all the objectives at a given level.
3.  When the group is stuck, switching organizational viewpoints can be helpful. Some groups get caught in a loop. Switching organizational viewpoints can break an individual out of the loop.
4.  Statements should be changed to reflect the positive and beneficial aspects implicit in the statement. For example, a statement of increasing profit or decreasing cost can be changed to provide a product or offer a service implicit in the initial statement.

At this point, a hierarchy of objectives has been created. The final step selects an objective in the hierarchy that will be used to develop the plan, using one of the voting techniques discussed next.

## ▲   THE CHOICE PHASE

In the choice phase priorities are set for the problems or objectives. Priorities can be set in one of two ways. Either a global assessment can be made or an index of merit can be constructed that combines the rankings made by applying several criteria. Useful techniques to help a group set priorities include ARS, paired comparisons, rank weight, distribute points, pooled rank, VDV, and Q-sort.

### Choice Mode

The choice mode provides a structure for voting or ranking. Two techniques are discussed: vote-discuss-vote and Q-sort.

## Vote-Discuss-Vote

To set priorities in a group, both reconsideration and reflection should be encouraged. Initial views of group members can be influenced by uncertainty in both their position and the position of others. To overcome these problems, a group sets priorities without discussion, using any of the voting techniques described in the following section of this chapter. Average values, representing the initial consensus, are computed and displayed to stimulate discussion. Discussion is directed toward defending or critiquing the initial priorities. The group considers these views as they emerge during discussion. After discussion, the group prioritizes the items again. The average weights that result represent an informed group consensus that show more agreement than the initial weights. This procedure, called vote-discuss-vote, or VDV (Nutt, 1984b), can be summarized as

1. Solicit individual priorities
2. Pool individual priorities into a mean score, to specify the initial group consensus
3. Discuss initial group consensus
4. Reconsider initial priorities by ranking the items a second time.

VDV is a useful way to organize the setting of priorities. A planning group often wants time to reflect and regards all choices as preliminary, pending more information. Reconsideration helps to reduce uncertainty about each member's position. The VDV technique brackets discussion with ranking. Discussion allows for informal lobbying that encourages disclosure and mutual adjustment among the group members. An initial priority will always shift after group members share information.

The VDV procedure was developed to obtain parameter estimates from groups for tasks in which a precise estimate was required. VDV was found to be a very accurate way to make these estimates (Gustafson et al., 1973). The procedure works for several reasons. First, it allows the current group consensus to be criticized, not an individual. Second, VDV simulates what a group typically does when faced with setting priorities (Nutt, 1977). In most situations, a planning group wants time to reflect. Groups typically treat their initial choices as preliminary, subject to change pending more information on how members feel and the facts they offer. Third, public voting by the show of hands, or through open discussion, subjects a member of a group to social pressure by other members. Members of a group that feel less knowledgeable are reluctant to take a position until they see how others are voting. Public voting will entice some members of a group to vote in ways that differ from how they would vote without knowledge of these sentiments. The initial ranking step gets each member to think through his or her preferences, avoiding the pressures to conform. After the initial ranking, changes are more apt to stem from the persuasiveness of the other members' arguments than from their status or personality (Huber and Delbecq, 1972).

## Q-Sort

A group process, survey, or public hearing often produces many ideas. The members of a planning group are often called on to set priorities for more than 60 items, such as problems. Priority setting with this number of items often becomes unreliable. Because of their sheer number, items are difficult to rank. The situation is complicated by the value-laden, complex, and partially overlapping nature of problems and the like that are contributed by a number of people. The Q-sort technique (Kerlinger, 1967) provides a way to reduce the information processing demands that improves the reliability of a priority list of items.

The Q-sort improves reliability by having a group member first look for the most important item in a pool of items and then the least important ones, switching back and forth until all items have been categorized. The number of items considered on each pass is equal. The items considered in all the sorts have the approximate shape of a normal distribution.

Three steps are required to rank a list of items. First, using the Q-sort procedure, items are prioritized. The second step repeats the first to ensure that the ranking can be reproducible, creating reliability. In the final step, items are ordered applying one of the ranking procedures discussed in the next section.

The Q-sort technique can be used for item pools ranging from 30 to 130. Below 30 and above 130, reliability declines (Kerlinger, 1967). When fewer than 30 items are to be screened, the direct assignment technique (discussed later) can be used because the information processing demands are manageable. Above 130, the task becomes tedious and items tend to be overlooked in the sorting process.

*The Sorting Procedure.* The first step in a Q-sort calls for items to be written on index cards, along with a brief definition. To begin a sort, an individual or the members of a group read through the items to be ranked. The simplest sort is to put the items into three categories of importance such as "important," "unimportant," and the residual. The residual will be made up of items that have an intermediate level of importance.

To illustrate the procedure, consider an example with 55 items to be ranked (Brown and Coke, 1977). The rater selects the 3 most important items from the 55 and enters a code number for each item under the +5 column. (Figure 10-9 provides a scoring sheet, useful in capturing the ratings.) Next, the rater selects the 3 least important items and enters them under the −5 column. The rater then selects the 4 most important items from those that remain. These items are listed under the +4 column. Four unimportant are selected next and put under the −4 column. The rater continues, adding items with each pass until 7 items remain. These remaining items are located under the 0 column. The sorting process is repeated until the same sets of items begin to appear in each category. This type of ranking takes from one-half to three quarters of an hour the first time that the procedure is used, and considerably less time thereafter (Brown, 1980).

*Sorting Schemes.* Different scoring schemes are needed for different-sized item pools. These distributions should be normal or as close to a normal distribution as possible to impose desirable statistical properties on the sort. Several such distributions (Kerlinger, 1967) are shown here:

$N = 80$

| Scoring: | −5 | −4 | −3 | −2 | −1 | 0 | +1 | +2 | +3 | +4 | +5 |
|---|---|---|---|---|---|---|---|---|---|---|---|
| Number Selected: | 2 | 4 | 6 | 9 | 12 | 14 | 12 | 9 | 6 | 4 | 2 |

Instructions: After sorting, insert the category number for each card in the appropriate box below. Be sure each category contains the specified number of cards.

Subject: _____ Sorter: _____

Information: _____ Date: _____

| 1 | 2 | 3 | 4 | 5 | 6 | 7 | 8 | 9 | 10 | 11 | 12 | 13 | 14 | 15 | 16 | 17 | 18 | 19 | 20 |
|---|---|---|---|---|---|---|---|---|----|----|----|----|----|----|----|----|----|----|----|
|   |   |   |   |   |   |   |   |   |    |    |    |    |    |    |    |    |    |    |    |

| 21 | 22 | 23 | 24 | 25 | 26 | 27 | 28 | 29 | 30 | 31 | 32 | 33 | 34 | 35 | 36 | 37 | 38 | 39 | 40 |
|----|----|----|----|----|----|----|----|----|----|----|----|----|----|----|----|----|----|----|----|
|    |    |    |    |    |    |    |    |    |    |    |    |    |    |    |    |    |    |    |    |

| 41 | 42 | 43 | 44 | 45 | 46 | 47 | 48 | 49 | 50 | 51 | 52 | 53 | 54 | 55 | 56 | 57 | 58 | 59 | 60 |
|----|----|----|----|----|----|----|----|----|----|----|----|----|----|----|----|----|----|----|----|
|    |    |    |    |    |    |    |    |    |    |    |    |    |    |    |    |    |    |    |    |

| 61 | 62 | 63 | 64 | 65 | 66 | 67 | 68 | 69 | 70 | 71 | 72 | 73 | 74 | 75 | 76 | 77 | 78 | 79 | 80 |
|----|----|----|----|----|----|----|----|----|----|----|----|----|----|----|----|----|----|----|----|
|    |    |    |    |    |    |    |    |    |    |    |    |    |    |    |    |    |    |    |    |

| 81 | 82 | 83 | 84 | 85 | 86 | 87 | 88 | 89 | 90 | 91 | 92 | 93 | 94 | 95 | 96 | 97 | 98 | 99 | 100 | 101 |
|----|----|----|----|----|----|----|----|----|----|----|----|----|----|----|----|----|----|----|-----|-----|
|    |    |    |    |    |    |    |    |    |    |    |    |    |    |    |    |    |    |     |     |     |

| Category value | 1 | 2 | 3 | 4 | 5 | 6 | 7 | 8 | 9 |
|---|---|---|---|---|---|---|---|---|---|
| Number of items in category | 5 | 8 | 12 | 16 | 19 | 16 | 12 | 8 | 5 |

Note: A value of 9 indicates "most important;" a value of 1 indicates "least important."

**Figure 10-9 ▲ Q-Sort Record Sheet**

Reprinted from Nutt (1989a).

| Scoring: | | −4 | −3 | −2 | −1 | 0 | +1 | +2 | +3 | +4 | |
|---|---|---|---|---|---|---|---|---|---|---|---|
| Number | | 4 | 6 | 9 | 13 | 16 | 13 | 9 | 6 | 4 | |
| Selected: | | 4 | 6 | 10 | 12 | 16 | 12 | 10 | 6 | 4 | |

$N = 70$

| Scoring: | −5 | −4 | −3 | −2 | −1 | 0 | +1 | +2 | +3 | +4 | +5 |
|---|---|---|---|---|---|---|---|---|---|---|---|
| Number | 2 | 3 | 5 | 8 | 11 | 12 | 11 | 8 | 5 | 3 | 2 |
| Selected: | 2 | 3 | 4 | 9 | 11 | 14 | 11 | 8 | 4 | 3 | 2 |

$N = 60$

| Scoring: | −5 | −4 | −3 | −2 | −1 | 0 | +1 | +2 | +3 | +4 | +5 |
|---|---|---|---|---|---|---|---|---|---|---|---|
| Number Selected: | 2 | 3 | 4 | 7 | 9 | 10 | 9 | 7 | 4 | 3 | 2 |

*Scoring.* Scoring schemes typically use a ±5 scale or a ±4 scale. For 80 items with ±5 scale, 2 items are initially selected, and with the ±4 scale 4 items are selected in the first sort. Any other scoring scheme with frequencies similar to the classic bell-shaped curve of a normal distribution can be used. To set up a scoring system, a set of index numbers can be created that specifies each category's value. For instance, for the 5-item scale,

| | Least important | | | | | | | | Most important | | |
|---|---|---|---|---|---|---|---|---|---|---|---|
| Scale | −5 | −4 | −3 | −2 | −1 | 0 | +1 | +2 | +3 | +4 | +5 |
| Category Value | 1 | 2 | 3 | 2 | 5 | 6 | 7 | 8 | 9 | 10 | 11 |

and for the 4 item scale,

| | Least important | | | | | | | Most important | |
|---|---|---|---|---|---|---|---|---|---|
| Scale | −4 | −3 | −2 | −1 | 0 | +1 | +2 | +3 | +4 |
| Category Value | 1 | 2 | 3 | 4 | 5 | 6 | 7 | 8 | 9 |

A Q-sort permits one or more participants to determine carefully their attitude toward a large number of items.

*Finding Coalitions.* Divisions of opinions about priorities among group members can yield important insights. Factions in a group can be isolated by comparing sorts to identify disagreements among the raters. The items supported by each faction suggest potential disagreements that should be addressed before consensus is sought.

Assume there were four panelists who provided the problem ratings shown in Table 10-3. In this example, panelists A and B and panelists C and D rank the problems much alike. To demonstrate the similarity, correlation between the values assigned by each panelist can be computed. Panelists A and B have a very high degree of linear association ($R = .92$). Panelists C and D also have considerable

## Table 10-3 ▲ A Q-Sort for a Ten-Problem, Four-Person Panel

| Problem Code Number | Panelist | | | |
|---|---|---|---|---|
| | *A* | *B* | *C* | *D* |
| 1 | 2* | 2 | 1 | 1 |
| 2 | 1 | 1 | 0 | 0 |
| 3 | 0 | 0 | 3 | 4 |
| 4 | 2 | 2 | 4 | 2 |
| 5 | 2 | 1 | 3 | 3 |
| 6 | 1 | 2 | 2 | 2 |
| 7 | 3 | 3 | 2 | 2 |
| 8 | 2 | 2 | 2 | 2 |
| 9 | 4 | 4 | 2 | 3 |
| 10 | 3 | 3 | 1 | 1 |

*Score based on category value.
Reprinted from Kerlinger (1967).

similarity ($r = .75$). No other pairs are similar. This suggests that two *coalitions* have formed among the participants. (The coalition would be inadvertent in a survey or a Delphi group.) The three highest-ranked items by panelists A and B and by C and D can be pooled. Comparing the two pooled lists indicates areas of agreement and disagreement. When disagreement is noted, further discussion to resolve the dispute may be warranted, a procedure that merges the VDV and the Q-sort techniques.

In large-scale applications, Kerlinger (1967) recommends using ANOVA statistical techniques to identify discrete item classes. In a one-way ANOVA, the item classes are the fixed effects and the panelist rankings from the Q-sort provide the variance to be explained. For example, behavioral scientists create definitions of "types," such as aesthetic, theoretical, economic, social, political, and religious. Instruments are devised to test the extent that religious items are selected by ministers, aesthetic items by artists, and economic items by business men and so on, which tests the instrument's reliability. Planners can also build up categories that define or describe problems and validate them in the same way. Surveys are constructed with brief statements based on the disaggregated items from a past Delphi survey or several NGT meetings. For example, assume that 70 items must be considered using the following Q-sort:

| | Least important | | | | | Most important | | | |
|---|---|---|---|---|---|---|---|---|---|
| Number to be Selected: | 2 | 4 | 6 | 13 | 20 | 13 | 6 | 4 | 2 |
| Category Value: | 1 | 2 | 3 | 4 | 5 | 6 | 7 | 8 | 9 |

The respondent is asked to look through the list and place a 9 next to the two most important problems and then a 1 next to the two least important problems. These problems are then crossed out to ease subsequent search. Next the respondent looks for the four most important problems scoring them with an 8 and the four least important scoring each with a 2. These problems are then eliminated and the rankings are repeated two additional times. A scoring sheet is shown on Figure 10-9, see p. 271. The scores from each problem are placed into their category and tested with a one-way ANOVA.

In the previous example, a single criterion was used to pool the problem statements. In practice, several criteria are often required. For instance, problems could be considered by the level of need each implies, the discovery implicit in each, and the prospects for resolution. Important problems would have high need, innovation, and feasibility. In this case, each panelist would do a Q-sort using each criterion. The criteria can be weighted to create a composite list, using the ranking techniques that are discussed in the next section.

*The Merits of Q-Sort.* Ranking tends to be quite subjective, and so divisions of opinion may yield important insights. Q-sort permits each participant to construct carefully his or her attitude toward a problem list. The technique is ideally suited for large ranking tasks (above 50 items) and can be quickly administered and scored. Coalitions can be isolated and points of disagreement quickly identified. Although Q-sort does not indicate the proportion of people in a coalition, it does suggest

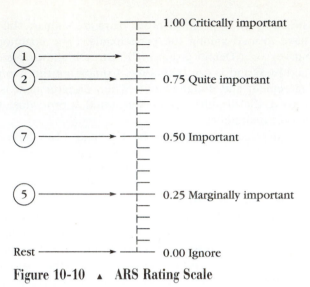

**Figure 10-10** ▲ **ARS Rating Scale**

the problems being supported (and not supported) by each coalition group so the sponsor can explore the substance of the disagreement.

## Ranking Techniques

Within each choice mode a ranking technique can be used. They include anchored rating scales, paired comparisons, rank-weight, direct assignment, and pooled-rank techniques.

### Anchored Rating Scales

Anchored rating scales or the ARS technique can be used to elicit the ranking of problems, objectives, and other items from a planning group or others that a sponsor wishes to poll. The technique is easily understood and can be applied quickly, making it useful in a survey and when fairly precise discriminations among items are needed. A continuous scale with descriptors at several points along the scale is constructed to help to define the scale's increments and the end points (Nutt, 1980a). The annotations help the group member (or survey respondent) to visualize the meaning of scale intervals and scale end points. A variety of scale sizes can be used including 0 to 100, minus to plus infinity, and 0 to infinity. A scale anchored with a 0 is used for items that have natural 0 points, such as cost. A negative end point can be used for items in which negative values are possible, such as profit. Positive or negative infinity end points convey the notion of no theoretical limits to item values. To use a scale with positive and/or negative infinity as end points, log increments are required. To simplify the scale, linear increments with −100 to +100 end points are recommended for applications in which values can be very large or very small. In most cases a 0 to 100 linear scale can be used, as shown in Figure 10-10.

To illustrate how ARS scales can be used, assume that a planning group wishes to set priorities for a problem list the group has uncovered. The problems are presented to members of the group with a numbered list. Each group member selects the number associated with each of the problems and draws an arrow from the number signifying a problem to a point on the scale that indicates his or her view of the problem's importance. These scale values are normalized to convert them to percentages. For example, if a line were drawn from the cost problem to .80 and from the quality to .60, the cost problem would be weighted as

$$\frac{.80}{(.80 + .60)} = .57$$

and the quality problem as

$$\frac{.60}{(.80 + .60)} = .43$$

This computation provides a rank or priority that establishes the relative importance of the items being compared. An average value, indicating the consensual views of a planning group (or group being polled), is determined by averaging the percentage scores for each group member.

The technique can be applied when priorities for a number of criteria (e.g., importance, feasibility, and political impact) are required by creating a rating scale, such as that shown in Figure 10-10, for each criterion. Each member rates each item (problem) using each criterion. These values can be combined into a consensual rating by averaging across group members and the criteria.

### Paired Comparisons

The paired comparison technique helps members of a planning group make comparisons that yield a very precise picture of priorities. Considering items, such as problems or objectives, in pairs permits a group member to concentrate on the difference between any two items, reducing the information processing demands. Consider an example in which members of a group are asked to prioritize five problems. To apply paired comparisons, the facilitator lists all combinations of the five problems two at a time. Group members are asked to compare the two problems (more generally, items) in each pair and indicate which is more important. Assume that the following choices were made by a group member:

| "Pairs" | Choice |
|---|---|
| Item 1 or Item 2 | Item 1 |
| Item 1 or Item 3 | Item 3 |
| Item 1 or Item 4 | Item 4 |
| Item 1 or Item 5 | Item 5 |
| Item 2 or Item 3 | Item 3 |
| Item 2 or Item 4 | Item 4 |
| Item 2 or Item 5 | Item 5 |
| Item 3 or Item 4 | Item 3 |
| Item 3 or Item 5 | Item 5 |
| Item 4 or Item 5 | Item 5 |

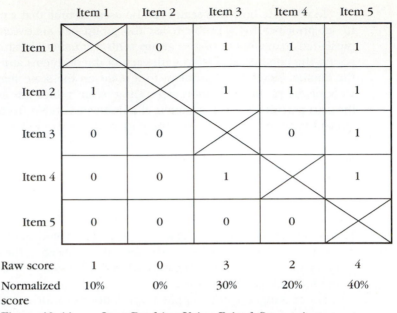

|  | Item 1 | Item 2 | Item 3 | Item 4 | Item 5 |
|---|---|---|---|---|---|
| Item 1 |  | 0 | 1 | 1 | 1 |
| Item 2 | 1 |  | 1 | 1 | 1 |
| Item 3 | 0 | 0 |  | 0 | 1 |
| Item 4 | 0 | 0 | 1 |  | 1 |
| Item 5 | 0 | 0 | 0 | 0 |  |
| Raw score | 1 | 0 | 3 | 2 | 4 |
| Normalized score | 10% | 0% | 30% | 20% | 40% |

**Figure 10-11** ▲ **Item Ranking Using Paired Comparisons**

The chart shown in Figure 10-11 is used to tabulate a weight for each item. First, the first column and first row are used. Item 1 is more important than item 2, so a 1 is entered in the first column and the second row, adjacent to item 2, and 0 under item 2 in the first row in Figure 10-11. Item 1 is less important than the other items, so a 1 is entered in the first row under items 2, 3, 4, and 5 and 0's under column 1. Now the first column and row have been filled out and can be eliminated from further consideration. The remaining cells in the second row and column are considered, scoring each cell in the same manner. These steps are repeated for the remaining columns and rows. The totals in each column are then summed for each group member to create an average panel score for each item.

The totals in each column are normalized to define a ranking for each problem, as shown in Figure 10-11. In most cases, an average value, indicating the consensus of the planning group, is determined by averaging the rankings of each member.

When multiple criteria are used, a paired comparison is made with each criterion. The results can be averaged or combined according to the importance accorded each criterion, producing a weighted index. In some cases the ratings for each criterion are kept separate so the planning group can appreciate differences that can arise as problems, objectives, and the like are prioritized from different perspectives, such as importance or feasibility.

### Rank-Weight Techniques

This approach has group members first rank each item (e.g., problems, objectives, etc.) and then specify its importance. Ordering the items in terms of their importance and then weighting them eases the information processing demands of the task, which improves reliability. Each item is placed on an index card. The group member first orders the items and then weights the items. One of the several approaches can be used to carry out the weighting. The odds procedure has the group member compare the items to the top-ranked item one at a time, recording times more important (Nutt, 1980a). The most important item is given a value of 1. If the first item was found to be twice as important as the second, a value of $\frac{1}{2}$ is assigned to the second item. The odd ratios are normalized to convert to percents. Priorities can also be assigned using linear scales of $-100$ to 100 and 0 to 100, log scales, or index numbers. The consensus view of the group is determined by averaging the values obtained from each group member, as described previously. The procedure can be repeated for criteria, such as feasibility and importance, to create ratings according to each of these notions of priority.

### Distribute Points

The distribute points technique is useful in prioritizing large numbers of items. The procedure can be carried out with or without anchors. Using the technique *with anchors* calls for three steps: selecting labels, recording item names on cards, and classifying the items according to the labels. Labels and values can be assigned as shown here:

| Label | Value |
|---|---|
| Most important | 10 |
| Highly important | 8 |
| Important | 6 |
| Somewhat important | 4 |
| Marginally important | 2 |
| Not important | 0 |

As the number of intervals increases, precision increases, but the ease of designation declines, leading to blurred discriminations. Five to ten intervals are typically selected. Item names are then recorded on index cards. Each group member sorts the cards into piles associated with each label. The sorts are repeated several times. This step helps to ensure that the items have been reliably placed into categories.

To speed up priority setting in a group the direct assignment of ranks can be used. In this case, the integers can be associated with descriptors, such as 10 = most important and 1 = least important, and assigned to each item to describe its importance. Scales, such as $-5$ (least) to $+5$ (most) or $-10$ to $+10$ are also widely used. These scales should be anchored by end-point descriptors (e.g., most/least)whenever possible to increase ranking precision.

### Pooled Rank

The pooled-rank technique is simple and quick, but violates additivity assumptions needed to create averages. First, each member ranks the items from 1 to 5. (Five is arbitrary, but often cited in the group process literature.) For example, assume that 20 items were generated from a group session. Each of the five members of the group ranked the items where 1 is most important and 5 is least, as shown:

| Rank | Weight | Member 1 | Member 2 | Member 3 | Member 4 | Member 5 |
|------|--------|----------|----------|----------|----------|----------|
| 1 | 5 | 20* | 1 | 2 | 4 | 9 |
| 2 | 4 | 11 | 3 | 4 | 3 | 8 |
| 3 | 3 | 9 | 4 | 7 | 6 | 7 |
| 4 | 2 | 8 | 6 | 6 | 7 | 20 |
| 5 | 1 | 7 | 7 | 1 | 1 | 1 |

* Item number.

The values assigned for item number 1 (5 + 1 + 1 + 1) are divided by 5 (the panel size) for an average value of 1.6. The remaining items are computed in the same way:

| Item | Values | Average Value |
|------|--------|---------------|
| 1 | 5, 1, 1, 1 | 1.6 |
| 3 | 4, 5, 4 | 2.6 |
| 4 | 2, 3, 5 | 2.0 |
| 6 | 2, 2, 3 | 1.4 |
| 7 | 1, 1, 3, 2, 3 | 2.0 |
| 8 | 2, 4 | 1.2 |
| 9 | 3, 5 | 1.6 |
| 11 | 4 | 0.8 |
| 20 | 5, 2 | 1.4 |

This leads to the following priorities:

| Priority | Item |
|----------|------|
| 1 | 3 |
| 2/3 | tie 4, 7 |
| 4/5 | tie 1, 9 |

Items 2, 5, 10, and 12 to 19 received no support. Items 6, 8, 11, and 20 received too little support to be considered a priority.

### Comparison of Methods

Each voting technique has strengths and weaknesses. Table 10-4 summarizes some of the characteristics of each to aid in selection. None of the techniques fully satisfies the additivity assumption. The pooled-rank technique makes no attempt to quantify the relative difference between items, so it ranks low on precision and satisfying assumptions. However, when the purpose of ranking is to sort several higher-ranking items from the rest, this procedure provides an adequate result. When a more precise value is needed, another technique must be used.

Paired comparisons have the best precision, but this technique is not practical for large numbers of items. When paired comparisons are used to compare ten or more items, the procedure becomes very time consuming. Using paired comparisons in conjunction with a survey can also create difficulties. The respondent may not see how the ranks will be computed and become suspicious that he or she is being manipulated.

### Table 10-4 ▲ Comparison of Priority-Setting Techniques

| Technique | Speed | Precision | Assumptions |
|---|---|---|---|
| 1. ARS scales | Moderate | Moderate | Moderate |
| 2. Paired comparisons | Moderate (for more than ten items) | High  Moderate | Moderate/high  Moderate |
| 3. Rank weight | Moderate | Moderate | Moderate |
| 4. Distribute points | High | Low | Low |
| 5. Q-sort | Low | High | Moderate |
| 6. Pooled rank | High | Low | Low |

Rank-weight techniques can be used in meetings, but the technique is cumbersome in a survey. In a meeting, rank-weight is superior to ARS scales and direct assignment because of its precision and relative speed. ARS scales are best in surveys when ranks with interval scale properties are needed because the instructions can be brief and easy to understand. This approach is the easiest for most respondents to grasp without a face-to-face explanation.

The distribute points technique works best in an individual, rather than a group, setting. The ranker can sort and then resort several times with relative ease, compared to the other techniques.

## ▲ Key Points

1. The formulation stage involves discovery and structure in which problems are uncovered and objectives are set.
2. The importance of formulation stems from the dilemmas of selecting a direction to guide planned change. For any direction that is selected there are many others that cannot be considered that, if followed, could yield better results. To reduce the chance of selecting an unproductive direction, sponsors go through steps of uncovering problems and setting objectives. Uncovering problems reduces the chance that planned change will deal with symptomatic and misleading signals. Objectives with an appropriate scope direct energies in useful directions.

## ▲ Cases

### The Elevator Case*

The manager of a large office building has been getting an increasing number of complaints about its elevator's slow service, particularly during rush hours. Several important tenants have threatened to move out unless service is drastically improved. To deal with the situation, the manager inquired into the possibility of adding one or two new elevators. Although feasible, the only elevator company in

---

* Courtesy of Roger Volkema, Ph.D.

the area has a six-month backlog of orders. As an assistant to the manager you were asked to come up with a plan to get new elevators installed in three months. You must present your ideas at the staff meeting tomorrow.                                    ▲

## The Emergency Room Case

This project deals with an emergency room in a 900-bed acute care hospital with a teaching program. The hospital has recently moved to a new facility. The move to the new facility was made amid considerable dissatisfaction with the emergency department. Concerns of excessive wait time were regularly voiced by members of the medical staff, physicians, employees of the department, and patients. It was assumed that the new facility would solve these problems.

The hospital administrator appointed a planning group when the old building could no longer be used as a scapegoat. The planning group was made up of eight physicians drawn from the various departments that often admitted or treated patients in the emergency room. Another eight were appointed: seven from the administrative staff and an operations research consultant.

The planning group held several meetings, making little progress until the OR consultant suggested an evaluation using a queuing model to verify wait times. Study isolated wait times by three patient categories: emergency, patients with life-threatening problems; urgent, patients with a problem that is not life threatening; and primary, patients needing only routine care.

The study showed that the emergency care patient waited approximately 40 minutes to see a physician after arriving in the treatment area, the urgent patient waited 44 minutes, and the primary patient waited 50 minutes. Needed tests were not performed until a physician saw the patient. The patient waited until test results were available and the physician could make a final diagnosis. The total time in the ER was determined to be 98 minutes. Ninety percent of the classifications given by the receptionist agreed with the physician or overclassified the patient. However, 10 percent of the patients were underclassified, which could lead to problems.

The study also showed that the laboratory and X-ray services were sluggish in responding to emergency care patients, creating a backlog. The queuing model determined that 10 minutes could be shaved from the average composite time if X-ray and laboratory could keep up with the patient arrival rate and avoid queuing.

Several proposals were made to avoid test queuing. All involved having a registered nurse perform triage and, under certain circumstances, ordering lab tests and X rays so they would be available when the patient was initially seen by the physician. Standard operating procedures were developed to direct the nurse in this ordering. An electrowriter was installed in the lab so test results could be communicated to the ER as soon as the test was completed. Finally, norms were established for the service areas. This included time between patient arrival and when first seen by the physician, time between lab test ordered and specimen taken, and time between ordering and results. Also, X-ray and ECG norms for turnaround times were established.

The program was installed as a pilot to determine the impact of new procedures on wait time. The wait time analysis was repeated to determine if wait time had been decreased and whether individual service norms were being met.

The results of the study indicated that 10 minutes had been shaved off total time in the emergency room; however, the time between arrival and seeing a physician had increased from 40 to 45 minutes. The sponsor was unsure how to interpret this information and reactivated the planning group. The physicians, after reviewing the information, objected. Because there was a bigger log jam in the treatment area waiting to see a physician, it was thought that patients would blame the physicians and not the hospital. Physicians also pointed out that no complaints had been received recently, suggesting that the planned change process may have been unnecessary. This led to the reinstitution of the old system. ▲

## ▲ Exercises

1.  What underlying problem was motivating planned change in the emergency room case? Was this problem a symptom or misleading? Why or why not?
2.  Develop a function expansion for the elevator case. Include at least six objectives in the hierarchy.

# The Concept Development Stage of Planned Change

**11**

▲ ▲ ▲    ▲ ▲ ▲ ▲ ▲ ▲ ▲ ▲ ▲ ▲ ▲ ▲ ▲ ▲ ▲ ▲

This chapter offers techniques that can be applied to carry out the concept development stage of a planned change process. The concept development stage is devoted to developing options or alternatives for planned change. To develop options, creativity, structuring, and choices are required. The creativity phase aids in the search for options. Structuring provides both aids for option search and synthesis. The choice phase organizes the analytical activities to separate potentially useful options, that merit further exploration, from the rest. The techniques presented in this chapter help sponsors and planners carry out the search, synthesis, and analysis needed to identify options that will be detailed in the next stage of the process.

As described in Chapters 4 and 5, sponsors initiate searches to find options that satisfy the objectives developed in formulation. Objectives and not problems guide this search to allow participants the widest possible latitude when looking for options. By opening up search in this way, the prospect of innovation is greatly increased. Innovation increases the prospect that the options considered in planned change will provide distinctive benefits to the organization (Nutt, 1984a; Damanpour and Evan, 1984; Foster, 1986). Innovation in product development can offer a company distinctive advantages in the marketplace or even launch a new firm. For instance, Rollerblade, Inc., introduced a roller skate with a single row of wheels that has launched a new sport called "blading." Its inventors envisioned a roller skate with the action of an ice skate. The product was perfected by using a ski boot atop a blade of polyurethane wheels. The initial market niche of off-season training for hockey players has grown rapidly to become a national craze. Innovation took place in several ways: imagining a new product, developing ideas that made the product a reality, and finding a market niche. The company that introduced rollerblades in 1980 now has two-thirds of its $50 million market, indicating how innovation can spark success.

## ▲  THE VALUE OF MULTIPLE OPTIONS

The literature relevant to planned change stresses the value of *multiple options*. Beginning with Dewey (1910), philosophers of science have called for multiple options. The rationale stems from the warrants cited for Kantian and Hegelian inquiring systems (IS) (see Chapter 2). Multiple options give the sponsor a way to compare and contrast the features of each option. Often these features can be merged to create a hybrid option with superior performance. Without examining multiple options the opportunities for enhancing an option would be lost.

Simon and Newell (1970) and Hogarth (1980) cite extensive research on problem solving that also supports the value of developing multiple options. Solutions improve when several different solution seeking tacks are maintained at the same time. Each tack offers a unique view and increases the chance one will provide particularly valuable results.

In practice, planned change seldom considers more than one alternative or option in any depth. People, left to their own devices, use a "progressively deepening" approach, which limits the range of options that are considered (Simon and Newell, 1970). Results improved when several ideas are dealt with simultaneously. This led

Simon and Newell to propose a "scan and search" approach in which several potentially viable options are considered at the same time. Synthesizing the best aspects of independently produced plans improves planned change results. This practice has been particularly useful when innovation is a desired plan feature. For instance, the Department of Defense routinely obtains several detailed designs for its aircraft, weaponry, and early warning systems. Considering several competing alternatives in a planned change process improves the prospects of innovation.

## Identifying Options

Approaches that can be applied to *identify options* stem from the literature in engineering, architecture, management, cognitive psychology, philosophy of science, social psychology, and still others. These literatures call for four distinct approaches called idea, search, adaptation, and design.

The *idea* approach is advocated by some management and social psychology literatures. Action research scholars, as noted in Chapter 4, assume that fully developed ideas can be found within an organization. The notion that ideas are lurking about and that knowledgeable sponsors are aware of these ideas is a common theme in the organizational development literature. Organizations are thought to have a vast store of yet-to-be-implemented plans seeking an adopter. Studies by Cohen, March, and Olsen (1976), Feldman and March (1981), and other finds that needs, ideas, and choice opportunities flow through organizations. By managing the timing of this flow a sponsor can get his or her ideas adopted. The idea theme is also found in the strategic management literature. Entrepreneurs are expected to have what Schendel and Hofer (1979) call a "key idea" when they seek financing. Founders and key executives are expected to shape organizations according to their own visions (Eisenhardt and Bourgeois, 1988). Lewin and Stephens (1990) cite John Scully of Apple and Jack Welch of General Electric as examples. As noted in Chapter 6, idea approaches have several notable limitations.

The *search* approach assumes that vendors, consultants, suppliers, and the like have ready-made solutions (Mintzberg et al., 1976). The sponsor aggressively shops for these ideas. Proposals from vendors can be compared and the best available idea adopted. As noted in Chapter 6, the search approach can produce useful ideas. This approach to option development can be dramatically improved by cyclical searches.

*Adaptation* looks for historically successful ideas (a template) that can be modified to fit the needs of the moment. Nystrom and coworkers (1976) and Hedberg (1981) note that sponsors find this approach to be pragmatic and timely, minimizing risk and cost. The template is identified using site visits to high-status organizations to find practices that can be emulated. Occasionally a key person is literally hired to install a desired practice or plan. Chapter 6 finds this approach to be useful when the best features of several templates are merged and fit the new setting.

Planners prefer, because of both inclination and training, to *design* a new scheme rather than adapt an existing system. The planner hopes that the sponsor's premises allow for innovation in operations, just as the architect hopes a building project will permit originality in creating the building envelope. When the sponsor's premises give the planner room to maneuver, the development of custom-made options is possible, which often leads to innovation. Because innovation is a key ingredient in the design approach, new ideas are sought. Creativity techniques are helpful in constructing innovative options.

Design is advocated by literature found in engineering, architecture, and cognitive psychology. Design approaches seek custom-made plans hoping that innovation will improve quality over what can be found by applying idea, search, or template approaches. As noted in Chapter 6, design is frequently carried out with little knowledge of creativity techniques. This chapter seeks to fill this void. The techniques that are offered concentrate on the development of custom-made options. These techniques also can be used to enhance the features of templates and to suggest how the ideas from a search can be melted into an improved idea, for which new proposals can be sought. The need for multiple options should be recognized in each of the three preferred approaches.

## ▲ TECHNIQUES USEFUL IN CONCEPT DEVELOPMENT

Table 11-1 identifies techniques that can be applied to devise options for planned change. Concept development has three phases: creativity, structure, and choice. Creativity techniques are applied to help participants uncover new ideas. New ideas must be nurtured in a formal way to ensure that options will be considered that have novel features. Free association creativity techniques (synectics and lateral thinking) help the participants of a planned change effort open up to new ideas and stimulate the individual's creative potential. The group process techniques discussed in Chapter 10 can also be used to develop ideas for plans, with experts as group members. Alternatively, the silent reflection group process steps can be used to manage group activities in synectics or lateral thinking.

### Table 11-1  ▲  The Sequence of Steps in Concept Development

| Creativity Techniques | Structuring Techniques |
|---|---|
| Silent reflective group process | Creating contexts |
| • NGT | • Scenarios |
| • Brainwriting | • Snowball |
| • Delphi | Identifying options |
| • NI | • Morphology |
| • Kiva | • Input-output |
| Group-based techniques | • Tree structures |
| • Synectics | |
| • Lateral thinking | |
| • Brainstorming | |
| Techniques for individuals | |
| • Attribute listing | |
| • Checklists | |
| • Relational algorithms | |

In the structural phase, ideas are organized and made explicit. The scenario technique creates a variety of important and plausible contexts in which contingency plans could be useful. Options are fashioned for each context or contingency using the morphology, relevance tree, or input-output technique. The sponsor or group then selects among these options with the techniques described for choice in Chapter 10.

Techniques useful in concept development can be merged in several ways, producing hybrids. For instance, a silent reflective group process was suggested to manage group activities in synectics and lateral thinking. Snowball can be added to derive themes in solution ideas to create options. Merging techniques in this way creates hybrids that can be selected for particular kinds of applications (see Chapter 13).

The creativity and structural phase can be carried out by individuals or groups. Groups are preferred, because groups have more creative potential, if properly managed. However, circumstances may arise that call for individuals to devise options.

## ▲ THE CREATIVITY PHASE

Creativity is often an important part of option development. Pioneers in creativity find that combining and recombining past experiences and distortions of that experience create new patterns, configurations, and arrangements that provide better solutions (Whiting, 1958). The creative process is not perceived by the individual and so it is not communicated to others (Weber, 1985). Although there is no accepted theory of creativity, creativity can be stimulated. Creativity techniques have been successfully applied for many years (Summers and White, 1986).

The record of creativity techniques is impressive. The 13 fastest-growing companies in the United States use formal programs to encourage creativity. General Electric uses formal creativity techniques routinely in product design, after finding that graduates of creativity courses had three times as many patents as nongraduates. Many believe that the crucial problem of the next decade is to connect innovation with a firm's products and markets. Fresh ideas are becoming a precious commodity. Nevertheless, there is no evidence that creativity techniques are routinely used in planned change because there is little knowledge of these techniques in most organizations.

Summers and White (1986) make several claims about the role of creativity. These claims are adapted to planned change and summarized as follows:

1. An increase in the number of options improves the prospect of finding a good one.
2. The typical planned change process does not develop unusual or novel ideas without external stimulation.
3. Identifying unusual ideas for planned change makes plan innovation more likely.
4. Challenging preconceived notions in planned change is risky in most organizations. Creativity techniques help people challenge the status quo.
5. People use only a small fraction of their intellectual skills and creativity techniques aid the individual to tap more of his or her potential.

Despite these advantages there are several impediments to using creativity techniques. Not all people are equally receptive to the environment that must be created by the leader or the openness that it facilitates. To behave in nontraditional ways is risky. To be seen as silly or naive is to be avoided at all costs in most organizations. At the onset, these behaviors seem to be encouraged so creativity techniques can be viewed with considerable mistrust. Some people lack the needed openness and others lack the intellectual skills needed to be effective participants. As a result, it is essential to select people to participate in a creativity session with care. Creativity sessions must be properly sanctioned by top management to lower the legitimate fears of the participant. When the organization formally sanctions the process, people are less likely to worry about being seen as a critic or troublemaker when being critical of the status quo.

Stein (1975) finds that people adopt one of three postures to the pressure for conformity: rebellion, creative individualism, and acceptance. Rebels are intolerant of the organization's standards, values, and aspirations. People with these characteristics either shift to one of the other postures or leave the organization. Conformity is often the norm because it is easy to justify. It is easy to accept the organization's demands and the many incentives to conform that are implicitly offered. The creative individual accepts pivotal values and standards and works for change within this context. This type of individual should be sought out for membership in a creativity group.

## Leader Selection

To ensure success, the sponsor should carefully prepare for a creativity session. (Often, it is desirable to use outside consultants skilled in applying creativity techniques.) Each technique requires particular aids and sanctions, and each session has some general requirements. First, the leader must be carefully selected or a consultant used. The planner should not take the leadership role unless he or she has, or can create, a peer relationship with members of the group. Typically, planners serve in a staff capacity to a group leader who has the required peer relationship.

Gueschka, Shaude, and Schlicksupp (1975) identify several behavioral requirements for the leader:

1. Show interest in the task.
2. Be prepared to offer insights when group activity begins to slow. Challenge the group by posing specific but difficult questions.
3. Maintain a vigorous pace of activities.
4. Encourage full participation by drawing out nonparticipants and stimulating the more reserved members.
5. Be sure suggestions are not seen as attempts to steer the group.

If not a creativity expert, the leader should be coached in the necessity of these requirements.

The session should be conducted in a location where phone calls and other distractions can be minimized or eliminated. A retreatlike atmosphere can be useful, as can a quiet and isolated room near the workplace.

## Group-Based Creativity Techniques

Several techniques have been devised to enhance the inherent creativity of people. Each stimulates an individual's mental processes, making it easier to draw on his or her creative resources. The creative process opens when the mind becomes receptive to novel ideas and closes when the mind assesses ideas (James and Libby, 1982). According to Stein (1975) jumping from one to the other is undesirable. Creativity is stimulated when people move through the following steps:

1. Problem sensing
2. Problem definition
3. Incubation
4. Insight
5. Selection

Two kinds of techniques are often used: free association and group process (Table 11-1). Under the group process category, techniques such as kiva, Delphi, brainwriting, NI, and NGT can be used. The creative phase would be carried out in the same manner as described for formulation in the last chapter, except that the nominal question deals with creating new ideas, rather than identifying priority problems or objectives. Experts, rather than users, make up the kiva, Delphi, brainwriting, NI, or NGT groups in concept development.

Free association techniques that have a particular value in developing novel options are brainstorming, synectics, and lateral thinking. The brainstorming technique, described in Chapter 10, can be used in concept development to identify solution ideas with experts as group members. The discussion that follows describes the synectics and lateral thinking techniques and how they can be used to develop novel ideas.

## The Synectics Technique

The synectics technique was devised to promote creativity for situations in which new ideas are essential (Gordon, 1961). The facilitator uses the technique to get a group of experts to visualize a new perspective and purge preconceived notions. Participants study analogies or metaphors to come up with innovative ideas. In the final step, ideas are modified to make them feasible. Velcro fasteners were identified using this procedure. Their widespread use in apparel stemmed from a proposed, but impractical, application for space suits.

In synectics, creativity stems from the use of analogies and metaphors in a systematic framework to deal with both strange and familiar problems. To enhance comprehension, a metaphor or an analogy is used to make the unfamiliar familiar. Obvious responses cause people to embrace quickly the conventional and not seek the innovative. In such instances, the metaphor or analogy is used to move the problem the distance needed to visualize innovative ideas, making the familiar unfamiliar.

In planned change, synectics can be applied to discover new options, solutions, or remedies. The use of analogies in carrying out these excursions is the heart of the procedure used in synectics. The process of innovation is both emotional and intellectual. Synectics seeks to engage a person's preconscious and unconscious to draw out emotional and nonrational linkages through the use of metaphors.

An analogy or a metaphor has been the key to many important discoveries. For example, Einstein used an image of himself riding on a ray of light to develop the theory of relativity. Composers, such as Mozart and Tchaikovsky, were found to have drawn on images from dreams before composing their best work. Handel claimed to have had visions of God before he wrote "The Messiah." Mental rehearsal has become a key aid in improving athletic performance (Garfield, 1985). Olympic diving coaches have divers repeatedly think through each motion that they will use, concentrating on producing a perfect score for each dive. Other uses include the relief of chronic pain and fear management. Images have been used to help cancer patients decrease pain intensity and to reduce fears in patients with phobias.

Several innovative organizations have sprung from imaging a new way to do things. For example, Banana Republic found new ways to sell clothing using a catalog. Analogies (the popularity of movies, such as Out of Africa) were used to identify what they thought would sell (safari clothing). They also found out what sold at flea markets and used clothing stores and reproduced these items for sale by catalog. Analogies were also used to find new ways to present their wares. Catalogs were thought to all look alike: glossy photos of glossy people in glossy clothes. The founders looked for something that would speak to a buyer. They tried writing and art, using analogies to their disciplines of journalism and illustration: the ability to get things done fast and to get to the bottom of things. In five years the operation has grown from a cottage industry to one of the most demanded stores in malls today.

The 3M Company in Minneapolis asks employees to devote 15 percent of their work schedule to nonjob related tasks, called "skunk work duty." Skunk work ideas created "Post-it" notes, three-dimensional magnetic tape, and disposable masks that have led to new products. 3M has set a goal of 25 percent revenues from such ideas in the next five years, indicating the importance attached to creativity by this company.

Hewlett-Packard is spending two years and $40 million to create a factory of the future. Employees will be hired according to their creative potential. Clearly creativity will be an important facet in the armament of well-run companies in the future.

### Synectics Teams and Facilitators

To be successful, synectics teams should have expertise, motivation, and willingness to seek new ideas. A key criterion is expertise, including only people able, both psychologically and intellectually, to deal with the demands of new ideas. Group members should have a high energy level and flexibility. Those with demonstrated ability to generalize, seeking the broader picture in a problem, make good group members. In addition, appropriate education and job training are essential. Some potential members are excluded because they have vested interests or a low tolerance for ambiguity and others because they lack up-to-date knowledge. The synectics participant should be acquainted with all steps in the process. The typical session lasts up to four hours.

The synectics facilitator should have four characteristics: optimism, a grasp of the environment, a capacity to maintain control over personal involvement so others can participate, and a clear understanding of the synectics technique. The last requirement is key, often demanding some training.

Synectics, like brainstorming, involves the generation of ideas under conditions of suspended criticism. Attempts are made to get participants to take a trip (mental excursion) to see where their thoughts will lead. The synectics procedure directs members of the team to focus their thoughts using several approaches that can create analogies and metaphors. The excursion is charted by guideposts that aid members in visualizing responses in new ways.

### The Technique

The facilitator begins by first carefully explaining what is wanted. The synectics process is then carried out to make the *strange familiar* or to make the *familiar strange*. The mind tends to draw on a person's experiences and to force these experiences, even when strange, into recognizable patterns. Often one becomes distracted by the detail, in part because the detail can be rationalized more easily than a new experience. In this case, the synectics team is forced to generalize to bring the original (strange) image back. To make the familiar strange, distortion, inversion, and transportation are attempted. The familiar has been made strange when a workable analogy is found. Four mechanisms are used to create analogies.

1. *Personal analogy*. Members attempt to identify with elements in a problem statement. Each member tries to become the thing on which he or she is working. The identification metaphor stems from the group attempting to "relate" to the problem. The critical element in personal analogy is empathy, not role-playing. For example, to understand how a debt collection system might work, team members would be asked to imagine that they were various types of nonpayers, such as low-income people or bill shirkers, and imagine what would force payment from them. In mechanical systems, the team members put themselves in place of the system. For example, in the design of a system to reduce float on a bank, team members would imagine that they were a financial transition and move through all steps in a process from activation to various points of data entry, and finally, to termination: data storage. The personal analogy is then tested to see if it can improve the efficiency and effectiveness of operations.

   Four degrees of involvement can be attempted for personal analogs.

   *First-person factual description*. The identification rests on a mere listing of facts. For instance, imagine that your VISA card minimum had not been paid and you were contacted about the nonpayment by your bank. The bank uses a "sweet young voice" to verify that you, the nonpayer, are on the phone and then plays a recording that presents veiled threats about bank action if payment is not received. Play this situation through your mind and imagine your reaction. Does it sound like a good tactic? Why or why not?

*First-person emotional description*. The lowest order of personal identification stems from some form of emotion. The team members could imagine their reaction to the VISA office contact under various conditions, such as being unable to pay or just forgetting to pay.

*Empathetic identification*. The true personal analogy is based on kinship and attachment. Team members think about how they would feel after being contacted by the VISA office when they could have paid but had not.

*Empathetic object identification*. The identification is shifted to a nonliving object. The synectics team member visualizes the place of residence of a VISA non-payor. The personal analogy exercise helps the group become more cohesive. Good personal analogies make the other steps easier.

2. *Direct analogy*. The basic mechanism used in synectics is the direct analogy. To construct a direct analogy, facts are placed side by side and are compared. The comparison seeks to extract the similarity or likeness of one thing with another. Facts, knowledge, or technology from one field are translated to another. Things that have closely corresponding purposes or tendencies make excellent analogies. For example, knowing how certain activities or purposes are achieved in biological organisms has provided a basis for extrapolation. Bell used the human ear to design the telephone. The Wright brothers designed a stabilizing system for the *Kitty Hawk* after watching a buzzard fly. Darwin drew his natural selection theory from husbandry, realizing that selection could be random as well as planned. Laplace used the human body's self-healing processes to visualize the equilibrium found in celestial mechanics. Biological systems are a good source of direct analogies. Most operating systems must work in equilibrium, so homeostatic analogies can be useful.

   Gordon (1971) distinguishes between cognitive strain introduced by the analogy's distance and inventive elegance. For example, a new form of radar may be designable, recognizing that pigeons are sensitive to the earth's magnetic field or that blind African freshwater fish create an electrical field that can distinguish between predators and prey and can communicate to others of its species. This degree of elegance is often hard to achieve. When using synectics for the first time, analogies that have a small psychological distance from the problem are best. For difficult problems, a greater distance is desirable. As the distance increases the chance for an innovative leap also increases.

3. *Symbolic analogies*. A symbolic analogy is created when the generalized image from the first step is used. A symbol is anything that stands for something else, such as an organization's logo. Firms recognize the importance of a logo and strive to make them daring, original, and modern. Imagine the logos used by Sun Oil, CBS, Olivetti, Westinghouse, and IBM and note how they conjure up images of heraldry in our modern age.

   Labeling creates another type of symbol. For example, calling management information system (MIS) options, "people-people," "superscore," and "microscope" creates distinct images about the data to be collected by each option. The idea is to create a new inference that opens up new thought patterns.

To use a symbolic analogy, a person seeks analogy that is aesthetically appealing, if not an accurate representation. The analogy compresses the problem disregarding some, or even many, of its elements. A paradoxical or even a controversial analogy is often sought.

4. *Fantasy analogy*. Fantasies can be used to create images that offer solutions. Gordon (1971) sees them as a link between problem and solution because a new mechanism is required. The fantasy can be any unreal image or illusion, including any strange notion or whimsical suggestion. For example, Goddard's fantasies about travel to Mars, stimulated by attending the lectures of Percival Lowell at the turn of the century, led to modern rocketry. Goddard formulated the basic components of propulsion that are used today while sitting in a large cherry tree staring at the moon and imagining each step in such a trip. Einstein thought up paradoxes concerning the behavior of light and created "thought experiments" that he solved while walking in rural Italy where he worked as a patent clerk. Runners who think about winning can run faster. A fantastic analogy often emerges while the group is attempting to draw on other analogies. It may create a dead end, but it can lead to productive new directions of inquiry.

The synectics leader moves through one or several of these analogy producing steps and lists the ideas that flow from the group.

The synectics procedure has seven steps:

1. Problem as given
2. Analysis
3. Purge
4. Problem as understood
5. Excursion
6. Force fit
7. Viewpoint

*Step 1: Problem as Given*. The first step begins with a description of the problem and objective. The description should conjure up obstacles so an "opportunity to solve" posture is created.

*Step 2: Analysis*. The analysis step begins with a review of the information generated in previous stages of the planned change process. In presenting the information, the group is asked to discuss what is central or essential. For example, when the intent is to reduce the costs of billing, the group could discuss the meaning of a "bill," attempting to make the familiar strange. When the objective has uncertainty, the leader initially attempts to make the strange familiar. For example, if the group was attempting to design a management information system, the group could begin by discussing information thought to be key to decision making. In each case, the group tries to come to grips with the problems and reveal some of its elements.

*Step 3: Purge*. Immediate suggestions often stem from step 2. While seldom useful they should be verbalized. This purges the group of off-the-shelf responses and allows them to consider other possibilities. Experts in the group are called on to point out the limitation of ideas that persist, which serves as a basis to purge them. A by-product is a further clarification of the group's mission.

*Step 4: Problem as Understood.* The new group aim becomes "the problem as understood." Each person is called on to describe the problem as they see it and to offer a wishful solution. These problems-idealized solutions are recorded by the leader on a flip chart. After discussion, a direction is selected, often an amalgam of those in the list. The leader then asks the group to dismiss the problem and begin a mental excursion.

*Step 5: Excursion.* Excursion marks the beginning of the creative process. Various analogies are used to make the familiar strange. The facilitator questions each member and tries to get a response. The participants are asked to make analogies further and further from the problem. The excursion process usually takes the following course:

1. *First direct analogy*—asking for a similar analogy in a comparable field
2. *Personal analogy*—each member personally identifies with the direct analogy
3. *Symbolic analogy*—form an abstract or seemingly contradictory idea from the personal analogy
4. Second direct analogy
5. Repeat

After the analogies are listed, some can be selected for further examination. Selection can be based on inherent interest or analogies very detached from the problem or seemingly irrelevant, or the group may have information to elaborate the analogy. This is a critical step and demands both facilitator skill and insight into the problem.

*Step 6: Forced Fit.* A force fit in which the results of the final estrangement step are connected to the problem ends the inquiry for a particular analogy chain. Several such chains are used.

The analogy and the problem are connected. Members are given considerable latitude in responding, so any connection, no matter how seemingly farfetched, is permitted. The forcing stems from the link between analogy and the problem. A fantasy force fit is followed with a practical force fit. In this step, the group substitutes a practical force fit with fantasy. For instance, assume participants are working with a Trojan horse analogy to design a superior mousetrap. The fantasy force fit to this analogy is to "leave something about which mice will covet so they will put it into their nests" (Stein, 1975). For the practical force fit the group must identify materials which the mice can use to build a nest that can be treated to be lethal to mice, but not house pets or children.

*Step 7: Viewpoint.* The terminal step in the technique is the discovery of an interesting idea or a better problem understanding. To have a viable solution viewpoint, one must begin to see how to create a viable solution. The viewpoint associated with this discovery is the basis to build a solution model or to return to step 5 for another excursion, hoping to elucidate the now somewhat better understood problem.

Prince (Stein, 1975) uses a somewhat different approach, which compresses the first six steps into four: happening, forced metaphor, forced fit, and connection. In step 1, the group selects an association to get started, called a "happening." If no one can make an association, the leader returns to one of the analogies and suggests a happening. This association is dropped as soon as a participant makes a viable suggestion. In the forced metaphor step, the group considers the element to be force fit to make a dynamic connection. No limits can be used, unlimited resources are assumed, and the group attempts to make the idea work. In the next step, each person is asked to write down his or her own forced fit, with the stipulation that no practical ideas are allowed. After each person has made some type of connection, practicality is introduced.

The steps in the synectics process are summarized in Table 11-2.

## The Lateral Thinking Technique

Lateral thinking was developed by de Bono (1970, 1971, 1972) to stimulate creative thought in people. Lateral suggests a sideways movement that attempts to create new patterns of thought, avoiding the conventional patterns in straight-ahead thinking. Groups are formed following the maxims of synectics, stressing expertise, and tolerance for ambiguity.

The word "Po" is used in a brainstorminglike group to signify that the group should abandon customary thinking patterns. During this period, customary communication patterns, constraints, and logic cannot be used. Po signals the need for radical and new suggestions. Po can be used by any member of the group, or the leader, when he or she feels that the discussion has become bogged down in a traditional solution or premature assessment. Each group member must feel free to stop the group by saying "Po," and the group must agree to stop and consider the direction of discussion. The purpose of Po is to bring about a provocative arrangement of information free of value judgments. Po is the opposite of no, replacing the question of feasibility with one of fanciful speculation.

## Table 11-2 ▲ Consolidated Steps for a Synectics Group

| Creative Process | Expected Outcome | Steps |
|---|---|---|
| Step 1. Problem exploration | The unknown becomes familiar by a review of the results of problem listing and objective setting. A further reformulation of the project is possible. | Explore the initial statement of needs and opportunities and the problem definition and the objective selected. |
| Step 2. Getting away from the problem | Move away from the problem via synectics techniques that cause local and temporal distance, change of activities, or physical relaxation. | a. Direct analogies<br>b. Personal analogies<br>c. Symbolic analogies |
| Step 3. Producing problem connections | Aspects of strange notions are brought into connection with the problem by subconscious comparisons and associations. | a. Analysis of analogy<br>    b. Force-fit analogy to part of the problem |
| Step 4. Spontaneous ideas | New ways to solve the problem arise. | Solutions drawn from the connection between the problem and the analogy. |

Lateral thinking is based on the restructuring of insight; Po is a critical notion in carrying out this approach. Po and no are opposites. de Bono sees *no* as the essence of logical (linear) thinking because logic hinges on rejection or disapproval of a relationship. Lateral thinking is intended to rearrange information for the purpose of breaking out of rigid patterns. Po is what de Bono calls the basic "language tool" in this operation. It is a construction and patterning device, but never a judgment device. The function of Po is to rearrange information into new patterns or at least to modify the structure of old patterns of thought.

### Steps in Lateral Thinking

Intermediate impossible, random juxtaposition, and challenge for change are the three steps often found in lateral thinking sessions. One, two, or all three of these steps can be used.

*Step 1: Intermediate Impossible*. The first phase is similar to brainstorming. The group members are asked to suspend judgment, avoiding the tendency to evaluate or attach value judgments to ideas as they are suggested. The rationale cited in the brainstorming literature applies. New ideas are more likely in a setting free of premature evaluation where people avoid making value judgments about one another's ideas. Even when ideas are silly, a person's critique discourages others to contribute, thereby thwarting potentially viable ideas. People often suggest several silly, unworkable, or politically naive ideas before offering one that is highly creative.

The habit of instant evaluation can be broken by just asking people to suspend judgment and discourage those who inadvertently slip into this posture. First, the leader briefs the group on the benefits of creativity and how premature evaluation and value judgments stifle it. Get the group to agree on the premise; this gives the leader the sanction needed to discourage evaluative behavior when it occurs.

The new twist offered by lateral thinking is to have the group consider the situation in the most outrageous way possible to see where it leads. The stage can be set in a variety of ways, including the synectics technique. For example, one of the four analogies can be used to create a new context for thinking. The leader can come prepared with several ways to view the problem and offer one to start the session, shifting to the others as needed. For example, to improve the speed of admitting in a hospital, the leader could ask the group to imagine patients on a moving belt and ask the group members how they would get needed information from the patients. Another view could eliminate all people from the admitting process and imagine instructions that allowed patients to complete the forms themselves. The basic ideas are made more elastic by gradually slowing the moving belt or inserting people into the admitting process, first to check the forms and then to deal with exceptions (e.g., the senile or incapacitated patient).

*Step 2: Juxaposition*. Step 2 seeks to create new arrangements or information patterns. This step in the process can be likened to the synectics approach to make the familiar strange. The leader attempts to force a new relationship by reversing the logic of an idea. For example, in nonrandom juxtaposition, the group could be asked to imagine the hospital without an admitting department and asked to list the problems that would occur. After listing each problem, the more important, such as no insurance (billing information) and no attending physician, must be dealt with, assuming that the admitting department has been disbanded.

Such a process provides a starting point for discussion different from the typical approach that would attempt to patch up problems in admitting that were identified in the formulation stage. The random juxtaposition approach assumes that the linkup of solutions and problems is more apt to be innovative when new entry points into thinking about the problem are forced. A new entry point is more apt to tap the brain's vast store of information. This store must be tapped in a new or unique way to avoid stereotypical responses.

Alternatively, this approach can be used by asking members of the group to make the juxtaposition. The random juxtaposition occurs when a person dissociates traditional values in a producer-product relationship and asks for a new view of a problem. For example, automation may be suggested to reduce company cafeteria costs. The leader asks the group to think of other ways cafeteria costs can be reduced *and* increased. Those things that increase cost are candidates for minimization, and those that decrease costs are candidates for synthesis into a solution.

*Step 3: Challenge for Change.* The leader conducts a direct attack on dogmatic suggestions and the assumptions behind them. The leader challenges each idea, but does not reject it, asking the group to alter it in some way to make it innovative. The response to the challenge may also be challenged by the leader or any group member. The challenge must be interpreted as agreeing that the original idea is good, but it may lack innovation. For instance, assume that the formulation stage identifies improving poor information flow in the hospital as the project objective. Someone in the group suggests that all information sources in the hospital should be merged and computerized. This suggestion can be challenged, contending that computerization would have little value because medical records are little more than physician control systems. For instance, a patient in a surgical intensive care unit has his or her respiration, spirometry, temperature, pulse, blood pressure, and a host of other factors recorded every hour or so, so that a physician can verify that the nurse looked in on the patients, not because this information has much intrinsic value. The idea of records computerization can be retained only by deleting all physician control information.

The leader asks what information remains in the medical record. This information is also challenged, leading to a parsimonious list of important information, such as laboratory results and treatment procedures that demand the immediate attention of hospital personnel. Important information, with intermediate speed requirements, such as billing, and important information with modest need for speed, such as budget variances, can be placed in a "nonreal-time" category, being extractable perhaps monthly. The solution has two dimensions: (1) information items, showing how treatments and laboratory information must flow to billing, which, in turn, provides the basis for (2) retrospective management review of revenue and cost performance.

De Bono lists four guidelines for facilitators carrying out lateral thinking:

1. New pattern creation
2. Old pattern challenge
3. Pattern disruption
4. Provocative information merger

### New Patterns

Our everyday experience puts everything into a pattern. When faced with a problem, we search our memory for a pattern or look for a pattern in the environment that leads to a solution. Po disrupts information from memory and the environment, forcing the use of different information sources. To create new patterns, four techniques are applied:

1. Juxtaposition
2. Random words
3. Disconnected jumps
4. Construction

*Juxtaposition.* The simplest use of Po is to force an interaction between two apparently unrelated things. No relationship is implied—indeed, there is no reason to put them together except to create a flash of insight. For example, De Bono suggests "computers Po omelettes." This juxtaposition stimulated computer cooking with a central store of recipes that could be dialed by telephone.

*Random Words.* Instead of linking two unrelated words, a random, unrelated word is introduced into a stream of logic. To be effective, the choice of the word should have no apparent rationale.

The leader introduces the concept by indicating the need to eliminate cliched patterns of thought and stimulate new ideas. The random word is selected to break the old pattern and attempt to provoke new ideas. Suppose the word "chaos" is selected. When the leader says, "Po chaos," the word is used as a point of departure in the discussion.

*Disconnected Jumps.* In learning, thinking jumps are sequential. Lateral thinking fills in gaps as the disconnected jump is being made. The word Po is used to signal the disconnected jump.

*Construction.* Any framework can be constraining. In lateral thinking artificial constructions are eliminated. For example, consider a plan to improve management practices. The group could be asked to imagine a society without supervisors. Altering the problem in this way forces the group to deal with nontraditional means of management.

The lateral thinking group is allowed to arrange information in any way its members choose. Attention is shifted from the rationale behind something to the gestalt of the statement—its contextual influences. During such a session, the leader attempts to deal with doubt, error, and premature judgment. Doubt blocks creative thinking. Denial behavior must be discouraged. The fear of being wrong or making what proves to be an error keeps the group members from switching attention from why something seems wrong to how it can be insightful. Finally, Po can be used to withhold judgment as well as to protect "wrong" ideas.

### Challenge Old Arrangements

A second use of Po is to challenge established patterns, question the validity of these patterns, disrupt the pattern, and restructure the pattern. Several steps are used:

1. Cliche patterns
2. Focusing
3. Alternatives
4. No counteraction
5. Divisions

*Cliches*. De Bono sees all patterns as cliches because their value inevitably leads to overuse. A *cliche* is defined as some building block that is seen as basic. For example, accepting that all treatment stems from a physician's diagnosis or that hospital administrators are resource coordinators because they lack control over the terms of hospital inputs and outputs (patient admitting and discharge) are cliches in health care industry. The manager may not always be right, but he or she is always the manager is a cliche frequently offered to block change in industry. Po breaks the cliche. The most "useful" pattern has the highest priority for being broken up.

*Focus*. The challenge to the cliche must be specific. The challenge repeats what is being questioned and prefaces the remark with Po. For instance, "Po managers being right" or "Po physician-based treatment." Po is used to focus on something being taken for granted in discussion.

*Alternatives*. Unreasonable alternatives, those that seem unsatisfactory or even absurd, can be used when a current system is unsatisfactory and the group continues to use it as an analogy. Po is used as an invitation to use another image in proposing a solution.

*Counteraction*. The use of no is prohibited. Po is used whenever the no logic crops up in the discussion. Po is used to move beyond the correctness labeling, which is implicit in the no statement. For example, someone contending that we must consider the manager's views can be dismissed with a directive to proceed (Po the manager) as if the manager could be replaced at will.

De Bono points out that people often make what prove to be untenable assumptions. For instance, man was thought to be unable to fly because all airplanes are heavier than air. He cites one expert who claimed that putting men on the moon would require a million-to-one ratio of rocket to payload. New fuel technology changed the ratio.

*Divisions*. De Bono claims that divisions is the first step toward rigidity. Divisions, classifications, and categories are rigid pigeonholes that become permanent and implicit assumptions about a problem structure. Po is used to challenge all divisions so a full consideration is possible.

### Pattern Disruption

The walls that have been built up between concepts should be torn down. The level of development of an old idea is compelling because its structure is well developed, compared with a new idea. However, this structure often limits creative thought. Po forces multiple ideas.

In this context of old patterns, Po becomes a generative mechanism. It is used when cliche patterns, premature focusing, tired alternatives, artificial divisions, or singular concepts emerge in discussion. It is never used as a negation or an evaluation. Instead, it signals the need to sidestep a direction and take a new tack. It permits the leader to challenge information use and to introduce new information at will. It provides an escape from the rigidity of assumptions about solutions that limit the scope of inquiry and stabilizes the discussion by making the bizarre not only possible but desirable. This sanctions new patterns that have been found to generate new ideas. Once a new pattern has emerged, it is developed with vertical thinking until conventionalism emerges. This signals a return to the Po tactics until restrictive assumptions are again cleared away. The facilitator moves between Po and no tactics to draw out a new representation of the planned change problem.

### Merger

The techniques of merger are provocation and rescue. To be provocative, the juxtaposition and random word techniques are used. To rescue, the leader protects the innovation idea or theme.

De Bono sees creative thinking as a skill that can be developed and improved by using lateral thinking. A group leader with this skill stimulates attitudes and habits that promote innovation.

## ▲ CREATIVITY TECHNIQUES FOR INDIVIDUALS

The idea generation techniques discussed to this point are applied by groups. The benefits of using groups for developing options are compelling, suggesting that groups should be used whenever feasible. In those cases in which groups cannot be used, due to time constraints or limited access, techniques that can be applied by individuals are provided. These techniques can be applied in place of or as an adjunct to the efforts of a group. As with group techniques, creativity can be applied to uncovering problems, identifying objectives, and establishing criteria, as well as generating solutions.

Attribute listing, checklist, and relational algorithm techniques are described. Each has features that can enhance group techniques but were developed to help the individual working alone.

### The Attribute Listing Technique

Attribute listing has been used for nearly 60 years (Crawford, 1954). It is similar to the juxtaposition step of lateral thinking. The technique is built on the assumption that most ideas are based on previously devised ideas that are modified in some fashion. Van Gundy (1981) shows how a ratchet screwdriver was developed by changing the attribute of power from turning to power by pushing to drive a screw.

The procedure calls for the following steps:

1. Conduct a problem and objective review
2. Make a list of component parts of the problem, objective, object, or problem-related idea
3. List attributes of each component
4. Systematically modify the attributes to meet the objective or deal with the problem

To develop an improved hammer (the objective), for example, components that deal with primary functions are considered. These could include the hammer's handle, head, head-handle attachment but not its color (Van Gundy, 1981). Attributes for each component are then listed. For the head, shape and composition are considered, such as fiberglass, and plastic combined with ways to shape the handle to fit the human hand. Other attributes for the head and attachment of head to handle could also consider shape and composition to create new options for a hammer. Attributes can be considered one component at a time or jointly, as in this example. The options could be evaluated against performance criteria such as split resistance for the handle, ease of use, and the handle's resistance to loosening from the head.

Variations on this technique have been used by inventors to get ideas for new products. One attribute at a time is attacked, allowing any substitutes, no matter how outrageous, to be used in place of a traditional attribute. Rabino (1988), who at one time had more U.S. patents than any other inventor, uses a variation of this technique, systematically working through key components by changing key attributes. For instance, his automatic headlight dimmer was devised by concentrating on ways to distinguish between the oncoming headlights of another car and other sources of light and reflections.

## The Checklist Technique

Checklists are widely advocated in engineering (e.g., Hall, 1977, Chap. 4). Applications of the technique have been limited to new product development, but could also be applied to services and still other applications.

The technique calls for a list of ideas that are checked against a problem or objective. Various checks are then suggested. For instance, to carry out product improvement, the following list is used to stimulate new ideas (Davis and Scott, 1978):

1.  Add or subtract something
2.  Alter color
3.  Change material
4.  Rearrange components
5.  Alter shape
6.  Change size
7.  Vary style or design features

Osborn (1963) suggests a more general list:

1.  *Adapt*—determine what other product (service, operation, etc.) is similar.
2.  *Modify*—list ways to change the product, service, or operation.
3.  *Magnify*—list ways to add to the product, service, or operation.
4.  *Minify*—list things that can be removed from the product, service, or operation.
5.  *Substitute*—list ways to eliminate the product, service, or operation.
6.  *Rearrange*—list ways to alter the composition of the product, service, or operation.

7. *Combine*—list components that could be combined to form a new product, service, or operation.
8. *Reverse*—list ways to deal with a reversal of the problem or objective (e.g., how can we decrease sales or reduce utilization). The "reverse list" suggests things to avoid or ideas that could be modified to have a reverse effect, such as changing features of the organization that lower sales force morale and reduce sales to features that can increase morale and sales.

Checklists are simple to use and help one to identify variations of existing ideas that might easily go undetected. They are less likely to produce breakthroughs because the technique uses a current idea or solution to launch the study of improvements. This technique can also be used to supplement another technique, such as synectics, that has fewer restrictions.

## The Relational Algorithm Technique

This technique compensates for limitations in human memory that make it difficult to compare several things at the same time. To stimulate the identification of new ideas, Crovitz (1978) suggests several lists of relational words:

| | | | | |
|---|---|---|---|---|
| about | before | near | out | 'til |
| across | between | not | over | to |
| after | but | now | round | under |
| against | by | of | so | up |
| among | down | off | still | when |
| and | for | on | then | where |
| as | from | opposite | though | while |
| at | if | or | through | with |
| because | in | | | |

Van Gundy (1981) extends the list as follows:

| | | | | |
|---|---|---|---|---|
| above | behind | beyond | past | upon |
| along | below | during | since | within |
| amid | beneath | except | throughout | without |
| around | beside | into | toward | |

To use the words, the technique calls for

1. Conducting a problem/objective review.
2. Inserting a relational word between each problem/objective element pairs.
3. Examining for ideas.

Consider the hanging ropes problem (Drucker, 1945). There are two ropes hanging from the ceiling, some distance apart. There is a small hook at the end of one rope on a small ring at the end of the other. The task is to connect the ropes. The distance between the ropes makes it impossible to reach both at the same time. Considering the components of rope and hand, combinations of rope-rope and rope-hand are formed. The rope-rope combination yields "rope across rope,"

"rope under rope," and "rope to rope." The rope-hand combination yields "rope against hand," and "rope in hand." Such combinations suggested the solution of swinging one rope and then grabbing it to attach the other.

The technique is tedious to apply, but it does force one to consider systematically ideas that are often overlooked. To decrease the tedium, Van Gundy (1981) suggests that the relational word be applied in units of ten or so and that a competition be created in which two people try to use the same set of ten words and compare their results.

# ▲ THE STRUCTURAL PHASE

Creativity techniques identify ideas that may serve as a solution or remedy. The structural phase assembles these ideas into a picture or a workable structure and teases out logical extensions that also provide new ideas. Structuring techniques describe the novel relationships and eliminate inconsistencies. These techniques are classified as holistic and reductionist. A "holistic" approach guides the breakdown of a focal system by decomposing an existing or imagined system (Weiner, 1945; Singer, 1959; Ackoff and Emery, 1972). To preserve important synergistic elements, the system is split at places where interactions among its components are the weakest (Simon, 1969). For example, in many large companies, the recruitment, retention, training, assignment, and performance evaluation of engineers have many synergistic relationships in a planning system for human resources.

A holistic technique is concerned with dependence and synergism. Synergy occurs when the whole is greater than the sum of its parts. Synergism stems from dependencies among components, such as the need to share information that describes plans for salesperson training and product advertising. Viewed structurally, when systems are subdivided, something is lost. The holistic approach attempts to deal with the largest possible system to preserve its synergistic nature.

Holistic thinking also contends that the solution to one problem has much to do with the solution to another (Churchman, 1979). Put differently, during planned change one must account for the interconnected and overlapping nature of problems identified in formulation. To think about a system, one first considers its purpose and then asks what are its constituent elements, not the other way around. The objective imposes constraints, determines resources, suggests components, and indicates how to manage.

In the Aristotelian or "reductionist" view, the whole is assumed to equal the sum of its parts or to provide an adequate approximation. Analogs to existing systems are applied to identify components that are assembled to create options. These analogs are often based on careful analysis of existing problems in operating systems. For example, when faced with a need to plan a quality-control unit, the typical sponsor visits organizations thought to be similar to visualize how such a program operates. Each control system that is observed serves as an analog.

Two processes can then be applied: enrichment and association (Morris, 1967). Enrichment is based on the elaboration of very simple models. Association stems from an analogy to previously developed solutions. To refine the working model of a quality-control unit, enrichment and association techniques begin with a composite of several related facilities and operating procedures and gradually shape the plan to fit perceptions of local needs. The planned change process becomes a learning experience.

Others build an analog model by specifying the input, output, and transform for each component of an existing or related system. For example, a quality-control program can be designed, using an input-output approach by specifying quality standards (outputs) and inspection procedures (transforms) for each test that is needed (inputs). Aggregated, the proposed inspection procedures provide a descriptive model of the quality-control program. Techniques like "input-output" describe existing systems to suggest alternative plans. Simon (1969) calls this the "in-out" strategy, which he contrasts with decomposition strategies that rely on an "out-in" approach to develop the conceptual model.

A holistic technique takes "out-in" perspective, emphasizing the big picture. A reductionist technique has an "in-out" perspective and builds up an argument through the matching of logic flows. Techniques that fall into each category are presented. Scenarios and morphology (holistic techniques) and tree structures and input-output (reductionist techniques) are discussed. These techniques can be used by individuals and groups, when aided by a group process (see Chapter 10). Scenarios and snowball (see Chapter 10) are useful to create contexts in which idea development can occur. Morphology, trees, and input-output are helpful to describe options within a given context.

## The Scenario Technique

Scenarios were developed to explore the plausible implications of military, diplomatic, and sociotechnical crises. For example, Kahn and Weiner (1967) laid out the features of a postindustrial society in their work "Toward the Year 2000." In this study, the emergence of the Organization of Petroleum Exporting Countries (OPEC) was not anticipated, making much of Kahn and Weiner's speculations invalid, pointing out the importance of valid assumptions in a scenario. Assumptions must be teased out and verified whenever possible. For example, in the "limits-to-growth" argument Meadows and his group (1972) extrapolated high, medium, and low resource use per capita, with various growth assumptions, in both the developing and developed countries. Each assumed level of resource use creates an alternative future with certain implications. In this case, the projections found that growth cannot continue at is present pace without the infusion of vast new sources of energy.

Today, both government and private industry are finding it necessary to devise scenarios to visualize alternative futures as a basis to plan. Each scenario specifies a variety of political-technological situations that define contingencies to be considered in planned change. This approach reduces the risk inherent in carrying out planned change with just one future in mind. Scenarios explore several futures that may occur and raise important issues that must be considered in the planned change process. In this sense, most planning is contingency based because it is done in the face of a turbulent and partially understood environment.

A scenario describes environments or situations in which the systems to be planned have to operate. In writing a scenario, a search for likely and significant future events is made. One typically starts with a current situation and extrapolates to identify other possibilities. Plausible future events are identified, but predictions are not made. To justify the construction of scenarios, the planned change process must have considerable importance and be faced with uncertainty, after problems and objectives are identified.

Waddington (1977) describes a scenario constructed to indicate how war could break out in central Europe. The steps were as follows:

1. Unrest leads to violent incidents in East Berlin.
2. General agitation in the populace increases and spreads to East Germany.
3. The Berlin wall is opened at several points by East German insurgents.
4. Limited intervention by West Germany "volunteers" occurs.
5. Soviets deliver warnings to West Germany and NATO.
6. And so on.

Note how each step is a plausible outgrowth of the previous one. Also note how the triggering event is no longer possible, which makes the entire chain of events implausible. Pivotal assumptions call for considerable testing to ensure that they are both likely to occur and significant if they do.

The technique helps one to explore the development of a crisis, suggesting which situation could benefit from a contingency plan and what contingencies should be present to activate the plan. Scenarios also lay out several social-technological futures for which plans should be constructed. For example, a scenario could be used to identify future city traffic possibilities in order to plan public transportation for the city.

The search for solutions can become quite complex when conditions facing the organization are difficult to visualize. Scenarios are used to deal with this complexity by windowing the search for solutions. Each "window" in the scenario provides an arena in which to do search, focusing, and simplifying the hunt for responses. Scenarios provide a way to *frame* the search.

Scenarios are constructed as a contingency framework that specifies how various possibilities combine to produce a variety of political, technological, or external event situations in which planned change may have to function (Vanston et al., 1977). Different options emerge when each of these possibilities is used as context for planning. Organizations use scenarios to pick out contexts for contingency planning. For instance, what if Medicaid began to reimburse using the local Blue Cross plan's rates or Medicaid payment delays double? Or what if key suppliers of petroleum-based raw material increase their prices because deranged despots in the Middle East wage war against each other and threaten oil supplies? The "what if" question is the most basic form of scenario construction, and it often stops with a "business as usual" condition. This provides several situations to consider. The status quo is included as a baseline to gauge the implications of the other situations.

### Illustrating Scenarios

The simplest form of a scenario is constructed by contrasting high and low levels of two crucial factors. For example, several types of organizations, such as mental health centers and publicly funded hospitals, like those in the state of Mississippi, face contingencies that can be defined in terms of prospects for new clients and the amount of support for local levies. The two-by-two representation in Figure 11-1 identifies four situations. The best case scenario—successful marketing to new clients and the enactment of a levy—calls for a "generic user" strategy. The focus of such a strategy is to identify new programs or services that fit within the aims of the mental health center or hospital. Fee-for-service and publicly funded poverty patients must coexist under any proposed strategy. Coexistence and new initiatives become the frame within which plans are sought. If neither marketing nor efforts to increase the levy size are successful, a worst case situation results, calling for "cutback" management. Priorities are set for clients' needs. Low-need, nonpaying clients would be dropped along with their providers. "Reimbursement" plans are sought that maximize revenue from sources that provide publicly supported care. Programs and services can be offered if they produce additional revenues or if reimbursement from third-party payors (e.g., Medicaid) will be sufficient to cover the costs of the other services offered.

The other cells of Figure 11-1 produce mixed outcomes, in terms of desirability. A "public service" approach would be adopted if the levy increases the level of support and marketing fails. The plan would call for the expansion of free care. Attention would be directed toward high-need groups that lack means, such as the severely retarded that are educable for a mental health center. A second mixed case occurs when the levy increase fails but marketing suggests that new fee-for-service clients can be obtained. A "lean and mean" context results in which plans would stress cost-effective responses to new users. Industry-based programs are tested to ensure that these new services and programs, such as mental health education and drug testing services, will be revenue producers and low cost. Such a plan would dramatically change the makeup of the center, calling for retraining and a substantial number of new hires.

EFFECTS OF MARKETING ON DEMAND

|  | Small | Large |
|---|---|---|
| Small | Cut back management | Lean and mean |
| Large | Public service | General user |

LEVY SIZE

Figure 11-1  ▲  Defining Scenarios for Growth

Adapted from Nutt and Backoff (1992).

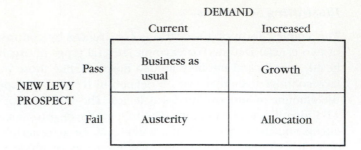

**Figure 11-2** ▲ **Defining Scenarios for Decline**
Adapted from Nutt and Backoff (1992).

The sponsor can look for the common threads in these four plans and treat the remaining as options that could be used if the contingencies shown in Figure 11-1 occur.

By altering the definition of the factors slightly, new interpretations emerge. For example, consider the scenario shown in Figure 11-2. In this example, the levy prospects can be treated as pass/fail. This situation applies to many public organizations that face the loss of public funds and seek to maintain their mission, such as libraries or publicly funded children's services. The levy could fail or pass and demand could grow or remain constant. The current situation creates a BAU or "business as usual" context in which to search for options. Levy failure–current demand and levy failure–increased demand create "austerity" and "allocative" planning contexts. Only the passage of a levy and increases in demand would permit a "growth" context in which to devise options.

A scenario applicable to a variety of organizations is shown in Figure 11-3. The categories apply to utilities, nonprofit hospitals, many banks, and other organizations in which the economic situation is expressed in terms of regulatory control of markup, limits on profit allowed, or caps to charges or budgets. These organizations are facing key environmental contingencies, given by the prospect of changes in markup and by changes in the demand for their services. In a utility, the economic situation is determined by a "public utility commission" that sets rates and other policies, such as shutoffs, that influence the level of recoverable costs. The impact of these rulings produces an economic situation in which plans must be devised. A second crucial factor is expected demand. When a "business as usual" attitude prevails and increases in the demand for power are forecasted, a best case scenario results that allows the utility to engage in capacity enhancement. In no other situation is capacity enhancement relevant as a plan. The worst case is observed when the acts of regulators result in reduced markups and increases in demands for power occur. Cost reduction programs may be needed to deal with this contingency. New programs or initiatives are needed when normal markup is maintained in the face of conservation that leads to reduction in use. Advertising—showing the benefits of using a particular form of power—is one kind of response. Allocative and adjustive strategies are called for when profits are squeezed. Who gets what becomes a key issue, calling for an allocative strategic response.

ENVIRONMENT

|  | | Business as usual | Change |
|---|---|---|---|
| DEMAND PROSPECTS | Increase | Capacity enhancement | Austerity plans |
| | Decrease | New program initiatives | Adjustive and allocative |

| Segment | BAU* | Change |
|---|---|---|
| Government | Flat budget | Decreased budget |
| Utilities | Old arrangements | Projected profit shortfalls |
| Banks | Stable discount rates | Increases in cost of money |
| Hospitals | Reimburse on charges | Reimbursed on costs with deductibles |

\* Business as usual, signifying a forecast or prior experience.

**Figure 11-3  ▲  Scenarios Relevant to Several Types of Organizations**

Adapted from Nutt and Backoff (1992).

Ways to treat BAU and change situations in several other industry segments are also shown in Figure 11-3. For instance, governmental agencies such as the National Aeronautics and Space Administration or the National Science Foundation may face flat or falling budgets. Other examples include utilities with profit shortfalls, banks facing increases in the cost of money, and nonprofit hospitals dealing with prospective reimbursement rates.

Three-by-three and more complex representations of future conditions that depict intermediate levels of crucial factors can be desirable. An example is shown in Figure 11- 4. In this case, a company is introducing a new product line that depends on petroleum-derived raw materials. Taking advantage of unrest in the Middle East, U.S. petroleum producers often increase their prices overnight. The sharp increase, when it occurs, is not matched with a comparable decrease when the crisis abates. As a result, a sharp price increase can occur at any time and will drive up costs for an extended period of time. Assume that past crises have increased raw material costs to a level that the product would barely break even. However, OPEC had been unable to keep its greedy members from overproducing, which can drive down the price of raw materials. Some forecasters call for significant price declines by the time the product is introduced because of a worldwide oil glut. Others see no change in price. This creates a price increase, business as usual,

DEMAND

|  |  | Low | BAU* | High |
|---|---|---|---|---|
| RAW MATERIAL PRICES | Decline | New marketing | Protect profit windfall | Capacity enhancement |
|  | BAU | Evaluate marketing | BAU | Back-order and lost sales tracking |
|  | Increase | Product suspension or termination | Cut-back management | Cost reduction |

\* Business as usual, signifying current experience.

Figure 11-4 ▲ Scenarios for a Petroleum-Based Product Line

or price decrease as possibilities for raw material prices in the scenario for the product.

The other factor concerns demand. Assume that economic conditions and consumer preferences combine to suggest that demand for the product line could be comparatively strong or weak, leading to dramatic shifts in revenues. In this example, demand can be termed pessimistic or low, current or forecasted, and optimistic or high. The nine contingencies in Figure 11-4 identify potentially important contexts to devise plans for the company's product line.

Combinations of the extreme values for raw material price and demand merit exploration as contingencies during planning. Increased prices and low demand create a worst case or loss situation in which a cutback in production and layoffs would be required. Plans for the temporary or permanent suspension of the product line would be needed if this contingency arises. If the oil glut continues, prices will fall, calling for plans to bolster sales, such as marketing. This mixed case contingency calls for plans to deal with demand enhancement.

High demand coupled with a decline in prices creates the best case contingency in which capacity enhancement plans could be drawn. Plans could consider two- and three-shift operations and ways to bring new production capacity on-line. High demand with high raw material prices create a mixed condition calling for cost-reduction tactics. Ways to lower costs form the basis for this contingency plan.

Four other contingencies can also arise in which only one factor exceeds or falls below forecasts. Low demand with expected prices may call for an examination of marketing tactics. High demand and expected prices create the need for a backlog system in which orders are taken and delivery dates negotiated with customers. Plans would be made to track lost sales to determine when capacity changes might be needed. Expected demand and price changes identify the final two contingencies. A drop in raw material price with expected demand creates a profit windfall. Defensive tactics may be needed to keep shareholders and others from demanding a share of what may be a temporary profit increase. Plans that target the windfall for long overdue capital expenditures is one option. An increase in raw material prices at expected demand calls for cutback management in which a lean and mean operating plan is fashioned to ride out the profit squeeze.

### Scenario Construction

The principal ingredients in a scenario are its construction, form, level, and credibility. To construct a scenario, the logic proceeds, step by step, linking happenings by causal arguments that lead to plausible futures. However, there is no clear-cut procedure that can be followed, partly because of the nature of the desired result. For instance, the demise of a Soviet-controlled Eastern Europe ushered in a new era. This may lead to new opportunities for U.S. firms to make investments in countries starved for the goods available in the West. But, if inflation soars due to oil price gouging, a cost-containment strategy is likely to be adopted. The scenario adds detail to these events to elaborate each of the four contingencies.

A scenario is no better than the information used and the knowledge applied to detail the causal links in the argument. When done well, it can be quite valuable. For example, the scenario on limited war in Iran, done by the Rand Corporation, proved to be particularly prophetic for the final days of the Carter administration. A scenario can guide the search for likely events or extreme conditions. Both are useful to gauge the value of alternatives in a plan.

Steps that can be followed to create a scenario are as follows:

1. Purpose specification
2. Team organization
3. Data gathering
4. Factor listing
5. Factor selection
6. Theme selection
7. Factor grouping
8. Defining present situation
9. Most probable future
10. Alter factors
11. Alternative scenario
12. Check
13. Revise

*Steps 1 and 2: The Initial Activities.* Steps 1 and 2 are covered by formulation and the initial phase of concept development in a planned change process. The purpose of the scenario is given by the problem and objective statements that emerge from formulation. These, along with the resources available, suggest the scope and the level of detail required in the scenario. Often, the number of scenarios and the detail of each are dictated by resource constraints. For instance, contracts let by the Department of Defense specify the number and scope of scenarios desired.

A team is drawn from the sponsor's staff to construct the scenario. Scenarios for pivotal planned change efforts with highly uncertain futures demand relatively wider participation. The scope of the effort dictates who should participate. For instance, a large construction project should involve top executives and support staff, and members of the board. Planning for a new product would include people with useful expertise in engineering, technological developments, marketing, finance, and production.

*Steps 3, 4, 5: Data and Factor Listing and Selection.* The listing of factors should be broad in scope. The list should include social, political, economic, and technological factors that may influence the future environment. For instance, trends, such as the influence of governmental action on revenues, must be understood to plan for an oil company. Trends in opening or closing new areas for oil exploration illustrate factors that make the situation favorable or unfavorable in the future. When the team is unfamiliar with the topic, the team must become familiar with useful material or involve experts to help.

To carry out steps 3–5, a formal structure is desirable. The data gathering, factor listing, and factor selection steps can be carried out by using one of the group processes described in Chapter 10. For instance, NGT, brainwriting, or Delphi can be used to organize data resources and come up with a priority list of factors. Synectics and lateral thinking can be used to elaborate scenarios when innovative factors seem essential. For example, the question posed to a group (the nominal question in NI, NGT, or brainwriting session) could be: "What factors restrict or give special opportunities to the growth of the company's capacity?" For a complex planning problem, several group processes should be used, one each to identify social, political, economic, and technical factors. Prioritization of factors can be done with inside experts (as a part of the group process) or with consultants. Choice of evaluators hinges on the uncertainty and the importance of the topic. When uncertainty is felt by insiders, consultants are desirable.

*Step 6: Theme Selection.* Selecting themes is the single most important step in scenario construction. There are many ways to visualize an environment and just a few can be detailed. Generally, three to six are used. One is the most probable; the others move away from the most probable in plausible but different ways. The themes place an approximate bound on the futures that have a fundamental influence on the organization's welfare. For instance, demand or utilization themes are often useful. Key management in the organization should have a role in theme selection.

One useful approach is to use several study groups, chaired by a sponsor, asking each group to devise a theme. The groups should use a formal group process or creativity techniques in theme identification and selection. A frequently recurring or generic theme can serve as starting points for group discussion. Examples of such themes for an oil company are the following:

1. *Import taxes.* The introduction of more restrictive import taxes to curb the use of foreign oil.
2. *Conservation emphasis.* Consumers buy energy-efficient autos, appliances, and other big-ticket items in unprecedented numbers.
3. *Regulatory change.* Environmentally sensitive areas are opened up to limited exploration, pending environmental impact studies.
4. *Governmental action.* Congress passes a bill calling for energy independence through alternative energy sources by 2010.

5. *International trade.* The blossoming East European economy demands more oil than expected, driving up the prices of crude bought on the international market.

6. *Political backlash.* The volatile price of gas at the pump calls for legislation to be passed creating an agency to regulate gas prices.

*Step 7: Factor-Theme Merger.* Key factors are identified for each theme. (Again, group processes such as NGT are useful in factor identification.) Factors are sought that make the theme consistent. The factor set is winnowed once again. Some factors may prove to be irrelevant and others may be added. Topics within the themes are identified by the winnowed factor set. For instance, consider regulatory change as the theme in an oil company's strategic plan. Factors like demand, capacity planning, and cost can be elaborated to define the themes of expanding, declining, or maintenance in the face of regulatory change.

*Steps 8 and 9: Most Likely Scenario.* These steps assign values to each factor for the current situation. Each factor is measured in terms of the current state of affairs, which serves two purposes. First, the implications of each factor are drawn out in a comparatively well-understood environment as a training exercise. Second, the factor levels serve as a baseline to measure the direction and magnitude of changes needed in the other themes. For instance, in the oil company's strategic plan, values for actual demand and their initial expectations, capacity enlargement problems, and cost forecasts are sought from experts. Values for these factors are used to prepare a statement (narrative or outline) about the present state of affairs. The statement includes relevant historical events and trends that give rise to the current practices of the company. Graphics (to display historical trends) are useful.

The current state can be used to define the most probable future state (step 9). Alternatively, forecasts can be made of each factor to make a judgment on its future value. For instance, will demand for oil products rise or fall? By how much? Formal techniques, like mathematical simulation (see Chapter 12), can be used for complex projections. The most likely scenario is composed of the forecasts made for each factor. Key assumptions should be cited.

*Step 10: Alter Factors.* The impact of each factor on each theme is considered next. Each theme is dealt with separately (or by one of the distinct scenario groups). Changes in factor level can be positive, negative, or zero. For instance, ending limits posed to oil drilling have no influence on demand but may muddy the supply picture because fewer restraints on market entry would be imposed. Following a trend that is reasonable, the factor should be changed to the point where different organizational actions result and where the factor's level is still reasonable. For instance, could supply increase to the point prices at the pump fall by 10 or 20 percent, and what are the profit implications of such changes?

*Step 11: Alternative Scenarios.* Scenarios like the most probable are prepared around each theme. Each should use the same presentation format so differences can be easily visualized. One useful approach would limit the presentation to themes where distinct differences in the factors crop up. Another would describe how the themes change with each factor. Assumptions must be clearly stated.

*Steps 12 and 13: Checking and Modification.* The final steps deal with the assessment of each scenario. The check deals with internal consistency and consensual support rather than validation. Completeness and apparent precision are checked. Modifications that improve these attributes are incorporated in the final product.

### Form

A scenario can take many forms that encompass computer language at one extreme and essays at the other. In the former, facts are extrapolated; in the latter, mood and tone become the operant descriptors. The priority problem suggests the most useful form of a scenario. If the form is quite general, broad options that are low in detail but high in their description of political and social forces are useful. If the priority problem is quite specific, one could forecast the parameters of relevant usage rates or demands and their likelihoods as required by the evaluation stage (Chapter 15). The middle ground between these extremes calls for various combinations of specific estimates and tonal descriptions of the environment.

### Levels

Operations, tactics, systems, and policies are four levels where scenarios can be constructed. *Operational* scenarios tend to focus on efficiency questions and deal with technological breakthroughs, such as scanners in hospitals that use strong magnetic fields, or the introduction of new man–machine systems, such as computer-aided design and computer-aided manufacturing.

*Tactical* scenarios consider new programs, such as a new type of management engineering department or new product-market niche in a firm, and trace out its consequences under particular assumptions. The assumptions could deal with the behavior of the organization's competition by offering the same product or service and the response to each as the organizations enter the market.

*Systems* are usually comprised of several tactical plans. For instance, the oil company's capacity plan must be merged with personnel planning, cost control, and managerial issues. A system-based scenario must tease out the market for new products, plausible problems in completing capacity enlargement on time and within budgets, and the interrelationship of the market and program components.

*Policy* level scenarios deal with the consequences that flow from key options seen as open to the executive staff of an organization. They usually involve one or more systems (e.g., a new product or service) and the reaction to the systems by key power centers in the organization's domain (e.g., its benefactors and endowers, the regulators, the reimbursers, stockholders, and the community).

Typically, one works at one of these levels. The level is usually implicit in the prescriptions for the planned change process developed in the formulation stage.

### Credibility

Validation of a scenario is both important and never fully achievable. The scenario's credibility stems from its logic and its assumptions, which depend on the effort expended in its creation. Its developer hopes that the scenario is realistic and captures the environment, but can only judge it by its face validity.

Several tests can be applied that help to tease out a scenario's credibility. One is *consistency*. Are assumptions consistent? If a company assumes that OSHA or EPA reviews will be terminated, what makes it reasonable to believe that more (or less) stringent programs will be put in their place? Another is *behavioral realism*. Good scenarios capture the most likely responses of key power centers. Asking experts if the anticipated behavior is plausible is a good check. The "would-ought" dichotomy is another test. "Would" is an imperative; for example, future governmental regulation would be less stringent. "Ought" is a hope; the government ought to enact less stringent regulation. The two are often confused, which confuses the argument.

The most quantitative evaluation can be made when a forecasting procedure is used. For instance, alternative techniques of forecasting, such as exponential smoothing or Box-Jenkins, can be used. The results suggest a range of probable outcomes. The midpoint can be selected and compared with most probable scenarios, or the extremes can be used to conduct alternative scenarios. The entire range of the forecast can be used to force the sponsor to think in nondeterministic ways. For example, if price increases at the pump are projected to be 10 percent by one technique and 30 percent by another, the range is used, not the 20 percent midpoint.

A scenario is never fully validated during a planned change process. Its value stems from the new situations discovered and the contingency plans stimulated for each.

## The Morphology Technique

The morphology technique creates many different options for systematic assessment. The technique is similar to "attribute listing" but is more comprehensive. For example, Zwicky (1968) was able to identify scores of new design ideas for a washing machine by taking all combinations of ways to provide power, agitation approaches, and rinsing (flushing).

Morphology has also been successfully used to identify alternate solutions for product design, technological innovation, market research, and social problem solving. The technique identifies potentially interesting options by dividing a problem or objective into major components and then subdividing the components further into elements. Various combinations of the elements are listed and examined as options that may provide a good response to an objective. Theoretically, the number of components and elements can be quite large, although three or four components each with three or four elements creates a large number of options to ponder.

The morphology technique is often used in product design. Consider the problem of packaging a food item (Van Gundy, 1981). The objective is to develop a package that is durable and easily opened and prevents spoilage. The components are material, shape, and closure. Elements for each are:

| *Material* | *Shape* | *Closure* |
|---|---|---|
| cellophane | square | adhesive |
| waxed paper | rectangular | snaps |
| aluminum foil | round | tabs |
| cardboard | cylindrical | clips |

A total of 64 solutions are created by this morphology. Each option can be evaluated to determine how well it meets the objective. Some, such as round cardboard containers, may have no value, but others may offer new ways to think about packaging (e.g., aluminum foils with snaps).

Turley and Richardson (1975) show how morphology was used to identify alternatives in order to meet the health needs in a large metropolitan community. Preliminary analysis found that the following components were vital:

1. Patient
2. Care type
3. Urgency of the care
4. Source of service
5. Ownership
6. Reimbursement

Elements from each component were identified. The patient was designated as privately insured or indigent. The type of care could be acute, chronic, rehabilitative, or custodial, and each type was further subdivided by its nature: convenience, urgent, or emergent. The organizational bases for the service included physicians' offices, contact centers (referral organizations), ambulatory care centers, free clinics, community health centers, hospitals (inpatient/outpatient), physician-owned clinics, nursing homes, and so on. Bases of ownership include public or governmental, private nonprofit, private profit, religious, physician, and user. Reimbursements could be based on fee-for-service or contracted annual payment.

Figure 11-5 illustrates how one can array these components and their elements in a morphology. In all, there are 2336 new community health system programs

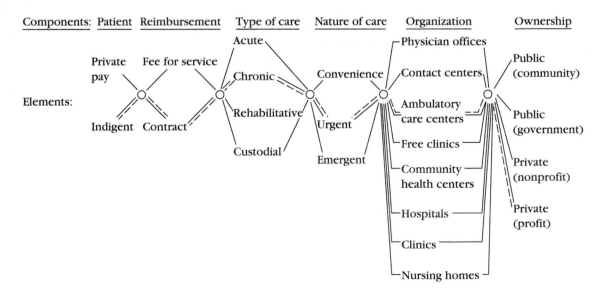

* The chart identifies 2 × 2 × 4 × 3 × 8 × 4 or 2336 options to be considered.

**Figure 11-5 ▲ Morphology Used to Derive Community Health Plan**

identified, some of which will be innovative. The dashed line in Figure 11-5 identifies one of these programs. Indigent patients served by contract could be treated for chronic conditions that are urgent in an ambulatory care center privately organized to operate for a profit. Some of these paths will have gone undiscovered. They provide a new look at how to provide a given type of care or suggest how alternative systems should be maintained to provide this care.

Wiseman (1988) developed a "strategic option generator" by applying morphology. Components critical in strategy formation for firms were found to be

1. Strategic targets
2. Thrusts against the target
3. Strategic mode
4. Thrust direction
5. Information systems

Elements for each component were then identified. Strategic targets could be customers, suppliers, or competitors. Strategic thrusts to use against the target include differentiation, cost, and innovation. Strategic modes are offensive and defensive. Directions can be usage and provision. Finally, information system skills can include processing, storage, and transmission.

Figure 11-6 (arrangement 1) illustrates how to array these components and their elements in a morphology. There are 108 ($3 \times 3 \times 2 \times 2 \times 3$) strategic options generated by the morphology.

By altering how the elements and components are defined, changes can be made, as shown in arrangement 2, Figure 11-6. In this arrangement strategic thrusts of growth and alliance are added to differentiation, cost, and innovation and are plotted against targets that add distribution channels to suppliers and customers. Competitors can be the enterprise, suppliers, channels, and customers, as well as rivals. Several such arrangements should be constructed, experimenting with the insights that are obtained before selecting strategic options for further development.

### Steps in the Technique

The morphology procedure has six steps:

1. *Performance gap*. Consider the problems defined in formulation and review the objective that was selected and the performance gap to be narrowed.
2. *Elements and component identification*. Identify elements and components upon which the objective and the performance gap depend. The components are conceptual in nature and frame the problem or set its scope. Elements identified for each component should be independent of one another. The search for elements and components can be carried out with the aid of a group process, like NGT or brainwriting, or a formal creativity technique, such as synectics or lateral thinking.
3. *Elements and components testing*. List components and elements on cards. Sort them and look for components that can be merged or separated and redundant elements or elements that are missing. Synthesize to create a parsimonious set.

Arrangement 1*

| Components: | Targets | Thrusts | Mode | Direction | Information |
|---|---|---|---|---|---|
| Elements: | Suppliers | Differentiation | Offensive | Usage | Processing |
| | Customers | Cost | Defensive | Provision | Storage |
| | Competitors | Innovation | | | Transmission |

* The chart identifies $3 \times 3 \times 2 \times 2 \times 3$ or 108 strategic options.

Arrangement 2*

| Components: | Thrusts | Targets | Users |
|---|---|---|---|
| Elements: | Differentiation | Suppliers | Enterprise (internal) |
| | Cost | Channels | Suppliers |
| | Innovation | Customers | Channels |
| | Growth | Rivals | Customers |
| | Alliance | | Rivals |

* The chart identifies $5 \times 4 \times 4$ or 80 strategic options.

**Figure 11-6 ▲ Morphology Applied to Generate Strategic Options**

Reduce the number of minor or irrelevant combinations. This can be done with or without a group process.

4. *Chart construction*. Elements and components are arranged in a chart to be systematically investigated. An alternative arrangement, suggested by Allen (1982), would cut the morphology into vertical strips, one per component. The strips can be moved to line up elements horizontally to identify options.

5. *Option search*. Identify the options. Useful options can be recorded by drawing a line on the chart through its elements. Some elements can be ruled out. Other elements are assembled around the organizing theme.

6. *Assess*. Evaluate the feasible combinations. First, the criterion of innovation is applied. All combinations that suggest a new practice are sought. This list is pruned by eliminating those combinations that are impractical or politically unwise.

### Application Issues

The key questions in morphology are the number of categories and subcategories and how to find and name them. The concept of "distance" is suggested to sort out the categories. First one lumps, then separates, to see if elements belong together. If a merger is possible, an attempt to fill in the void is made; if not, the elements are renamed. The renaming process is not trivial. The images suggested by a label often help to visualize solutions. Labels that conjure up a new representation are particularly useful. Carefully selected labels are more apt to suggest creative options.

### Merits of the Technique

Morphology has several advantages and some disadvantages. A key advantage is the structure that allows one to work systematically and quickly through a large number of options. Warfield and Hill (1972) cite the benefits of morphology as

1.  A comprehensive list of program possibilities
2.  Known components that are combined in unique ways
3.  Storing ideas for systematic analysis

They sum up by noting that, whether by inclination or lack of education, people seldom carry out systematic inquiry without external aids. The morphological chart provides an easy-to-access record of features to be examined. All possible features can be examined. Enumeration of all relevant options, which fall within the previously selected scope of inquiry, coaxes one to consider options that may otherwise be overlooked or prematurely dismissed as unworkable. Often, upon closer examination, one finds that some of these options are viable, or can be made viable with minor modifications. Gaps in service or technology become apparent, identifying goals for future work.

There are several limits to the technique. Technology is one problem. Morphology assumes that technology is available. In some instances, the innovative options depend, in part or totally, on developing new capabilities. For instance, it is hard to imagine clinics providing emergency care without new triage procedures and perhaps more automation (Figure 11-5).

A more important limitation is the necessity of having considerable content area knowledge before applying the technique. Using a creativity technique or a group process with experts helps to overcome knowledge limitations.

Proper listing of elements and components is essential. When either is superficial or nonexhaustive, a nonoptimal set of options results. There is no practical way to ensure that the components and the elements are exhaustive or that those selected are the best set to deal with the performance gap.

## Techniques Using Tree Structures

Tree structures have a hierarchy like that found in society and nature. They have a recognizable ordering of components where the components at a given level produce something unique at the next higher level. The technique is used to describe the relationships among planned change activities.

The key concept is a tree that joins elements with line segments to create a hierarchical pyramid. The tree has just one path between any two vertices, giving rise to a structure like that shown in Figure 11-7. The value of a tree is its ability to represent a wide variety of things as levels and associations between levels. Every vertex represents a concept (like an objective) and the line segment connecting the levels often represents a relational linkage. There are four types of trees: objective, activity, decision, and relevance.

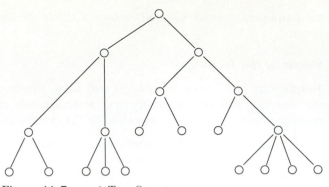

**Figure 11-7** ▲ A Tree Structure

### Objective Trees

All vertices in a objective tree are specified by objectives. The lower-level objectives contribute to the achievement of the higher-order objective. An objective is defined in the same manner as in Chapter 10 and should follow the infinitive action verb format used by function expansion technique, also discussed in Chapter 10. The objective hierarchy derived from function expansion is one of several paths through the objective tree.

To construct an objective tree, one starts at any vertex and expands both horizontally or vertically. The analyst uses logic and knowledge of the planning topic to suggest objectives and the links between them. The procedure used in the function expansion technique can be used. Like function expansion, the highest-level objective is often devoted to satisfying the higher-level needs of people. An example of an objective tree is shown in Figure 11-8.

### Activity Trees

The activity tree is constructed by using an objective tree or its equivalent as a guide to link objectives and activities to achieve them. The correspondence between activities and objectives need not be one to one. For example, the objective "decrease costs" does not require an enumeration of all conceivable cost reduction activities at the next level. Each vertex represents an activity, with several lower-level activities linked to each higher-level activity.

A typical use of an activity tree is to delineate responsibility. The highest level may be a hospital's quality assurance (QA) program. The next level can be QA projectlike activities, such as hospital utilization review, and the tissue and infection control communities. This level could be followed by information gathering, storage, and retrieval tasks. Regularly performed tasks, such as performance monitoring, and committees' developmental tasks, such as norm setting, would be shown at the next lower level. The tree is expanded until a fundamental unit is identified.

### Decision Trees

The decision tree is a graphic aid that helps to organize a complex set of consequences, each leading to various outcomes. There are three types of vertices: choice,

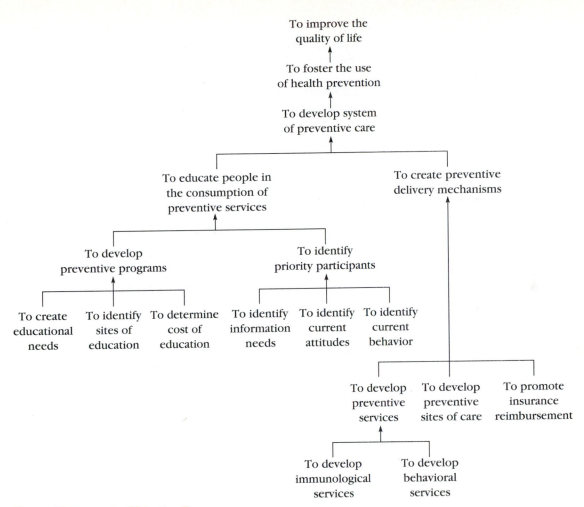

**Figure 11-8** ▲ **An Objective Tree**

consequence, and outcome. The choice vertex depicts the alternatives. The consequence vertex lays out external events that can affect the outcome, such as product or service demand being high or low. The outcome gives a utility, cost, or some other indicator of consequences for each branch in the tree. The decision tree will be described in Chapter 15.

### Relevance Trees

A relevance tree is a hierarchically ordered network that relates an overall objective to intermediate actions. As a result, the relevance tree has different types of vertices at each level in the tree hierarchy. Warfield (1990) calls this a hybrid tree because of the mixed nature of its items, moving from one level to the next. Connections from one level to another are based on the relevance one level has for another. Broader issues fall at the top of the hierarchy, narrower issues are in the middle, and very specific issues are located at the bottom of the tree. The highest level states the problem to be solved or the objective to be met. The adjacent level could enumerate the environment in which the problem must be solved, with vertices enumerating elements of the environment. The tree many terminate with lists of specific actions.

The usefulness of a relevance tree can be illustrated with an example drawn from the U.S. space program. Figure 11-9 illustrates how NASA was able to reduce the complexity of planning by enumerating activities to be accomplished. Eleven levels were used, each with several vertices, which led to the identification of over 2300 specific planning activities needed to meet our space objectives. Figure 11-10 shows a relevance tree for air pollution (Waddington, 1977). The tree is expanded to the point where practical issues that merit investigation are identified. The first step in the construction of a relevance tree is to take the higher-order objectives and

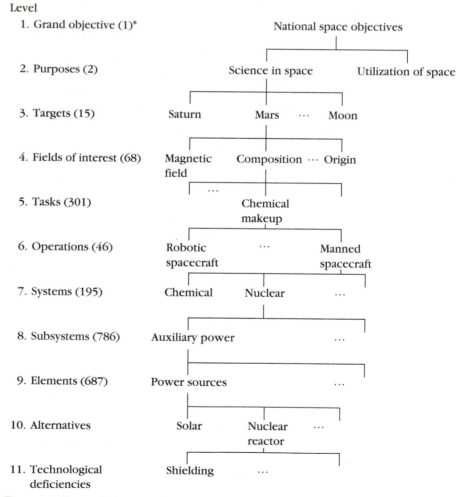

**Level**

1. Grand objective (1)*

2. Purposes (2)

3. Targets (15)

4. Fields of interest (68)

5. Tasks (301)

6. Operations (46)

7. Systems (195)

8. Subsystems (786)

9. Elements (687)

10. Alternatives

11. Technological deficiencies

**Figure 11-9  ▲  A Relevance Tree for NASA**

Reprinted from Warfield (1990).

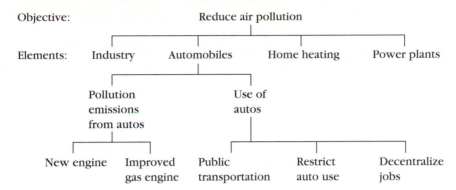

**Figure 11-10** ▲ **A Relevance Tree for Air Pollution**

Reprinted from Waddington (1977). Copyright ©1977 by the estate of the late C.H. Waddington, and Yolanda Sonnabend.

relate alternative courses of action that contribute to meeting that objective. The network identifies various pathways that permit the achievement of the objective. In the detailing stage the more promising paths are developed further. The treelike structure does not solve problems; rather, its value stems from a framework that permits the enumeration of alternatives for detailed exploration.

### Summary

The tree structures provide an insightful way to identify options for planned change. These techniques allow one to trace the implications of various options and frame policy questions and their consequences for the sponsor to ponder.

The limitations of these techniques stem from their subjectivity in creating components and estimating their importance. The subjectivity can be reduced by using the Q-sort of the vote-discuss-vote decision structure. Ranking techniques help to lower the information processing demands. Nevertheless, the value of tree techniques depends on the active participation of experts. Lack of attention to detail may plague one during tree construction, and personal biases can be hard to set aside.

## The Input-Output Technique

Input-output analysis is a technique advocated by many systems engineers and systems analysts. The basic components of a system are identified and treated like a "black box." The inputs and outputs of the component are carefully identified, but the transforms, the procedures used to convert inputs to outputs, are ignored. The input-output technique was intended to help in the design of physical devices, but is also suitable to identify the nature of key connections among components in a variety of social planning, human relations, and service sector applications.

The basic steps are

1. Specifying desired output
2. Specifying needed inputs
3. Noting limiting conditions that outputs must meet

4. Sorting out input and output relationships (outputs matched to particular outputs)
5. Linking input and output sequences until desired output is achieved, with transforms as "black boxes" (e.g., unspecified)

The input-output technique is often used to describe an *existing* system so the system can be used elsewhere. The options that are described depict various alternatives. The logic structure can also be applied to create new or *innovative* options, as the following example illustrates.

Consider the design of a fire-warning device (Whiting, 1988). The desired output is a warning and the input a fire. Constraints include size, cost, and sensitivity level of the device. Outputs linked to a fire are heat, light, and several types of gases that arise from combination and smoke. By treating the outcomes of a fire as first-order inputs, new outputs such as light and smoke emerge. The inputs converted into outputs that seem best to create a fire-warning device are used to describe the device. For instance, smoke-sensitive chemicals or something that melts below the boiling point of water could be used to trip a circuit and sound an alarm.

To describe an existing system one visits a company and describes a system or procedure of interest. Consider a hospital that needs to redesign its admitting department. To represent an admitting department in a hospital, the analyst first identifies inputs—in this instance, patients. Elaborations of the input, such as patient characteristics, may be required, but are never detailed at this point. Then what the admitting department produces, that is, its outputs are identified. As shown in Figure 11-11 several outputs are created, such as a bill, bed assignment, nursing instructions, and schedules for services (e.g, laboratory, radiology, and pharmacy). One recognizes that the admitting department uses several procedures to create these outputs, but ignores them at this point.

The "black box" approach is a useful way to model options. To illustrate the technique, assume that a sponsor stipulated the need to reduce admission time in a large, acute care hospital. The planner traces the input-output process well beyond the affected department (admitting) to determine the origin and final destination of essential inputs and outputs. The flow that follows a simplified representation of the process is shown in Figure 11-12. In each component the transforms are ignored,

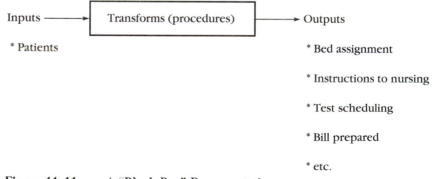

**Figure 11-11** ▲ A "Black Box" Representation

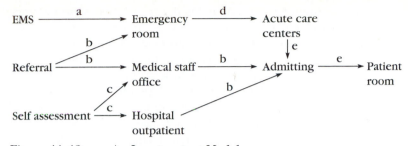

**Figure 11-12** ▲ **An Input-output Model**

Input-output codes: a, attendent judgment; b, physician judgment (outside); c, self-diagnosis; d, physician judgment (inside hospital).

and the essential inputs and outputs are enumerated. Note that the outputs to one work unit often become the inputs to others. The planner matches these inputs and outputs to trace the logic of the admissions system.

Not all components fall under the jurisdiction of the hospital. Delays in admission can stem from physicians who take the patient directly to an acute care center. For example, hospitals with a significant trauma population will experience admission delays because many patients are routed to acute care centers for immediate treatment. This suggests that the planner should look for other ways to initiate the admission procedure. Two approaches can be taken: creating an information input from the emergency room or developing procedures to do admitting locally, along with the acute care center's normal operations. This illustrates how one identifies "detailing questions" to consider in the next stage of the planned change process.

In other instances, constraints emerge. Delays in admissions can stem from doctors' offices that fail to notify the hospital of their admission plans for patients. Delays with such an origin can be reduced, but probably not eliminated, because the hospital lacks jurisdiction. The input-output model identifies these constraints so they can be dealt with during detailing. For example, forms that the physician gives a patient can be developed so information is in order at the time of admission. As similar analysis would be done for the local emergency medical service (EMS) and the hospital's outpatient personnel.

Finally, the input-output model identifies problems that stem from the transform. The input-output model suggests that a mechanism to update bed use is needed. This helps one to visualize requirements and in systemlike terms, such as the reservation approach used by airlines. To keep beds full, using the reservation system as a model, one enumerates the information inputs required and outputs that can be provided. Inputs are checked to see if the needed information can be collected and outputs tested to see how they can be used. The list of empty beds can be kept current with discharge information. If physicians make a daily list of planned discharges, the probable number of empty beds can be forecasted.

The final step has the planner develop models for essential transforms, those transforms controlled by the sponsor and found to induce system problems. In our example, transforms in the emergency department and acute care centers would be investigated. In each instance, procedures that create essential outputs would be questioned and alternative procedures posed for further study. These outputs become inputs to the admission department. New procedures in the admissions department are needed, both to process the new inputs and to reduce delays inherent in the procedures used to process essential information.

Input-output analysis captures the linkages between any set of system components, such as departments in a hospital. Rather than attacking the admitting procedures in seeking to reduce delays, the input-output technique considers how the departments can alter their outputs or provide more relevant ones to speed admissions. To change outputs, changes in the procedures used by some departments are identified for attention during detailing. Rather than viewing inputs as constraints, inputs would be modified whenever possible. Tracing patient movement reveals points at which constraints can and cannot be relaxed. For instance, patients must be moved directly to acute care centers, but information flow to admitting could be improved. The movement of the key inputs traces out a pattern of relationships that must be investigated. This trace identifies which components (e.g., departments) must be assessed in detail in subsequent planning activities.

### Summary

In large-scale applications, input-output analysis is often invaluable. The complexity of a planning effort can be overwhelming. By focusing on a pattern that traces the relationships among components of primary interest, important synergistic relationships are revealed. Also, the input-output model reduces complexity. The disadvantage of the input-output technique stems from its reliance on an existing system as a model. Templates limit innovation, as described in Chapters 4 and 6. The analysis of components of a system focuses attention too quickly. Much time can be wasted dealing with the wrong problem. Finally, a component view focuses on existing procedure, making marginal changes when more pervasive change is both desirable and possible. Nevertheless, analysis of an existing system or procedure can be a useful exercise. When many processing steps are required, breaking these steps down can be a useful way to attack systematically aspects of a procedure needing change. This attack can be assisted by applying one of the creativity techniques discussed in this chapter.

## ▲ Key Points

1. Innovation brings special advantages to an organization. Innovation creates new products (e.g., rollerblades), new internal operations (e.g., procedures for quality control or billing), and new policies (e.g., sick time rules) that improve an organization's competitive position and its effectiveness.
2. Planned change is more successful when multiple options are developed. Both the quality and innovation of a planned change is improved by considering more than one option in the planned change process.
3. Techniques useful in identifying innovative options for planned change stress creativity. Techniques are also needed to add structure to describe an option.
4. Techniques used for option identification and development can be combined to bring out a particular benefit and for specialized uses. Group process techniques

can be used with synectics, lateral thinking, and other techniques that rely on groups. Creativity techniques can be applied with morphology, relevance trees, and input-output techniques. Finally, scenarios create a variety of contexts in which options can be sought applying techniques that have been combined in various ways.

5. The group leader or facilitator, knowledgeable of the range of techniques that are available, can combine techniques in still other ways. This creates a repertoire of hybrid techniques that can be used to meet the special circumstances that arise in a particular planned change effort.

## ▲ Cases

### *The Lost Charges Case*

A lost charges program was initiated by a cost-containment committee in a large university hospital. The committee was appointed by the hospital's CEO. It had representatives from nursing, data systems, material management, industrial engineering, personnel, pharmacy, and the business office. The committee met monthly to discuss various aspects of hospital operations where cost-containment efforts could be identified. Available data suggested that lost charges, stemming from supply items used in patient care and not billed to the patient, may be a problem. The committee decided to launch a formal campaign to reduce lost charges.

A financial audit identified lost charges as shown:

64 percent (49 cost centers) averaged more than $100 per year

52 percent (40 cost centers) averaged more than $300 a year, or $25 monthly

43 percent (33 cost centers) averaged more than $600 a year, or $50 monthly

31 percent (24 cost centers) averaged more than $1200 a year, or $100 monthly

30 percent (23 cost centers) averaged more than $1800 a year, or $150 monthly

14 percent (11 cost centers) averaged more than $5000 a year, or $416 monthly

4 percent (3 cost centers) averaged more than $10,000 a year, or $830 monthly

More than a 2-to-1 relationship existed between lost charges and revenues. For example, the past study has found that $140,000 of lost charges could have generated revenue of $370,000. The lost charges appeared to be sufficiently widespread and of sufficient magnitude to justify a project to reduce them.

The concept of employee incentives was introduced. The idea was based on a plan that had worked in another setting where direct employee compensation for lost charge reduction was possible. Analysis of the idea concluded that no direct compensation could be made. A group reward idea was selected. A cost center (e.g., nursing unit) would be given a lump-sum based on the actions of all the nurses in that unit. The funds were to be used to provide a travel budget, to be drawn upon by the nurses for professional purposes.

The development of an incentive schedule dominated activities in the detailing stage. It was decided to give 10 percent of the value of the lost charge reduction back to the cost center for a one-third reduction in lost charges, 20 percent for a 50 percent reduction, and 30 percent for a 75 percent reduction. The committee selected implementation steps of quarterly computation and immediate feedback to the various units.

Program cost was projected, which suggested that a budget of $10,000 was needed. In addition, it was decided to exclude all small offenders, defined as those with $300 per year or less in lost charges. This decision kept 89 of the 173 cost centers from participating.

The cost-containment committee took action by establishing a budget for the program and announcing it with a memo. Field performance was determined by monitoring lost charges. In the first quarter of operation, a total of $90 in rewards was distributed and the magnitude of lost charges *increased*.                   ▲

### The Strategic Management of a Pediatrics Department in a Medical School Case

Assume that a strategic action of "increase growth and provide funding to support growth" has been derived by using the snowball technique from categories of

1. Increased funds
2. Financial allocations
3. Management
4. Patient volume
5. Increased services
6. Promotion and tenure
7. Research money

The top ranked theme of "increase funds" was identified by the snowball from the following individual action suggestions:

1. Seek endowments.
2. Redefine the budget process.
3. Increase teaching tied to budget subsidies.
4. Decrease teaching not tied to budget subsidies (e.g., physical exams).
5. Increase residents' time to the satellite hospital.
6. Increase grant funding.
7. Tie university hospital budget subsidy to admission from departments' satellites.
8. Increase subsidy from state legislature.
9. Reduce all faculty to part time to reduce costs of liability insurance.
10. Allow faculty moonlighting for a salary reduction proportional to time off.
11. Increase residents' time at satellite hospitals (where it *is* compensated) and reduce time at university hospital.
12. Get College of Medicine to take over debt in the practice plan.
13. Give faculty a personal discretion budget linked to money raised in grants.
14. Seek money from special programs offered by the university regents.
15. Have new chairperson negotiate an increase in faculty salary support to reduce pressure to provide patient care and to pay employee salaries.          ▲

## ▲ Exercises

1. Count the number of windows in your house or apartment. After you have finished, write down the steps you followed to do the counting.

2. How would you pack your trunk for a family vacation? Write down the steps that you would take.

3. Design a new package for golf balls by using the checklist, attribute listing, and relational algorithm techniques. Compare your results.

4. Develop a scenario for a planned change in an organization with which you are familiar. Select two factors, each with two levels, and sketch four conditions under which planning might be attempted.

5. Do an input-output analysis of some aspect of a job that you have done. Choose something that is small and accessible such as bill collection, customer complaints, cooking hamburgers, or a hospital discharge.

6. Consider the lost charges case. Critique what was done and offer suggestions.

7. Consider the strategic management case. Apply the morphology and relevance tree techniques to the actions that make up the "increase funds" theme. Compare your results. What did you find?

# 12 The Detailing Stage of Planned Change

▲ ▲ ▲     ▲ ▲ ▲ ▲ ▲ ▲ ▲ ▲ ▲ ▲ ▲ ▲ ▲ ▲ ▲ ▲

The purpose of the detailing stage is to describe how potentially viable planned change options will function. Options are developed by specifying their inputs, outputs, procedures, and other key features.

Detailing is done for both comparative and elaborative purposes. Frequently, several options are identified that appear to have potential. The operating features of these options must be sketched to discover those with the greatest merit. For instance, in the previous chapter, the morphology technique was used to identify several designs for a washing machine. A partial detailing of each potentially viable option would be necessary before the sponsor would have a basis for selecting among the options. Detailing also helps to rule out some options. For example, safety program options may appear promising, but the sponsor must imagine how each program would be carried out, including staffing and other considerations, to determine which are workable. Options must be developed to the point that operating procedures can be imagined to make these assessments. This chapter discusses techniques that can be used to carry out the detailing stage in a planned change process.

## ▲ TECHNIQUES USEFUL IN DETAILING

The detailing stage has constructive and interrogative phases. The interrogation phase applies techniques that rely on a representation. The representation usually takes the form of a detailed description of a particular plan. The plan is investigated to determine how changes in resources, personnel, and the like influence its efficiency and effectiveness. The ability of an interrogation approach to describe a plan is vitally important. A good representation has a good fit to the plan. Simulation, optimization, waiting lines, interpretive structural modeling, and the program evaluation and review technique (PERT) are interrogation techniques that have these features.

There are far fewer useful construction techniques in the literature. Most construction techniques are exhortive, recognizing the need to detail a solution but failing to offer concrete steps to follow. Other techniques mistake an interrogative approach for a constructive one. Advocates of simulation, for example, stress procedures that test the plan being considered (e.g., Monte Carlo techniques) rather than how the plan that the simulation is to test can be constructed. The plan is taken as a given. Even systems approaches often tend to emphasize the analysis of an existing plan. In its most advanced form, a construction technique can be used to devise a innovative or creative plan without reference to existing plans or practices.

Both search and synthesis activities are essential in the construction phase. Group process and creativity techniques can be applied in many of the steps called for by a construction technique. Some synthesis and selection is carried out by applying an interrogation technique. The construction phase looks for ideas and shapes them. The interrogation phase fine-tunes the idea and evaluates it.

A construction technique attempts to devise the features of a plan. The means of evaluating these procedures are often left implicit. Interrogation techniques represent the plan with a model to make evaluations and comparisons. The model permits the analyst to manipulate key components. For example, procedures for a plan are detailed to see if they work. The emphasis in a construction technique is on devising the procedure while an interrogation technique is concerned with testing the merits of a procedure. To apply an interrogation technique, one must devise the procedure before it can be tested. But the emphasis is on testing. Because little help is provided to create the procedure to be tested, one is implicitly coaxed to use a current plan or practice as a model, which lowers innovation. Also, by placing testing before development, the purpose of the detailing stage is deemphasized. Interrogation techniques are best used when applied with a construction technique.

## Merging Techniques

The merging of techniques for detailing can be complex. Creativity techniques and group processes can be used during each step in construction technique. This approach to detailing calls for one technique to elaborate, refine, explain, or document the results that stem from another technique. Some detailing techniques are not compatible. Furthermore, not all techniques available to detail a plan match up well with techniques in the concept development stage. If, for example, a relevance tree were used in concept development, the techniques applied in detailing must be able to recognize and deal with information arrayed in a treelike structure. For instance, relevance tree information is quite useful in interpretive structural modeling. Discussion in this chapter is limited to detailing techniques that can be matched with the techniques proposed for concept development in Chapter 11.

## Creating Hybrids

Figure 12-1 identifies techniques that can be applied to detail a plan. Each hybrid is made up of techniques drawn from the construction and the interrogation phases. Interrogation may require a path analysis as well as a structural test. All combinations of the constructive and interrogative techniques define several ways to carry out the detailing stage that specify the sequence of steps to be followed. These options are summarized in Figure 12-1.

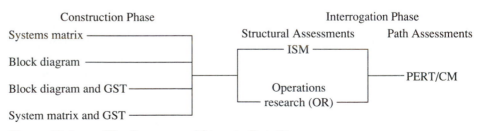

**Figure 12-1 ▲ The Sequence of Steps in Detailing**
Adapted from Nutt (1982).

# ▲  THE CONSTRUCTION PHASE

In the construction phase, the operating features of a plan for an option are sketched. Three techniques are considered: the systems matrix approach, the block diagram technique, and general systems theory. These techniques are discussed in the next three sections of this chapter.

## The Systems Matrix Technique

The "systems matrix" technique presents a "systems design" procedure for detailing a plan (Nadler, 1970, 1981; Nadler and Hibino, 1990). The systems matrix technique provides a way to detail a plan when its objective is known or can be specified. When the objective is unclear, it must be clarified. For example, the loading dock component of a firm's storage system can be developed when the purpose of storage is clear (e.g., hold finished goods, supplies, work-in-process, and various combinations). If not, an objective is identified by using the function expansion technique described in Chapter 10.

The systems matrix technique has considerable flexibility. It can be used to detail plans for options described by any of the concept development techniques. The systems matrix technique can be used to detail ideas defined by a morphology or a relevance tree. In the latter case, the technique develops a system for each component found in the tree. These systems are then merged to form the overall plan. The details of the plan at operational level are worked out with successive iterations of the systems matrix technique. This permits the systems matrix technique to be used for many types of projects that vary considerably in scale.

When techniques used in concept development give a less precise structure, as in a scenario or the nominal group technique, the overall system is defined as the first step in the detailing stage. The function expansion technique is used to begin the planning activities in detailing, identifying an objective for each systems component found in a relevance tree or a scenario.

### Systems Matrix Development

The systems matrix technique uses a system definition and a design procedure to identify the operating characteristics of the plan. The systems definition specifies what must be considered during detailing. The hierarchy of functions defines several systems that are to be detailed by the systems matrix technique. Each of the system components identified by morphology or in a relevance tree can also be detailed with the technique.

### Systems Definitions

A system is composed of elements. Each element has several dimensions, as shown in Figure 12-1. Nadler contends that the same elements must exist in all systems. The system elements are the objective or function, inputs, outputs, sequence, environment, physical catalysts, and human agents.

*Objective*. The objective is synonymous with the function, mission, or aim, which should guide the system to be planned. The objective describes the system's purpose. The hierarchy developed by the function expansion technique is one way to identify the objective for the system or system component to be planned (see Chapter 10).

*Output*. Outputs describe the products to be produced by the system. They show how the purpose of the system will be met. For example, a billing service for physicians could have a mailed statement of charges to Blue Cross, the patient, or the Medicaid program as an output. The purposes of a billing system are broader than bill preparation. It is important to distinguish outputs from purposes. Several outputs may be needed to achieve the purpose. Purpose emphasizes the desired result, whereas an output is one of the many ways to meet a system's purpose. For example, the billing service for physicians could have a purpose to "serve physician needs." Billing would be just one of many needs. To specify an output, its physical features are described. For instance, the bill can be specified by enumerating the information it contains, the level or detail in the explanation of charges, its format, its weight (mailing cost), and the like.

Consider the airlines reservation system. One output is a record of the travel booking that is stored in the system. Another is a confirmation sent to the traveler or a travel agent. Still another is a bill sent to the payor that may activate various types of billing mechanisms (e.g., a credit account or a credit card) that is sent to the traveler or a third party. The purpose of the system is to process transactions. Each output is described according to the information needed, means of storage or handling, and other relevant requirements.

Some outputs are unwanted such as scrap, polluted water, and the like for which disposal arrangements must be made. As disposal has costs, attempts should be made to minimize or reduce unwanted outputs or to find ways to recycle them. For instance, Eastman Kodak reclaims the silver in black and white film emulsion during developing to be used again in filmmaking.

*Input*. Inputs include all the things necessary to produce an output. For example, in an airline reservation system inputs include choice of flights and means of payment. When patients are treated in the emergency room, inputs include the patient as well as tangible items, such as surgical supplies, and information, such as medical history and current physiological parameters. Inputs always include clients in service systems. For those systems that guide the organization's operations, the inputs can be information and physical items. Most systems have a wide variety of inputs.

Some outputs become inputs elsewhere in the organization. The flight selected by a traveler provides an input to systems that measure capacity. The output sent to another system must be considered before the specifications of inputs are altered. For example, surgical supplies are outputs of a purchasing system. Before altering supply specifications, purchasing rationale, such as standardization, must be considered. This illustrates how the systems of surgery and purchasing interface. Similarly, the airline reservation system must interface with systems that measure capacity of each aircraft as each booking is made. Interfaces identify important sources of information for the planning process.

Thus, inputs raise several concerns in the detailing stage. Inputs represent an important source of cost in the system that one seeks to minimize.

*Sequence*. Sequence describes procedures and other mechanisms that are used to convert inputs to outputs. Sequence is a critical systems element because it specifies key activities in the input-output conversion process. The sequence can be complex, with both series and parallel channels that diverge and then converge to produce a single output. For example, the airline reservation system converts requests for travel to aircraft utilization such as type of space available (e.g., first class, tourist, free ticket) using computer software. A trauma center may receive a comatose person as its basic input. The trauma center then generates information (more inputs) that describes the patient's status (e.g., cause of injury, site of injury via a CT scanner, body function, and prospects for survival), which dictates a treatment process. These treatments can be sequential, awaiting patient response before deciding on the next action to be taken.

*Environment*. The context in which the system operates is defined as its environment. For example, an airline reservation system must operate under conditions of intense use that occur when weather grounds planes and strands passengers, delaying flights at airports across the country. The environment includes technology and its limitations in updating available space, stressed-out passengers and airline clerks, decision rules that reroute aircraft low on fuel, and the like. A trauma center's environment includes the technology available, economic conditions, and behavioral dimensions of the setting in which the system must operate. A trauma center may be planned for a hospital that lacks available technology, such as a CT scanner. The hospital may have limited resources because it is located in a low-income area. Both poor collection prospects for self-pay patients and Medicaid's reimbursement rates, which are below cost, make the financial environment precarious for a hospital servicing a low-income population. (Nevertheless, trauma centers are badly needed in low-income areas because socioeconomic conditions in these areas seem to create considerable demand for trauma services.) Behavioral features of the environment include provider attitudes and the morale of treatment personnel that would be common in ghetto hospitals.

Culture can be a key environmental feature. For instance, Japanese firms do not build factories with a northeast entrance, considered to be the "devil's gate." The U-Haul company relies on homegrown executives pulled from former blue-collar employees that have intense company loyalty. The logic of such practices can seldom be questioned without challenging the tenets on which an organization was built, and thus must be considered as a feature of the environment.

*Physical Catalysts*. A catalyst is a resource that aids in the input-to-output conversion without becoming part of the output. Equipment and facilities are the most common examples. For an airline reservation system, physical catalysts include computer terminals, software that updates flights over long time periods, and means to store bookings as they occur. A hospital's trauma system requires physical catalysts that include office furniture, examining rooms, X-ray equipment, laboratories, monitors, computers (hardware and software), and reusable supplies. Some catalysts can be interchangeable with inputs and outputs, depending on the system. For example, hospital bed sheets are reusable (catalysts), except in contagious areas where they are destroyed after use, making them inputs to the treatment process. Computers can be a catalyst, an input, an output, or part of the sequence. Along with inputs, catalysts describe resources that the system uses to create outputs. Like all resources, they are subjected to careful study during planning to minimize their costs.

*Human Catalysts*. Human agents are also catalysts who aid the transformation of inputs to outputs and do not become part of the output. The airline reservation system must be staffed by people who operate computers, repair them, and deal with demands when the reservation system is inoperative. In service organizations, people are both acted on (the inputs) and used in carrying out a service (human agents). Most systems require human agents at key points to extract information from inputs, carry out procedures, requisition supplies, and monitor outputs. In a surgical intensive care unit (SICU), nurses, the house staff, and the attending physician are the key human agents. The nurses record observations from monitors and the patient. Patient responses, such as clammy skin and sallow complexion, and readings, such as an arrhythmia measured by an ECG monitor, are collected to determine the need for various actions by human agents. Using these inputs, various procedures can be evoked. The procedures (sequence) come from the attending physician's standing orders and SICU's standard operating procedures, indicating when house staff should be summoned and what to do until they arrive. After a patient is stabilized and exhibits normal reactions for a certain time interval, he or she is discharged by a human agent to a standard hospital bed for less intensive treatment. The attending physician makes the judgment about discharge.

Human agents also represent an important cost element in most systems. However, reductions in the cost of staffing a system can create nasty trade-offs. For example, reducing the entry-level qualifications of airline clerks can cut costs but may increase training and turnover and produce poor customer relations that reduce airline profit. Substituting lower-cost personnel in an SICU offers cost savings but may damage the output, measured in mortality rates. Trade-offs of resources with the output is serious business and must be approached with care. Nonetheless, proof of the deleterious effects caused by cost cutting should be required before the opportunities for cost savings are dismissed.

To define each system element fully, its four dimensions—a description, measures, control, and target—are described (Figure 12-2). To plan the system, each system element is defined by using each of the dimensions.

*Descriptive*. This dimension acts as an identity; it identifies the characteristics of a particular element. The characteristics of system elements are described by the form in which they are most typically observed. For instance, an input for an airline reservation system is described by the types of information needed to make a reservation. An input in an SICU identifies parameters of particular interest in monitoring a patient. For sequence, the process to be used in converting inputs to outputs would be traced.

The descriptive dimension also indicates how each system element interfaces or links up with other systems. For example, the airline reservation system must interface with decision makers who set rules for the allocation of frequent flyer space (free tickets) among flights. Shifts in demand can be accommodated by reducing this space for flights that have an unexpected increase in bookings. Discharges from

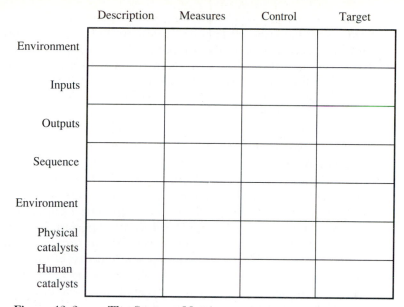

**Figure 12-2** ▲ **The Systems Matrix**

Adapted from Nadler (1970, 1981).

the SICU (an output) require a hospital bed. The patient's intrahospital transfer activates another system. The SICU inputs come from the emergency room or the local emergency medical service. On occasion, these systems must be changed before changes in the system being planned can be accommodated. These changes are called *interactions,* and their link to the focal system is called an *interface*. (An interface column can be put in Figure 12-2 after the descriptive dimension to capture complex interface relationships.)

*Measures*. This dimension provides measures of each characteristic of the system elements. Measures are often based on time, cost, or capacity. For instance, the capacity of a system for airline reservations is critical to avoid lost business. Capacity indicators suggest when more equipment or people are needed or when changes in procedure should be considered. Cost measures indicate system staffing expenses. Air traffic controllers must be rotated periodically to reduce fatigue, indicating staffing requirements and cost. Utilization figures express cost absorption in a system. Unit cost measures of inputs concern (among other things) consumable supplies used in a manufacturing process.

Measures are also expressed in normlike terms. Outputs, such as bookings, indicate demand for flights in an airline. Inputs, like supplies, can be specified using targets for their expected cost or level of use. Also, norms for information are often needed, for example, specifying how quickly reports of use are needed by top management for performance review.

Some measures are contained in the descriptive dimension and others must be teased out by indirect methods, including evaluation. For instance, the need to measure demand and system staffing is clear, but error rates may go unreported. The need to measure patient characteristics in a trauma unit is obvious, but the norms for the frequency of these measurements are not. Nurses contend that they are required to take readings on spirometry, blood pressure, urine output, and a host of other factors just so the attending physician, who is only on the scene briefly each day, can be assured that his or her patient has been "looked in on." But the subjective side of the patient (coloration and behavioral features, such as apparent respiratory difficulties) may be more important than objective measures, such as urine output, in specifying patient condition and dictating an intervention.

To determine the need for monitoring, objective measures and the rationale behind monitoring them must be teased out by consulting the literature or, when conditions permit, formally evaluating their need.

*Control*. The control dimension specifies how the system, once operating, will be maintained. A general model of a control system is shown in Figure 12-3.

The control system (Figure 12-3) monitors output in the system's domain with various sensors. The sensors document performance factors, such as cost or utilization. Expectations set objectives that, in turn, set norms for system operation, indicating desirable or required levels of cost or utilization. The discriminator (e.g., the accounting department) compares norms and performance and creates a report that is given to the system monitor. The monitor decides if corrective action is needed. The effector (often a manager) is activated when corrective action is needed, which moves the manager back into the system's domain to make necessary changes. Whether or not corrective action is taken, expectations are exposed to feedback that describes performance experience. This experience may or may not alter objectives and norms.

The control dimension creates an analog for each term in Figure 12-3 that dictates how the system will be controlled. Typically, performance measures and norms (drawn from the measures for each system element) are compared. The control dimension specifies how the performance information is to be collected, acceptable deviations of performance from norms, and discretionary actions that can be used by a manager when unacceptable deviations are observed. The comparison of norms and performance can be done automatically by a computer; through delegation, as when the nurse monitors a patient; or by the responsible manager, such as the review of various departments' cost-variance reports by their managers. In inventory control systems, the corrections are done automatically. When inventory falls to a certain level, a modern computer system initiates an invoice. When performance-norm deviations are large enough, many segments of the organization may be activated. For instance, a work-related death in a company should evoke a review of both procedure and circumstances surrounding the death, with the participation of top management.

The control dimension is detailed by asking how the system will ensure that inputs, outputs, and other system elements are adequate. Effective control mechanisms make precise and rapid modifications for an out-of-control system element. Precision is ensured by monitoring more frequently until performance and norms match. The need for speed of the modification depends on the nature of the system element. When speed is essential, lags should be shortened, and vice versa. For example, when clerks (human agents) that operate an airline reservation quit, this action turns up in monthly turnover figures (the personnel department's system).

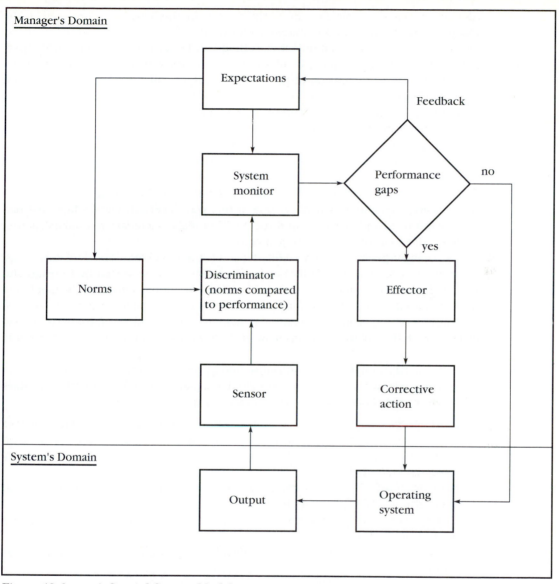

**Figure 12-3** ▲ **A Control System Model**

A revamped control system that is more timely does not seem to be needed in this case. Similar conclusions can be drawn about costs; however, during the early phases of system operation, cost may be monitored closely because less is known about cost behavior.

*Target*. The target dimension forecasts the basic features of a system. This is vital in planned change because the plan should describe a *future* (likely or desirable) state of affairs. Even when planning operations, such as billing, the system must be created in phases. The present system is moved toward the target. In other instances, the description dimension identifies features of the plan, and the target dimension describes the system of the future. In this case, the target gives the planner a way to provide for system evolution.

Provisions for periodic objective setting can be used to determine if the purpose of the system has changed sufficiently to call for replanning. To activate such a study, the target dimension of the objective might call for a function expansion session every several years. Obsolescence, technological change, and organizational growth create the need for planned change before dsyfunctions occur. This approach forces an organization into action before a crisis sets in.

The systems matrix provides a means to collect and sort information in a meaningful manner. For instance, Nadler and Hibino (1990) used this approach to help air force intelligence personnel deal with the huge accumulation of information that flows in to them from the four corners of the globe. Incoming information was sorted using the system matrix. Sorting in this way revealed relationships that had been overlooked and provided air force decision makers a means to establish action plans on the basis of intelligence gathered.

A manager planning a new facility faces a similar problem. The demands, ideas, preferences, wants, and wish lists of facility users must be sorted in a meaningful way to identify requirements and conflicts that must be managed. By tabulating these requests as objectives, inputs, desirable and undesirable outputs, sequences, environments (e.g., cultural dictates), human agents, and physical catalysts, a road map is created to help the sponsor in dealing with system users and other stakeholders.

The matrix highlights relationships among elements and ensures that each of the required elements have been considered in a plan. The systems matrix organizes information that describes the system being planned. It provides

1. *A language*. Language, such as inputs, outputs, and sequence, provides images and concepts that suggest ideas useful in the plan. The complexity of most planned change efforts can be reduced by using a set of terms that identify essential system elements.
2. *Specifications*. The system matrix suggests what a solution must consider to meet the needs of planned change.
3. *Documentation*. The systems matrix provides a record of each plan option and its distinctive features.
4. *Focus*. The essential aspects of plan development are kept in mind as a plan is formulated.

Spelling out the details of a system early in the process reduces risk and errors. This step makes it harder to plan high-quality activities that are nonessential and tests the advisability of policies. Nadler and Hibino (1990) show how the Caterpiller Company tested its policy to provide an engine or engine parts worldwide in 48 hours by examining its manufacturing, warehousing, sales, and accounting systems in this way.

### The Minimal Limitations Concept

Innovation stems from the concept of an "ideal system," one that has minimal restrictions. Detailing systems with limitations leads to unimaginative plans. The ideal system is shaped by reality after its basic design features have been laid out.

The key ingredient in ideal system development is the notion of "minimal limitations." Restrictions of any kind will hamper a planned change effort. Nadler requires that such restraints be laid out beforehand. Two steps are used: list and attempt to eliminate. The planner, sponsor, or planning group lists restrictions and then attempts to negate them. Requirements by management, demands by regulators or a legislature, and demands of experts are listed to determine how they limit the plan. For instance, licensure makes personnel substitution in a hospital impossible in some instances. Many firms have sacrosanct practices, such as U-Haul's promotion from the ranks and Avis's refusal to have a public relations department. The list is reviewed to seek out ways that each limitation can be eliminated.

Limitations can be present in all the system elements. Each should be tested separately by following "list" and "negate" steps. For example, inputs can be checked by noting opportunities to relax their specifications. More stringent specifications often lead to increased cost and may not yield superior system performance. All such input restrictions are listed, hoping to negate them. Similarly, sequence may have unwarranted restrictions that mandate processing steps justified by tradition rather than need. The systems planner seeks to eliminate all possible sequence restrictions. Unused outputs, such as computer reports, create waste. These and other nonessential output restrictions are identified to seek permission to eliminate them.

Environment is made up of company values, the demands of accreditation agencies, organizational policy, regulators, and government, to name a few. Some pose restraints that can be relaxed, or at least kept in the background until the merits of a plan can be considered without these restrictions.

Assumption about physical catalysts and people to staff the system can be overly restrictive. Restrictions about using old equipment should be probed. Substitution—considering the use of cheaper forms of labor—should be tolerated, except where firm legal prohibitions exist.

### Steps in the Planning Procedure

To detail an ideal system, the system matrix shown in Figure 12-2 is filled in. A six-step procedure is proposed:

1. Purpose verification
2. Regularities
3. System features
4. Elaboration
5. Ultimate and feasible systems
6. Long-range plans

*Step 1: Purpose Verification.* The first task is to attempt to eliminate the purpose of the system to be planned. Without a purpose, no system is needed, which is always the least costly option. Recall that the intent of formulation was to select the planned change objective. In concept development options were identified by specifying key components. These system components are eliminated, unless there is a compelling reason to retain them. For instance, the laboratory component of a company could be contract managed, or tests could be done by another organization on a purchased basis, eliminating the need for the laboratory.

If the planner cannot eliminate the objective, attempts are then made to combine it with another objective. For instance, merging the billing and sales departments may offer important ways to improve information management in a company. Also, simplifying and rearranging the objective can yield important benefits.

*Step 2: Regularity.* Regularity defines the most frequently occurring conditions that dominate the system. The regularity principle keeps the unusual or bizarre situation (which creates only vaguely understood consequences) from dominating a planned change process. For instance, business travelers who care more about convenience than cost make up the bulk of an airline's business. Catering to this segment of the business by stressing fast and efficient service is suggested. Similarly, an SICU should be planned to meet the needs of the open heart and kidney transplant patients, if these patients represent the bulk of the SICU cases. All other conditions (i.e., types of patients) are considered as exceptions. Only in the final phases of detailing is the system shaped to deal with all the conditions one can imagine.

A regularity unit is defined by the occurrence frequency for each minimal limitation in each system element. For example, reservation systems can be geared to deal with business travelers and their needs for information. If a trauma unit is required to treat all arriving patients, the categories of patients that occur most often would be selected to guide the detailing stage. At least one regulatory unit is specified for each limitation. For example, the most commonly used procedures to meet the needs of the business traveler and each type of trauma patient are laid out. If possible, these procedures are merged into a single sequence of activities.

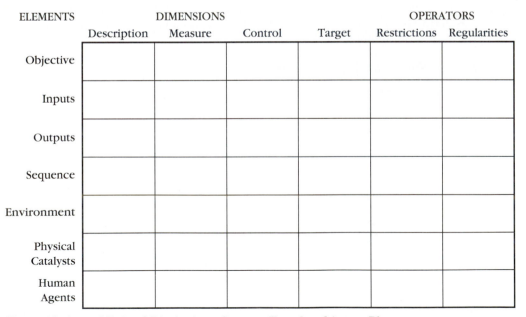

ELEMENTS | DIMENSIONS | | | | OPERATORS |

| | Description | Measure | Control | Target | Restrictions | Regularities |
|---|---|---|---|---|---|---|
| Objective | | | | | | |
| Inputs | | | | | | |
| Outputs | | | | | | |
| Sequence | | | | | | |
| Environment | | | | | | |
| Physical Catalysts | | | | | | |
| Human Agents | | | | | | |

**Figure 12-4**  ▲  **Minimal Limitations Concept Translated into a Plan**
Adapted from Nadler (1970, 1981).

Figure 12-4 illustrates the process. Two operator columns are added to the systems matrix. The minimal limitations are listed in the first of these columns. Regularities are then derived and put into the regularity column.

*Input Expansions.* Regularities are derived from each of the minimum limitations by constructing an expansion of each system element. First, an input expansion is carried out for each input restriction. If aluminum is required as an input in a product manufacturing plan, the rate of its arrival may create a limitation.

In the example shown in Table 12-1, a trauma center has a single input restriction: it is required to treat all patients who present themselves for treatment. (This is a reasonable expectation for trauma centers in large urban areas.) Input expansion in this example leads to a definition of the hospital's catchment area and then to making historical and latent demand forecasts. The catchment area is profiled to reveal demographic patterns, such as age, income, education, and migratory patterns. These patterns are correlated with patient profiles to tell which population group makes what type of demands. A historical demand forecast extrapolates present relationships, assuming particular migratory patterns. A latent demand forecast considers population groups that have not used the trauma center, but may in the future. For example, if current usage stems mostly from victims of knife and gunshot wounds, future usage may also include chest and head injuries from auto

## Table 12-1 ▲ Regularity Units for a Trauma Center

| Restrictions | Regularity Units | Basis |
|---|---|---|
| **Input** | | |
| Past patients | 1. Frequency of patients in various categories<br>2. Severity of patient condition in each category | More severe conditions occur frequently so use proportions |
| Catchment area | Same | |
| Demand forecast (historical) | Same | |
| Demand forecast (latent) | Same | |
| **Output** | | |
| Expired patients | | |
| Stabilized patients | Transfers to non-I.C. hospital bed | |
| **Sequence** | | |
| Treatment procedures for each category | Common procedures in trauma treatment | |
| **Environment** | | |
| None | | |
| **Catalysts** | | |
| Existing OR and ER facilities | Current equipment and facility capacities | |
| **Human agents** | | |
| Physicians manage process | 1. House staff<br>2. General surgeons | House staff does most of treatment |

accidents, if other area hospitals drop their category IV emergency room rating which classifies a hospital as having full-service treatment.

Inputs arise from programs, policies, target populations, market trends, prices, user/customer preferences, raw materials, growth projections, and outputs from other systems. In each case restrictions are reviewed to determine if the restriction can be eliminated. Selecting the least restrictive input is desirable, using the procedure described for function expansion (see Chapter 10).

*Regulatory Units*. After the input expansion has been made, regulatory units are listed. In the trauma unit example, two options are provided: severity and occurrence frequency by category. The basis for the selection is summarized in the last column of Table 12-1.

In practice, many other descriptors may be needed. Volume, status, utilization, and time are often used, in addition to severity and frequency.

*Other System Elements*. Regularity units are developed for all other system elements. Referring to Table 12-1, *output* restrictions recognize that some trauma patients will not survive. Also, trauma centers are restricted to stabilizing the patient. Once vital signs and behaviors return to acceptable ranges, the patient is transferred to an appropriate care area in the hospital; the regularity unit is those transfers. Parenthetically, transfers also define a boundary between the SICU and the regular acute care system in the hospital. This interface would be explored in step 3.

Output expansions, following the function expansion procedure (Chapter 10), help to eliminate unnecessary restrictions. The strong link between inputs and outputs frequently translate from the more to the less restrictive of the two. For example, if one wishes to eliminate an expensive raw material but retains features of an output that calls for the superior features of the dropped input, one or the other must be changed.

Returning to the trauma example, restrictions on the *sequence* are limited to physicians' descriptions of the treatment procedures for each of the frequently occurring categories of patients (Table 12-1). A regulatory unit is defined as the steps common to these procedures. Resource restrictions may include using existing emergency and operating room facilities and equipment. Constraints of this type are common. They stem from sponsors who seek to minimize the cost of implementing the plan and from the limitations in the growth of capital investment that regulatory agencies have levied on the health care industry. The capacity of current equipment and facilities represent a system regularity that is often folded into the plan.

The restriction on *human agents* can be illustrated by the tradition that physicians must control all aspects of a treatment process. The planner must determine a way to work within these constraints, producing sufficient staffing to meet the demands made by the trauma patients. House staff and general surgeons can be used, but only the former can be made available on demand basis. Often, a trauma system is planned so it can function with house staff initiating treatment, with appropriate specialists on call.

In many other plans staffing poses restrictions. People cannot be released from work, hiring standards are treated as sacrosanct, and skill levels (often dictated by academic degree) are difficult to question. However, staffing in the least expensive manner is more apt to be discovered if these restrictions are set aside (e.g., listed in Table 12-1) during plan development.

Restrictions for *physical catalysts* often stem from restrictions to work with existing equipment and facilities. This restriction also merits probing. To avoid missing the significant advantage that can stem from technological innovations or a rearranged work flow system suggested by a new facility, this restriction is set aside by listing it in Table 12-1.

Step 2 is completed when a full list of regularity items has been identified. Considering only regularities that are based on essential limitations improves the final plan. Without the regularity step, current systems act as templates that bring tradition and not innovation to the detailing stage. The restrictions that remain after this step are more likely to be basic.

*Step 3: Ideal System Development.* To detail the system, ways to deal with each system element are posed. The procedure calls for the following substeps:

1. Ignore the limitation.
2. Fill out the system matrix.
3. Employ creativity techniques.
4. Find multiple solutions.
5. Identify missing information.
6. Recycle for each contingency plan.

To initiate the process, the limitations that were derived in the last step are ignored. This permits the planner to create an ideal system that is used as a benchmark. First, the objective of the plan (or system component) is listed in the systems matrix. The planner proceeds from this point to list an ideal input, output, and so on for each system element.

The matrix can be completed by the planner, in a dyad with another planner or the sponsor, or with the aid of a group. If a group is used, the importance of the leader's role in the detailing process should be noted as discussed in Chapter 10.

Creativity techniques are useful to detail the plan. For a planner working alone, attribute listing, checklists, and the relational algorithm can be applied. Brainstorming, synectics, and laterial thinking help a group to break out of restrictive patterns and develop new ideas. Group processes like kiva, nominal-interaction technique (NI), nominal group technique (NGT), and brainwriting are also useful. Although each group must be properly charged, such group processes allow for the reflection often necessary to come up with new ideas. For example, NGT can be used to list ideal inputs, outputs, and every other system element in each dimension. In all, 28 group processes would be needed to fill the system matrix.

This step often requires an extended period of time to complete. Time is needed to carry out creativity techniques, to use group process, or merely to come up with several solutions. Multiple solutions (each defined by an ideal system matrix) are desirable. The best aspects of each solution are eventually merged.

The final consideration in ideal system development is to search for unanswered questions. Even with the aid of creativity techniques and group processes, additional information is often needed. *Only* essential information is collected.

At this point, an idealized version of a system has been created. To complete step 3, attempts are made to collect essential but missing information. Collection of information from traditional sources is delayed until the planner is sure of its usefulness. This tactic eliminates much of the useless information collected in the typical planning project.

Finally, the entire process is repeated for each contingency plan. Frequently several planning teams are formed and carry out development under each important contingency.

*Step 4: Elaborate the Ideal System.* To initiate activities in step 4, the planner has several systems matrices, each representing a unique plan. Each plan has the *same* objective but should differ in all other aspects. To provide more detail, creativity and group process techniques are used again. Different groups can be formed to get a fresh approach or previous groups can be used. Each group is asked to add detail to the dimensions of each system element. As before, NGT can be used to improve the management of the group process and synectics to improve creativity.

The planner, armed with the information from group process, creativity techniques, or introspection, constructs models of each element. For example, a flow diagram can be used to illustrate sequence. Lists usually suffice for the other system features.

*Step 5: Developing Feasible Systems.* The ultimate system often represents one that cannot be implemented due to limits in technology and other constraints. The feasible system is workable with present technology or adhering to current conditions or constraints that cannot be relaxed. Solutions are sorted into these categories. A synthesis of the best features of several workable plans, as defined by the various systems matrices, is sought. The limitations laid out at the start of the process are now incorporated into the system details. The planner makes an element-by-dement comparison of limitations to the ideal formulation of that element. Some limitations can be relaxed at this point, and others must be incorporated into the alternative plans. These alternatives represent the detailed system solutions for evaluation in stage 4 of the planned change process.

*Step 6: Long-range Plans.* The final step is to form the ultimate system into a long-range plan. The plan provides a goal-like statement about the hoped-for state of the system. Its usefulness depends on changes in technology and other factors that limited its feasibility in step 5.

*Summary.* The systems matrix technique is both elegant and highly usable. It represents one of the few systems design approaches that can be readily used to detail a system. The systems matrix technique draws on its internal logic for justification. The steps in its procedure have been verified by experience. Nonetheless, the case studies used to substantiate the value of the systems matrix approach must be interpreted with care as they rely heavily on testimonials.

## The Block Diagram Technique

Systems analysis is widely used to detail plans. Systems analysis techniques attempt to capture the essential features of a practice or procedure useful in a plan to refine or fine-tune them. One of the more useful applies a graphical approach to identify system features, components, and their relationships. A diagram is used to show blocks, and the relationships among each block, that describe steps called *functions*, used to transform input to outputs in the system being planned. The "functional block diagram" defines and summarizes this set of functions and their relationships.

Blocks in the diagram must meet necessity and sufficiency requirements. Every functional block must be *necessary* in a sequence of events that converts input(s) to output(s). Functions that can be deleted save operating cost. An exception to this rule is made when redundant blocks are needed to ensure safe or reliable system operation. The *sufficiency* requirement demands that only one functional block be used for each process step.

One of several equivalent block arrangements can be adopted. Two arrangements are equivalent when each accepts inputs and creates outputs that have the same requirements. The equivalency definition does not extend to the transforms used in a functional block, which allows the planner to propose alternative ways to convert inputs to outputs for each block.

The advantages of the block diagram technique stem from the logic shown in the graphical representations. The flow of steps helps to make processing ideas tangible so they can be checked and improved. The block diagram does not list all the needed information. Inputs and outputs are *not* always shown, in part because the logic pattern often becomes cumbersome. Similarly, redundant blocks (functional blocks used to verify or safeguard) are not shown if the processing time demands that are implied can be represented in the diagram.

### Principles of the Block Diagram Technique

*Categories of Blocks.* Wilson and Wilson (1970) identify five categories of blocks. As shown in Figure 12-5, blocks are defined by the number of inputs and outputs that each requires. Functional blocks can be described as follows:

Class 1. Neither input nor output

Class 2. Either an input or an output

Class 3. One input and one output

Class 4. One input with several outputs or one output with several inputs

|  |  | OUTPUTS | | |
|---|---|---|---|---|
|  |  | None | One | Several |
| **INPUTS** | None | Class 1 | Class 2 | Class 6 |
|  | One | Class 2 | Class 3* | Class 4* |
|  | Several | Class 6 | Class 4* | Class 5* |

\* The asterisks indicate block classifications frequently used in planned change.

**Figure 12-5** ▲ **Defining Categories of Blocks**

Class 5. Several inputs and several outputs

Class 6. Lacking an input with several outputs or vice versa

The block called "class 1" has neither inputs nor outputs. Such a block has no value in planning. Class 5 can be represented by one of the class 4 blocks and class 6 by one of the class 2–type blocks. In practice, classes 3, 4, and 5 are frequently used.

*Inputs and Outputs.* An object or the potential to create an object is represented by inputs and outputs. For example, the output of a step in a billing system can be information drawn from a computer that indicates unpaid balance and new charges used to create a bill. The bill is the object and information the potential. In each step of the process (each block), resources are used so each block represents an operation (a computer program) or inputs (information validation and merger) to create an output (a bill). Inputs and outputs can be wanted or unwanted. For example, the computer may produce a master list of information that the billing clerk must review to find the unpaid balance or new charges information.

*Types of Blocks.* Blocks can serve as combiners (multiplexers), sinks, discriminators, or operators (converters). Blocks acting as a *combiner* merge inputs. For instance, some computer systems' procedures create bills, order inventory, update accounting reports, and perform other functions. Retail stores tie registers that record sales to accounting, inventory control, customer billing (if store charge is used), third-party billing (e.g., VISA), and customer contact by direct mail. In hospitals computers take raw data on medical procedures performed, lab work, hospital room, and location to compute a daily charge by applying logic (e.g., multiplying a semiprivate room cost by days in residence) to merge information. *Sinks* can be thought of as storage devices. *Discriminators* make comparisons. For example, retail stores can make comparisons of current sales rates to seasonal expectations or determine the impact of promotions. In hospitals a comparison of length of stay (LOS) to an LOS norm can be made. Discriminations are key points of a control system, as described in the previous section. *Operator* blocks alter the input. For instance, a report can be created from raw information used to construct the output (e.g., a bill). Most operator blocks are class 4 (several inputs–one input).

*Connecting Blocks.* By stringing together blocks that act as combiners, sinks, discriminators, or converters, the planner models a system that the blocks represent. The planner looks for the simplest possible way to convert inputs to outputs in the process, attempting to eliminate blocks by substituting others that are less costly and/or more reliable. Three basic arrangements often crop up that can be related to electrical engineering principles: tandem, parallel, and bridge (Figure 12-6). These basic arrangements of blocks can be combined in various ways to create a system model.

### The Block Diagram Procedure

The block diagram technique locates all functions required, determines at least one way to carry out each function, and ensures that the functions work together in the block arrangement. The following procedure is used to meet these requirements:

1. Crystallization
2. Ideation
3. Synthesis
4. Analysis
5. Representation
6. Selection

Each of these steps will be discussed in some detail.

*Step 1: Crystallization.* The basic steps to form the block diagram are as follows:

1. Performance requirements
2. Output and input lists
3. Constraints

The performance requirements are divided into "musts" and "wants." The listing and ranking can be done using the group process and ranking approaches discussed in Chapter 10. Outputs and inputs are usually obvious, by consulting the way options were represented in the concept development stage. In addition,

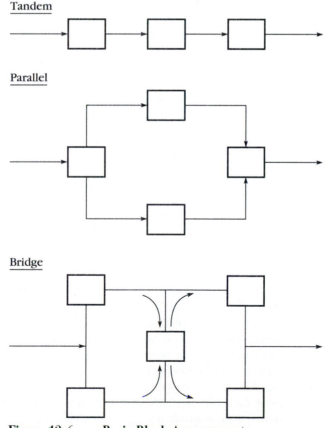

**Figure 12-6** ▲ **Basic Block Arrangements**

unwanted side effects (outputs not desired) are listed. For instance, drugs used for chemotherapy convert an input (an unstable tumor) to a desired output (tumor shrinkage) but also cause skin rash, hair loss, and nausea. Side effects may become sufficiently severe to render particular drugs unusable. Most product manufacturing creates scrap as well as produce air and water pollution.

Input and output lists can be created in three ways. First, existing systems (e.g., how bills are processed) can be captured with a flowchart to identify inputs and outputs. Second, creativity techniques with or without a group process can be used to develop novel ideas. Third, a combination of system models and creativity can be used. An existing system's procedures and processing steps can be used to suggest types of inputs and outputs that seem needed. Changes can be devised using creativity aids and/or a group process.

Constraints take several forms, including accepting inputs from other systems, using an existing conversion process for the block (e.g., computer system), and working with a limited planned change process budget. Other limitations include using the ideas of others and taking existing facilities as givens. Tolerances are demanded for the performance features of inputs and outputs, such as bills sent within two to three days of incurring an expense or making a sale.

*Step 2: Ideation.* The identification of functions represented by each block is a key step in the block diagram technique. The description of an option developed in the concept development stage guides the activities by framing the scope of inquiry. Group process (NGT, NI, and brainwriting) and creativity techniques (synectics, lateral thinking, and checklists) are useful to list the blocks, test the blocks' functions, and propose alternatives for each function. Several group process and/or creativity sessions may be needed to list, test, and prune the functions.

The planner uses the option (devised in the concept development stage) to guide the listing of functions. The planner then traces the flow of activities through a system. For instance, Figure 12-7 depicts a block diagram for case finding. A patient's flow through activities that begin with identification and end with treatment is traced. This trace ensures that processing includes all the steps needed to recognize, diagnose, and treat. Better ways to do each are then sought. (Note that Figure 12-7 has a bridge arrangement; see Figure 12-6.)

*Step 3: Synthesis.* In this step, the functions are merged into a block diagram. The diagram provides a picture that can be assessed and revised. In early versions of the diagram, deliberate simplifications are often made. After verification, these preliminary diagrams are enlarged to encompass all functions (see Figure 12-8.)

The synthesis step begins by posing three questions. In the first, the planner asks, "Why do it at all?" The emerging plan must respond to the objectives set in the formulation stage of the planned change process. Periodic checks are used to verify that original aims are being met by proposed activities or that more appropriate aims are now being served. Second, the planner asks, "Why do it now?" This question also verifies that the imperative to act, which prompted the planned change effort, still exists. Finally, the planner asks, "Why do it this way?" Alternative ways of carrying out each function, identified in step 2 (ideation), are tested to see which set provides viable alternatives.

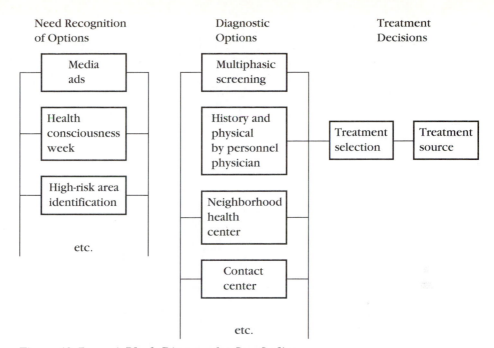

**Figure 12-7** ▲ **A Block Diagram for Casefinding**

The principle behind the third question is to avoid unnecessary and overly elegant processing. For instance, computers, for all their virtues, may be overkill for certain activities and for organizations that lack the sophistication to use them to their potential. The functional blocks are arranged in various ways to improve performance features. Complex systems require that the planner trace the inputs and outputs using a "single-thread" analysis. This analysis verifies the logic of processing steps and precedes simplification activities.

Several block diagrams should be prepared in this way, representing basic options. Each tentative plan is then analyzed to discover latent weaknesses and to identify several apparently superior arrangements for the next step to assess.

*Step 4: Analysis.* After the synthesis step, several alternatives will have been prepared. In step 4, these arrangements are carefully checked. The analysis step requires considerable attention by the planner. A checklist helps the planner ensure that key questions have been answered:

1. Are all functional blocks in the diagram required?
2. Do blocks perform all required functions?
3. Are the blocks correctly ordered?
4. What are the effects of unwanted outputs on performance?
5. What is the effect of poor or untimely inputs?
6. How can the system fail?
7. What constitutes a partial failure?
8. Does the diagram describe how the system must interface with other systems?

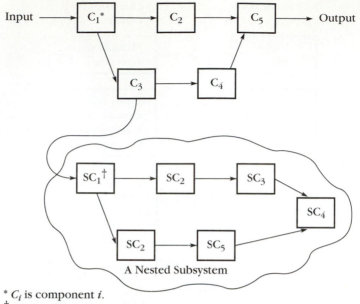

* $C_i$ is component $i$.
† $SC_i$ is subcomponent $i$.

**Figure 12-8** ▲ **Nesting in a Block Diagram**

In addition, several key determinations must be made:

1. *Capacities.* Each block has capacity that should be fully utilized. Multiples can often be proposed. For instance, a second small computer or time sharing could be substituted for a large computer with underused capacity.
2. *Sequencing.* Each of the block functions must be integrated. Blocks that act as a sink, a multiplexer, discriminator, or operator must work appropriately in the sequence.
3. *Demand.* Each option can be tested to see how it behaves under high and low demands.
4. *Cost.* Costs must be estimated to verify that each alternative falls within budget constraints.

Trade-offs also help in finding ways that an alternative can be improved. For instance, managers who want "real-time" information but do not use this information in decisions drive up costs unnecessarily. Physician demands for extensive information and rapid turnaround of analyses in a surgical intensive care unit monitoring system may create prohibitive costs. The cost-turnaround and cost-monitoring relationship could be explored to see where changes can be made.

The analysis step poses questions that lead to revision of the block diagram to accommodate trade-off compromises, capacities, and sequences. Each diagram now represents a feasible alternative.

*Step 5: Representation.* Each viable alternative is carefully depicted as a functional block diagram. To point out salient differences among the options, common blocks can be shown with a particular color or using some common referent.

*Step 6: Selection.* The assessment of alternatives is based on the degree that the project's objectives have been met and the ability of each alternative to create desirable outcomes and minimize the undesirable. Selection among the alternatives is carried out in the evaluation stage of the planned change process.

### Types of Synthesis Problems

The synthesis step is both demanding and complex. To aid the planner in visualizing how to carry out a systems synthesis, synthesis problems are classified according to whether outputs, inputs, or transforms are known or not. Recall that an output captures what is wanted in an input, an input indicates what is needed to produce an output, and transforms identify procedures that convert inputs to outputs. The problems can be described as one of eight cases, as shown in Table 12-2. Cases 1, 2, and 3 have two unknowns. Case 1 is a *production problem.* Knowing a desired output, a procedure and appropriate input is needed. An example would be an alcoholism treatment center. The output is clear (rates of abstinence). The planner searches for treatment procedures, noting how well each procedure can deal with particular types of alcoholics.

Case 2 is called the *use problem.* An input is given and systems synthesis is used to turn it into a useful output. This occurs when some procedure produces a by-product. For instance, a sewage disposal facility creates by-products that require expensive disposal. By processing these by-products, such plants have produced lawn fertilizer that can be marketed to help defray the costs of waste disposal.

Case 3 is called the *capacity problem.* A procedure is available that is unused (no current inputs and outputs), and the task is to find a suitable use for this excess capacity. This situation arises when there is unused production capacity in a firm. A search is made to find a new product that can be manufactured. The inputs and outputs for the new product are sought in the capacity problem. Similarly, unused beds in a hospital stimulate proposals of alcoholism, mental health, and other programs.

Cases 4, 5, and 6 are less demanding because only one component is missing. Case 4 calls for a way to transform inputs to outputs, which is called the *conversion problem.* Determining the best way to bill suppliers or customers is an example of a conversion problem.

### Table 12-2 ▲ Types of Synthesis Problems

| Case | Output | Input | Transform | Category |
|------|--------|-------|-----------|----------|
| 1 | Given | Unknown | Unknown | Production |
| 2 | Unknown | Given | Unknown | Use |
| 3 | Unknown | Unknown | Given | Capacity |
| 4 | Given | Given | Unknown | Conversion |
| 5 | Given | Unknown | Given | Requirements |
| 6 | Unknown | Given | Given | Performance |
| 7 | Unknown | Unknown | Unknown | Undefined |
| 8 | Given | Given | Given | Resolved |

In case 5, the input is missing, which is called a *requirement problem*. The planner must determine what is needed to produce an output and seeks the lowest-cost inputs that can satisfy the transform and its output requirements. For instance, the reservation system for an airline should seek the minimal amount of information to update status (e.g., purchased, committed, or empty).

Case 6 defines a *performance problem* because a procedure exists, but it is unclear how to use some aspects of it. This often occurs after a turnkey system (e.g., a management information system or financial analysis system) has been installed. More planning is needed to realize the system's full potential. Performance problems also occur when new technological advances are recognized but their value to the organization is unclear. A search is made to determine how the innovation can be effectively used.

Case 7 is undefined because there are no clues. Without some inkling as to needs, requirement, or unused conversion capability, no problem can be defined. Case 8 is also trivial because it represents a solution to one of cases 1 to 6, so a problem no longer exists.

*System Synthesis.* In cases 1, 2, and 3, a two-step process is needed. In step 1, finding an input converts a production problem, case 1, to case 4, a conversion problem. In step 2, the conversion problem is solved, converting case 4 to case 8 (problem resolved). The sequences that can occur are shown in Table 12-3.

The sequence of case 1 to case 4 to case 8 (denoted 1-4-8) is more desirable than 1-5-8 because it is best to define inputs before defining transforms. Sequences 3-5-8 and 2-4-8 are preferred because performance should be considered before conversion problems or requirements are dealt with. The required steps call for dealing with outputs or what is needed, then dealing with inputs or what is used to create outputs, and then dealing with ways to create outputs from inputs.

*The Black Box.* In the preceding section, the need to define inputs and/or outputs prior to considering the transform was explained. The transform is dependent on inputs (requirements or constraints) or outputs (performance) to aid in its specification. The transform must wait until requirements, constraints, and performance factors are defined before it can be planned. During this process a "black box" is used to represent the transform.

The black box technique poses the basic question in a systems synthesis by specifying inputs and outputs and asking how to convert one to the other. Figure 12-9 describes several synthesis situations that can exist. In each case, a search is mounted to find a conversion that eliminates the unwanted output while meeting

Table 12-3 ▲ Synthesis Procedure

| Conversion Sequence | Problem Sequence |
| --- | --- |
| 1-4-8[a] | Production to conversion |
| 1-5-8 | Production to requirements |
| 2-4-8[a] | Use to conversion |
| 2-6-8 | Use to performance |
| 3-5-8[a] | Capacity to requirements |
| 3-6-8 | Capacity to performance |

[a] Preferred sequences in system synthesis.

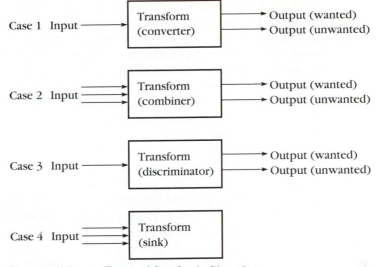

Figure 12-9 ▲ Types of Synthesis Situations

the performance requirements implicit in the output and considering constraints and other input demands.

Case 1 (Figure 12-9) describes the search for a conversion transform or operator. An example would be computer options for data processing in a laboratory. The unwanted output might represent the unneeded tests in an auto analyzer. In this example, a planner searches for conversion options that create outputs (needed tests) and minimize unneeded tests.

Case 2 describes the search for a combiner (or multiplexer) that can merge several inputs. The Bayesian diagnostic programs, which merge several cues into diagnosis, exemplify such a transform. Ernst and Young, Arthur Anderson, and other accounting firms provide financial analysis packages that merge accounting information into various types of reports for control systems.

Case 3 requires a discriminator. The transform compares performances with a norm, such as a control system that uses cost-variance data or reviews sales rates. The desired output is a judgment on the adequacy of costs or sales. The unneeded output can identify nonessential information in the discrimination.

Case 4 is a sink, a terminal processing mode, often taking the form of a storage-retrieval system. Libraries and company archives are examples.

The typical synthesis problem has a vast array of these cases. They are merged in series (tandem), parallel, and bridgelike logic so the outputs of one become the input to another.

### Supporting Block Diagram Development

Facts and relations that describe block functions are sought in the crystallization, ideation, and synthesis steps. The following aids are provided to help along the discovery process.

*Thinking.* Divergent and convergent types of thinking can be used. To diverge, many ideas are generated. To converge, ideas are selected and merged. A divergent strategy is used to get ideas and a convergent strategy to synthesize and evaluate. Steps 1 and 2 in the block diagram technique use divergent approaches, and convergent approaches are preferred for steps 3, 4, and 5.

*Divergent Techniques.* In steps 1 and 2 (crystallization and ideation), techniques that create a wide range of ideas for functions and their relations are required. To aid in this process, group methods, including NGT, NI, kiva, and brainwriting, or creativity techniques, such as synectics or lateral thinking, can be used. The previous two chapters should be consulted for details.

*Convergent Techniques.* Synthesis requires a reordering of information combining it into a new pattern that yields a tentative solution. For instance, knowing the ultimate picture sought and the shape of the puzzle pieces helps to complete a picture puzzle. This process is called *pattern recognition.* It describes a combinatorial problem, one with so many possibilities that it is difficult to find a starting point. Initial search patterns in puzzle construction call for edge search because one can match pieces that have the edge characteristic more easily than merely enumerating all pieces. Later on, search is based on color and shape cues. Pattern recognition is also used to solve many math problems. Search procedures are used, hoping to cause a flash of insight that makes the problem tractable. For example, people learn factoring skills to break down math problems in creative ways.

Another helpful tool is *analogy.* The planner tries to recall some other problem that resembles the current one and draws cures from it. The manner in which that problem was solved provides a guide that can be adapted to current circumstances. These cues provide ways to extract ideas useful in identifying essential functions.

In summary, the synthesis step is aided by factoring and analogy. By repeatedly factoring representations of options from the concept development stage (e.g., a morphology), essential functions can be identified. Analogies are sought to suggest how to fill gaps that emerge. Just like the puzzle, a solution gradually becomes easier to specify as more functions are found.

*Other Types of Searches.* Several types of function searches can be used. In addition to factoring, a *heuristic* search can be used. Heuristics usually have a "cut and try" format. This type of search relies on the human mind to create viable hunches and eureka-like closure on a transform.

An enumeration approach can be used to trace several pathways through various combinations of the black box cases, using a tree structure. Such an arrangement is shown in Figure 12-10. Each block in Figure 12-10 is represented by a node in the network, and each line segment represents a possible outcome. More than one choice of transforms may be needed to be sure that a good outcome is obtained. (The superior outcome can be evaluated with a decision tree, to be described in the next chapter.) Once identified, the path connects all desirable transforms, tying them together in a system. (Note that Figure 12-10 also shows why it is best to identify outputs and inputs before searching for a transform.) Enumeration searches list all imaginable transforms and trace all possible paths (see Figure 12-10). The enumeration approach, while comprehensive, can become cumbersome because of the large number of feasible pathways that must be assessed.

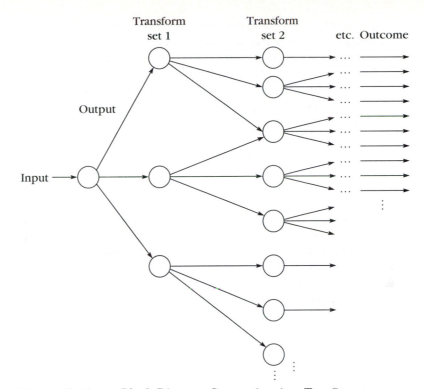

Figure 12-10   ▲   **Block Diagram Connectives in a Tree Structure**

## General Systems Theory

General systems theory (GST) was created by scientists who became disenchanted with the artificial boundaries that had been erected around traditional disciplines (e.g., Weiner, 1945; Boulding, 1956; Ashby, 1963; von Bertalanffy, 1968; Buckley, 1967; Miller, 1978; Prigogine, 1982). They sought to identify insights and unifying principles that could bridge these disciplines, thereby synthesizing and integrating them. The unifying theme became the notion of a "system," defined as a set of objects and relationships between these objects or their attributes. All disciplines deal with systems, so uncovering the basic concepts that lie behind a "general system" was seen as a way to create the basis for a general theory.

An isomorphic assumption underlies all GST thinking. The features of systems are assumed to have comparable structures and operating properties. Principles (e.g., the economists' notion of supply and demand) were also thought generalizable. A metalevel set of principles that governed the behavior of all systems was sought. By synthesizing these structures, properties, and principles, a generalized system seemed definable and uncovering properties of the "general system" feasible.

### Systems Thinking

GST thinking draws sharp distinctions (indeed, overly sharp) to pose pointed questions (Weinberg, 1985). For example, the study of economics or any other field quickly submerges the student in particular paradigms, such as production-possibility curves and diminishing returns. Systems define words such as stability, behavior, state, noise, and adaptation, which can be used to translate and generalize the principles of a specialist. The production-possibility curve in economics becomes a "line of behavior in two-dimensional state space," which permits sharp questions to be posed. Similarly, the law of diminishing returns becomes the law of limiting factors. The genesis of many of these general laws has been dependent on economic and other theories to provide ideas to generalize.

The GST has been directed toward particular topics such as information systems, work systems, incentive systems, and health systems, to name just a few. Applications to disciplines like engineering, political science, and management, are often made. For instance, treating such subjects from a systems point of view has been the organizing theme of many textbooks.

Finally, GST has had some use in the creation of new laws or principles. None, however, makes any pretext of providing straightforward rules for planning. Although such rules can be inferred, the planned change process implied by GST is, of necessity, incomplete.

### Uses of GST

The GST is a montage of observations about how systems tend to operate. These concepts have had only limited and sporadic use, in part because GST does not lay out a procedure that can be used to construct a system. Instead, it offers a description about how most (if not all) systems work. These systems descriptions have some normative uses. In this chapter, GST ideas will be used as a checklist to verify that the plan has considered the key features of most systems, how systems maintain their operation or change, and the way in which systems deal with breakdowns. The key to application is rooted in explanations and predictions of how systems tend to operate. Planners can use these explanations and predictions to determine ways to buffer predictable changes, anticipate certain types of failure, and use inherent system features to suggest or improve system operations.

GST features and operating principles can be classified as system descriptors, system regulation, system change, and how systems malfunction.

### Systems Properties

Systems have two generic properties: boundaries and environment (Young, 1984). Also, systems have key features that include openness, integrating forces, components, dependencies, interaction, centralization, state, and equifinality (see Table 12-4).

*Boundaries.* A system boundary determines what is included and excluded, helping the planner define the scope of the problem being addressed. Things that have special features or identities can be separated by a boundary. For instance, a system boundary can de defined by the actions of a clerk using a computer to schedule a flight for an airline. A clear boundary exists between the clerk and the computer because they represent things that are fully distinguishable. The planner can plan the clerical or the computer system. A clear specification of system boundaries helps the planner to visualize what should be included in the planning process.

**Table 12-4  ▲  General System Descriptors**

| Plan Scope Specified by Defining | Check for the Presence of the Following Basic System Features |
|---|---|
| Boundaries | Openness |
| Environment | Integrative forces |
| | Dependencies |
| | Interaction |
| | Centralization |
| | State |
| | Equifinality |

*Environment.* The environment is all things not defined as part of the system that can influence system operation. Environmental definitions also aid the planner by delimiting the planning problem. Every system can be seen as part of a larger system. In a firm, a manufacturing department has an environment that includes support services (e.g., purchasing), supply departments, and upper management. Each metasystem includes both the focal system and parts of this system's environment. If the manufacturing department is the focal system, the metasystem includes that department, the firm, relevant competitors, governmental relations, and regulation. Every focal system has a metasystem.

### Key System Features

Key features of a system give the planner insights and guides to check on the plan as it evolves. These features are described in the discussion that follows.

*Openness.* An open system has an environment that influences system operation. Closed systems are isolated. The environment has no important effects on its operation and can be ignored. A closed system functions without any significant information, cues, or demands from the environment. Rather, cues and demands are generated internally. For example, a company cafeteria with a captive set of patrons, a readily available supply of labor, reliable equipment, and dependable source of supplies has little environmental contact. Closed systems operate as though they are largely self-maintaining units. The operations of a hospital illustrates an open system strongly influenced by benefactors, regulators, third-party payors, the medical staff, and still other elements of its environment. Defense contractors, a symphony orchestra, and departments of state government also operate in an open environment. Open systems are more difficult to plan because the environment creates complex demands that can be hard to understand, let alone predict. As a result, planners are faced with a difficult task in open system planning because adaptability and flexibility must be designed into system operation.

The planner can think about optimizing performance in a closed system. Such a system can be optimized because it is possible (if not desirable) to define procedures that consider key contingencies. Operations research techniques (discussed later in this chapter) are particularly useful in closed system planning.

*Integration.* Mechanisms and principles that bind a system together provide integrating forces. A disaggregated system is differentiated, whereas a tightly bound system is integrated. Planning can be aided by recognizing the degree of integration that seems feasible or to decide if a current degree of integration is desirable. A hospital medical staff illustrates a disaggregated system; its members are primarily bound together by their admitting privileges. The radiology department of a hospital or the department making film containers for Eastman Kodak has more integration because the system is bound together by reward systems for its employees, activities, processes and procedures, and still other principles and mechanisms. The prospects of increasing the integration in a medical staff are desirable but low. In contrast, high integration is both possible and desirable in a department engaged in manufacturing film containers.

*Components.* All systems have components, which can be called *subsystems.* For example, an R & D department's components can be defined as various types of procedures, labor, equipment, and so on. Each system component has a distinct role in system operation. Furthermore, components can have a special purpose or general purpose. Some components, such as quality control activities, play a specialized role in system operation whereas others, such as manpower, have systemwide implications.

Planners define components to reduce complexity, as discussed in Chapter 11. By completely enumerating components using a relevance tree or a similar device, a system can be completely specified. Thus, components represent a fundamental concept used by planners in constructing a plan.

*Dependence.* Systems have components that influence each other. Changes in a system create perturbations so every part of a system tends to respond to every other part. The influence can be major or minor. For instance, if procedures are changed in an R & D department, technicians must learn new ways of operating, equipment schedules may change, supervisory practices (e.g., appraisal) can be affected, and so on.

Planners use the notion of dependence to divide systems into components. The division is made where the influence among components are weakest. The planner must recognize that components seldom operate independently and must enumerate the interface communications that are likely to occur between components.

*Interaction.* When two or more systems mutually affect one another's actions, they are said to be interacting. The interacting systems can be of either similar or dissimilar size, and such systems may operate in relative isolation from other systems. The operation of mutually dependent departments, such as purchasing, distribution, inventory control, and fabricating departments, illustrates interacting systems. Few systems are fully isolated, although many have few important intersystem transactions. For instance, a firm's housekeeping department provides services that are largely routine and repetitive, involving few contacts with others except the evaluation of its work by external agents.

Planners must define communication between systems to specify fully system operation. The demands of one system (e.g., product recall) can influence inputs of another (e.g., quality control) by indicating what tests are required and when. Outputs indicating performance can also be intersystem generated, as, for example, when the product rejection norms are set or when management sets error limits for quality control tests. Specifications for key inputs and outputs often have their origins beyond the system being planned. Planners define system interactions to understand these specifications and their prospect for modification.

*Centralization.* In a centralized system, one component has a dominant role in system operation. This component tends to dictate the system's product. To predict the product, one must also predict the state of the component. For instance, a defense contractor has but one client: government. Predicting what government wants is the key to the contractor's success. Also, many hospitals have medical staffs with a few members who do the bulk of the admitting. These people are the key consumers for the hospital because they dictate its financial success. For example, to predict financial performance, medical staff admissions are forecasted. Age and other factors that describe the high physician admitter indicate important features of the medical staff system component.

A key system component emerges as a central feature that predicts system outcome. For instance, the medical staff composition periodically changes. The addition of more loyal and aggressive physicians can dilute the influence of the current high admitters on the medical staff. Predicting the magnitude and nature of the next generation of weapon systems is the key task of a defense contractor.

Centralized systems ease the task of a planner. In such a system, relatively fewer factors can be used to predict an outcome, so the planner can focus on them and exclude others. Decentralized systems are more complex. Knowledge of the behavior of one part says little about how the system as a whole will respond. A decentralized system demands more time and resources to plan.

*State.* The condition of a system at any point in time is called its state. For example, the state of fabrication department can be described by its work-in-process. Often a state is maintained using control systems. For instance, inventory control systems maintain safety stocks and order when the inventory of a supply item (its state) falls below a predetermined level.

The states of dominant system features often must be controlled, suggesting that a control system is required in most plans. Thus, state-controlled systems suggest to the planner the need to enumerate control features needed in their operation.

*Equifinality.* Equifinality applies principally to open systems. It requires that the same final state is reached, regardless of the route taken through the system or antecedent conditions. No matter how a system is activated or what environmental forces are acting on it, this type of system will reach a particular final state. For instance, if the same results are expected for a quality-control test that can be initiated and conducted in several ways, the test is an equifinal system. Planners use the concept of equifinality to determine if a system has (or can develop by the addition of feedback) equilibrium. Equifinality offers several advantages that can be exploited during planning. Systems with such a capability need less aggressive (if any) control mechanisms. Van Gigch (1979) contends equifinality seldom occurs outside of the living system, but that feedback can be used to help all systems to acquire this highly desirable property.

### System Regulation

System maintenance is an important aspect of system operation. System performance is influenced and maintained in several ways. Factors useful in system regulation are equilibrium, stability, communication, feedback, homeostasis, control,

**Table 12-5** ▲ **Factors That (1) Regulate and Maintain Systems, (2) Involve System Change, and (3) Lead to System Failure**

| Factors That Regulate and Maintain Systems | Factors That Involve System Change | Factors That Lead to System Failure |
|---|---|---|
| Devise ways to control system operation using the following principles: | Seek ways to incorporate: | Create ways to buffer: |
| Equilibrium | Adaptation (elastic or plastic) | Positive entropy |
| Stability | Learning | Overloads |
| Communication | Change directionally | Stress (internal and external) |
| Feedback (positive and negative) | Growth | Disturbances |
| Homeostasis (self-regulation) | Imposed process modification | Decay |
| Control | | |
| Negentropy | | |
| Regeneration | | |

negative entropy, and regeneration (see Table 12-5). Planners use some of these features to suggest how a control system can be created. These systems' features identify tendencies that need to be monitored in any control procedure.

*Equilibrium.* Equilibrium can be thought of as the opposite of disorder. Systems with equilibrium have a rest state that the system gravitates toward, such as 98.6°F for a person's body temperature. This rest state is always sought after a disturbance, such as a sickness. All systems with equifinality also have equilibrium.

Equilibrium can also be defined in physical systems where disruptions tend to be damped and the system returns to its original state. For instance, a car traveling on a bridge causes a slight deflection in the bridge, which returns to its original position if the bridge is maintained in equilibrium. Operating systems, such as a fabrication department, also have equilibrium states, but they are not as clearly defined and must be maintained by feedback.

Forrester (1961, 1968) used the notion of equilibrium to model the operations of an organization that draws inputs and produces outputs in a series of transactions that couple the activities needed to produce a final product. Such an organizational system has components that draw inputs and produce outputs that are internally used or consumed. The system operates in equilibrium when its demands for inputs and outputs are met. Inventories are maintained and other devices used so shortages do not develop that disturb this equilibrium. To create equilibrium in a system, the planner often mimics the equilibrium processes in living systems, devising or creating feedback.

*Stability.* A system is termed stable if it tends to remain within certain limits. Systems can display stable characteristics in some parameters and instability in others. Stability is defined in terms of the parameters that are kept in relative equilibrium. The upper and lower boundaries of these parameters identify a domain of stability. Systems able to stay between these boundaries are called *resilient*. For example, a quality-control test must be accurate within a certain tolerance. Upper and lower boundaries for errors can be used to define expected performance. However, to maintain a very low error rate in a quality-control program demanding many independent tests can be prohibitively costly.

In social systems, stability can be an undesirable property when, for example, managers seek to change behavior in an attempt to alter cost or performance. When change has been successful, the new expectations for cost or performance create a norm, which defines a new plateau of stability. Control systems are then activated to ensure that the norm is embraced and then maintained (made stable). Planners use the concept of stability to define acceptable variations in performance for operating systems.

*Homeostasis.* A homeostatic system is self-regulating. The homeostatic system changes its components in the face of environmental changes (Ackoff, 1971). The state of the system is maintained as its environment changes by internal adjustment. The home heating system's thermostat is an example. Living organisms also have this capability. Homeostatic control is used to maintain body temperature and other parameters within ranges demanded by the body so it can function.

Planners can make good use of the concept of homeostatic control. This type of control is used by a manager to review cost-variance reports. For example, when performance (e.g., cost) falls outside acceptable ranges, a set of actions (plans) can be automatically evoked. Homeostatic control embodies both the control system and a set of actions to be used, if the system is found to be out of control.

*Feedback.* Feedback is the most commonly cited system feature and the most misunderstood. It occurs when the output, behavior, or a final state of a system is used to modify future system operations. The modification can be negative or positive. *Negative feedback* attempts to counteract or reduce the output. In positive feedback, the output is amplified (Kim, 1975). Performance monitoring in a control system uses a negative feedback concept, comparing performance with norms in an attempt to narrow the performance gap. Negative feedback is difference reducing. *Positive feedback* can describe a growth process. For instance, federal investments in education and health have been made to create an impetus or direction, hoping to stimulate a deviation-amplification process. The expectation is that a modest investment will highlight opportunities or needs, which others can be enticed to fill. Much of economic growth theory also relies on a positive feedback principle. However, in underdeveloped countries, the growth in income for the wealthy was found to be matched by a decline in income for the poor, nullifying the growth effect.

Feedback can also deal with objectives, monitoring progress toward the objective's achievement or changing the objective through learning. For instance, firms often use the average performance of their key competitors (e.g., market share or return on investment) as an objective to be met or exceeded. Feedback is objective seeking in this example. If the objective changes given current beliefs about acceptable performance, the feedback becomes objective modifying.

These examples identify three types of gaps that are considered in a feedback process. First, objectives can be compared with performance. Second, initial and final performance outputs can be compared (e.g., investments compared with returns). Third, performance in one system can be compared with performance in another comparable system. Each offers the planner tips on ways to devise control mechanisms for a plan.

*Communication.* The information generated through system operations is called communication. The communication can be formal or informal. For instance, a raw material receiving system communicates internally to order tests and to assign lots to inventory, using various codes. The same system communicates informally by its actions, and the implications people draw from these actions.

Some types of system communication can be used by a planner to provide positive or negative feedback for the operation of homeostatic or other types of control systems. Other forms of communication must be kept confidential. Illustrations include patient status in a hospital and employee performance appraisals in a firm. The planner must devise ways to keep this type of system communication confidential during normal system operation. Lists of communications generated by a system are reviewed to see if they must be placed in a restricted access or other categories.

Permanent records are seldom needed for the remaining types of system communications. Eliminating nonessential records is a valuable cost reduction tactic.

*Control.* Control makes up the set of actions taken to meet some objective in system operation, using feedback information. The set of routines, SOPs, or procedures used to reach objectives is *positive control*. The actions taken to avoid threats are termed *negative control*.

The planner considers the need to construct both positive and negative control features into the plan. Negative control may use feedback in a homeostatic framework to manage system performance. Positive control includes contingency plans that can be enacted when certain conditions arise. For instance, the threat of a strike entices firms to make plans to increase finished goods inventories or to stockpile raw materials.

*Steady State.* The term "steady state" describes a system in equilibrium, often with a balance between inputs and outputs (e.g., raw materials and finished goods, hospital admissions and discharges). Systems moving from one operating state to another, such as increasing capacity, are transient, showing a growth or decline in outputs with a certain level of inputs. New systems often go through transient phases to reach a steady state. Control activities often have steady-state operation as their objective. Open systems show equifinality if they can attain a steady state of operation.

The properties of a system's steady state suggest norms for a control system. For instance, planners study how a comparable system functions to deduce the characteristics of steady-state operation. Simulations give similar insights by investigating the operating features in the analog of a system not yet designed.

*Negative Entropy.* Disorder in a closed system is called entropy. Negative entropy (negentropy) implies increased order. Negative entropy can be informational, such as the reduction of message uncertainty (Shannon and Weaver, 1949). Negative entropy can also describe the acquisition of knowledge. For an open system to survive, it must have negentropy, which occurs when the system reduces uncertainty and increases the predictability of operation. Many managerial systems attempt to acquire this quality.

Planners identify and build in mechanisms that create negative entropy in system operation. Systems that allow the practitioner to learn and modify procedures in the face of performance have this feature.

*Regeneration.* Regeneration occurs when a component of a system is replaced or repaired. Analogs can be drawn from biology. Biological systems can be observed doing repair, which suggests they have a built-in signal indicating the need to regenerate a part of their structure (Ashby, 1962).

When planning a system, it is often desirable to use mechanisms that can signal the need to replace or recharge components. Planners use this principle when they establish preventive maintenance programs that replace or repair worn components before they are predicted to fail.

### System Change

Systems respond to their environment and to internal pressures that suggest obsolescence. System change is a fundamental planning notion. Factors and concepts important to system change are adaptation, learning, growth, directionality, and process (see Table 12-5). Planners use these concepts to plan systems that can respond to change while minimizing declines in performance.

*Adaptation.* The adaptive process is called *plastic* when it does not return to its original configuration and *elastic* when it does. Strains can occur that exceed the limits of system elasticity, causing rupture or even destruction of the system. Systems can be planned so they have a high or low capability to adapt to change.

Adaptive systems respond by changing internally or by modifying the environment. Ackoff (1971) defines four types of adaptation that have an interesting symmetry in the location of the disturbance and what is modified to respond to it.

*Class 1 (environment-environment).* The system responds to an external change by environmental modification. For instance, in a class 1 adaptation, a manager would set higher prices when the costs of supply, labor, and the like rise. Home building contractors and oil companies rely on this approach.

*Class 2 (environment-system).* Responding to the environment, the system makes internal modifications in a class 2 adaptation. For example, a cost-control program can be mounted in the face of reduced sales.

*Class 3 (system-environment).* Predicted changes in an operating system are used as the rationale to try to make modifications in the environment. A class 3 adaptation is illustrated by a company CEO who expects lower profits because operating costs are expected to increase and tests the market to see if a price increase will be accepted.

*Class 4 (system-system).* Actual changes in the system are measured and used to modify the system, such as initiating methods improvement and cost control when poor financial performance is observed.

Planners can devise control and regulating systems, as well as contingency plans, that draw their rationale for changes in the ways described. Integrated approaches measure performance changes, induced both internally and externally, and consider both environmental and system modifications as responses.

*Learning.* Modifications made in the face of performance information is a special case of adaptation called *learning*. Ackoff (1971) defines learning as seeking to improve performance in the pursuit of objective under changing environmental conditions. The ability to modify system's behavior and its memory are key elements in system learning.

Planners should consider ways to construct plans that have sufficient flexibility to permit learning. Such plans are particularly useful when the system is open, tends to be unstable, and faces a shifting environment.

*Change Directionality.* Change can be reversible or irreversible. Reversible change describes a perturbation that moves through a system but leaves it in its original state. An irreversible change causes the system to move to another state. For example, the pricing of products may or may not respond to the increased cost for supplies, labor, or other factors.

The direction of a change creates a special problem for the design of control procedures. An irreversible change has priority because it causes more important problems than does a reversible change. For example, soft drink and chocolate bar producers experimented with price changes (a reversible change) and reducing product size (a less reversible change) to determine consumer acceptance. These companies were wary of reducing the size of a soft drink bottle or a candy bar package because such a change is more costly and disruptive. Identifying and categorizing changes likely to occur and their directionality suggests priority concerns in planning system controls.

*Growth.* A basic system feature is growth. It occurs when a capacity is enlarged (e.g., a building program), capability is increased (e.g., new products), ability is enhanced (e.g., management expands its skills), and in other ways. Growth can be a desirable feature of a system, and provisions for it are often demanded in a plan. For instance, building programs pay attention to both current and future needs, often identifying several of the growth phases that are expected. The facility is designed so it can accommodate the anticipated growth.

*Process.* A system process captures the steps taken to produce some outcome or to meet an objective. Each step or behavioral act in the process is intended to bring the process closer to producing some product. Ackoff and Emery (1972) identify four types of systems processes:

*Type 1: State maintaining.* This type of process responds to the negative feedback. A type 1 process is often thought of as a control system, such as process seeks negentropy, reducing variety, and exceptions.

*Type 2: Purposive.* This type of process seeks several objectives that have a common attribute (e.g., cost). The system's process is fixed by past practice or external agents and cannot be altered. An example is a personnel policy and other SOPs in an organization.

*Type 3: Purposeful.* This type of process modifies objectives and its procedures, in the light of new conditions, to meet new norms. An example of a purposeful process is a planning group.

*Type 4: Ideal.* The ideal-seeking system is a special case of a purposeful system that chooses more stringent objectives when an objective has been met. Such a process defines the new objective evolving a concept of "perfection" and pursues this concept to evolve toward an ideal state. This type of system procedure is often variety enhancing, hoping to introduce new concepts that have value in improving results.

Planners use various combinations of these process types to check and refine system procedures. Purposive systems are tested to see if they can become purposeful and to determine what benefits might be realized from such a change.

### System Failure

Systems breakdown stems from excessive disruptions, disintegration of its components, and failures in performance. Adaptations can be stretched beyond feasible limits when disruptions become excessive. Also, the system can gradually lose its cohesion and become fragmented. For example, when the best people in an organization resign and are replaced by people who are less competent, the process of fragmentation begins. Ultimately, such a system can fail because it no longer provides sufficient value to its users. Factors that cause system failure are stress, disturbance, overload, positive entropy, and decay (see Table 12-5).

*Positive Entropy.* System planners can overestimate the performance potential of a system when they fail to account for the gradual movement toward less predictable system operation. Many systems have such a feature, which is called *positive entropy*. Such a system gradually loses cohesion among its key components or shows a gradual decline in the reliability of its performance. For example, many counseling programs depend on a hospital for backup psychiatric services. The relationship shows positive entropy when delays in getting patients admitted gradually increase. The relationship between the hospital and the counseling agency gradually deteriorates, caused by perceptions of overuse or misuses held by key hospital people, and beliefs by the counselors that the hospital does not live up to its commitments. Such views cause positive entropy to develop.

Some performance factors also have positive entropy. For example, the initial enthusiasm of counselors can be buffeted by disinterested administrators, gatekeeping behavior, and excessive layers of bureaucracy that make needed action difficult. The counselor's zeal declines, and performance becomes less predictable. Difficult cases can be abandoned because the counselor loses his or her willingness to fight a system that seldom responds to legitimate needs.

Positive entropy creates transient system performance. A new steady-state performance often follows learning, adaptations to environmental change, routinization, and the moderation of zeal held by system operators. Planners should consider the initial period of operation as a transient condition and not use this level of performance as a norm.

*Overload.* When demands on a system are gradually or abruptly increased, overloads can occur. System planners should be concerned about the limits to the capacity of their plan. For example, a power overload in an electrical circuit can cause system failure. Traffic continues to move through a highway interchange until an overload occurs and a traffic jam results where no movement of traffic is possible. In each case, the system can be designed to allow for more capacity to avoid overload, often causing increased cost. System planners are concerned about capacities attempting to predict when an overload will occur and how much should be spent to alter capacity so that an overload is rare.

Systems with human operators can also have overloads. For example, the queue in an emergency room after a disaster can become so long that rules for triage no longer apply. The emergency care patient may have to wait so long that he or she becomes treated like a patient with a self-limiting condition. System breakdown occurs unless there are procedures available to activate alternative treatment sites.

*Stress.* System stability can be threatened by stress. System planners devise ways to dissipate stress within a system to ensure its stability.

Stress can be internal or external. Internal stress can stem from conflicts over goals, unacceptable performance, and new directions or programs. For instance, periodic changes in operations can stress an organization, requiring people perpetually to learn new procedures and tasks. The organization can become more unstable if change comes faster than it can be absorbed and routinized. To deal with such a situation, managers reject plans with merit because of the disruption that would stem from their implementation.

External system stress is imposed by the environment. For instance, repeated budget cuts imposed on a state department of natural resources create stress by gradually eroding the department's ability to provide quality services. Philanthropy and research grants can soften the impact of these cuts. Mechanisms to buffer predictable external and internal stresses should be planned as part of the system.

*Disturbance.* A disturbance can move a system from one state to another (Rapoport, 1986). System planners attempt to design systems that can cope with a variety of disturbances.

Typically, disturbances have their origin outside a system. For example, Iowa corn farmers were recently faced with corn prices of $1 per bushel when it cost them $3 per bushel to produce it. Similarly, government price controls on hospital services drive down revenues. Medicaid can (and often does) reclassify a nursing home from a skilled to an intermediate skilled facility (ISF), reducing the cost-per-day reimbursement rate. Such disturbances can lead to stress, causing instability and eventually overloads. System procedures should be able to dampen predictable disturbances. For instance, nursing homes facing a change in classification from skilled to ISF should have contingency plans to modify nurse staffing in the home. The contingency plan could use the staffing change either as a negotiating position with Medicaid enforcers or to balance costs and revenues in the facility.

*Decay.* Many systems have key components that gradually lose their energy or competence. Competence can deteriorate or the component can simply wear out. Decay is different from positive entropy, which also causes performance to decline. In decay, the components fail rather than lose their cohesion. System planners devise repair routines to cope with decay. For example, the people who control the system can be periodically assessed using performance appraisal and other managerial tools.

### Operating Principles in Systems

Principles that govern the operation of systems can be enumerated to aid the planner in thinking about systems procedures and modeling them. These principles are as follows:

1. Indifference
2. Complementation
3. Invariance
4. Indeterminability

They often become an overlay to issues of system stability, survival, and viability.

*The Indifference Principle.* To say that an observation is correct, the observational or notational process must be validated. The principle of indifference states that outcome of an observation must be independent of the observational process. For instance, naming or categorizing something must not depend on who is the observer. The problem often arises in the diagnosis of both mental and physical problems. For example, psychiatrists often disagree on a patient's diagnosis. However, it does not matter if a schizophrenic is or is not a multiple personality if the treatment is the same. To illustrate, Gustafson (1969) developed a program to diagnose thyroid disease and hyperthyroidism only to find the treatment did not depend on which diagnosis was made; it was the same for either. The principle of indifference is violated in these examples.

The indifference principle requires that the basis for putting things in categories must be clear. For example, a malpractice study used data, provided by a hospital survey, of closed malpractice claims where the hospital was a defendant. The respondent was to classify each claim by specifying the severity of the injury, in addition to claimant factors, settlement amount, and other factors. Note that the basis for selecting one category depends, to a degree, on the observer's interpretation, which violates the indifference principle.

A superobserver (Weinberg, 1985) can cross-reference two other observers who view things in different ways, as shown in Figure 12-11. In system planning this type of capability is essential.

*The Complementary Principle.* No matter how carefully a representation is constructed, complementation can never be ensured. For instance, two observers of an organization applying organizational development (OD) principles may develop

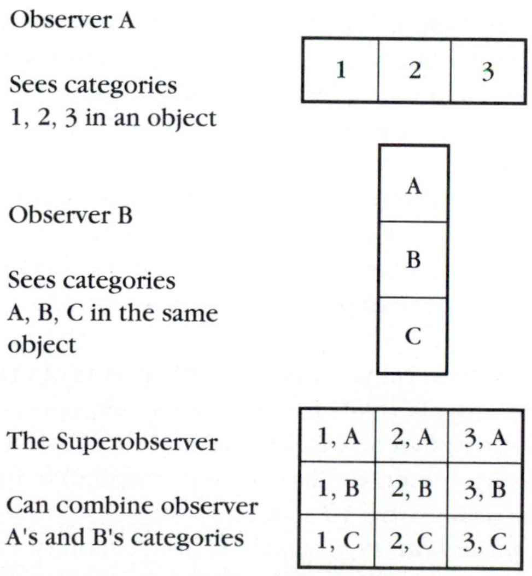

**Figure 12-11** ▲ **The Superobserver**

different views about the necessity for and type of action that seems needed. These views are called complementary when one is completely reducible to the other.

Dissimilarity in the prescriptions is caused by the inability of OD measurement tools to eliminate bias and misclassification, no matter how carefully they were applied. Further, the OD specialists are not independent observers because their ideas were derived from the same system. To be complementary, the two points of view must be reducible to essentially the same position. When observers make infinitely refined observations (e.g., those with unlimited levels in a relevance tree), their points of view become complementary.

Most observers do not care if their views fail to be fully complementary. Planners who have different disciplines can construct different plans, even though they are based on the same definition of a performance gap. Each plan is based on the same information that defines needs, but the plans will never be fully reconcilable. The planned change process should preserve these views as options for further study and perhaps synthesis.

*The Principle of Invariance.* System attributes are called *qualities*. A quality should be original or a priori, not derived, although many qualities are defined in terms of another attribute. Qualities can be extensive or intensive. Assume that a system, such as accounting, is divided into two pieces. If each subsystem can still operate, the operation has an intensive quality. An extensive system split in half can no longer operate because some of its activities (e.g., coordination of a supervisor) cannot be divided. One of the parts cannot be allocated to a portion of the split system. There are two ways to partition a system: one that preserves its ability to function and one that fails to preserve it.

To be useful, naming portions of system, such as public-private, centralized-decentralized, and the like, must help the planner think about the categories that are produced by these divisions. If the principle of invariance holds, a transformation would not modify the meaning of these categories.

*The Indeterminability Principle.* The final state of most systems cannot be predicted by knowing its inputs. Thus, most systems of interest to the planner do not have the property of equifinality. Even if the structure of the transform is known (a glass box), the planner must wait until an output is produced to see if its features are desirable.

The indeterminability principle contends that the output can be due to a constraint of the environment as well as the system. For instance, researchers who developed morphine as a painkiller were unable to tell if location of the injection (e.g., near source of pain) or a person's physical characteristics were factors in drug effectiveness.

The indeterminability principle points out that the number of untested assumptions in any plan will be enormous. Sometimes a constraint or even peculiarities in the environment can be the key to effectiveness, and not the plan. Simulation techniques (described later in this chapter) help to identify the reliability of system outputs, if not what produced them.

*Application Principles.* System stability, survival, and viability are used to apply the system principle. Stability may or may not be a desirable quality, as discussed previously. Assuming that it is desirable, the principle of invariance can be applied. The principle asks why the system or its components remain unchanged. The answer suggests ways to incorporate stability into the plan.

Survival deals with why systems continue to exist. Systems with this property are often thought to be particularly useful as templates for a planning process, as discussed in Chapter 4. Considerable energy is often consumed in modeling systems that are survivors. The principles of indifference and completeness apply. What observational process is used to classify the system as a survivor? Is it accurate? Does survival mean the system also has admirable qualities? Answers to these questions are essential before adaptation of a system by another user can be undertaken.

To be viable, a system must be able to function in various environmental conditions by adapting to these changes. This often calls for an ability to devise new procedures that can improve performance. Adaptations of this type were described in the system operation discussion.

### Summary

General systems theory does not offer planning principles. Although not useful as a planning technique, GST can be used in conjunction with other techniques to identify factors and concepts that can aid the plan by improving its operations.

Construction techniques can be merged in two ways: system matrix GST and block diagram GST. In each case, GST poses a checklist of considerations for the the planner to ponder, such as determining if environmental factors have been accounted for and if the system to be planned has been fully defined. The checklist also enumerates methods of control, provides responses to predictable change, and specifies how decline and breakdown can occur. The systems matrix approach creates a system that can be checked by GST principles. In the block diagram technique, existing systems can be interrogated to see how the system deals with control and other system features.

## ▲  THE INTERROGATION PHASE

Most interrogation techniques focus on how inputs are transformed to an output. These techniques offer ways to describe a sequence in the system matrix or transforms in the block diagram technique to shape system procedures. The construction phase of the detailing stage identifies several ways to convert inputs to outputs for each component in the structure. Several options in transformation procedures were required. The interrogation phase is used to improve and fine-tune the operating principles of these transforming mechanisms.

### Interpretive Structural Modeling

Interpretive structural modeling applies graph theory to create a network that describes the relational properties among a set of elements. The ISM procedure has two key steps: constructing an element set and specifying relations among the elements. The elements correspond to *nodes* in a network, and the relationship between elements is denoted graphically by a line segment.

Transforming mechanisms, such as the procedure used to manufacture a product or provide a service, require steps that can be arranged in a sequence. The human mind is limited in its ability to deal with tasks that require many elements having complex relationships. One has some notion about the steps in a process but is often stymied trying to enumerate and understand all the relationships. To aid this process, Warfield (1990) contends that the "mental model" should be exchanged for one that allows relationships to be viewed comprehensively. With such a model, the planner can focus attention on the logic of each relationship, questioning and fine-tuning it. The ability to interrogate the model without losing sight of the overall structure is a key benefit of ISM.

For example, Wallen (1975) points out that a human's learning apparatus is composed of sight, sound, and cognitive steps. Because auditory channels are weaker than the visual, there is a relation between these steps in a learning process. The "weaker than" relation is one of several relationships that can be described by ISM. Assigning values to each relationship allows a process to be modeled. The model aids the planner first in understanding and then in manipulating the process. The philosophical basis and analytical details for ISM can be found in Warfield (1976; 1990) and the mathematical background in Norman and Cartright (1975) and Elmaghraby (1964).

### Steps in the ISM Technique

A procedure used by the ISM technique is shown in Figure 12-12. The ISM procedure develops a matrix and from it a digraph that provides the interpretive structural model.

The ISM procedure begins by linking one's view (mental model) of the procedural elements with a matrix. This approach merely exchanges the mental representation for another. Although not fully isomorphic (the structures are *not* identical), the matrix seeks to document and preserve key relations. For example, imagine communication between departments in an organization. Let 1 designate such an information flow and 0 designate no information flow. Figure 12-13 describes how departments 1, 2, and 3 in the hypothetical organization communicate. The matrix is filled in by asking, "Does department 1 use its own information?" (Or is it consumed internally as well as externally?) If yes, a 1 is entered at the first row-column intersection. Department 1 does not provide information to department 2, so a 0 is entered in the second column for row 1. The analyst continues in this fashion, documenting the relationship between all departments, or in general terms, ele-

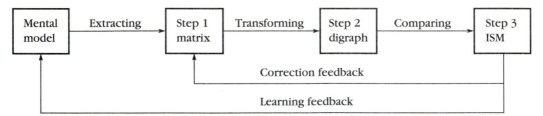

**Figure 12-12** ▲ The ISM Procedure

FROM

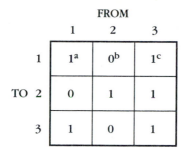

Key: ᵃ, Department 1 creates information for internal use;
ᵇ, Department 2 does not send information to department 1;
ᶜ, Department 3 sends information to department 1.

**Figure 12-13** ▲ **Capturing Departmental Communications in the Matrix**

ments or steps, under consideration. The matrix is used to record the answers to these queries. The paired comparison technique described in Chapter 10 is used to organize the task of making comparisons. Several types of relationships can be documented in this way, including precedence (which is done first), subordination, severity, and importance.

The mathematical laws of transitivity may or may not apply to the digraph that is created. In precedence or importance relations, transitivity must hold. (See the discussion on cyclical majorities in Chapter 10.) Transitivity is not a factor in other relationships. For instance, in a precedence relation, if A precedes B, and B precedes C, then A must also come before C. Other relationships may not be symmetrical. For example, department A may send information to B and B may send to C, but logic does not require C to send information to A.

The next step creates a digraph. The relationships shown in the matrix are displayed graphically. Figure 12-14 provides a digraph for the information in Figure 12-13. Departments 1 and 3 have a reciprocal relationship. Department 2 receives information from department 3 but not 1. Each department creates information that is consumed internally, shown by the arrow that starts and ends in the same department.

Computer programs have been devised to construct a digraph from a matrix. They are needed when the number of elements or steps become large. The digraph

**Figure 12-14** ▲ **A Digraph for Departmental Communications**

provides a convenient picture that allows the planner and others to grasp quickly the structure of the transform, procedure, or sequence. It is particularly useful when faced with a complex situation or when comparing competing alternatives.

Several types of processes can be represented with a digraph. For instance, the digraph in Figure 12-14 could be *actual* information flow, which could be compared with *needed* information flow to identify gaps. The digraph could compare various ways to fabricate a product, provide a service, or carry out a procedure (e.g., billing) by documenting their steps. Any set of procedures can be compared using digraphs.

### Modeling a Treatment Process

Wallen (1975) offers an example of using ISM to capture steps in a treatment procedure for learning disabled children. Remedial measures are selected to deal with learning impediments, after specifying each child's learning needs and their relationships. Impediments to learning for a learning disabled child appear in Table 12-6. (For convenience, these procedures have been assigned an alphabetical code.)

The ISM technique can be applied in several ways. For example, ISM can be used to contrast evaluations made by treatment professionals. Comparing the ISM digraphs forces conflicts into the open. To work out a mutually agreeable treatment plan, those involved in the treatment process must consider and resolve these conflicts over diagnosis. The vote-discuss-vote sequence can be used to aid in resolving disputes in diagnosis, shown by the digraphs. The VDV procedure can be used to build a consensus digraph. The points of disagreement among the treatment team can be captured by the matrix using percentages drawn from each individual response. Resolving conflicts concerning each individual's needs creates a treatment plan with high acceptance and one with superior quality, because it incorporates the views of several professionals (e.g., psychologists, psychiatric social workers, and others).

### Table 12-6 ▲ Learning Impediment Categories

| | |
|---|---|
| A. | Auditory reception |
| B. | Visual reception |
| C. | Auditory association |
| D. | Visual expression |
| E. | Verbal expression |
| F. | Manual expression |
| G. | Grammatic closure |
| H. | Auditory closure |
| I. | Sound blending |
| J. | Visual closure |
| K. | Auditory sequential memory |
| L. | Visual sequential memory |
| M. | Visual-motor coordination |

### The Matrix Development Step

The treatment professional working with the analyst fills in the matrix shown in Figure 12-15. In this example, the relationship between learning impediments was expressed in terms of severity, each pair of impediments was judged to determine which is more severe for a given child. To construct the matrix, each row is considered by moving across it asking if learning impediment denoted A is a more severe problem than B, C, and so on, for a particular child, using the paired comparison technique. In Figure 12-15, A (auditory reception) turned out to be subordinate to all other learning impediment categories for this patient, so a 0 was entered in each column across row A. Also, B (visual reception) was not a severe problem for this child, so all 0's are found in row B. In row C, auditory association was a more important problem than A or B. C was found to be less severe impediment to learning than F and I, so a 0 was entered under these heading in row C and a 1 entered elsewhere. (Note that F is more important than C, and C more important than A or B, so it is demanded, by the symmetry of importance judgments, that F be more important than A or B.)

A large value in the total column in this example indicates a severe impediment. A *small value* suggests a minimal impediment and indicates a good means to use when teaching the child.

IMPEDIMENT CODE

| | A | B | C | D | E | F | G | H | I | J | K | L | M | Total |
|---|---|---|---|---|---|---|---|---|---|---|---|---|---|---|
| A | | 0 | 0 | 0 | 0 | 0 | 0 | 0 | 0 | 0 | 0 | 0 | 0 | 0 |
| B | 0 | | 0 | 0 | 0 | 0 | 0 | 0 | 0 | 0 | 0 | 0 | 0 | 0 |
| C | 1 | 1 | | 1 | 1 | 0 | 1 | 1 | 0 | 1 | 1 | 1 | 1 | 10 |
| D | 0 | 0 | 0 | | 0 | 0 | 0 | 0 | 0 | 0 | 0 | 0 | 0 | 0 |
| E | 0 | 0 | 0 | 0 | | 0 | 0 | 0 | 0 | 0 | 0 | 0 | 0 | 0 |
| F | 1 | 1 | 1 | 1 | 1 | | 1 | 0 | 1 | 1 | 1 | 1 | 1 | 11 |
| G | 1 | 1 | 0 | 1 | 1 | 0 | | 0 | 0 | 1 | 1 | 1 | 0 | 7 |
| H | 1 | 1 | 0 | 1 | 1 | 0 | 1 | | 0 | 1 | 1 | 1 | 1 | 9 |
| I | 1 | 1 | 1 | 1 | 1 | 0 | 1 | 1 | | 1 | 1 | 1 | 1 | 11 |
| J | 0 | 0 | 0 | 0 | 0 | 0 | 0 | 0 | 0 | | 0 | 0 | 0 | 0 |
| K | 1 | 1 | 0 | 1 | 1 | 0 | 0 | 0 | 0 | 1 | | 1 | 0 | 6 |
| L | 0 | 0 | 0 | 0 | 0 | 0 | 0 | 0 | 0 | 0 | 0 | | 0 | 0 |
| M | 1 | 1 | 0 | 1 | 1 | 0 | 1 | 0 | 0 | 1 | 1 | 1 | | 8 |

(Left label: IMPEDIMENT CODE)

Figure 12-15 ▲ Matrix for the Learning Disabilities Example

The Digraph

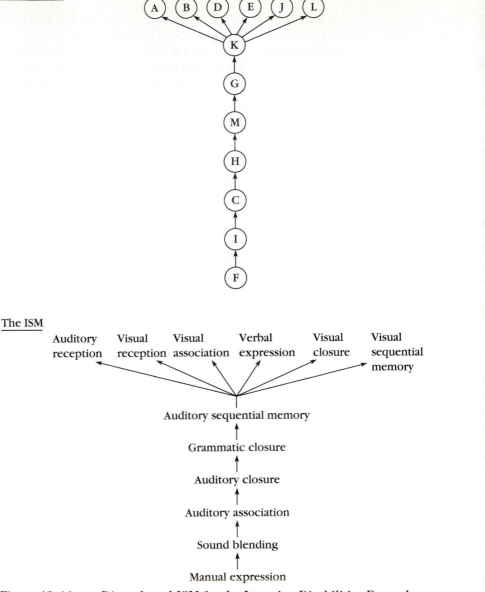

The ISM

Figure 12-16 ▲ Digraph and ISM for the Learning Disabilities Example
Reprinted from Wallen (1975).

### *The Digraph Step*

The matrix (Figure 12-15) shows that A, B, D, E, J, and L have all 0's in their rows. They are the least severe impediments so they represent the child's strongest learning channels. The digraph (Figure 12-16) decodes the relationship shown in the matrix with a graph that depicts the hierarchical relationship. Severity can be quickly determined by counting the number of 1's in each row. (This procedure is the same as the tallying approach for the paired comparison technique discussed in Chapter 10.) The totals are shown in the last column of Figure 12-16.

Rows A, B, D, E, J, and L represent impediment codes that are the least severe, so they are located at the top of the digraph. Rows F and I represent the most severe impediment. To break the ties, note that F is judged more severe than I when they were directly compared, placing F at the bottom of the digraph with I immediately above F. The remaining impediments are sorted in the same way, creating the structure shown in Figure 12-16. The interpretative structural model is created by substituting the learning impediments for the codes (Figure 12-16). The arrows on the digraph indicate the direction of *decreasing* severity, pointing toward the strongest learning channels.

*Confirmational Steps.* The ISM chart is given to the professional for confirmation. This step is essential because of the following three problems that crop up when the paired comparison technique is used to capture human judgments:

1.  Reflexivity
2.  Asymmetry
3.  Transitivity

The actual number of comparisons may be less than the multiple of elements (13 × 13 in the learning desirability example) because an element may not be comparable to itself. This situation is called *reflexivity*. It was true in the learning disabled example, but not true for the information flow example in the previous section. Information can be used internally as well as externally. Hence, internal use must be counted when describing a relationship based on either precedence or frequency of use.

*Asymmetry* occurs when a person judges A to be more important (or severe) than, say, F, and when getting to element F, contends it is more important than A. Such illogical choices stem from people's information processing limitations and recall problems. By checking the matrices for symmetry, the planner can identify where conflicting choices are made and get them straightened out before building the digraph. Ties (elements with equal importance or steps that must be done concurrently) are represented by a 1 at both intersections in Figure 12-15 (see Chapter 10).

*Transitivity* poses a more serious problem. For instance, if item A is judged more important than B, and B more important than C, but C is seen as more important than A, it creates a "cyclical majority." Cyclical majorities and procedures to deal with them are discussed in Chapter 10. The planner must recognize transitivity problems and attempt to resolve them through questioning the expert making the judgments. When the planner deals with symmetry, transitivity, and reflexivity problems, discussion of seemingly illogical choices can lead to new insights.

Developing a digraph using the scoring system in Chapter 10 is relatively fast and keeps a meeting moving along. Experts required less than 15 minutes to complete the matrix after training for the learning disabilities example. Although complex structures (more than 13 elements) will take longer, the time demands on experts are modest, in view of the value of the information obtained.

### Types of ISM Applications

The ISM technique is easy to understand and can be used to represent any procedure. The model of the procedure is shaped through interrogation. For instance, the manufacturing procedure that a firm seeks to copy can be captured with ISM. Steps in the hospital treatment of patients with end-stage renal disease can be modeled by tracing the sequential relationships among elements in the treatment process. The "boarding process," in which cancer patients are prospectively reviewed to select treatment, can be represented with ISM. The ISM technique can be used to lay out relationships among steps in a billing procedure, as well as other systems and procedures used by an organization. In each case, two steps are required. First, expert (e.g., the product engineer or the nephrologist) judgments are checked and fed back to fine-tune the procedure being modeled. Second, differences among ISM representations (e.g., between engineers or nephrologists) are explored. These differences may stem from individual views or the operating systems each has seen in use. The VDV technique (Chapter 10) helps experts resolve the differences through discussion.

ISM has many applications. The technique has been used to determine priorities among objectives created by a city council. Using ISM to sort out the conflicting demands made in a management by objectives program can also be envisioned. Similarly, the relational aspects in a problem list from an NGT or a brainwriting group could be modeled. NGT and the other group processes produce many ideas with an implicit relationship. ISM makes these relationships explicit. In strategic management, order and causality relationships among issues and strategies, identified using a group process, are captured with ISM (Nutt and Backoff, 1992). Warfield (1990) describes a hypothetical application, using ISM to set national objectives. Malone (1977) describes an ISM application that determined investment barriers in an inner city, considering the relative importance of vandalism, property taxes, the neighborhood's appearance, land cost, security problem, and the like. Also, ISM can be used to deal with decisions, process steps, and a wide variety of other phenomena, to clarify the relationships among steps in the procedure.

## Path Techniques

Path techniques can be used to control, manipulate, or study a sequence of well-defined activities. They can be used in tandem with the ISM technique or separately to fine-tune the sequence of activities in a transform or procedure.

### Charting Techniques

Laying out the time relationship among activities helps to find gaps in the logic. Two simple devices are often used: Gantt charts and milestone charts. The Gantt chart is used to plan, control, and demarcate progress toward a goal. As a planning device, bars are placed on a chart to describe all events needed to convert inputs

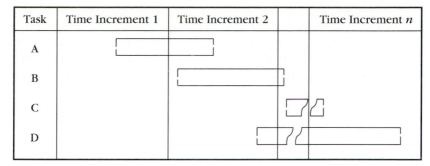

**Figure 12-17** ▲ **A Gantt Chart**

to outputs, against processing time. An example is shown in Figure 12-17. The total processing cycle in this case would be *n* time increments. In this example, there are four tasks. C is dependent upon the completion of B while B and D can begin earlier.

Milestone charts are used to show the control and reporting points within a sequence of activities, providing refinements to Gantt charts. Milestone charts are used primarily to show when needed control reports should be provided and to suggest information that should be contained. An example is provided in Figure 12-18.

### Network Techniques

Networks can be used both to represent and analyze a sequence of tasks to fine-tune them or reduce cost. Program evaluation and review technique and the critical path method (CPM) consider the time needed to carry out steps in a sequence of activities, constructing a network that links the steps. For example, the steps for food preparation in a cafeteria can be laid out by observing the food service activities (or those in comparable organizations). The network finds the "critical path" of steps. To reduce food preparation time, activities along this path are studied in an attempt to shorten them.

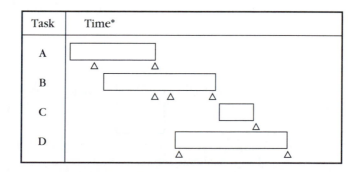

\* Triangle designates a control point.

**Figure 12-18** ▲ **A Milestone Chart**

The two procedures, PERT and CPM, were introduced at approximately the same time (Wattell, 1964; U.S. Department of the Navy, 1958). Each can be used to represent the steps used to convert input(s) to output(s). The steps are called *activities*. The CPM activities, as shown in Figure 12-19, are denoted by circles and the dependencies by arrows (Woodgate, 1964). In PERT, activities are denoted by arrows and the circles that connect the arrows are called *events*, representing points in time when an activity is completed (Cook, 1971). A typical PERT diagram is shown in Figure 12-19. PERT on occasion must use "dummy" activities (arrows) to show the dependency of one step on another. The CPM does not

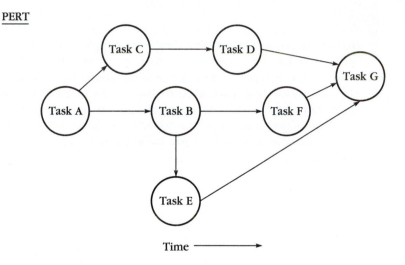

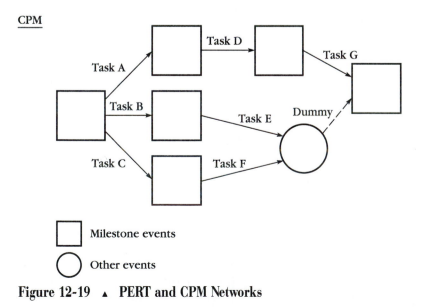

Figure 12-19 ▲ PERT and CPM Networks

use dummy activities, which some consider an advantage. However, tracing paths through the network is harder with CPM because the linkages are not as clear. PERT networks will be described in this chapter because they are somewhat more useful in representing a procedure or sequence.

## PERT

A PERT diagram has four basic features: the network, activities, events, and constraints. The *network* is a graphical representation of all steps in a sequence of activities that make up a procedure. (Recall that a system's procedure is described by sets of transforms that convert inputs to outputs in the block diagram technique and by a *sequence* in the systems matrix technique.) The sequence illustrates the dependency and relationship among the steps in a procedure. Most procedures are unidirectional, with the flow from left to right (see Figure 12-19). Alternative system procedures can be described also by a network.

*Activity* describes the individual steps in a system's procedure. Each step embodies both time (to complete) and costs (to carry out) so steps consume both time and money. The steps can be defined specifically or quite generally, but they are usually tied to a procedure. Steps are shown by arrows. Typically, the length of the arrow is *not* related to time or resources, to make drawing the network easier. Less often, a network is "time scaled" so the length of an arrow *does* correspond to the time needed to carry out the step.

*Events* represent the points in time when each step in the procedure is finished. They do not use either time or money but merely locate the beginning or the end of activities in a procedure. Circles designate most events, with squares used for special events, such as those meriting a control activity (e.g., an interim report). An interface event connects one procedure with another and is designated by a triangle.

*Constraints* indicate that a given step cannot begin until one or more other steps are finished. If step A constrains step B, A usually precedes B. When one step constrains another, because the second cannot begin until the first is completed, a dummy constraint is used (Figure 12-20). The dummy activity requires no time (or money). The dummy is shown with a dotted line in Figure 12-20.

### PERT Time Estimates

Completing the processing faster can pay important dividends. To identify ways to shorten processing steps, the following time-dependent data are required:

1. Step duration
2. Earliest time an event can begin
3. Last permissible time an event can end

Time estimates can be made using means or means and variances. A variance estimate recognizes the stochastic nature of most activities.

In most cases, an 8-hour day, 40-hour work week is assumed. Also, work loads are ignored. The analysis seeks to find the pathway that consumes the most time (or cost) and slack, or free time, in the pathway. Ways to cut time (or cost) from the pathway by eliminating or combining steps are sought.

Simple Constraint

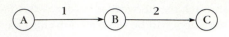

Complex Constraint

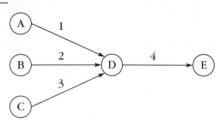

Dummy Constraint

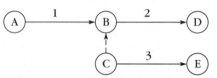

**Figure 12-20** ▲ **Constraints in a PERT Network**

### Step Duration Estimates

Typical PERT practice obtains the most likely, optimistic, and pessimistic estimates for the duration of each activity. It is conventional to combine these estimates as shown:

$$T_E = \frac{a + 4m + b}{6}$$

where $a$ and $b$ are the extreme values, and $m$ is the most likely value. (The most likely time $m$ can also be used to estimate $T_E$.) $T_E$ is used to scale the distance between events which mark the beginning and end of an activity (or a step in a procedure). A crude measure of uncertainty, called the "step-time variance," is computed by

$$s^2 = \frac{(b - a)^2}{6}$$

The variance can be used to identify steps that have considerable uncertainty, for potential modification. The variance is used to identify range of time that may be required to complete processing in the system or the likelihood of completing processing to meet a schedule.

### Start and Completion Times

Times are assigned that place boundaries on when an event can take place. The earliest and latest time an event can occur without delaying another event is determined. The resulting analysis is used to identify the critical path and slack time.

The critical path identifies the most time-consuming path through the network, indicating how long it will take to complete the procedure. Slack time determines available time in the network.

The earliest event time ($T_E$) and the latest event time ($T_L$) are determined by the same procedure. In Figure 12-21 a hypothetical PERT diagram is shown. The calculation of $T_E$ is made by moving from left to right in the network, adding activity time estimates for various pathways. To compute $T_E$ at the beginning of all events, a value of 0 is assigned (Figure 12-21). For events D and G, two arrows converge on a single event. The time for A-B-D equals 7, but A-C-D is 3. The constraint is 7, so this value is selected. The same approach is used for event G. Three pathways must be checked (A-B-D-E-G, A-C-D-E-G, and A-C-F-G) to find the most time-consuming pathway. Adding values one finds

| Pathway | Time |
|---|---|
| A-B-D-E-G | 3 + 4 + 6 + 1 = 14 |
| A-C-D-E-G | 2 + 1 + 6 + 1 = 10 |
| A-C-F-G | 2 + 7 + 3 = 12 |

Pathway A-B-D-E-G is the critical path. It is shown by a double arrow in Figure 12-21. The earliest completion time is given by the $T_E$ value at G.

To compute, $T_L$, the latest allowable time, one starts at the right of the network and works to the left subtracting. Employing the path activity rule in this case

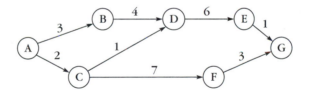

(a) Network with $T_E$

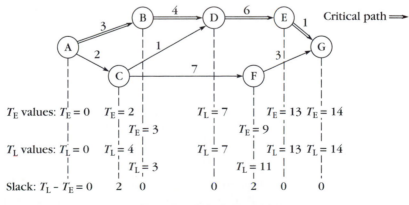

(b) Network with $T_E$ and $T_L$

**Figure 12-21 ▲ PERT Time Calculations**

requires that the smallest value obtained be assigned $T_L$. For instance, for event C, there are two paths: G-E-D-C and G-F-C. The computational process is

| Pathway | Time |
|---------|------|
| G-E-D-C | $14 - 1 - 6 - 1 = 6$ |
| G-F-C | $14 - 3 - 7 = 4$ |

$T_L$ for event C is 4. For event F, $T_L$ is $14 - 3$, or 11, and so on.

To compute slack for each event, $T_E$ is subtracted from $T_L$. Slack was found for event C and F, two units in each case. To compute slack, all events along a pathway are added and subtracted from $T_E$.

| Pathway | Slack |
|---------|-------|
| A-B-D-E-G | 0 |
| A-C-D-E-G | 2 |
| A-C-F-G | 4 |

The pathway with no slack is the critical path. The term *float* is used for slack in CPM; both terms have the same meaning.

When dummy events are used, the computational procedure changes somewhat, as shown in Figure 12-22. If the step between events D and C had a time requirement, it would influence $T_L$, $T_E$, and the slack at event D, reducing the slack in path A-D-C-E (Figure 12-22).

### Adjusting Network Times

When a completion time is known in advance, it can be substituted for $T_L$ in the last event. The latest *start date* is then $T_L$ less the critical path time. Resources can be added that reduce the step time between any two events. As a result, the critical path may change. Trade-offs can be made, balancing costs against shrunken completion

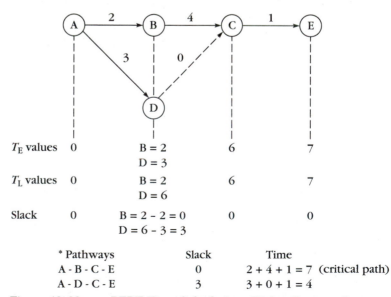

Figure 12-22 ▲ PERT Time Calculations With a Dummy Step

times. Another strategy to alter the critical path is to redefine the step to shorten its time. Steps with long times on the critical path are targeted for investigation. One of two approaches can be used: *paralleling* or *elimination*. By paralleling, sequential steps are changed so they can be decoupled, permitting them to be done at the same time. Elimination substitutes one set of activities for another that take less time to complete.

### Estimating Completion Likelihoods

PERT can also be used to manage the implementation stage of planned change, such as construction projects. This application of PERT is used to illustrate how to estimate the chance of meeting deadlines, and ways to reduce the time requirements in the critical path in order to improve the likelihood of finishing a project on time. For example, assume that the activities in Table 12-7 are required to construct a new facility that increases production capacity. The time for each activity in days is also shown in Table 12-7. Assume that the project manager has been requested to finish the project in 70 days. The PERT diagram in Figure 12-23 shows the order of activities proposed by the contractor to complete the project.

First, the computations for $T_E$ and $s$ for the activities are made, using the data in Table 12-7. (The formulas for $T_E$ and $s$ were used in these computations.) These computations yield the following:

| Activity | $T_E$ | $s$ |
|---|---|---|
| 1 | 10.0 | 1.0 |
| 2 | 17.5 | 4.2 |
| 3 | 12.5 | 1.5 |
| 4 | 10.5 | 2.2 |
| 5 | 20.5 | 2.2 |
| 6 | 10.5 | 1.2 |
| 7 | 5.0 | 0.7 |
| 8 | 6.5 | 0.8 |

### Table 12-7 ▲ Activities in a Construction Project

| Code | Activity | Times in Days | | |
|---|---|---|---|---|
| | | $a$ | $m$ | $b$ |
| 1 | Survey ground and dig basement | 7 | 10 | 13 |
| 2 | Order steel | 5 | 15 | 30 |
| 3 | Pour footers and basement | 9 | 12 | 18 |
| 4 | Grading for building and parking lot | 5 | 10 | 18 |
| 5 | Frame and enclose the upper level | 15 | 20 | 28 |
| 6 | Landscape | 8 | 10 | 15 |
| 7 | Install lights in parking lot | 3 | 5 | 7 |
| 8 | Blacktop parking lot | 4 | 6 | 11 |
| 9 | Plumbing | 6 | 8 | 10 |
| 10 | Electrical | 10 | 12 | 14 |
| 11 | Dummy | | 0 | |
| 12 | Finish Interior | 16 | 20 | 24 |
| 13 | Paint exterior | 3 | 4 | 5 |

| Activity | $T_E$ | $s$ |
|---|---|---|
| 9 | 8.0 | 0.7 |
| 10 | 12.0 | 0.7 |
| 11 | — | — |
| 12 | 20.0 | 1.3 |
| 13 | 4.0 | 0.3 |

Next, the earliest and latest completion times and slack for each event in Figure 12-23 are computed. The results of these computations are as follows:

| Event | $T_E$ | $T_L$ | Slack $T_L - T_E$ |
|---|---|---|---|
| A | 0.0 | 0.0 | 0.0 |
| B | 10.0 | 10.0 | 0.0 |
| C | 22.5 | 22.5 | 0.0 |
| D | 20.5 | 69.5 | 49.0 |
| E | 43.5 | 43.0 | 0.0 |
| F | 25.5 | 74.5 | 49.0 |
| G | 55.0 | 55.0 | 0.0 |
| H | 55.0 | 55.0 | 0.0 |
| J | 75.0 | 75.0 | 0.0 |
| K | 79.0 | 79.0 | 0.0 |

The critical path in Figure 12-23 is 1-3-5-10-11-12-13 (survey, pour cement, frame, electrical, finish, and paint). The contractor proposed to finish the parking lot and landscaping in parallel with construction. Steel is to be ordered in parallel with site preparation, and the plumbing and electrical work are to be done at the same time. The minimal expected completion time with this schedule is 79 days.

Each of these activities has stochastic properties. The likelihood of meeting the 70-day constraint is determined by calculating the area under a normal curve beyond a $Z$ statistic, which is computed by

$$\frac{Scheduled\ time\ -\ Expected\ time}{Sum\ of\ the\ critical\ path\ standard\ deviations} =$$

$$\frac{70 - 79}{(1.0 + 1.5 + 2.2 + 0.7 + 1.3 + 0.3)} = \frac{-9}{7.0} = -1.285$$

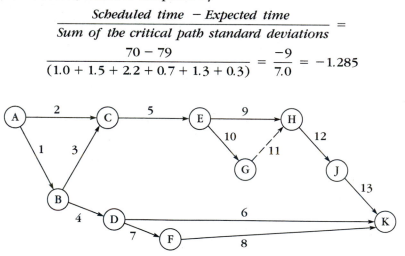

\* Letters designate events and numbers activities.

**Figure 12-23 ▲ The PERT Chart for the Construction Project**

The *Z* value (found in any statistics text) indicates that the probability of meeting the 70-day constraint is less than 10 percent.

The project manager finds that the prospect of finishing on time is remote. To speed up the construction, three types of actions can be taken: paralleling, increased sequencing, and the elimination of some tasks. To parallel, the manager can require that the work of the electrical subcontractor must be divided into two activities: electrical (designated activity 10A) and cooling (10B), which can be done at the same time. To increase sequencing and redefine tasks, a quick spray can be substituted for roller painting (13) and more money spent to get the plumber (9) to finish sooner than called for in the subcontractor's contract.

The new activity times are:

| Activity | a | m | b | $T_E$ | s |
|---|---|---|---|---|---|
| 10A Electrical | 4 | 6 | 8 | 6 | 0.7 |
| 10B Cooling | 4 | 6 | 8 | 6 | 0.7 |
| 13 Spray paint | 1 | 1 | 1 | 1 | 0.3 |
| 9 Plumbing | 4 | 6 | 8 | 6 | 0.7 |
| 11A Dummy | | | | 0 | 0 |
| 11B Dummy | | | | 0 | 0 |

The revised PERT diagram is shown in Figure 12-24. The critical path is now 1-3-5-9-12-13. The computations for earliest and latest completion dates and slack are as follows:

| Event | $T_E$ | $T_L$ | Slack |
|---|---|---|---|
| A | 0.0 | 0.0 | 0.0 |
| B | 10.0 | 10.0 | 0.0 |
| C | 22.5 | 22.5 | 0.0 |
| D | 20.5 | 48.0 | 27.5 |
| E | 43.0 | 43.0 | 0.0 |
| F | 25.5 | 53.0 | 27.5 |
| $G_1$ | 49.0 | 49.0 | 0.0 |
| $G_2$ | 49.0 | 49.0 | 0.0 |
| H | 49.0 | 49.0 | 0.0 |
| I | 32.0 | 59.5 | 27.5 |

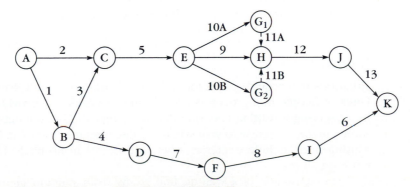

**Figure 12-24 ▲ The Revised PERT Chart**

| Event | $T_E$ | $T_L$ | Slack |
|-------|-------|-------|-------|
| J | 69.0 | 69.0 | 0.0 |
| K | 70.0 | 70.0 | 0.0 |

The critical path is now 70 days, which meets the constraint. Because these completion times can very, a likelihood must be computed as before. The $Z$ value is

$$\frac{Schedule\ time\ -\ Actual\ time}{Standard\ deviation\ of\ critical\ path} = \frac{70 - 70}{(1.0 + 1.5 + 2.2 + .7 + 1.3 + .3)}$$

$$= \frac{0}{7.0} = 0$$

The probability given by a statistics table is 50 percent, indicating that there is a 50/50 chance of finishing on time. To increase the likelihood further, still more changes in activities must be made.

### Summary

The PERT technique can be used to represent operations (such as food service) or one-of-a-kind projects (such as construction). The PERT chart represents the sequence of activities that is analyzed in an attempt to minimize completion time and thus cost. The PERT is also very useful in the identification of processing bottlenecks. By paralleling or modifying their activities, the critical path identifies steps in a procedure that merit redesign. Thus, in large, complex systems, PERT is useful in isolating trouble spots and for making realistic estimates of the time needed to finish a project or a sequence of events in a procedure.

## Operations Research

Operations research (OR) makes up a body of techniques that apply mathematical principles to solve problems. Used in a planned change process, these techniques determine the consequences of particular courses of action, which suggests how to improve the plan. In the detailing stage, OR techniques permit the planner to fine-tune proposed solutions.

The list of OR techniques and their applications is long, which prohibits a detailed discussion. A few techniques will be presented to illustrate purpose and possible applications. Details will not be presented. The interested reader is referred to operations research texts.

### Waiting Lines

Situations that require a wait for service are common in our everyday experiences. Lines of people in a grocery store waiting to check out provides one illustration. By observing a waiting line, one discovers that the line's length changes and that some customers refuse to wait when the line becomes too long. Examples that have waiting lines include cafeterias, operating rooms in hospitals, bill processing, and fast-food stores.

The existence of a waiting line stems from random elements in the needs for service and its provision. Either the patterns of arrivals or the service time, or both can vary. Even when the average service capacity is sufficient to meet demand, waiting lines will occur because both arrival patterns and service time have a random behavior. Waiting lines have three primary components:

1. *Arrivals.* Customer or user types and the time pattern that describes how each customer type arrives
2. *Queues.* The behavior of customers waiting for service
3. *Service.* How long it takes to serve each customer type and the number of servers

*Arrivals.* The times between customers who arrive for a service are used to describe arrivals. If these times are constant, arrivals are called *deterministic*. If not, the pattern in arrival times can usually be represented by some distribution, a negative exponential (because it is easy to manipulate), Erlang, and others. A homogeneous arrival pattern is one with a constant, average arrival rate. Nonhomogeneous patterns have increasing, decreasing, or cyclical changes.

*Queues.* Queues can be managed in various ways, including

1. First in, first out (FIFO)
2. Last in, first out (LIFO)
3. Priority
   a. Preemptive (customers who can interrupt service)
   b. Nonpreemptive

Queue organization is dictated by which of these disciplines is followed. Constraints also organize a queue. For example, multiple queues can have limits, such as telephones that give busy signals when all incoming lines are busy.

*Service.* Service is described by number of servers and service time characteristics. Service time is described by its average and its distribution. Deterministic, negative exponential, and other distributions are used.

In most cases, the pattern of arrivals (e.g., people who arrive at a fast-food store) cannot be scheduled. The server must always be ready to receive a new arrival (the customer). In such cases, the server will fall behind at some times and be idle at other times.

*Applications.* The variety of waiting line configurations is summarized in Figure 12-25. Mathematical techniques allow an exact solution to many of these waiting line systems. Solutions to waiting lines have several important uses, which can be summarized as follows:

1. Permitting an orderly examination of which waiting system has the best features (e.g., least average wait time or least operating cost) among those that can be used
2. Indicating how additions to service can reduce waiting, determining a cost–waiting time trade-off
3. Investigating how scheduling to reduce arrival variations can reduce waiting time, cost, and idle capacity
4. Considering the cost impact of various priorities that preempt service that can be demanded by the "special" customer
5. Determining if service can be improved by changes in the processing procedures

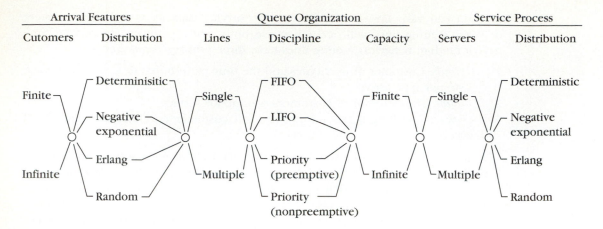

* There are $2 \times 4 \times 2 \times 4 \times 2 \times 2 \times 4$ or 1,024 types of waiting lines.

**Figure 12-25** ▲ **Waiting Line Configuration**

Waiting lines offer the planner an opportunity to explore various plans in the abstract, without the expense and disruption of altering an operating system to make measurements.

### Simulation

Simulation is another OR technique that can be used to investigate the properties of a plan in the abstract. A simulation is an easy-to-manipulate construct that resembles the plan to be studied. Simulations are widely used. Examples include mock fire or disaster drills, training using role-playing, field exercises in the military, and training apes to smoke cigarettes in order to study the effects of massive doses of tar and nicotine. The plan is represented by something with similar properties that can be constructed and/or controlled for less cost and with less difficulty than a direct manipulation of the system under study.

Simulation is also used to capture the behavior of systems that exhibit random behavior. Typically, a model is constructed that generates performance and other types of data that are similar to data from an operating system.

Useful forms of simulation are based on an analytical model, expressed by a set of equations. Also, a set of rules can be used that dictates what will occur under certain conditions. The role-playing exercise for union bargaining in which conditions are introduced by an outsider altering economic conditions and other factors to gauge the bargainer's ability to cope provides an example. The outcome is determined by the preset rules. Simulation is typically used to investigate a specific case or set of cases that can be traced by hand calculation or with the aid of computers.

*The Stimulation Framework.* A simulation is made up of elements, attributes, activities, plans, and time. *Elements* are the things interacting in a system. For instance, in disaster planning, they would include transport vehicles, site treatment teams, communication, dispatch, full-service hospital emergency departments, hospital treatment teams, and the like.

*Attributes* define properties of the elements. Transport vehicles have capacities, speeds, and locations. Site treatment teams can deal with some, but not all, types of injuries. Communication equipment has a capacity as does the hospital emergency room, hospital treatment teams, and so on. Some attributes, such as the numbers or injury types, hospitals, and transports (called parameters), are systematically altered during the simulation.

*Activities* depict rules that indicate what will happen under particular circumstances. To illustrate, site treatment can be authorized when a hospital emergency room is full or when movement would create unacceptable risks. Such an event can be triggered in a simulation by the coordinating physician who specifies this condition to measure performance. This permits the simulator to see how well treatment would be rendered under this type of condition.

Plans can be *micro* or *macro*. They can, at the micro level, refer to protocols that specify how treatment will be given at particular sites and for particular types of injuries (e.g., head, chest, fractures). Protocols can also represent system strategies, specifying number of vehicles, deployment patterns, and the like. Macro plans are seldom reducible to a simple response mode, but the simulation captures salient elements and treats them as constraints.

The *time* element controls the other elements. For instance, a disaster creates a variety of events that mix together and cause a wide range of injury profiles with which one must deal. An interval or an event approach can be used to capture the impact of the time element. The *interval* approach segments time into equal periods. The system's progress (e.g., disaster response) is examined period by period. Profiles of occurrences and consequences (e.g., deaths) are measured. An *event* simulation poses various situations to see how the system responds. Various plans can be tested to see their effects. For instance, the disaster could cause a particular spatial profile of injuries to which the emergency medical system would have to respond. An event simulation is more useful than an interval approach because it allows the simulator to try out various plans and measure their effects.

*Monte Carlo and Expected Value Methods.* Simulation can also trace the effects of probabilistic events. For instance, emergency vehicles can be delayed in transit, treatment time can be extended due to complications, and so on. *Expected value* models take a chance event, determine its most likely effect, and fold it into the analysis. For example, if vehicle delay in transit has a probability of 30 percent, the performance of the emergency medical service system is estimated, assuming that 70 percent of the vehicles arrived.

In *Monte Carlo* methods, the number of vehicle delays is determined by chance and requires a computer solution. In this example, the computer generates a random number between 0 and 10. If the number is greater than 3, the vehicle is assumed to have arrived. A single computer run provides one sample. Several runs are needed to predict how the system would respond to a given set of conditions.

Both expected value and Monte Carlo methods are useful. The expected value model can be used to make crude judgments among plans. The Monte Carlo approach finds stable operating regions in a given plan. It is used when the precision of estimates has overriding importance.

*Level of Detail.* Simulation is widely used because it can be applied at many levels of detail. An inexpensive test of several plans can be made using models that range from simple to elaborate. For instance, the U.S. Department of Defense tested and refined its early warning systems, SAGE and NORAD, against various Russian battle plans to see how they would perform.

A checklist for the construction of a simulation is:

1. Determine the objective of the simulation (see formulation stage, Chapter 10).
2. Establish scope (see formulation stage, Chapter 10).
3. Identify key components (see concept development stage, Chapter 11).
4. Apply the functional block diagram technique to develop each component and its element, attributes (parameters), and activities.
5. Identify relationships in each block.
6. Establish values for parameters.
7. Check logic by tracing events through the flowchart to ensure proper operation and representation.
8. Tie together components in a consistent manner.
9. Computerize (optional).
10. Test, comparing against known behavior of the system under study.
11. Compare the merits of plans using an interval or an event approach.

*Advantages and Limitations of Simulation.* Simulation requires the creation of a model that represents the system under study by capturing its salient features. Developing such a model and generating the data to test it can be time consuming and costly, with considerable risk of failure. This is particularly true when the simulation is tested using Monte Carlo methods to form a distributionlike picture of performance. Both data collection and validation of the prediction can be very difficult. Most simulations string together many casual relationships among factors that have a judgmental, rather than an empirical, base. The validity of these relationships, let alone their synergistic effects, is seldom, if ever, tested.

Simulation can be used quite effectively when a plan seems to satisfy the assumptions that experts would be willing to make about the system under study. However, there is seldom a way to validate these assumptions to determine if they are realistic, or even representative. As a result, simulation should be used when no other convenient way exists to represent the system and manipulate it. Because this is often the case, simulation is widely used.

Simulations has several important advantages:

1. Exposing and resolving inconsistencies in the plan that remain after the construction phase of detailing
2. Fine-tuning, to illuminate omissions and errors that may have been overlooked
3. Discovering the merits and consequences of several alternative plans prior to implementation
4. Using sensitivity analysis (Chapter 15) to reveal key factors that make a plan unstable

### Optimization Techniques

Optimization techniques try to find the arrangement of variables that best meets a specific objective. These techniques have three principal characteristics: a quantifiable objective function, the ability to express alternatives in terms of a set of variables, and solving an equation that gives a value for each variable that optimizes function, considering necessary restrictions on these same variables.

Many plans have multiple objectives that must be balanced. For example, U-Haul locates sites and vehicles to be offered according to expected demand. To place a government-supported service in a region, a location is sought that has the optimal combination of travel time, cost, and level of utilization. The objective function is made up of various components like those mentioned to give an overall measure of performance.

Optimization techniques find an ideal value for each variable that optimizes an objective function, adhering to constraints. For example, variables in the service location problem include the location of potential sites, the capacity of each site, and the type of services that can be provided at each site. For a burn care service, both secondary treatment sites (used to stabilize and identify severe burns) and tertiary treatment sites (used to provide acute and long-term restorative care to severe burn patients) are needed. The location and the capacity of each site and its ability to provide particular services becomes a key variable in the location decision. Constraints in this example could represent candidate sites that cannot provide secondary care or tertiary care for burn patients. The ideal location would minimize travel time and cost, giving each potential site all the business it is qualified to receive.

*Types of Optimization Techniques.* A particular optimization technique is used for problems that have a given structure. *Linear programming* is used for problems in which the objective function can be represented as a linear function of variables and constraints. If variables were restricted to take on integer values, the problem would be solved by *integer programming*. To illustrate, integer restrictions on the variables occur in a staffing problem. Problems with several decision steps, such as the allocation of a fixed number of fast-food stores in a region, demand the use of techniques called *dynamic or goal programming*. These techniques permit the measures of multiple objectives to be traded off considering a limited number of decision variables and simple constraints. *Unconstrained* optimization problems place no constraints on values of the variables.

*Limitations and Cautions.* When a problem can be represented with a mathematical programming format, an optimal arrangement of resources or parameters can be determined. The importance of optimization techniques stem from this feature. No other techniques can offer such definitive guidance in determining what makes a particular alternative operate in an optimum manner. However, when the representation of the problem is incomplete or unrealistic, misleading recommendations can result. The assumptions must be religiously adhered to. Optimization techniques are useful only in a situations that adhere to their linear, integer, and goal assumptions.

Typically, the sponsor must hire an OR expert to determine which technique is appropriate and to carry it out. The sponsor provides interpretive skills. The sponsor must be trained to recognize when an optimal solution can be provided, understand the solution to extract its policy implications, and translate the solution into terms that can be understood by management.

### Summary

Operations research techniques can be effectively used in a planned change process, with the sponsor as a coordinator. This role allows the sponsor to interpret the problem, define constraints, and point out values that must be considered, providing a focus for the OR application. The interpretation of results is clarified because it is focused on improving each evolving plan's arrangement of resources.

In most instances, OR techniques are applied to a special type of planning problem, termed *well structured*. These problems are often tactical because the solution is given, or at least suggested, by the problem definition made in the formulation stage. Examples include work loads for a PBX telephone system, allocating capacity, or reducing inventory costs.

When the problem is recognized as a certain type, such as a waiting line, it can be represented or modeled as a queue. This linkage of problem and evaluation model implicitly assumes that the OR technique provides a good representation of the problem. A good representation captures all (or at least many) salient aspects of the problem. It also assumes that fine-tuning the system being modeled provides as good a solution as seeking out new ideas.

Many planning problems are multifaceted and ill structured, even after formulation, making a representation by a mathematical model incomplete, which will render its analysis misleading. OR techniques work for well-structured planning problems that have a clear match to a mathematical model. OR techniques provide insightful evaluative observations, not creative ones. For example, a waiting line makes the sponsor think through a particular set of trade-off questions, in both economic and service terms. Capacity is considered by examining the consequences of waiting for a customer and the costs of idle capacity. This forces the sponsor to equate the guarantees of service with economic realities. Such an analysis does not offer a novel way to deal with a customer, which can reduce costs while preserving space that can be converted to other uses. An OR technique would not lead the planner to such a conclusion. Rather, OR would describe how to balance competing demands with existing capacity.

OR techniques cannot supplant the planning activities of the detailing stage; they merely support these activities. When used to support the detailing stage's activities, OR techniques have an interrogation role, showing how changes can produce operating benefits in a given alternative.

## ▲ Key Points

1. In the detailing stage, several plans are developed to extract the policy implications from each. Creativity is an essential aspect of detailing if innovative plans are expected.

2. The detailing stage has construction and interrogation phases. The construction phase is used to describe the operating characteristics of plans, and the

interrogation phase provides a means to refine and compare the plans. The interrogation phase often requires structuring and path techniques.

3.  The construction phase creates plan details. Three detailing techniques were discussed: systems engineering, general systems theory, and current systems models. The systems matrix technique was derived from systems engineering principles. The technique has two unique features: its systems definition (a matrix of seven elements and four dimensions) and its procedure to detail the system. Each element and dimension in the matrix are defined to detail a plan. Current system modeling (also called system analysis) enumerates how a reference system operates. The block diagram technique was described that traces the transforms needed to connect all inputs to outputs. The plan is enriched by synthesizing the best aspects of several current systems. General systems theory is used with the other two techniques. It offers a generic description of system features. By enumerating the traits of the system to be planned, a checklist is provided that aids in detailing.

4.  Most interrogation techniques treat the system as a "glass box," fine-tuning how inputs are to be converted into outputs. This transformation process is modeled and then refinements are made. The structuring aspect of the interrogation phase offers a way to fine-tune the plan. Two types of techniques can be used: networks and operations research techniques. ISM and PERT are network techniques that help to sort out steps in a procedure. They have particular value in describing the implicit procedures used by people, seeking to improve the reliability of these procedures. PERT can also be used to find the optimal (or constraining) pathway. Simulation, waiting lines, and optimization techniques were discussed. These techniques are termed interrogative, because each requires an operating system to model, making them reactive rather than proactive planning tools.

▲ Cases

### The Fraudproof Credit Card Case

A recent rash of stolen credit cards prompted a large oil company to require the clerk selling goods to record the license number of the automobile along with purchase information whenever a credit card was used. To force compliance, the company would not reimburse the dealer for credit slips that did not have the license plate number recorded. The company believed that this additional information would limit the use of stolen credit cards and thereby lower the oil company's uncollectable charges.

The company operates a large number of gas stations, and all have self-service and full-service pumps. A company audit revealed several disturbing problems. Self-service customers who make up the bulk of the business must bring their card into the building for processing. In 75 percent of the cases monitored, customers became irritated because they didn't know their plate number and gave the clerk a bogus number to avoid going out to the car to check. The clerk never checked the number for accuracy. When this problem was brought to the clerks' attention, they claimed to be too busy to check plates, except for full-service customers, because they can easily get the full-service customer's tag number as they provided service. The audit revealed that full-service customers were nearly all high income and not likely to have a stolen credit card.

The company wants to reduce its losses from stolen credit cards, but is willing to admit that recording the license number has little effect, except to irritate paying customers.                                                                                           ▲

### The Patient Origin Case

The planning of a patient origin information system was initiated in a new, 100-bed, university-based, teaching hospital. The hospital had been open for six years but was using just half of its allocated beds. In an attempt to demonstrate that the hospital was becoming a major center for comprehensive care, and thereby increase its utilization, the hospital undertook a patient origin study. To do such a study, both the referring physician and patient origin must be recorded at the time of admission. It is also desirable to have the transferring community hospital and attending physician in the data base.

Patient origin information collection was quite simple. The admitting department was asked to pull the necessary information from the patient chart and record it on a hospital log. The system became suspect when the physicians' morning report (which contained patient name, sex, admitting physician's name, and diagnosis made by the referring physician or hospital) was compared against the log. The log was found to be incomplete in places and appeared to be incorrect in others. Statistical tests were conducted that raised further questions about the data base's reliability.                                                                                           ▲

### The Roll Film Spool Case

Eastman Kodak, a large film manufacturing company, had been receiving complaints from professional photographers about its 120 professional film. This film fits Hasselblad and Rollei cameras that use a 4" × 5" negative format. The larger format gives much more resolution than the 35mm. format of most cameras, which allow enlargements that can be made into commercial ads and billboards. This film, unlike amateur film, has numbers on the edges so professionals can keep accurate records of subjects, conditions of shot, f-stops, and shutter speed. According to the complaints, edge fog has been obliterating these numbers. The cause of the edge fog was attributed to paint blobs on the flange of the spool that holds the 120 film. According to this theory, the blobs made it impossible for a paper cover to seal the edges of the film from exposure when loading and unloading a camera.

The manufacturing process for the spool calls for a light-gauge metal to be slit into two size strips. One strip is fed through a punch press to create round flanges. The other is fed into a machine that folds the metal into a tube on which the flanges are welded. The welding process is largely automated. Flanges and tubes drop into containers that are linked to a vibrating bowl that aligns the flanges and a tube and positions the spool for welding. The finished spool drops into a wire basket, 1 foot in diameter and 2 feet deep. These baskets are picked up by a conveyor that moves them through a spray operation in which a thin coat of black paint is applied to the spools. The spray paint device applies the coating from six directions (top and bottom and the four compass points). After painting, the baskets are dumped into containers and shipped to the roll film division. This division slits the strips of film, winds them on a film spool, and seals it in a paper cover in low-light conditions.

The division manufacturing spools claims that welding operation has very high quality. Checks of samples of spools reveal that miswelds are very rare, and when they occur they are easy to spot because they jam the automatic welder. The paint operation appears to be the cause of the problem. To improve quality, inspectors have been added to roll 100 percent of the spools down a gauge after painting. A spool is expected to jam when it has a paint blob. To keep the costs of inspection as low as possible, management has installed an incentive pay system in which inspectors are paid on a piecework basis.

The engineer assigned to the project claims that the inspectors get frustrated when spools get stuck and push them through the gauge to keep their wages high. A sample of the spools was carefully examined. This inspection revealed that spools pushed through the gauge tend to have blobs, but also have welds that fail to meet specifications.

Management believes the paint machine is at fault. Engineering has put cones, and other devices to find out where paint may become top heavy and run, creating blobs. These tests are inconclusive. Paint appears to be applied uniformly by the machine. Even spools at the bottom of the basket have no more blobs than those at the top. ▲

## ▲ Exercises

1. Apply the systems matrix technique to the patient origin, fraudproof credit card, or the roll film spool case. Complete the matrix by identifying each of the 28 system elements and its dimensions. Add the operator columns to trim out unnecessary limitations.

2. Using Figure 12-3 as a guide, design a control system for the roll film case. How would you insure that the system emphasized exceptions?

3. Apply the input-output technique (Chapter 11) and the block diagram technique, discussed in this chapter, to do a systems analysis, such as a billing procedure, getting a patient admitted in a hospital, or an assembly line. Draw a diagram that captures the flow of inputs and outputs and how inputs are transformed to outputs in your system. Identify blocks that serve as combiners, sinks, discriminators, and operators. Suggest *one thing* that can be done to cut cost or increase precision in the system. (Efficiency examples include simpler ways to do transforms, eliminating outputs, and reducing the complexity of inputs. Precision could mean more accurate outputs or better transforms.) What type of synthesis problem does your suggestion pose?

4. Apply the systems matrix technique to your planned change problem in exercise 3. Compare your results. What are the key differences?

5. Reconstruct the paired comparisons for the learning disabilities example in Figure 12-15.

6. Assume that a strategic management project created four strategic themes: expand customers, new methods of manufacture, contain costs, and stabilize revenues. Interview an entrepreneur and have him or her determine the order and causality of these strategies for his or her company. Have the respondent show priority for the order relationship, and estimate the strength and directions of the causality relationship with a 5-point +/− scale. Construct the paired comparisons, matrix, and digraph for both relationships.

7. Interpret the digraphs in Exercise 4. What do they suggest to the person that you interviewed?

8. Change the event times by 1 unit in Figure 12-23. Carry out the necessary computations to interpret the PERT diagram.

# *Part V*

# FORMING HYBRID PLANNED CHANGE METHODS

▲ ▲ ▲ ▲ ▲ ▲ ▲ ▲ ▲ ▲ ▲ ▲ ▲ ▲ ▲ ▲ ▲ ▲ ▲ ▲ ▲ ▲ ▲ ▲ ▲ ▲ ▲

*The creative aspects of planned change arise in formulation, concept development, and detailing. In Part Five guidelines are offered to select among techniques to fashion hybrid methods of planned change for these three process stages. Guidelines stem from two sources: the requirements posed by sponsors and the posture adopted by the sponsor in guiding the planned change process. In Chapter 13, the "requirements approach" is described. Guidelines stem from expectations for quality, innovation, acceptance, and preservation in the results expected for projects or strategic planning efforts. Chapter 14 describes the "role approach." Guidelines stem from devising supportive working relationships between planners and sponsors. Planning techniques that will be accepted by sponsors who take one of several roles in process management are identified.*

*Planners (facilitators) and sponsors select among techniques that balance working relationships with expected outcomes. Should these guidelines suggest techniques that differ significantly (e.g., one calls for stakeholder involvement, the other does not), sponsors should recognize that their leadership role is incompatible with their expectations. One or the other should be modified.*

# 13

# The Requirements Approach: Technique Selection Based on Sponsor Expectations

▲ ▲ ▲    ▲ ▲ ▲ ▲ ▲ ▲ ▲ ▲ ▲ ▲ ▲ ▲ ▲ ▲ ▲ ▲ ▲

This chapter offers a way to fashion a method for planned change (Nutt, 1982a, 1984c). A method has two distinguishing features: process and technique. Process, as noted in Parts One and Two, spells out stages of activity and how these stages are ordered. Technique provides a way to carry out the activities called for by each process stage. A method for planned change is specified by its process and supporting techniques.

A process has been identified in Part Two that calls for particular stages of activity for all types of planned changes. To introduce efficiency and tailor the process to particular types of applications, process stages should receive various degrees of emphasis, depending on the *requirements* imposed by the sponsor. A tailored process produces a hybrid method with techniques selected according to these requirements. Hybrid methods are defined by "technique strings" that are best able to meet the requirements imposed by sponsors.

Technique strings for the planned change stages discussed in the previous three chapters are summarized in Figure 13-1. The strings are made up of techniques that can be applied to deal with the activities called for by formulation, concept development, and detailing. Each of these technique strings identifies a hybrid method. Selecting a technique string according to the requirement imposed by a sponsor makes the resulting hybrid method contingency based, selected according to expected results.

Discussion is limited to the creative aspects of planned change. During formulation, concept development, and detailing, which set directions, identify options, and fashion plans, the features of a planned change are established. These features and how they are established determine a plan's acceptance and innovativeness, as well as its costs and benefits. Evaluation and implementation are also important but do not alter a plan's features. Implementation tactics stress gaining acceptance, as discussed in Part Three. Evaluation involves measurement and making valid comparisons and will be discussed in a later chapter.

Choices are also required in each process phase. The choices set priorities, winnow ideas, and select among ideas for development. The techniques for decision making are selected according to the needs for precision and speed, following the discussion in Chapter 10.

The guidelines should not be used to make decisions for sponsors. They are provided to help sponsors think carefully about their needs and how these needs will influence the conduct of planned change.

## ▲ REQUIREMENTS

Four types of requirements identify criteria that can be applied to determine a sponsor's expectations. Three of these criteria are useful for both project and strategic planned change efforts. Expectations for high performance call for *quality*. A quality plan or strategy has desirable performance features, such as cost, benefit, or effectiveness. *Acceptance* deals with the subjective views of people who can block or covertly subvert both the planned change process and its product. A plan with high acceptance has the support of key groups. An *innovative* strategy is derived

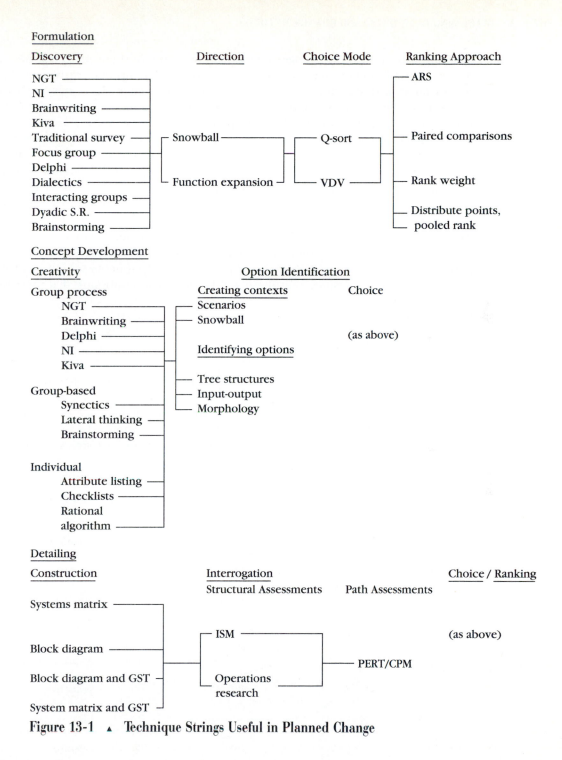

**Formulation**

**Discovery**       **Direction**     **Choice Mode**     **Ranking Approach**

NGT
NI
Brainwriting
Kiva
Traditional survey    Snowball    Q-sort    ARS
Focus group                                 Paired comparisons
Delphi
Dialectics        Function expansion   VDV    Rank weight
Interacting groups
Dyadic S.R.                                Distribute points,
Brainstorming                               pooled rank

**Concept Development**

**Creativity**           **Option Identification**

Group process    **Creating contexts**   Choice
  NGT           Scenarios
  Brainwriting     Snowball
  Delphi
  NI                       (as above)
  Kiva           **Identifying options**

Group-based
  Synectics       Tree structures
  Lateral thinking   Input-output
  Brainstorming     Morphology

Individual
  Attribute listing
  Checklists
  Rational
  algorithm

**Detailing**

**Construction**      **Interrogation**         **Choice / Ranking**
               Structural Assessments   Path Assessments

Systems matrix

               ISM                 (as above)
Block diagram                         PERT/CPM
Block diagram and GST  Operations
               research
System matrix and GST

**Figure 13-1** ▴ **Technique Strings Useful in Planned Change**

from ideas not previously recognized, hoping that some of these ideas will offer a decisive advantage. For example, an innovative plan in a nonprofit organization has the organization deal with unfamiliar interest groups, new clientele, or new services. In the for-profit setting, innovation seeks ideas that offer market advantages (e.g., rollerblades), ways to increase sales, or procedures that trim costs.

Strategic planned change efforts introduce a fourth criterion: *preservation*. Preservation recognizes that requirements to maintain current arrangements and to work within them are often imposed on strategy development. Examples include sacrosanct procedures, policies, programs, products/services, or relationships, as depicted by an organization chart, that the organization does not want to challenge or change. The organization seeks to retain this order in the face of the disruption that strategic planned change may bring. These commitments become real values to which the organization commits itself, not merely constraints, and thus become performance expectations in their own right. These commitments set out an arena in which people can assume that there will be order and continuity that preserve certain values.

## ▲ PROJECT AND STRATEGY TYPES

Types of planned change *projects* are defined by a sponsor's expectations for quality, innovation, and acceptance, as shown in Figure 13-2. *Comprehensive* projects call for quality, innovation, and acceptance. This type of planned change project poses extensive expectations, which suggests that techniques should be selected that encourage a broad search for ideas. *Traditional* projects do not stress innovation

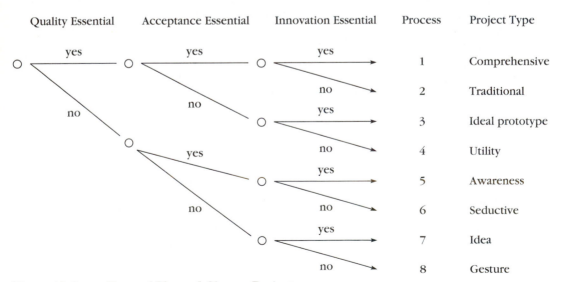

**Figure 13-2** ▲ **Types of Planned Change Projects**
Reprinted from Nutt (1982a).

but do call for quality and acceptance. Although the demands for creativity in plan development are lowered, the need for good results that are readily accepted calls for techniques that allow for a carefully executed planned change process. *Ideal prototypes* demand innovation and quality, but not acceptance. Techniques that stress creativity when fashioning plans are more important than are those that garner acceptance. *Utility* projects stress quality. This type of plan is often sought during short-fuse crisis situations by sponsors who are empowered to take decisive action. Techniques that stress quality in plans are sought. *Awareness* projects call for acceptance and innovation. Such projects are carried out to investigate people's reaction to new technology and practices. Planning techniques are used to find out what must be invested in overcoming resistance to change, to take advantage of new developments. The *seductive* project calls for acceptance. This type of project installs the visions and pet ideas of sponsor and others with significant power in the organization. Techniques that promote acceptance are preferred. *Idea* projects stress innovation and investigate the merits of new technology or practices to determine which offers the organization a useful advantage. Techniques are selected that can help the organization develop or transfer technology and new practices for local use. Finally, *gesture* projects have no expectations. Such efforts are mounted to impress people that something is being done when no action is contemplated. Techniques that minimize effort are used for this type of project.

Key types of *strategic plans* can be identified by the importance accorded to quality, acceptance, innovation, *and* preservation by the sponsor. The types of strategy that result are indicated in Table 13-1. The comprehensive, traditional, ideal prototype, utility, awareness, seductive, and idea strategies have motivations similar to those suggested for projects. By adding preservation, each type becomes *constrained*. For each of these strategies, techniques must be able to introduce these constraints subtly into the deliberations of key bodies during strategy development.

Table 13-1 ▲ Types of Strategy

| Performance Expectations | | Process Type |
|---|---|---|
| Quality, acceptance, and innovation | 1. | Comprehensive |
| Quality, acceptance, innovation, and preservation | 2. | Qualified comprehensive |
| Quality and acceptance | 3. | Traditional |
| Quality, acceptance, and preservation | 4. | Constrained traditional |
| Quality and innovation | 5. | Ideal prototype |
| Quality, innovation, and preservation | 6. | Constrained prototype |
| Quality | 7. | Utility |
| Quality and preservation | 8. | Quality utility |
| Acceptance and innovation | 9. | Awareness |
| Acceptance, innovation, and preservation | 10. | Constrained awareness |
| Acceptance | 11. | Seductive |
| Acceptance and preservation | 12. | Constrained seductive |
| Innovation | 13. | Idea |
| Innovation and preservation | 14. | Constrained idea |
| Preservation | 15. | Ratification |
| None | 16. | Gesture |

The *gesture strategy* has motivations, much like the gesture project. Adding preservation changes this strategic type to one of *ratification*. A current strategy is often examined merely to ratify it, without seeking a review of its quality, acceptance, or innovative features. Such a step is followed by university departments after an accreditation site visit and by firms when CEOs reaffirm the fitness of past practices.

The planning literature was reviewed to identify techniques that can produce quality, innovation, and acceptance and allow sponsors and/or facilitators to introduce constraints that preserve valued practices. The guides that are offered were derived from a completion of research findings, analyses of the technique's features, and years of experience in practical application.

## ▲ HYBRID METHODS FOR PLANNED CHANGE PROJECTS

In project planning, the plan can call for quality, acceptance, or innovation. All combinations of these requirements identify eight types of projects. A hybrid method identifying a technique string is proposed for each of these projects, as shown in Table 13-2.

### Comprehensive Projects

Comprehensive projects make the most stringent demands, requiring quality, acceptance, and innovation in the plan. This type of project is seen as critically important by its sponsor. Examples include the design of a new program for revenue recovery in the financially distressed hospital or profit enhancement in a firm. Projects that modify or introduce new products/services, internal operations, policies, and the like often have all three requirements.

As shown in Table 13-2, discovery in which the sponsor searches for hidden problems, concerns, and difficulties prompting action is carried out using a silent reflective group process (SRGP). One of these techniques is preferred because each stimulates disclosure, innovation, and acceptance (Van de Ven and Delbec, 1977; Nutt, 1976b, 1977). Each of these techniques has these three attributes, so selection among them can be based on circumstances. For instance, in situations of high conflict, nominal interaction (NI) is preferred. For planners working alone, dyadic reflection would be used.

Acceptance is vitally important in comprehensive projects to ensure that the organization benefits from plans that are developed. Acceptance of such projects can be enhanced when it is clear that the need for change is real and compelling. Debating need from two perspectives, such as two positions on consumers or costs, can be carried out to make this point. The Kiva group process can be modified to draw out these positions by having the first ring take one position (e.g., customers are a problem) and the second the reverse position (customers are *not* a problem), with the outside ring being made up of a planning group.

Function expansion is applied to establish direction. The identification of objectives would be carried out with a SRGP selected as has just been noted. Using nominal group technique (NGT), or another SRGP, to identify objectives retains all the benefit of function expansion and helps to manage group activities.

**Table 13-2 ▲ Methods for Planned Change Projects**

| Project Type | Formulation | | | Concept Development | | | Detailing | |
|---|---|---|---|---|---|---|---|---|
| | Requirements | Discovery | Direction | Creativity | Option Identification | Construction | Interrogation |
| 1. Comprehensive | Quality, acceptance, innovation | Silent reflective group process (SRGP) with snowball and dialectics | Function expansion (FE) | Synectics with SRGP | Scenarios and morphology | Systems matrix and GST | ISM, PERT, and OR |
| 2. Traditional | Quality and acceptance | SRGP and snowball | FE | SRGP and snowball | Scenarios and relevance trees | Block diagram and GST | PERT and OR |
| 3. Ideal prototype | Quality and innovation | Delphi or focus groups | None | Lateral thinking | Morphology | Systems matrix and GST | ISM and OR |
| 4. Utility | Quality | Interactive | FE | None | Input-output | Block diagram and GST | PERT or OR |
| 5. Awareness | Acceptance and innovation | Delphi and Kiva | None | Interacting groups or NI | None | Systems matrix | None |
| 6. Seductive | Acceptance | Interacting group with "plants" | None | Interacting group | None | Systems matrix | None |
| 7. Idea | Innovation | Delphi survey | None | Lateral thinking or synectics | Morphology | Systems matrix with NGT and synectics | None |
| 8. Gesture | None | Interacting group | None | None | Input-output | Block diagram | None |

Comprehensive projects can have considerable uncertainty. Scenarios deal with uncertainty by specifying contingencies so several plans can be proposed for plausible future conditions. An SRGP, such as the NGT, was selected to manage the creativity phase of option identification for two reasons. First, an SRGP can clear away uncertainty by identifying priority factors for the scenario to consider. Second, an SRGP stimulates acceptance and has been shown to be innovative. Delphi can also creative innovative ideas and can be substituted for an SRGP if logistics make meetings difficult. To identify options, the recommended approach merges synectics with morphology. Morphology gives a quick, concrete representation of options. A synectics exercise opens up the option identification process and should be used to identify the morphology factors. Synectics is recommended because the technique seems better matched to morphology than is lateral thinking. However, selection of a creativity technique should depend on participants' familiarity with it and their acceptance of it. Familiarity and personal preference can be used as a selection criteria in this case. If neither is acceptable (a possibility due to their unusual approach), an SRGP such as NGT can be used. Planned change efforts without planning groups can adopt one of the creativity techniques for individuals (see Figure 13-1).

For the detailing stage, the systems matrix approach combined with general systems theory (GST) is recommended for the construction phase along with interpretive structural modeling (ISM), operations research, and PERT charts for the interrogation phase. This technique string seems best because only the systems matrix technique strives for innovation and can build in acceptance through participation (Nadler, 1981). The GST identifies generic issues, such as the necessity for feedback, for the planner to ponder. The ISM complements the systems matrix approach by testing the viability of the procedures that are discovered. Operations research models may be needed to refine the solution, adding to its quality. PERT charts are used to make important procedures more efficient.

Priorities are needed at several points in this process to determine problems to be addressed, objectives to be followed, options to be developed, and plans to be proposed for pilot testing. Because group process is used, techniques that work quickly are needed. To speed priority setting, vote-discuss-vote (VDV) and a ranking technique that can be carried out quickly, like distribute points, are recommended. If increased precision is essential, the paired comparison technique can be substituted for distribute points. In some instances, separate priorities are set for problems, objectives, options, and plans for each requirement (quality, innovation, and acceptance). These priorities are merged by establishing the relative importance of each requirement using the anchored rating scales (ARS) technique and combining the ranks (see Chapter 10 for the mechanics). To speed the process, a global assessment of problems, objectives, options, and plans can be made with the understanding that all of the requirements should be met.

## Traditional Projects

Projects that do not demand innovation are called "traditional" because the typical planning effort does not seek innovation (e.g., Cyert and March, 1963; Nutt, 1984a).

The sponsor of such a project prefers to mimic the programs used by high-status organizations.

A silent reflective group process is used to discover problems and objectives during formulation. An SRGP is preferred because of its ability to promote acceptance. A function expansion aided by an SRGP is applied to select a direction for the project (Nutt, 1977). Silent reflective group process is added to the function expansion process to stimulate acceptance. Function expansion has been found to provide quality results but does not create much acceptance. As noted, using an SRGP session to identify objectives retains the benefits of function expansion and manages the group efforts.

In concept development, options are sought that do not require innovation. A relevance tree coupled with an SRGP such as NGT is a good way to identify options. The group process stimulates acceptance while defining the priority elements to be included in the tree. Several NGTs may be needed to identify levels for the relevance tree and entries for each level. A relevance tree is needed for each of several scenarios. The scenario is created using an SRGP, as has been noted.

In the detailing stage, the block diagram approach along with GST can be used to detail the plan. Quality in the solution can be enhanced by one of several operations research techniques. A PERT chart may be needed to capture and fine-tune key procedures.

Priorities for problems, objectives, options, and plans can be set following the same guides offered for comprehensive projects, with one exception. Only quality and acceptance are essential so priorities are set using these two requirements, merging the results as discussed for comprehensive projects.

## Ideal Prototype Projects

The ideal prototype project demands quality and innovation. The ideal prototype creates a benchmark against which other plans will be gauged. It is similar to an architect's first rendering or the automotive designer's mockup. Consulting firms develop such plans to provide ready-made solutions to their prospective client's problems. Many clients expect the consultant to have ideas, making ready-made plans essential for the consultant.

The preferred formulation process for an ideal prototyping project uses either a Delphi survey or a focus group. Because acceptance is less of an issue, a Delphi survey is used to tap outside experts who have relevant knowledge. If insiders are used, a focus group may be desirable. Each involves people thought to have relevant information and places less emphasis on the participation of organizational representatives. These techniques are preferred because each produces innovation through a new view of the problem. Directions are obvious so directions need not be considered beyond making the objective of finding new developments explicit.

In concept development, ideas are identified that can benefit the organization. In this situation, a free association creativity technique should be used to identify these ideas. Lateral thinking is suggested because it offers the widest possible latitude of inquiry. Morphology is used to capture the ideas developed by lateral thinking.

It is unwise to use current systems models for detailing because this technique uses current arrangements as a template, which lowers innovation. Systems matrix and GST are used because the former stresses innovation and the latter improves quality by questioning with checklists. Both these outcomes are essential for the ideal prototype project. The ISM is used to ensure that the mechanisms that transform inputs to outputs are logically constructed. Operations research (OR) is used to test feasibility and fine-tune solutions.

Choices among problems, objectives, options, and plans are made by applying the requirements of innovation and quality. In this type of process many possibilities often emerge from Delphi and focus groups, calling for the rank-weight techniques to winnow the possibilities. When a larger number of ideas is uncovered, two Q-sorts can be used, one for innovation and one for quality. Paired comparisons can be used to set priorities. The VDV and merged ranking are applied with these techniques following the steps outlined for comprehensive and traditional projects.

## Utility Projects

Neither innovation nor acceptance is crucial in a utility project. Utility projects merely seek a good way to close the performance gap. Sponsors of such projects want a pragmatic solution to the problems calling for action.

The traditional form of function expansion with an interacting group process is suggested. Function expansion, with an interacting group, offers quality and modest levels of acceptance in identifying an objective (Nutt, 1976b, 1977). An interactive group process is preferred because it is faster than using NGT. A traditional survey can also be used to list the objectives, with the sponsor finishing the hierarchy. The synthetic group could vote on which objective should be adopted, using the paired comparison strategy in a second survey.

For concept development in a *utility* project, the creativity phase is skipped because neither acceptance nor innovation is needed in the plan. Input-output models are used to represent the malfunctioning system. Because innovation is not necessary, tracing important relationships in an existing system is quick and often identifies ways to meet the objective. Quality is enhanced if synergistic elements and appropriate details of the system are identified.

In the detailing stage, the block diagram technique and operations research techniques are sufficient to detail the plan. PERT can be used to fine-tune procedures and enhance efficiency.

The VDV and distribute points techniques can be used to set priorities according to a quality. The procedures outlined for comprehensive projects would be followed.

## Awareness Projects

For the remaining processes in Table 13-2 quality is not an issue. Awareness planning is undertaken to influence project acceptance of innovation. Such a project postures an organization for change and readies it to consider innovative ideas. Because quality is unimportant, several phases can be skipped, which reduces the cost of planned change.

A Delphi and a Kiva group process can be used to discover ideas and create acceptance. First, a Delphi is used to obtain the views of outside experts. Delphi has several benefits that can be exploited if the sponsor has the time to apply it. Delphi creates a wide range of information because it can tap many different experts for ideas, and Delphi can be inexpensive. Van de Ven (1976) estimates the out-of-pocket cost of Delphi to be less than that of a group process, assuming that participant cost is comparable. Second, a Kiva is used to study and reflect on the results of the Delphi survey. These steps subtly introduce new ideas and uncover sources of resistance to their adoption. The intent of the project is often described as uncovering new ideas, with an implicit objective of promoting understanding and acceptance.

When acceptance and innovation are required, the systems matrix technique is used to detail plans. The systems matrix technique is preferred because it promotes innovation and because a group process can be used with it that stimulates acceptance. Several groups of stakeholders can participate in finding ways to use ideas. The systems matrix documents these efforts. Interrogative techniques are not needed because quality is not essential. The detailed plans have two purposes. First, they demonstrate that an idea is workable. Second, the plans pave the way for the acceptance of change that would come from using it. Awareness projects do not seek an airtight plan.

To select among the ideas or to set priorities, an interactive discussion of the ideas is used in the concept development stage. To promote more integration of the ideas or to manage conflict filled situations, an NI group process is recommended. Somewhat elaborate prioritizing schemes are often needed, such as combining a Q-sort with VDV and ARS (see Chapter 10). Two Q-sorts are required: one sort for acceptance and one for innovation. The criteria are weighted by the ARS approach. The criteria weights are normalized to convert them to percentages. The weights are multiplied by each item's rank from the Q-sorts. The rank-weight product is added for each item to combine the lists. A debate among key people in a study group is started. The debate is focused on the merged rankings from the Q-sorts. After discussion, the Q-sort can be used again and the final ranks are computed in the same manner as described.

## Seductive Projects

When only acceptance is needed, the project is called *seductive*. Such projects try to gain acceptance for a sponsor's or key individual's pet ideas or visions.

The sponsor hopes that key people during formulation will "discover" the merits of the idea or vision, suggesting an interacting group. The interactive group must have "plants" who will offer problems consistent with the sponsor's ideas. An interacting group is preferred because it is less apt to stimulate new ideas that may challenge the preconceived solution. This makes silent reflecting group processes undesirable for seductive projects.

An interacting group process is recommended to aid concept development for the "seductive" project. A silent reflective group process should *not* be used for the reasons given earlier. As in formulation, "plants" are used. In concept development, the "plants" are coached to offer ideas drawn from the preconceived plan. The option identification phase is not used.

Careful detailing is not required for all the seductive project. An adaptation of the systems matrix technique is recommended. Participation is used as a cooptative device. Stakeholders are asked to define a system using the matrix. The systems matrix aids the participants by guiding them through the steps required for detailing planning. (Used in this way, the systems matrix technique may also yield interesting insights into the demands of key constituents.) "Plants" in the group can be used who are prepared to offer ways to fill in each cell in the matrix consistent with the sponsor's idea. The interrogation phase is not used.

To select among acceptable problems and options, the VDV with an ARS or distribute points techniques are recommended.

## Idea Projects

When innovation is stressed, an idea project results. These projects are used to explore ways to deal with thorny problems without committing to implementation. No steps are taken to enhance adoption prospects.

A Delphi coupled with a Q-sort can be used to initiate activities in formulation. This technique string creates a large and well-prioritized information pool, using innovation as the sole criterion. An extraorganizational group of experts should be used in a Delphi because they are more likely to be innovative than are local experts. If Delphi surveys produce a large number of ideas, they can be sorted according to their innovativeness with a Q-sort. Paired comparisons can be used to select options with innovative potential for detailing.

A free association technique is recommended for the concept development stage. Lateral thinking can be used for a small group, and synectics can be used if the planning group must be somewhat large. The first assumes the planning team is made up of coworkers who can work out de Bono's process at some length. The second is used when a formal planning group must be assembled. For projects without planning groups, techniques that stimulate creativity in individuals would be applied. Options would be captured with the morphology technique.

Innovation is required in plan details. Only the systems matrix technique creates an environment in which innovation is possible. Synectics and NGT with experts can be used to provide the definitions for each cell in the matrix. This improves the prospect that fresh and pertinent ideas will be identified. Individuals working without planning groups should use one of the creativity techniques for individuals to provide cell entries. Because quality and acceptance are not needed for this type of project, interrogation techniques merely add to planning costs and are not required.

## Gesture Projects

Projects that make no demands are termed *gesture*. If neither quality nor acceptance nor innovation is important, questions can be raised about the need for planning. Projects initiated under these conditions are often postures, carried out to create the trappings of objectivity (Nutt, 1984e). Sponsors can be acting rationally in creating a gesture planning effort. For example, higher-ups may initiate a planned change effort to demonstrate to organizational critics that "something is being done." When planning is demanded without clear justification by a sponsor's superior, "pseudoplanning" results (Nutt, 1984d).

When faced with a gesture project, sponsor claims are used to define problems. No formal technique is recommended because none would be helpful (Table 13-2). The appearance of objectivity is often sought by discussing needs and opportunities in various meetings.

If concept development is initiated by pronouncements with no formal activity in formulation, the chances are good that the planned change effort is a smoke screen set up to create the aura of objectivity. Under these conditions, the input-output approach should be used to replan an existing system. When the system to be planned does not currently exist, a historical model (someone else's system) provides the ideas which are captured by the input-output technique. Realistically, little effort is called for, and the planner should allocate as much time as possible to other activities.

The block diagram technique is recommended to detail a current system. Gesture projects demand the appearance of planning to deflect attention for various reasons. A planning outcome is often required. The sponsor is under duress and must have tangible evidence that something was done, which justifies a cursory description of the current system. In most cases, the description has little real value, but construction of system flowcharts demonstrates that planning was attempted. Just a single problem and a single option are considered, eliminating the need to establish priorities.

## ▲ HYBRID METHODS FOR STRATEGIC PLANNED CHANGE

Strategy, unlike project planning, activates only the formulation and concept development stages of a planned change process. To develop an organizational strategy, strategic planning is used to identify goals and broad options. Concept development is undertaken to create strategic options consistent with the goals set in formulation. Implementation is carried out by several project planning efforts, which follow the prescriptions presented in the previous section of this chapter.

Like projects, strategy development can emphasize quality, acceptance, and innovation or make less stringent demands. Unlike project planning, a requirement for preservation may be introduced. Types of strategy under 16 conditions, defined by various combinations of quality, innovation, acceptance, and preservation, are identified. Planned change methods useful for creating strategic options are shown in Table 13-3. Table 13-3 also lists technique strings that are fashioned into a hybrid method for each type of strategy.

Group process is particularly essential in most strategic planning activities to get the board of directors or other key groups to "buy into" the process and its product. Typically, organizations use members of a board of trustees or directors and

**Table 13-3 ▲ Methods for Strategic Planned Change**

| Project Type | Requirements | Formulation | | Concept Development | |
|---|---|---|---|---|---|
| | | Discovery | Direction | Creativity | Option Identification |
| 1. Comprehensive | Quality, acceptance, innovation | Silent reflective group process with snowball and/or dialectics | Priority goals | Synectics and lateral thinking with SRGP | Scenarios and morphology and/or dialectics |
| 2. Qualified comprehensive | Quality, acceptance, innovation with important constraints | Brainwriting with snowball and/or dialectics | Priority goals | Synectics and lateral thinking with brainwriting | Scenarios and morphology and/or dialectics |
| 3. Traditional | Quality and acceptance | NI with snowball | Priority goals | NI with snowball | Scenarios and relevance trees |
| 4. Constrained traditional | Quality and acceptance with important constraints | Brainwriting with snowball | Priority goals | Brainwriting with snowball | Scenarios and relevance trees |
| 5. Strategic prototypes | Quality and innovation with important constraints | Delphi | None | NGT with synectics | Morphology and relevance trees |
| 6. Constrained prototypes | Quality and innovation with constraints | Focus group | None | NGT with synectics | Morphology and relevance trees |
| 7. Utility | Quality | None | Implicit goals | None | Focus group |
| 8. Qualified utility | Quality with important constraints | None | Implicit goals | None | Focus group with NI |
| 9. Awareness | Acceptance and innovation | Delphi and morphology | Implicit goals | NI | Inferred from priorities |
| 10. Constrained awareness | Acceptance and innovation with important constraints | Delphi and morphology | Implicit goals | Kiva with brainwriting | Inferred from priorities |
| 11. Seductive | Acceptance | NI | Prioritized goals | None | Interacting group |
| 12. Constrained seductive | Acceptance with important constraints | Brainwriting with advocates | Prioritized goals | None | Brainwriting with advocates |
| 13. Idea | Innovation | Delphi with morphology | Inferred goals | Focus group | Interacting group |
| 14. Constrained idea | Innovation with constraints | Delphi with morphology | Inferred goals | Focus group | Interacting group |
| 15. Gesture | None | None | None | None | Interacting group |
| 16. Ratification | Recognizing important constraints | None | None | None | Brainwriting with advocates |

other key people to form a strategic planning committee that guides and monitors strategy development.

Strategy development requires a somewhat different approach from that outlined for project planned change. The strategic planned change process is built using sets of techniques that differ from those recommended for project planned change.

## Comprehensive Strategy

*Comprehensive strategies* require quality, acceptance, and innovation without constraints. The strategist has considerable latitude of action, but the strategy that is sought has several expectations. This type of strategic planned change process would be initiated when an organization makes a commitment to consider significant changes in its services and clientele or products and markets. Typically, a key body in the organization is assigned the responsibility of developing strategy. The group processes used for discovery should engage this group of key executives in far-reaching considerations. As a result, one of the silent reflective group processes is recommended because it stimulates both innovation and acceptance. Structure is added with a snowball to find themes in the group's ideas. Several group process sessions are required. The first identifies goals.[1] Goals are broad missionlike statements that indicate directions the organization will take. Goals typically take the form of provide (make or seek), maintain (continue or remain), carry out (operate), or support (aid or participate), followed by a specific action. Table 13-4 illustrates some goals that have been devised by hospitals, and Table 13-5 lists goals devised for firms. The objectives shown under each goal have project implications, each with the potential to guide a project planned change process as discussed in the previous section of this chapter.

To generate goals, the two initial steps of a silent reflective group process, such as NGT, are emphasized: silent listing and round-robin recording. (Note, however, that a preliminary prioritization of the goals is a useful way to get closure in an initial meeting.) Subsequent group processes define objectives for each goal. In the typical meeting, between 15 and 20 goals are suggested. The group is divided into five-member subgroups and assigned goals according to their expertise. Between two and five goals are considered by the subgroups, requiring four to five additional group processes to lay out objectives for each goal. In these last group processes, all the NGT steps are used.

When time is short, the process can be streamlined by using a modified brainwriting procedure. Two people with comparable expertise are drawn from the strategic planning committee. Each is assigned goals within their area of expertise and asked to come to the next committee meeting with a list of possible objectives

---

[1] There is considerable confusion over the definition of the terms goals and objectives. In some of the literature, a goal is treated as subservient to an objective. Goals are thought of as having measurelike properties, while objectives are broad and missionlike in character (see, for example, the arguments cited in Chapter 10). The reverse is true in other writing on the subject. In this book, the term "goal" will be used to identify broad statements of intent that the organization seeks to achieve over extended periods of time. "Objectives" will be used to identify the intent of projects initiated to meet these goals. Planned change projects are carried out to meet an objective and strategic planned change to set goals and ways to achieve them.

for each goal assigned to them. (For a group of ten members, about two goals per person would be assigned.) As a first step in the meeting, the two people exchange lists and comment on each other's objectives. Next, they consolidate or merge the objectives into one list.

Note that the goals in Tables 13-4 and 13-5 do not indicate norms. For example, margins (profits) are sought for goal 3, but expectations are not specified. Additional time can be spent making each goal measurable, specifying the following:

1. Market or target group
2. Expected performance level
3. Time horizon

## Table 13-4  ▲  Illustrative Goals and Objectives for a Hospital's Strategic Plan

Goal 1:    Provide leadership for our community (e.g., hospitals that are part of a
           multihospital system)
           Objective 1: Expand management contracting
           Objective 2: Investigate hospital acquisition
           Objective 3: Offer backup services to hospitals in service area

Goal 2:    Improve medical staff
           Objective 1: Seek balance and eliminate gaps
           Objective 2: Offer programs that attract high physician admitters

Goal 3:    Improve institutional financing
           Objective 1: Provide margins that allow for replacement and expansion
           Objective 2: Ensure reasonable third-party reimbursement
           Objective 3: Seek new and maintain existing endowments
           Objective 4: Seek funding for research projects

Goal 4:    Enhance institutional resources
           Objective 1: Create efficiency through resource sharing
           Objective 2: Ensure balance in resources made available to service
                        departments
           Objective 3: Ensure adequate return on investment of resources

Goal 5:    Provide leadership to others in health delivery and public policy
           Objective 1: Develop new concept in health care delivery
           Objective 2: Promote public policy that ensures survival and well-being of
                        the industry
           Objective 3: Act with others to serve under or in unserved regions
           Objective 4: Become the leader in particular services

Goal 6:    Supplement and aid in the educational process of health professionals
           Objective 1: Provide residency training (list)
           Objective 2: Maintain and develop new medical education programs (list)

Goal 7:    Increase size of service area (market management)
           Objective 1: Create a management contract capability
           Objective 2: Establish ambulatory care centers
           Objective 3: Provide new tertiary care services (list)
           Objective 4: Enlarge medical staff in existing services

Goal 8:    Streamline governance
           Objective 1: Improve organization structure
           Objective 2: Speed communication and decision making

**Table 13-5  ▲  Illustrative Goals and Objectives for a Firm's Strategic Plan**

| | |
|---|---|
| Goal 1: | Expand market share for key products |
| | Objective 1: Increase product use by current customers |
| | Objective 2: Promote brand switching |
| | Objective 3: Find new customers |
| Goal 2: | Develop new products |
| | Objective 1: Identify market niches |
| | Objective 2: Match products to niches |
| Goal 3: | Improve profit |
| | Objective 1: Provide retained earnings that allow for replacement and expansion |
| | Objective 2: Competitive salaries for key people |
| | Objective 3: Seek new and maintain old sources of revenue |
| | Objective 4: Seek capital for key projects |
| | Objective 5: Improve return on investment |
| Goal 4: | Reduce cost of operation |
| | Objective 1: Explore the efficiency of operations |
| | Objective 2: Find and eliminate slack |
| Goal 5: | Become a market leader |
| | Objective 1: Develop new product ideas |
| | Objective 2: Promote products that ensure survival against foreign competition |
| | Objective 3: Become the industry leader in at least one product |
| Goal 6: | Improve communications |
| | Objective 1: Improve the flow of information |
| | Objective 2: Speed communication and decision making |

Target group specifies the users or consumers to be addressed. For example, in Table 13-4, goal 3 addresses improved financing, which organizational units (e.g., contract managed hospitals) are to improve. The target group is all contract managed hospitals in the multihospital system. Continuing with this example, performance level would specify the expected increase in revenue less expenses and time horizon, over what time period the increases are expected. In Table 13-5, goal 4 must determine where cost-reduction efforts in a firm will be directed. The goal to improve medical staff (2 in Table 13-4) could be elaborated using objective 2. Target group defines what is meant by "high admitters": their characteristics and where they can be found. Performance level indicates what number of physicians of this type is to be sought in a given time period.

In Table 13-5, goals 1 and 3—market share and profit—can be given targets based on the industry leader. In the automobile industry, General Motors' market share is targeted by others in the industry as a norm for which they can reach. Ford's profit is used in a similar fashion. Both goals and objectives can be elaborated in this way. Goals are typically considered first. Often the target group or market, expected performance, and time horizon of key objectives are detailed as well.

The VDV technique is used to elaborate goals and objectives. First, target groups, performances, and horizons are written down for each goal silently without discussion. Staff summarizes the consensus position on each, which serves as a focus for discussion. After discussion, members consider if they wish to revise their initial views and respecify target groups, performances, and time horizons. Strategic planned change often must treat its goals and/or objectives in detail.

The criteria of quality, acceptance, and innovation are used to prioritize the goals. For large numbers of goals, a Q-sort is conducted for each criterion. When ten or fewer goals are to be considered, a paired comparison strategy is used and repeated three times, one for each criterion. The VDV technique allows for discussion during the ranking process. The average ranking from the paired comparisons or the Q-sort is computed and used to stimulate discussion prior to the final ranking. The ARS technique is used to weight the criteria, providing a basis to merge the three lists. A set of priority goals, with objectives that define broad programmatic options, results.

The priority goal sets are used to search for strategic options in a series of group processes, using a silent reflective group process such as an NGT. Each priority goal is assigned to a subgroup drawn from the strategic planning committee (SPC). The assignment is based on expertise, with insiders or outside consultants knowledgeable about the goal's subject matter added to each group as needed. Subgroups of between five to seven members are desirable. For instance, the goal to improve institutional margin in a service organization, such as a hospital, could involve the SPC members who are knowledgeable about finance and reimbursement. An expanded educational service program goal calls for the participation of physicians knowledgeable about the creation and management of such programs and their impact on the hospital. A manufacturing company would involve financial experts, R&D personnel, market specialists, and other authorities in such a group.

Each subgroup of the SPC takes a goal and the objectives and suggests ideas that seem consistent with that goal, using the lateral thinking or synectics techniques. For example, a profit goal group would be asked to propose ways to increase profit. The objectives, such as new sources of revenue, act as initial guides. Groups in the silent reflective phase identify projects the organization can consider to meet the profit goal. The projects identified for each goal are then prioritized. Either the Q-sort or paired comparison approach is used in the VDV format. In strategic planned change, dialectics can be used to create contingency plans using scenarios. Each goal can be examined with two factors such as favorable and unfavorable product demand and capital financing in firms or endowments and ticket sales for a symphony. Subcommittees are assigned to develop ideas under each set of conditions, using the approach just outlined.

The subcommittees use the contingencies to frame their search for new ideas and then plans for each idea. Two group processes are used. In the first, new ideas are developed, and in the second, plans are suggested for each idea. Subgroups of the strategic planning committee are matched to ideas in which they have special knowledge or expertise. Subgroups with five members are desirable. The membership of the SPC is augmented by outsiders who have special knowledge of the ideas being considered. For instance, a subgroup charged to identify ways to carry out a marketing idea could add a local consultant with expertise in marketing.

In each case, the idea (e.g., income creation) and its components (e.g., vertical integration, marketing, recruitment of staff) are added to and elaborated upon, creating a list of program options. To simplify and shorten the process, NGT without synectics can be used in the idea and component discovery process.

Morphology is used to organize these plans and identify gaps. Morphology sorts the plans to find coherent ideas. The strategic option generator described in Chapter 11 can be used. Options identified by morphology, for each contingency, are reviewed by the SPC and then prioritized. To aid in setting priorities a dialectic can be created in which each subgroup presents its ideas and argues for their adoption. When options are numerous, Q-sorts are used. The paired comparisons ranking approach is used for ten or fewer options. Three sorts are made: one each for quality, acceptance, and innovation. The criteria weights, set in the formulation stage using the anchor rating scales technique, are used to weight the ranks in each sort. The vote-discuss-vote technique is used to guide the prioritization, allowing the initial priorities to be discussed before a final vote is taken by the SPC. When time is short, the prioritization of plans can be done with a global criterion, which allows the VDV steps to be carried out in a single meeting. If all criteria are used, two meetings are called for, permitting staff the time to merge the lists between meetings.

Giving SPC members the time to reflect between meetings is crucial. To improve the final judgments, a variation on the nominal-interacting (anteroom lobbying) group process can be used. The importance of strategy development to an organization calls for a time commitment commensurate with its importance. A number of meetings and time to reflect between the meetings is highly desirable.

The product of strategic planned change process is several strategic options, each made up of several goal-like statements and prioritized options for each goal that the organization can pursue using planned change projects. The time frame and performance expectations set for each goal provide the basis for periodic appraisal of the overall strategy.

The imposition of constraints calls for a *qualified comprehensive strategy*. A broad search is undertaken, but core values that the organization will attempt to preserve must be introduced into the process. When constraints are present the brainwriting technique can be used to introduce subtly their requirements both during goal formation and, again, as options are developed. Brainwriting is used to manage discovery and creativity phases. This step helps to preserve quality and acceptance and retains some degree of innovation, as constraints are introduced. Directions are set and options are derived following the steps called for to create a comprehensive strategy (see Table 13-3).

## Traditional Strategies

*Traditional strategies* do not stress innovation but require quality and acceptance. Such a strategic planned change process could be mounted as a quick fix to perceived problems. Also, many organizations do not see the need for innovative strategies, preferring to mimic the posture of respected competitors.

A silent reflective group process, such as NI, is preferred to identify goals because it promotes both quality and acceptance in the SPC. Structure is added by finding important themes in the goals, like those shown in Tables 13-4 and 13-5. The NI format allows time between formal meetings for informal lobbying among SPC members.

To prioritize large numbers of goals, two Q-sorts are conducted: one for quality and one for acceptance. Paired comparison is used to set priorities among the goals. The ARS technique is used to specify the relative importance of quality and acceptance, allowing the list of priority goals to reflect both requirements.

An SRGP is used by the strategic planning committee to identify options for each goal that suggest ideas that can be pursued by a project planning process. Snowball is applied to find themes in the ideas. These themes and their components are structured using the relevance tree technique. The relevance tree is used to elaborate each option and find gaps in logic that can be closed.

Scenarios are often useful to guide the search for options. The NI or other SRGP is applied by subgroups of the SPC that seek options under one of several assumed conditions. For instance, a low-demand–high-capital-cost or worst case condition would be assumed by one group to suggest ways in which markets could be expanded. The other groups would consider markets (and the other goals) under conditions of high demand–high capital cost and low demand–low capital cost (mixed conditions) and high demand–low capital cost (best condition). Such a step reduces risk and ensures that options fashioned under a variety of conservative and nonconservative assumptions are considered.

The VDV or NI format is used to manage the priority steps. First, goals and then options are prioritized for each goal, using two Q-sorts (or paired comparisons), one for quality and one for acceptance. These criteria are weighted using the ARS technique by the SPC. The lists are merged by multiplying the criteria weight by the rank and averaging. The group discusses these priorities and then reranks them. In the NI format, time is allowed for formal lobbying between meetings after the initial priority list has been published. The VDV structure is used under conditions of extreme time pressure.

When constraints are imposed, the strategy is called *constrained traditional*. The quick fix has constraints. The sponsor seeks to introduce values that reflect personal or organizational practices that are not to be changed. Brainwriting is substituted for NI to introduce these constraints in discovery and option identification. The other process stages are carried out by following the steps outlined for traditional strategies.

## Strategic Prototypes

The *strategic prototype* calls for quality and innovation. The prototype creates a benchmark to gauge future efforts. Such a strategic plan could be sought by consulting firms to specify the range of strategic alignments that make sense for their current and/or projected clients. Because acceptance is not an issue, Delphi surveys are recommended. The surveys are designed to tap people with state-of-the-art information, by involving individuals inside and outside the firm. The Delphi survey is used to dredge up ideas for consideration. The initial search is focused on seeking out salable ideas. Goals are not needed until the ideas are proposed for a specific use or user. The intent is to find potentially useful ideas. These ideas (and their supporting arguments) are sorted into quality and innovative categories by two Q-sorts. No ideas are selected, so this importance ordering is sufficient. The idea list that results provides a range of strategic options for the organization to ponder.

Option development is preceded by a review of the ideas gleaned from the delphi. To identify options from this information an NGT group process is used with synectics. Morphology is used to organize the ideas gleaned from the NGT. Components in the morphology are defined by the features of both strategies and environments. The features of these strategies and environments are mixed to create new strategic environmental alignments. For instance, stable demand environments may not use marketing strategies, and consumer-dominated environments may have emphasized service at the expense of profit. These new strategic-environmental alignments are then pruned to select those that seem useful. Each feasible alignment is elaborated using a relevance tree. The tree is matched to one of the ideas. The idea theme (e.g., marketing or profit) is progressively elaborated in each level of the tree. The relevance tree provides a picture of a strategy that seems feasible.

A focus group is used to ensure that ideas the sponsor wants considered get introduced to a strategic planning group in a *constrained prototype*. For example, strategic positions open to various types of organizations facing environments that may have competitors are identified. Focus groups are used to bring in experts knowledgeable about each environment to present strategies that have worked in these settings. Delphi is not desirable. An in-depth quizzing of each expert by the consultant's key staff should follow their presentation of a strategy and its features. Both the strategy and environmental features, as well as indicators of success, should be carefully enumerated.

To identify options from the focus group discussion, a nominal group technique with synectics is used. The remaining steps follow the procedure outlined for strategic prototypes (see Table 13-3).

## Utility Strategies

Strategies devised to seek only quality are called *utility*. This type of strategy is preferred when organizational leaders are both powerful and relatively independent of their board and regulatory agents. Not-for-profit organizations with fee-for-service revenue generation could adopt such a posture. Examples include consulting firms, such as RAND, and some state organizations, such as departments of natural resources, that can charge for licenses or inspections mandated by law. Both profit or not-for-profit multihospital systems, in states that have little in the way of rate control or capital expenditure regulation, could adopt such a posture. Firms that are dominated by a small number of shareholders (e.g., Ford) or a proprietorship (e.g., U-Haul) can adopt such a strategy. To seek such a strategy a proactively inclined leader operates in a highly autonomous manner. When such a leader (e.g., CEO) is less interested in "what's new" than "what works," a utility strategy can be pursued.

The CEO does nothing in the formulation stage, skipping to the concept development stage and using a *focus group*. No formulation techniques are used because goals are inferred after the concept development stage has been completed.

For utility strategies, activity is concentrated on option development using the template approach. To create a utility strategy, a focus group is formed as in process 6 (Table 13-3), with one difference. The sponsor seeks presentations about environments that are strictly comparable to the organization. For instance, several consultants can be hired to point out strategies that have proved to be useful in settings like the sponsor's. The consultant would not be asked to create strategy for the organization. Also, noncompeting CEOs and academics can offer useful insights about strategic alignments that have worked in comparable environments.

The sponsor appoints key organizational constituents to hear these presentations. To extract implications for the organizations, discussion groups are formed around themes, such as marketing or product lines, recognized by the CEO. The membership of the group is expanded to include inside and outside expertise thought by the CEO to be useful in project identification. These groups identify projects for each theme. The product is a set of projects that the CEO can ponder. Project planning is activated around projects seen by the CEO as particularly useful, applying criteria that are external to the planning process.

A *qualified utility strategy* is devised when an organizational leader, acting as a sponsor, recognizes the need to affirm some of its current practices. The markets, customers, products, and organizational arrangements to be preserved can be introduced by "plants" during the focus group sessions. The NI process offers a further opportunity for "plants" to introduce cautions should these markets, customers, products, and arrangements seem threatened by an emerging consensus.

## Awareness Strategy

An *awareness strategy* is carried out to inform key individuals, such as a board, about possibilities and to seek acceptance to act on possibilities that seem particularly relevant. Organizations that seek to coopt key stakeholders into exploring possibilities would use this type of strategy. A Delphi survey is used with organizational insiders and/or outsiders who would have insights into new ideas that merit exploration. Participants are drawn from consultants, the organization's auditor, research and development, engineering departments, data processing, manufacturing or fabrication, and the like. Morphology is used to flesh out the ideas, identifying options that are implied by the Delphi results. These options serve as a starting point for discussion by a key group, like the organization's executive committee or its board of directors. This group uses an NI group process to identify options that the organization should consider, adding their own ideas. The informal lobbying opportunities permit key stakeholders to develop a consensus about opportunities, creating implied goals. The decision body creates a prioritized action plan using Q-sort to identify potentially valuable options and the paired comparison technique to prioritize the strategic options.

*Constrained awareness* strategies also seek the acceptance of strategic possibilities but impose constraints on the search. For instance, a utility could use such a process to get top management to see new vistas for the organization recognizing key constraints, such as avoiding nuclear power or soft coal in power generation. A Delphi is used to identify ideas, and morphology is applied to fashion the ideas into options, following the steps outlined for awareness strategy. Differences arise in promoting acceptance while introducing constraints. Key stakeholders consider these ideas using a kiva. Each round is carried out with a brainwriting group process, to introduce key constraints. The first kiva circle has representatives of the executive committee and/or board of directors. The outer rings have representatives from lower levels of management. At least two kiva circles are recommended. By reflecting on how people who must implement new ideas see these ideas and their benefits and motivations, members of a key discussion group develop a deeper understanding of the barriers and dangers as well as the benefits of strategic action.

*The kiva experience* develops both a commitment to act and an acceptance of constraints in key groups, such as a board. The rationale for each emerges from the kiva groups. A prioritized action plan is produced using Q-sort to winnow the list of options and paired comparisons to create a priority list of strategic options.

## Seductive Strategy

For the *seductive strategy,* only acceptance is important. Such strategy can arise when leaders are confronted by board members who insist that the organization devise a strategic plan. For example, business representatives on a school board may be content that schools without a formal strategy are run by the "seat of the pants." The school superintendent may have a strategy, but prefers to keep it under wraps, for example, because of threatened desegregation litigation, or may not see the merit of a strategic planned change process. In either case, only acceptance would be sought. Preferred techniques get people to think that something was accomplished, but do not limit the leader's ability to maneuver.

The nominal interactive process is recommended to elicit goals, with closure by a formal vote. In the first step, each member of a board or executive committee silently lists candidate goals. Next, a sequential listing and ranking of the goals is carried out. Ranking should be done using a procedure that gives the appearance of sophistication, to promote acceptance, such as paired comparisons. The group is given the initial goal priorities and asked to discuss them with groups members and others. Meeting rooms are arranged where members can mingle and lobby one another.

The final meeting begins with an open discussion of the goal priorities and ends with another vote to create goal priorities. The sponsor (leader) resists the development of goal measures (performance, horizons, or target groups) because this level of specificity can hamper his or her maneuverability.

Seductive strategies seek the acceptance of individuals who are important to the organization, usually in the form of support or endorsement. These individuals are gathered in a group by the CEO. Themes in the goals identified in formulation specify the discussion topics for the group. Experts (consultants, other CEOs, academics) are asked to describe to the group workable strategies that deal with each goal. The group prioritizes possible projects for each goal using the paired comparison technique. The result is program ideas organized around consensual goals for the organization that the leader can pursue selectively at his or her leisure.

*Constrained seductive* strategies arise when leaders are wary of an open discussion of strategic options, fearing being hemmed in by projects that they may not favor. Such a leader makes a list of his or her interests. The leader then forms a group composed of people whose support is essential and advocates that can be trusted to argue for the leader's interests. Goals are then set by this group using a brainwriting session. The starter ideas introduce goals that the leader wants adopted and others that group members are known to support that do not conflict with the leaders. Strategic options are identified in this way as well. Priorities for goals and options are set by using the paired comparison technique.

## Idea Strategies

*Idea* strategies develop possibilities for contemplation, not action. Hospitals that explore ways to replace revenue losses due to reimbursement caps may develop such strategies to inform themselves about possibilities without the need to make assessments of quality or acceptance. The process is initiated to show a key body, such as a board of directors or trustees, what can be done and ready it for a more comprehensive process of strategic planned change.

A Delphi process similar to that described for awareness strategy is initiated. The Delphi findings are structured with a morphology. The options that result are then described to key bodies using a focus group approach. The focus group is made up of experts that participated in the Delphi who were found to have particularly insightful ideas. These individuals are brought together to debate the options in terms of their comparative merits and possible benefits. A key body, such as a board, is asked to listen to the debate and discuss possibilities for action in a subsequent meeting.

A *constrained idea* strategy is carried out in the same fashion as an idea strategy with one exception. Ideas that conflict with organizational values are dropped from Delphi options that are uncovered.

## Gesture and Ratification Strategies

A *gesture strategy* is created when the process to derive strategy is mounted merely to impress or appease third parties. Such a process may be rational when regulatory or legislative bodies give special consideration to organizations that carry out strategic planning or appear to have produced a new strategy. For example, health regulators require evidence of a strategic plan before capacity expansion plans of a hospital will be considered. Accreditation agencies call for strategic plans before they will accredit academic programs in colleges and universities. In both illustrations, there is no obligation to use the plan, merely to have it.

A "friendly" group that can be controlled by the leader is established. The leader presents a synthesis of the strategies that others have successfully used, showing how the proposed strategy is consistent with historical goals previously identified or why inconsistencies can be tolerated. The group is asked to support the proposed strategy. Urgency, such as needing a strategic plan for a certificate of need (CON) submission or an impending accreditation review, is usually cited as the reason to support the staff-dominated strategic planning approach. The product is a document resembling a strategic plan that the organization can effectively ignore. The leader may even share these intentions with boards or executive committees, if there are sufficient trust and confidence between the leader and the members of such groups. This sets the stage for an interactive discussion to elicit ideas to be included in the gesture strategy.

A *ratification strategy* arises when an organization must form a gesture strategy *and* protect sensitive negotiations. If revealed, negotiations could collapse or the organization may lose an important competitive advantage. As a result, steps are taken to keep outsiders from learning about (continuing with the foregoing example) plans for mergers and buyouts or management contracts of smaller hospitals. Also, the organization may wish to posture about aims, such as hospitals that dramatize indigent care programs as they argue for the approval of high-cost services, such as open heart surgery, to regulators. In such a situation, the leader activates a brainwriting group with advocates as members, following the arguments offered for constrained seductive strategies. In this case, the advocates are present to rule out options that would reveal or call attention to sensitive plans not ready for public discussion. The list of ideas used to initiate the brainwriting session would include options that convey an image the organization wants to project.

## ▲ THE TOTAL PLANNED CHANGE PROCESS

The product of a strategic planned change process is prioritized goals and program options that alter an organization's mission, products, services, markets, clients, and policies. Many project planning activities are carried out to shape options described by a strategy into viable programs of planned change for the organization. Strategic planned change is carried out periodically, responding to the successes and failures of project plans. Feedback on plan success is used to modify goals and programmatic initiatives.

### The Process for Strategic Planned Change

Strategic planned change has two essential stages: formulation and concept development. Project planned change develops options that flow from strategic initiatives, and assessments stem from measurements or organizational performance, as shown in Figure 13-3. This framework is similar to that offered by strategists such as Glueck (1980) who see objectives and options as "strategic management elements" and the "strategic management process" encompassing the stages of analysis and diagnosis, choice, implementation, and evaluation. Project planned change is similar to Glueck's strategic management, with performance assessed through the organization's control activities. Strategic planned change focuses on the creative acts of formulating intentions and conceptualizing options.

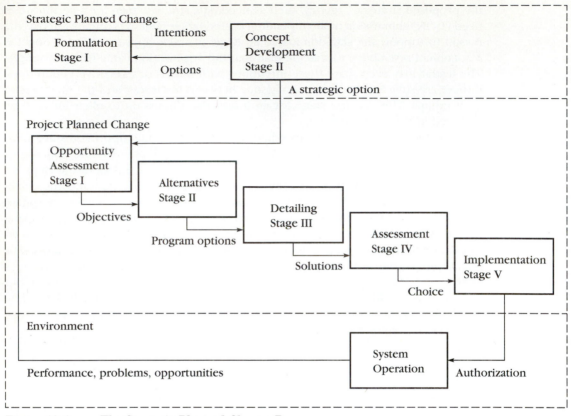

**Figure 13-3** ▲ The Strategic Planned Change Process
Adapted from Nutt (1984e).

### Strategic Planning

In a given strategic planning cycle, information is exchanged between the formulation and concept development stages. In formulation, the issues confronting the organization are clarified and expectations are set out for discussion and analysis. Formulation draws on and collates environmental assessments that have identified trends in regulation, politics, and technological breakthroughs that, taken together, create opportunities for action or threats. The formulation stage typically produces a prioritized set of goals and elaborating objectives.

The concept development stage identifies opportunities. It draws on and reconciles formal and informal audits of resources that identify the organization's administrative capability, marketing expertise, and programs that have distinctive or useful competencies that can deal with perceived needs and opportunities. In the concept development stage, sufficient detail is provided so strategic options can be described, compared, and prioritized.

Considerable movement between the formulation and concept development stages should occur. Goals and objectives are added or modified, given the implications of strategic options, and goals and objectives direct the search for options. The strategic planning process moves back and forth between formulation and concept development until a strategic plan emerges that meets predetermined requirements. These requirements define planning methods that can be used to create the types of strategies shown in Table 13-3. The techniques identify planning methods that can be used to create each type of strategy are summarized in the table.

### Project Planning

Strategic planned change identifies opportunities that are investigated by project planning, as shown by Figure 13-3. A strategy specifies an option that can energize several project planning activities. Stages 1 and 2 in project planning are similar in purpose to formulation and concept development in strategic planning. The opportunities implicit in the strategic options are considered in the formulation stage and serve as the basis to set objectives. In concept development, alternatives within a candidate strategy are explored, creating program options. Specifics are added to seemingly desirable alternatives in the detailing stage. The evaluation stage provides the basis to select an alternative, and the implementation stage sets in place the favored alternative.

### The Planning Cycle

The success of projects activated by strategic planned change, the general level of organizational performance, environmental pressure, and the like provide signals that indicate when another round of strategic planning activity is needed. Some organizations periodically (e.g., at five-year intervals) repeat a strategic planning process to see if new opportunities surface. Others wait for explicit and implicit signals, and still others seem remarkably oblivious to the need for strategy revision.

## ▲ Key Points

1. Hybrid planned change methods are created by merging planning techniques in creative ways. Some of these combinations were described in Chapters 10, 11, and 12, but still others are possible. The process facilitator who becomes familiar with these techniques can fashion still more hybrid methods, tailored to his or her specific needs.

2. Types of strategy were defined by whether or not quality, acceptance, innovation, and preservation is required. Each strategy was matched to technique strings to create a planned change method that can be used to deal with the activities called for in each process stage and produce the desired results.

3. Planning methods for planned change projects were defined by techniques to carry out the formulation, concept development, and detailing stages of the process. Planning methods are made up of techniques selected for the three stages, and within stage phases. Two steps were taken to create planning methods. First, techniques were fit to the phases of each stage of the process. Candidate planning processes were made up of techniques for the discovery and direction phases of the formulation stage, for the creativity and option identification of

phases in the concept development stage, and for the construction and interrogation phases used to detail the plan. Together, technique strings for these stages and phases define a planning method. Second, the desired outcome of planned change was used to devise guides that can be used to select a planning method for a particular application.

4.  Strategic planned change requires knowledge of process, techniques that support the demands of the process, and ways to combine techniques into hybrid methods that meet the special needs of strategic planned change under a variety of conditions.

## ▲ Cases

### *The Same-Day Testing Case*

This project was conducted in a large university hospital with a massive referral outreach program that provides tertiary care services to some 30 counties both within and outside the state. The hospital is typical of large, university settings with several managerial levels.

The CEO had toyed with the idea of same-day testing for some time. His motives stemmed from the traditional and seemingly inefficient pattern of admissions in which people were first taken to their rooms and then moved back to various departments for X rays, lab work, and other types of routine services. The same-day testing idea has all testing done before patients are moved to their rooms.

The same-day testing idea was used to initiate the planned change process. After dreaming up the idea, the sponsor had staff people list the opportunities that stem from same-day testing and suggest objectives. They identified two: speeding the testing process and reducing admission costs.

The sponsor asked a systems analyst and an architect to develop the same-day testing idea. They responded by providing layout and a flowchart of a new admitting department. The layout and flowchart were revised three times in response to sponsor questioning. First, the number and types of services were questioned. This led to a revised building configuration. The expanded role of admitting in this second layout raised questions about premises of admitting: Whether it should orient patients or merely coordinate the provision of services. This led to the second revision. In the third cycle, the sponsor questioned the timing and privacy of services. For instance, pap smears must be provided in an area that can be sealed off to normal flows of personnel and patients. The final revision was subjected to an evaluation to explore how changes in assumptions might influence the plan.

A simulation of the operation of the admitting department was made, making several assumptions about patient volume to determine effectiveness and potential acceptability. (Acceptance was based on the notion that patients eased into the hospital environment through a better coordination and centralization of activities that were often fragmented would improve their attitude toward their hospital stay.) These simulations led to further evaluation of the building's configuration and modification of the plan. ▲

## The Customized Travel Vehicle Case

A proprietorship providing customized travel vehicles had grown to 5 million sales in just a few years. The company began by converting buses to provide luxury transportation for country and western singers to travel between their engagements. Business grew from this point by word of mouth. Lorretta Lynn bought the first vehicle. The list of customers now includes John Madden, the NFL football analyst, and others who fear flying but must travel long distances for their work.

Recently profits have leveled off. The CEO is concerned that the market for expensive customized vehicles may have become saturated, with new sales being largely replacements or rehabilitations, that have a smaller profit margin. He is wondering about new businesses, but is unsure of how to proceed.  ▲

## The Family Medicine Department Case

A large university medical school has a family medicine department that has failed to meet the dean's expectations of bringing in large federal grants. The department was founded 20 years ago with federal and state funds provided to encourage family medicine concepts in medical school curriculums. The medical school, like countless others across the United States, was skeptical of the value of family medicine but wanted the money.

The department has become an embarrassment because none of its faculty members has been promoted. The "tenure" decision for a faculty member is made at six years of service, based on the amount of money that is raised by the individual's grants from federal agencies and foundations. Normally, faculty that are not promoted are given a one-year terminal contract.

Each faculty member in family medicine provides considerable revenue for the medical school through patient care and through their oversight of urgent care facilities, spread throughout the city. These urgent care centers also provide a large number of referrals to the university hospital. The loss of one faculty member would have an immediate impact on medical school revenues. Faculty members contend that these responsibilities keep them from writing grants.

By claiming that he cannot hire replacements, the department chairman has been able to block the termination of faculty. Instead of a terminal contract, each faculty member has been tenured at the assistant professor level. This action precludes any further advancement, but does save the faculty member's job.

Department faculty have become upset at these developments. With the resident supervision work load and oversight responsibilities, none of the faculty believes that he or she has any chance of being promoted.  ▲

## ▲ Exercises

1. Consider the outpatient registration case in Chapter 1. What requirements did the sponsor implicitly impose? Identify the planning method that is recommended for these requirements. (Consult Table 13-2.) Compare the recommended steps and the steps actually carried out. What did you find?

2. Review the same-day testing case. What requirements did the sponsor seem to impose? Identify another set of requirements that seem reasonable for this case. Compare the planning methods suggested for each. What did you discover?

3. Go to Chapter 5, and review the data processing case. Answer the questions posed in Exercises 1 and 2.

4. Consider the customized vehicle case. What requirements seem paramount? Use these requirements to select a planning method. Assume that the leader is to do most of the work and cannot use groups. Suggest techniques that can be used by the leader in place of the group techniques that are called for by the planning method you have selected.

5. Review the family medicine case. How must strategic planned change be carried out in this setting? What requirements are implied? Identify a planning method for this case and compare it to the one selected for the customized vehicle case. What are the similarities and differences? Why do these differences arise?

# The Role Approach: Technique Selection Based on the Style of Process Management

**14**

▲ ▲ ▲   ▲ ▲ ▲ ▲ ▲ ▲ ▲ ▲ ▲ ▲ ▲ ▲ ▲ ▲ ▲ ▲

The results of a planning process are heavily dependent upon a dialogue between the sponsor who sanctions and manages the process and the planner, individuals subordinate to the sponsor, who carries it out. The word "dialogue" is chosen to characterize the discussions that take place between planner and sponsor. This dialogue can be somewhat chaotic and irrational rather than a sequential rational exchange of information implied by the process ideas presented in this book.

Several roles that sponsors take when managing planned change during its developmental stages are described in terms of the expected exchanges between sponsors and planners. To capture the planned change process as a dialogue, these exchanges are treated as arguments, using the approach suggested by Toulmin (1979) and Nutt and Backoff (1986). The form of the argument and the resulting patterns in the exchanges between sponsor and planner strongly influence the effectiveness of planned change.

Arguments are used to specify the expected behavior of planners confronted with a sponsor who is acting out a given role. The preferred and ideal planning techniques for each role while coping with the demands of formulation, concept development, and detailing are identified. The preferred technique is consistent with the sponsor's beliefs and biases. Such a technique is likely to promote good sponsor-planner relations. The recommended technique is one that complements the strengths and ameliorates the weaknesses inherent in a particular role taken by a plan sponsor and can improve planning results. This technique is acceptable to a sponsor, in a particular role, but will not be used without action by the planner. It represents a compromise between sponsor acceptance and producing good results. This chapter identifies planned change techniques that cater to the idiosyncracies of the sponsor for the purpose of promoting sponsor support.

## ▲  SPONSOR ROLES

Sponsors guiding a planned change process are often described as rationalists who have neutral attitudes toward planning. However, one's everyday experiences suggest that the role played by a sponsor can be positive or critical, in addition to taking a posture of neutrality. A variety of roles can be imagined that take on different shades of these views (Nutt and Backoff, 1986).

Figure 14-1 shows how sponsor directives during planned change, described in Chapter 5, are influenced by sponsor attitudes toward planning and the roles that can be played. The positive, neutral, and critical postures that can be struck by a sponsor in a planned change process are summarized in Table 14-1. Each role is described in terms of the rules of conduct applied as well as the sponsor's behavior, motives, and expectations of how the process is to unfold. Process expectations are described in terms of the procedures to be used and the plan's expected appearance, as well as the plan's adoption prospects and expected consequences.

The dialogue between a sponsor and a planner is shaped quite differently, depending upon which of these roles is taken. Critics, such as a devil's advocate, play the role of judge. Skeptics require many comprehension recycles. Critics demand comparative certainty in prediction and assessments. Others strike a neutral

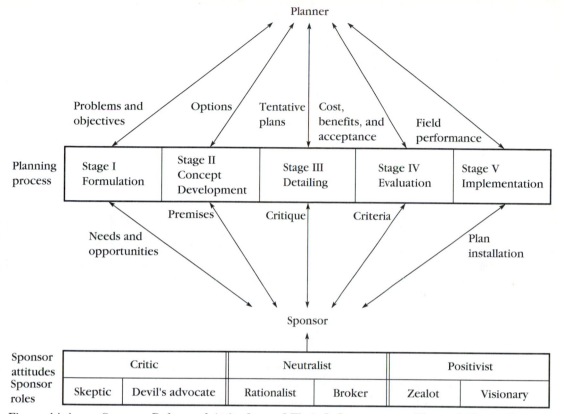

**Figure 14-1**  ▲  **Sponsor Roles and Attitudes and Their Influences on a Planned Change Process**

posture. The broker takes the evolving plan and attempts to play a pivotal role in negotiating acceptance. Rationalists, in contrast, see themselves as providing a logic for choice. Each sees the importance of information as it emerges from the planning process differently. Positivists adopt still different tactics. The visionary pushes for innovation. A new idea is likened to a better idea without the necessity to test its merits. Zealots also try to ensure that something is done, but that something is often strikingly similar to one of their pet ideas.

These sponsor roles are intended to be caricatures, in part because managers are unlikely to display such pure behavior in practice. Further, managers may adopt different roles as new opportunities emerge. External circumstances surrounding the planned change effort demand that sponsors be adept at taking a variety of postures. This leads a sponsor to switch from one role to another during a planned change. A devil's advocate may revert to a broker when the prospects of plan approval have been demonstrated. Similarly, brokers may become skeptics if the planned change process fails to produce outcomes that seem viable. Because some roles have more affinity than others, some of these shifts are more likely than others.

Table 14-2 illustrates role shifts that are likely during planned change. The devil's advocate becomes less critical if the planner is able to fend off the questions

Table 14-1 ▲ The Features of Sponsor Roles

| Approach to Monitoring by Sponsor | Critic | | Neutralist | | Positivist | |
|---|---|---|---|---|---|---|
| | Skeptic | Devil's Advocate | Rationalist | Broker | Zealot | Visionary |
| Rules of conduct | Question in great detail | Impose stringent standards | Sufficient information to decide if performance gap can be closed | Agitation for change creates a performance gap | Attributes of pet idea create process requirements | Provide broad outline of grand scheme |
| Behaviors | Challenge the wisdom of change | Ask embarrassing questions | Suspends judgment | Seek a compromise solution | Single-minded commitment to a pet idea | Use plan gestalt to direct inquiry |
| Motives | Status quo preferred | Challenge improves the plan | Create a logic for choice | Power stems from negotiating plan acceptance | Get pet idea adopted | Stimulate innovation |
| Expectations of the planner | Understand that all contingencies must be explored | See merit in hard questioning | Produce realistic options, documented so merits can be verified | Incorporate wishes of power centers into evolving plan | Help put pet idea in best possible light and provide new justifications | Detail the vision by adding specifics |
| Process expectations: 1. Role in the process | Interrogate the planner | Interrogation of the plan | Review and advise | Bargain and compromise | Gradually providing details to pet idea | Guiding the gradual increase in understanding |
| 2. Plan's appearance | Detailed description of all contingencies | Airtight and defensible | Meet original need | Acceptance by key power centers | The pet idea | Grand scheme with some detailing |
| 3. Adoption prospects | Dismal, without outside intervention | Mixed | Yes, if cost effective | Yes, if compromise soution politically feasible | Yes, if pet idea can be preserved | Yes, with tactical planning |
| 4. Plan consequences | Negative, resistance to change expected | Somewhat negative, some important problem always overlooked | Mildly positive, if rational process has been followed | Mildly positive, if inconsistencies caused by bargaining can be worked out | Positive, if pet idea properly used | Positive, if other can appreciate vision |

Table 14-2  ▲  Role Shifts During Planned Change

| | Change to | | | | | |
| | Critic | | Neutralist | | Positivist | |
| Change from | Skeptic | Devil's Advocate | Rationalist | Broker | Zealot | Visionary |
|---|---|---|---|---|---|---|
| Skeptic | X | | | | | |
| Devil's Advocate | | X | X | X | X[a] | |
| Rationalist | | X | X | X | X | |
| Broker | | X | X | X | X | |
| Zealot | | | | | X | |
| Visionary | | | | | X | X |

X designates a feasible role shift.
[a] Rarely.

posed, adopting either a broker or a rationalist's posture, and may even become a true believer, adopting the posture of a zealot. A sponsor who is a skeptic tends to retain this posture, as does the zealot. Skeptics and zealots tend to retain their initial commitments partly because of the extremity of these views, which makes them hard to abandon. The visionary may become a zealot when his or her grand scheme becomes an obsession. George Romney's premature commitment to compact cars is an example.

Neutral sponsors are often adaptable. The rationalist and the broker can be enticed into all but the skeptic and visionary roles, as shown in Table 14-2. The broker can be seduced, becoming a zealot, when the wishes of a power center are clear and unambiguous and the broker sees the opportunity to gather social credit by embracing these wishes. When power centers have conflicting views, and each is important, the broker may become a rationalist or even a devil's advocate, to explore the ramifications of pursuing various options. The rationalist may become a broker when it is clear that acceptance must be negotiated. When an idea emerges that seems certain of success, the rationalist may adopt it as his or her own, beginning to take on the trappings of a zealot. When ideas seem less viable, the rationalist and the broker may behave like a devil's advocate to locate the reasons.[1]

## ▲  DIALOGUE DURING PLANNED CHANGE

A sponsor and a planner engage in a debate during the planned change process. In this debate, the sponsor and planner take up sides and defend their positions. The stance toward process control and the outcome of this stance is described in Figure 14-2. The planner can play either an acquiescing or a proactive role and the sponsor can strike a reflective or a directive posture.

---

[1]  Roles can also vary if the planned change effort deals with an ill-structured, as opposed to a well-structured, problem. There are many other factors that shape the dialogue between the planner and sponsor. They include, but are not limited to, the intensity of the planning effort, the resources available, the difficulty of information exchange due to the cognitive style of the planner and sponsor, and the relative power of the sponsor and planner within the organization.

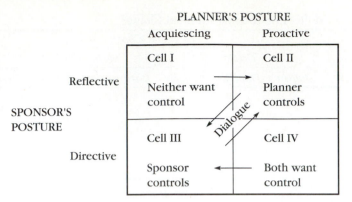

Figure 14-2  ▲  Shifts in Stance Toward Process Control

## Unstable Conditions

Cells I and IV in Figure 14-2 represent unstable conditions. In cell I, neither the planner nor the sponsor is willing to take control. This often occurs when planned change is motivated by foggy problems. Both the sponsor and planner are inclined to grope in an attempt to elicit a deeper understanding of the problem. Given an insight, either can take the initiative. Without it, no dialogue occurs, and eventually, the planned change process is aborted. Groping also occurs when the sponsor has a hidden agenda. The skilled planner fences with the sponsor, attempting to elicit an expectation or a preference. The legitimacy of the request for direction by the planner can force the sponsor to become directive (even if the direction is misleading), moving to cell III, or to abandon the effort, perhaps by calling it low priority.

In cell IV, both the planner and the sponsor want control. Confrontations of this type are typically caused by naive planners because the planner will lose. In most organizations the sponsor will have the right to decide. Any dialogue in cell IV will be brief, moving quickly to cell III.

## Stable Conditions

The dialogue that occurs along the arrows shown in Figure 14-2 is usually initiated by a sponsor's directive. Sponsors can activate planned change in cell III with statements of need, perceived opportunities, or performance gaps, as described in Chapter 5. The planner is expected to respond. When the sponsor is in a nondirective mode (e.g., listening), the planner activates the process, and the dialogue moves from upper right (cell II) to lower left (cell III) and back. Examples include expert testimony to a legislative committee or problem analysis submitted by members of an organization's staff. The equilibrium state for the dialogue is defined as planner and sponsor switching their postures, moving between cell II and III in Figure 14-2.

## ▲  TOULMIN'S APPROACH TO ARGUMENTATION

A dialogue is required when process control is in equilibrium—moving between cells II and II in Figure 14-2. During the dialogue, the sponsor and the planner engage in "arguments." The components of an argument are drawn from the work of Toulmin (1972) and Rescher (1968) who show how claims are developed. Toulmin's model has been further elaborated by Mitroff and Mason (1981) who apply it to the arguments made by managers and by Dunn (1981), who shows how policy-making is linked to argumentation. In this chapter, a still further refinement is offered, showing how argumentation can explain the debates between planner and a sponsor that occur during planned change.

The approach is summarized in Figure 14-3. A claim is the overt statement of a needed action. For example, some policymakers contend that the United States

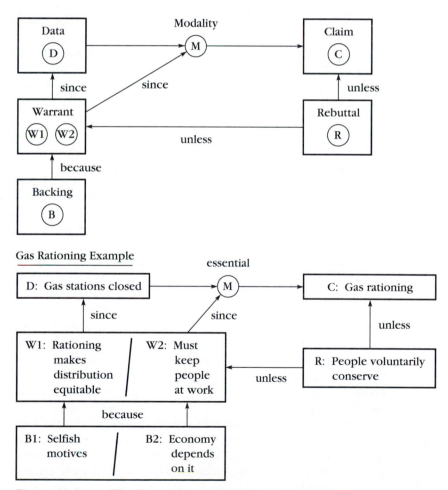

**Figure 14-3**  ▲  **The Form of Argumentation**

must have gas rationing contingency plan to avoid severe economic problems if oil shipments from the Middle East are interrupted. A claim is based on *data* or grounds that provide the evidence used in the factual content of the argument. In the gas rationing example, data could be based on observing that many gas stations have closed or have limited their hours of service when gas supplies were reportedly tight. The link between a claim and data is through a *modality*. The modality describes the perceived strength of the relationship. Gas stations can be seen terminating service, making rationing essential, or merely desirable, depending upon the strength of the warrant that is thought to support the data. *Warrants* can be defined as principles, rules, or premises that lie behind any data used to make a claim or to collect data. These rules are often little more than fuzzy sets of propositions that give inferential license. Those who support gas rationing may believe, for instance, that rationing is the only way to ensure equitable distribution of gas supplies in times of crisis.

Behind every warrant is a *backing*, which is waiting to come to the warrant's defense. All warrants have taken-for-granted assumptions, and the backing is used to certify and rationalize these assumptions. The gas rationer's backing may stem from a belief that basic selfishness in people makes equal distribution to all the only fair scheme. Warrants are linked to data with a "since" statement, and backings are linked to the warrants with a "because" statement. The rationer argues that since gas stations are closed, equitable distribution is essential. The rationer believes that because people will behave in a self-serving manner, assurances of an equitable distribution will be essential.

Finally, *rebuttals* act as safety valves, identifying conditions in which the warrant fails to hold. Sometimes rebuttals are face-saving devices; in other cases they serve as fallback positions. For instance, the rationer may qualify his or her conclusion by pointing out that people accepted the need to lower their gas consumption in World War II and may do so again if properly sold on the need for rationing. Rationing should be our policy, unless people accept the need to conserve voluntarily.

The warrant moderates both the data-claim relationship (the conclusions drawn using the data) and the generation of data (Figure 14-3). Several data collections can be initiated, and each can have a different warrant. For example, the researcher uses a warrant that calls for the use of experiments to collect data and tests of internal validity to certify the data-claim relationship. Multiple warrants can be evoked in a given data collection activity, such as using both expert or personal opinion and tests of generalizability to validate a data-claim relationship. The situation can become quite complex. There may be several pieces of data buttressing a claim, several warrants for a given set of data, multiple backings, and rebuttals for each warrant.

Only the claim is stated with completeness and clarity. The remaining elements are seldom fully articulated. During a debate, one hears a claim justified by what seems to be incomplete, inconsistent, or even biases processes of reasoning. This is particularly true in planned change where considerable uncertainty surround the early process stages.

## ▲ ARGUMENTATION AND THE PLANNED CHANGE PROCESS

Discussion considers just the early stages of planned change. Because the formulation, concept development, and detailing stages are creative, they can be dramatically influenced, for better or worse, by the sponsor's involvement. The evaluation and implementation stages have a conformational role. The sponsor is less likely to role-play when faced with the need to assess the product of planning or to select a way to implement the plan.

### Types of Claims

One type of claim is always made by the planner and by the sponsor in each of the creative stages of the planned change process, as shown in Figure 14-4. For instance, planned change is activated by definitions of opportunities or needs, in formulation. These stipulations vary in terms of specificity but do identify the sponsor's overt beliefs. The planner interprets beliefs about needs or opportunities by identifying problems and possible objectives for the planned change effort to address (Figure 14-4). In the concept development stage, the sponsor's premises, which indicate

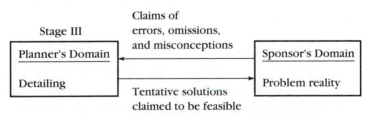

**Figure 14-4** ▲ **Argumentation During Planned Change**

attributes of a solution and an arena of action, become claims. The planner takes these premises and creates options that codify the themes that are implied. In the detailing stage the planner's claims describe plans that seem feasible, and the sponsor makes claims about the errors, omissions, and misconceptions in these same plans.

The following discussion illustrates how argumentation, which lies behind the formation of one's claims, can differ. The Toulmin framework will be used to identify the nature of the arguments made and the likelihood that conflict will stem from these arguments. Planners often fail to understand or appreciate the arguments of sponsors, partly because sponsors use a variety of basic arguments and even change them as the planned change process unfolds. There are many roles that sponsors can play, and they often shift roles for reasons that are obscure to planners. By the same token, sponsors are postulated to expect planners to demonstrate more flexibility in their mode of argumentation than, in fact, occurs.

## The Basis of Conflict

Planners with methodological training, which covers many practicing planners, use a fixed mode or argument. The argument made in each stage of planned change does not change as the planner confronts the issues posed by each process stage. The planner exhibits very predictable behavior at the same time that the sponsor expects more situationally responsive behavior. The reverse is also true. The planner expects the sponsor's arguments to be congruent, or at least responsible to his or her own. Thus, a careful examination of how the planner's fixed mode or argument compliments or contradicts arguments made by the sponsor at each stage of a planned change process provides a basis to evaluate the exchange. As understanding between planner and sponsor increases, the prospects of success grow. A mutually understandable exchange promotes learning, enables a synthesis of ideas, enhances the prospects of innovation, and promotes process efficiency. These benefits reduce the chance of an abort and improve the chance of achieving a desirable result.

Failing to manage the conflict may doom a planned change effort or at least reduce its effectiveness. To manage the conflict, the planner and sponsor must reconcile their expectations. An adjustment by either party, or a mutual adjustment, lowers the conflict and heightens understanding. By understanding the argumentation process used by sponsors, the planner learns to be more flexible, anticipating the range of sponsor arguments and possible shifts in position.

## The Planner's Mode of Argumentation

During the formulation stage of the planned change process, the sponsor interprets signals calling for action. The sponsor's interpretations yield needs and opportunities that become stipulations, as shown in Figure 14-4. The planner is charged with applying an appropriate technique to translate these stipulations into problems and objectives.

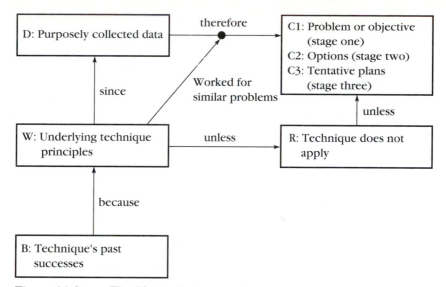

**Figure 14-5** ▲ **The Planner's Argument**

The planner's information base differs dramatically from that of the sponsor. The planner's mode of argument is consistent throughout the planned change process, as shown in Figure 14-5. For example, the claim advanced by the planner stems from information that was purposefully collected following the tenets of a planning technique. In formulation, a particular planning technique is used to provide data for problem definition and objective specification. In concept development, options are produced, and plans are proposed in detailing.

Problems and objectives, options, and plans are the claims made by planners. These claims are thought to be correct because the planner believes in the underpinnings of the technique used to produce them (the warrant) and because the technique has worked before, in general or for a similar problem (the backing for the warrant). These arguments will always be advanced to defend the claims made by the planner unless circumstances suggest that the technique does not apply (the rebuttal). The rebuttal that the technique does not apply or that a different technique should be used *may* be advanced by the sponsor. This is unlikely in practice because sponsors typically lack sufficient expertise to challenge the technique's workability. Further, a sponsor who has confidence in the planner seldom asks for a defense of a technique prior to or following its use. However, when forced to, planners can only certify the appropriateness of their results by advancing the underlying principles of the technique that produced them (the warrant). The technique's track record of successful application is used to certify and rationalize the technique's assumptions (the backing).

For example, consider the program planning method (PPM) and its nominal group technique (NGT) discussed in Chapters 4 and 10, respectively. NGT used in the formulation stage creates a ranked list of problems, provided by clients, using a structured group process. There is considerable evidence that the NGT has worked and can be applied in settings in which a diffuse but potentially responsive set of clients must be served. NGT's backing stems from the behavior of people working in interacting groups. People in these groups tend to focus on just a few ideas, making marginal changes, and tend to react rather than suggest—evaluation dominates ideation. Thus, the backing for the warrant stems from an understanding of how people behave in groups and how to improve their performance. To rebut the use of NGT, one identifies conditions where the technique should not be applied, such as when groups are to be composed of superiors and subordinates. This rebuttal can be turned aside if a previous application of the technique, under these conditions, has been successful. If this argument fails, research findings can be advanced to demonstrate that the dominating presence of supervisors in a planning group can be somewhat neutralized by the silent reflection phase of NGT.

### Behavioral Implications

Planners use a single form of argumentation. Sponsors, however, react quite differently. The dialogue between sponsors and planners in each phase of the planned change process plays an important role in determining if the process will have a successful outcome. Creative conflict can lead to improved results. Conflict can also create misunderstandings leading to communication breakdown, which limits the effectiveness of the planned change effort.

In the following discussion, the dialogue stemming from the six sponsor roles is described for each phase of the planned change process.

## ▲ THE RATIONALIST SPONSOR

The rationalist has a neutral attitude toward planned change, viewing the process as an attempt to deal with needs or opportunities important to the organization. No a priori position is taken on the prospects of a positive or a negative outcome. The rationalist expects the force of the argument to come from facts that document the costs and benefits that stem from closing the performance gap.

To manage the planned change process, the rationalist sponsor seeks sufficient information to ensure that the plan can close the performance gap (see Table 14-1). Behaviorally, the rationalist suspends judgment and waits for information to accumulate. Motivation is based on providing the organization with a logic for choice. The rationalist expects the planner to provide realistic options, documented in sufficient detail so analysis can verify the merits of the case. He or she expects the planner to demonstrate sophistication in areas of ideation and analysis. The rationalist prefers a linear sequence of events in which review and advice is provided. The proposal is expected to embrace realistic options that meet the originally stated need. Adoption prospects and consequences are seen in a positive manner, if cost-effectiveness can be demonstrated. A cost-effective outcome is believed to be more likely if planned change follows a rational process.

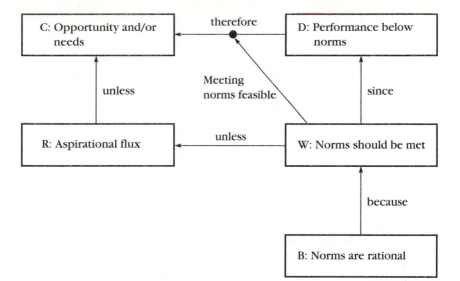

Figure 14-6 ▲ The Rationalist's Argument During Formulation

## The Rationalist During Formulation

### *The Argument*

Figure 14-6 shows the rationalist's argument for formulation. For the rationalist, opportunity and needs stem from a comparison of observed performance with norms. When performance falls below norms, assuming that the information describing performance and norms is seen as accurate, the performance gap so defined creates a claim that planned change is required, as described in Chapter 5. The rationalist sponsor's warrant stems from the belief that norms should be met, because to do otherwise would be irrational. If it seems feasible to meet the norms, planned change is called for. The backing for the rationalist sponsor's warrant is that to operate any enterprise rationally, norms are required that define expectations. For these reasons, the rationalist sets in place management information systems that can compare performance with norms to define performance gaps.

Data from management information systems and other types of objective information are used to define performance gaps. One example would be a review of cost-variance reports to determine if departments are performing within budget. Those that do not are candidates for a planned change effort, unless there are extenuating circumstances. For instance, a planned change process may not be initiated when resources are not available or when there are other activities that have a larger performance gap (March and Simon, 1958).

The rationalist sponsor also recognizes that he or she cannot deal with every performance gap: one must have sufficient social credit to initiate a process and sufficient time and resources to carry it out. Aspirations rise and fall as the rationalist assesses the prospects for change. The flux of (realistic) aspirations provides the rebuttal for a claim of an opportunity or need.

### *The Dialogue*

Rationalist-planner dialogue during formulation is amicable because planned changed is initiated by a performance gap, making expectations clear cut. The nature of the dialogue is highly compatible with the planner's notion of direction. The major difficulty is that this dialogue may lack the creative tension necessary to identify problems. When the problem is described as a performance gap, it strikes a responsive cord with the planner; hence, there seems to be no need to consider a change. However, as Mitroff (1974) and others have pointed out, this may lead to solving the wrong problem. Delbecq (1977, 1989) contends one must stay "problem centered," reviewing and reflecting on the performance gap and expanding the scope of inquiry to a point where it can be the most effective. The planner, with an explicit and clear-cut definition of either opportunity or need, is inclined merely to rephrase the statement in terms of an objective, applying no planning techniques to aid in this effort.

The rationalist-planner dialogue during the formulation coaxes the planner to abandon his or her technique orientation because the stage seems unnecessary. The planner uses the sponsor's definition of a performance gap to define a project's objective. The dialogue is one way: Sponsor stipulates and planner codifies. In effect, formulation tends to be skipped. The planner and the rationalist sponsor are likely to reflect similar (e.g., quantitative) values. This leads to mutual understanding and often creates a positive relationship. The rationalist-planner dialogue is adequate when problem symptoms can be readily interpreted, as in well-structured, low-uncertainty problems. The dialogue may be inadequate for ill-structured problems.

The juxtaposition of the planner's and the rationalist's arguments are shown in Figure 14-7.

## Technique Guidelines

Two guidelines are offered for each sponsor role, in a given stage. First, the sponsor's preferred technique is identified. The preferred technique calls for action that is consistent with the sponsor's role. Using this technique is likely to promote positive planner-sponsor relations but often not the best results. Next, the recommended technique is suggested. This technique complements the sponsor's strengths, rather than reinforces his or her weaknesses. Although sponsors would not have selected this technique, they will find it to be acceptable.

Guidelines 1 and 2 describe the preferred and best techniques when dealing with a rationalist during formulation.

1. *Rationalist technique preference.* Techniques that translate the performance gap into an explicit objective are preferred by the sponsor. To seek still more detail, objective trees, which show relationships between objectives or activities that support the dominant objective, can be used.
2. *Technique recommendation.* Objective setting using NGT and function expansion is preferable because it opens up search.

Quantifying objectives by defining expectations, performance norms, time, and budget constraints and elaborating them with an objective tree often supersedes all

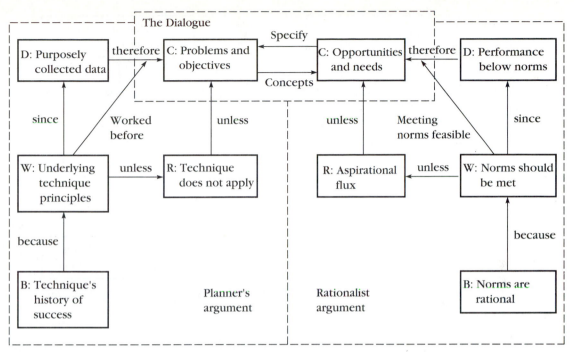

**Figure 14-7** ▲ **The Dialogue During Formulation with a Rationalist Sponsor**

other concerns. The compatibility of sponsor and planner views may focus effort on symptoms or narrowly defined problems, increasing the prospect of solving the wrong problem.

Objective-setting, using a group process like NGT, opens up the search for problems upon which objectives can be based, which often leads to innovation. The involvement of clients, users, or experts outside the routine contacts of the sponsor in the NGT session helps to open up the planned change process to new ideas. The objective hierarchy developed by function expansion allows the rationalist sponsor to consider several alternative directions for the project.

## The Rationalist During Concept Development

The rationalist is proactive, offering premises that define ideas, which the planner is expected to form into a set of options in the concept development stage. The planner considers the sponsor's premises and offers various ways to deal with the planned change objective. A dynamic interaction between these premises and the planner's options is expected.

### The Argument

The rationalist's argumentation process for concept development is shown in Figure 14-8. The rationalist often behaves like a pragmatist, with premises based on analogies to operating systems that seemed to work, called *templates* in Chapter 4.

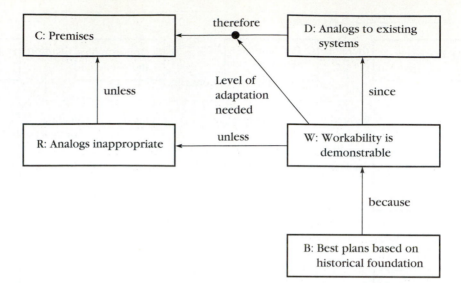

**Figure 14-8** ▲ **The Rationalist's Argument During Concept Development**

An operating system is used because it is tangible. The planner who concentrates on the level of adaptation needed in an existing system often has a positive relationship with the rationalist. Premises are based on what the rationalist thinks would be practical in the work situation.

The rationalist's warrant stems from the adage that what has worked in the past will work in the future. This warrant is backed by anecdotes and war stories that call for plans to be put on a firm, historical foundation. The best plans are thought to follow careful field evaluation. A nova plan is believed to take too long and be inappropriate when the practices of others can be adapted to make them workable. Obviously, this warrant can be rebutted if there are no analogies from which the sponsor can draw. Also, the level of adaptation may be extensive, which drives up costs. When these circumstances arise, the rationalist will support a nova planned changed effort.

### The Dialogue

The planner has considerable latitude in working with a rationalist. It is understood that the template must be adapted to fit the new circumstances. If the planner understands the origin of the sponsor's premises, a process of template enrichment can be used. The planner trims out the restrictive assumptions made by the sponsor and gradually moves the plan toward a better fit with current circumstances. Planner-rationalist dialogue can be mutually satisfying because each takes a posture that can be understood by the other, providing a basis for communication.

The rationalist role in concept development works best when innovation is unimportant. The rationalist-planner dialogue can be unproductive, particularly when creative tension is missing. Without this tension, the planner may even have trouble convincing the rationalist sponsor of the need to enrich the template.

### Techniques

Guidelines 3 and 4 indicate the preferred and recommended technique when dealing with a rationalist sponsor during concept development.

3. *Rationalist technique preference.* The rationalist will prefer to have his or her premises modeled with a input-output technique, which combines the best features of systems thought to be relevant to outline a plan.
4. *Technique recommendation.* A scenario as a dialectic offers an ideal structure for the planner-rationalist dialogue in concept development because it makes premature plan closure unlikely.

The input-output technique describes useful system analogies but will offer few new ideas and thus little innovation. To break the rationalist out of the confines of the practices of others, a scenario can be used to create a plan-counterplan dialectic. This approach creates two (or more) plan alternatives with the opposite assumptions. For example, if the practice being considered assumes a no-growth environment, the counterplan assumes growth. The options are derived from a synthesis of the ideas that stem from the plan and counterplan.

## The Rationalist During Detailing

In detailing, the rationalist sponsor often takes a reactive role. Tentative plans are offered by the planner. The rationalist's review is to find errors, omissions, and misconceptions. These findings are used to fine-tune the plan.

### The Argument

The rationalist determines omissions, misconceptions, and errors by comparing the plan's features against the plan's objective, as shown in Figure 14-9. Features that limit the achievement of the objective are identified for the planner to consider. According to the rationalist's warrant for detailing, planning is done to meet a prescribed objective, so this aim must be met. To certify the assumptions (backing) for this type of argument, the rationalist would contend that although planned change processes are pulled in many directions and even manipulated, it is not rational to do so. The rationalist will hold to this warrant unless a superior modifies the objective. Because a rationalist is also a realist, the new objectives will be adopted, which can cause questioning to vary from the predictable course.

### The Dialogue

Questioning by the rationalist sponsor is seldom misunderstood by the experienced planner. The dialogue is expected to focus on deviations of solutions from the plan's initially prescribed path and the planners with experience come prepared to rationalize these changes. If changes can be defended, they are likely to be adopted. The rationalist seldom probes beyond the apparent fit of the plan to what was initially agreed upon as the need to be met or the opportunity to be captured. The planner-rationalist dialogue concentrates on deviations of the tentative plan from the prescribed objective, so little refinement occurs. To simulate plan refinement, cycling with an expanded dialogue must be encouraged.

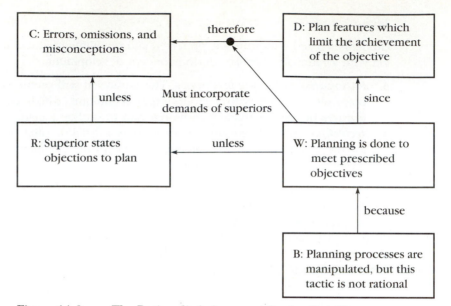

**Figure 14-9** ▲ **The Rationalist's Argument During Detailing**

### Techniques

Guidelines 5 and 6 identify the preferred and recommended techniques when dealing with a rationalist sponsor during detailing.

5. *Rationalist technique preference.* The rationalist reviews the plan to see if the performance gap can be closed, prematurely evaluating the plan rather than refining it. Any evaluative technique can be selected.

6. *Technique recommendation.* Rationalist sponsors should be confronted with ideas that interpret the needs of users, which can be determined by a silent reflective group process, with plan users as members. These ideas serve as a checklist to provide constructive modifications, leading to plan refinement using a block diagram.

The preference of the rationalist to evaluate in detailing should be discouraged. Premature evaluation distracts the sponsor from checking the plan to ensure its internal integrity. The planner must often conduct the systems design without rationalist-sponsor participation. To aid the sponsor's review of the plan, a checklist of desirable features from users, determined by using brainwriting or some other silent reflective group process, is recommended. This points out the need for review and gives the sponsor a basis for conducting it. These ideas are then captured with the block diagram technique.

## ▲ THE BROKER AS A SPONSOR

The broker is also neutral toward planning (Table 14-1). The broker, like the rationalist, does not take a personal position about the preferred outcome of the planned change process. However, brokers and rationalists approach process management in different ways. The rationalist expects the force of the argument to come from facts that document the costs and benefits in closing the performance gap. The broker sees the performance gap as perceptual, which may or may not have factual base. To close the perceived gap, the broker deals with perceptions and the rationalist deals with facts, leading them to stress the acquisition of quite different information.

The broker questions to extract information that indicates where compromise and barter will be essential. For instance, when considering the prospects for change, the broker lists the centers of power that will be affected by implementation. The broker makes an internal assessment of his or her social credit with these power centers, and the current values of people in them, and then elicits information to help judge expected reactions. The broker believes that all needs or opportunities stem from people agitating for change, which creates a *perceived* performance gap, and that planned changed must create a compromise response. A broker believes that power stems from negotiating plan acceptance so brokers posture to acquire this power. Brokers expect the planner to understand the necessity of incorporating the needs of the power centers into the evolving plan: objectives may be reconsidered and alternatives discarded because they cannot be adapted to fit the needs or desires of key individuals and groups.

The dominant procedure used by a broker is bargaining. This leads to a proposal made up of an amalgamation of the ideas, desires, and demands of key people in the organization. The broker sees adoption prospects as positive if the plan proves to be politically feasible. Similarly, the consequences of the plan are seen as positive if the internal inconsistencies caused by the bargaining process can be worked out in subsequent planned change activities.

## The Broker During Formulation

### *The Argument*

The broker's argument during formulation is illustrated in Figure 14-10. For the broker, opportunities or needs are couched in terms of a subjective comparison of performance with norms. If important reference groups within the organization *believe* that improvements are possible, this belief serves as the data or grounds for the broker's claim that an opportunity or a need exists. These claims by power centers can be inconsistent with objectively measured performance or with each other.

The broker uses a warrant that equates personal and organizational opportunity. Meeting the expectations of important reference groups in the organization offers personal opportunity. The broker gains the center stage by managing the process and assumes (sometimes tongue-in-cheek) that the powerful in an organization know what they are doing. The broker believes that if the needs seem real to protagonists they must be acted on, even when their needs do not seem all that compelling to others.

If the time is ripe for change, a process is engaged. The backing for this warrant stems from the broker's belief that meeting the expectations of organizational power centers expands the social credit of those involved. Drawing on caches of social credit is thought to be the basis for change. Thus, meeting the powerful's expectations can always be justified.

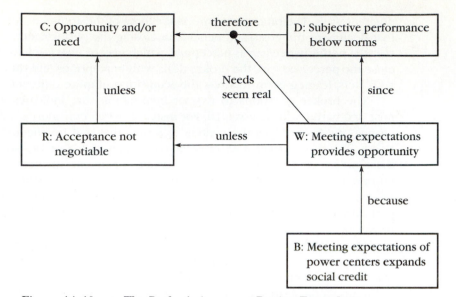

**Figure 14-10 ▲ The Broker's Argument During Formulation**

The rebuttal stems from the often cluttered picture of how social credit can accumulate. If acceptance appears to be partially nonnegotiable, the advantage of meeting expectations declines. For example, there may be disagreement between power centers over the type of action that should be initiated, or indeed whether action is necessary. Disagreement will reduce imperatives that lie behind the opportunities or needs that a broker will specify.

### The Dialogue

The broker's dialogue with a planner during formulation is complicated by the planner's skill at reading of the political tea leaves. Planners often fail to recognize the importance of being responsive to organizational power centers and lack information sources to appreciate the imperatives that accompany a stipulation of opportunities and needs. Furthermore, most planners view plan quality as more important than plan acceptance, which is inconsistent with the views of the broker. Third, planners seldom believe that building the sponsor a store of social credit is part of their role.

The dialogue between a broker and a planner can break down as the opportunity or need is explored. The planner's motives in carrying out this exploration tend to be misunderstood, so that a redefinition may not be viewed by the sponsor as helpful. On the other hand, sponsors may be unwilling to give the planner full access to the power centers that are dictating change, which limits the planner's understanding of what is wanted.

Brokers will resist modifying the performance gap because it requires them to seek acceptance of the change from one or more power centers in the organization. As a result, the dialogue between broker sponsor–planner may create tension, particularly when the planner also has access to the power centers in the organization. Sponsors tend to limit this access because to do otherwise will reveal information that they hope to manage. This leads to several comprehensive cycles, which are necessary to fully understand the sponsor's definition of the performance gap. In spite of these difficulties, a brokerlike role can be useful, particularly when acceptance is a key criterion for plan success.

### Techniques

Guidelines 7 and 8 suggest the preferred and recommended techniques for the planner to use when working with a broker during formulation.

7. *Broker technique preference.* The nominal interaction (NI) technique allows time between formal sessions for lobbying and logrolling among key constituents, permitting bargaining to take place before the choices regarding project direction are made.
8. *Technique recommendation.* Kiva is the preferred planning technique because it identifies and works with important power centers and attempts to reconcile their views.

Brokers call for compromise among competing claimants and their claims. The broker believes that a stipulation of the claim hinders the negotiation process. As a consequence, informal, unstructured discussion allows for the needed mutual adjustment as problems and objectives are identified. The NI technique is preferred because it adds the anteroom lobby to a structured process, thereby providing the arrangements for the bartering preferred by the broker.

The kiva technique adds more structure to the bargaining process, attempting to understand and reconcile the views of the partisans. However, the negotiations in a kiva can be drawn out and hard to predict. As a result, brokers may find this technique harder to use in some situations. Acceptance can be enhanced by a demonstration, showing how the kiva technique can uncover potential misunderstandings and head off conflict.

## The Broker During Concept Development

### The Argument

The broker derives premises from the views and the desires of power centers (Figure 14-11). The broker is positioned to get and interpret information from these centers of power. The broker becomes the bartering agent and the planner must rely on the broker for information. The broker's warrant is simple: acceptance is the key to success. The backing, which ratifies this assumption, contends that most plans fail because they lack acceptance, not because they lack quality. The acceptance warrant will be used unless it becomes clear that people in centers of power fail to have an idea for a plan with defensible quality. The broker will not use this rebuttal unless controversy arises, which makes planned change infeasible.

### The Dialogue

In concept development, a broker is particularly effective when power centers have preconceived demands that must be incorporated in the final plan to ensure accep-

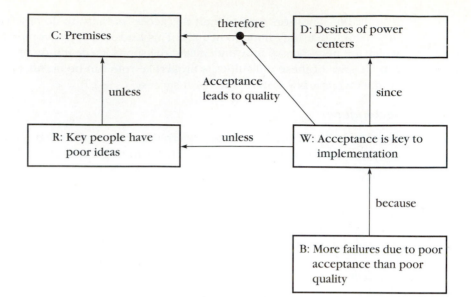

**Figure 14-11** ▲ **The Broker's Argument During Concept Development**

tance. The broker-planner dialogue in concept development provides information about the wants and needs of users and those who can block implementation. Options are uncovered during the comprehension cycles needed to take in these demands. If the planner can interrogate the users directly, or with the broker, both the timeliness and quality of the plan will be improved.

### Techniques

Guidelines 9 and 10 suggest the preferred and recommended techniques for the planner to use when working with a broker during concept development.

9. *Broker technique preference*. The nominal-interaction (NI) technique permits the protagonists to meet, share views, and negotiate conflicting elements of the plan. The sponsor uses these discussions to derive premises.
10. *Technique prescription*. NI coupled with dialectics, with the sponsor in a leadership role, will improve the results. The group process ends with a dialectic debate between the options that represent the view of each power center. This approach is preferred because it creates a basis for compromise and provides a synthesis of competing ideas.

As in formulation, the broker prefers an unstructured discussion to ferret out competing ideas. However, unstructured discussion provides little detail, leaving the sponsor and the planner unsure of premises that are essential. The structure of the NI technique allows the bargaining to take place but also captures the agreements struck. The dialectical debate among options brings out the merits of alternative plans and creates a basis to select the best elements of each.

## The Broker During Detailing

### *The Argument*

The broker takes the plan to various power centers in the organization and elicits their objections. These serve as the basis (data) for identifying a tentative plan's omissions, misconceptions, and errors. As shown in Figure 14-12, the warrant and backing for the broker's behavior are exactly the same as in concept development, with a different rebuttal: A power center may have (or develop) an incentive to make the plan fail. As the broker attempts to rationalize the conflicting aims of power centers, descriptions of omissions, misconceptions, and errors will be couched in terms of the importance of each and the incentives of various parties to be positive or critical of the plan. Thus, some criticisms are weighted differently than others.

### *The Dialogue*

Planner-broker dialogue can be productive when the broker is candid about the origins of the criticisms to the tentative plan. If the planner can appreciate how various parties are likely to react and how their support is critical to implementation, changes offering a compromise to affected parties can be sought. This information is critical if the planner is to tailor the plan to enhance its acceptance. The sponsor always stands ready to withdraw his or her support if a compromise plan does not emerge. When planners fail to appreciate the importance of these power centers or the nature of their objections, the prospects of a compromise plan declines.

The effectiveness of the planner-broker dialogue is determined by the planner's appreciation of the objections raised by power centers. A plan is fine-tuned by

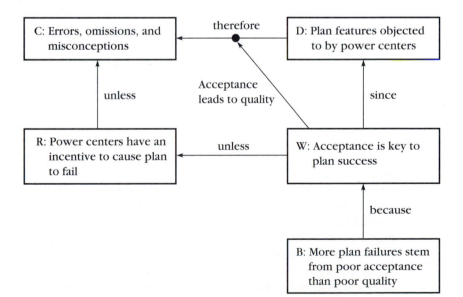

**Figure 14-12** ▲ **The Broker's Argument During Detailing**

incorporating the needs and wants of each power center. Cycling occurs until at least one option meets the acceptance test.

### Techniques

Guidelines 11 and 12 suggest the preferred and recommended techniques to use when a planner is working with a broker during detailing.

11. *Broker's preferred technique.* The broker prefers to identify trade-offs without the aid of formal techniques, which leads to an incomplete synthesis due to information overloads.

12. *Technique recommendation.* A quasi-interrogative representation, such as interpretive structural modeling (ISM), permits the broker to specify and compare the merits of procedures being pushed by each power center. The NI technique is used to seek consensus in a group, to create a synthesis plan.

The broker prefers to ponder the claims of the various parties affected by the plan. When several parties are involved, making the claim quite complex, an incomplete assimilation and the prospect of overlooking an important demand or condition may result. Structure is needed to document these claims, seeking to compare and rationalize them. The ISM allows each partisan's claim to be documented in terms of procedure. These procedures are then merged at common points to find areas of procedural agreement. The NI group process can be used to seek a workable consensus as the ISM technique is carried out.

## ▲ THE ZEALOT AS A SPONSOR

The zealot promotes an idea. Such a sponsor is at home in innovative organizations that are rule abhorrent, decentralized with small difference in pay and prestige, stressing quality, and lacking incentives to be overly cost conscious (see Chapter 9). Consulting firms often behave as zealots when they are paid to legitimize what their client wants. Consumer-dominating planning is likewise hamstrung, albeit by design. The objectives of planned change are dictated by what people say they want. The activist planner summarizes the results and gives them back as needs.

The zealot has a pet idea, and the purpose of planned changed (as the zealot sees it) is to translate the pet idea into practice. Rules of conduct are adopted to ensure that details in the sponsor's pet idea become the requirements that will be used to judge success (see Table 14-1). The pet idea creates norms for the planned change effort. As a result, the zealot's hidden agenda may become quite transparent as the planned change process unfolds. Zealots single-mindedly sustain the face of all forms of criticism, such as the snide remarks from peers and bemused nonsupport from superiors. Their motive is, quite simply, to get their pet idea adopted. Hyman Rickover and his nuclear navy provides an example.

The zealot expects the planner to aid him or her in putting the pet idea in the best possible light and to provide new rationalizations for its adoption. This leads to a one-sided procedure through which the zealot gradually reveals more and more details of the pet idea to the planner. If the plan closely resembles the zealot's pet idea and it is implemented without alteration, the zealot believes the plan will have a good prospect of adoption. Negative plan results would be interpreted as improper use of the plan, which led to unfair performance expectations.

## The Zealot During Formulation

### *The Argument*

Zealots are sponsors who engage the planned change process to push a specific idea. The zealot reveals information to the planner to coach him or her into adopting the "preferred" outcome.

The argumentation is shown in Figure 14-13. First, the preconceived plan is used by the sponsor to identify the unique opportunities and/or needs that it can serve, which are advanced as rationales for the planned change process. The zealot's behavior is often self-serving, but zealots believe in their idea and see it as "the one best way."

The plans are often held in waiting until the organization seems prepared to accept a diagnosis that change is needed, derived from the arguments consistent with broker or rationalist logic. However, when the zealot manages the planned change process, a preconceived plan becomes the rationale that guides the process. Backing stems from the zealot's belief in his or her track record and the benefits of the plan. The warrant stems from past successes in which the zealot's pet ideas proved to be useful. These beliefs are clung to unless the idea proves unacceptable to power centers, as its features are gradually revealed (the rebuttal).

Unlike the other sponsor roles, the zealot uses the *same* form of argumentation for each stage of the planned change process. The only change is that the

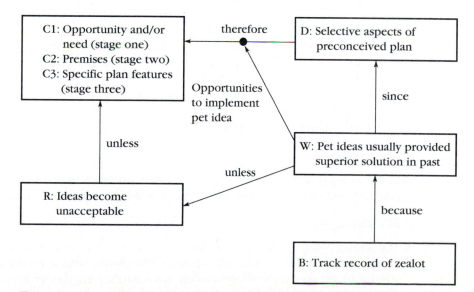

**Figure 14-13** ▲ **The Zealot's Argument During Planned Change**

information derived from the preconceived plan differs with each process stage, as shown in Figure 14-13.

### The Dialogue

The planner-zealot dialogue has many potential pitfalls. The zealot will resist making changes in his or her stipulation during formulation because there is too great a risk that problems will be defined that the preconceived plan cannot deal with. Seldom is the planner-sponsor relationship strong enough for the sponsor to share these views, and even if it is, such an approach can be politically unwise. As a result, the manipulative behavior of the zealot makes it difficult for the planner to understand the rational behind the needs and opportunities that are provided. The dialogue is one way and used by the zealot to make clear his or her view of the needs and opportunities to the planner. The zealot may resist giving any information beyond a perfunctory examination of the performance gap during formulation. During formulation the zealot's dogmatic behavior begins to damage planner-sponsor relations.

### Techniques

Guidelines 13 and 14 suggest how a planner can work with a zealot during formulation.

13. *Zealot's technique preference.* The zealot expects his or her needs and/or opportunities to be accepted as stated. The use of formal planning techniques is resisted because it may change the stipulation, which may invalidate the zealot's preconceived solution idea.

14. *Technique recommendation.* The optimal approach of opening up new vistas will not work. No planning technique will alter the zealot's behavior.

In formulation, problems and opportunities are to be accepted as given. No attempt to examine them will be permitted because the results may invalidate the preconceived plan. In effect, the zealot forces the planner to skip formulation. As shown in Figure 14-2, the planner who attempts to be proactive when the sponsor is being directive must, ultimately, give way to sponsor control. Experienced planners realize they must acquiesce to the sponsor. Protracted debates will not change the sponsor and may well damage the planner's relationship with the sponsor. A zealot-initiated planned change process is single-minded and beyond the influence of the planner.

## The Zealot During Concept Development

### The Argument

In the concept development the zealot offers premises drawn from his or her preconceived plan. The argumentation process shown in Figures 14-13 applies.

### The Dialogue

The zealot-planner dialogue in the concept development is used to create an image of the zealot's preferred solution. Discussion with a zealot is carried out strictly to aid planner comprehension. Each further encounter between the planner and the zealot provides more of the details of the plan. Soon it becomes clear to the planner that the sponsor had a plan in mind all along and that the process is a sham. Some planners may go along in this situation and others may confront the sponsor. In either case, the planner-sponsor relationship is damaged.

### Techniques

Guidelines 15 and 16 are proposed to help a planner who is working with a zealot during concept development.

15. *Zealot technique preference*. The zealot tightly controls the process so the planner must use a reactive (reductionist) planning technique, such as the input-output approach, in an attempt to capture the salient elements of the sponsor's idea.

16. *Technique recommendation*. The optimal technique of considering several solution options will be resisted. The planner must adopt zealot's technique preference.

The input-output approach creates a model of the sponsor's plan. The technique forms the zealot's ideas and sets the plan in relief. By making the plan tangible, the zealot can begin to fine-tune it, a process that begins in concept development and extends through detailing. For zealot-initiated planned change, the distinction between these stages is seldom clear. As in formulation, no planning technique can be expected to overcome a domineering zealot, so none was suggested.

## The Zealot During Detailing

### The Argument

The zealot's form of argumentation remains the same as in formulation and concept development, as shown in Figure 14-13.

### The Dialogue

During solution development, the zealot-sponsor looks for coaching from the planner. Their roles as planner and sponsor are reversed. The planner offers the omissions, misconceptions, and errors for a plan that in reality have been proposed by the sponsor. The zealot requires this role reversal hoping the planner will provide a careful critique of the internal consistency of his or her idea. The planner is often asked to fix up the concerns that are identified, causing still further tensions. Zealot sponsor-planner dialogue becomes ineffective when the sponsor requires the planner to raise concerns and then find ways to overcome them.

Several comprehensive recycles occur, with the dialogue always sponsor to planner. This often leads the planner to see the sponsor as abdicating responsibility to guide the process, after systematically manipulating it in the earlier stages.

### Techniques

Guidelines 17 and 18 help a planner who is coping with the zealot during detailing.

17. *Zealot technique preference*. The block diagram technique helps the planner document the demands of the sponsor and identify inconsistencies. Collaboratively, the sponsor and planner work out plan details.

18. *Technique recommendation.* The planner must serve as a collaborator, adopting the sponsor's technique preference.

As a zealot controlled planning process comes to a close, the planner becomes a paid critic. The block diagram technique is preferred because it helps the planner define each aspect of the pet idea and offer a thoughtful critique. The purpose is not to create a new plan but rather to rationalize and make marginal changes in the sponsor's idea as it emerges.

# ▲ THE SPONSOR AS A VISIONARY

The visionary is a positivist who, like the zealot, promotes change. Even change for change's sake is appealing to the visionary (Table 14-1). Such sponsors find support in innovative organizations that have a concentration of well-educated and yet diverse disciplines. Visionaries can be illustrated by Edison and his idea for the electrification of cities, Ford and his assembly lines for manufacturing, and IBM's former chairman Tom Watson and his notion of an information society.

The visionary tends to be expansive, defending his or her ideas for change by giving a sketch of the scaffolding necessary to make it work. The visionary is committed to a grand scheme with which he or she can be identified. The rules of conduct for the dialogue call for the planner to react to a broad outline of the grand scheme. The visionary provides a gestalt, and the planner is expected to grasp the nature of the vision. No specific questions are posed; rather, the planner is expected to provide the details of the sponsor's vision. Planners who fail to understand the vision are greeted with, "You don't think too big, do you?"

The visionary is motivated by a desire to innovate. The planner is expected to see the big picture that the sponsor creates and fill in the voids. A partial outline of the grand scheme is expected, with some specifics to satisfy critics and functionaries. Adoption prospects are viewed as good, with the understanding that additional tactical planning will be needed. Further, visionaries believe that the outcome of the planned changed will be positive, unless implementation distorts the grand scheme. In the visionary's terms, the "great unwashed" may fail to grasp the opportunities that the vision offers and, by their demand for justification and premature evaluation, may ruin the effort.

## The Visionary During Formulation

The visionary, like the zealot, is a protagonist. The visionary is in love with change, but has fewer notions about the specifics of the change. As a result, the visionary offers planners a considerable opportunity to exercise their planning skills.

### The Argument

The visionary's argument during formulation is shown in Figure 14-14. Opportunities and needs are taken from the visionary's "strategic plan" for the organization, which may or may not have formal organizational sanction. Opportunities and needs are often stated in broad and general terms. The visionary relies on a "growth is

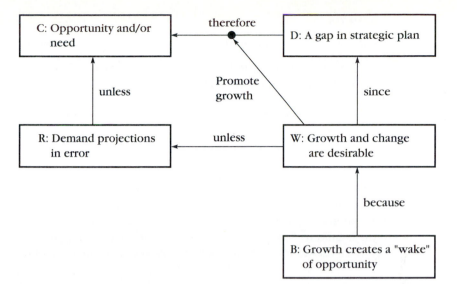

**Figure 14-14** ▲ **The Visionary's Argument During Formulation**

good" or a "more is better" type of warrant, based on analogies to other organizations that have experienced dramatic growth. In this context, advancement stems from growth and the sponsor attempts to eliminate inconsistencies in the growth argument.

Organizational and personal growth are equated. The backing for such a belief is that growth creates a wake of organizational opportunity. To clean up the wake, many jobs are created and the sponsor's resulting visibility creates still other opportunities. The "change is good" syndrome, when carried to the extreme, leaves an organization constantly stirred up. The rebuttal to the visionary's argument stems from financial propriety. For example, if demand or use forecasts are inconsistent with proposed increases in capacity, the "growth is good" argument can be negated.

### The Dialogue

The visionary sponsor offers the planner considerable opportunity to apply his or her planning expertise. The commitment to action creates perpetual sanction for planning, and there is plenty of room for the planner to add structure by specifying the details of what is to be done. The dialogue between the sponsor and the planner can be positive if the planner is able to provide needed specifics for the visionary's grand scheme.

The planner must be aware of the visionary's argument to determine how to provide a response to the visionary's stipulation. Problem restipulation is possible, even desirable, if the planner offers a new direction that is consistent with the "change is good" argument. As a result, visionary-planner dialogues can be quite beneficial as long as the planner provides an insightful objective or a problem definition that adds salience. This type of dialogue is particularly beneficial in formulation, because innovation is valued.

### Techniques

Guidelines 19 and 20 help the planner to cope with a visionary during formulation.

19. *Visionary technique preference*. The visionary wants the planner to take the initiative, allowing the planner the freedom to choose any technique that can add structure.
20. *Technique recommendation*. Function expansion leading to a hierarchy of possible objectives for the plan offers the visionary an ideal structure to sort out an arena of action.

The visionary expects the planner to use any technique that will add specifics to his or her notions of needs and opportunities. A technique is seen as desirable as long as it can create new insights into an arena of action. Function expansion gives the visionary just what is desired: a series of possibilities with increasing scope to choose among. This lets the visionary sponsor contemplate which objective offers the best way to frame his or her understanding of needs and opportunities.

## The Visionary During Concept Development

### The Argument

In contrast to the zealot, the visionary offers little direction. Premises are based on a very-broad-scope description of the sponsor's vision (Figure 14-15). This description is often vague and expansive so the premises lack specificity. The planner is left to fill in the details.

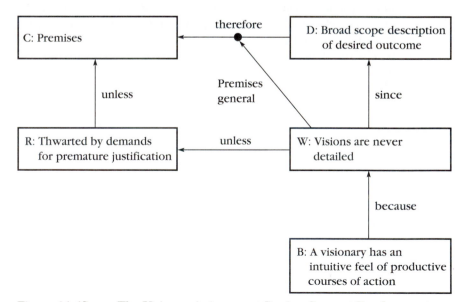

**Figure 14-15** ▲ **The Visionary's Argument During Concept Development**

The warrant stems from the visionary's beliefs that his or her role is to give direction, not details. Specifics are left to detail-oriented functionaries. The backing for the vision stems from the sponsor's belief in his or her own cleverness and track record. The visionary sees himself or herself as having an intuitive feel for courses of action that will prove to be superior. In other words, this type of sponsor can take the position, "I've been successful in translating my visions into practice in the past, and there is no reason why I cannot be successful in this effort as well."

Rebuttals stem from a resistance to the vision that was not recognized in prior stages of the process. In visionary's terms, the the "Luddites"[2] may get wind of the idea and try to thwart it. Plans can also be thwarted by nitpickers whose demands for detail are inappropriate during the early stages of planned change.

### The Dialogue

The visionary in concept development needs help in "fleshing out" his or her idea. If the planner is reluctant to offer structure, little direction will be provided. However, structure is just what the visionary hopes for: someone to fill in the gaps and rationalize disparate aspects of his or her idea. The visionary sponsor often believes that he or she could offer this structure, but just lacks the time. Visionaries see their value as being conceptual, not synthetic or analytic. Planners are valued when they complement the visionary sponsor by adding ways to develop an idea that can turn a vision into a reality.

The visionary-planner dialogue produces beneficial results when the planner creates concrete representations of the idea for the visionary sponsor to ponder. The visionary will discourage looping because additional cycles create depth. The visionary sponsor sees this as a focus on details rather than scope, which is preferred. This creates an incentive for planners to provide a rather complete representation of the visionary's idea in their first attempt.

### Techniques

Guidelines 21 and 22 help the planner understand and deal with a visionary during concept development.

21. *Visionary technique preference*. The implications of the visionary's ideas rather than details are preferred. Expert opinion is solicited to verify the innovative nature of the scheme, tending to ignore the premises' internal consistency.
22. *Technique recommendation*. The most appropriate technique develops means-ends strings, using a planning technique such as a relevance tree.

A relevance tree helps the planner trace and verify the logic behind the visionary's grand scheme. Experts, after having verified the scheme's innovation, can be asked to critique the relevance tree. The tree helps the planner fill in gaps and appreciate and reconcile aspects of the visionary's scheme.

---

[2] The term Luddites is from Ned Lud, a feeble-minded man who smashed labor-saving devices in the nineteenth century thinking they would lead to reduced wages. A Luddite opposes new ideas.

## The Visionary During Detailing

### The Argument

The visionary's critique is based on features of the plan that appear to lack innovation. Again, the warrant for this approach stems from the belief that new ideas revitalize an organization. Novel approaches give the organization visibility and thus become an indispensable attribute of any plan. This warrant is backed by the view that organizations that fail to innovate will stagnate. This warrant is adhered to unless change is coming too fast for the organization to absorb. The argument is summarized in Figure 14-16.

### The Dialogue

Dialogue with a visionary during detailing is often difficult because the visionary is not prone to study the plan and pick out its internal inconsistencies. Review is perfunctory. The visionary-planner dialogue in the detailing stage is often ineffective because the visionary dislikes conducting a detailed review. As a result, little plan refinement occurs when a visionary controls plan development. Guidance is seldom offered, particularly when the plan seems innovative and opportunities seem to have been capitalized upon.

### Techniques

Guidelines 23 and 24 help the planner understand and cope with the visionary during detailing.

23. *Visionary technique preference.* The visionary will prefer to delegate system detailing to the planner or to a trusted colleague. If this proves to be impossi-

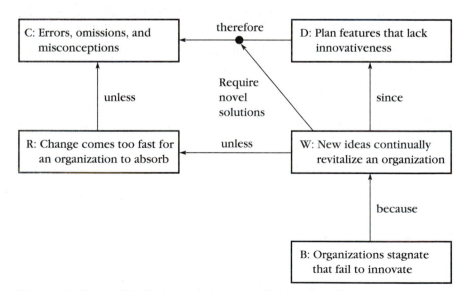

Figure 14-16 ▲ The Visionary's Argument During Detailing

ble, the visionary will attempt to verify the innovativeness of the plan, tending to ignore its internal consistency.

24.  *Technique recommendation.* The systems matrix is an ideal technique to detail the visionary's plan. The ISM aids the planner in tracing the logic inherent in the plan.

The systems matrix approach gives the sponsor a broad-scale representation of the plan, while preserving its detail for others to check. The plan's comprehensiveness and broad scope appearance give it legitimacy, from a visionary sponsor's point of view. The dialogue in detailing involves experts or program users to certify the plan's veracity. The true visionary is happy to delegate these details and will typically accept any modification that does not detract from the innovative thrust of the plan.

## ▲  THE CRITIC DURING FORMULATION

Sponsors who play the role of a critic accept the stipulations of others and do not initiate planning. Sponsors taking devil's advocate and skeptic roles become active in the second stage of a planned change process. A manager acting out these roles will either accept need or opportunity statements by the other sponsor types or shift to a role that can activate a planned change process. Either a neutral or a positive role is needed to initiate planned change.

## ▲  THE SPONSOR AS A DEVIL'S ADVOCATE

Devil's advocates adopt a critical posture toward planned change, viewing the process as inherently risky. They believe that every recommendation should be subjected to considerable scrutiny. The devil's advocate becomes a critic by digging for inconsistencies in a plan.

The information sought has a decidedly negative cast because the devil's advocate believes that questioning must be intense to ensure that a plan is defensible. Intense questioning is believed to make sweeping contributions in shaping the plan as it emerges. The devil's advocate makes a conscious effort to ask embarrassing questions, motivated by the belief that challenge stimulates quality results. The questioning is hard, but thought to be essential because the case must be airtight. The devil's advocate believes that he or she must avoid advocating what turns out to be a poor-quality plan, and the only way to do so is to carefully scrutinize the process and to impose stringent standards. Thus, this type of sponsor expects planned changed to be interactive, believing that interaction can lead to a proposal that may be defensible. The devil's advocate expects the planner to understand the merits of using these tactics.

Even with intense interaction, the adoption prospects are often viewed as mixed. The devil's advocate sees the prospects for implementation pessimistically, believing that there are always overlooked problems, even when the level of scrutiny during plan development has been intense.

The devil's advocate posture is summarized in Table 14-1.

## The Devil's Advocate During Concept Development

In concept development, the planner translates sponsor premises to lay out options that deal with problems (Figure 14-5). During option development, sponsors who behave as critics react rather than suggest. The devil's advocate insists that the planner offer the broad outline of a feasible plan, which is used as the basis for the critic to define premises. Planners are expected to have prepackaged solutions. The critic provides advice on the feasibility of the ideas and ways to tailor the idea so it fits the political climate. This approach seems disarming, but often leads to controversy.

### *The Argument*

The argumentation used by the devil's advocate during concept development is shown in Figure 14-17. Premises are claims compiled from criticisms of the planner's ideas. Various plausible situations that make each idea infeasible are brought to the planner's attention and serve as the grounds or data for the sponsor's argument. The devil's advocate's warrant is that experience and insight help expose the planner's ideas to practical concerns. Underlying this view is the devil's advocate's belief that the best steel comes from the hottest furnace. The planner will be forced to defend every action every step of the way in the planned change process. Using this approach, the devil's advocate hopes to learn if the plan has any merit and, if so, how to defend it at higher levels of the organization. The backing for the warrant used by the devil's advocate is that sponsors must gauge the idea's fit to reality. If the planner lacks competence, such a warrant can be rebutted because incompetent planners would devise plans that are not worth critiquing.

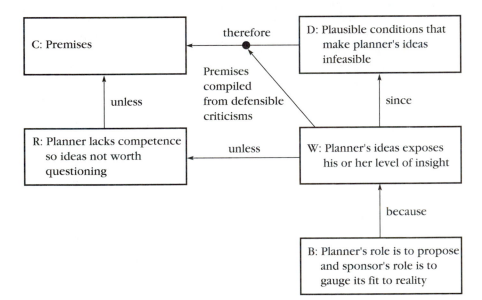

**Figure 14-17  ▲  The Devil's Advocate's Argument During Concept Development**

## The Dialogue

The planner often becomes defensive under the intense interrogation of a devil's advocate. Particularly in the early stages of the planned change, ideas cannot be foolproof. The planner also resents having to anticipate the sponsor's every objection and then refute them one by one. Often the sponsor's concerns and objections are not seen by the planner as being central to discovering potentially viable ideas for detailed planning. The need to reassure this type of sponsor and to help improve his or her level of comprehension is seldom appreciated by the planner.

Planner–devil's advocate dialogue is likely to cause considerable refinement (cycling) leading to options that have a high level of detail. As a result, dialogue with a devil's advocate is often stressful for the planner. The devil's advocate approach to managing the process can be effective when there is considerable residual uncertainty after formulation and when the planner has enough experience with comparable problems to offer potentially viable ideas.

## Techniques

Guidelines 25 and 26 indicate the preferred and the recommended techniques for a planner to use when working for a devil's advocate during concept development.

25. *Devil's advocate technique preference.* The devil's advocate will prefer a checklist of important factors that can be used to identify potential concerns or difficulties with the idea under consideration. This approach helps this sponsor to see concerns and difficulties.
26. *Technique recommendation.* Techniques that open up option identification, such as morphology and scenarios, are preferred because they suggest vistas that the devil's advocate is likely to overlook.

The devil's advocate prefers to draw his or her argumentation from a tangible system. Checklists are preferred because they can be specific and detailed. However, the checklist is based on current practice and will tend to overlook opportunities. Checklists tend to thwart innovation because they limit the sponsor's view of potential solutions.

New vistas provided by a morphology fit to the conditions identified in a scenario offer new options for the sponsor to ponder. Without these techniques, the concept development stage closes too quickly, drawing premises from current operations rather than possibilities. Premature closure on a solution concept is the cause of many planned change failures.

## The Devil's Advocate During Detailing

In the detailing stage, the devil's advocate sponsor takes a reactive role. Tentative solutions are offered by the planner and the sponsor critiques these solutions. The argument used by the devil's advocate is based on errors, misconceptions, and omissions in the plan.

### The Argument

The argument is summarized in Figure 14-18. The devil's advocate will look for negative features of the plan and use them as grounds or data in the argument. As before, this approach is believed to be proper because the sponsor must defend the plan to higher-ups. This warrant of defensibility supersedes all other concerns, such as apparent innovativeness. The devil's advocate defends his or her posture by noting that failures in an organization are weighted many times higher than successes. Such a backing stems from past contacts with superiors who are perceived as demanding low-risk solutions, even when they have low-payoff prospects. Reacting (or perhaps overreacting) to these views, the devil's advocate becomes a staunch proponent of the status quo.

These grounds can be circumvented only when the planner can refute the challenges offered one by one. Intensive questioning will dominate the dialogue, unless the planner has stumbled onto a solution that has powerful advocates. In this case, the number and specificity of the negative features will be discounted, and a more positive relationship between planner and sponsor will emerge, although motivated by concerns unrelated to the plan's features. The devil's advocate bends when power can be used as a rebuttal.

### The Dialogue

The dialogue flows from the planner's responses to the sponsor's views of errors, omissions, and misconceptions. During option identification, the planner often becomes put off by the sponsor's persistent questioning. The planner is likely to view the past interrogations as nitpicking, which creates a poor foundation for discussion in the detailing stage. However, in this stage, a devil's advocate posture has consid-

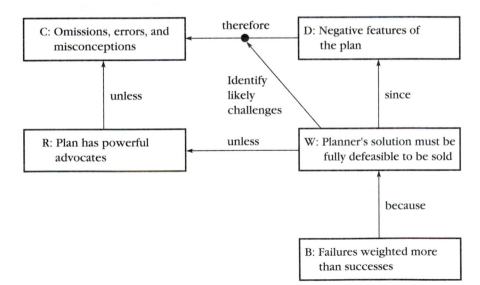

Figure 14-18 ▲ The Devil's Advocate's Argument During Detailing

erable value. Poking holes in a tentative plan identifies critical problems to which attention must be given. However, the intensity of prior questioning can undermine repeating this tactic when applied during detailing.

### Techniques

The devil's advocate–planner dialogue in detailing can be beneficial if conflict, stemming from friction that often develops in the prior stage, can be managed. Intense questioning has benefit because progressive refinements often lead to improved plan quality. Gradually refining the plan tidies up loose ends, which leads to improved quality and acceptance.

27. *Devil's advocate technique preference.* Planning techniques that allow the devil's advocate to ask evaluative "what if" questions, such as sensitivity analysis, are preferred because they permit the sponsor to explore plausible assumptional changes that can render a plan unworkable.
28. *Technique recommendation.* A constructive technique, such as systems matrix, coupled with an interrogative technique, such as interpretive structural modeling, brings the devil's advocate into the planned change process in an ideal way, providing a means for this sponsor to focus systematically on plan details, increasing both plan quality and acceptance.

The devil's advocate prefers to probe at perceived weak spots, coaxing the unwary planner to respond to these probes with analysis. Sensitivity analysis responds to the sponsor's "what if" questions but does not draw on the sponsor's ability to see weak spots in a plan. The best approach has the planner detail a plan using the systems matrix approach, before submitting it for a critique. The systems description of the plan gives the devil's advocate plenty of details and effectively draws on this sponsor's strengths as a critic. Similarly, the ISM technique graphically details the procedure to be used, again giving the devil's advocate a way to visualize how to rearrange steps to negate the objections of affected parties, pick out bad practice, or both.

## ▲ THE SKEPTIC AS A SPONSOR

Another type of critic is the skeptic (Figure 14-1). A skeptic takes the view that planned change is unwise because one cannot hope to understand the uncontrolled, sociological forces that are moving the organization toward a particular course of action. To the skeptic, complete understanding is essential before one can proceed. Because complete understanding is never possible, planned change is viewed as being foolhardy. This view is often not expressed directly to the planner, but rather seeps into the skeptic's reaction to the results of each phase of a planned changed process.

The skeptic believes that a perfectly complex problem demands a perfectly complex solution, which creates an impossible situation, so nothing useful can result from planning. The problem's complexity conjures up a mosaic of contingencies in the mind of the skeptic that must be explained. Sponsors with this belief will manage the planned change process by questioning in great detail. In the early stages of planned change, answers to questions about various contingencies are often, of necessity, vague, giving the skeptic the opportunity to reaffirm his or her view that change should occur by means other than planning. The status quo is seen as low risk and understandable, as compared to the results of a planned change process, which are viewed as uncertain and opaque. The skeptic's behavior makes it very difficult for a planner to get the necessary commitments.

The skeptic expects the planner to see the need for perfect information and to explore all contingencies. The skeptic demands constant reporting and monitors by using checklists of objections derived from past planned changed incidents he or she experienced, or just heard about. This behavior is similar to the behavior of a salesperson peddling commodities, such as encyclopedias. Armed with a list of arguments and counterarguments, the salesperson uses them to try to wear down an individual's sales resistance.

The skeptic anticipates that the plan will be incomplete and will contain impractical and infeasible features that are politically unwise or unacceptable. Improvement seems unlikely, so the perceived consequences of planned change are believed to be negative. As a result, adoption prospects are seen as dismal, and high resistance to change is expected if one tries to implement the plan, unless a higher authority intervenes (see Table 14-1).

## The Skeptic During Concept Development

### The Argument

Like the devil's advocate, the skeptic plays a reactive role in option identification. He or she, however, does not really believe that planned change is possible and is poised to disprove the planner's proposed solutions. The skeptic believes that the planner's ideas must account for all the stochastic properties that exist in the environment. In Boulding's terms, a plan must be able to take in and rationalize all the disorder found in the environment (Pondy and Mitroff, 1982). Because option descriptions built in concept development are often deterministic, the skeptic sees all such representations as incomplete.

As shown in Figure 14-19, the skeptic's argument for concept development leads him or her to articulate premises that appear to demand that the planner's ideas consider all possible contingencies. Skeptics adopt this warrant because they believe that small incremental changes with minimal personal risks have the best track record of success (Lindblom, 1965). Rebuttals stem from the one-in-a-million project in which key factors are sufficiently clear to model them deterministically. In the mind of the skeptic, this rebuttal is so seldom evoked that it can be disregarded.

### The Dialogue

The skeptic-planner dialogue is similar to the dialogues between the devil's advocate and the planner but the similarities are deceptive. The level and purpose of questioning are quite different. The skeptic offers a critical, but more comprehensive

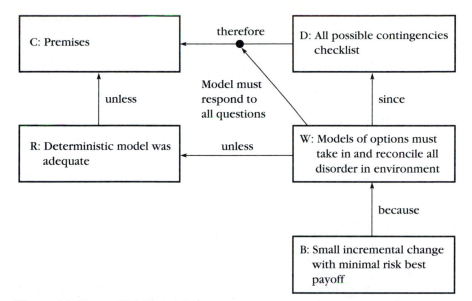

**Figure 14-19** ▲ **The Skeptic's Argument During Concept Development**

list of requirements than does the devil's advocate. The devil's advocate will pick away at the weak spots in the plan, whereas the skeptic requires the planner to deal with one level of detail beyond what is reasonable for the current process stage. Detailing information is requested (plan specifics) to build options during concept development. As a result, the planner-skeptic dialogue leads to incorporating considerable detail, in the form of contingencies, into each option. Dialogue with a skeptic creates considerable option refinement, much of which is unproductive in concept development.

### Techniques

The skeptic's behavior makes it difficult for planners to cope during concept development.

29. *Skeptic technique preference.* The skeptic will prefer a technique that highlights the functions of an operating system and identifies a few problems for remedial action. A variation of Lindblom's (1965) partisan mutual adjustment (PMA) approach is preferred, which points out a few areas in which the sponsor can make marginal adjustments through remedial action.
30. *Technique recommendation.* Planned change techniques like NGT with experts that expose the skeptic's concerns and find clues that reveal what is good about current system operations provide the basic ingredients to define options. These ingredients are enriched by incorporating desirable features from other systems and redefining system components using a morphology.

The skeptic prefers remedial action and will support a technique, like partisan mutual adjustment, designed to produce small changes. Unlike the PMA strictures, a one-time small change is sought. No evolution toward a goal would be embraced. To break the skeptic away from this fixation, a careful exposition of options is needed. One such set of techniques would merge NGT with experts and morphology. Experts give the process credibility, making the result potentially defensible to the skeptic. The NGT process is undertaken to identify components that will be merged by morphology. Some innovative arrangements of the components can be retained for detailing in the next stage, along with the skeptic's problem-based critique.

## The Skeptic During Detailing

### The Argument

In the detailing stage, the skeptic identifies omissions, misconceptions, and errors in terms of the plan's ability to deal with stock concerns. The argumentation is summarized in Figure 14-20. Over a period of years the skeptic develops an elaborate checklist that describes situations and conditions that have cropped up and hindered the success of previous planned change efforts. These are trotted out as a basis on which to test the new plan, whether they are applicable or not. The backing for the checklist stems from war stories and anecdotes that describe the benefits derived from each checklist item or problems that developed because someone did not carefully check a particular item in the past. This warrant and backing holds unless contextual factors conclusively show that a particular item on the checklist is irrelevant.

### The Dialogue

The skeptic-planner dialogue is damaged by past questioning tactics. In this case, the antiplanning sentiments of the skeptic limits his or her effectiveness in probing

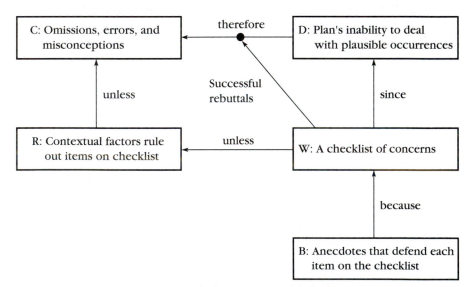

Figure 14-20 ▲ The Skeptic's Argument During Detailing

for ways to improve the plan's integrity. Answering challenges to the plan that lack relevance or importance tends to destroy the sponsor's credibility. Contentiousness between sponsor and planner often results with each becoming frustrated with the perceived inability of the other to be constructive. As a result, planner-skeptic dialogue often creates considerable tension.

### Technique

Guidelines 31 and 32 indicate the preferred and recommended technique to help a planner work with a skeptic during detailing.

31. *Skeptic technique preference*. A systems description that details a single plan will be demanded so the skeptics can apply each item in the universal checklist. Processing concerns, translating inputs to outputs, will be emphasized, suggesting the ISM technique.
32. *Technique recommendation*. A Q-sort or ranking of sponsor checklist items is useful. The trimmed-down list of items is more manageable and focused on the project, allowing the planner to identify the features that should be considered.

To move the skeptic away from his or her marginal change preference, the solution space must be opened up. First, the planner deals with the checklist, helping the sponsor reduce the information overload inherent in the list, and tailors the checklist to fit the current effort. A Q-sort is useful for large-item lists and ranking techniques like paired comparisons for the rest. The resulting criteria are applied to the solution concepts from concept development. At least two are selected for detailing, and one should have innovative features. Detailing is done using a systems approach and ISM. This provides one option with innovative features.

## ▲ Key Points

1. A planned change episode was treated as a debate. The dialogue between conflicting claims of sponsors and planners provide ideas for each stage of a planned change process. The chains of reasoning that stimulate these ideas have several implications. First, the sponsor may abort the planned change effort. Second, the debate may lead to a large number of exchanges, causing all parties to the planned change effort to become frustrated. Third, a particular stage of the process may be skipped. Fourth, the purpose of a given stage in the planned change process may be distorted to meet the needs of the sponsor.
2. The behavior of sponsors, when they take on one of the six roles, can be assessed to determine the benefits and difficulties that flow from planner-sponsor dialogue. Techniques that a planner can use when dealing with a sponsor who takes on one of these roles are summarized in Table 14-3. The recommended technique complements the sponsor's strengths and will be accepted by them. The sponsor's preferred technique caters to the sponsor's biases and expectations.
3. The guidelines offered in this chapter help the planner cater to the sponsor. A basis was provided to select techniques that promote positive relations with

Table 14-3 ▲ Planning Techniques That Cater to Sponsor Roles

| | Rationalist | Broker | Zealot | Visionary | Devil's Advocate | Skeptic |
|---|---|---|---|---|---|---|
| **Formulation** | | | | | | |
| Preference | 1.[a] Objective trees | 7. NI | 13. Take needs opportunities as given | 19. Any | Stage not activated by sponsor | Stage not activated by sponsor |
| Recommendation | 2. NGT to set objectives | 8. Kiva | 14. No technique | 20. Function expansion | | |
| **Concept Development** | | | | | | |
| Preference | 3. Input-output | 9. NI | 15. Input-output | 21. Expert opinion | 25. Checklists | 29. PMA adaptation |
| Recommendation | 4. Plan-counterplan dialectic in a scenario | 10. NI with dialectics | 16. No technique | 22. Relevance trees | 26. Morphology and scenarios | 30. NGT with experts and morphology |
| **Detailing** | | | | | | |
| Preference | 5. MAU evaluation | 11. Trade-offs | 17. Block diagram | 23. Delegation | 27. Sensitivity analysis | 31. Systems description and ISM |
| Recommendation | 6. Brainwriting with block diagram | 12. ISM with NI | 18. No technique | 24. Systems matrix and ISM | 28. Systems matrix and ISM | 32. Q-sort to prioritize checklist items |

[a] Numbers in text

the sponsor or help sponsors overcome weakness inherent in various styles of process management.

4. In Chapter 13 another set of guidelines was offered, basing technique selection on expected plan results (quality, acceptance, innovation, and/or preservation). To reconcile plan results against the need to work with its sponsor, determine the result-based and management-based prescriptions and compare them. Disagreements are likely for comprehensive projects or comprehensive strategies managed by skeptics and zealots. When dealing with skeptics and zealots, it is wise to promote sponsor acceptance that limits the techniques that can be used (see Table 14-3). The other sponsor roles allow more latitude in the selection of planning techniques.

## ▲ Exercises

1. Apply the argumentation ideas to describe how two parties to a plan develop their claims. If possible listen to people making their claims in a meeting to collect this information. Possibilities include C-Span coverage of legislature hearings, a local school board, or a faculty meeting. Develop the arguments of each party and analyze them indicating how insight into the warrants, backing, rebuttals, and data are used to form claims can provide insight into the bargaining and negotiation that takes place.

2. Consider the same-day testing case (last chapter), the outpatient registration case (Chapter 1), and the data processing case (Chapter 5). What role best describes sponsor behavior in these cases. Form a planning method according to the guidelines in Table 14-3. Contrast the recommended techniques with those selected using plan requirements in the last chapter. Propose a planning method for each case. Justify your answers.

3. Review the customized vehicle case and the family medicine case in the last chapter. What role could the leader adopt in each case to promote strategic planned change? Contrast the planning method that results with the one selected using requirements in the last chapter. Propose a method for each case and justify your answers.

4. Consider each of the sponsor roles. Which role creates ethical problems for the sponsor? How could a subordinate deal with a sponsor taking a role that is ethically suspect? What role shifts should a subordinate recommend, assuming the subordinate has a trust relationship with the sponsor? Reconcile your answer with the feasible role shifts noted in Table 14-2.

# *Part VI*

▲ ▲ ▲  ▲ ▲ ▲ ▲ ▲ ▲ ▲ ▲ ▲ ▲ ▲ ▲ ▲ ▲

# CHOOSING AND
# REFLECTING

▲ ▲ ▲ ▲ ▲ ▲ ▲ ▲ ▲ ▲ ▲ ▲ ▲ ▲ ▲ ▲ ▲ ▲ ▲ ▲ ▲ ▲

*Part Six discusses ways to choose and reflect about planned change. Choosing involves evaluation. What is needed are ways to evaluate options to determine their merits. Subjective, qualitative, and quantitative techniques are presented to show how each can be used to determine the merits of planned change options.*

*Reflecting on planned change suggests ways to change practice. Practice that leads to "pseudoplanned change" is identified to suggest problem areas. Key points in the book are summarized to remind the reader of planned change principles. If followed, these principles provide ways to overcome dilemmas that arise when planned change is attempted.*

# 15 The Evaluation Stage of Planned Change

The purpose of the evaluation stage is to identify the costs, benefits, acceptance, and other features that influence the adoptability of each alternative that survives the detailing stage. Evaluation information provides the basis to select a plan from among these alternatives.

# ▲ EVALUATION INFORMATION

Evaluative information can be obtained in one of three ways: by pilots, by simulations, and subjectively.[1] Pilot programs produce estimates of performance in fieldlike conditions. Simulations evaluate with mock-ups of the alternatives. Subjective approaches use expert opinion and qualitative techniques to determine levels of criteria present in each alternative.

## Pilot Programs

The essential components of a pilot evaluation are described in Figure 15-1. A stratified sample is drawn from potential plan users and divided into comparison group. One type of comparison group is called *experimental*.[2] The members of this group (e.g., people in work units) are exposed to the plan in a fieldlike situation. The members of the other comparison group, termed the *control,* are exposed to a placebo or the current program. The members of the comparison groups are exposed to the same measurement process to document the effects of performance for each plan alternative. A comparison of these effects is made using tests of statistical significance.

There are three essential activities in a pilot study: constructing equivalent comparison groups, exposing these groups to the alternatives, and the defining and measuring effects.

### Measuring Effects

A pilot evaluation weighs the importance of factors and conditions that lead to success. A careful definition of what marks success is drawn from the objectives set during formulation. Each alternative may produce a variety of subsidiary results. The evaluation examines the alternatives to measure the consequences of their use, both positive and negative.

The process of measurement follows the dictums of clinical investigations, often using blind or double-blind observational arrangements and placebos. Placebos are used to control the symbolic power of many formal activities that can alter the

---

[1]   As described in Chapter 12, operations research provides several evaluation techniques that link detailing and evaluation. The means to fine-tune and to evaluate the plan are developed at the same time. Each alternative is modeled with a stock representation, such as a waiting line. The representation is manipulated to reveal the merits of each alternative. A comparison of these merits suggests which alternatives should be adopted.
[2]   The example illustrates the comparison of a single alternative to a baseline derived from current practices. Similar procedures can be used to assess several options. The experimental group is subdivided so groups are created for each alternative to be assessed. A complete discussion of these procedures is beyond the scope of the book.

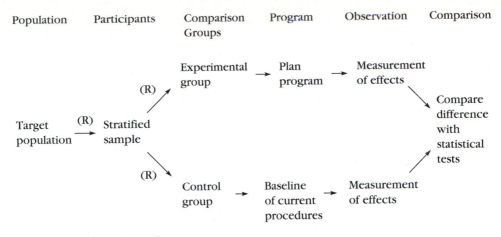

| Population | Participants | Comparison Groups | Program | Observation | Comparison |

Principal ingredients in a pilot:

1. Construct equivalent comparison groups
2. Administer the intervention and current procedure to the comparison groups
3. Define and measure effects

**Figure 15-1 ▲ Components of a Pilot Evaluation**

views, behavior, and performance of people. Blind measurement ensures that the evaluation participants do not know whether they will be exposed to the current or a proposed practice. In a double-blind evaluation, neither the participant nor the observer (or even the evaluator in certain types of studies) knows whether a participant has been exposed to a new or current practice.

Statistical tests are used to compare the effects that stem from each comparison group. The calculation procedures needed to assign both operational and statistical significance to these comparisons are described in statistical textbooks.

### Protocols

Each alternative must have a protocol that documents procedures, staff qualifications, and the environment in which the alternative is proposed to operate. The protocol is carefully defined so each alternative plan can be carried out in the same way at different points in time and in different settings. When doing pilot testing, several causal factors must be accounted for to determine the association between each factor and the performance measures. Evaluation becomes cumbersome, and even impossible, if the pilot is carried out in a different way at different sites or evolves during the collection of evaluation data, making evaluation data impossible to interpret.

### Comparison Groups

Comparison groups are drawn from the target population of the plan (Figure 15-1). The target group is defined by those the plan will act on or serve. For example, the users of information are served by a management information system (MIS).

Statisticians call the target group the "population" or the "universe." When the number of potential users is large, economy dictates that a sample is drawn to represent a subset of the population. This sample must be drawn in such a way that the evaluator can make valid assertions about the performance of this program when applied to all its intended users.

Randomization ensures that the participants in an evaluation will tend to match the target group, eliminating various types of selection biases. Bias occurs when evaluation studies select participants who are easy to work with or sympathetic to the aims of the plan (Suchman, 1967). Cooperative volunteers will provide few insights into the behavior, preferences, or performance of the larger population because these potential or former users may be apathetic or even antagonistic toward the plan. (Randomization is denoted by an "R" in Figure 15-1.)

Formal rules for the selection of participants (sample size) require a historical measure of the variability of performance for the target group, which is seldom available. Without this information, the sample size is based on the number of strata to be considered and the anticipated size of the effect. Many population subgroupings or strata lead to large samples. Sample size is frequently dictated by practical necessity, considering the cost of data acquisition and the availability of participants.

The evaluator draws from the pool of users to set up comparison groups that are equivalent. In well-controlled situations, participants can be assigned to comparison groups by a random process, such as a coin flip. Comparison groups are formed, making the individuals in each group as much alike as possible. The plan is applied in the *experimental groups*. The control groups are not exposed to the plan and may receive a placebo. Control groups establish a baseline indicating the attitude, behavior, or performance of those *not* exposed to the plan.

Comparison groups are constructed by controlling their membership. For example, to judge the effects of a new service, patients would be randomly assigned to the new service (experimental group) and the old service (control group) categories. People often respond in unique ways to identical stimuli. Randomization ensures that capricious responses are equally likely to occur in each comparison group. For example, suggestibility, resistance to change, natural immunity, and a host of other factors may dictate how people will react to treatment programs. Like people, organizations often exhibit unique responses to an intervention. For instance, administrators cannot pilot test a new appraisal program in just one department of an organization and obtain a good indication of the program's value. Randomly selecting departments or people in them to participate in a pilot study controls for these differences.

In some instances, random assignment is impractical or impossible, and other methods must be adopted. For example, some administrators of human service programs have restricted or eliminated the use of control groups. They fear that people who find they were in a control group will perceive that they have been denied benefits, even if these benefits have yet to be demonstrated. The target populations of the Great Society programs expressed such views, believing that control groups would deny them benefits or keep them from participating. In certain settings, these criticisms became so intense that control groups have been prohibited.

In other situations, structural limitations prohibit the use of randomization. For instance, it is not feasible to *assign* people to health maintenance organizations (HMOs) or private practitioners in order to compare these modes of health care delivery. The evaluator has no control over people's choices.

When randomization is prohibited, matched or naturally occurring groups or time-series data are used to provide the comparison groups. A *matched group* equates the profiles of comparison groups across a series of factors thought to cause behavior or performance to differ. *Naturally occurring* groups often represent independent organizations, work groups, or programs that, by virtue of their distinct origin or history, can be assumed independent. *Time-ordered performance data* track important performance indicators prior to and following plan use to see if trends are favorable. The before and after data sets become the comparison groups. By extracting trends, cycles, and other patterns in the data, the performance in the before and after data can be compared.

Quasi-experimental designs use one or more of these principles and combine them in various ways with randomization to create quasi-experimental data collection devices that can be used for a particular pilot situation. (See, for example, Campbell and Stanley, 1966.) For instance, naturally occurring groups provide several independent observations for an evaluation. An intervention with a plan alternative in one setting often goes unnoticed in the other environments. If these environments are carefully matched so their characteristics are similar, both a control for differences among the environments and independence in the observations are provided. Randomization within a naturally occurring or a matched group is often possible, even if the groups themselves were not selected by a random process, which enhances the validity of evaluation findings.

Selection of a data collection device should be based on the special needs of the evaluation study as well as the opportunities inherent in the evaluation environment. For instance, naturally occurring groups provide an inexpensive and useful way of making performance comparisons. When uncontrollable processes, such as learning or maturation, take place during an evaluation, time-series or time-ordered data often can be useful. Finally, the concepts of matching can be used to check the comparability of naturally occurring environments, or to construct an environment for an evaluation study. For specific examples of quasi-experimental data collection devices, see Cook and Campbell (1979) and Nutt (1982b).

Finally, alternatives can be tested in a scaled-down fashion to measure their merits. Either natural or pilot variations can be used. The pilot variation approach imposes a plan whereas the natural variation merely observes how groups implement a plan.

## Simulations

Simulated evaluations make estimates of merit by using mock-ups devised to capture salient aspects of plan performance. The simulation approach can be illustrated best through an example. To evaluate the merits of surgical intensive care unit (SICU) monitoring equipment, replicas of each system's displays are prepared. Physicians are asked to select courses of action by looking at information that each of the candidate monitoring systems provides. The best system provides the most guidance in selecting an appropriate response for an SICU patient in distress.

To produce such a test, two types of information are needed: the capabilities of each system and case histories of, in the example given, SICU patients. A sample of SICU patients that reflects the 30 percent mortality found in an SICU unit that deals with a difficult case mix would be selected. Each of these patients would be profiled using the information that *can* be collected and displayed by a monitoring system. For instance, if a particular monitoring system had a 24-hour trending capability for arrhythmias, this information would be made available in the system's mock-up. Each monitoring system alternative would describe all patients in the sample using its unique capabilities. Physicians would examine the information provided by each monitoring system and make treatment decisions. The decisions made for each patient would be correlated with patient needs, as reflected by their history found in the medical record. The monitoring equipment that aids physicians selecting the most appropriate treatment with the fewest delays is the best system.

The process of simulation is particularly useful when pilot testing is infeasible or prohibitively expensive. Optimization techniques and waiting lines are also useful in predicting costs or benefits prior to implementation. (Refer to Chapter 12 for a discussion of these techniques.)

### Subjective Estimates

Expert opinion provides the third basic type of information in an evaluation. Most, if not all, choices have a sizable degree of subjectivity. It is desirable to capture the subjective aspects of a plan's merits in a way that minimizes bias.

There are a number of approaches for sorting out alternatives. Simple ranking has each decision maker list his or her preferred alternatives in a priority order, using a particular criterion. These techniques are widely used when options must be reduced to a manageable number. Distribute points or rank-weight techniques can be used when there are large number of alternatives to be ranked. These techniques have the sponsor place each alternative in one of several discrete categories. Between 5 and 11 categories are recommended. Q-sorts merged with ranking techniques, such as paired comparisons (described in Chapter 10), are also useful to winnow the list of alternatives.

## ▲ MULTICRITERIA EVALUATION

The choice between alternatives seldom depends solely on the level of a single criterion. Typically, several criteria are important, such as cost, various effectiveness measures, and user satisfaction. Examples include the location of a distribution center, selecting between expansion plans that focus on new products, or an increase in capacity for current products. In such cases, time, cost, the satisfaction of key power centers, need, and still other criteria are important in the choice among alternatives. This type of evaluation is called *multicriteria*.

Each alternative may also have several unique features with intrinsic value. A comparison of these values also helps to identify the option with the best performance. For example, personal computer options may have unique attributes, such as color graphics, touch update, or memory.

The steps in multiple-criteria evaluation are criteria identification, weighting, and aggregation, and considering environmental factors. The values for the criteria, such as the level of cost in an alternative, are provided by the techniques just discussed: pilots, simulations, and subjective estimates.

The basis for selecting among alternatives is drawn from the planned change objectives. For instance, the impetus to replan a firm's customer service division could be motivated by cost, customer complaints, or errors in explaining the use or repair of company products. In this example, the criteria for judging new customer service procedures would be based on satisfaction, the precision of information, and costs.

Although evaluation criteria are suggested by planned change objectives, criteria must be identified in the evaluation stage. Changes in needs often occur as planning reveals opportunity during detailing. With these changes, carefully considering the appropriateness of each criterion implied by the objective is essential. Two steps are used: a listing and a reappraisal of the criteria implicitly called for by the objectives. To carry out this appraisal, several categories of people are consulted who have a stake in the outcome, including the system user, the experts, and its managers. There are two steps: criteria listing and the appraisal of value.

### Step 1: Criteria Listing

Evaluation criteria can be identified by using one of the group processes discussed in Chapter 10. Users or customers, experts, managers, and others can be polled by survey, using a traditional or a Delphi format. Also, the nominal group technique (NGT) or brainwriting can be used when it seems necessary to reflect on the implications of each criterion implied by the objectives. The criteria listing step is carried out for each group separately because experts will tend to stress quality ideas, users' acceptance measures, and managers' cost concerns. Experts tend to suggest measures that are plan specific. For example, a given MIS plan may have unique features, such as speed or precision, that help to discriminate among the alternatives. A merger of unique features and generic attributes provides a comprehensive set of criteria to consider during evaluation.

### Step 2: Appraisal of Value

The listing step typically provides an unwieldy set of criteria that must be merged and winnowed. The discussion and voting steps in brainwriting, nominal interaction, or NGT can be used to cull the candidate criteria. For example, to select criteria, NGT could be merged with vote-discuss-vote (VDV) or Q-sort and the ranking procedures discussed in Chapter 10. Planner-sponsor discussion may be sufficient to select a workable set of criteria in other instances.

The prerogatives of users, experts, and managers suggest which of these tactics should be used. For example, if a particular manager is empowered to make the choice among alternatives, his or her criteria will dominate. When power is diffused, involving several individuals who can influence the implementation of the alternative, groups are essential. A group process is used to manage the selection of a parsimonious set of criteria that are acceptable to the group's members. The planner should help the group keep the criteria mutually exclusive or independent. (When two criteria measure the same concept, the group should be asked to select the more important of the two.)

## ▲ SUBJECTIVE APPROACHES

A number of subjective approaches exists that can quickly winnow alternatives. Each has the virtue of speed, but each lacks the precision that is often required to compare options carefully. These techniques are often used as a screening device when large numbers of alternatives must be compared or in short-fuse situations.

### The Advantage-Disadvantage Technique

The simplest and most commonly used technique lists criteria (or attributes) and examines the advantages and disadvantages of available options. Consider an example in which two locations for a new plant are being compared, as in Table 15-1. The alternatives are assessed by comparing them with each criteria. The winner gets a checkmark. By counting the number of checks for advantages and disadvantages, a crude comparison of sites can be made (Van Gundy, 1981).

Note that much information has been discarded by this technique. An actual comparison of level of costs and the like is possible and would give a clearer picture of the relative advantages of the sites. Also, some criteria seem more important than others, so merely totaling checkmarks can give a misleading assessment of options.

Table 15-1 ▲ The Advantage-Disadvantage Technique

| Criteria | Advantage | Disadvantage |
|---|---|---|
| **Alternative A: Dallas, Texas** | | |
| Quality of water | | ✔ |
| Cost of land | | ✔ |
| Taxes | ✔ | |
| Unionization history | ✔ | |
| Average labor cost | | ✔ |
| Schools | | ✔ |
| Climate | | ✔ |
| Total | 2 | 5 |
| **Alternative B: Columbus, Ohio** | | |
| Quality of water | ✔ | |
| Cost of land | ✔ | |
| Taxes | | ✔ |
| Unionization history | | ✔ |
| Average labor cost | ✔ | |
| Schools | ✔ | |
| Climate | ✔ | |
| Total | 5 | 2 |

Adapted from Van Gundy (1981).

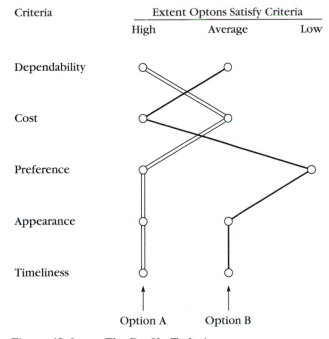

**Figure 15-2** ▲ **The Profile Technique**

Adapted from Souder (1980).

## The Profile Technique

The profile technique compares each alternative subjectively, using several criteria. The sponsor can make these judgments, or they can be left to a group.

Figure 15-2 provides an example of the profile technique. Each decision maker rates each option using several criteria. The result permits the decision maker(s) to compare alternatives across several criteria and pick out the highest performers by its profile. In the example shown in Figure 15-2, the criteria of dependability, cost, preferences, appearance, and timeliness were used to judge computer options. In this illustration, option A seems preferable. Although cost is better for option B, A is selected because it scores higher on the other criteria.

The profile technique cannot be used unless one assumes that the criteria have equal importance. Such an assumption can be unrealistic, particularly when a plan has been drawn to overcome several problems seen as important by the organization. The objectives suggest criteria as does the performance features of each alternative. Criteria derived from objectives are usually more important than are criteria based on performance features.

## The Scoring Technique

A somewhat more sophisticated technique asks the decision maker to distinguish options by indicating the degree to which they satisfy each of the criteria. The following scale could be used:

+4 Ideal

+2 Above average

 0 Average

−2 Below average

−4 Unacceptable

The decision maker selects a value that indicates his or her view of the degree that each option meets each of the criteria. One then adds the scores to determine which options seem preferable. An example of comparing personal computer options with this technique is shown in Table 15-2.

The technique can be used to winnow options, with a certain score as a cutoff. Those that survive are subjected to more detailed analysis. This technique also assumes that criteria have equal importance, which limits its value.

## The Weight-Rank Technique

The weight-rank technique can deal with criteria that have different importance. To obtain a weight, criteria are ranked. The weight is proportional to the rank. (Alternatively, Q-sort and VDV, coupled with anchored rating scales, rank-weight,

**Table 15-2 ▲ The Scoring Technique**

| Criteria | +4 | +2 | 0 | −2 | −4 | |
|---|---|---|---|---|---|---|
| **Option A** | | | | | | |
| Dependability | | | | X | | |
| Cost | | X | | | | |
| Preference | | | X | | | |
| Appearance | | X | | | | |
| Timeliness | X | | | | | |
| Total | | | | | | 6 points |
| **Option B** | | | | | | |
| Dependability | X | | | | | |
| Cost | | | X | | | |
| Preference | | X | | | | |
| Appearance | X | | | | | |
| Timeliness | | | X | | | |
| Total | | | | | | 10 points |
| **Option C** | | | | | | |
| Dependability | | | X | | | |
| Cost | | | X | | | |
| Preference | | X | | | | |
| Appearance | | | X | | | |
| Timeliness | | X | | | | |
| Total | | | | | | 4 points |

*Column headers span "Criteria Levels" across +4, +2, 0, −2, −4.*

Adapted from Souder (1980).

or pooled-rank techniques, can be used to weight the criteria.) Assume that the criteria to evaluate computer equipment were ranked as follows:

|  | Rank | Weight |
|---|---|---|
| Timelines | 1 | 5 |
| Cost | 2 | 4 |
| Preference | 3 | 3 |
| Dependability | 4 | 2 |
| Appearance | 5 | 1 |

The analyst assigns weights, as shown, and then multiplies the weight by a score assigned to each option by the decision maker. The result is shown in Table 15-3. By weighting the criteria, option A becomes preferable to options B and C.

The weight-rank, scoring, and profile techniques are useful in separating long lists of alternatives into categories. A more sophisticated analysis is often needed to identify the best alternative from the highest-ranked options.

## Hybrid Techniques

By combining some of the subjective techniques, some of the disadvantages of these techniques for screening options can be overcome (Hamilton, 1974). First,

Table 15-3   ▲   The Weight-Rank Technique

| Criteria | Criterion Weight | Criterion Value[a] | Score[b] |
|---|---|---|---|
| **Option A** | | | |
| Dependability | 2 | −2 | −4 |
| Cost | 4 | +2 | 8 |
| Preference | 3 | 0 | 0 |
| Appearance | 1 | +2 | 2 |
| Timeliness | 5 | +4 | 20 |
| Weighted score | | | 26 |
| **Option B** | | | |
| Dependability | 2 | 4 | 8 |
| Cost | 4 | 0 | 0 |
| Preference | 3 | +2 | 6 |
| Appearance | 1 | +4 | 4 |
| Timeliness | 5 | 0 | 0 |
| Weighted score | | | 18 |
| **Option C** | | | |
| Dependability | 2 | 0 | 0 |
| Cost | 4 | 0 | 0 |
| Preference | 3 | +2 | 6 |
| Appearance | 1 | 0 | 0 |
| Timeliness | 5 | +2 | 10 |
| Weighted score | | | 16 |

[a] As taken from Table 15-2.
[b] Criterion weight × criterion value = score.

### Table 15-4　▲　The Hybrid Technique: Applied to Site A

1. Culling Criteria
   a. Saturated with units?
   b. Turnover rate less than 10%?
   c. Area population more that 100,000?

   *Pass to next stage.*

2. Rating Criteria

| | | Yes | No |
|---|---|---|---|
| a. | Required site size available? | X | |
| b. | Land development costs meet norms? | | X |
| c. | Site near one-third of market? | X | |
| | Minimum score is 2 | 2 yes | 1 no |

   *Pass to next stage.*

3. Scoring Criteria

| | | Poor | Fair | Good | Weight | Minimum Score |
|---|---|---|---|---|---|---|
| a. | Return on investment? | 1 | (2) | 3 | 4 | 8 |
| b. | Cost overrun prospects? | (1) | 2 | 3 | 3 | 6 |
| c. | Projected market growth? | 1 | 2 | (3) | 2 | 4 |
| | | | | | | 18 |

Actual score $= 8 + 3 + 6 = 17$[a]

*Site fails.*

Adapted from Hamilton (1974).
[a] Determined by $(2 \times 4) + (1 \times 3) + (3 \times 2)$ or the minimal criterion value multiplied by the criterion's weight and adding.

one develops "culling" criteria to act as first-cut screens that can be answered in a yes/no fashion. Next, rating criteria are applied as a second-cut screen. Finally, scoring criteria are applied.

An example is shown in Table 15-4, which uses the screens to compare apartment development sites (Van Gundy, 1981). The *minimum score* is determined by multiplying the minimal acceptable value for each criterion (shown by the values in parentheses in Table 15-4) by the weight assigned to that criterion and adding up the results. The actual score is determined by an evaluation of a site (poor, fair, or good) for each criterion multiplied by the criterion's weight. This technique allows individuals to visit a number of sites and apply a comparable basis of assessment. Sites that survive the final screen can be examined more carefully.

The same approach can be applied to examine equipment options, managers for an important executive position, or vendors that supply a critical raw material. In each case, a large number of alternatives are available, and the sponsor wants a wide search to be sure that a good option has not been overlooked.

## ▲　QUALITATIVE APPROACHES

Qualitative techniques introduce difficult-to-measure criteria that go beyond economic considerations to deal with political and ethical issues. The balance sheet and stakeholders techniques offer a way to get at these issues.

## The Balance Sheet Technique

This technique provides a format for exploring alternatives and estimating the political and ethical as well as economic benefits and costs of each (Janis and Mann, 1977; Janis, 1989). Four categories of expected consequences are considered.

1.  Tangible gains and losses that identify how the sponsor is effected by each of the alternatives.
2.  Tangible gains and losses for others that indicate who else can be a winner or loser and the nature of these losses and gains.
3.  Self-assessments that call for the sponsor to imagine his or her standards and how they will be affected if an alternative is adopted.
4.  Social assessments that call for the sponsor to imagine how he or she will appear to others if an alternative is adopted

First, a balance sheet like that shown in Table 15-5 is constructed. To apply the technique, select an alternative that has survived a screening, like that depicted in the hybrid technique, and think of the positive and negative points for self, others, self-perception, and social credit. All cells must be filled out for each alternative examined in this way. Compare the sheets for the most important alternatives. Rule out alternatives that create unacceptable losses for self or others. Rule out alternatives that produce ethical dilemmas for self or create image problems. Select among the alternatives that remain using economic criteria.

The balance sheet technique forces a sponsor to examine alternatives carefully with a variety of considerations. The format encourages a search for consequences that are economic, political, *and* ethical. As a result, the technique draws out information often overlooked in evaluation. It gets sponsors to examine carefully who is a winner and who is not. This assessment may reveal important figures who will

**Table 15-5 ▲ The Balance Sheet Technique**

| Alternative | Positive Anticipations | Negative Anticipations |
| --- | --- | --- |
| 1. Self | | |
|   a. Tangible gains | | |
|   b. Tangible losses | | |
| 2. Others | | |
|   a. Tangible gains | | |
|   b. Tangible losses | | |
| 3. Self-image | | |
|   a. Enhanced | | |
|   b. Diminished | | |
| 4. Social credit | | |
|   a. Enhanced | | |
|   b. Diminished | | |

Adapted from Janis (1989).

resist a plan alternative, making it infeasible even if it is economically desirable. Also, the technique makes sponsors reflect on how they will appear to self and others. These insights can identify potentially troublesome ethical issues that are often overlooked when alternatives are compared purely in terms of economic considerations. By considering the choice from these perspectives, postdecision stress is reduced. This technique gets sponsors to develop considerable commitment to the alternative selected. When an alternative meets economic, political, and ethical criteria a persuasive argument to support the planned change called for by the selected alternative can be made.

Although developed for individuals, groups can apply the balance sheet ideas as well. The silent reflection group process techniques are particularly useful in adding pertinent ideas that are high in disclosure and innovation to each of the cells in Table 15-5.

## Stakeholder Techniques

The attempt to initiate planned change sweeps in far-ranging considerations. In addition to the typical concerns about customers or clients and employee views of the change political, legal, and ethical implications are also important. Stakeholder techniques have been developed to deal with this broader set of considerations (e.g., Mason and Mitroff, 1981; Freeman, 1984; Nutt, 1984b; Nutt and Backoff, 1987). To carry out these techniques, the sponsor determines how important parties, called stakeholders, will affect or will be affected by the planned change. People (and interests they represent) with political, financial, managerial, and professional stakes in the alternatives being considered are identified, and their position is assessed.

### Identifying Stakeholders

Sponsors typically wish to target key stakeholders: people whose stakes are particularly important. This listing frequently includes customers or users of services, key suppliers, cooperating units or departments, professionals such as R&D teams and the providers of services, founders, members of a board of directors or trustees, benefactors or endowers, key members of the management team, and trusted staff people, among others. This information is often collected by survey or by a group process (see Chapter 10).

### Rating Stakeholders

Following listing, stakeholders are rated in terms of importance and their position on one of the planned change alternatives. The rating can be done by the sponsor or the planning group mobilized to manage the planned change effort. Each stakeholder is rated in terms of his or her importance on a 0 (least) to 10 (most) scale. This rating is followed by an assessment of each stakeholder's view of each alternative, using a +5 (support) to a −5 (oppose) scale. In a group, the VDV technique would be applied to seek consensus on the ratings.

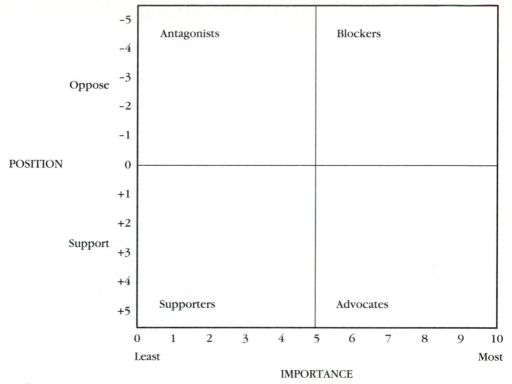

**Figure 15-3** ▲ **Classification of Stakeholders**

The ratings are plotted on a grid (see Figure 15-3). The grid is segmented into four regions: blockers, antagonists, supporters, and advocates. Alternatives can be evaluated by the proportion of stakeholders in each category.

Several kinds of profiles can result, as shown in Table 15-6. If one of the alternatives has many advocates and the others many blockers, an unambiguous selection can be made on *political* grounds. The ethics and the pragmatics of this choice can be questioned if a client group that the organization is expected to serve becomes a blocker stakeholder. This assessment suggests that one should examine the alternative to see if it can be altered to make it acceptable to clients, without losing its appeal to others.

Similarly, if supporters clearly outnumber antagonists, the alternative with the preponderance of supporters can be selected on *pragmatic* grounds. Implementation is more apt to be successful when supporters outnumber antagonists and the stakeholders who are antagonists have little importance (see Figure 15-3). When advocates favor an alternative and the others have antagonists, a similar argument can be made (see Table 15-6).

A clear-cut choice among the alternatives can be made if one has advocates and the others have supporters or when one has advocates and the other antagonists (Table 15-6). Such a choice would be made using a *consensus* rationale.

Table 15-6　▲　Interpreting the Stakeholder Grids

| Alternative 1 | Alternative 2 | Rationale | Action |
|---|---|---|---|
| Blocker | Advocate | Political | Choose 2 |
| Blocker | Antagonist | None | Choose neither |
| Blocker | Supporter | Satisficing | Choose 2 |
| Antagonist | Advocate | Consensus | Choose 2 |
| Antagonist | Supporter | Pragmatics | Choose 2 |
| Supporter | Advocate | Consensus | Choose 2 |

An alternative that has supporters when others have blockers can be selected on a *satisficing* basis. It is better to satisfy unimportant stakeholders than it is to encourage blockers to move against the planned change process.

There is no basis for a choice if all alternatives have either blocker or antagonist stakeholders. In this case, additional alternatives must be sought by reverting to an earlier stage of the planned change process.

When more than one of the alternatives have a favorable stakeholder profile, another basis for selection must be adopted to select among these options. Several approaches can be applied. First, one can count the number of favorable stakeholders in the advocate category. Another tactic is to narrow the advocate category by drawing lines at 7 for importance and +3 for position on Figure 15-3, and then counting the number of advocate stakeholders for the remaining alternatives. Finally, one can apply the hybrid or balance sheet technique to select among the remaining alternatives.

## The Assumptional Analysis Technique

Another technique that gives a qualitative assessment of alternatives deals with assumptions that lie behind each alternative. This technique is based on sorting out faulty assumptions to create a basis to choose among alternatives. Information and warrants (see Chapter 14) provide a way to make a choice among planned change options. Selecting the appropriate set of information upon which to base a choice poses significant difficulties. Neither the sponsor nor key stakeholders can be relied upon to provide this information. Both make assumptions that are tacit and hard to tease out. This technique draws out these assumptions and examines and tests them. The procedure requires that at least two groups be assigned to assess an alternative.

An adaptation of the SAST (strategic assumption stating and testing) procedure devised by Mason and Mitroff (1981) is presented. SAST has four phases:

1. Identify assumptions on which an alternative is based
2. Produce alternative assumptions
3. Critique each assumption in terms of its implications
4. Choose an assumption set to guide the evaluation

The technique focuses on the evaluation activities where taken for granted "givens" are derived. The technique extracts knowledge about an organization to determine the extent this knowledge is firm, widely understood, and agreed upon. The rationale is:

▲ Few premises are widely agreed to.
  ▲ Some are inconsistent.
  ▲ Some are contradictory.
  ▲ Others are implicit.
▲ People talk about preferences (e.g., for information) but seldom expose *assumptions* on which these preferences are based.
▲ Assumptions are treated as claims for an argument to include (or exclude) specific types of information.
▲ To evaluate a plan, these assumptions must be exposed and tested.

The procedure has five steps, which are presented in the following discussion.

### Step 1: Group Formation

The group formation step can follow one of several tactics. Groups can be created that include or exclude people in conflict. The conflict can be personal, but preferably based on the group member's support for one of the alternatives. Because groups in conflict over ways to solve the planning problem are likely to form unique assumptions, their preferred plans can be used in a subsequent step to create a dialectical debate.

Differences in preferred alternatives among the stakeholders can be inferred. One way to get this information is through a survey. For example, stakeholders can be asked to indicate which of the alternatives being discussed that they prefer.

### Step 2: Assumption Surfacing

To begin discussion, an initial list of assumptions can be introduced and discussed. Members of the group are told to add assumptions that make the alternative a priority. In this instance, a brainwriting approach would be used to uncover assumptions (see Chapter 10).

The group is given examples of assumptions to stimulate thinking. Consider plan alternatives to raise or lower prices in the pharmaceutical company. The facilitator asks what must be assumed to make a plan (e.g., raise price) valid. For instance, to raise price, one has to assume that physicians will remain price insensitive in spite of the government's cost-containment attempts. More generally, assumptions about materials, suppliers, current customers, creditors, stockholders, production, employers, the marketing force, unions, communities in which plants are to be built, capital markets, new technologies, governmental alliances/support, competitors, R&D capability, company know-how, and corporate staff are often made. Each represents a claimant inside or outside the organization that has a vested interest in the alternative. The support or opposition to an alternative makes assumptions about the current and the future behavior of these claimants.

To help uncover these assumptions, the facilitator (sponsor or planner) asks what must be assumed about the claimants to make the alternative an ideal solution to the planned change problem. A brainwriting, NGT, NI, or Kiva group process can be used to identify the assumptions. Examples of assumptions that often arise include beliefs about the existence of stockholders demanding high returns, the ability to make changes called for by a plan, the cost of energy sources, suppliers prices, the ease acquiring funds from capital markets, the skills of key staff in production departments, lax oversight by regulatory bodies such as OSHA or the EPA, and the availability of essential technology. After the assumptions-listing step, the group tests the assumptions.

### Step 3: The Within-Group Dialectic

This step ferrets out irrelevant concerns and seeks to avoid the tendency for groups to concentrate on a few narrow issues. The group is asked to attempt to negate or make invalid each assumption listed in step 2. For example, the group is asked what would happen if the reverse were true? If nothing would happen, the assumption can be ruled out. To illustrate, stockholders demanding high returns cannot be negated. It is likely that the demands of retirement plans and others holding large blocks of stock for high dividends will continue. However, one can negate an assumption about new competitors if market entry is difficult, so this assumption is not confirmed.

Generally, several assumptions are dropped after this form of scrutiny. Some assumptions about reliability of the suppliers, directors or trustees, energy sources, capital financing, competition, and regulations are often ill-founded and can be negated.

### Step 4: Assumption Ranking

To accept an assumption, it must meet two criteria: certainty and importance. To be certain, an assumption must seem plausible. The link between the assumption and some consequence should be clear and apparent. An important assumption also has intrinsic virtue. It should have a significant bearing on the plan's outcome.

To create a ranking of the assumptions, each member of the group compares each assumption to every other using the paired comparison technique. The facilitator numbers all nonnegated assumptions for identification purposes. Each member of the group compares all pairs of assumptions, first in terms of their importance and then in terms of their certainty.

Figure 15-4 illustrates the procedure. Each pair of assumptions is compared to determine which seems to be the more important. When assumption 1 is more important than 2, a checkmark is placed in column 1. If the assumptions have equal importance, a checkmark is made at the row-column intersection for the pair. The checkmarks in each column are then tallied to give an importance index, following the paired comparison procedure described in Chapter 10.

The assumption's certainty is determined by using another chart identical to the one in Figure 15-4. Again, each pair of assumptions is compared, this time asking which of each pair of assumptions seems more plausible or reasonable than another, or more likely to hold in the future. The results are scored in the same way.

The weights are then converted to percentages. For example, assume the following scores in which "6" is the largest number that can occur:

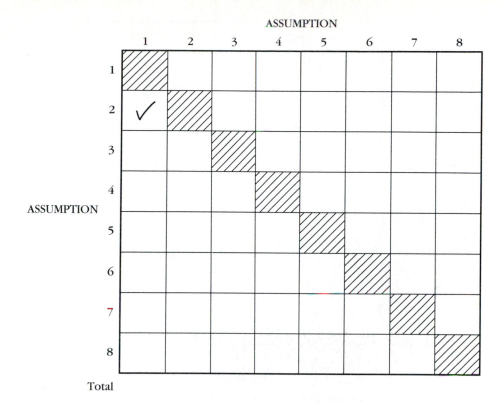

Steps: (1) ✓ = assumption 1 is more important than assumption 2.
(2) Tally number of checks in each column.

**Figure 15-4 ▲ The Assumption Testing Chart**

| Assumption Code No. | Importance | Value |
|---|---|---|
| 1 | 5 | 5/6 = .83 |
| 2 | 4 | 4/6 = .67 |
| 3 | 0 | 0 |
| 4 | 4 | 4/6 = .67 |
| 5 | 2 | 2/6 = .33 |
| 6 | 2 | 2/6 = .33 |

The importance-certainty chart is used to summarize the ratings. The normalized values from the importance and certainty scores define a coordinate for each assumption. They are plotted on a chart like that shown in Figure 15-5. Assumptions falling in quadrants 3 and 4 are ignored. In quadrant 3, the assumptions are plausible, but unimportant, making them candidates for elimination. Quadrant 4 contains the unclear and unimportant assumptions. If the uncertainty can be cleared up, these assumptions would move to quadrant 3 so they can also be ignored. Quadrant 1 is high importance–high certainty forming unambiguous issues. Quadrant 2 contains assumptions that are important, but the planning group does not fully understand their implications. They represent candidates for careful study. For example, an

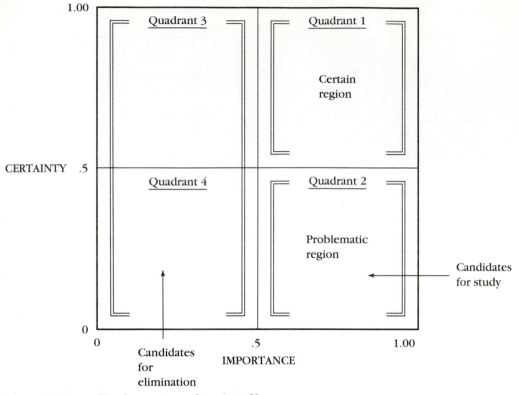

**Figure 15-5** ▲ **The Importance Certainty Chart**
Reprinted from Mitroff and Emshoff (1979).

assumption about the ability of a metals company to make a transition from producing raw material to manufacturing high technology fell into quadrant 2. After study, some assumptions in quadrant 2 may move into quadrant 1. Assumptions in quadrant 1 make up what are called the "pivotal assumptions."

Priorities are implicit in the rankings. In the study of the metal processing firm, both capital markets and new technology fell into quadrant 2, but capital ranked higher on the importance scale, suggesting an investigation of capital before exploring new technology (Mason and Mitroff, 1979). In this case, investment bankers and other types of financiers could be consulted to collect more data. Market research, operations research, competitor analysis, and PIMS data provide other ways to clarify assumptions.

### Step 5: The Between Group Dialectic

An issue that is systematically examined from several points of view creates a dialectic. To improve a final judgment, the assumptions are subjected to a critical review. To provide such a review, the planning groups are asked to debate the merits of each other's work. The debate begins with a presentation by each group, followed by a discussion. The debate seeks to spell out the implication of each alternative and to challenge it by exposing its underlying assumptions. To force closure, a vote can be taken.

A dialectic is not created by merely comparing two competing alternatives. Instead, the basic assumptions that lie behind the alternatives must differ. Consider the comparison of plans for a United Way agency. A debate initiated to choose between a supply-based plan (more funds) and an allocation plan (who gets the funds) is not a dialectic. Supply and allocation are not dialectical plans but, rather, components of any reasonable United Way strategy in which the assumptions about supply and allocation must be teased out.

Each presentation begins with each group's importance-certainty chart that identifies the assumptions believed to be pivotal. Next, the alternative plan is presented. In the discussion, issues implicit in the assumptions are considered.

Groups often identify similar assumptions for alternatives, but rate them differently. A revision of the certainty-importance chart can help to resolve conflict. A new group can be formed to reconsider the assumptions in quadrant 1. Alternatively, all the pivotal assumptions could be used as a starting point for a new evaluation.

When conflict persists after the discussion and no common ground emerges, each assumption can be treated as an argument, as discussed in Chapter 14. The claim for each assumption can be explored in the hopes of revealing issues that require validation. This procedure forces hard evidence to surface. For example, the grounds for a transition from raw material to high technology stemmed from instances where management had dealt successfully with high technology and where managerial innovation created market advantages (Mason and Mitroff, 1979). If no consensus is reached, the issue should be sent off for study. Typically, the basis to proceed emerges from the first five steps. If not, the consensual assumptions become the premises for further evaluation.

The assumptional analysis technique has several benefits. First, the debate forces consideration of a wide range of information. Pet ideas are subjected to careful and systematic scrutiny by noting how key people would view them. This leads participants to develop a fuller appreciation of one another's rationales.

The technique will not work when a choice is well structured or when key administrative people fail to understand and endorse the technique. The conflict it produces can be dangerous if not resolved and there is no guarantee that a resolution is possible. The technique must be carried out by someone who is at home with groups and has little to lose by a failure. It may be a consultant's paradise and the staff person's nightmare to carry out.

## ▲ QUANTITATIVE APPROACHES

Quantitative approaches determine how well each alternative meets important criteria, taking into account the importance of these criteria. Three approaches are considered. Decision trees are used to factor the impact of chance events and the importance accorded to criteria into quantitative information. Sensitivity analysis is applied to cope with the risk that arises when dealing with uncertain and value-laden information. The elimination-by-aspects technique offers an efficient and reliable way for a sponsor to cope with large amounts of evaluation information and a large number of alternatives in a quantitative manner.

## The Elimination by Aspects Technique

The elimination by aspects technique calls for the sponsor to scan the alternatives using the evaluation criteria one at a time (Tversky, 1972). Consider an apartment seeker's decision. The apartment seeker can prepare a spreadsheet that lists criteria as row headings and apartment alternatives as column headings. Several criteria are important in the apartment decision, such as rent, location (safety), contract length, pool and other facilities, amount of security deposit, work commuting time, and access to downtown. Each apartment option is valued with each of these criteria in the spreadsheet. The would-be renter then scans all the apartment alternatives to rule out the unacceptable using the most important criterion first. In our example, alternatives with unacceptably high rent could be eliminated first, followed by those with unsafe locations, and so on.

Site selection tactics used by oil companies for gas stations and fast-food chains for their restaurants illustrate how elimination by aspects can be applied. The preferred site must meet several criteria. For example, fast-food restaurants, such as Wendy's, apply 17 criteria in categories that describe the area, site features, and competition.

The criteria are as follows:

*Area Characteristics*
1. Retail activity
2. Employment
3. Traffic
4. Population density
5. Population growth
6. Income
7. Overall activity

*Site Features*
8. Lost size
9. Viability
10. Ingress/egress
11. Convenience
12. Cost

*Competition*
13. Number of units
14. Location of units
15. Volume of units
16. Lunch business
17. Dinner business

Car counts and proximity to intersections give an indication of traffic. The volume of retail activity in competitive fast-food outlets, such as McDonald's or Burger King, being at least 20 percent above their national average provides a norm for projected volume. Cost is measured in dollars per square foot and is limited to no more than $2 per square foot above the average prices in the area. Convenience is measured by proxies such as time to turn through traffic to get to a site and time to get back into the flow of traffic from the site. Demographic data from census tracts identify population growth, income, and local business activity. Market research firms provide the remaining information. Market research for Wendy's estimated that 70 percent of its volume is determined by retail activity and employment in the area, making these factors the dominant criteria. No other criterion accounts for more than 10 percent of the volume.

If Wendy's is faced with choosing among a large number of sites, elimination by aspects would be a useful way to eliminate sites systematically until the best site alternative emerges. The criteria are ranked to consider the most important first, as shown in Table 15-7. This is done with a large chart on which the proposed sites (alternatives) are numbered and listed across the top and the 17 criteria down the left side. The sponsor deals with the criteria one at a time, applies a norm, and draws a line through all sites (more generally options) that fail to meet the norm. In the Wendy's case, sites with unacceptably low business volume projections would be ruled out first. Next, sites with competitors doing below 20 percent more than

**Table 15-7 ▲ Using Elimination by Aspects to Select a Restaurant Site**

| | Site 1 | Site 2 | Site 3 | Site 4 | Site 5 | Site 6 | ... | Site n |
|---|---|---|---|---|---|---|---|---|
| *Area Characteristics* | | | | | | | | |
| 1. Retail activity | | | | | | | | |
| 2. Employment | | | | | | | | |
| 3. Traffic | | | | | | | | |
| 4. Population density | | | | | | | | |
| 5. Population growth | | | | | | | | |
| 6. Income | | | | | | | | |
| 7. Overall activity | | | | | | | | |
| *Site Features* | | | | | | | | |
| 8. Lot size | | | | | | | | |
| 9. Visibility | | | | | | | | |
| 10. Ingress/egress | | | | | | | | |
| 11. Convenience | | | | | | | | |
| 12. Cost | | | | | | | | |
| *Competition* | | | | | | | | |
| 13. Name of units | | | | | | | | |
| 14. Location of units | | | | | | | | |
| 15. Volume of units | | | | | | | | |
| 16. Lunch business | | | | | | | | |
| 17. Dinner business | | | | | | | | |

Reprinted from Nutt (1989a).

their national average volume would be ruled out. The process continues until one site remains.

The technique can be repeated several times with different stakeholders to reveal their views of criteria importance and norms that should be applied. For instance, some people in the organization may rule out sites that have to compete with a Ponderosa steak house, thinking that Wendy's would be more apt to lose business to a steak house than to other fast-food outlets. This procedure unobtrusively reveals the extent to which this view is shared by others.

When several criteria are applied in this way, the list of alternatives can be quickly narrowed in a simple and efficient manner. The technique is good for minimizing both evaluation cost and time. The disadvantage stems from its inability to consider trade-offs. The elimination by aspects technique is called noncompensatory because compensating criteria values are not considered in the choice among alternatives.

## The Decision Tree Technique

An important factor in the choice among alternatives is future conditions. The best alternative under current conditions can fare poorly if conditions change. Some of these changes stem from managerial action, and some are imposed by factors outside the manager's control. For instance, a marketing program can be designed to increase sales, hoping to change the level of demand for the firm's products. The likelihoods associated with various levels of success for the marketing effort create several situations in which an alternative can be evaluated. Other changes can be caused by the actions of third parties. For example, a sharp increase in interest rates will alter the merits of expansion alternatives. In such a situation, the alternatives should be evaluated under "increase" and "no-increase" future conditions.

The analytical approach incorporates key future conditions by linking them to data that describe the value of alternatives (von Neumann and Morgenstern, 1947). This approach has four components:

1. *Alternatives*. The planned change process provides a set of alternatives from which the sponsor must choose.
2. *Future conditions*. To make a choice, the sponsor must consider how conditions under which the alternatives must function can alter the alternative's value. For instance, when deciding on the desirability of a new product, consumer demands are considered. Very high (or very low) sales can make one of the products more desirable than another.
3. *The likelihood of future conditions*. Future conditions are made up of plausible events that can occur. Each future condition has a probability that indicates its chance of occurring. Since only one condition will occur, the sponsor can consider only the condition's likelihood when the decision is made. For instance, forecasts of sales can be made based on past experience. The likelihood that demand will be high (150 percent of the projection) or low (50 percent of the projection) can be used to define the probabilities. To collect this information, the records of comparable companies could be reviewed to detect their sales rates, creating a frequency distribution that describes the range of demand. Subjective information can also be used to estimate these probabilities. When

relevant forecasts cannot be made, the probabilities are estimated by experts, aided by the tools of the subjective estimation.[3]

4. *Criteria*. Criteria are used to link each alternative to each future condition and to describe the option's value. Values for criteria are also dependent on future conditions. For example, equipment options can be evaluated in terms of cost and quality. The strains created by the increased use associated with high demands may hike costs, such as maintenance, and lower quality, due to equipment malfunction that increase the rate of rejects. The weights assigned to the criteria reflect the sponsor's values.

An index describing the value of an alternative is made up of objective information (level of cost and quality for each alternative for a given future condition) and subjective information (the relative importance or weight attached to the cost and quality criteria). This approach requires the acquisition of objective and subjective information. The sponsor, assisted by others, identifies future conditions that can occur, estimates the likelihood that each condition will occur, and provides a set of criteria that can be used to evaluate each alternative, considering the alternative's intrinsic value and the influence of environmental factors, such as level of demand. For example, several levels of usage for a management information system are conceivable. Evaluation must consider how different use rates may influence cost, client satisfaction, and other criteria.

### The Analytical Framework

To illustrate the analytical framework, consider a department store's staffing plans in which a sponsor must select among ways to deal with increased work load during periods of heavy demand, such as sales and Christmas. The department store is considering alternative ways to deal with increases in demand such as temporary help, restricting vacations, overtime, or ignoring the situation. Future conditions under which these alternatives must be evaluated depict the amount of business that the store anticipates during the peak period, say, 25 percent and 50 percent more than normal. The criterion used to evaluate options could be cost. (Ways to deal with other relevant criteria, such employee resistance to increased work during a holiday, will be considered later in the chapter.) Each of the four alternatives would be evaluated under each of the three conditions (normal and 25 percent and 50 percent above normal) by estimating its cost. The best alternative is identified by trading off gains against losses for each plausible future condition. The likelihood of these conditions identifies assumptions about uncertainty that are made to evaluate the alternatives.

The merit of each alternative is determined by the average cost savings for each future condition, weighted according to the likelihood that these conditions will occur. The estimated savings in cost for each alternative is the weighted average of cost savings that could be realized under the relevant future conditions of current and increased demand. This calculation applies what is called the "expected value" decision rule to deal with the uncertainty in the choice among alternatives.

---

[3] The probabilities are assumed to be independent of the alternatives selected. When the distribution of probabilities is continuous, rather than discrete, a more complicated formulation is required.

### The Decision Tree Format

Evaluation information is usually captured with a decision tree. The tree provides a flow diagram with its branches depicting significant chance events that can occur. At each fork these events are described so they are mutually exclusive and exhaustive. The likelihoods at this point must always sum to one. The tree depicts the order of possible acts by a sponsor and outcomes flowing from these acts governed by chance. The forks in the tree distinguish between choice and chance events by designating a choice juncture with a *square* and a chance juncture with a *circle*. The branches of the tree terminate with a payoff. Only one of these payoffs will be realized, but all are plausible when a choice among alternatives is made by a sponsor.

The decision tree has three features: nodes, branches, and payoffs. Nodes describe choices and outcomes. Branches depict alternatives and the consequences that stem from adapting an alternative. Figure 15-6 illustrates this idea for the choice among department store staffing plans. The expected value for each alternative is determined by weighting each payoff according to its chance of occurrence. Note that this value will never be realized, because one of the payoffs in Figure 15-6 *will* occur. The expected value provides a sponsor with a means to compare the payoffs taking into account chance events that can influence these payoffs.

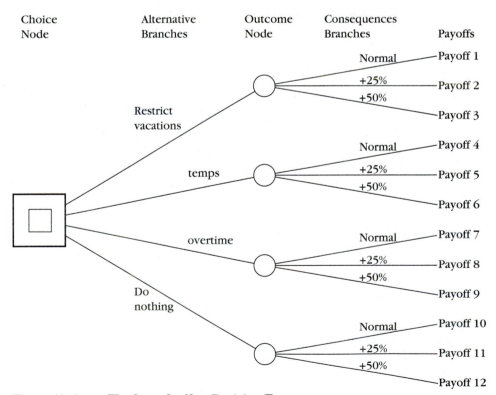

**Figure 15-6**   ▲   **The Store Staffing Decision Tree**

Decision trees have several advantages. The tree can depict multiple chance events and sequential choices. Several chance and choice nodes can be described, such as alternative marketing efforts and their likelihood of simulating sales during Christmas, by listing these choices and consequences in the order they occur. One of two approaches can be used to deal with choices with several criteria. First, several trees can be used, one for each criterion (e.g., cost, quality) that is deemed important. Alternatively, an index that measures the weighted value of several criteria (cost and quality) can be substituted for the payoffs in Figure 15-6. The maximum expected value of this index suggests the alternative with the greatest merit.

## A Numerical Example

Assume that a firm is considering replacing its robot welder with an updated version. The new robot welder's purchase cost may be offset by lower operating cost. The alternatives are replacing or retaining.

The following data have been collected:

|  | Current Robot Welder Alternative | New Robot Welder Alternative |
| --- | --- | --- |
| Purchase cost | $ 0 | $4,000,000 |
| Operating cost | $2,000,000 | $1,000,000 |
| Salvage value | $ 400,000 | $ 0 |
| Expected life | — | 5 years |

The present worth technique can be used to determine the payoff of each alternative. This approach determines the time-discounted present value of all savings and compares them to the capital outlay for each alternative. If the discounted savings exceed the capital requirements, the purchase of the new robot welder would provide cost savings. The option with the largest amount of "savings less outlays" would be selected.

The present worth of savings attributable to the new robot welder is

$$\text{Present worth} = \frac{\text{Salvage}}{\text{value}} + \frac{\text{Annual}}{\text{savings}} \times \frac{\text{Present}}{\text{worth}}$$
$$\text{cost} \qquad \text{factor}$$

The present worth factor can be determined by consulting tables (see, for example, Grant and Ireson, 1980). Assume that the firm has been seeking a 15 percent return on equipment changes. Applying this assumption, the present worth (PW) of the new equipment alternative with a 5-year life and a 15 percent interest rate is

$$\text{PW} = \$400,000 + [(\$2,000,000 - \$1,000,000)(3.3352)] = \$3,752,000$$

The cost savings associated with each alternative would be:

$$A_1 \text{ (Retain)} = \$0$$
$$A_2 \text{ (Purchase)} = \text{Discounted return} - \text{Initial cost}$$
$$= \$3,752,000 - \$4,000,000$$
$$= -\$248,000$$

The new equipment would not be purchased, as indicated by the operating cost savings for the alternatives.

$$A_1 \text{ (Retain)} = \$0$$

$$A_2 \text{ (Purchase)} = -\$248,000$$

Unlikely events, estimated to have a 1 in 10 chance of occurring, could increase the demands placed on the welding operation by 50 percent. Assume that the division manager (planned change sponsor) is concerned about costs in the welding operation should an increase in demand occur and wants to factor the implications of increased demand into the evaluation. In this situation there would be two future conditions: one reflecting the current demand ($P_1 = .90$) and the other a 50 percent increase ($P_2 = .10$). Each alternative must now be evaluated under the increased demand condition to compare with the current demand condition.

The change in demand can influence the operating cost of both the purchase and retain alternatives. If the old robot welder is fully utilized, no additional capacity could be created in the current system should demand increase. Assume that the only feasible way to increase capacity is to contract out work at a 50 percent increase in cost. This increases operating cost by $1,500,000 and results in a total operating cost of $3,500,000. (A 50 percent increase in activity would increase costs from $2,000,000 to $3,000,000, and a 50 percent increase in unit cost for this $1,000,000 increase would add another $500,000 for a total of $3,500,000.) The purchase option could deal with the increased demand with a 25 percent increase in operating cost, resulting in an operating cost of $1,250,000. Present worth would be computed to reflect the changes in cost caused by the higher level of demand. The present worth of the cost savings of the new equipment would be

$$PW = \$400,000 + [(\$3,500,000 - \$1,250,000)(3.352)] = \$7,942,000$$

The discounted cost savings of each alternative under this condition (a 50 percent increase in demand) would be

$$A_1 \text{ (Retain)} = \text{Increase in operating cost}$$

$$= -\$1,500,000$$

$$A_2 \text{ (Purchase)} = \text{Discounted return} - \text{Purchase cost}$$

$$= \$7,942,000 - \$4,000,000$$

$$= \$3,942,000$$

Selecting the alternative with the greatest value is no longer clear cut. A significant increase in cost can occur for each alternative. The retain alternative results in a $1,500,000 increase in cost when demand is high, but the purchase alternative results in a $248,000 cost increase under a current demand assumption, as shown here:

|  | $C_1$<br>*Current Demand* | $C_2$<br>*50% Increase in Demand* |
|---|---|---|
|  | $P_1 = .90$ | $P_2 = .10$ |
| $A_1$ *(Retain)* | $ 0 | $ −1,500,000 |
| $A_2$ *(Purchase)* | $ −248,000 | $ 3,942,000 |

An expected value rule is used to capture the compensatory aspects of cost savings that can occur. To apply the rule, the analyst weights the savings for each option according to the likelihood of each future condition:

$$\text{Expected value} = \begin{array}{c}\text{Likelihood} \\ \text{of current} \\ \text{demand}\end{array}(\text{savings}) + \begin{array}{c}\text{Likelihood} \\ \text{of increased} \\ \text{demand}\end{array}(\text{savings})$$

Using these data, the calculations are

$$A_1 \text{ (Retain)} = .9(0) + .1(-\$1,500,000) = -\$150,000$$

$$A_2 \text{ (Purchase)} = .9(-\$248,000) + .1(\$3,942,000) = \$171,000$$

By folding in the unlikely prospects of an increased demand, the purchase alternative would be preferred.

## Sensitivity Analysis

When one is unsure about the likelihood of future conditions, it is desirable to make the best possible estimates and then treat these estimates as assumptions. Using sensitivity analysis, a sponsor can pose "what if" questions to determine the implications of making various assumptions about future conditions. Sensitivity analysis is a technique that progressively relaxes important assumptions to determine how these assumptions influence the choice among alternatives. The magnitude of a change in the likelihood of future conditions that would lead to a different choice is determined. Sensitivity analysis can be applied to all types of subjective information and to objective information (e.g., cost) that can have large measurement errors.

To use sensitivity analysis in the robot welder decision, each alternative is evaluated by treating the likelihood of the future conditions as an unknown. Applying the Hurwicz principle (Raiffa, 1970), the likelihood of increased demand is represented by an unknown, designated as $P$ in the expected value format, as shown:

$$A_1 \text{ (Retain)} = (1 - P)(0) + P(-\$1,500,000)$$

$$A_2 \text{ (Purchase)} = (1 - P)(-\$248,000) + P(\$3,942,000)$$

Simplifying, these equations reduce to

$$A_1 = -\$1,500,000P$$

$$A_2 = -\$248,000 + P(\$4,190,000)$$

The payoffs can be plotted by having $P$ take on values of 0 and 1 (see Figure 15-7).

|       | $P = 0$      | $P = 1$      |
|-------|--------------|--------------|
| $A_1$ | $ 0          | −$1,500,000  |
| $A_2$ | $ −248,000   | $3,942,000   |

The break-even value of $P$, where operating cost savings are the same for both alternatives, is found by setting the equations equal and solving for $P$.

$$-\$1,500,000P = -\$248,000 + P(\$4,190,000)$$

$$\$248,000 = P(\$4,190,000 + \$1,500,000)$$

$$P = \frac{\$248,000}{\$5,690,000} = .044$$

This computation shows that the purchase alternative is the less risky of the two options. Even if one assumes that the prospects of increased demand are very unlikely (e.g., $P < .05$), the purchase choice has a greater payoff (operating cost savings). The plot of the linear relationship in Figure 15-7 provides visual appreciation. Note that the cost savings of the purchase alternative is greater than the cost savings for the retain alternative for nearly all assumptions that can be made about increases in volume, which makes it easy to defend purchasing the equipment.

### Sensitivity Analysis Applied to Criteria

Assume that a second type of robot welder (system 2) is uncovered during planning. The chief engineer claims that system 2 improves product reliability. The following cost savings data were collected for the two types of robot welders:

|                   | Current Demand | 50% Increase |
|-------------------|----------------|--------------|
| $A_1$ (system 1)  | $ −248,000     | $3,942,000   |
| $A_2$ (system 2)  | $ −1,000,000   | $ 500,000    |

The following data were collected for the robot welders in a pilot test, expressed as the percentage of nondefective welds:

|       | Current Demand | 50% Increase |
|-------|----------------|--------------|
| $A_1$ | 99%            | 97%          |
| $A_2$ | 99%            | 98%          |

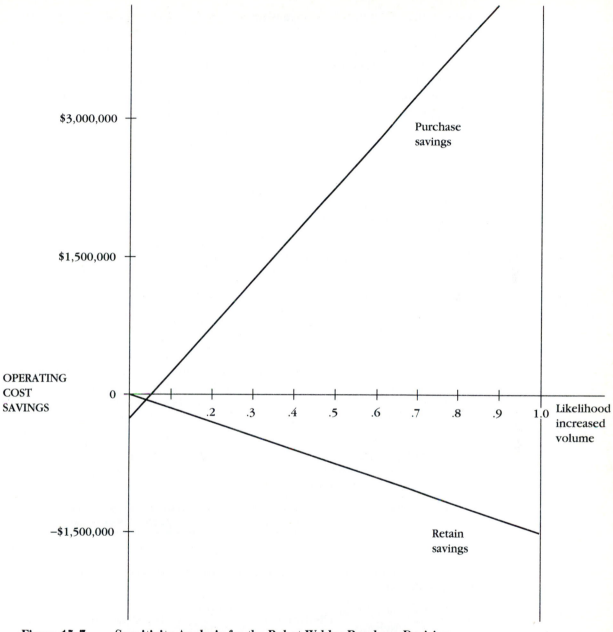

**Figure 15-7 ▲ Sensitivity Analysis for the Robot Welder Purchase Decision**

Assume that the firm has no means to carry out 100% inspection and remain competitive. Because defective welds can lead to a loss of business, the chief engineer claims that quality is twice as important as cost savings and calls for the adoption of $A_2$. Accepting the chief engineer's criteria weighing for the moment, the analyst converts cost savings to the same scale as reliability by a linear transformation in which the lowest-cost value ($-\$1,000,000$) becomes zero and the highest ($\$3,942,000$) becomes 1.0. The intermediate values are

$$\frac{(\$1,000,000 - \$248,000)}{(\$1,000,000 + \$3,940,000)} = .152$$

$$\frac{(\$1,000,000 + \$500,000)}{(\$1,000,000 + \$3,940,000)} = .304$$

The rescaled cost saving values are:

|       | Current Demand | 50% Increase |
|-------|----------------|--------------|
| $A_1$ | .152           | 1.00         |
| $A_2$ | 0              | .304         |

If the chief engineer claims that no robot welder could be sold with less than a 95 percent reliability, the relevant scale for reliability runs from 95 percent to 100 percent. Because the reliability scale has no relevance below values of 95 percent reliability, data must also be rescaled, as shown:

|       | Current Demand | 50% Increase |
|-------|----------------|--------------|
| $A_1$ | $(99 - 95)/(100 - 95) = .80$ | $(97 - 95)/(100 - 95) = .40$ |
| $A_2$ | $(99 - 95)/(100 - 95) = .80$ | $(98 - 95)/(100 - 95) = .60$ |

Now the reliability and cost savings values have comparable scales and can be combined as shown:

$$\text{Payoff} = \frac{\text{Weight for}}{\text{Reliability}} (\text{Reliability}) + \frac{\text{Weight for}}{\text{Cost Savings}} (\text{Cost Savings})$$

$$A_1 \ (\text{Current Demand}) = 2/3(.8) + 1/3(.152) = .584$$

$$A_1 \ (\text{Increased Demand}) = 2/3(.4) + 1/3(1.0) = .600$$

$$A_2 \ (\text{Current Demand}) = 2/3(.8) + 1/3(0) = .533$$

$$A_2 \ (\text{Increased Demand}) = 2/3(.6) + 1/3(.304) = .501$$

The outcomes that combine cost with reliability are as follows:

|  | Current Demand ($P = .9$) | 50% Increase ($P = .1$) |
|---|---|---|
| $A_1$ | .584 | .600 |
| $A_2$ | .533 | .501 |

The expected value rule yields

$$A_1 = .9\,(.584) + .1\,(.6) \quad = .59$$

$$A_2 = .9\,(.533) + .1\,(.501) = .53$$

Shown these results, the chief engineer refuses to accept them, claiming that reliability is too important to ignore regardless of how it was initially weighted.

To deal with this situation, the analyst treats the criteria weights as unknowns and applies sensitivity analysis. By letting $b$ equal the weight attached to reliability and $1 - b$ the weight of cost savings in the expected value formulation yields

$$A_1 = [(b).8 + (1 - b).152].9 + [(b).4 + (1 - b)1.0].1$$

$$A_2 = [(b).8 + (1 - b)0].9 + [(b).6 + (1 - b).304].1$$

Solving for the weight attached to reliability, $b$, in each equation yields

$$A_1 = .523b + .237$$

$$A_2 = .750b + .030$$

The break-even point is determined by setting the payoffs equal and solving for $b$:

$$.52b + .24 = .75b + .03$$

$$.21 = .23b$$

$$b = \frac{.21}{.23} = .91 \text{ (the weight attached to reliability)}$$

$$1 - b = 1 - .91 = .09 \text{ (the weight attached to cost savings)}$$

This calculation shows that cost savings must have little importance for the chief engineer's robot welder ($A_2$) to be preferable. The analysis indicates how cost savings has been disregarded by the chief engineer and how the division manager can defend the choice of the robot welder with the greater cost savings by showing how quality considerations were taken into account. The firm must subordinate cost savings to a 1 percent reduction in defective welds before the chief engineer's robot welder would be preferred. In most cases, this argument would put proponents of system 2 with the poorer cost savings on the defensive because the savings could be put to use elsewhere. It would be hard for the chief engineer to argue against saving money without seeming provincial.

### Determining the Value of Additional Information

Sponsors are often confronted with a choice of whether or not to seek information that clarifies the alternatives before a selection among alternatives can be made. The sponsor must decide what to pay for the clarifying information. For example, in the robot welder decision, assume that the company's strategic plan calls for an expansion of the welding operation. In the plan new contracts are to be sought that will increase demand by 50 to 100 percent. The chief engineer, citing the plan, claims that the more reliable robot welder (system 2) is now justified considering only cost savings. Potential cost savings for the new alternatives are as follows:

|       | 50% Increase ($P = .6$) | 100% Increase ($P = .4$) |
|-------|-------------------------|--------------------------|
| $A_1$ | $1,000,000              | $4,000,000               |
| $A_2$ | $ 500,000               | $7,000,000               |

The division manager is dubious and is considering proposing a market study. The division manager must estimate how much the company can justify paying for such a study before proposing it to top management.

The expected value rule applied to these values yields

$$A_1 = \$1,000,000(.6) + \$4,000,000(.4) = \$2,200,000$$

$$A_2 = \$\ 500,000(.6) + \$7,000,000(.4) = \$3,100,000$$

These data make the chief engineer's robot welder seem preferable.

Sensitivity analysis is applied to the likelihoods because the division manager is skeptical of the chief engineer's likelihood estimates. Treating these values as assumptions, the analyst makes the likelihood of a 50 percent increase in demand an unknown, designated as $P$, thereby making the likelihood of a 100 percent increase $1 - P$. The expected values for the payoffs are written as

$$A_1 = \$1,000,000P + \$4,000,000(1 - P)$$

$$= -\$3,000,000P + \$4,000,000$$

$$A_2 = \$500,000P + \$7,000,000(1 - P)$$

$$= -\$6,500,000P + \$7,000,000$$

Setting the payoffs equal and solving for $P$ yields

$$-\$3,000,000P + \$4,000,000 = -\$6,500,000P + \$7,000,000$$

$$P = \frac{30}{35} = .857$$

The likelihood of a 50 percent increase in demand must be at least 85 percent to justify the chief engineer's system. This analysis gives the division manager considerable incentive to clarify the market situation. All the division manager has to go on are the estimates provided by the chief engineer, which seem overly optimistic. The division manager must decide how much the company can justify to pay for a market study that clarifies the choice among the alternatives.

The notion of lost opportunity, called "regret," is applied to determine what to pay for the market study. First, the analyst determines what will happen if a 100 percent increase in demand is realized and calculates the lost opportunity for that outcome by subtracting the largest payoff under this condition from the others. The lost opportunity for $A_1$ is $7,000,000 − $4,000,000 or $3,000,000 and the lost opportunity for $A_2$ is $7,000,000 − $7,000,000 or zero. The same logic is applied, assuming that a 50 percent increase in demand *will* occur. The largest payoff is $1,000,000, which is subtracted from the others. For $A_1$ lost opportunity is $1,000,000 − $1,000,000, or zero, and $A_2$ is $1,000,000 − $500,000, or $500,000. The failure to realize an additional $500,000 savings creates a $500,000 regret should a 50 percent increase in demand materialize. These values are shown here as the lost opportunity for cost savings:

|  | 50% Increase (P = .6) | 100% Increase (P = .4) |
|---|---|---|
| $A_1$ | $ 0 | $3, 000, 000 |
| $A_2$ | $500, 000 | $ 0 |

The expected values for the lost opportunity are

$$A_1 = 0(.6) + \$3,000,000(.4) = \$1,200,000$$

$$A_2 = \$500,000(.6) + 0(.4) = \$300,000$$

The minimal expected loss is $300,000, which specifies the maximum amount that can be spent for additional information. The company can justify up to $300,000 for the market study, assuming that the study can provide accurate information.

### Dealing with Unknown Payoffs

A form of sensitivity analysis can also be used to estimate unknown payoffs, such as the amount of insurance to purchase given various assumptions about the prospects of a loss. This type of analysis can also be applied to investments in flood control, provision of spare machines or spare parts, cross-training of people in a work group, and inventory accumulations under the threat of strike. To illustrate the procedure, assume that a company is considering the purchase of a safety device for its welding machines that eliminates injury if correctly used. Experience suggests that when an injury occurs, it will produce litigation. The company has decided to self-insure against such incidents because of the exorbitant premiums insurance carriers impose on firms operating this type of equipment that have had no history of large, or indeed any, claims. Should an injury occur, it would be paid for by drawing on company profits.

Assume that the safety device installed on all machines costs $1,000,000, including all needed assistance to put the device into operation, and can prohibit injury. An injury can occur only if the safety device has been disconnected. Experience suggests that the courts typically dismiss lawsuits for injuries sustained when safety devices have been disconnected by the claimant. If the safety device is not installed and an injury occurs, the company will have to install the safety device to show OSHA and others that it can head off future injuries. The unknowns are the prospect of at least one injury and the cost of an injury. Most companies have no way to estimate these values.

The alternatives can be described as

$$A_1 = \text{purchase the saftey equipment}$$

$$A_2 = \text{delay purchase until an injury occurs}$$

The future conditions are

$$C_1 = \text{no injury}$$

$$C_2 = \text{at least one injury}$$

The data shown next provide an example. In the example, $X$ stands for the cost of an injury, including the costs of litigation and the amount paid. Because the device eliminates an injury when conditions that can create an injury arise (e.g., operator inattentiveness), the cost $X$ occurs only with the delay alternative under injury-provoking conditions.

|  | $C_1$<br>No Injury-<br>Provoking<br>Conditions | $C_2$<br>At Least One<br>Injury-Provoking<br>Condition |
|---|---|---|
| $A_1$ (Purchase) | $1,000,000 | $1,000,000 |
| $A_2$ (Delay) | $      0 | $1,000,000+X |

The likelihood of an injury-provoking condition is treated as an unknown. The chance of avoiding this condition is designated $P$, so the likelihood of conditions that could produce an injury is $1 - P$. The alternatives are assessed by applying the expected value rule as follows:

$$A_1 \text{ (Purchase)} = (P)\$1,000,000 + (1 - P)(\$1,000,000)$$

$$= 1,000,000$$

$$A_2 \text{ (Delay)} = (P)(0) + (1 - P)(\$1,000,000 + X)$$

$$= (1 - P)(\$1,000,000 + X)$$

The purchase decision is preferred when the cost for $A_2$ (delay) is greater than $A_1$ (purchase). This can be represented as follows:

$$A_2 > A_1$$

Substituting payoffs for each alternative yields

$$(1 - P)(\$1,000,000 + X) > \$1,000,000$$

Solving for $X$ yields

$$X > \frac{P}{1 - P}(\$1,000,000)$$

Assigning a value of zero to $P$ represents a pessimistic view, assuming that there is no chance of avoiding an injury. Such a position may have merit if workers are enticed to take risks because their pay is based on incentives tied to piecework. Substituting $P = 0$ reduces the equation to $X > 0$. Even a very small prospect of an injury will make the safety equipment seem justifiable. The optimistic or risk-taking view assigns $P$ a value of 1, taking the position that there is no chance that an injury will occur. Letting $P = 1$ in the equation reduces the equation to $X > \infty$. The cost of an injury would have to be infinitely large before an investment in the safety equipment would be made.

These extremes bracket postures that can be adopted. If the prospect of an injury is thought to be 50 percent, contending that there is one chance in two of experiencing an injury, investing in the safety equipment will create a break-even condition: $X = [.5/(1 - .5)]\ \$1,000,000 = \$1,000,000$. If the prospect of a claim is greater than 50/50, investment in the safety equipment is justified from a cost perspective. (Social responsibility provides a second criterion, which also argues for the purchase of the safety equipment.)

### Sensitivity Analysis with Several Future Conditions

Many evaluations require assumptions about several future conditions. Two approaches can be used. In the first, all future conditions but one are treated in expected value terms. The future conditions are then explored one at a time, applying the same procedure that was illustrated in the first example. For the second approach, future conditions are treated as unknowns and examined together. To demonstrate the analysis for the second case, assume that a company is considering expanding its welding operation because of a steady increase in successful bids for its welding business. The cost of leasing space, buying fixtures, and other related expenditures is $1,000,000. Experience shows that such funds, once committed, are not recoverable. Leases cannot be broken, fixtures have little salvage value, and unused capacity cannot be resold. The standard practice of the firm is to bid on a large number of contracts and select one of two approaches to promote its bid with potential customers. In the past two public relations firms have been used that offer different promotion plans. Experience suggests that promotion improves the prospect of a successful bid. Payoffs in this illustration are expressed as the present worth of profits, determined by discounting an income stream of revenues expected under each alternative less operating costs needed to operate at the demand level produced by promotion. Data that summarize the present worth of profit estimates for a capacity expansion using the two promotional plans are as follows:

| Level of Promotion | Promotional Cost | Demand | Prospects | Profits (present worth) |
|---|---|---|---|---|
| Major | $100,000 | Large | $p = .6$ | $ 10, 000, 000 |
| | (firm 1) | Small | $p = .4$ | $-1, 000, 000 |
| Minor | $ 50,000 | Large | $p = .2$ | $ 5, 000, 000 |
| | (firm 2) | Small | $p = .8$ | $ -500, 000 |

The firm has a competitor. The competitor is small but offers high-quality work that attracts considerable following. The competitor carefully selects bids to insure that each has a high profit potential. The competitor does not compete with

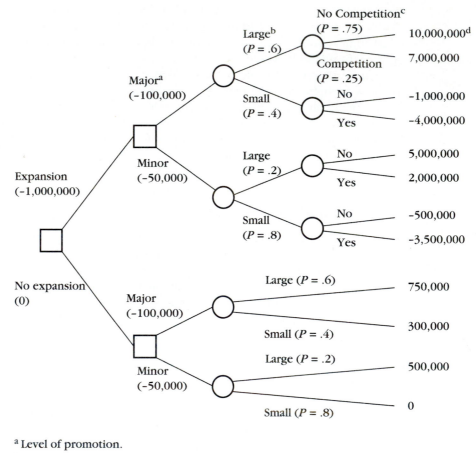

[a] Level of promotion.
[b] Utilization.
[c] Competition in bidding.
[d] Operating profit.

**Figure 15-8 ▲ Decision Tree for Expansion Decision**

all of the firm's bids but when it does compete, the competitor always manages to capture all the work it bids on. For one in every four previous bids made by the firm the competitor also bid on the work and took volume valued at $3,000,000 in present worth terms, no matter what steps the firm used to counter by offering concessions. To reflect the impact of competition when it occurs, $3,000,000 must be subtracted from the profits that result from the two promotion programs.

The CEO does not want to bid on work on which the competitor is also bidding. However, the time needed to increase capacity requires that the firm bid contracts before it finds out whether the competitor has also decided to bid on this work. The CEO has no way to determine whether the competitor has decided to bid before it must make its own commitments. To make matters worse, the competitor seems to have inside information on the firm's plans. The firm's CEO hopes that its market strategy leaks have been plugged. As a result, the CEO believes that there are no good data on the prospect of competition.

The CEO can choose to concentrate promotion on current clients, which creates a "no expansion" alternative. However, for this alternative, promotion would have a smaller impact because of limited capacity in the current facility. The payoffs for the no expansion alternative are also expressed as the present worth of profit increases forecasted when promotion is used. The payoffs are:

| Level of Promotion | Promotion Cost | Demand | Prospects | Payoff |
|---|---|---|---|---|
| Major | $100,000 | Large | $p = .6$ | $ 750,000 |
| | (firm 1) | Small | $p = .4$ | $ 300,000 |
| Minor | $ 50,000 | Large | $p = .2$ | $ 500,000 |
| | (firm 2) | Small | $p = .8$ | $ 0 |

The decision is summarized by the decision tree shown in Figure 15-8.

### Estimation of Payoffs

The decision tree in Figure 15-8 is collapsed using the expected value format:

Payoff $= -$Expansion cost $-$ Promotion cost

$$+ \begin{matrix} \text{Large demand} \\ \text{prospects} \end{matrix} \left[ \begin{matrix} \text{No competition (Profit)} \\ \text{prospects} \end{matrix} + \begin{matrix} \text{Competition (Profit)} \\ \text{prospects} \end{matrix} \right]$$

$$+ \begin{matrix} \text{Small demand} \\ \text{prospects} \end{matrix} \left[ \begin{matrix} \text{No competition (Profit)} \\ \text{prospects} \end{matrix} + \begin{matrix} \text{Competition (Profit)} \\ \text{prospects} \end{matrix} \right]$$

Using the best estimates of future conditions (large demand = .6, small demand = .4; competition = .25, no competition = .75) and profits produces the following evaluations:

$$\text{Expansion and major promotion} \quad = -\$1,000,000 - \$100,000$$
$$+ .6\,[.75(\$10,000,000)$$
$$+.25(\$7,000,000)]$$
$$+ .4[.75(-\$1,000,000)$$
$$+.25(-\$4,000,000)]$$
$$= \$3,750,000$$

$$\text{Expansion and minor promotion} \quad = -\$1,200,000$$
$$\text{No expansion and major promotion} \ = \$470,000$$
$$\text{No expansion and minor promotion} \ = \$\ 50,000$$

The expected values suggest that expanding capacity with a major promotional package is the best alternative. However, the CEO worries that if the strategy leaks have not been plugged, the chance of competition may increase above 1 in 4. The CEO also believes that the historical impact of promotion may have been eroded because everyone has adopted promotional tactics, which may have diluted its impact.

Each of the four options can be subjected to a sensitivity analysis that treats the likelihoods of both future conditions as unknowns. The most favorable option, calling for expansion and major promotion, is selected for sensitivity analysis. This option with the likelihoods expressed as unknowns is

$$\text{Target profit} = -\$1,100,000 + P[p(\$10,000,000) + (1-p)(\$7,000,000)]$$
$$+ (1-P)[p(-\$1,000,000) + (1-p)(-\$4,000,000)]$$

$P$ represents the prospects of a large demand and $p$ the likelihood that the firm can avoid competition. Simplifying the equation in terms of the unknowns yields

$$\text{Target profit} = -\$5,100,000 + \$11,000,000P + \$3,000,000p$$

Solving for $P$ yields

$$P = \frac{(\$5,100,000 + \text{Target profit}) - \$3,000,000p}{\$11,000,000}$$

To carry out sensitivity analysis with three unknowns and one equation, the value of $P$ is determined by selecting feasible values for target profit and all possible values for $p$, the chance of avoiding competition. The maximum profit (in present worth terms) that the expansion can produce is $8,900,000, the $10,000,000 maximum profit less the $1,000,000 in expansion cost and $100,000 in promotional costs. For the purpose of exploration, the analyst sets profit at zero, beginning with the smallest target value of any interest.

Setting the target profit at zero reduces the equation to

$$P = \frac{\$5,100,000 - \$3,000,000p}{\$11,000,000}$$

Now let $p$, the prospect of avoiding competition, take the extreme values of zero and one. Letting $p = 0$, or making competition a certainty, yields:

$$P = \frac{\$5,100,000 - \$0}{\$11,000,000} = .4636$$

Letting $p = 1$, making no competition a certainty, yields

$$P = \frac{\$5,100,000 - \$3,000,000}{\$11,000,000} = .191$$

Considering target profit in \$1 million increments and solving for extreme values of $p$ produces the following values for $P$, the prospect of a large demand:

| Target Profit | Values of P when | |
| --- | --- | --- |
| | $p = 0$ | $p = 1$ |
| \$        0 | .464 | .191 |
| 1,000,000 | .545 | .282 |
| 2,000,000 | .645 | .372 |
| 3,000,000 | .736 | .464 |
| 4,000,000 | .820 | .554 |
| 5,000,000 | .920 | .645 |
| 6,000,000 | | .736 |
| 7,000,000 | | .827 |
| 8,000,000 | | .918 |

A family of straight lines results that can be plotted on a grid for the unknowns $P$ (prospects of a large demand) and $p$ (prospects of avoiding competition), as shown in Figure 15-9.

*"What If" Questioning.* Figure 15-9 can be subjected to "what if" questioning by the CEO. To conduct a sensitivity analysis, the sponsor notes that the previous estimates of $p$ and $P$ were .75 and .6, respectively. Entering these values in Figure 15-10 produces the expected value for profit of between \$3,000,000 and \$4,000,000. A more conservative estimate would be to assume a 50/50 chance of avoiding competition and having a large demand. Using Figure 15-9 and entering $p = .5$ and $P = .5$, the CEO discovers that profit for this contingency would be about 2.0 million. Using this kind of logic, the CEO can carry out various kinds of "what if" questioning. For instance, assume that the prospects of a large demand is clarified by experts who contend that it falls between .4 and .6. Drawing vertical lines at these points on Figure 15-10 allows the CEO to explore the implications of making a range of supportable assumptions about the competitor. To make these assumptions clear, the payoff lines outside the expected demand region are shown as dashed lines (see Figure 15-10) to rule out payoff possibilities outside the .4 to .6 region.

To conduct sensitivity analysis, the CEO entertains various assumptions about competition. Competition must be quite likely (80 percent) to push profit to zero, shown as the lowest horizontal line in Figure 15-10. A 50/50 competition assessment results in a minimum profit of nearly \$1,000,000 and a maximum profit of \$3,000,000. If the competitor's past history is used as a guide (75 percent chance of no competition), a zero profit results only when the prospect of a large demand falls below 25 percent, well below the demand thought to be attainable by experts. A *very* conservative, 1 in 5, estimate of no competition produces a profit range of \$0 to \$2,000,000.

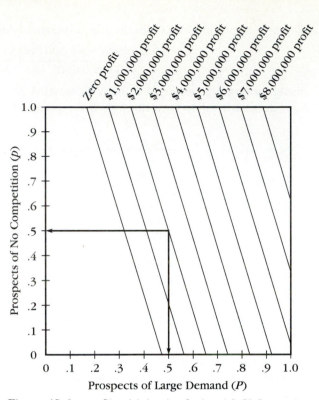

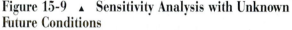

**Figure 15-9** ▲ **Sensitivity Analysis with Unknown Future Conditions**

Reprinted from Nutt (1989a).

The prospects of competition can be given a similar treatment. A range of values of .20 to .75 for no competition is bracketed by the top and bottom horizontal lines in Figure 15-10. For these values, prospects of a high demand above .4 will avoid losses and can produce profits of up to $8,000,000.

This assessment shows that the CEO need not be concerned with the competitor's plans. Not enough revenues are syphoned to make the expansion strategy unprofitable, even when very conservative estimates of future demand are made.

The best option identified by an expected value analysis is usually selected for multiple sensitivity analysis. However, the same type of analysis can be applied to all options. In this example, the options identified by the expansion, minor promotion, and use of existing capacity with each promotion package could also be subjected to sensitivity analysis. If the computations produce different choices, the sponsor can assess the choices by treating the prospects associated with all future conditions as unknowns. The analysis is used to prune the options, as well as to reassure the sponsor about how payoffs can be changed by chance events.

## Weighting the Criteria

Several techniques can be used to weight criteria. Most of the ranking techniques were presented in Chapter 10, so this discussion will show how each can be used

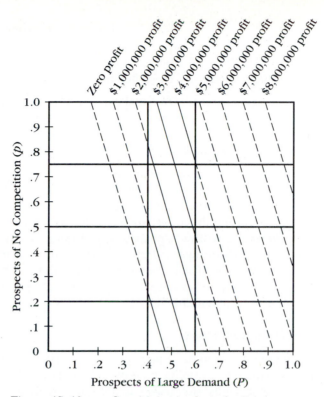

**Figure 15-10**  ▲  **Sensitivity Analysis for Ranges of Expectations**

Reprinted from Nutt (1989a).

to weight criteria. For example, consider an agency such as the American Heart Association or the National Heart Institute in the National Institutes of Health (NIH) evaluating potential program areas. To develop project priorities, criteria such as target group size, disability relieved, quality of life, years of life gained, and cost are used (Nutt, 1980a). These criteria are defined as follows:

| | |
|---|---|
| Net target group | The total number of people affected defines the population of risk. The net target group is the target group times the expected survival rate following treatment. |
| Disability relieved | The change in the level of disability after treatment is defined by a disability level. The levels are defined by: |

| | |
|---|---|
| Class I: | People with no symptoms and no limitations |
| Class II: | People with problems suffering no limitations where physical activity would cause fatigue |
| Class III: | People with problems that cause a slight limitation that occurs with strenuous activity |
| Class IV: | People with problems that cause a marked limitation, experienced when engaging in mild forms of ordinary activity |

| | |
|---|---|
| Class V: | People with problems that cause severe limitations that occur with any physical activity and at rest |
| Quality of Life | Defined as the residual disability after treatment |
| Years of life gained | The difference in years of survival, with and without treatment |
| Cost | The total expenditures per individual to apply the best available treatment |

### Anchored Rating Scales

The ARS approach uses a continuous scale with descriptors that elaborate the scale, defining the scale's increments and the zero point. To illustrate the ARS, criteria recommended to select projects for the health care funding agency could be presented to a sponsor using the format shown in Figure 15-11.

Criteria can be listed alphabetically or randomly to avoid placement biases. The sponsor or decision maker draws an arrow from each of the criterion to a point on the linear scale that indicates his or her view of its importance. The assigned values are normalized in order to convert them to percentages. These values would be averaged to determine the weight assigned by a group.

### Paired Comparisons

Considering the criteria in pairs permits the sponsor to concentrate on the differences between two criteria, thereby reducing the information processing demands. The sponsor or decision maker is presented with all criteria combinations. He or she considers each pair of criteria and indicates which is more important. Using the example that has cost, disability relieved, quality of life, target group size, and years of life gained as criteria for the selection of projects by a funding agency, assume that the following choices were made:

| Pairs | Choice |
|---|---|
| Cost versus disability | Cost |
| Cost versus quality | Quality |
| Cost versus target group | Target group |
| Cost versus years | Years |
| Disability versus quality | Quality |
| Disability versus target group | Target group |
| Disability versus years | Years |
| Quality versus target group | Quality |
| Quality versus years | Years |
| Target group versus years | Years |

The chart shown in Figure 15-12 is used to tabulate a weight for each criterion, following the procedure described in Chapter 10.

### Rank Weight

This technique requires the sponsor or decision maker first to rank the criteria and then to specify their importance. Each of the criteria is placed on an index

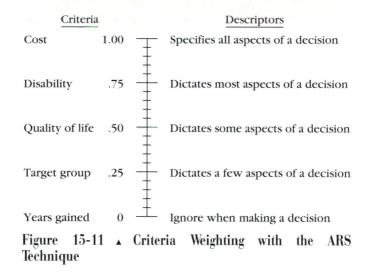

| Criteria | | Descriptors |
|---|---|---|
| Cost | 1.00 | Specifies all aspects of a decision |
| Disability | .75 | Dictates most aspects of a decision |
| Quality of life | .50 | Dictates some aspects of a decision |
| Target group | .25 | Dictates a few aspects of a decision |
| Years gained | 0 | Ignore when making a decision |

**Figure 15-11 ▲ Criteria Weighting with the ARS Technique**

card. The sponsor ranks the criteria by ordering the cards and then recording the times more important on each card. An odds procedure can be used. The most important criterion is given a value of one. Each of the remaining criteria is compared with the most important and a times more important value is recorded. If the second criterion is seen as twice as important as the first, a value of one-half is recorded for the second criterion. The odds ratios are normalized to convert them to percentages, indicating the value of a criterion weight. The rationale for the odds

| | Cost | Disability Relieved | Quality of Life | Target Group Size | Years of Life Gained |
|---|---|---|---|---|---|
| Cost | ✕ | 0 | 1 | 1 | 1 |
| Disability Relieved | 1 | ✕ | 1 | 1 | 1 |
| Quality of Life | 0 | 0 | ✕ | 0 | 1 |
| Target Group | 0 | 0 | 1 | ✕ | 1 |
| Years | 0 | 0 | 0 | 0 | ✕ |
| Raw Score | 1 | 0 | 3 | 2 | 4 |
| Normalized Score | 10% | 0% | 30% | 20% | 40% |

**Figure 15-12 ▲ Paired Comparisons Used to Determine Criteria Weights**

procedure was described in Chapter 10. Ranking with index numbers (e.g., 1 = unimportant and 5 = critically important), a linear scale like that used in the ARS technique, or a log scale can be used in place of the odds procedure.

### Direct Assignment

To weight large numbers of criteria, integers can be associated with descriptors, such as 10 = most important and 1 = least important, and assigned to each criterion to describe its importance. These values, when normalized, give a weight to each criterion in terms of a percentage. Six to eight intervals and index numbers are typically used. With large numbers of criteria, it is helpful to put each on an index card and have the decision makers sort the criteria into several piles associated with each label. Typically, several re-sorts occur and should be encouraged. Each pile has a value assigned and a label:

| Label | Value |
|---|---|
| Most desirable | 10 |
| Highly desirable | 8 |
| Desirable | 6 |
| Somewhat desirable | 4 |
| Marginally desirable | 2 |
| Undesirable | 0 |

### Reconsideration in Groups

Groups should use the VDV approach discussed in Chapter 10. First, an initial judgment is made. Next, the group's initial consensus value for each criterion's weight is presented. The initial consensus is used to provoke discussion. Each member can argue for a higher or a lower criterion weight by citing his or her past experience and facts. After discussion, the weights are reestimated and used to reflect the consensus of the group.

## Making Subjective Estimates of Future Conditions

The previous section illustrates how to collect information that weights the criteria. This section illustrates how to make subjective estimates of the likelihoods of future conditions. Many of the same techniques can be used.

### Anchored Rating Scales

The ARS technique helps the sponsor to make fine discriminations for the probabilities assigned to each future condition. As with criteria weighting, the descriptors help the sponsor select a likelihood value that is congruent with a mutually understood concept. The scale is similar to that used for criteria weighting, with future conditions listed in place of the criteria. In this example, 250 percent of past demand, 100 percent of past demand, 75 percent of past demand, and 50 percent of past demand is used. The decision maker draws a line from each future condition to the scale to indicate its likelihood of occurring. A scale like that shown in Figure 15-13 is used. The probabilities are drawn directly from the scale.

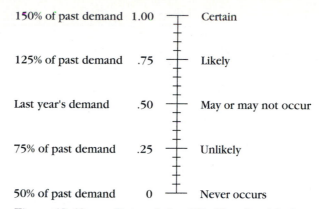

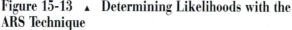

**Figure 15-13** ▲ **Determining Likelihoods with the ARS Technique**

## Paired Comparisons

Paired comparisons can sort out likelihood values for the future conditions by asking the sponsor which of two conditions is more likely. Consider an example where demand is forecasted to be 200 percent, 150 percent, and 50 percent of last year's demand. (Finer discriminations are desirable but unnecessary for purposes of illustration.) Assume that the following choices are made:

| *Pairs* | *More Likely Outcome* |
|---|---|
| 200 versus 150 | 150 |
| 200 versus 100 | 100 |
| 200 versus 50 | 200 |
| 150 versus 100 | 150 |
| 150 versus 50 | 150 |
| 100 versus 50 | 100 |

The probabilities for each condition are sorted out in Figure 15-14.

## Rank-Weight

Each future condition is placed on an index card. First, the sponsor sorts the cards to rank the conditions in terms of their likelihood. Next, the sponsor places an odds ratio on each card, indicating the times more likely one condition is than the next. After normalizing, these values can be used as probability estimates. (Groups would also use the VDV approach.)

## Direct Assignment

To estimate probabilities, values and labels would be created as shown on the next page:

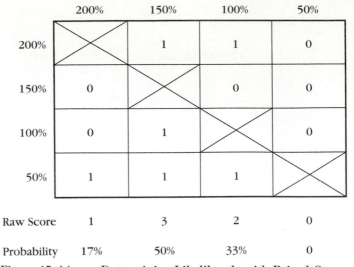

| | 200% | 150% | 100% | 50% |
|---|---|---|---|---|
| 200% | ✕ | 1 | 1 | 0 |
| 150% | 0 | ✕ | 0 | 0 |
| 100% | 0 | 1 | ✕ | 0 |
| 50% | 1 | 1 | 1 | ✕ |
| Raw Score | 1 | 3 | 2 | 0 |
| Probability | 17% | 50% | 33% | 0 |

**Figure 15-14 ▲ Determining Likelihoods with Paired Comparisons**

| *Label* | *Value* |
|---|---|
| Certain | 10 |
| High certainty | 8 |
| Considerable certainty | 6 |
| Some certainty | 4 |
| Little certainty | 2 |
| No certainty | 0 |

When large numbers of future conditions are to be compared, each is placed on an index card. The sponsor sorts them into piles with labels. Considerable sorting and re-sorting are desirable until the conditions found in each pile stabilizes, indicating that reliable designations have been made. The probabilities are estimated by normalizing the values assigned to future conditions in this way.

## ▲ CARRYING OUT EVALUATIONS

The techniques discussed in this chapter are used to develop evaluation information. These techniques are summarized in Figure 15-15. The demands for sophistication in the collection and aggregation of evaluation data are dictated by the importance of the planned change effort.

The selection among sources of evaluative information is governed by both opportunity and the need for precision. Some evaluative situations may prohibit pilot testing, forcing simulated performance data to be gathered. In other situations, subjective estimates must be used because neither simulations nor pilots can be carried out. Although generalizations are difficult to make, precision is generally greatest with a field test or pilot, declines somewhat with a simulation, and falls considerably when subjective estimates are used. When a planned change effort is

EVALUATION INFORMATION SOURCES

|  | Pilot Programs | Simulation | Subjective Estimation |
|---|---|---|---|
| **Subjective Techniques**<br><br>1. Advantage-disadvantage<br>2. Profile<br>3. Scoring<br>4. Hybrids |  |  |  |
| **Qualitative Techniques**<br><br>5. Balance sheet<br>6. Stakeholder analysis<br>7. Assumptional analysis |  |  |  |
| **Quantitative Techniques**<br><br>8. Elimination by aspects<br>9. Decision trees<br>10. Sensitivity analysis |  |  |  |

EVALUATIVE APPROACHES

**Figure 15-15  ▲  Evaluation Approaches**

seen as having critical importance, the evaluation of alternative plans should attempt to use performance data from pilot programs when possible and simulations in other instances. Subjective data are less desirable.

Techniques that aggregate and draw out the implications of evaluation data also depend on the importance that plans have to their sponsor. During some stages of planning, subjective techniques were recommended because they could sort quickly among large numbers of alternatives. For instance, in the concept development stage, morphology generates a large number of options that can be screened using the profile or scoring techniques. If the assessment is somewhat more demanding, the weight-rank or hybrid technique can be used. Factoring the evaluation task into its constituent elements prior to an assessment will improve the reliability of most subjective estimates.

When fewer alternatives must be compared, and the choice has considerable importance to the organization, a quantitative technique should be used. As the implications of the choice for the organization grow, environmental factors must be considered using decision trees to aggregate criterion values for each alternative. Sensitivity analysis helps the sponsor and others to take steps to deal with risk according to what is knowable about the choice among alternatives. When faced with the need to make a short-fuse choice and many criteria are deemed relevant, sponsors can apply the elimination-by-aspects technique. This technique has quantitative precision and improves a sponsor's consistency in applying large numbers of criteria.

Sponsors confronted with alternatives that have criteria and/or attributes that resist quantification should apply one or more of the qualitative techniques. Balance sheet and stakeholders techniques can deal with political and ethical issues that are important but difficult to quantify with criteria. Assumptional analysis draws out the implications of political and ethical issues and suggests areas that merit study before a choice among alternatives is made.

Finally, the choice among planned change alternatives may effect a number of people. In this type of situation, a consensus is sought using a group process technique combined with a technique that can help to rank the alternatives. This approach exposes the range of views in key power centers and explores evaluation information as it emerges. An adroitly managed group will note who objects and the rationale behind these objections before choosing among alternatives.

Evaluation is an essential ingredient in a planned change process. Although some techniques are better than others, a formal evaluation is essential. As Bennis (1989) points out, "Only art is its own verification."

## ▲ Key Points

1. Evaluative information drawn from pilots, simulations, or subjective estimates is used to determine the merits of alternatives that survive the detailing stage of a planned change process.

2. Subjective techniques help the sponsor and other key parties make judgments about the extent alternatives meet relevant criteria, pooling these judgments across the criteria and decision makers. These techniques are used when alternatives need to be screened to shorten the list of options, when the sponsor lacks the time needed to make quantitative comparisons, and when quantitative information is prohibitively costly or suspect.

3. Qualitative techniques help the sponsor to deal with criteria that resist quantification, such as ethical and political concerns posed by the choice among alternatives.

4. Quantitative techniques determine the value of an alternative by applying criteria, such as cost and quality, and considering how the criteria are influenced by the level of demand and other future conditions. The value of each alternative is weighted according to the likelihood of these future conditions and the extent to which it satisfies the criteria. Elimination-by-aspects can be used to efficiently deal with large numbers of criteria. This technique can be used to shorten a list of seemingly viable options by applying quantitative norms.

5. Several types of sensitivity analyses can be used to manage the uncertainty that often arises when selecting among alternatives in a planned change process. To cope with the uncertainty in future conditions, the analyst determines what

must be assumed about uncertain future events, such as inflation, that can make one course of action better than another. If inflation must be kept below historically observed levels to make an option viable, this option becomes high risk. Criteria such as cost and quality are often used to argue for the selection of an alternative. Both are important but, like most criteria, resist precise weighting. Sensitivity analysis can be used to identify the trade-offs between key criteria to determine how much weight must be attached to each to justify the adoption of an alternative. This approach gives the sponsor a means to pose questions about trade-offs, such as how much importance can be accorded to cost to cater to the demands for quality stemming from a firm's sales force. Unknowns, such as what to pay for market research, can also be determined. The alternative with the smallest expected value of lost opportunity identifies how much can be spent to gather additional information.

## ▲  Case

### *The Iranian Rescue Mission Case*

The overthrow of the shah of Iran created a backlash of intense anti-American feeling in Iran. For reasons still not clear, the titular leaders of Iran authorized the taking of American diplomats as hostages, violating a previously ironclad principle of diplomatic immunity for embassy personnel stationed in a foreign country, a principle officially adhered to by every country on the globe. The nightly spectacle on the evening television news programs of lunatics menacing Americans supposedly protected by diplomatic immunity galvanized the country. Enormous pressure was brought to bear to free the hostages, no matter what the cost.

Responding to this pressure, President Carter authorized a rescue mission. Helicopters were flown from an aircraft carrier to a remote spot in the Iranian desert. The plan called for the helicopters to assemble in the desert, fly to the Iranian capital of Tehran, some thousand miles away, land in the center of a populous and crowded city, take the hostages, by force if need be, and return the way they came. A sandstorm intervened before the second leg of the flight that was to carry the rescuers to Tehran could begin. One helicopter's engines, fouled by sand from the storm, malfunctioned on take-off. With its pilot blinded by the storm, the helicopter collided with a transport plane that was to carry out the hostages, killing eight of the would-be rescuers. Calls to the aircraft carrier revealed that there were no functional backup helicopters. In the ensuing chaos, the rescue was aborted, and the surviving members of the rescue team returned to the carrier.

The decision to rescue was vehemently criticized. Critics claimed that, even with good weather, such a rescue was sure to fail because of impossible logistics. The distance to the Iranian capital, finding nearly a hundred people who might have been dispersed, and ferrying them out of a crowded city made the rescue attempt seem foolhardy at best. According to some critics, the helicopter accident was grimly fortuitous because it averted a nearly certain larger loss of life had the rescuers reached Tehran. The sorry state of the helicopters' level of readiness, which was revealed in subsequent TV news stories, made the rescue attempt seem even more ill-advised.

The Iranian rescue decision was riddled with conflict. Speculation about the leadership of Iran was futile because information was either lacking or contradictory. Beliefs about who was in control and who could act as a spokesperson resulted in heated disagreement. All conceivable responses seemed to have undesirable consequences for U.S. foreign policy and little chance of freeing the hostages.    ▲

## ▲  Exercises

1. Apply the hybrid technique to a choice among apartments. Use the following criteria: rent, bus line access, pets, deposit amount, children, security, maintenance, lease terms on damage, pool, spa and sauna, party room, tennis court, parking garage, extra storage, washer-dryer hook-up, laundry nearby, gas or electric, cable TV, number of square feet, number of bedrooms, number of bathrooms, distance to work, distance to downtown. State your preferences and set up a format, like that in Table 15-4, to realize your preferences. Use three criteria in each screen. How would you pilot test your format?

2. Set up the elimination-by-aspects technique to select an apartment, using the criteria in Exercise 1. Evaluate two apartments and compare your results to that obtained in Exercise 1. Are your choices alike or different? Why?

3. Former President Carter initiated a rescue mission to extract U.S. embassy hostages taken captive by Iran in 1979. Review the Iranian rescue mission case and then examine this option using the balance sheet technique. Fill out all the cells in Table 15-5.

4. Consider the Iranian rescue mission case and apply the stakeholder technique to the alternatives of "rescue" and "diplomatic initiative." Identify the stakeholders. Rank them according to your values. Interpret your ratings. What would you do? Why?

5. Apply the stakeholder technique to the supply management, the community health center, or the telecommunication cases that follow Chapter 9. Assume that one option is to do nothing and compare this option to the one considered in the case. Deal with at least three of the stakeholders in the case you select. Select an option and defend your choice.

6. Apply the assumptional analysis technique to the Iranian rescue mission case. What assumptions must you make about each stakeholder for the alternatives of "rescue" and "diplomatic initiatives"? Assume that you are a decision maker and rate these assumptions using the procedure described in the book. What would you recommend after examining the importance-certainty charts for the options?

7. Apply the assumptional analysis technique to the supply management case, the community health center case, or the telecommunications case that follows Chapter 9. As in Exercise 5, assume that one option is to do nothing and contrast this option with the one considered in the case. Take the role of

the sponsor. Uncover two assumptions for each stakeholder found in Exercise 5 and then rate these assumptions, following the procedures for assumptional analysis found in the book. Review the importance-certainty charts for each option. Which option would you choose? Defend your position.

8. The chief engineer in a firm wants a new flexible manufacturing system and has presented the CEO with the following data on cost savings:

|  | $C_1$ Current Demand | $C_2$ 50% Increase |
|---|---|---|
| $A_1$ (Old system) | $ 0 | $-300,000 |
| $A_2$ (New system) | $-500,000 | $ 400,000 |

a. Assuming that the likelihood of current demand is 80 percent, make the choice using the uncertainty decision rule.

b. Is this decision rule compensatory? Why?

9. Assume that the chief engineer contends that the decision cannot be made with just cost savings data and offers the following data on reliability that compares the two systems in Exercise 8.

|  | Current | 50% Increase |
|---|---|---|
| $A_1$ | 99% | 97% |
| $A_2$ | 99% | 98% |

a. Do a sensitivity analysis on the reliability data. What did you find? Do we need to merge the savings and reliability data?

b. Assuming that merging the reliability and cost savings data were needed, how would you do it? Carry out the computations. What does the index mean? Do a sensitivity analysis on $b$, the weight of the reliability data.

10. Assume that a company is considering establishing a reference laboratory and to do so must purchase one of two testing systems. The director of R&D prefers $A_2$, the more elaborate system, and claims that demand justifies the added expense. Cost savings estimated for the two systems for 50 percent and 100 percent increases in demand are:

|  | 50% Increase ($P = .7$) | 100% Increase ($P = .3$) |
|---|---|---|
| $A_1$ | $100,000 | $300,000 |
| $A_2$ | $ 50,000 | $600,000 |

The CEO thinks that the demand for the laboratory is too optimistic.

a. Do a sensitivity analysis and interpret the results. Assume that the firm is in a hostile market for lab services. If the market becomes favorable for a lab (e.g., competitors leave), what decision would you make?

b. How much can the CEO justify paying for a market study that clarifies demand prospects?

# 16 Practicing Planned Change and Changing Practice

▲ ▲ ▲　▲ ▲ ▲ ▲ ▲ ▲ ▲ ▲ ▲ ▲ ▲ ▲ ▲ ▲ ▲

In this chapter difficulties with process management that lead to "pseudo" planned change are considered. This assessment is followed by a discussion of planned change principles. If followed, these principles can overcome many of the difficulties that prompt pseudoplanned change.

# ▲   PSEUDOPLANNED CHANGE

Some forms of planned change leave the process undermanaged. In other cases, the process can be misdirected. When sponsors manipulate the process or ignore its management, pseudoplanned change or pseudoplanning results (Nutt, 1984d).

Pseudoplanning has three sources: approach, behavior, and monitoring. Approach-based pseudoplanning results when a project is carried out in an unstructured manner or stresses analysis. Behavioral pseudoplanning stems from sponsors who intervene capriciously with the process. Pseudoplanning is monitoring based when the sponsor exercises too little or too much control over the process. Various forms of pseudoplanning in each of these categories are described to illustrate how planned change can malfunction through poor leadership or poor practice.

## Behaviorally Based Pseudoplanning

Behavioral problems occur when the sponsor makes errors in prescribing what the process is to do. These errors stem from inappropriate assumptions about needs or opportunities that are specified by the sponsor. Six types of pseudoplanning can occur.

### What's the Problem

A common form of pseudoplanning occurs when the sponsor fails to give a thoughtful problem diagnosis. The formulation stage in planned change is skipped or finessed by the sponsor, who sees all statements about objectives as obvious. Attempts to set objectives are resisted. Such sponsors are likely to misdirect the process and to solve the wrong problem.

Problem misperceptions can stem from anecdotes, conflict, and outright misrepresentations. *Anecdotes* represent isolated incidents that provide a poor basis to make an assessment of need or opportunity. Even if an anecdote does identify a significant concern, its use gives antagonists a basis to resist plan adoption, as pointed out by the outpatient registration case in Chapter 1.

*Conflict* can be stimulated when a problem is vague and misunderstood, as illustrated in the branch bank case (Chapter 1). The failure to specify whether the objective of the branch bank was security, convenience, or coopting bank representatives on the board of trustees led to the plan being scuttled. In other instances, unresolved disagreements about need and opportunity can abort the process before it begins.

*Misperceptions* arise through poorly thought out need or opportunity claims. When staff people fail to challenge these claims, the results can be bizarre. Recall the emergency room case in Chapter 10. In this project, the planner failed to see how the practice of using on-call physicians caused the waiting line model to represent the wrong problem. Scheduling was attacked when the true bottleneck was the decision to use on-call, rather than full-time, emergency room physicians. Also note that the assumed problem of lost charges may or may not have been present in the lost charges case.

Wrong problem planned change is invariably disastrous, typically resulting in failed plans. A key reason for failure stems from skipping the formulation stage.

### The Omnipotent Expert

Some sponsors expect experts to provide an idea. The sponsor activates planned change by defining a need and then looks for someone who has a plan. Typically consultants are used. This practice skips the concept development stage and parts of the detailing stage. Most consultants have a single "prepackaged" solution for certain types of problems that is tailored (somewhat) to fit the new setting. When extensive shaping is required, the ready-made plan may be a poor way to deal with the organization's problem.

Delegation of solution seeking can be creative when several consulting firms are asked to offer their plan. This gives the sponsor the chance to select the most appropriate plan or to create a synthesis. This almost never occurs in practice. Rather, a single firm is selected, typically without carefully checking the features of its canned solution. Chapters 1 and 4 illustrate off-the-shelf consultant plans for a management information system and a parking project. In both cases, the consultant presented a single option to the sponsor.

### Transported Ideas

This type of pseudoplanning lets the new make way for the old. As shown in Figure 5-3, the premises offered by the sponsor in the concept development stage stem from ideas developed by others. Concepts drawn from these procedures and practices are used as a template for planned change. For example, when faced with a problem, sponsors often visit organizations thought to be high prestige for the purpose of copying their practices. If trips are made to several organizations to assess the merit of their systems, a synthesis can be tailored to fit the new setting. However, these evaluations are seldom carried out with care. When differences between the organization and its environment are not accounted for, exporting a plan can lead to considerable cost in shaping it to fit the new setting. Pseudoplanning results when plans are taken from a single source without an evaluation of its local merits, let alone a test of the plan's applicability to the new setting.

Borrowing ideas from others is very common, as has been illustrated by many of the cases. These include the renal dialysis center (Chapter 1), which copied the features of the for-profit center's facility; the outpatient registration project (Chapter 1), which copied the procedures used by other hospitals for admitting; and many others. Transporting ideas seldom leads to innovation and often creates unanticipated planned change costs that are incurred to fit the plan to its new setting.

### Pooled Ignorance

The planning committee is another common planned change practice. The committee is assigned an oversight function, replacing the sponsor at the center of the transactional process diagram as shown in Figures 5-14 and 5-15. The committee can be beneficial as an implementation tool, when full participation of those affected by the plan is possible, and as an idea generator when knowledgeable people participate. However, using committees without such rationales assumes that "pooled ignorance leads to wisdom." Committees create a form of pseudoplanning when its members do not represent legitimate interests or provide a knowledge base. The committee acts as gatekeeper rather than an idea generator. This approach often provides unclear or misleading stipulations and forces the planner to justify everything prematurely, including the planned change process.

Examples of pooled ignorance were described in the lost charges case (Chapter 1) and the medical records case (Chapter 4). In each case, the planning committee misdirected the process, which caused plan failure. Key issues that regulate the prospects of implementation were not discovered during planned change. Failure occurred because the planning committees did not understand the values that were held by key people who could block a change.

### "Do It My Way"

Planning can be used to gain sanction for the pet idea of the sponsor. The concept development and detailing stages are managed by the sponsor to state premises that imply solutions and thereby manipulate the process. Although pet idea planned change is always self-serving, the sponsor may be pushing a visionary or an enlightened plan. In other instances, the pet idea may not be in the best interests of the organization.

The pet idea creates a solution-driven process. When the time seems right and success seems likely, the sponsor initiates a planned change process and adopts a zealot role. Examples include the same-day testing case (Chapter 13) and the community lab case (Chapter 5).

The self-serving behavior of the sponsor is often transparent, which undermines the credibility of the planned change effort. People dislike being manipulated and often resist the resulting plan merely because of its identification with the sponsor, as in the supply management case (Chapter 9).

### Change as Given

This type of pseudoplanning skips or treats superficially the implementation stage. Plans are created without giving careful consideration to how the required changes are to be made. Problems occur when cooptation is incomplete, when edicts don't work, and when the wrong sponsor guides planned change.

*Cooptation* fails when a planning committee has the wrong members. As pointed out in the medical records plan (Chapter 4), one cannot coopt when key people do not have a voice in the process. However, this level of participation can be cumbersome, and even impossible. The active involvement of all university medical staff would have been a tactical nightmare. Nevertheless, a better understanding of their values in the process may have salvaged the medical records plan.

The sponsor uses power to force change in an *edict*. Such a tactic can be unwise when the sponsor's prerogatives are not clear or when more palatable tactics can be used. The supply management case (Chapter 9) illustrates how sabotage can follow an unpopular edict. Participation would have been a better approach.

Following the procedure in Chapter 7, sponsors are sought out. If the sponsor lacks the power to manage the implementation process it results in *wrong sponsor* pseudoplanning. The telecommunication system case (Chapter 9) experienced lengthy delays because it had a divisional vice president as its sponsor. The company's CEO would have been a better choice. Apparently, sponsors cling to their projects, perhaps because they fail to interest a superior in championing their cause. This may be due to the "not-discovered-here" syndrome or the subordinate's inability to penetrate the superior's agenda.

## Pseudoplanning Stemming from the Monitoring Approach

Pseudoplanning can result from the approach used to monitor the planned change process. An overly aggressive posture drives out the ideas of others. An overly passive approach may let an expert's parochial interests prevail.

### Surrender

Some sponsors allow the planned change process to follow the path shown in Figure 5-2. Experts develop the plan without sponsor participation. The case studies in Chapters 4 and 5 reveal that such tactics are rare, occurring far less often than the literature would suggest. Surrender is unlikely because most sponsors find it in their best interest to act far more aggressively than the literature acknowledges. In those cases where it occurs, the expert was found to have more power than the sponsor, or the sponsor treated the project as low priority. Behaving as if the project was low priority is often traceable to sponsor ignorance. Two tactics can be used. First, several comprehension cycles in the detailing and the evaluation stages can be demanded by such sponsors so they can appreciate how the plan is to function and what are its merit. Second, when participation would reveal a sponsor's lack of knowledge, a safe tactic is to delegate to an expert. What appears to be benign neglect is in reality, delegation through fear. Planned change efforts that lack priority may also be carried out through delegation.

High-power experts often crop up in equipment selection projects, such as the computer case (Chapter 5) and the MRI scanner case (Chapter 5). By demanding comprehension recycles, the sponsor learns to appreciate the plan's implications.

### Takeover

Takeover is the opposite of surrender. The sponsor postures himself or herself to receive all pertinent information, often sharing it as narrowly as possible. Sponsors adopt these tactics when a planned change effort is perceived as critical to their future. For instance, building projects often conjure up the need for tight control. In such a situation, the sponsor's values dictate all choices. The cash flow project (Chapter 5) and the same-day testing case (Chapter 13) provide illustrations.

## Approach-Based Pseudoplanning

The approach used to manage the process can be drawn from inappropriate sources. Two types of pseudoplanning are described: sciencism and empty phases.

### Sciencism

This approach stresses analysis at the expense of search and synthesis. Analysis focuses on "what is." New ideas are seldom developed because search and synthesis activities, required to create innovative options, are not carried out.

Analytic traditions often dictate this type of planned change process, as illustrated by the pharmacological dosing project (Chapter 4). In this case, assessment was the key activity. The project experienced lengthy delays because its sponsor could not find out how to proceed. The inability to identify a process to follow nearly sunk a beneficial idea.

### Empty Phases

Practitioners are often exhorted to use a checklist. Checklists offer little help in dealing with planned change, as pointed out in Chapter 4. For example, the approach used by parking and building consultants is force fitted to every project and seldom, if ever, practiced in a contingency framework. The parking project cited in Chapter 1 provides an example.

# ▲ PRINCIPLES OF PLANNED CHANGE

Sponsors who follow the principles of planned change set in motion a process which avoids difficulties that can lead to pseudoplanning. These principles call for sponsors to manage the planned change process, to include both planning and change activities during process management, to use planned change for strategic and nonstrategic efforts, to stress search and synthesis, to uncover and explore problems, to set clear directions, to promote innovation, to seek multiple alternatives and alternatives broadly defined, to make careful evaluations, to deal with the barriers to implementation, to select techniques according to expected results, and to recognize and cope with the role taken to manage the process of planned change. Adhering to these principles improves the prospect that a plan with merit will be adopted by the sponsor's organization.

## 1. Ensuring That a Responsible Leader Manages the Planned Change Process

To be successful, planned change must have someone in authority take charge. The authority figure should demonstrate why needs or opportunities are important and call for action by the organization. This leadership typically comes from managers with line authority in the organization. Sponsors who abdicate this responsibility are less successful in getting plans adopted.

## 2. Dealing with Both Planning and Change

Planning activities create ideas. Change activities are carried out to get the ideas adopted. A planned change process guides thinking about action and taking action. The process is not a substitute for either thinking or action taking. It helps sponsors recognize needed activities and provides a way to direct ones thinking about complex change attempts. Learning the stages of planned change and their purpose liberates rather than constrains a sponsor. Knowing the stages of planned change cues sponsors, helping them introduce, at an appropriate time, considerations that can be overlooked.

## 3. Using Planned Change for Strategic and Nonstrategic Efforts

Planned change can have strategic, nonstrategic, or strategic and nonstrategic purposes. "Strategic planned change" is carried out to fashion new directions for an organization and initiates a number of project efforts. "Project planned change" is narrower in scope but is also important because this type of effort is continually underway at all levels of the well-run organization.

## 4. Stressing Search and Synthesis

Search and synthesis as well as analysis steps are essential for all of the stages of planned change. Search and synthesis during formulation help sponsors uncover and articulate problems meriting attention and objectives that can guide the planned change effort. Analysis is used to select among problems and objectives to focus attention. Search in concept development uncovers ideas. Synthesis takes the best features of these ideas and blends them into options. Analysis is used to select viable options for detailing. Search is useful in detailing to identify plan features, in evaluation to select criteria and norms, and in implementation to isolate political and social barriers to change. Synthesis combines these features in useful ways, and analysis picks the more important. As a result, search and synthesis are far more important than is analysis in a planned change effort.

## 5. Uncovering Problems

The signals and events that attract attention are frequently the symptoms of other concerns, misleading, or more urgent than important (Kolb, 1983). Because problems create a window that directs attention, symptomatic, misleading, or unimportant problems will misdirect the planned change effort. Careful probing, however, often reveals underlying concerns. This probing is done with techniques to introduce a variety of concerns and difficulties for reflection and assessment. Sponsors who explore their perceptions of needs and opportunities in this way develop a deeper and more defensible understanding of what should be done and why. This provides both a defense of actions taken and a stronger appreciation of the issues meriting attention.

## 6. Setting Directions

Planned change efforts should be guided by objectives that indicate what is wanted, not problems that suggest what is wrong or who to blame. Objectives provide targets that open up the search for ideas in the developmental phase of planned change. Objectives also suggest criteria to measure the merits of alternatives and provide indicators of success following implementation.

## 7. Promoting Innovation

Organizations that seek innovation or radical innovation (ideas new to their industry) are more successful. Alternatives with innovative features must be nurtured because tradition and imitation dominate most planned change efforts. Sponsors must give innovation a special legitimacy to avoid having conventional ideas drive out thinking about new ones.

## 8. Seeking Multiple Alternatives

Developing several competing alternatives improves the plan that is ultimately adopted. The discarded alternatives are not wasted. They provide a confirmation that the best plan was selected and offer ways to improve it. Frequently, the plan that is adopted draws several of its features from the other alternative. A synthesis of the best features of competing plans frequently improves planned change results.

## 9. Developing Alternatives "Broadly Defined"

Broadly defined options are identified by examining a broader and a narrower objective, along with the objective currently being considered to guide planned change. These options are useful because they go beyond the point at which the organization is focused to raise questions about things that must be done to get at the objective of interest. The narrower objective identifies solutions to problems that are stepping stones to get at the selected objective. The broader objective introduces more sweeping ideas. These ideas may suggest more significant ways in which to direct the organization's energies. Adopting them can dramatically alter the organization's priorities. Testing plans as they emerge in this way keeps the organization focused on possibilities and prevents premature closure on a conventional and less beneficial plan.

## 10. Making Careful Evaluations of the Alternatives

The value of an alternative is often hidden in features that are poorly understood. An evaluation reveals these features and makes comparisons that suggest which alternative best meets the objective of planned change. Economic, political, *and* ethical rationality provides the basis to make a choice among alternatives. Techniques that explore the alternatives from these three perspectives are essential. Both quantitative and qualitative evaluation techniques must be applied to get these insights.

## 11. Dealing with Barriers to Action

Implementation calls for the identification and management of factors that can doom a planned change effort. These factors arise as stakeholders examine the emerging plan and assess how they will affect and be affected by the change called for by the plan. Techniques that allow sponsors to anticipate who will object, why they may object, and the intensity of their position provide a diagnosis. The climate of the organization or work unit offers additional cues. Finally, the sponsor's freedom to act and the need for consultation suggests how to organize the planned change effort. Together these diagnoses suggest an implementation process and implementation techniques that enhance the prospects of plan adoption.

## 12. Selecting Planning Techniques According to Requirements

A hybrid planned change method is created by selecting techniques according to the requirements imposed on the process by its sponsor. Sponsors who can identify these requirements and select techniques accordingly adjust the cost of planned change to its requirements. Selecting techniques in this way ensures that the hoped-for outcomes of planned change will be realized in an efficient manner.

## 13. Recognizing and Coping with Sponsor Roles

Zealot and devil's advocate roles can be adopted by planned change sponsors. Sponsors who adopt these roles are apt to develop plans that are less valuable than they could be. This occurs because a planner is motivated to use techniques that cater to the zealot and devil's advocate styles of process management and not according to the needs prompting the effort. Zealot and devil's advocate roles lead the sponsor down a path that creates resentment and fails to offer sound process management. Sponsors who are prone to adopt these roles make poor candidates to manage planned change. Well informed planners also adapt to sponsors in critic, visionary, rationalist, and broker roles. This adaptation, however, is less apt to draw the planner away from using techniques deemed essential for the creative stages of planned change.

## ▲ Key Points

1. Pseudoplanned change occurs when sponsors manipulate the process or ignore its management.
2. The principles of planned change help to overcome the concerns raised by pseudoplanning and improves the prospect that a plan with merit will be adopted by the sponsor's organization.

# REFERENCES

▲ ▲ ▲ ▲ ▲ ▲ ▲ ▲ ▲ ▲ ▲ ▲ ▲ ▲ ▲ ▲ ▲ ▲ ▲ ▲ ▲ ▲ ▲

Abernathy, W. J., and R. S. Rosenbloom (1969), "Parallel Strategies in Developmental Projects," *Management Science,* Vol. 16, no. 6.

Acar, W. (1987),"Organizational Processes and Strategic Postures: Cross-classification or Continuum," *Proceedings of the General Systems Society,* pp. J70–J84.

Ackoff, R. L. (1981), *Creating the Corporate Future.* New York: John Wiley.

Ackoff, R. L. (1974), *Redesigning the Future.* New York: John Wiley.

Ackoff, R. L. (1971), "Towards a System Concept of Systems," *Management Science,* Vol. 17, no. 11, pp. 661–671.

Ackoff, R. L., and F. E. Emery (1972), *On Purposeful Systems.* New York: Aldene-Atherton.

Alexander, L. D. (1985), "Successfully Implementing Strategic Decisions," Long-Range Planning, June, pp. 85–94.

Alexander, T. (1977), "The Deceptive Allure of National Planning,"*Fortune,* March.

Allen, M. S. (1962), *Morphological Creativity.* Englewood Cliffs, N.J.: Prentice Hall.

Allison, G. T. (1969), "Conceptual Models and the Cuban Missile Crisis," *American Political Science Review,* Vol. 63, no. 3, September, pp. 689–719.

Ansoff, I. (1984), *Implementing Strategic Management.* Englewood Cliffs, N.J.: Prentice Hall.

Archer, L. B. (1969), "Systematic Method for Designers," *Design,* pp. 173 ff.

Argyris, C. (1976), "Single-Loop and Double-Loop Models in Research on Decision Making," *Administrative Science Quarterly,* Vol. 21, pp. 363–375.

Armstrong, S. (1982), "The Value of Formal Planning for Strategic Decisions," *Strategic Management Journal,* Vol. 3, pp. 197–211.

Asch, E. (1951), "Effects of Group Pressure upon the Modification and Distortion of Judgments." In H. Guetzkow, ed., *Groups, Leadership, and Men.* Pittsburgh, Pa.: Carnegie Press.

Ashby, R. W. (1963), *An Introduction to Cybernetics.* New York: John Wiley.

Ashby, W. R. (1962), "Principles of the Self Organizing System." In H. Forrester and G. Zopf, eds., *Principles of Self Organization.* New York: Pergamon Press.

Asimow, M. (1962), *An Introduction to Design.* Englewood Cliffs, N.J.: Prentice Hall.

Backnell, H. M. (1966), "The Local School System and Change." In R. Miller, ed., *Perspectives on Educational Change.* New York: Appleton-Century-Crofts.

Backoff, R. W. (1976). "Organizational Design: Problem Formulation," OSU mimeo, The Ohio State University, Columbus.

Backoff, R. W. and P. C. Nutt (1989), "A Process for Strategic Management with Special Application for the Non-Profit Sector." In J. Bryson and R. Einsweiler, eds., *Strategic Planning.* Chicago: Planners Press.

Bardach, E. (1977), *The Implementation Game.* Cambridge, Mass.: MIT Press.

Ben-David, J. (1982), "Scientific Productivity and Academic Organizations in the Nineteenth Century." In B. Barber and W. Hirsch, eds., *The Sociology of Science,* pp. 305–328. New York: Free Press.

Bennis, W. (1989), *Why Leaders Can't Lead.* San Francisco: Jossey-Bass.

Bennis, W., and B. Nanus (1985), *Leaders.* San Francisco: Jossey-Bass.

Betaque, N., and A. Gorry (1971), "Automating Judgmental Decision Making for a Serious Medical Problem," *Management Science,* Vol. 17, no. 8, pp. B421–B434.

Blake, R. R., and J. S. Mouton (1964), *The Managerial Grid.* Houston: Gulf.

Blake, R., J. Mouton, L. Barnes, and L. Greiner (1964), "Breakthrough in Organizational Development," *Harvard Business Review,* November/December.

Blau, P. (1985), *The Dynamics of Bureaucracy: A Study of Interpersonal Relations in Two Government Agencies.* Chicago: University of Chicago Press.

Block, J. (1961), "The Q-Sort Method." *In Personality Assessment and Psychiatric Research.* Springfield, Ill.: Charles C. Thomas.

Blum, H. L. (1974), *Planning for Health: Development and Application of Social Theory.* New York: Human Sciences Press.

Boone-Young Final Report (1978). Washington, D.C.: U. S. Department of Health, Education, and Welfare, December.

Bouchard, T. J., Jr., and M. Hare (1970), "Size, Performance, and Potential in Brainstorming Groups," *Journal of Applied Psychology,* Vol. 54, no. 4, pp. 338–341.

Boulding, K. (1956), "General Systems Theory: The Skeleton of a Science," *General Systems,* Vol. 1.

Bourgeois, L. J. (1990), "Strategic Decision Processes in High Velocity Environments: Four Cases in the Microcomputer Industry," *Management Science,* Vol. 14, pp. 816–835.

Bourgeois, L. J. (1990), "Strategy and Environment: A Conceptual Integration," *Academy of Management Review,* Vol. 5, no. 1, pp. 25–39.

Bright, J. R., ed. (1968), *Technological Forecasting for Industry and Government.* Englewood Cliffs, N.J.: Prentice Hall.

Bristol, L. H., Jr. (1958), "The Application of Group Thinking to the Problems of Pharmaceutical Education," *American Journal of Pharmaceutical Education,* Vol. 22, pp. 146–156.

Brown, S. (1980), *Q-Sort Analysis.* New Haven, Conn.: Yale University Press.

Brown, S. (1968), "Scenarios in System Analysis." In E. S. Quade and W. I. Boucher, eds., *Systems Analysis and Policy Planning.* New York: Elsevier.

Brown, S. R. (1974), "The Composition of Microcosm," *Policy Sciences,* Vol. 5, pp. 15–27.

Brown, S. R., and J. G. Coke (1977), "Public Opinion on Land Use Regulation," Urban and Regional Development Series, No. 1. Columbus, Ohio: Academy of Contemporary Problems.

Bryan, S. E. (1964), "The TFXA—A Case in Policy Level Decision Making," *The Academy of Management Journal,* March.

Bryson, J. (1988), *Strategic Planning for Public and Non-Profit Organizations.* San Francisco: Jossey-Bass.

Buckley, W. (1967), *Sociology and Modern Systems Theory.* Englewood Cliffs, N.J.: Prentice Hall.

Burns, T., and G. M. Stalker (1961), *The Management of Innovation.* London: Tavistock.

Campbell, D. T., and J. C. Stanley (1964), *Experimental and Quasi-experimental Designs for Research.* Chicago: Rand McNally.

Cannell, C., and R. Kahn (1953), "A Collection of Data by Interviewing." In L. Sestinger and D. Katz, eds., *Research Methods in the Behavioral Sciences.* New York: Holt, Rinehart and Winston.

Catron, B. L. (1983), "Ethical Postures and Ethical Posturing," *American Review of Public Management,* Vol. 17, nos. 2, 3, pp. 155–159.

Christensen, P. R., J. P. Guilford, and R. C. Wilson (1957), "Relations of Creative Responses to Work Time Instructions," *Journal of Experimental Psychology,* Vol. 53, pp. 82–88.

Churchman, C. W., (1971), *The Design of Inquiring Systems: Basic Concepts of Systems and Organization.* New York: Basic Books.

Churchman, C. W. (1979a), *The Systems Approach,* rev. ed. New York: Dell.

Churchman, C. W. (1979b), *The Systems Approach and Its Enemies.* New York: Basic Books.

Churchman, C. W. (1975), "Theories of Implementation," In R. Schultz and D. Sleven, eds., *Implementation Operations Research and Management Science.* New York: Elsevier.

Clark, B. R. (1965), "Interorganizational Patterns in Organizations," *Administrative Science Quarterly,* Vol. 10, no. 2, pp. 224–237.

Clark, B. R. (1972), "The Occupational Saga in Higher Education," *Administrative Science Quarterly,* Vol. 17, pp. 178–184.

Cobb, R. W., and C. D. Elder (n.d.), "Problems and Prospects in the Study of Political Symbolism," mimeo, University of Pennsylvania, Philadelphia.

Coch, L., and J. French, Jr. (1948), "Overcoming Resistance to Change," *Human Relations,* Vol. 1, August, pp. 512–532.

Cohen, M. D., J. P. March, and J. P. Olsen (1976), "A Garbage Can Model of Organizational Choice," *Administrative Science Quarterly,* Vol. 17, pp. 1–25.

Collins, B., and H. Guetzkow (1964), *A Social Psychology of Group Process for Decision Making.* New York: John Wiley.

Cook, D. L. (1971), *Educational Project Management.* Columbus, Ohio: Charles E. Merrill.

Cook, T. J., F. P. Scioli, Jr., and S. R. Brown (1975), "Experimental Design and Methodology: Improving the Analysis of Attitude Change," *Political Methodology,* pp. 51–76.

Cook, T. O., and D. T. Campbell (1979), *Quasi-experimentation: Design and Analysis Issues for Field Settings.* Chicago: Rand McNally.

Crawford, R. P. (1954), *Technologies for Creative Thinking.* Englewood Cliffs, N.J.: Prentice Hall.

Crosier, R. A., and J. C. Aplin (1980), "A Critical View of Dialectical Inquiry as a Tool for Strategic Planning," *Strategic Management Journal,* Vol. 1, pp. 343–356.

Crovitz, H. G. (1978), *Galton's Walk.* New York: Harper & Row.

Cummings, L. L., G. P. Huber, and L. Arndt (1974), "Effects of Size and Spatial Arrangements on Group Decision Making," *Academy of Management Journal,* Vol. 17, pp. 460–475.

Cyert, R. M., and J. B. March (1963), *A Behavioral Theory of the Firm.* Englewood Cliffs, N.J.: Prentice Hall.

Daft, R. L., and S. W. Becker (1978), *Innovation in Organizations.* New York: Elsevier.

Daft, R. L., and S. W. Becker (1973), *Innovation in Organizations.* New York: Wiley-Interscience.

Dalky, N. (1968), "Simulation." In E. S. Quade and W. I. Boucher, eds., *Systems Analysis and Policy Planning.* New York: Elsevier.

Dalky, N. (1967), *Delphi.* Santa Monica, Calif.: The Rand Corporation.

Dalton, G. W. (1970a), "Influence and Organizational Change." In *Organizational Change and Development,* pp. 230–259. Homewood, Ill.: Richard D. Irwin-Dorsey Press.

Dalton, G. W. (1970b), "Patterns of Organizational Change." In G. W. Dalton, P. R. Lawrence, and L. E. Greiner, eds., *Organizational Change and Development.* Homewood, Ill.: Richard D. Irwin.

Damanpour, F., and W. M. Evan (1984), "Organizational Innovation and Preference," *Administrative Science Quarterly,* Vol. 29, pp. 392–409.

Davidoff, P. (1965), "Advocacy and Pluralism in Planning," *Journal of American Institute of Planners,* Vol. 31, no. 4, November.

Davis, G. A., and J. A. Scott, eds. (1978), *Galton's Walk.* New York: Harper & Row.

de Bono, E. (1972), *Po: A Device for Successful Thinking.* New York: Simon & Schuster.

de Bono, E. (1971), *New Think.* New York: Avon.

de Bono, E. (1970), *Lateral Thinking: Creativity Step by Step.* New York: Harper & Row.

DeGreen, K. (1973), *Sociotechnical Systems,* p. 210. Englewood Cliffs, N.J.: Prentice Hall.

Delbecq, A. (1989), *Sustaining Innovation as an American Competitive Advantage,* Institute for Urban Studies Monograph Series Number 7. College Park: University of Maryland at College Park.

Delbecq, A. (1977), "The Management of Decision Making Within the Firm: Three Strategies for Three Types of Decision Making," *Academy of Management Journal,* Vol. 10, no. 4, pp. 329–339.

Delbecq, A. (1968), "The World Within the Span of Control," *Business Horizons,* Vol. 11, pp. 47–56.

Delbecq, A. (1967), "The Myth of the Indigenous Community Leader," *Academy of Management Journal,* Vol. 11, pp. 11–26.

Delbecq, A., and A. Van de Ven (1971), "A Group Process Model for Problem Identification and Program Planning," *Journal of Applied Behavioral Science,* Vol. 7, no. 4, pp. 466–492.

Delbecq, A., A. Van de Ven, and D. H. Gustafson (1986), *Group Techniques for Program Planning.* Middleton, Wisc.: Greenbrier.

Dewey, J. (1910), *How We Think.* Lexington, Mass.: D. C. Heath.

Doktor, R., and D. M. Bloom (1977), "Selective Lateralization of Cognitive Style Related to Occupation as Determined by EEG Alpha Asymmetry," *Psychophysiology,* pp. 385–387.

Down, A. (1967), *Inside Bureaucracy.* Boston: Little, Brown.

Dramanpour, F., and W. Evan (1984), "Organizational Innovation and Preference: The Problem of Organizational Tag," *Administrative Science Quarterly,* Vol. 29, pp. 392–409.

Drucker, K. (1945), "On Problem Solving," *Psychological Monographs,* Vol. 58, no. 5.

Dunn, W. N. (1981), *Public Policy Analysis,* Chap. 4, "Modes of Policy Argument." Englewood Cliffs, N.J.: Prentice Hall.

Eastlack, J. O., and P. R. MacDonald (1980), "CEO's Role in Corporate Growth," *Harvard Business Review,* Vol. 42, no. 3, May/June.

Ebert, R. J., and T. R. Mitchell (1975), *Organizational Decision Processes.* New York: Crane, Russak.

Eckenrode, R. T. (1965), "Weighting Multiple Criteria," *Management Science,* Vol. 12, no. 3, pp. 180–192.

Edwards, W., H. Lindman, and L. D. Phillips (1967), "Emerging Technologies for Making Decisions." In H. Lindman, ed., *New Directions in Psychology.* New York: Holt, Rinehart and Winston.

Eichholtz, G., and M. Rogers (1964), "Resistance to the Adoption of Audiovisual Aids by Elementary Teachers." In M. Miles, ed., *Innovations in Education.* New York: Columbia University Teacher's College Press.

Eisenhardt, K. M., and L. J. Bourgeois (1988), "Politics of Strategic Decision Making in High Velocity Environments: Toward a Mid-Range Theory," *Academy of Management Journal,* Vol. 31, pp. 737–770.

Elmaghraby, S. A. (1964), "An Algebra for the Analysis of Generalized Activity Networks," *Management Science,* Vol. 10, no. 3, pp. 494–514.

Emshoff, J. R. (1980), *Managerial Breakthroughs: Action Techniques for Strategic Change,* p. 211. New York: AMA–AMACOM.

Feldman, M. S., and J. C. March (1981), "Information in Organizations as Signal and Symbol," *Administrative Science Quarterly,* Vol. 26, pp. 171–186.

Fiedler, F. (1965), "Engineering the Job to Fit the Manager," *Harvard Business Review,* Vol. 43, pp. 115–122.

Filley, A., R. House, and S. Kerr (1976), *Managerial Process and Organizational Behavior,* 2nd ed. Glenview, Ill.: Scott, Foresman.

Fischer, G. W. (1978), "Utility Models for Multiple Objective Decisions: Do They Accurately Represent Human Preferences," *Decision Sciences,* Vol. 10, no. 3, mspp. 451–470.

Fleishman, A. (1957), "Leader Behavior Descriptions for Industry." In R. M. Stogdill et al., eds., *Leader Behavior: Description and Measurement,* Monograph 88. Columbus: Bureau of Business Research, The Ohio State University.

Forrester, J. W. (1971), *World Dynamics.* Cambridge, Mass.: Wright Allen.

Forrester, J. W. (1969), *Urban Dynamics.* Cambridge, Mass.: MIT Press.

Forrester, J. W. (1968), *Principles of Systems.* Cambridge, Mass.: Wright Allen.

Forrester, J. W. (1961), *Industrial Dynamics.* Cambridge, Mass.: MIT Press.

Foster, R. (1986), *Innovation: The Attackers Advantage.* New York: Summit.

Fox, A. (1971), *The Sociology of Work and Industry.* London: Collier-Macmillan.

Freeman, R. W. (1984), *Strategic Management: A Stakeholder Approach.* Boston: Pittman.

French, J., Jr., and B. H. Raven (1959), "The Bases of Social Power." In D. Cartwright, ed., *Studies in Social Power.* Ann Arbor, Mich.: Institute of Social Research.

French, W. (1969), "Organizational Development: Objectives, Assumptions, and Strategies," *California Management Review,* Vol. 12, no. 2, Winter.

Fryback, D.G., D. H. Gustafson, and D. E. Detmer (1978), "Local Priorities for Allocation of Resources: Comparison with the IMU," *Inquiry,* Vol. 15, September, pp. 265–274.

Galbraith, J. R. (1971), "Matrix Organization Designs," *Business Horizons,* February, pp. 20–40.

Galbraith, J. R., and R. K. Kazanjian (1986), *Strategic Implementation: Structure, Systems, and Process.* St. Paul, Minn.: West Publishing.

Garfield, C. (1985), *Peak Performance.* New York: Warner Books.

Ghiselli, E. E. (1971), *Exploration in Managerial Talent.* New York: Goodyear.

Ginsberg, A. S., and F. L. Offensend (1968), "An Application of Decision Theory to a Medical Diagnosis-Treatment Problem," *IEEE Transactions on Systems and Cybernetics,* Vol. SSC-4, no. 3, September, pp. 335–362.

Glueck, W. F. (1980), *Business Policy and Strategic Management.* New York: McGraw-Hill

Gordon, W. J. J. (1971), *The Metaphorical Way.* Cambridge, Mass.: Porpoise.

Gordon, W. J. J. (1961), *Synectics.* New York: Harper & Row.

Grant, W. G., and E. Ireson (1980), *Principles of Engineering Economy,* rev. ed. New York: Ronald Press.

Greenblat, K. S., and R. D. Duke (1981), *Principles and Practices of Gaming Situations.* Beverly Hills, Calif.: Sage Publications.

Gregory, S. A. (1966), "Design Science." In W. S. Gregory, ed., *The Design Method.* New York: Plenum.

Greiner, L. E. (1970), "Patterns of Organizational Change." In G. W. Dalton, P. R. Lawrence, and L. E. Greiner, eds., *Organizational Change and Development.* Homewood, Ill.: Richard D. Irwin.

Gueschka, H., G. R. Shaude, and H. Schlicksupp (1975), "Modern Techniques for Solving Problems." In *Portraits of Complexity,* Battelle Monograph Series. Columbus, Ohio: Battelle Memorial Institute.

Guetzkow, H. (1960), "Differentiation of Roles in Task-Oriented Groups." In D. Cartwright et al., eds., *Group Dynamics: Research and Theory.* Evanston, Ill.: Row-Peterson.

Guetzkow, H., and W. R. Dill (1957), "Factors in the Development of Task-Oriented Groups," *Sociometry,* Vol. 20, pp. 175–204.

Guetzkow, H., and H. Simon (1950), "The Impact of Certain Communication Nets upon Organization and Performance in Task-Oriented Groups," *Management Science,* Vol. 21, pp. 233–250.

Gustafson, D. H. (1969), "The Evaluation of Probabilities Information Processing in Medical Decision Making," *Organizational Behavior and Human Performance,* Vol. 4, pp. 20–34.

Gustafson, D. H., G. K. Pai, and G. G. Kramer (1971), "A 'Weighted Aggregate' Approach to R&D Project Selection," *AIIE Transactions,* Vol. 3, no. 2, pp. 22–31.

Gustafson, D. H., R. Shukla, A. Delbecq, and G. Wallester (1973). "A Comparative Study in Subjective Likelihood Estimates Made by Individuals, Interacting Groups, Delphi Groups, and Nominal Groups," *Organizational Behavior and Human Performance,* Vol. 9, April, pp. 280–291.

Gustafson, D. H., et al. (1978), "Methodology for Severity Index Development," Center for Health Systems Research and Analysis, University of Wisconsin, Madison, March.

Hage, H., and H. Aiken (1970), *Social Change in Complex Organizations.* New York: Random House.

Hall, A. D., III (1977), "Methodological Framework for Systems Engineering." In A. P. Sage, ed., *Systems Engineering: Methodology and Applications.* New York: IEEE Press.

Hall, A. D., III (1969), *A Methodology for Systems Engineering.* New York: Nostrand.

Hall, A. D., and R. E. Jaeger (1956). "Definitions of a System," *General Systems,* Vol. 1

Halpin, A. W. (1960), "The Leadership Behavior and Combat Performance of Airplane Commanders," *Journal of Abnormal and Social Psychology,* Vol. 61, pp. 350–354.

Hamilton, H. R. (1974), "Screening Business Development Opportunities," *Business Horizons,* August, pp. 13–17.

Harary, F., Z. Norman, and D. Cartwright (1975), *Structural Models: An Introduction to the Theory of Directed Graphs.* New York: John Wiley.

Harrigan, K. (1981), "Barriers to Entry and Competitive Strategies," *Strategic Management Journal,* Vol. 2, pp. 395–412.

Harringdon, K. (1981), "Barriers to Entry and Competitive Strategies," *Strategic Management Journal,* Vol. 2, pp. 395–412.

Havelock, R. G. (1973), *Planning for Innovation Through Dissemination and Utilization of Scientific Knowledge.* Ann Arbor, Mich.: CRUSK, The Center for Research Utilization of Scientific Knowledge.

Health Services Research Group (1975), "The Development of an Index of Medical Under-service," *Health Services Research,* Summer, pp. 168–180.

Henderson, B. (1979), *Henderson on Corporate Strategy.* Cambridge, Mass.: Basic Books.

Herbert, T. T., and E. B. Yost (1979), "A Comparison of Decision Quality Under Nominal and Interacting Consensus Group Formats: The Case of the Structured Problem," *Decision Sciences,* Vol. 10, no. 3, July, pp. 358–370.

Hester, T., Jr., and E. Sussman (1974), "Medicaid Prepayment: Concept and Implementation Issues," New York City Health Services Administration, Office of Program Analysis.

Hill, J. D., and J. N. Warfield (1977), "Unified Program Planning." In A. P. Sage, ed., *Systems Engineering: Methodology and Applications.* New York: IEEE Press.

Hinton, B. L., and H. J. Reitz (1971), *Groups and Organizations: Analysis of Social Behavior.* Belmont, Calif.: Wadsworth.

Hofer, C. W., and O. Schendel (1978), *Strategy Formulation: Analytical Concepts.* St. Paul, Minn.: West Publishing.

Hogarth, R. (1980), *Judgment & Choice.* New York: Wiley-Interscience.

Holloman, C. R., and H. W. Hendrick (1972), "Adequacy of Group Decisions as a Function of the Decision Making Process," *Academy of Management Journal,* Vol. 15, pp. 175–184.

Hoos, I. R. (1972), *Systems Analysis in Public Policy: A Critique.* Berkeley: University of California Press.

Houston, P. (1986). "Northwest's Merger Has Its Passengers Fuming," *Business Week,* November 24, p. 64.

Huber, G. P. (1982), "Organizational Information Systems: Determinants of Their Performance and Behavior," *Management Science,* Vol. 28, no. 2, pp. 138–155.

Huber, G. P. (1980), *Managerial Decision Making,* p. 66. Glenview, Ill.: Scott, Foresman.

Huber, G. P. (1974), "Multi-attribute Utility Models: A Review of Field and Field-like Studies," *Management Science,* Vol. 20, no. 10, June, pp. 1393–1402.

Huber, G. P., and A. Delbecq (1972), "Guidelines for Combining the Judgments of Individual Members in Decision Conferences," *Academy of Management Journal,* Vol. 15, pp. 159–174.

Huber, G. P., V. Sahney, and D. Ford (1969), "A Study of Subjective Evaluation Models," *Behavioral Science,* Vol. 14, November.

Hubka, V. (1982), *Principles of Engineering Design.* London: Butterworth Scientific.

Huse, E. F. (1975), *Organizational Development and Change.* St. Paul, Minn.: West Publishing.

Ireson, G. (1980), *Principles of Engineering Economy.* New York: Ronald Press.

James, B. J., and W. L. Libby, Jr. (1962), "An Experimental Curriculum for Studies in Administrative Innovation," *Education for Innovative Behavior of Executives,* Project 975. Washington, D.C.: U.S. Department of Health, Education, and Welfare, Office of Education, August.

Janis, I. (1989). *Crucial Decisions.* New York: Free Press.

Janis, I., and L. Mann (1977), *Decision Making.* New York: Free Press.

Jantsch, E. (1967), *Technological Forecasting in Perspective.* Paris: OECD.

Jerrell, S. L. (1980), "Political Contexts and Strategic Execution Skills," Midwest Division of the Academy of Management Conference, Cincinnati, Ohio, April 10–12.

Johnson, E. M., and G. Huber (1977), "The Technology of Utility Assessment." In A. P. Sage, ed., *Systems Engineering Methodology and Applications.* New York: IEEE Press.

Johnson, R. C. (1978), "The Power Broker—Prototype of the Hospital Chief Executive," *Health Care Management Review,* Vol. 3, no. 4, Fall.

Jones, J. L. (1983), *Conference on Design Methods.* New York: Macmillan.

Kahn, A. J. (1969), *Theory and Practice of Social Planning.* Washington, D.C.: Russell Sage.

Kahn, H., and A. J. Weiner (1967), *The Year 2000.* New York: Macmillan.

Kahn, H., and A. J. Weiner (1969), "The Next Thirty Years: A Framework for Speculation." In D. Bell, ed., *Toward the Year 2000.* Boston: Beacon Press.

Kast, F., and J. Rosenzweig (1970). *Organization and Management: A Systems Approach.* New York: McGraw-Hill.

Keeney, R. L., and H. Raiffa (1978). *Decision with Multiple Objectives.* New York: John Wiley.

Kerlinger, F. N. (1967), *Foundations of Behavioral Research,* 2nd ed. New York: Holt, Rinehart and Winston.

Kerr, S., C. Schriesheim, C. J. Murphy, and R. M. Stogdill (1974), "Toward a Contingency Theory of Leadership Based on Consideration and Interaction Structure Literature," *Organizational Behavior and Human Performance,* Vol. 12, pp. 62–82.

Kim, J. (1975), "Feedback in the Social Sciences: Toward a Reconceptualization of Morphogeneses." In R. D. Rubin and J. Kim, eds., *General Systems Theory and Human Communication,* pp. 207–221. Rochelle Park, N.J.: Hayden.

Kneppreth, N. P., D. H. Gustafson, J. H. Rose, and R. P. Leifer (1973), "Techniques for the Assessment of Worth." In R. Berg, ed., *Health Status Indexes.* Chicago: Hospital Research and Education Trust.

Kolb, D. A. (1983), "Problem Management: Learning from Experience." In S. Strivastva and Associates, *The Executive Mind: New Insights on Effective Thought and Action.* San Francisco: Jossey-Bass.

Krick, E. V. (1965), *An Introduction to Engineering and Engineering Design.* New York: John Wiley.

Laswell, H. (1985), "The Policy Sciences of Development," *World Politics,* Vol. 17, pp. 286–309.

Laswell, H. (1974), *A Preview of Policy Science.* New York: American Elsevier.

Laswell, H. (1965), "The Policy Sciences of Development," *World Politics,* Vol. 17, no. 2, pp. 286–309.

Laswell, H. (1960), "The Technique of Decision Seminars," *Journal of Political Science,* Vol. 4, pp. 213–236.

Laswell. H. (1956), "The Decision Process: Seven Categories of Functional Analysis," Bureau of Governmental Research, College of Business Administration, College Park, Maryland.

Lawrence, P.R., and D. Dyer (1983), *Reviving American Industry.* New York: Free Press.

Leavitt, H. J. (1975), "Beyond the Analytic Manager," *California Management Review,* Vol. 17, no. 5, pp. 1–12.

Levin, C. H., R. W. Backoff, A. R. Cahoon, and W. J. Stiffen (1975), "Organizational Design: A Post Minnowbrook Perspective for the New Public Administrator," *Public Administration Review,* July/August.

Lewin, A., and C. U. Stephens (1990), "The CEO as a Determinant of Organizational Design." In *The CEO as a Pygmalion: Do CEOs Shape Organizations in Their Images?* Academy of Management Meeting, Organization and Management Theory Division, San Francisco, August 12–15.

Lewin, K. (1958), "Group Decisions and Social Change." In J. E. Maccoby, T. W. Newcomb, and E. Hartley, eds., *Readings in Social Psychology.* New York: Holt, Rinehart and Winston.

Lewin, K. (1951), *Field Theory in Social Science.* New York: Harper & Row.

Likert, R. (1967), *The Human Organization.* New York: McGraw-Hill.

Lindblom, C. E. (1965), *The Intelligence of Democracy: Decision Process Through Adjustment.* New York: Free Press.

Lippitt, M. E., and K. D. Mackenzie (1976), "Authority Task Problems," *Administrative Science Quarterly,* Vol. 21, no. 4, pp. 643–660.

Lippitt, R., J. Watson, and B. Westley (1970a), *The Dynamics of Planned Change.* Reading, Mass.: Addison-Wesley.

Lippitt, R., J. Watson, and B. Westley (1970b), "Intervention Theory." In C. Argyris, *Intervention Theory and Method.* Reading, Mass.: Addison-Wesley.

Lippitt, R., J. Watson, and B. Westley (1958), *The Dynamics of Planned Change.* New York: Harcourt.

Lorange, P. (1980), *Corporate Planning: An Executive Viewpoint.* Englewood Cliffs, N.J.: Prentice Hall.

Lyles, M. (1980), "Political Processes and Organization Problem Formulation," Midwest Academy of Management Conference, Cincinnati, Ohio, April 10–12.

Mackenzie, K. D. (1978a), "A Process Based Measure for the Degree of Hierarchy in a Group. I: The Measure," *Journal of Enterprise Management,* Vol. 1, pp. 153–162.

Mackenzie, K. D. (1978b), "A Process Based Measure for the Degree of Hierarchy in a Group. III: Applications to Organizational Design," *Journal of Enterprise Management,* Vol. 1, pp. 175–184.

Mackenzie, K. D. (1978c), "A Theory of Group Structure. II: Empirical Tests," *Journal of Enterprise Management,* Vol. 1, pp. 163–174.

Mackenzie, K. D. (1976), *A Theory of Group Structure,* Volume I, *Basic Theory.* New York: Gordon and Beach Science.

Maier, N. R. F. (1970), *Problem Solving and Creativity: In Individuals and Groups.* New York: Brooks-Cole.

Malone, D. W. (1977), "An Introduction of the Application of Interpretive Structural Modeling." In A. P. Sage, ed., *Systems Engineering: Methodology and Applications,* pp. 70–78. New York: IEEE Press.

Mann, F. C., and C. K. Williams (1960), "Observations on the Dynamics of a Change to EDP Equipment," *Administrative Science Quarterly,* Vol. 5, pp. 217–256.

March, J. G. (1981), "Footnotes to Organizational Change," *Administrative Science Quarterly,* Vol. 26, no. 4, pp. 563–577.

March, J. G., and H. Simon (1958), *Organizations.* New York: McGraw-Hill.

Margulis, N., and J. Wallace (1973), *Organizational Change: Techniques and Applications.* Glenview, Ill.: Scott, Foresman.

Mason, R. O. (1969), "A Dialectical Approach to Strategic Planning," *Management Science,* Vol. 15, no. 8, pp. B403–B444.

Mason, R. O., and I. I. Mitroff (1981), *Challenging Strategic Assumptions: Theory, Cases, and Techniques.* New York: Wiley-Interscience.

Mason, R. O., and I. I. Mitroff (1979), "Assumptions—Making of Majestic Metals: Strategy Through Dialectics," *California Management Review,* Vol. 23, no. 2, pp. 80–88.

Mason, R. O., and I. I. Mitroff (1973), "A Program for Research on Management Information Systems," *Management Science,* Vol. 19, no. 5, pp. 475–487.

Mayo, E. (1933), *The Human Problems of Industrial Civilization.* New York: Macmillan.

Meadows, D. H., D. L. Meadows, J. Randers, and W. W. Behrens (1972), *The Limits to Growth.* New York: Universe Books.

Mendelson, M. A. (1984), *Tender Loving Greed.* New York: Alfred A. Knopf.

Miles, R. (1982), *Coffin Nails and Corporate Strategy.* Englewood Cliffs, N.J.: Prentice Hall.

Miles, R. E., and K. Cameron (1982), *Coffin Nails and Corporate Strategy.* Englewood Cliffs, N.J.: Prentice Hall.

Miles, R. E., and C. C. Snow (1982), "Organizational Strategy, Structure, and Process." New York: McGraw-Hill.

Miles, R. E., C. C. Snow, A. D. Meyer, and H. S. Coleman, Jr. (1978), "Organization Strategy, Structure, and Process," *Academy of Management Review,* Vol. 2, no. 3, pp. 546–562.

Miller, D., and P. H. Friesan (1978), "Archetypes of Strategy Formulation," *Management Science,* Vol. 24, no. 9, pp. 921–922.

Miller, J. G. (1978), *Living Systems.* New York: McGraw-Hill.

Minor, J. B. (1977), *Management Policy and Strategy.* New York: Macmillan.

Mintzberg, H. (1987), "The Strategy Concept. I: Five P's for Strategy," *California Management Review,* Vol. 30, pp. 11–24.

Mintzberg, H. (1981), "What Is Planning Anyway?" *Strategic Management Journal,* Vol. 2, pp. 319–324.

Mintzberg, H. (1979), "Beyond Implementation: An Analysis of the Resistance to Policy Analysis." In K. B. Haley, ed., *IFORS Proceedings.* New York: North Holland.

Mintzberg, H. (1978), "Patterns in Strategy Formation," *Management Science,* Vol. 24, no. 9, pp. 934–948.

Mintzberg, H. (1976), "Planning on the Left Side and Managing on the Right," *Harvard Business Review,* Vol. 54, pp. 49–58.

Mintzberg, H., D. Raisinghani, and A. Theoret (1976), "The Structure of 'Unstructured' Decision Processes," *Administrative Science Quarterly,* Vol. 21, no. 2, pp. 246–275.

Mitroff, I. I. (1977) "Teaching Managers to Do Policy Analysis: A Case in Corporate Bribes," *California Management Review,* Vol. 20, pp. 47–54.

Mitroff, I. I. (1974), "On Systematic Problem Solving and the Error of the Third Kind," *Behavioral Science,* Vol. 19, pp. 383–393.

Mitroff, I. I., and J. R. Emshoff (1979), "On Strategic Assumption Making: A Dialectical Approach to Policy and Planning," *Academy of Management Review,* Vol. 4, no. 1, pp. 1–12.

Mitroff, I. I., J. R. Emshoff, and R. H. Kilmann (1979), "Assumptional Analysis: A Methodology for Strategic Problem Solving," *Management Science,* Vol. 24, no. 6, pp. 583–593.

Mitroff, I. I., and R. Kilmann (1976), "An Organizational Story: An Approach to the Design and Analysis of Organizations Through Myths and Stories." In R. Kilmann, L. Pondy, and D. Sleven, eds., *The Management of Organizational Design: Strategies and Implementation.* New York: Elsevier.

Mitroff, I. I., and R. H. Kilmann (1978), "On Integrating Behavioral and Philosophical Systems: Towards a Unified Theory of Problem Solving," *Annual Series in Sociology,* Vol. 1.

Mitroff, I. I., and R. O. Mason (1981), *Challenging Strategic Planning Assumption.* New York: John Wiley.

Mitroff, I. I., and R. O. Mason (1980), "Structuring Ill-Structured Issues: Further Explorations in a Methodology for Messy Problems." *Strategic Management Journal,* Vol. 1, pp. 331–342.

Mohrman, S. (1979), "A New Look at Participation in Decision Making: The Concept of Political Access," *The Academy of Management Proceedings,* August.

Morris, W. T. (1979), *Implementation Techniques for Industrial Engineers.* Columbus, Ohio: Grid.

Morris, W. T. (1967), "On the Art of Modeling," *Management Science,* Vol. 13, no. 12, August.

Murray, E. A., Jr. (1978), "Strategic Choice as a Negotiated Outcome," *Management Science,* Vol. 24, no. 9, pp. 960–971.

Nadler, G. (1981), *The Planning and Design Approach.* New York: John Wiley.

Nadler, G. (1971), "The Effect of Design Strategy on Productivity," *International Journal of Production Research,* Vol. 9, no. 1, pp. 83–94.

Nadler, G. (1970a), *Work Design: A Systems Concept.* Georgetown, Ontario, Canada: Irwin.

Nadler, G. (1970b), *Work Design: A Systems Approach.* Homewood, Ill.: Richard D. Irwin.

Nadler, G. (1967), "An Investigation of Design Methodology," *Management Science,* Vol. 13, no. 10, pp. B642–B655.

Nadler, G., and S. Hibino (1990), *Breakthrough Thinking.* Rocklin, Calif.: Prima.

Naraynan, V. K. (1980), "Political Process and Strategy Making," Midwest Academy of Management Conference, Cincinnati, Ohio.

Newcomb, T. W. (1958), "Attitude Development as a Function of Reference Groups." In J. E. Maccoby, T. Newcomb, and E. Hartley, eds., *Readings in Social Psychology.* New York: Holt, Rinehart and Winston.

Newman, W. H. (1971), "Selecting Company Strategy," *Journal of Business Policy,* Vol. 2, no. 2, pp. 60–71.

Nutt, P. C. (1992a), "Formulation Processes and Tactics," *Organizational Science* (in press).

Nutt, P. C. (1992b), "The Influence of Formulation Tactics on the Success of Organizational Decision Making," *Decision Sciences* (in press).

Nutt, P. C. (1991a), "Solution Development in Decision Making," *DSI International Conference Proceedings,* Brussels, Belgium, June 24–26.

Nutt, P. C. (1991b), "Formulation Tactics Used by Decision Makers," *Decision Sciences* (in press).

Nutt, P. C. (1989a), *Making Tough Decisions.* San Francisco: Jossey-Bass.

Nutt, P. C. (1989b), "Selecting Tactics to Implement Strategic Plans," *Strategic Management Journal,* Vol. 10, pp. 145–161.

Nutt, P. C. (1987), "Identifying and Appraising How Managers Install Strategic Changes," *Strategic Management Journal,* Vol. 8, no. 1, pp. 1–14.

Nutt, P. C. (1986), "The Tactics of Implementation," *Academy of Management Journal,* Vol. 29, no. 2, pp. 230–261.

Nutt, P. C. (1984a), "Types of Organizational Decision Processes," *Administrative Science Quarterly,* Vol. 29, no. 3, pp. 414–450.

Nutt, P. C. (1984b), *Planning Methods.* New York: John Wiley.

Nutt, P. C. (1984c), "Planning Process Archetypes and Their Effectiveness,"*Decision Sciences,* Vol. 15, no. 2, pp. 221–238.

Nutt, P. C. (1984d), "Pseudoplanning," *Technological Forecasting and Social Change,* Vol. 25, no. 2, pp. 91–108.

Nutt, P. C. (1984e), "A Strategic Planning Network for Organizations," *Strategic Planning Journal,* Vol. 5, no. 1, pp. 57–77.

Nutt, P. C. (1983), "Implementation Approaches for Planning," *Academy of Management Review,* Vol. 8, pp. 600–611.

Nutt, P. C. (1982a), "Hybrid Planning Methods," *Academy of Management Review,* Vol. 7, pp. 444–454.

Nutt, P. C. (1982b), *Evaluating Concepts and Methods.* Jamaica, N.Y.: Spectrum.

Nutt, P. C. (1981), "The Acceptance and Accuracy of Decision Analysis Methods," *Omega, The International Journal of Operations Research,* Vol. 9, no. 6, pp. 619–632.

Nutt, P. C. (1980a), "Comparing Methods for Weighting Decision Criteria," *Omega, The International Journal of Operations Research,* Vol. 8, no. 2, pp. 163–172.

Nutt, P. C. (1980b), "On Managed Evaluation Process," *Technological Forecasting and Social Change,* Vol. 17, pp. 313–328.

Nutt, P. C. (1979a), "Calling Out and Calling Off the Dogs: Managerial Diagnosis in Organizations," *Academy of Management Review,* Vol. 4, no. 2, pp. 203–214.

Nutt, P. C. (1979b), "On the Acceptance and Quality of Plans Drawn by Consortiums," *The Journal of Applied Behavioral Science,* Vol. 15, no. 1, Winter.

Nutt, P. C. (1979c), "The Influence of Decision Style on the Selection of a Decision Approach," *Technological Forecasting and Social Change,* Vol. 14, no. l, June, pp. 77–93.

Nutt, P. C. (1977), "An Experimental Comparison of the Effectiveness of Three Planning Methods," *Management Science,* Vol. 23, no. 4, pp. 449–511.

Nutt, P. C. (1976a), "A Field Experiment Which Compared the Effectiveness of Design Methods," *Decision Sciences,* Vol. 7, no. 4, pp. 739–758.

Nutt, P. C. (1976b), "The Merits of Using Experts and Consumers as Members of Planning Groups," *The Academy of Management Journal,* Vol. 19, no. 3, pp. 378–394.

Nutt, P. C., and R. W. Backoff (1992), *The Strategic Management of Public and Third Sector Organizations.* San Francisco: Jossey-Bass.

Nutt, P. C., and R. W. Backoff (1987), "The Strategic Management of Public and Third Sector Organizations," *The American Journal of Planning,* Vol. 53, pp. 44–57.

Nutt, P. C., and R. W. Backoff (1986), "Mutual Understanding and Its Impact on Formulation During Planning," *Technological Forecasting and Social Change,* Vol. 29, pp. 13–21.

Nutt, P. C., and S. Beatty (1981), "Cross-validating Decision Analysis Models," *Decision Sciences Institute Proceedings,* Vol. 13, November.

Nutt, P. C., and S. M. Emswiler (1979), "Factors Influencing the Size of Malpractice Awards in Hospitals," *The Midwest Academy of Management Proceedings,* Vol. 22, April.

Nystrom, P., L. Hedberg, and W. Starbuck (1976), "Interacting Process as Organizational Design." In L. Poudy and D. Sleven, eds., *The Management of Organizational Design.* New York: Elsevier.

O'Donnell, C. (1974), *Essentials of Management.* New York: McGraw-Hill.

Osborn, A. F. (1957), *Applied Imagination,* 3rd ed. New York: Scribners.

Parker, A. W. (1970), "The Consumer as Policy Maker—Issues of Training," *American Journal of Public Health,* Vol. 60, pp. 2139–2153.

Parkinson, C. H. (1962), *Parkinson's Law and Other Studies in Administration.* Boston: Houghton Mifflin.

Parnes, S. J. (1961), "Effects of Extended Effort in Creative Problem Solving," *Journal of Educational Psychology,* Vol. 52, pp. 117–122.

Parnes, S. J., and A. Meadow (1959), "The Effects of Brainstorming Instructions on Creative Problem Solving by Trained and Untrained Subjects," *Journal of Educational Psychology,* Vol. 50, pp. 117–122.

Parsons, T. (1960), "On the Concept of Influence," *Public Opinion Quarterly,* Vol. 27, pp. 37–62.

PERT, Program Evaluation Research Task, Summary Report, Phase I, Special Projects Office, Bureau of Naval Weapons, U.S. Department of the Navy, Washington, D.C., July 1958.

Polanyi, M. (1966), *The Tacit Dimension.* Garden City, N.Y.: Doubleday.

Pondy, L. (1977), "Leadership Is a Language Game." In M. McCall and M. Lombardo, eds., *Leadership: Where Else Can We Go?* Durham, N.C.: Duke University Press.

Pondy, L., and I. I. Mitroff (1979), "Beyond Open System Models of Organization." In *Research in Organizational Behavior,* Vol. I. Greenwich, Conn.: JAI Press.

Porter, M. E. (1985), *Competitive Advantage.* New York: Free Press.

Porter, M. E. (1980), *Competitive Strategy: Techniques for Analyzing Industries and Competitors.* New York: Free Press.

Pounds, W. (1969), "The Process of Problem Finding," *Industrial Management Review,* Fall, pp. 1–19.

Prigogine, I. (1982), *Self-organizing and Dissipative Structures.* Austin: University of Texas Press.

Quade, E. S., and W. I. Boucher, eds. (1968), *Systems Analysis and Policy Planning: Applications in Defense.* New York: Elsevier.

Rabino, J. (1988), "Design Theory and Method Workshop," address to the National Science Foundation, September 18.

Rader, L. T. (1965), "Road Blocks to Progress in the Management Sciences and Operation Research," *Management Science,* Vol. 11, pp. C1–C5.

Raiffa, H. (1970), *Decision Analysis.* Reading, Mass.: Addison-Wesley.

Rapoport, A. (1986), "Mathematical Aspects of General Systems Analysis," *General Systems,* Vol. 11, pp. 3–11.

Raven, B. H. (1965), "Social Influence and Power." In I. Steiner and M. Fishbein, eds., *Current Studies in Social Psychology.* New York: Holt, Rinehart and Winston.

Rescher, N. (1968), *Topics in Philosophical Logic.* Dordrecht, Holland: Reidel.

Rhemon, E. (1968), *Industrial Democracy and Industrial Man.* London: Tavistock.

Ritti, R. R., and G. F. Funkhouser (1987), *The Ropes to Skip and the Ropes to Know.* New York: John Wiley.

Rodgers, E. M. (1962), *The Diffusion of Innovation.* New York: Free Press.

Sagan, C. (1980), *Cosmos.* New York: Random House.

Sagan, C. (1975), *Broca's Brain.* New York: Random House.

Schein, E. H. (1964a), "The Mechanisms of Change." In W. Bennis, E. Schein, A. Stelle, and B. Berlow, eds., *Interpersonal Dynamics,* pp. 362–378. Homewood, Ill.: Dorsey.

Schein, E. H. (1964b), *Process Consultation.* Reading, Mass.: Addison-Wesley.

Schein, E. H., et al. (1961), *Cohesive Persuasion.* New York: W. W. Norton.

Schendel, D., and C. Hofer (1979), *Strategic Management.* Boston: Little, Brown.

Schlesinger, L., S. M. Jackson, and J. Butman (1960), "Leader-Member Interaction in Management Committees," *Journal of Abnormal and Social Psychology,* Vol. 61, pp. 359–354.

Schreisheim, C. J., J. M. Tolliver, and O. C. Behling (1980), "Leadership: Some Organizational and Managerial Implications." In P. Hersey and J. Stinson, eds., *Perspectives in Leader Effectiveness.* Athens, Ohio: Center for Leadership Studies.

Schultz, R. L., and M. J. Ginsberg, eds. (1984), *Management Science Implementation.* Greenwich, Conn.: JAI Press.

Schultz, R. L., and D. P. Sleven (1975), *Implementing Operations Research and Management Science.* New York: Elsevier.

Selltiz, C., M. Jahoda, M. Deutch, and S. Cook (1959), *Research Methods in the Social Sciences.* New York: Holt, Rinehart and Winston.

Selznick, P. (1957), *Leadership in Administration.* Evanston, Ill.: Row-Peterson.

Shannon, C. E., and W. Weaver (1949), *The Mathematical Theory of Communication.* Urbana: University of Illinois Press.

Simon, H. A. (1977), *The New Science of Management Decision,* rev. ed. Englewood Cliffs, N.J.: Prentice Hall.

Simon, H. A. (1969). *The Sciences of the Artificial.* Cambridge, Mass.: MIT Press.

Simon, H. A., and A. Newell (1970), "Human Problem Solving—The State of the Art in 1970," *American Psychologist,* February.

Singer, E. A., Jr. (1959), *Experience and Reflection*, ed. C. W. Churchman. Philadelphia: University of Pennsylvania Press.

Slovic, P., B. Fishoff, and S. Lichtenstein (1977), "Behavioral Decision Theory", *Annual Review of Psychology*, Vol. 28, pp. 129.

Snyder, N., and W. Glueck (1980), "How Managers Plan—The Analysis of Managers' Activities," *Long-Range Planning,* February, pp. 70–76.

Snyder, R. C., and G. D. Paige (1958), "The U.S. Decision to Resist Aggression in Korea: The Application of an Analytical Scheme," *Administrative Science Quarterly,* pp. 341–378.

Soelberg, P. (1967), "Unprogrammed Decision Making," *Industrial Management Review,* Spring 1967, pp. 19–29.

Sorensen, R. E. (1975), "Improving the Implementation of OR/MS Models by Applying the Lewin-Schein Theory of Change." In R. Shultz and D. S. Levin, eds., *Implementing Operations Research/Management Science.* New York: Elsevier.

Souder, W. E. (1980), *Management Decision Methods for Managers of Engineering and Research.* New York: Van Nostrand Reinhold.

Souder, W. E. (1987), *Managing New Product Innovations.* Lexington, Mass.: D. C. Heath, 1987.

Stein, M. I. (1975), *Stimulating Creativity,* Volume 2, *Group Procedures.* New York: Academic Press.

Steiner, G. (1979), *Top Management Planning,* rev. ed. New York: Macmillan.

Stephenson, W. (1953), *The Study of Behavior.* Chicago: University of Chicago Press.

Stogdill, R. M. (1969), *Individual Behavior and Group Achievement.* New York: Oxford University Press.

Stogdill, R. M. (1974), *Handbook of Leadership.* New York: Free Press.

Stogdill, R. M., and A. E. Coons, eds. (1957), *Leader Behavior: Its Description and Measurement,* Monograph 8. Columbus: Bureau of Business Research, The Ohio State University.

Suchman, E. A. (1967), *Evaluation Research: Principles and Practice in Public Service and Social Action Programs.* Washington, D.C.: Russell Sage.

Sudman, S., and N. M. Bradburn (1982), *Asking Questions: A Practical Guide to Questionnaire Design.* San Francisco: Jossey-Bass.

Summers, I., and D. D. White (1976),"Creativity Techniques: Toward Improvement of the Decision Process," *Academy of Management Review,* Vol. 1, no. 2, pp. 99–107.

Sussman, L., and R. P. Herden (1985), "Dialectic Problem Solving," *Business Horizons,* Vol. 20, pp. 1–15.

Thelen, H. A. (1967), "Concepts of Collaborative Action-Inquiry." In G. Watson, ed., *Concepts of Social Change.* Washington, D.C.: NTL Institute.

Thompson, J. D. (1967), *Organizations in Action: Social Science Bases of Administrative Theory.* New York: McGraw-Hill.

Thune, S. S., and R. H. House (1970), "Where Long-Range Planning Pays Off, Business Horizons," Vol. 13, pp. 81–87.

Toulmin, S. (1979), *Knowing and Acting: An Invitation to Philosophy.* New York: Macmillan.

Toulmin, S. (1972), *Human Understanding: The Collective Use and Evaluation of Concepts.* Princeton, N.J.: Princeton University Press.

Toulmin, S., R. Riecke, and A. Janick (1979), *An Introduction to Reasoning.* New York: Macmillan.

Townsend, R. (1970), *Up the Organization.* New York: Fawcett.

Turley, R. E., and W. E. Richardson (1975), "Morphological Analysis for Health Care Systems Planning." In M. M. Baldwin, ed., *Portraits in Complexity: Applications of Systems to Social Problems.* Columbus, Ohio: Battelle Memorial Institute.

Tversky, A. (1972), "Elimination by Aspects: A Theory of Choice," *Psychological Review,* Vol. 79, pp. 281–299.

Utterback, J. M. (1971), "The Process of Technological Innovation in Firms," *Academy of Management Journal,* Vol. 14, no. 1, March, pp. 75–87.

Van de Ven, A., and A. Delbecq (1977), "The Effectiveness of Delphi, Interacting and Nominal Groups in Decision Making Processes," *Academy of Management Journal,* Vol. 17, no. 4, pp. 605–619.

Van de Ven, A., and A. Delbecq (1974), "Nominal vs. Interacting Group Process Effectiveness for Committee Decision Making," *Academy of Management Journal,* Vol. 14, no. 2, pp. 203–217.

Van Gigch, J. P. (1979), *Applied General Systems Theory,* 2nd ed., p. 41, New York: Harper & Row.

Van Gundy, A. B. (1981), *Techniques of Structures Problem Solving.* New York: Van Nostrand Reinhold.

Vanston, H. J., Jr., W. P. Frisbe, S. C. Lopreato, and D. L. Poston, Jr. (1977), "Alternative Scenario Planning," *Technological Forecasting and Social Change,* Vol. 10, pp. 159–180.

Volkema, R. (1983), "Problem Formulation in Planning and Design," *Management Science,* Vol. 29, no. 6, pp. 639–652.

Volkema, R. (1986), "Problem Formulation as a Purposive Activity," *Strategic Management Journal,* Vol. 7, no. 3, pp. 167–179.

von Bertalanffy, L. (1968), *General Systems Theory.* New York: G. Braziller.

von Neumann, S., and O. Morgenstern (1947), *Theory of Games and Economic Behavior.* Princeton, N.J.: Princeton University Press.

Vroom, V. H., L. P. Grand, and T. J. Cotton (1969), "The Sequences of Social Interaction in Group Problem Solving," *Journal of Applied Psychology,* Vol. 54, no. 4, pp. 338–341.

Waddington, C. H. (1977), *Tools for Thought.* New York: Basic Books.

Wade, J. W. (1977), *Architectural Problems and Purposes.* New York: Wiley-Interscience.

Wallen, R. J. (1975), "Applications of Interpretative Structural Modeling in the Management of the Learning Disabled." In M. M. Baldwin, ed., *Portraits in Complexity,* Battelle Monograph No. 9. Columbus, Ohio: Battelle Memorial Institute.

Warfield, J. N. (1990), *A Science of Generic Design.* Salinas, Calif.: Interscience.

Warfield, J. N. (1976), *Societal Systems Planning, Policy, and Complexity.* New York: John Wiley. Reprinted Salinas, Calif.: Intersystems.

Warfield, J. N. (1973), *An Assault on Complexity,* Battelle Monograph No. 3. Columbus, Ohio: Battelle Memorial Institute.

Warfield, J. N., and J. D. Hill (1972), *A Unified Systems Engineering Concept,* Battelle Monograph Series. Columbus, Ohio: Battelle Memorial Institute.

Warfield, J. N., and J. D. Hill (1971), "The Delta Chart: A Method for R and D Project Portrayal," *IEEE Transactions on Engineering Management,* Vol. EM-18, no. 4, November, pp. 132–139.

Wattell, H. L., ed. (1964), *The Dissemination of New Business Techniques: Network Scheduling and Control Systems (CMP/PERT),* Hofstra University Yearbook, Vol. II. Hempstead, N.Y.: Hofstra University Press.

Watts, R. D. (1966), "Elements of Design." In W. S. Gregory, ed., *The Design Method.* New York: Plenum.

Weber, R. A. (1975), *Management.* Homewood, Ill.: Richard D. Irwin.

Weinberg, G. M. (1985), *An Introduction to System Thinking.* New York: John Wiley.

Weiner, N. (1961), *Cybernetics,* 2nd ed. New York: John Wiley.

Weiner, N. (1945), *Cybernetics.* New York: John Wiley.

Weisman, C. (1988), *Strategic Information Systems.* Homewood, Ill.: Richard D. Irwin.

Wheeler, T. L., and J. D. Hunger (1989), *Strategic Management and Business Policy.* Reading, Mass.: Addison-Wesley.

Whiting, C. S. (1988), *Creative Thinking.* New York: Reinhold.

Wildavsky, A. (1966), "The Political Economy of Efficiency: Cost-Benefit, Systems Auditing, and PPBS," *The Public Administration Review,* December.

Wildavsky, A. (1979), *Speaking Truth to Power.* Boston: Little, Brown.

Wilson, I. G., and M. E. Wilson (1970), *From the Idea to the Working Model.* New York: John Wiley.

Woodgate, H. A. (1964), *Planning by Network.* New York: Brandon Systems Press.

Young, O. R. (1984), "A Survey of General Systems Theory," *General Systems,* Vol. 9, pp. 61–67.

Zaltman, G., R. Duncan, and J. Holbeck (1973), *Innovation and Organizations.* New York: Wiley-Interscience.

Zand, C. E. (1974), "Collateral Organization: New Change Strategy," *The Journal of Applied Behavioral Science,* Vol. 10, no. 1, pp. 64–89.

Zwicky, F. (1969), *Discovery, Invention, Research Through the Morphological Approach.* New York: Macmillan.

# INDEX

▲ ▲ ▲ ▲ ▲ ▲ ▲ ▲ ▲ ▲ ▲ ▲ ▲ ▲ ▲ ▲ ▲ ▲ ▲ ▲ ▲ ▲ ▲ ▲